THE DIARY OF GEORGE LLOYD
(1642–1718)

THE DIARY OF GEORGE LLOYD (1642–1718)

edited by
DANIEL PATTERSON

CAMDEN FIFTH SERIES
Volume 64

CAMBRIDGE
UNIVERSITY PRESS

FOR THE ROYAL HISTORICAL SOCIETY
University College London, Gower Street, London WC1 6BT
2022

Published by Cambridge University Press on behalf of The Royal Historical Society
Shaftesbury Road, Cambridge CB2 8EA, United Kingdom
One Liberty Plaza, 20th Floor, New York, NY 10006, USA
477 Williamstown Road, Port Melbourne, VIC 3207, Australia
314–321, 3rd Floor, Plot 3, Splendor Forum, Jasola District Centre,
New Delhi – 110025, India
103 Penang Road, #05–06/07, Visioncrest Commercial, Singapore 238467

© The Royal Historical Society 2022

First published 2022

A catalogue record for this book is available from the British Library

ISBN 9781009323413 hardback

SUBSCRIPTIONS. The serial publications of the Royal Historical Society, *Royal Historical Society Transactions* (ISSN 0080-4401) and Camden Fifth Series (ISSN 0960-1163) volumes, may be purchased together on annual subscription. The 2022 subscription price, which includes print and electronic access (but not VAT), is £229 (US $382 in the USA, Canada, and Mexico) and includes Camden Fifth Series, Volumes 63, 64 and Transactions Sixth Series, Volume 32 (published in December). The electronic only price available to institutional subscribers is £186 (US $310 in the USA, Canada, and Mexico). Japanese prices are available from Kinokuniya Company Ltd, P.O. Box 55, Chitose, Tokyo 156, Japan. EU subscribers may be required to pay import VAT at their country's rate on receipt of physical deliveries. EU subscribers for electronic deliveries who are not VAT registered should add VAT at their country's rate. VAT registered subscribers should provide their VAT number.

Subscription orders, which must be accompanied by payment, may be sent to a bookseller, subscription agent, or direct to the publisher: Cambridge University Press, University Printing House, Shaftesbury Road, Cambridge CB2 8BS, UK; or in the USA, Canada, and Mexico: Cambridge University Press, Journals Fulfillment Department, One Liberty Plaza, Floor 20, New York, NY 10006, USA.

SINGLE VOLUMES AND BACK VOLUMES. A list of Royal Historical Society volumes available from Cambridge University Press may be obtained from the Humanities Marketing Department at the address above.

Printed in Great Britain by Bell & Bain Ltd.

CONTENTS

PREFACE	vii
ABBREVIATIONS	ix
INTRODUCTION	1
EDITORIAL PRINCIPLES	35
THE DIARY OF GEORGE LLOYD	37
Autobiographical Preface	39
Colchester Diary, 1675–1678	41
London Diary, 1711–1712	295
SELECT BIBLIOGRAPHY	423
INDEX	431

PREFACE

A reconstruction of the life of George Lloyd, a person hitherto completely unknown to history, made up the basis of my doctoral work. I have, therefore, been living with George for quite some time and I am glad to be able to introduce him to my fellow scholars at last. I hope that others will go on to contribute to unlocking the diary's remaining secrets. The text, which covers almost every single day of nearly five years of Lloyd's life, contains a wealth of material touching on all manner of subjects of interest to scholars, most of which I have addressed only briefly in the present volume, and some of which I have not been able to cover at all.

I first transcribed the diary and carried out much of the initial research on Lloyd's life between 2014 and 2018, taking a brief hiatus in 2019 and resuming at the start of 2020. My endeavour to bring the diary to a wider readership, daunting enough in itself, took a strange and difficult turn in the March of that year, with the onset of the COVID-19 lockdown. I have spent the ensuing time in Belfast, Northern Ireland, carrying out much of my research remotely. This has been a challenging but highly rewarding experience but, while this volume is the result of a more solitary effort than it otherwise might have been, there are still a number of individuals and institutions without whom this project would not have been possible.

Firstly, I would like to thank the Camden Fifth Series, the Royal Historical Society, and Cambridge University Press, all of whom provided me with the opportunity to carry out such a special project at an early stage in my career. I am particularly grateful to Andrew Spicer, Siobhan Talbott, Philip Carter, and Miranda Bethell.

Whilst much of the work for this volume was carried out remotely, I am grateful to the staff of the National Archives, London Metropolitan Archives, Lambeth Palace Library, London Guildhall Library, the Essex Record Office, the Hampshire Record Office, Carlisle Archive Centre, and the British Library. I must also thank the staff of the Bodleian Library, Oxford, where the diary is held. I was fortunate enough to be offered a two-month Bodleian Visiting Fellowship to carry out the final stages of my research on the diary – unfortunately, the Fellowship commenced in March

2020. As a result, I was forced to break up my Fellowship into a series of shorter visits. Particular thanks must go to Rachel Naismith and Dr Alexandra Franklin for their flexibility and patience in facilitating my work – completion of this volume would have been impossible otherwise.

Above all, I must extend my heartfelt gratitude to Professor Chris Marsh at Queen's University, Belfast. Chris first convinced me of the fascinating richness of early modern diaries when he introduced me to the diary of Roger Lowe in 2014. His seemingly infinite generosity and patience as a supervisor and mentor has been invaluable to me over the years, and I can honestly say that my career as a researcher would not have been possible without him.

Special thanks also to Professor David Hayton, my undergraduate supervisor at Queen's. He inspired my interest in early modern history, for which I will be forever grateful.

I would also like to thank my colleagues at the University of Huddersfield. I was tremendously excited to take up my first real academic post at the English Literature department at Huddersfield at the end of 2019. Sadly, I have not been able to spend much time there since, but it has nonetheless been a great experience, not least thanks to my closest colleagues Dr Mary Chadwick and Revd Professor Jessica Malay, both of whom have been sources of much-needed advice and support.

Special thanks must also go to my friend Gerard Mc Auley. His constant encouragement and unfailing optimism stopped me from giving up many times. I am also grateful to John Wootton, Louise Dornan, Joe Miller, Peter Hunter, and to all the other friends and colleagues who have listened to me ramble or complain about Lloyd and 'my book' over the last couple of years, or have helped me out in one way or another.

I am also tremendously grateful to my family for their endless love and support – my mother, father, and my brothers Sam and Stephen. Finally, but above all, I thank my partner, Ali Campeau, who has been with me through all the highs and lows of trying to produce this book during an unprecedented global pandemic. This is for all of you.

ABBREVIATIONS

BL	British Library
BODL	Bodleian Library, Oxford
Cantabrigienses	Venn, John, and John A. Venn, *Alumni Cantabrigienses: A biographical list* ... (Cambridge, 1922–1954; 2011)
CCEd	Clergy of the Church of England Database
EHT	Ferguson, Catherine, Christopher Thornton, and Andrew Wareham (eds), *Essex Hearth Tax Return Michaelmas 1670* (London, 2012).
ERO	Essex Record Office
GHL	London Guildhall Library
HRO	Hampshire Record Office
Hist. Parl. 1660–1690	Henning, Basil Duke, *The History of Parliament: The House of Commons, 1660–1690*, 3 vols (London, 1983)
Hist. Parl. 1690–1715	Hayton, David, and Eveline Cruickshanks, *The History of Parliament: The House of Commons, 1690–1715*, 5 vols (London, 2001)
KRO	Kent Record Office
LCH	Lillywhite, Bryant, *London Coffee Houses: A Reference Book of Coffee Houses of the Seventeenth, Eighteenth and Nineteenth Centuries* (London, 1963)
LMA	London Metropolitan Archives
LPL	Lambeth Palace Library
OED	*Oxford English Dictionary*, online edition
ODNB	*Oxford Dictionary of National Biography*, online edition
Oxonienses	Foster, Joseph (ed.), *Alumni Oxonienses: The members of the University of Oxford, 1500–1714* ... (London, 1891)
Pepys	R. C. Latham and W. Matthews (eds), *The Diary of Samuel Pepys*, 11 vols (London, 1995)
TBE	Nikolaus Pevsner et al., *The Buildings of England* (see Bibliography)
TNA	The National Archives, Kew
VCHE	Janet Cooper (ed.), *The Victoria History of the County of Essex*, Vol. 9: *The Borough of Colchester* (Oxford, 1994)

INTRODUCTION

> A man is so vain, so unfixed, so perishing a creature, that he cannot long last in the scene of fancy: a man goes off, and is forgotten, like the dream of a distracted person.
>
> Jeremy Taylor, *The Rule and Exercises of Holy Dying* (1651)

On the afternoon of 21 August 1675, George Lloyd sat down in his room at the Three Crowns inn, Colchester, and made himself a little book. Paper in the 1670s was a fairly valuable commodity and he was not a wealthy man, so its pages were tiny. In a necessarily minute hand, Lloyd proceeded to carefully document his activities over the preceding two days, beginning with his early morning journey from London to Colchester on 19 August, right up 'to this place'. He scrupulously recorded little details, noting that he had stopped at the Essex village of Ingatestone at eleven o'clock and there dined with '2 gentell men and one woman', stopped again at Kelvedon at four, and arrived at Colchester a little after six. He stayed at the Three Crowns Inn and, clearly exhausted by his journey, went immediately to bed.[1] The entry for the following day offers an even more minute account of his comings and goings in an unfamiliar town. Times of appointments, places visited, people spoken to are all accounted for in a detailed, rational narrative which mirrors the linear temporality of a day recently lived and carefully remembered. Lloyd offered no moralistic or grandiose 'reason' for recording these minutiae or any rationale for his method of doing so. It was not an exercise in religious piety, an educational memento for his descendants, nor a record of important events for posterity. He did write a brief preface of sorts, which outlined his personal background, to which I shall return below. In terms of how he thought about the text I refer to as 'the diary of George Lloyd' (for the author never used these words), he offered few clues. He did, however, describe the book as a record of 'the most remarkable passages and alterations of

---

[1] This building still stands today at North Hill, Colchester, and was until recently used as a post office.

my life'. This introductory essay will set this life, and its diary, in historical context.[2]

I

Lloyd's diary is, in fact, anonymous, and has remained so despite a handful of brief citations in other works.[3] However, it contains identifying details which made it possible for me to identify the author for the first time. The volume begins with a brief 'account of the most remarkable passages and alterations of my life', in which the author states that he was born on 11 May 1642 'in the parsonage hous in the parlour at Wonston', suggesting that his father was a clergyman. Also bound into the back of the book is a page written in a distinctively different hand, containing a basic cypher using astrological symbols, and a signature – N. Floyd. These snippets of information turned my attention to Nicholas Lloyd [Floyd] (1630–1680), a notable but not famous clergyman and scholar, and the subject of a brief article in the *ODNB* – but clearly not the diary's author. Nicholas was born in the parsonage house at Wonston, Hampshire, the son of 'the Revd George Lloyd'. He had three brothers; John (1643/4–1682, a poet and clergyman, who also merited inclusion in the *ODNB*), Edward (d.1655), and George. John was born in Wonston in 1643/4, followed in Nicholas's footsteps to attend Wadham College, Oxford, 1662–1666, was appointed vicar of Holyrood,

---

[2] Due to restrictions of space, this introductory essay will not attempt an in-depth thematic or formal analysis of the diary text. However, elsewhere, I have published 'Writing time: Charting the history of clock time in seventeenth-century diaries', *Huntington Library Quarterly*, 83:2 (2020), 305–329, which focuses on Lloyd's use of 'clock time', unique in the seventeenth century, to punctuate his diary entries. I hope to publish articles examining Lloyd's religious practices in detail, and his evident interest in fashion and clothing, amongst other topics, in the future.

[3] The diary is recorded on the list compiled by William Matthews, *British Diaries: An Annotated Bibliography of British Diaries Written between 1442 and 1942* (London, 1950), 35. Otherwise, it has been cited four times by other scholars, so far as I am aware. In all of these cases, it is cited once, very briefly, by each author, and the diarist's identity is left undiscovered. These are: Jennifer Farooq, *Preaching in Eighteenth-Century London* (Woodbridge, 2013), 111, in which Lloyd's later diary is cited as 'sermon notes'; Richard Grassby, *Kinship and Capitalism: Marriage, Family, and Business in the English-Speaking World, 1580–1740* (Cambridge, 2001), 241, which uses the London Diary to show that property brokers often drank with their clients; Christopher Marsh, *Music and Society in Early Modern England* (Cambridge, 2010), 184, in which the diarist is compared to his contemporary Samuel Pepys, since both of them played the newly fashionable violin in their spare time in the late seventeenth century; and Kaspar von Greyerz, 'Spuren eines vormodernen Individualismus in englischen Selbstzeugnissen des 16. und 17. Jahrhunderts', in W. Schulze (ed.), *Ego-Dokumente: Annäherung an den Menschen in der Geschichte* (Berlin, 1996), 135, which cites the earlier diary as evidence of an emergent self-conscious self-discipline in the maintenance of a daily routine.

INTRODUCTION   3

Southampton, on 20 May 1675, and died at his living in 1682; he can also, therefore, be ruled out as the author.[4] This leaves us with George, a man totally forgotten by history, but whose distinctly unremarkable life left a surprising number of biographical and archival traces.

George Lloyd's diary did not survive as a result of its literary qualities or the exploits of its author. Rather, it almost certainly avoided the dustbin of history because Lloyd's brother Nicholas *was* the kind of man whose diary which might have been carefully preserved by antiquarians. A clergyman and academic, Nicholas occupied a number of prestigious positions throughout his career, mostly at his *alma mater*, Wadham College, Oxford. He was university rhetoric leader in 1665, and sub-warden of Wadham in 1666 and 1670. In addition, in 1665 he was appointed chaplain to Dr Walter Blandford, bishop of Oxford. His magnum opus, published in 1670, was a much revised and expanded version of the *Dictionarium historicum, geographicum, poeticum* of Charles Estienne's 1553 work. Nicholas was also a noted friend and companion to Anthony Wood.[5] His final years were spent apparently uneventfully as rector of St Mary Newington, a living to which he was appointed on 28 April 1673. When Nicholas died on 27 November 1680, George inherited the majority of his brother's estate, including most of his papers.[6] The 1719 edition of John Aubrey's *The Natural History and Antiquities of the County of Surrey*, following a very brief biographical sketch of the life of Nicholas Lloyd (in his capacity as Rector at St Mary Newington), suggests that

> much more might have been said of him and his Labours, had Mr *Lloyd* been pleased to communicate what he has left behind him, or his Brother, in whose Possession [Nicholas's] Papers were till lately, after his Death, they were retrieved from being made Waste Paper.[7]

In fact, this passage was written not by Aubrey (who died in 1697), but by the antiquarian and bibliophile Richard Rawlinson, who revised, updated, and published the manuscripts started but left unfinished by Aubrey. The papers discussed in this passage are held by the Bodleian today, as part of the Rawlinson Collection, the manuscripts bequeathed to the library by Richard Rawlinson

---

[4] *ODNB.*
[5] See Letters almost entirely written to Anthony Wood, 1657–1695, BODL, MS Wood F. 43.
[6] Will of Nicholas Lloyd, Rector of St Mary Newington Butts, St Mary Newington Butts, Surrey, proved 6 December 1680 LPL, VH 97/2/33v.
[7] John Aubrey, *The Natural History and Antiquities of the County of Surrey*, Vol. 5 (London, 1719), 140–141. George died at the very end of 1718, so whilst he is not explicitly named as the 'Brother' mentioned in the text, he was clearly the person referred to.

when he died in 1755.[8] In other words, George Lloyd preserved certain papers of particular significance pertaining to his brother, and Rawlinson appears to have personally acquired them after his death. Certainty here is impossible, but it seems likely that Rawlinson 'retrieved' the papers from Lloyd's widow Elizabeth, who survived him by some six months.[9] Whether Lloyd's inconspicuous little diary was passed to Rawlinson and then bequeathed to the Bodleian with any purpose, or whether it was a happy accident, is impossible to say. Perhaps the signature of Nicholas, bound upside down into the back of the volume, is the sole reason for its ultimate survival.

II

Perhaps unsurprisingly, therefore, this diary is not the only substantial but forgotten biographical text relating to the Lloyd family held in the Rawlinson Collection. The diaries of Nicholas and Edward Lloyd are lost, but the former composed and preserved two sermons in memory of his father, entitled 'Parenti parentatio', and accompanied them with a fairly rich and personal elegiac biography of the elder George Lloyd.[10] This short biography provides some insight into what it must have been like for the diarist growing up. Nicholas was an intelligent and sensitive man who greatly esteemed his father. The text, though undated, was probably written in the late 1650s, very shortly after the death of the elder George Lloyd (d.1658).[11] Its tone is reverent and even emotional at times, and it is clear that the anecdotes chosen to paint a picture of the elder Lloyd were designed to flatter him. However, as a source of incidental biographical information, it is very valuable and corroborated by other documents.

The elder George was born in Leckford, Hampshire, in 1597, the son of David Floyd and Anne Tainter. Anne, Nicholas informs us, was from Cricklade in Wiltshire, 'where some of the Family remain to this day in good fashion and Reputation'. David Floyd was also a

---

[8] BODL, MS Rawl. D. 32.

[9] Will of Elizabeth Lloyd, widow of St Dunstan in the East, City of London, proved in the Prerogative Court of Canterbury, 11 June 1719, TNA, PROB 11/569/85.

[10] Parenti parentatio, or funerall obsequies (in two sermons) by Nicholas Lloyd in memory of his ever honoured father Mr. Geo. Lloyd; together with some breife observations upon the chiefe passages of his life and death, 1658, BODL, MS Rawl. D.1301/4, fos 45–84. It is not linked to the diary in the Bodleian's catalogue.

[11] I have based this dating primarily upon incidental references to the political situation, which suggest (but certainly do not prove beyond doubt) that at the time of writing, the Restoration had not yet occurred.

clergyman, serving as vicar of Leckford from 1596 until his death in 1627.[12] The family used the names Lloyd and Floyd interchangeably, perhaps with an awareness that both were a 'corruption' (to use Nicholas's word) of the 'Native Pronunciation'. The elder George 'adher'd peremptorily to noe one' spelling, 'but was wont all waies, or for the most part to write his Name thus. Geo: Floyd.'[13] Nicholas also used 'Floyd' in this document and in his inscription in the back of the diary, but in 'official' sources he was always referred to as Lloyd. The diarist, on the other hand, invariably used Lloyd when he signed his name in a handful of other sources.[14] The family was indeed of Welsh extraction, and its roots in England were probably shallow; Nicholas suggests that David Lloyd was himself born and bred in Flintshire, Wales, but 'when he came over, and how long or where he abode before he came to Leckford' he could not be certain.[15]

George Sr was destined to follow in his father's footsteps. At the age of nine he was sent to Winchester College as a Chorister, and after suffering through 'a World of Hardness there under that Rigid Informator Dr Robinson',[16] he went up to Oxford, 'first To Trinity Coll[ege] [...] and fro[m] thence to Brazen Nose'.[17] After successfully taking his BA, Lloyd Sr returned to Hampshire to teach the sons of 'a Gentleman one Mr Helliar', before being called to the curacy of Hunton, part of the parish of Crawley, in 1622. This appointment signalled the beginning of a career characterized by hard work and scanty rewards. Nicholas continues,

> As his Means was but small, so his Work was not very great, the custome then being to preach but once a Month, wheras now in most places they preach twice a Day. He had been but few years at Hunton, but he was called to

---

[12] *Alumni Oxonienses*, ed. Joseph Foster, Vol. 3, 922; *CCEd* Person ID: 69019.

[13] Parenti parentatio, BODL, MS Rawl. D.1301/4.

[14] For instance, the original copy of his will: Bundles of original wills and sentences, surnames L–Z, proved January–February 1719, TNA, PROB 10/1569.

[15] Nicholas, clearly rather taken with the thought that his family descended from 'the Race of the old Britains', rebuked himself 'for not being more diligent' in inquiring about his grandfather's Welsh origins whilst his father was alive. He therefore 'leav[es] those things [...] as uncertain'. Indeed, he may have been mistaken, as *Oxonienses* gives his county of origin as Merioneth, Vol. 3, 922.

[16] Hugh Robinson DD (1583/4–1655) was made master of Winchester in 1613. He produced a number of textbooks for the use of pupils at the school, some of which enjoyed widespread popularity throughout the seventeenth century. A serial pluralist, he became canon of Lincoln in 1624/5 and archdeacon of Gloucester in 1634, before being ousted during the Civil Wars, *ODNB*.

[17] Again, this may be another error of Nicholas Lloyd's part. *Oxonienses* states that George Lloyd matriculated at Hart Hall on 20 June 1617, before proceeding to take his BA at Brasenose, Vol. 3, 924.

Officiate at Wonston hard by under Dr Love[18] Warden of the Colledge <neare Winton> and one of the Prebends there. Where as his stipend was more so also was his Work for he Preached not onely every Sunday once, but also Expounded, or preached a Lecture beside. In the year 1626. He took his degree of M[aste]r in the Arts – And In the year 1629 He was Married. Not long after which Dr Love died; and Dr Harris[19] succeeded him in the Wardenship, and might have so don also in his Parsonage, but that he preferred Mean Stoke[20] before it And therefore Dr Burby[21] Archdeacon of Winton had it by reason the Bishop[22] was his friend and after his kinsman.

This was to be the story of the elder George Lloyd's career; Nicholas paints him as a diligent and well-intentioned clergyman who never won the kind of preferment necessary for material success. Instead, he found himself trapped in margin and junior clerical positions, often subservient to younger men who purportedly treated him poorly. He remained a curate at Wonston for some twenty years, and 'was not negligent in his office', according to Nicholas, labouring to encourage his apparently recalcitrant parishioners in their observation of the faith. This proved to be a futile enterprise; like Saint Peter, Lloyd Sr 'toyled all night and caught nothing.'[23]

The travails of the Lloyd family worsened with the onset of the Civil Wars, during which the elder George Lloyd attempted to negotiate a path of judicious compromise between the warring factions, which seems to have attracted the enmity of both sides. He was deeply disturbed by the conflict and feared for the unity and preservation of the Church of England, so much so that 'upon a certain Fast-day praying for the Nation he burst out into Tears and could

---

[18] Nicholas Love DD (d.1630), rector of Chawton (1601), Meonstoke (1604), and Wonston (1615). As noted by Nicholas Lloyd, he was also headmaster and subsequently warden of Winchester College, and prebendary of Winchester Cathedral in 1610: see *Oxonienses*, Vol. 3, 940; *CCEd* Person ID: 84652. His son, Nicholas Love (1608–1682) was a regicide, *ODNB*.

[19] John Harris DD (1587/8–1658), warden of Winchester College (1630) and rector of North Crawley, Buckinghamshire (1621), prebend of Combe XII at Wells Cathedral (1622), and Meonstoke (1630): *ODNB*; *CCEd* Person ID: 13017.

[20] Meonstoke, Hampshire.

[21] Edward Burby or Burbie DD (d. *c*.1654), vicar of Canewdon, Essex (1627), rector of East Woodhay, Hampshire (1629), and Wonston (1631). He was also made canon and prebend of Winchester Cathedral in 1631: *Oxonienses*, Vol. 1, 211; *CCEd* Person ID: 89735.

[22] Richard Neile (1562–1640), an ally of Laud and holder of an unequalled six successive dioceses: Rochester (1608), Lichfield and Coventry (1610), Lincoln (1614), Durham (1617), Winchester (1628), and the archbishopric of York (1631), *ODNB*. Burby married one of his daughters, and as Nicholas Lloyd implies, enjoyed some preferment as a result.

[23] 'And Simon answering said unto him, Master, we have toiled all the night, and have taken nothing: nevertheless at thy word I will let down the net.' Luke 5:5.

INTRODUCTION 7

[pro]ceed no farther'. According to Nicholas, George Lloyd Sr was 'not Superstitious yet Loved to observe the Ceremonies of the church', was 'not profane, yet cared not for Innovation', and continued to wear his surplice and hood 'till they were both taken away'. In spite of this, he found himself accused of being 'against the King' – apparently a slander concocted by a disaffected parishioner. Then, when the living of the rector Dr Burby was sequestrated by the Parliamentarians – the parsonage house itself being used to billet troops – he 'suffered many things by the Parliament's Souldiers'. These trials and tribulations were too much for George Lloyd Sr, who had been 'alwaies before of a gracile and slender constitution', and he died of a fever on 20 November 1658, after catching a cold a few weeks earlier.

III

War, death, and civil unrest provided an uneasy backdrop for the upbringing of the Lloyd children. Beyond Nicholas and John, Lloyd had at least three more siblings. There was one more brother, Edward, who died of smallpox on 14 March 1655.[24] Very little information survives relating to Edward, but he was significant in one respect: he was the first Lloyd sibling to keep a diary. A page-long autobiographical memorandum written by Nicholas, preserved with his papers at the Bodleian, notes that in 1656 while visiting his family, he commenced a 'diarie, which I undertook by occasion of my Brother Edwards, who kept one of his' – perhaps in his memory.[25] Rather intriguingly, at the very bottom of the same page, there is a fragment of a diary entry, which reads '30 Augt within doing things in my Chambr. dined pd within at worke in my Chambr. after made a place for ye Ducks supt at pr. pd'. Who wrote these lines? This is the same system of abbreviations used by George Lloyd in his later London Diary; 'at pr.' means 'at prayers', and 'pd' means 'performed my devotion'. Perhaps the Lloyd brothers shared not only a tendency to keep diaries, but also a particular way of using abbreviation and narrating their experiences. Or,

---

[24] Interestingly, Nicholas Lloyd notes that Edward 'dyed at London of the Small Pox. He had before gon a great jorney for G[ene]rall Mountague into Walls [Wales] His death proved very greivous to his Father', BODL, MS Rawl. D.1301/4. Edward Montagu, 2nd earl of Manchester (1602–1671) had been a leading general on the Parliamentarian side during the First English Civil War. By 1655, however, he had long retired from public life after becoming disaffected with the Parliamentarian cause: Edward must have died serving him in a private capacity.

[25] BODL, MS Rawl. D. 32/1.

George Lloyd was making notes on Nicholas's papers – either way, it hints at a Lloyd diary which no longer survives. Work by Elaine McKay has found that early modern diarists rarely acted 'alone'; they usually began writing under the influence of family or wider social networks.[26]

George Lloyd also had an uncertain number of sisters, whose lives have unfortunately proven almost impossible to trace. Frustratingly, the births (and deaths) of Lloyd siblings are inconsistently entered in the Wonston parish registers; perhaps some were born elsewhere. The baptism of a Maria Floyd is recorded in the parish register for Wonston on 17 June 1632, but her funeral was subsequently entered on 27 April 1634.[27] Interestingly, there is one reference in the Colchester Diary to 'my sister Mary', presumably another sister born later and given the same name. Throughout the diary, Lloyd also makes reference to his correspondence with 'my sister Carless'.[28] This was almost certainly the surname of a married sister, or even a more distant in-law, since in the London Diary he regularly referred to in-laws in this way.[29] Another sister, Frances, is mentioned in a draft copy of Lloyd's will from 1717 as living in Cheriton, Hampshire in the early eighteenth century.[30] Most curious of all, however, is the fact the Lloyd wrote in his Colchester Diary about a 'sister' who appeared to be a small child. On a visit to Aynho, Northamptonshire, where he had temporarily resided before moving to Colchester, he described how he 'sate with my sister in my lap' whilst the rest of the household played at cards; two days later, he 'helpt dress my sister'.[31] This suggests that this 'sister' was very young indeed, but unfortunately he never provided any further explanation. It is, however, vanishingly unlikely that Lloyd's own mother, who had her first child in 1630, could have had young children in the 1670s. It is possible that she was a very young sister-in-law, or perhaps a cousin or niece. He also makes reference to a visit to 'my sister Mary' on the same trip.[32] The will of George's eldest brother Nicholas, who died on 27 November

---

[26] Elaine McKay, 'The diary network in sixteenth- and seventeenth-century England', *Eras*, 2 (2001), unpaginated.

[27] I am very grateful to Gina Hynard and Molly Hudson at the Hampshire Record Office for checking this source for me when I was unable to visit. Transcripts of the Wonston parish registers can be found at HRO, TRA348/1 and TRA348/2.

[28] Colchester Diary, **5 December 1677**.

[29] For example, see London Diary, **19 June 1712**. In this entry, he described going to meet 'Brother Walker', referring to his wife's brother, Richard Walker.

[30] Copy of the will of George Lloyd, of St Thomas, Southwark, gent., 15 May 1717, BODL, MS Rawl. D. 32, fos 24r–25v.

[31] Colchester Diary, **29** and **31 December 1676**.

[32] Ibid. **24 December 1676**.

1680, lists all of the surviving immediate members of the Lloyd family at that date. Unless Nicholas had seen fit to disinherit any close relatives, his (and George's) remaining family consisted of their brother John Lloyd, their sister Frances James with her son Nicholas (who was not yet of age), and somewhat surprisingly their mother, Jane Lloyd.[33] Unfortunately, the ultimate fates of most of these individuals remains obscure, but Frances is the only one of Lloyd's siblings who was still alive during his later diary in 1711.

Lloyd was educated at home by his father until 1651, when at the age of nine, he moved less than a mile to Hunton to attend the school where his father was master. In his teens, George followed his father and elder brother to Winchester College. One of the most intriguing and significant biographical facts about George Lloyd is that, of three brothers (leaving aside Edward, who died young), he was the only one not to be educated at the University of Oxford, attendance of which was a virtual family tradition. The reasons for this are unclear, but it is possible that, due to a combination of unfortunate circumstances, it was simply not convenient for him to attend university. The family's fortunes had been mixed for some years, and they certainly suffered with the death of the elder George Lloyd at the end of 1658; this was particularly bad timing for the diarist, since he was sixteen and approaching the age at which decisions about his future would have been made. In George's construction of his own lifestory, the death of his father was followed by the completion of his school studies, and immediately he 'designed to goe to Lond[on] to be an aprentice'.[34] Bad luck struck again, however; as a result of 'Richard Cromwell being out and times unsettled', Lloyd was forced to live at home with his mother until Michaelmas, 1659. He was then sent to nearby Crawley to live with Samuel Tomlins, a former chaplain of Richard Cromwell, who had been installed as rector there by the victorious Parliamentarians in 1655. According to Nicholas Lloyd, Tomlins had 'domineer[ed] over' George Lloyd Sr when he had served him as curate, making his final years a misery.[35] That the Lloyds turned to such an individual for help indicates just how difficult things must have been for the family. Lloyd remained with Tomlins until 1661, when, aged 18 or 19, Lloyd returned home 'in order to fitt me for a place for a Justices of the Peace his cleark

---

[33] Will of Nicholas Lloyd, LPL, VH 97/2/33v. The will also mentions that George Lloyd was living with Nicholas in 1680, nearly two years after the end of the Colchester Diary. Nicholas also made George the sole executor and overseer of his will.
[34] See [Autobiographical Preface], p. 39.
[35] BODL, MS Rawl. D.1301/4; Venn, John, and John A. Venn, *Alumni Cantabrigienses*, Vol. 1, part 4, 248.

but got none till October'. He then went to live with, and work for, one 'Mr May of Coldry'.[36]

Another explanation is that George was simply not a good enough student. John, a little over a year his junior, was able to go up to Oxford in 1662, and was fully admitted on 30 September 1663, at the age of nineteen.[37] Nicholas, more strikingly, had matriculated in May 1652, some two weeks short of his 22nd birthday. It seems unlikely, therefore, that the family would have considered George 'too old' to go to Oxford at the age of 19. Lloyd seems to have been the least intellectually distinguished of three Lloyd brothers.

In fact, there is a hint that George was self-conscious of this educational and even intellectual disparity. When, in 1682, John Lloyd found modest fame with the publication of his English verse rendering of the Song of Solomon, *Shir ha shirim, or, The Song of Songs*, George supplied a brief dedicatory poem – the only time, so far as I am aware, that he appeared in print. Its opening lines are suggestive:

Should my unhappy Muse Attempt to praise
Thy Sacred Poem, 'twould but harm thy Bays,
And blast that Laurel in its Virgin shew
Which Thunder, Storms, and Lightning ne'r could do.
Alas! my sorry, poor, thatcht-fence, about
Thy stately House, will Keep all Strangers out;
What Dainties can we there expect (they'l say)
Whither we'r led by Such an homely way?

Lloyd felt rather insecure about his social and educational status, and this insecurity is reflected in his diary. Throughout, an impression is formed of an individual preoccupied with self-improvement and the need to prove his social, cultural, and economic value. He seems to have relished his status as a highly literate citizen in Colchester, offering to teach adults in reading and writing at any opportunity, and even occasionally lecturing friends and neighbours on their moral[38] and religious choices, sometimes reading aloud from books to drive his message home.[39] At the same time, he obsessively strove to improve his physical appearance – on a budget – devoting hours

---

[36] See [Autobiographical Preface], p. 39. Almost certainly James May of Coldrey, Hampshire, son and heir of Sir Humphrey May and half brother to the more well-known Baptist May, a favourite of Charles II, *ODNB*.
[37] *ODNB*.
[38] **17 January 1676**.
[39] **25 March 1676**.

to mending and altering various garments, or making them almost from scratch himself, despite a lack of any formal training as a tailor. He was, in short, a man eager to telegraph his value, physically, intellectually, and culturally. In this respect, his diary bears comparison with other examples of life-writing produced by other ambitious young men in late seventeenth-century England, such as Roger Lowe,[40] or indeed Samuel Pepys.

Returning to the narrative of George Lloyd's life before the diary, he stayed with Mr May until February 1666, when he moved to London and 'lodged at Mr Eaglesfields by Warwick house near Chayring Cross'.[41] The diarist spent the next few years apparently in the employment of various gentlemen, and although it is unclear what exactly he was doing, it can be speculated with some confidence that he was a clerk to at least one JP, and perhaps later a servant, or private tutor. He mentions that he was once again employed by a Mr May; he was sent to live in his 'new house in St James's and took care of his things'. In August 1667, at the age of 25, he was afflicted with smallpox, and was apparently incapacitated until Christmas of the same year. His next move, after a brief lodging at Long Acre, was to Welham, Leicester, where he had gained 'a place with Mr Halford' in March 1668 'with the helpe of Mr Winsloe', probably as a servant. A few days after the diarist's arrival in Colchester in 1675, he mentioned recognizing the 'tapster' at the King's Head, who had been 'at Sir Will Halfords with Sir John Pretyman when I was with Sir Will'. The following day, the diarist 'wrote a letter to Sir Will Halford to let him know I woud wayt on him'.[42] Sir William Halford of Welham married Elizabeth Pretyman, daughter of Sir John Pretyman, 1st Baronet, in 1663; it seems plausible that he, or a relative, was the diarist's former employer.[43] In 1669, Lloyd went 'to live with Mr Cockain my Lord Cullens son at Harborough', probably as a tutor to Charles Cockayne, the future 3rd Viscount Cullen.

Lloyd stayed there until 1674 or 1675, and proceeded to stay with his brother Nicholas at Aynho, Northamptonshire, and at his new living at Newington Butts. During this time, Lloyd received tuition from the well-known calligrapher and mathematician Edward Cocker[44] (1631/2–1676) 'learning som knacks in writting and Arithmatic', and paid him the substantial sum of £10. On 19 August 1675, he

---

[40] William L. Sachse (ed.), *The Diary of Roger Lowe of Ashton-in-Makerfield, Lancashire, 1663–74* (London, 1938).
[41] See [Autobiographical Preface], p. 40.
[42] Lloyd, **25** and **26 August 1675**.
[43] G. E. Cokayne (ed.), *The Complete Baronetage*, Vol. 4 (Exeter, 1904), 195.
[44] *ODNB*.

set off from London to Colchester, from which point, in Lloyd's words, he provides 'a perfect account of my Actions etc.'

IV

The biographical catalyst for Lloyd's diary-keeping was his move to open a school in Colchester. The first thirty-three years of his life are rendered in a brief preface, whereas his life as a schoolmaster is documented on a daily basis for two and a half years. The nature and purpose of the school is, however, quite obscure. This is because the information provided in the diary relating to the school is almost impossible to corroborate due to a dearth of sources. Lloyd's school left no discernible documentary trace in the records of Colchester borough, and was also apparently unlicensed.[45] Going by what can be gleaned from Lloyd's educational background and the account provided by the diary, which depicts a fairly informal, small-scale arrangement which appears to have provided instruction in literacy and numeracy for young children (and perhaps calligraphy lessons for their parents and older siblings), I suggest that Lloyd's was probably a 'petty school', perhaps with a 'specialism' in calligraphy and penmanship.

In general, the quality of such institutions was not high: David Cressy has suggested that 'many petty teachers were little more than child-minders'.[46] Charles Poole, an experienced grammar school teacher writing in the 1630s, opined that

> The Petty-Schoole is the place where indeed the first Principles of all Religion and learning ought to be taught, and therefore rather deserveth that more encouragement should be given to the Teachers of it, then that it should be left as a work for poor women, or others, whose necessities compel them to undertake it, as a meer shelter from beggery.[47]

These were early 'elementary' educational institutions for younger children of 'middling' parents, which tended to be by their nature transient, informal, and, from the historian's perspective, often

---

[45] Lloyd, whose school in Colchester would have fallen under the jurisdiction of the Diocese of London, does not appear in the surviving lists of licences from the period: Diocese of London, Licensing papers, 1674–5, 1675–6, LMA, DL/A/B/051/MS10116/008, DL/A/B/051/MS10116/009. Lloyd is also absent from 'Abstracts of schoolmasters' licences from Vicar-General's books, 1627–1685', collated by J. A. Morris, esq., LMA, O/228/001.

[46] David Cressy, *Literacy and the Social Order: Reading and writing in Tudor and Stuart England* (Cambridge, 1980), 19.

[47] Charles Hoole, *A New Discovery of the Old Art of Teaching Schoole* (London, 1661), 28.

invisible, an issue which is exacerbated by the fact that most of their teachers gave 'fitful service'.[48] According to Cressy, 'school teaching could be a career, but it could also be undertaken begrudgingly as a lowly stopgap employment on the way to something else.'[49] Indeed, Lloyd is a perfect illustration of this; he stayed in Colchester from 19 August 1675, opened his school in September, closed for business on 28 September 1677, and left the town for good on 19 October, and may never have returned. The only source touching on Lloyd's school is his own diary, and he provides little context or exposition. In particular, he is peculiarly silent on what went on in the classroom. That said, he still includes a valuable account of the 'business' of running a seventeenth-century school. Whilst this section will serve as practical overview, designed to make the text of the diary more intelligible to readers, I believe that there is more material to be extracted by scholars primarily interested in the history of early modern education.

In Lloyd's own educational journey, the high point must have been his tuition under the famous writing master, Edward Cocker. One of Lloyd's particular 'specialities' appears to have been writing and calligraphy. It seems likely that his school was intended to fill a gap in the educational 'market', between the extremely basic literacy that a minority of children would have been able to acquire at home, and the more advanced learning available at the Colchester Free Grammar (now known as Colchester Royal Grammar School). The Grammar only admitted boys aged 8 and over, and required entrants to be able to read printed and written material and to write, and its teachers to have a university degree.[50] Interestingly, throughout the diary, Lloyd made no reference whatsoever to Colchester Grammar, nor to its master at the time, James

---

[48] Ibid. 52. See also Rosemary O'Day, 'Church records and the history of education in early modern England 1558–1642: A problem in methodology', *The History of Education*, 2 (1973), 115–132.

[49] David Cressy, 'The drudgery of schoolmasters: The teaching profession in Elizabethan and Stuart England', in W. Prest (ed.), *The Professions in Early Modern England* (London, 1987), 129.

[50] According to one source, in spite of the efforts of the borough assembly to protect Colchester Grammar from competition, by the later 17th-century dissatisfaction with that school's curriculum, its religious bias, and its low teaching standards prompted the opening of several boys' schools. It is possible, then, that Lloyd was attempting to fill a different gap in the market, and compete with the grammar school, *VCHE*, Vol. 9, 352. For a brief study of the history of Colchester Grammar with a focus on the eighteenth century, see David Tomlinson, ' "Young gentlemen are at a reasonable rate to be boarded": An account of the Free Grammar School, Colchester c.1690–c.1820', *The Transactions of the Essex Society for Archaeology and History*, 4th ser., 4 (2013), 158–176.

Cranston.[51] Lloyd probably did not consider the grammar to be 'competition': in fact, he may have provided some form of tuition (perhaps in calligraphy) to a handful of its pupils.[52] He did, however, take an interest in the work – namely calligraphic 'peeces' – and premises of other keepers of small schools.

Upon his arrival in Colchester, Lloyd immediately set about searching for premises for his school. At the same time, he also searched for private lodgings for himself, and this makes it difficult to disentangle the two projects. Whilst Lloyd's brother Nicholas appears to have known a member of the local clergy,[53] the diarist had no connection to Colchester, and no prior arrangements had been made for the foundation of his school. His efforts appear to have been informal, amateurish, and indeed rather stressful.[54] In the event, he opened his school in the room above a local shop of some sort, owned by a Mr Meadows, who 'let me his roomes for 5li the year for 6 months'. It is worth noting that by October of the same year, Lloyd had haggled Meadows down to £4 per annum, suggesting that barely more than a month into his project, finances were already a problem. On the same day that he secured a room, Lloyd went and 'bought 3 bords to make a table and 2 for formes and bespeake a frame for my peece'.[55] Several of the entries from this period refer to constant work on a 'peece', or 'peeces', – almost certainly works of calligraphy to advertize his skills – and a few days later, Lloyd ordered another frame, and then went to ask for official permission from the mayor 'to keepe a schoole'. He received the mayor's blessing, and two days later, he 'nayld my peeces of writing to the frames and hung one out at the doore of my schoole and the other at the Coffee house'.[56]

The school, it seems, got off to a slow start. It officially opened for business on 6 September 1675.[57] Early that morning, one 'Goodman Bell' brought his son for Lloyd 'to learne'; he made the boy a book, 'and began with him'. Two weeks later, Lloyd 'sent [his] scholler home' at the end of the day, and it appears he still had only a single pupil by 1 October. Uptake appears to have been picking up by January 1676, but, beyond Lloyd's scattered mentions of

---

[51] Geoffrey Martin, 'The history of Colchester Royal Grammar School', *The Colcestrian*, NS, 131 (1947), 17.
[52] Namely the sons of a William Coleman: see **31 October 1675**.
[53] **20 August 1675**.
[54] **23 August 1675**.
[55] **31 August** and **1 October 1675**.
[56] **2** and **4 September 1675**.
[57] Lloyd had arrived in Colchester on **19 August 1675**.

initial recruitment to his school, there is little reference to numbers of pupils, or the success of his enterprise in general, until much later in the diary. In June 1677, shortly before Lloyd closed the school, a 'fayre' was held at Colchester, and Lloyd complained that as a result, he 'had but 4 boys' to teach, and the following day only '5 or 6 boys' by the first recess at 11.[58] Since this must have been remarkably low turnout in order to elicit repeated mention by Lloyd, one can surmise that, after about a year and a half of operation, his school probably had pupils in the double digits – perhaps in the teens or twenties. This phrasing also suggests that, whilst Lloyd clearly tutored young women, the school itself was not co-educational.

This 'after hours' tuition probably focused either on more advanced skills in penmanship and calligraphy,[59] or on improving the basic literacy of local adults or adolescents. Less than a fortnight after his arrival in Colchester, Lloyd had agreed to teach Elizabeth Edlin to read for twenty shillings. She was presumably a relative of the joiner he had hired to build his tables and 'frame his "peeces" '. Since she solicited his services and bargained for a price herself, it seems likely that she was at least older than elementary school age, if not an adult, and Lloyd continued to teach other adults literacy skills of varying levels as a sideline during his time in Colchester.[60] Lloyd also gave regular lessons to his landlady, Mrs Stratton, in both reading and writing, and listening to her reading aloud each night (probably from a psalm or other scripture) almost seems to have become a kind of bedtime 'ritual'.[61] He also taught a number of other local people, and he seems to have taught as many (if not more) women than men.[62]

Ultimately, however, Lloyd's school was an unsuccessful enterprise. The reasons for this are not entirely clear, owing primarily to Lloyd's opaque style of diary-keeping, and his evident reluctance to document his failures and mistakes in detail. In brief, on 13 December 1675, Lloyd met a 'Mr Ardrey', and promised to 'learne

---

[58] **25** and **26 June 1676**.

[59] For instance, he taught italic and 'church' hand to an Isaac Bloome, **25 September**, **1** and **5 October 1677**. Lloyd first offered his services on **20 September**, after apparently only having met him a few days previously. Bloome was at least partially literate as he had seemingly written a play for Lloyd's pupils, **12 September 1677**.

[60] **2 September 1675**.

[61] The first instance of this occurred on **5 September 1675**. By the 26th, he was listening to his landlord's reading too. He also gave her some instruction in writing, **5 May 1676**.

[62] One such pupil was Susan Wheeler, for whom he wrote out 'peeces' to test her literacy, **7 April 1676**.

him to write'.[63] The two developed a friendship, with Lloyd spending more and more time visiting Ardrey's house. By April 1676, Ardrey had evidently proposed that they went into business together, and commenced searching for new (presumably larger) premises for a school,[64] and on 16 September 1676, they rented a new set of rooms. At the same time, Lloyd agreed to move out of his lodgings, and into Ardrey's house. This was a poor decision; by reneging on his agreements without notice with his domestic and commercial landlords (a Mr Stratton and Mr Meadows, respectively) he managed to infuriate both of them simultaneously. The following day, Stratton threatened to sue Lloyd, apparently over a mysterious dispute concerning a horse.[65]

This rather abrupt and ultimately disastrous move is, frustratingly, never adequately explained by Lloyd. Indeed, one fact makes it downright puzzling: Lloyd discovered, just before he moved his school and lodgings, that Mr Ardrey was in fact a violent and abusive alcoholic. Lloyd had to physically restrain him from murdering his wife and maidservant only a few days before he moved into Ardrey's home.[66] Diary entries from the period when Lloyd boarded with Ardrey regularly note, with evident displeasure, the drunken state in which he returned home in the evenings – or went missing.[67]

Lloyd's social and economic prospects in Colchester were clearly dimming. During this period, several of the names regularly mentioned in a social context in the first half of the diary appear with much less frequency: evidently, Lloyd had done damage to his

---

[63] This individual proved extremely difficult to identify. Ardrey is not a common name around Colchester (or anywhere) and I have found almost none of the usual identifying traces in or around Essex. On 14 September 1675, a girl named Margaret was baptized, and her parents were recorded as 'William Ardrey and Elizabeth' (ERO, D/P 138/1/7). In the diary, on **12 September 1677**, by which time Lloyd was living in the Ardrey household, Lloyd noted in passing that it was 'Peggis birthday'. Later, Lloyd also mentions reading a sermon 'of Mr Ardreys Father's (**30 June 1677**). It is likely therefore that the man Lloyd knew was William Ardrey, son of John Ardrey (d.1684), rector of Cliburn, Westmorland, from 1657 until his resignation in 1673, rector of Great Musgrave (1671–1684) and vicar of Kirkland, Cumberland, now Cumbria (1681–1684): see B. Nightingale, *The Ejected of 1662 in Cumberland and Westmorland: Their Predecessors and Successors*, Vol. 2 (Manchester, 1911), pp. 1118, 1243; *CCEd* Person ID: 61586. His will leaves £100 to 'Margratt Ardrey daughter to my son William Ardrey', but William himself is not otherwise mentioned, suggesting that he was dead or disinherited by 1684: see Will and inventory of John Ardrey, rector, of Great Musgrave, Westmorland, Carlisle Archive Centre, PROB/1684/WINVX4. Why Ardrey was in Colchester, and his ultimate fate, remains a mystery.
[64] **7 April 1676**.
[65] **29** and **30 September 1676**.
[66] **18 September 1676**.
[67] **20 November 1676**, **12 February 1677**.

INTRODUCTION 17

own reputation. On 1 January 1677, during a visit to his brother in Aynho, Nicholas gave him £5 and persuaded him to move to Newington Butts to stay with him. Lloyd appears to have reluctantly accepted, but ultimately returned to Colchester, perhaps to give things one final go.

At the same time, in 1677 Stratton did indeed commence proceedings against Lloyd.[68] He attempted to talk Stratton down, but to no avail.[69] After initial efforts to hire attorneys seemingly came to nothing, Lloyd and Stratton agreed to an informal process of mediation, and their case was never heard in court.[70] On 22 August 1677, at the home of a Mrs Jackson, a Mr King and a Mr Phillips arbitrated and determined that Lloyd should pay Stratton £20 for the disputed horse, '7^s and 6^d for other things', and settle an outstanding bill with another neighbour. This was the final straw. On 25 September, Lloyd visited another local schoolmaster, Mr Delight, 'and told him I was to leave the towne'. Then, rather dramatically, at the end of the school day on Friday 28 September, he 'broke of schoole and told my boyes I should never keepe schoole any more'. The ensuing days were spent attempting to collect payments from his pupils' parents. On 19 October 1677 he left Colchester for London.

V

The end of his school also spelt the end of Lloyd's Colchester Diary. It continued for a few months until 1 February 1678, by which time George had moved to Newington, Southwark, to reside with his brother Nicholas. Perhaps, since his attempt at establishing himself in Colchester seems to have ended in failure, he felt that there was no longer any point in documenting his actions. Perhaps life was simply too busy. The most tantalizing possibility, of course, is that he continued keeping a diary, which sadly no longer exists. Either way, Lloyd continued to make impressions in the historical record between his diaries, which allows us to trace the major developments of his life in these intervening years.

When Lloyd moved to Colchester and opened his school at the age of 33, he was (unhappily) a bachelor. By the time the diary ended, aged almost 36, he was still unmarried. Lloyd had, before and during

---

[68] **9 July 1677**.
[69] **11 July 1677**.
[70] **18 August 1677**. Cf. *Pepys*, Vol. 4, 351–352 for Pepys's out-of-court settlement of a Chancery case which he had waged against his cousin Thomas Trice; the venue here was a tavern.

his days in Colchester, attempted a number of courtships, with varying degrees of success. During the diary, he maintained a correspondence with his 'deare Mrs Gray' and paid visits to her in London throughout. Theirs was a rather tumultuous on-again-off-again relationship, probably owing to Lloyd's physical distance, and his wandering eye. According to a letter of 25 October 1676 they had 'miscarried', but by 10 November that year, Gray 'declared her affection' for Lloyd yet again. Later, in another letter received on 4 August 1677, Lloyd 'received a letter from Mrs Gray in which she tould me she understood all things were at an end betweene us'. Rather pathetically, however, when Lloyd arrived back in London after leaving Colchester, his first act was to deck himself out in a brand new 'Brusells Camlet Coate', purchase a barrel of oysters and a carnelian ring, and produce these tokens before Mrs Gray in an attempt to win her back.[71] He was at least temporarily successful; by 28 November 1677, by which time Lloyd was living in Newington, he 'stayd all night' with Mrs Gray.

It is worth noting here that the inconstancy of Lloyd resulted from his sudden proximity in Colchester to two single, and rather eligible, sisters who lived in the village of Dedham, Elizabeth and Mary Lynford. They were, in fact, the sisters of Thomas Lynford (bap. 1650–1724), a clergyman who would later be made Doctor of Divinity and chaplain-in-ordinary to William III.[72] Their father had died before the Restoration, and it seems they were living with a guardian in Dedham. Lloyd may have known the sisters before his move to Colchester, but he clearly knew he was acting rather dishonourably, frequently referring to the sisters, particularly their correspondences with him, using the slightly pretentious sobriquets *Philoclea* and *Pamela*, the daughters of the Duke Basilius in Sydney's *Arcadia* (1593).[73] Certainty is difficult, but there are some hints in the diary that 'Philoclea' (the primary subject of his affection) was Mary, while Elizabeth was 'Pamela'.[74] Whilst he was writing love-letters to Mrs Gray, Lloyd was fawning over the sisters, eventually managing to finagle his way into staying overnight at their home, culminating in this heady passage:

---

[71] **22 October 1677**.

[72] *ODNB*. In fact, Lloyd attended Thomas Lynford's sermons in his London Diary in 1712: **18** and **25 May 1712**. Thomas Lynford's will, proved 22 August 1724, was witnessed by a Philip Oddy; the same individual also witnessed Lloyd's will, being a distant in-law.

[73] The first use of this name is on **7 September 1675**, suggesting he probably already knew them. His first meeting with them (in the diary) was on **30 December 1675**, in Cambridge.

[74] See **1 August 1677**.

Thursday, 5 July [1677]: [...] went into the garden see [*sic*] them play at ninepins went in eat som super playd till after 10 [p.m.] and was about to com home but I stayd all night after 12 went to our chamber the young Ladys went in with us[75] I Kisst them both upon my bed I went to bed had but little or no sleepe at 4 I rose went into Mrs Lynfords chamber and stayd till almost 7 sate by her beds side and Kist her several times more than I ever did dressed myselfe performed my devotion eat som breakfast stayd till after 8 came home after 9 went to school stayd till after 11 came in lay downe till 12 went to diner

The evident significance of this night to Lloyd is evident in the fact that this is the only point in the diary, excluding major disruptions such as severe illness or travel by sea, that the orderly stream of daily entries is interrupted, and one day bleeds into the next. Lloyd's rather careless attitude toward both the young women he was pursuing, and to his school-teaching responsibilities, is difficult to ignore.

Lloyd energetically tried to impress and win the favour of the two sisters for several months, and the diary provides an interesting insight into aspects of courtship in the late seventeenth century, bearing comparison to texts such as the diary of Roger Lowe or the 'courtship narrative' of Leonard Wheatcroft.[76] Lloyd's diurnal style places a focus on the material side of courtship, with a particular emphasis on day-trips, holidays, and gifts.[77]

For reasons which are not entirely clear, however, Lloyd's courtship of Mary or Elizabeth (or both) floundered in the final months of the diary, with the latter sister marrying his acquaintance, an apothecary named Thomas Lardner.[78] Rather strangely, Lloyd wrote that he officiated at a kind of mock betrothal service. This failure may have been related to Lloyd's apparently social and economic fall from grace in Colchester more generally; notably, Lloyd's efforts to win the sisters' favour intensified during this period.

Failure to win the heart of either Lynford sister may not have mattered too much to the diarist. The evidence is not definitive, but on 2 January 1682, a George Lloyd married a Frances Graye at the

---

[75] It is not clear from the diary who else was in the room other than George, Mary, and Elizabeth.

[76] George Parfitt and Ralph Houlbrooke (eds), *The Courtship Narrative of Leonard Wheatcroft, Derbyshire Yeoman* (Reading, 1986).

[77] See, for instance, a trip to Ipswich on **25 July 1677**, or Lloyd's efforts to procure one of the sisters a watch, commencing **21 June 1677**.

[78] Thomas Lardner's will was proved in 1703, at which time Elizabeth was still alive; he appointed Thomas Lynford overseer. TNA, PROB 11/470/146. Elizabeth's own will was proved in 1723. Mary is unmentioned and had presumably predeceased her, TNA, PROB 11/594/278.

church St Mary, Newington Butts – the church where Nicholas Lloyd had ministered and was buried.[79] This may have been a coincidence, but I think it unlikely. Almost nothing can be known about the married life of George and Frances, except that it was brief, and ended in tragedy. On 27 September 1685, a child named Frances, daughter of George and Frances Lloyd, was baptized at the church of St Giles-in-the-Fields.[80] Sadly, on 2 October Frances Lloyd of Drury Lane was buried at the same church.[81] Then, on 29 October 'Frances of George Lloyd', of White Hart Corner on Drury Lane was also buried.[82]

Lloyd married again, at the age of 45. His wedding to Elizabeth Winter, née Walker, a widow, took place at the church of St Swithin, London Stone on 9 July 1687.[83] Elizabeth must have had at least one child from her first marriage, as she left her 'grandson George Winter Fifty pounds and my Silver Tankard' in her will, which was proved at the Prerogative Court of Canterbury.[84] Lloyd married Elizabeth almost a decade after the end of his first surviving diary, and more than two before the commencement of his second, so we know little about the early circumstances or nature of their marriage. However, all the evidence suggests that they never had any children, a fact which is not altogether surprising since this was a late-in-life marriage for Lloyd at least, and probably for his new wife also. Unfortunately, it seems that Elizabeth was rarely at the forefront of George's mind when he sat down to keep his diary, and she is merely referred to in passing as 'my wife' (never by name), when Lloyd saw fit to mention that he had taken her along on a social or business call. He never wrote in detail about the nature of their relationship, but it does appear to have been an affectionate and important one. The only 'deeper' references to his married life come in the form of expressions of regret and remorse when he and Elizabeth argued, and worried documentations of her physical ailments.[85]

---

[79] See parish register, St Mary, Newington Butts, 1668–1731, LMA, P92/MRY/007.
[80] Baptism register, St Giles-in-the-Fields, 1637–1924, P82/GIS/A/02.
[81] Burial register, St Giles-in-the-Fields, 1636–1859, LMA, P82/GIS/A/04.
[82] Ibid.
[83] Parish register of St Swithin London Stone with St Mary Bothaw, LMA, P69/SWI/A/002/MS04312, p. 173. Elizabeth's previous marriage was probably to a Richard Winter, and took place on 29 October 1668 at St Giles, Camberwell: Composite register, St Giles, Camberwell, 1557–1750, LMA, P73/GIS/125.
[84] Will of Elizabeth Lloyd, widow of St Dunstan in the East, City of London, proved 11 June 1719, TNA, PROB 11/569/85. The will also confirms Elizabeth's maiden name to be Walker.
[85] For instance, on **29 March 1711**, Lloyd had 'words with my Wife for Nothing to both our great griefe'. See also London Diary, **23 March 1712**, for another argument which caused Lloyd 'trouble and sorrowe'.

VI

Among Lloyd's other chief personal upheavals during this time were the deaths of his two surviving brothers, Nicholas and John, in 1680 and 1682 respectively.[86] The death of Nicholas, in particular, must have been deeply upsetting. Nicholas's will makes clear the strength of their relationship; 'my Brother George Lloyd now dwelling with mee' received almost all of his older brother's estate and was made sole executor and overseer, while John, who had a vocation in common with Nicholas, inherited a number of books, including a 'Polyglot Bible contaning six Volumes'.[87] The depth of George's grief is evident in his stern reply to a letter from Richard Berry, a clergyman whom Nicholas had previously helped to obtain a post at Lincoln Cathedral, but who had neglected to write to express his gratitude to his benefactor. When Berry eventually wrote to Nicholas not with thanks but with requests for yet more favours, his letter arrived after the latter's death on 27 November 1680. After rebuking Berry for his 'forgetfullness, or rather ingratitude' and the offence it caused Nicholas, George moves to vividly and emotively describe his brother's decline and death:

> ... toward the latter end of July he was seized with the feavour so Comon this sumer, and after a Moneth was a little recovered and able to goe abroad, but not often, and then he had the griping of the gutts very violently, and the yellow Jaundice which kept him in the most part of September and October and quite tooke away his stumack and at the beginning of November had an Ague and then the scurvey and as the Doctors say a dropsy in the stumack, (which I understand Not) for he was so far from any swelling, that he was wasted away to nothing, and for all that Month scarce eat tooke anything but what came from Doctors that so he was by degrees brought to that Condition that death had little to do, for on November 27th, Saterday morning about 11 he rendered his body to the power of death and his soule to the hands of his gratious Creatour and Mercifull Redeemer after 3 faint groans, sensibly speaking not above a Minute before and has left all his friends to bewayle the loss of so great a scholler so good a Man and true a Friend, but the assurance of our loss is his gaine is the only ingredient can help to sweeten so severe a dispensation of providence[88]

---

[86] The cause and circumstances of John's death are unclear, except that he died at Southampton on 31 August 1682, apparently without a will, *ODNB*.

[87] Will of Nicholas Lloyd, LPL, VH 97/2/33v.

[88] BODL., MS Rawl. D. 32, fo. 22. Whilst any kind of definitive historical 'diagnosis' is beyond me, Nicholas Lloyd's symptoms (fever, severe digestive problems, jaundice, and recrudescence), the timing of the onset of his illness (summer), and his living near a large, unsanitary body of water (the Thames) are all indicative of malaria, which was still a major cause of death in England in the seventeenth century. See P. Reiter, 'From Shakespeare to Defoe: Malaria in England in the Little Ice Age', *Emerging Infectious Diseases*, 6 (2000), 1–11.

Nicholas's death proved to be a watershed event in George's life. Now almost in his forties, Lloyd could no longer retreat beneath his older brother's wing: a dependable livelihood was required.

VII

To that end, on 22 February 1681, the diarist, styling himself 'George Lloyd, gentleman', petitioned the Treasury 'for the Office of Surveyor, Landwayter or Searcher or other Imploy in the Customs', and supplied a 'Certificate of his fitnesse'.[89] Work by John Brewer on the backgrounds and motivations of individuals who applied to work as revenue officers in the early modern civil service shows that Lloyd was, in fact, a typical candidate.[90] Applicants for positions in the revenue offices in the late seventeenth and eighteenth centuries were more often 'tradesmen who had fallen on hard times or members of that group best described as "shabby genteel" than men who had risen from the bottom of society.' It was, in other words, an 'escape route or fall-back'.[91] Lloyd had already lived an entire lifetime pursuing a different calling – service, tutoring, and teaching – and now he had decided to start from the bottom in a new profession.

Brewer's work shows that Lloyd's background placed him in an ideal position to apply. Most revenue officers needed to be skilled in 'penmanship, mathematics, and bookkeeping', since their job was based on (amongst other things) calculating and recording the taxable values of goods. Indeed, another eighteenth-century 'autobiographer' (for his texts did not quite constitute a diary), John Cannon (1684–1743), followed a career trajectory which was a mirror image of Lloyd's, using his basic, non-university education to become an officer in the Excise, and then, 'like so many others' according to Brewer, drawing on the same skill set to open a small local school and work as a scrivener when he was ejected from his post.[92]

---

[89] Treasury Reference Book of Applications, 1680–1682, TNA, T 4/1, p. 225.

[90] John Brewer, 'Servants of the public – servants of the Crown: Officialdom of eighteenth-century English central government', in J. Brewer and E. Hellmuth (eds), *Rethinking Leviathan: The Eighteenth-Century state in Britain and Germany* (Oxford, 1999), 127–147. Brewer's primary focus throughout the essay is Excise rather than Customs officers, and there were some key differences between the two roles. However, there were also many similarities, and most of the points Brewer makes also apply to Customs men.

[91] Brewer, 'Servants of the public', 129. For a classic account of the seventeenth-century 'pseudo-gentry', see Alan Everitt, 'Social mobility in early modern England', *Past and Present*, 33 (1966), 56–73.

[92] Brewer, 'Servants of the public', 132–133. Cannon's 'chronicle', which combines elements of diary-keeping and retrospective autobiography, has recently been published in

INTRODUCTION 23

Brewer points out that the abilities in basic literacy and numeracy were often emphasized in letters of recommendation for applicants to the service, and this was almost certainly true of Lloyd. Whilst the original copy of the petition he sent to the Customs no longer survives – likely casualties of a catastrophic Custom House fire in 1814, which destroyed almost all of the institution's records before this point – a copy of the 'Commissioners of the Customs Report' relating to his application for a post can be found in a Treasury 'Reference Book' from the period. The opinion of Commissioners Francis Millington, John Upton, and Charles Cheyne, the men who assessed the application of 'Mr Georg Lloyd' on 16 March 1681, was as follows:

> it appeares That the Petitioner is a person of great integrity and honesty and very well skilled in writing and the method of accounts and we judge him fitt for a land Carriage man Coast Waiter or a landwaiters place in an out port when a vacancy shall happen in either of the sayd imployments[93]

Ultimately, Lloyd was appointed to a position at London Port, rather than one of the less significant 'out ports', in March 1682.[94] He was appointed to the office of 'Coast Waiter', one of lesser seniority than those to which he had applied, but which provided a reliable income of £40 per annum, plus fees and gratuities.[95]

What was a Coast Waiter? A contemporary definition runs:

> These Officers take Care of the Coasting Vessels, as to the landing and loading of their Goods, in the same Manner as the Searchers, the Land- Waiters,

two excellent volumes edited by John Money. John Money (ed.), *The Chronicles of John Cannon, Excise Officer and Writing Master*, 2 vols (Oxford, 2010).

[93] Treasury Reference Book, TNA, T 4/1, pp. 507–508.

[94] Treasury book of out-letters to the Board of Customs and Excise, 1681–1684, TNA, T 11/8, p. 74. An 'out port' was any port at which shipping was subject to Customs outside the Port of London.

[95] Land Waiters – who dealt with goods imported from abroad – received the same salaries as Coast Waiters, but were far busier, and so hypothetically had higher earning potential through fees charged to merchants in the discharge of their service. There were, however, many more Land Waiters than Coast Waiters, increasing competition between officers; it was therefore a higher risk/reward position: Elizabeth Hoon, *The Organization of the English Customs System, 1696–1786* (New York, 1938), 141. Searchers were responsible for certifying the shipping of goods for export and ensuring that the correct duty had been paid; Hoon describes the Searchers as 'the central officer of the export department', an office which required 'the utmost skill and integrity', ibid. 145. There were many different types of surveyor in the Customs, and they were equivalent to something like a modern 'manager': thus, there were Surveyors of the Land Waiters, Tide Waiters, Coast Waiters, and so on. Typically, such officers were promoted from the ranks of the offices they were to oversee, Edward Carson, *The Ancient and Rightful Customs: A History of the English Customs Service* (London, 1972), 52.

and King's-Waiters, do of the Vessels exporting and importing the Goods to and from foreign Parts.[96]

To put it more simply, the primary responsibility of the Coast Waiter was to supervise the landing and shipping of domestic goods moved by vessels travelling along the coast, and ensure that these goods were not then surreptitiously redirected for foreign export, in order to evade paying the relevant duties. In the early eighteenth century there were seventeen Coast Waiters at London Port.[97] Whilst the revenues from duties on the movement of goods coastwise were small in comparison to those generated by foreign trade, the transport of such goods was still vitally important to the English (and after 1707 the British) economy. Coastwise trade to and from London was particularly significant as a result of the capital's role as the major centre for the distribution of goods and services around the rest of the country.[98] Lloyd, as one of only seventeen individuals supervising the bulk of coastwise trade around the British Isles at the beginning of the eighteenth century, was a man of some responsibility, albeit in a fairly junior role. In the scanty history of the daily workings of the early modern English Customs, only Elizabeth Hoon has provided anything resembling a detailed account of the primary duties of Lloyd and his fellows, which were too byzantine to fully recount here.[99] In sum, the office of Coast Waiter required literacy, numeracy, the ability to accurately assess the weights and qualities of diverse cargoes, and, perhaps most importantly, personal integrity – if this was lacking, the coastwise trade was vulnerable to fraud at multiple points. Lloyd was judged, rightly or wrongly, to possess all of these attributes.

This was to be Lloyd's primary employment for the rest of his life.[100] By the time of his London Diary he appears to have worked

[96] Anon., *Rules of the Water-Side, or, The General Practice of the Customs* (London, 1715), BL, C.194.a.962, p. 88.
[97] Carson, *Ancient and Rightful Customs*, 53.
[98] Hoon, *Organization*, 264.
[99] Ibid. 265–269. Hoon's account is based on Henry Crouch, *A Complete Guide to the Officers of His Majesty's Customs* (London, 1732), 11–17, 21–25, 28, and Thomas Daniel, *Ductor Mercatorius, or, The Young Merchant's Instructor with respect to the Customs* (Newcastle, 1750), 41–42, 44.
[100] With a minor blip: in 1688 Lloyd was one of many civil servants dismissed from his position for refusing to subscribe to James II's repeal of the Penal Laws. He was replaced by one Henry Keates, Surveyor at Barking: William A. Shaw and F. H. Slingsby (eds), *Calendar of Treasury Books, 1660–1718*, Vol. 8 (London, 1923), p. 1949. In January the following year, after the so-called 'Glorious Revolution', Lloyd and some former colleagues petitioned to be restored to their former posts, arguing that 'there being now vacant two landwaiters' and one deputy searcher's places, the persons in them "being unqualified by law, having not received the Sacrament and taken the oaths and Test" for which the

at a reduced capacity; he did not attend the Custom House or wharfs every day, or indeed anywhere near it. The diary provides only intermittent detail about the specifics of his work, but where it does, context and explanation are provided in the notes. Overall, Lloyd's diary paints a picture of a service characterized by informality, a lax work ethic, and frequent 'double-jobbing', or at least the swapping of official responsibilities. This is an aspect of Customs business which is by definition poorly covered by more official forms of documentation – at least from the perspective of the officers on the ground. Lloyd's diary is a new and valuable source for specialists in the area to find a fresh perspective on this neglected but important aspect of the history of the development of the British state. Aside from a spell in Gravesend from 31 May until 27 June 1711, Lloyd clearly carried out his Customs duties inconsistently, rarely describing the kinds of duties expected of a Coast Waiter, such as boarding ships and inspecting cargoes. Instead, he attended meetings about establishing a new office for the Coast Waiters,[101] supervised groups of London watermen,[102] and sat with his colleagues at a number of local taverns.[103]

VIII

By 1711 Lloyd was collecting the salary of a Coast Waiter and transacting certain official Customs duties, but, as mentioned above, readers will notice that his diary suggests he was not spending the majority of his time sitting at the wharfs waiting to 'take' ships. What, then, was he doing? Lloyd had a busy social life; he visited friends, relatives, coffee houses, and taverns. He also continued to pursue a rich spiritual life, and frequently attended churches around the City of London. Readers will also, however, find themselves confronted with a host of opaque references to ostensibly professional commitments and appointments which bear no relation to the work of the Customs. This is because, like many early modern 'middling' Londoners, Lloyd had a number of 'sidelines', chief amongst which was his role as a rent broker, primarily in the service of one 'Lady Mathews'.[104]

---

petitioners have brought informations against them', ibid. p. 2161. Note that Lloyd did not actually end up as a Land Waiter or Deputy Surveyor. He petitioned the Commissioners of the Customs to be 'restored' in April 1689, and was returned to his post, at the expense of Keates, in July of the same year, ibid. Vol. 9 (London, 1931) 87, 175.

[101] For instance **31 December 1711**; **1 February 1712**.
[102] **12 November 1711**.
[103] **4**, **8**, **13**, and **19 December 1711**, amongst other instances.
[104] The first reference to 'my Lady' appears on the second page of the London Diary, in the entry for **9 January 1711**.

The fact that Lloyd's employer was a woman is noteworthy in itself in the overwhelmingly patriarchal world of early eighteenth-century London. In this male-dominated society, even socially elite widows were proportionately much less likely that their male counterparts to own substantial real property, as moveable goods were considered to be more appropriate legacies for women.[105] That said, Peter Earle's examination of insurance policies taken out by the fairly small number of financially independent women who operated in London during the period shows that 'widows quite clearly dominate the female property market'. Earle goes so far as to argue that, in late seventeenth- and early eighteenth-century London, 'a woman as a landlady must have been a common experience'.[106] The widowed Lady Mathews, formerly Anne Wolstonholme, was one such woman.[107] Her husband, Sir Philip Mathews of Great Gobbions, Essex, died intestate in 1685, and the precise details of how his estate was settled remain unclear.[108] Their son, Sir John Mathews, 2nd Bt, died unmarried and without issue, killed in 1708 at the Battle of Oudenarde in Flanders, where he was a Colonel under Marlborough. Curiously his will, hastily drawn up before his departure for Flanders, does not make reference to any real property, or to his mother.[109] It is, however, worth noting that evidence from litigation makes clear that it was Anne herself who brought much of the real property into the Mathews family estate; her 'considerable marriage portion' included land, tenements, and messuages on 'Barbican Street' in St Botolph without Aldersgate and St Giles without

[105] William C. Baer, 'Landlords and tenants in London, 1550–1700', *Urban History*, 38 (2011), 250.

[106] Peter Earle, *The Making of the English Middle Class: Business, Society and Family Life in London, 1660–1730* (London, 1989), 166–174.

[107] Anne, later Lady Mathews, was the eldest daughter of Thomas Wolstonholme, 2nd Bt, and his wife Elizabeth, daughter of Phineas Andrews of Denton Court, Kent: see W. Betham, *The Baronetage of England, or, The History of the English Baronets* (London, 1802), 361–364. Examples can be found spelling her married name 'Mathews' and 'Matthews'. I have chosen the former since it is in line with the spelling used by Lloyd, and indeed other manuscripts dating from the period.

[108] The intestate death of Sir Philip Mathews unsurprisingly resulted in litigation from his erstwhile creditors. The answer to one such suit, which is unfortunately too damaged to be entirely readable, suggests that in the 1680s, Lady Mathews was maintained by her dead husband's estate to the tune of £300 per annum. It was charged that Mathews had 'much incumbred himselfe and his estate by debts and not having made any will or provision for the payment of his debts hee left his affaires in great confusion'. I have not determined exactly how his estate was eventually settled, but it is clear that Lady Mathews was a wealthy landowner in her own right by the time of the diary. Atkinson v. Matthews, 1681, TNA, C 6/365/53.

[109] Will of Sir John Mathews of Saint Martin in the Fields, Middlesex, 7 July 1708, TNA, PROB 11/502/272.

Cripplegate. All of this, along with property 'formerly purchased [...] of Sir Peregrine Bertie' by her father-in-law, John Mathews, was settled upon Anne by her husband 'in full [*sic*] of her Jointure and in lien[110] of her Dower'.[111] By 1711, then, Lady Mathews was a relatively wealthy and substantial landowner in London.[112]

How Lloyd came to work for Lady Mathews cannot be definitively established. One potential link might be found in the will of Sir John Mathews, who left all of his moveable goods (which included a very substantial quantity of plate, jewellery, and various other luxury items) to a widow named Susannah Bird. The identity of this individual remains obscure, but there are several references in Lloyd's diary to visits to a female 'Cousin Bird'.[113] The most likely explanation for their association is that Lloyd had a family or social connection to Mathews. Another, admittedly more tenuous hypothesis is that Lady Mathews's family appears to have had an ancestral connection with the Customs. Her grandfather and great-grandfather had been farmers of the Customs prior to its transformation into a more modern, professionalized government department in 1671.[114]

Lloyd appears variously to have been Lady Mathews's accountant,[115] tenant manager, a kind of bailiff, a supervisor of construction work,[116] and even, at times, little more than an errand boy. This variety meant that Lloyd often moved rapidly between very varied social groups and contexts: one day he might be visiting his Lady's mansion in Windsor, or rendezvousing with a lawyer at the Inns of Court, the next, he could be 'amongst the tenants', trying, and often failing, to 'get money'.[117] In addition, Lloyd managed dealings between Lady Mathews and the authorities and stakeholders in the parishes in

---

[110] 'A right to retain possession of property (whether land, goods, or money) until a debt due in respect of it to the person detaining it is satisfied', *OED*.

[111] Mathewes v. Stone, 1712, TNA, C 8/654/26.

[112] The will of Lady Mathews, proved on 24 March 1736 (TNA, PROB 11/676/196) is unremarkable, leaving the bulk of her estate to her four granddaughters. However, a newspaper noted at the time that this estate was worth £40,000, *Daily Post*, 25 March 1736, issue 5158, BL, *Burney Collection*.

[113] London Diary, **31 July**, **6** and **30 September 1711**; **9 June** and **28 August 1712**. The visit on **6 September 1711** confirms that Bird was a woman; Lloyd visited 'her house' in Islington.

[114] Anne's grandfather, Sir John, 1st Bt, was a farmer of the Customs, and held a patent as Collector-Outwards at the Port of London. He died in 1670. In addition, her father was chosen a baron of the Cinque Ports, after marrying into the Andrews family of Gravesend. Betham, *Baronetage of England*, 361–364.

[115] **15 March 1712**.

[116] **24** and **25 January 1712**.

[117] For example, on one occasion Lloyd 'went to the Temple and Mett Mr Rowlandson and talked about my Ladys business', before immediately reporting back to his mistress. London Diary, **24 April 1711**.

which she held interests.[118] The complexities with which Lloyd had to deal are readily apparent in the following passage:

> within all day and Mr Sandford was with me and we adjusted the Accounts betweene my Lady and him my Lady allowing him 13^l.11^s for repayres he allowd 1 yeare and ½ Rent and paid 4^{li}.10^s for Mr Harris for a yeares Rent and I gave him a Noate for 6.10^s and he gave me a Receipt in full for his Bill of 50^l.3^s:11½^d there being 30^{li} paid before, and he gave me a Receipt for 13:11 for Repayres.[119]

Lloyd was a figure of considerable responsibility, both in the more cerebral, financial side of Lady Mathews's affairs, and in the day-to-day running of more practical activities.

Lloyd functioned as a kind of proxy between Mathews and her often impoverished tenants. Early modern urban tenant–landlord relations is a badly neglected area of research, perhaps owing to evidential difficulties; it is hoped that this volume may prove valuable to scholars attempting to redress this.[120] One of Lloyd's tasks documented extensively in the diary serves as a useful case study in understanding his role; his dealings with a pauper tenant named Richard Hedges. By coincidence, Hedges is actually one of the 'lives' featured in Robert Shoemaker and Tim Hitchcock's *London Lives* project.[121] Put very briefly, Hedges and his family resided at Vine Yard, a property owned by Lady Mathews, off Goswell Street. Although he no longer lived in the parish of St Dionis Backchurch, Hedges received relief from its churchwardens, and the diary shows that Lloyd was responsible for collecting it. In 1711, Hedges fell ill, and also seems to have come into conflict with the churchwardens and/or Lady Mathews. His relief was halted, and Lloyd attempted to evict him and seize his 'goods', but was unable to as Hedges was bedridden with illness.[122]

---

[118] One example being John Sandford, a member of the vestry for the parish of St Botolph Aldersgate, in which Mathews owned property. Sandford was upper churchwarden for the parish in 1700, and was still very active in the vestry by the period of the diary: see vestry minute book, St Botolph Aldersgate, 1679–1717, LMA, P69/BOT1/B/001/MS01453/003, fos 70–76 and *passim*.

[119] **26 November 1711**.

[120] Baer, 'Landlords and tenants in London', 234–255.

[121] *London Lives* was funded by the Economic and Social Research Council (ESRC) and resulted in a website with an online database and a monograph, Tim Hitchcock and Robert Shoemaker, *London Lives: Poverty, Crime and the Making of a Modern City, 1690–1800* (Cambridge, 2015). The article on Richard Hedges appears only on the website: see https://www.londonlives.org/static/HedgesRichard.jsp (accessed April 2022).

[122] Lloyd obtained a 'Noate' from the churchwardens of St Dionis permitting the eviction on **29 May 1711**, but does not appear to have attempted to carry it out until **13 October 1711**.

Interestingly, at exactly the same time, Mathews was in the process of trying to sell Vine Yard to the Commission for Building Fifty New Churches and, yet again, Lloyd was doing much of the work in organizing this transaction.[123] Lady Mathews had a plan and appraisal of the property drawn up in 1712, estimating its value at £1306, 10s.[124] In a petition to the Commissioners dated 18 October 1711, pursuant to a request by the Commission on 4 October, the Churchwardens and Vestry of St Botolph Aldersgate gave an account of their parish, which contained 705 households, and an estimated population of 'about Six thousand; a great many of which are so poor, that they receive Alms from the Parish'.[125] The parish was too big to be sustainable, in other words, and a new church would have to be built to share the ecclesiastical and social burden. As a result, the leaders of the parish suggested a couple of sites, including 'Vine Yard [...] which is the estate of the Lady Mathews, and an Estate of Sir George Newlands adjoyning thereto [...] which we conceive may be proper places for the Sight of a Church'.[126] Newlands, then an Alderman of London, was also a member of the Commission.[127] Amongst the signatories of the letter (most of whom formed the parish vestry) are some familiar names, namely 'John Sandford', and a 'William Briscoe', who may have been the owner of a plot shown annexed to Vine Yard on the plan, labelled 'Mr Briscow's wast Ground to be sold'. The vestry minutes for the parish note that on 12 October 1711, a sub-committee had been established 'to Search and Give an Account of Ground for Building a New Church', of which Sandford was a member.[128] Lloyd also collected

---

[123] For instance **19 December 1711**.

[124] Valuation of land and houses adjoining Cripplegate belonging to Lady Mathews, widow of Sir Philip Mathews, Bt, 20 December 1712, LPL, MS 2714, fo. 239; Plan of Vine Yard fronting Goswell Street and Fan Alley belonging to Lady Mathews, 1712, LPL, MS 2750, fo. 36.

[125] Memorial by the churchwardens and vestry of St Botolph Without Aldersgate, 18 October 1711, LPL, MS 2712, fo. 148.

[126] Memorial by the churchwardens and vestry of St. Botolph Without Aldersgate, 18 October 1711, LPL, MS 2712, fo. 148.

[127] Michael H. Port (ed.), *The Commission for Building Fifty New Churches: The Minute Books, 1711–27, a Calendar* (London, 1986), xxxiv.

[128] Vestry minute book, St Botolph Aldersgate, P69/BOT1/B/001/MS01453/003, fo. 110r. Interestingly, the vestry minutes for St Giles Cripplegate show that 'a Comittee to find a peece of Ground to build one or More Churches' was also established in that parish on 27 September 1711. They decided that three new churches would be necessary, one in the 'Freedom' (the part of the parish within the City) and two in the 'Lordship' (in Middlesex). Vine Yard was not put forward as an option. See vestry minute book, St Giles Cripplegate, LMA, P69/GIS/B/001/MS06048/001, fos 168v–169v. Cf. Petition by the minister and churchwardens of St. Giles Cripplegate, 13 November 1711, LPL, MS 2714, fo. 210.

relief money for Hedges from Thomas Briscoe, churchwarden of St Dionis.[129]

Mathews's sale was ultimately unsuccessful, and Hedges continued to receive intermittent relief, dying in 1715. The whole affair does, however, provide an interesting insight into the networks of interest and obligation which operated beneath the surface of the housing system in early eighteenth-century London – and it forms just one small part of Lloyd's activities as a rent-gatherer. I have only been able to reconstruct a handful of these examples for the purposes of this volume; much potential remains in the pages of the diary.

IX

Lloyd's second diary ends as abruptly as his first, at the end of August 1712. His final years can only be glanced fleetingly through a small number of archival traces. It seems his health may have failed progressively; a draft copy of a will, dated 1717 and written in his own hand, can be found with the papers of his brother Nicholas at the Bodleian. It indicates that by this time, George and Elizabeth were living at St Thomas, Southwark, rather than in the City.[130]

Near the end of 1718, 'Nicholas Wade of London Citizen and Leatherseller' petitioned the Lord of the Treasury, claiming that

> at this time Mr George Loyd who has been Employ'd in the office of a Coast Waiter for severall Yeares being dangerously Ill in so much that there is no hopes of his life and your Petitioner's Misfortunes in the world still Increasing upon him, his Necessitys oblige him once more to Request the favour of your Lordships that he may succeed the said George Loyd in the said office of a Coast Waiter In Case he shall happen to die or that your Petitioner May have the next Vacancy that shall happen.[131]

Wade was, in fact, probably a friend of Lloyd's: his London Diary contains several references to purchasing fabrics from, or socializing with, a 'Mr Wade'.[132] Whether Lloyd encouraged Wade to apply for his position, or was too ill to know anything about it, we cannot know.

Either way, the prediction of the petition proved accurate; Lloyd died some time in late December, 1718. The original copy of his

---

[129] **2 March 1711**. Briscoe was Upper Churchwarden for 1710: see vestry minute book, St Dionis Backchurch, LMA, P69/DIO/B/001/MS04216/002, p. 326.
[130] MS Rawl. D. 32, fos 24r–25v.
[131] The Humble Peticon of Nicholas Wade of London Citizen and leatherseller, TNA, T 1/219, fo. 75.
[132] **25 January 1711; 14 April 1712**.

will, dated 22 December 1718, bears a very shaky signature and is endorsed with his seal, an image of Charles I, whose martyrdom Lloyd carefully observed by fasting in the Colchester Diary.[133] Describing him this time as a 'Gentleman of St Dunstan in the East', it is a plain document of little interest, lacking even the expressions of repentance and faith often found in wills of this period – something of a surprise, considering the piety and devotion evident in the diary.[134] However, the will, which was proved in the Prerogative Court of Canterbury, makes clear that Lloyd's geriatric double-jobbing had, to some extent, paid off; he was clearly a man of comfortable means. Lloyd left £30 to his one surviving sibling, his sister Frances James, £100 to her eldest son Nicholas (about whom he complains in the London Diary[135]), and £50 each to her four younger sons. The entire remainder of his estate was left to Elizabeth, though the precise value of the bequest is not specified.[136] In the slightly longer draft will mentioned above, Lloyd also left almost everything to Elizabeth, so that

> she may not only enjoy the benefit of the Interest and produce thereof dureng her Life, but may also if she hath Occasion made use of so much of the Principal as shall be necessary for her more Comfortable subsistance and Maintenance, for which reason I have not thought fitt to prescribe any particular sum to my said Wife haveing an entire Confidence in her prudence and discretion.

In spite of these good intentions, Elizabeth lingered on for just a few months after George's death. Her own will, dated 7 May 1719 and proved in the Prerogative Court of Canterbury on 11 June, asks that she be buried in the same grave as her 'dear husband', at Camberwell.[137]

It must have been in these intervening months that Rawlinson obtained from a grieving Elizabeth her late husband's diaries and

---

[133] Bundles of original wills, TNA, PROB 10/1569.

[134] Historians have long made use of, and disagreed over, the evidence of religious preambles in early modern wills as indicators of piety and denominational 'allegiance', beginning with A. G. Dickens, *Lollards and Protestants in the Diocese of York* (Oxford, 1959). This methodology can be problematic, however, as such preambles were often formulaic and did not necessary reflect the specific religious convictions of the testator; Lloyd's own will can be seen as evidence of this. See James Alsop, 'Religious preambles in early modern English wills as formulae', *Journal of Ecclesiastical History*, 40 (1989), 19–27.

[135] **26 March 1711**. Nicholas James lived out his life as a yeoman in Cheriton, Hampshire, dying in 1741: see HRO, 1741P/122.

[136] Will of George Lloyd, Gentleman of Saint Dunstan in the East, City of London, proved 29 January 1719, TNA, PROB 11/567/206.

[137] Will of Elizabeth Lloyd, TNA, PROB 11/569/85.

the papers of his brother, to preserve them for posterity. George and Elizabeth fell quickly and deeply into obscurity, however, and this long, detailed, and dense diary has sat virtually unnoticed by generations of historians. I hope that by presenting the diary in this volume, future scholars will find much of interest in the mundane and unexceptional life of George Lloyd.

Note on the Manuscript

The diary of George Lloyd is bound into a tiny volume measuring approximately 16 cm by 10 cm, containing 119 folios of text. The autobiographical preface takes up the first folio and the second folio is blank. The first part of the volume – fos 3–77 – referred to here as the Colchester Diary, covers the period of Lloyd's life from 19 August 1675 to 1 February 1678 with mostly consistent discrete daily entries. The second part – fos 89–119 – referred to as the London Diary, 'resumes' without any explanation on 1 January 1711, and there are again consistent, discrete entries for each day. The handwriting in the first volume is truly minute, with each page often containing entries for five days, each of which may have ten or more lines. Difficulty increases as the reader moves down the page; perhaps to save on the expense of paper, Lloyd seems to have been keen to cram in as much material as possible, and so the handwriting becomes almost impossibly small in the final entry on each leaf. The larger handwriting and slightly more generous margins found in the London Diary probably attest both to his advanced age (we know he wore spectacles and had eye problems[138]) and his more comfortable economic position.

Very occasionally, Lloyd uses a shorthand writing system or systems in his Colchester Diary. This system bears some resemblance to the Tachygraphy of Thomas Shelton (1600/1–50?), which was used by Samuel Pepys in the composition of his diary. Lloyd also occasionally interspersed this shorthand with pictograms, particularly in his rendering of Proverbs 28:14 in the entry for 22 August, 1675, wherein he denotes the word 'heart' with a heart-like symbol. Lloyd's rendering of the shorthand is also very untidy in places – namely at the top of fo. 3r – which makes interpretation even more challenging. The inscrutability of this shorthand only becomes seriously frustrating at fo. 58v, where Lloyd clearly uses it to obscure his account of a romantic encounter with his future wife, Frances Gray. In total,

---

[138] On **28 May 1711**, he visited one 'Lady Swan' 'about my Eyes', and on **17 December 1711**: 'got my Spectacles mended'.

shorthand and/or pictograms appear on fos 3r, 34r, 58r, and 58v, only ever for a few words at a time. It is my hope that any interest in the diary of George Lloyd generated by this edition may one day result in Lloyd's code being cracked!

It seems likely that these were originally two separate volumes which were bound together at a later time, as the folios for the second part are very slightly larger than the first. There are a few leaves between the two diaries; some are blank, others contain some untidy accounting, a note about the arrival and departure of a lodger or maidservant, and some handwriting practice.

EDITORIAL PRINCIPLES

This transcript has been edited in accordance with the recommendations of the Camden Fifth Series. The editorial method employed here has two primary objectives; to render the text easily comprehensible and useful to the modern reader, and to preserve, as far as possible, the character of the manuscript and putative intentions of the original author. This edition does not attempt to reproduce an exact facsimile of what is, at first glance, a very challenging manuscript.

The binding of the volume is very tight, particularly at the top of each page, partially obscuring some small parts of the text. The pages of the diary are, in places, damaged, stained, or torn away entirely, leaving a small number of passages illegible. Lloyd's tiny and rather messy hand serves only to compound this difficulty. Great effort has been made to accurately reproduce every letter of the manuscript here, but, of course, there are some words which remain either totally inscrutable or which cannot be transcribed with absolute confidence. In such cases, this is made clear in the text, either with an insertion of '[*illegible*]' or occasionally with a note explaining the uncertainty. In some cases, a word is partly or almost entirely obscured or missing as a result of tight binding or damage to the paper; where possible, I will 'restore' missing letters inside square brackets (e.g. 'chu[rch]'). Uncertainty or speculation in such cases will be indicated with a question mark (e.g. 'ch[?urch]').

Like many seventeenth-century writers, Lloyd's use of punctuation was idiosyncratic and inconsistent. Experienced readers of early modern prose will be used to spare or eccentric punctuation, but Lloyd's diary is composed of a particularly unforgiving series of unpunctuated, rambling clauses. Lloyd usually, but not always, neglected to begin his 'sentences' with capital letters or end them with full stops. I have tried to avoid retroactively adding these, however, since this would fundamentally alter the way in which Lloyd rendered his daily experiences – that is, in a spontaneous, almost 'stream of consciousness' style. Instead, the text is broken up into short daily entries – as laid out by the original author – so that even where punctuation is sparse, the writing never runs into a single, unintelligible block. However, where Lloyd has indicated the end of a sentence, I have added capitalization as appropriate. Like many of his contemporaries, Lloyd also added many 'unnecessary' and idiosyncratic capitalizations; these have largely been left unchanged, except where they are confusing.[1] Similarly some proper nouns have been capitalized for clarity where necessary. Additionally, I have occasionally inserted sparse punctuation where the lack of it makes it very difficult to understand the sense of the language. Elsewhere, Lloyd *did* employ quite extensive 'punctuation', usually to denote abbreviations, but also seemingly at random. Much of this irregular punctuation has been silently removed, as it renders the transcript untidy, confusing, and difficult to read. Likewise, idiosyncratic personal titles are standardized; for instance, 'S'' becomes 'Sir', 'mr:' becomes 'Mr', and so on. Lloyd was also a frequent user of symbols, especially the ampersand and other similar symbols (often something resembling a 'plus' sign) to denote 'and', all of which have been expanded.

Where I have expanded abbreviated possessive words, I have inserted a possessive apostrophe; Lloyd included these very infrequently. I have also added in possessive apostrophes where their absence would be confusing. Additions or amendments inserted into the text by Lloyd are enclosed in angle brackets, e.g. 'I went to my Chamber <performed my devotion> and read'.[2]

George Lloyd also made extensive use of abbreviations throughout the diary, some of which were idiosyncratic, and the vast majority of which have been silently expanded throughout. In situations where an unusual or semantically significant abbreviation is encountered, it has been left as Lloyd wrote it, and its conjectured meaning is rendered in a note. Like many of his contemporaries, Lloyd often treated the letters i/j and u/v/w as interchangeable. Where this might cause confusion, I have modernized spellings. Otherwise, Lloyd's original spelling has been left unaltered.

Lloyd used the 'Old Style' of dating, whereby the first day of the year is taken to be 25 March; thus, on this day, he would mark the beginning of a 'new year' of his diary. This edition uses the 'New Style', with the new year starting on 1 January.

Cross references to diary entries within the footnotes are indicated by dates in bold. The Select Bibliography contains a few titles I have used but not cited that are included as further reading.

---

[1] Yet another idiosyncrasy of Lloyd's hand was a tendency to begin some words with a larger lower-case letter, particularly in his London Diary in words beginning with 'N'. The result is occasional ambiguity with regard to transcription; in such cases, I have rendered these letters in lower case.

[2] **5 September 1675**, p. 53, below.

THE DIARY OF GEORGE LLOYD
(1642–1718)

[Autobiographical Preface]

[fo. 1r]

An account of the most remarkable passages and alterations of my life, being borne on Sunday May 11 1642 in the parsonage hous in the parlour at Wonston, where I livd and learned of my Father till the yeare 1651 with out any remarkable thing, then we went to Hunton to live where I went to schoole to my father till 1655 then John went to Winton Ma: 14 when my Brother Edward died, I was at home till 1657 then I was at Winton at schoole with Mr Kirby and borded at Mr Fiffelds 20 of November 1658 my Father dyed and I was a little at home and went a little againe to Winton to school till after Easter and was designed to goe to London to be an aprentice but then Richard Cromwell being out and times unsettled I was at home with my Mother till Michaelmas 1659 then went to Crawley to live with Mr Tomlins and stayd till the begining of 1661 a yeare and ½ then came home and was there in order to fitt me for a place for a Justices of the Peace his cleark, but got none till October 1661 then went to Mr May of Coldry and there I lived till February 1666, about 5 yeare then I went to London and first I lodged at Mr Eaglesfields by Warwick house near Chayring Cross at Lady day removed to the Harrow in St Martains Lane, stayd there till after Whitsontide then went to Mr Davis's in Charles Streete in St James's and in August 1667 I had the small pox lay there till near Christmas and was at Mr Mays New house in St James's and took care of his things and was a Month or more in the House, then went from there and lodged in Long Acer[1] about a Month or 6 weeks then by the helpe of Mr Winsloe got a place with Mr Halford at Wellham[2] whither I went in March 1667[3] at Michaellmas we went to Stockerston[4] and I livd there till Michaellmas 1669 then I went thence in October to live with Mr Cockain my Lord Cullens son at Harborough and boarded at Mr Herrns till Midsomer then Mr Bury bough[t] a house in the Lower end of the Towne and there we stayd till [?Eas]ter 1674 and then we went away [*illegible words*] at Rushton till [*illegible words*][5]

---

[1] Long Acre, Westminster, which runs from St Martin's Lane to Drury Lane.
[2] Welham, Leicestershire, four miles north-east of Market Harborough.
[3] Lloyd may have overwritten an '8' here, but either way he means March 1668 in the 'New Style'.
[4] A village about ten miles north-east of Market Harborough.
[5] Bottom line very faded and stained.

[fo. 1v]

which time we went to Dr Templers at Balsham[6] and there I stayd till Good Friday 1675. Then I came to Rushton and stayd there a weeke then bought me a horse of Clement Pope[7] at Harborrow and went to Dr Longmans[8] to my Brother stayd 10 dayes went to see a parsonedg of Mr Jamesons but my Brother liked it not then I went back to Rushton and got all my things put up and ordered to be sent to London by the Carrier (when I sent word) I left my Lord and went to Dr Longmans to my Brother and we went into Hamp[?shire][9] to my Mothers came back and I stayd at Aynhoe till Whitson Munday and came away being displeased with the Doctor for what he sayd the night before about Mrs Margaret I came the next day to the Red Lyon in Drury Lane and lay there 10 days then I came to Newington and lay at my Brother's House he came to me the beginning of August I was with Cocker learning som knacks in writting and Arithmatic for which I gave him 10^{li} and I stayd there till the 19 of August 1675 (my Brother being 4 or 5 dayes before gon to Aynhoe) I came to Colches[ter] from which time I have a perfect account of my Actions etc.

[6] John Templer, DD (d.1693), rector of Balsham, Cambridgeshire, 1654–1693: see *Cantabrigienses*, Vol. 1, pt. 4, 312; *CCEd* Person ID: 20475.
[7] Perhaps Clement Pope, BA Cantab. 1686/7, and later curate of Braybrooke (just outside Market Harborough), d.1698: see *Cantabrigienses*, Vol. 1, pt. 3, 380, or a relative of the same name.
[8] James Longman, DD (d.1677), rector of Aynho, Northamptonshire. Longman, a Royalist, supposedly gained the living by nefarious means. The living was controlled by Mary, widow of Richard Cartwright, and a Parliamentarian. Longman had her arrested and tortured to force her to grant him the living. He was subsequently deprived of the rectorship by the Parliamentarians and replaced with Robert Wild (*ODNB*), in turn ejected under the Act of Uniformity in 1662, and Longman was restored. See Susan Ransom, 'Squire Cartwright and parson Drope', *Cake and Cockhorse*, 4 (1969), 67–72; *Oxonienses*, Vol. 3, 938; *CCEd* Person ID: 8698.
[9] The tight binding of the pages has obscured the end of this word.

[Colchester Diary]

[fo. 3r]

1675 [*shorthand*] **Colchester**

Thursday, 19 August: Half an houer after 5 I took Coach at the King's Armes in Leadenhall Streete, about 9 bayted[10] at Hart Streete, about 11 came to Ingerstone[11] dined there with 2 gentell men and one woman after at 12 came out and about 4 stayd at a towne <Keldon>[12] 8 miles shorte of Colchester, and came thither a little after 6 to the Three Crownes[13] where I lay that night.

Friday, 20 August: Rose about 7 of the clock and stayd in my chamber till almost 9 went downe into the house and drunk my morning draught with my Landlord and talked with him till almost 10 and then went to Mr Smiths but not finding him at home went to walke in the north sid of the Towne, and came in a little after 11 went into my chamber and was finishing the peece of writing I began with Mr Cocker after my Brother about 1 I went againe to Mr Smith[14] and found him within and gave him the letter from

---

[10] 'Baited' (archaic), to stop briefly on a journey, originally to feed horses, *OED*.

[11] Lloyd refers here to the Essex village of Ingatestone, roughly halfway between London and Colchester.

[12] The village of Kelvedon, between Chelmsford and Colchester.

[13] This building still stands where Head Street becomes North Hill, facing down Colchester High Street, and until recently was used as a post office. Shani D'Cruze (ed.), *Colchester People*, Vol. 3 (Morrisville, NC, 2010), 28–29.

[14] John Smith, rector of St Mary-at-the-Walls 1662–1677 (*CCEd*). The church had been damaged in the siege in 1648, and so from this time until 1714, the rectors of St Mary's sequestrated Holy Trinity, ministering to both congregations and carrying out much of their business there. Smith was an author of at least one substantial Volume of Christian apologia, *Christian Religion's Appeal from the Groundless Prejudices of the Sceptick to the Bar of Common Reason* (London, 1675). At least one other work, namely *The Doctrine of the Church of England, concerning the Lord's Day* (London, 1683; 2nd edn 1694) is attributed to him, though his name does not appear on the title page. He is sometimes wrongly conflated with 'Narrative Smith', known for his narrative of the Popish Plot, who was from Walworth in Durham: see *VCHE*, 325; cf. John Smith, *The Narrative of Mr John Smith of Walworth* (London, 1679). *CCEd* Person ID: 166567.

my Brother who went with me to see for his son[15] about 2 we called at the Grayhound[16] neere St Butolfs Gate[17] stayd halfe an houer and drank one flagon of Beere where I saw Rose his writing, went thence to the Three Mariners[18] to enquire for Mr Smiths son who after an houer or there abouts came to us who went with me to see Delights[19] writing afterward went into Angell Lane[20] to see the house where John Laduke[21] kept schoole came home a little before 5 of the clock went to my chamber and was mending my peece of writing as long as I could well see and after a little perusing the beginning of the Rules in fractions and my devotion[22] I went downe and eate som bread and butter and dranke a Jug of beere, and after a little while setting Mr Smith came to me with whom I drank part of a Jugg of beere and stayd till nine of the clock and went then to my bed.

Saturday, 21 August: Rose about 7 trimed myselfe and af[t]er I was dressed and my devotion, mended som small faults in my peece till about 9 of the clock at what time young Mr Smith came to me with whome I went to enquire for a place for a schoole we

---

[15] This is a good example of Lloyd's poorly parsed and often confusing writing style; he is here describing accompanying Smith in search of his son, not his brother.

[16] This small inn stood at what is now 38 St Botolphs St., Colchester: D'Cruze, *Colchester People*, Vol. 3, p. 14.

[17] St Botolph's Gate, also known as South Gate, to the south-east of the centre of Colchester, near the church of the same name. Possibly Roman in origin, the Gate survived the Siege of Colchester in 1648. It was demolished in 1814.

[18] Also known simply as the Mariners, the building from which this tavern operated still stands at 111 Magdalen St., on the corner with Magdalen Green: D'Cruze, *Colchester People*, Vol. 3, p. 19.

[19] Probably Moses Delight, scrivener of Trinity parish, who died in 1717; for will, see ERO, D/ABW 82/179. He was assessed at three hearths in 1670, *EHT*, 294. Lloyd's diary tells us that he was also a schoolmaster: see **25 September 1677**.

[20] Just off West Stockwell St., in the town centre.

[21] A recently deceased Colchester schoolmaster. See Will of John Le Duke of Colchester, schoolmaster, proved 4 May 1670, ERO, D/AC W18/189.

[22] Here commences Lloyd's rigorous documentation of his thrice daily regime of 'devotion', which is consistently observed throughout the diary. In the manuscript, Lloyd renders this phrase using various abbreviations, usually 'per: my dt' or similar, and in the London Diary, simply 'pd'. Daily regimes of private religious devotion are recommended in a number of 17th-century devotional manuals, but I think it likely that Lloyd followed the prescription laid out by arguably his favourite divine, Jeremy Taylor. In *The Golden Grove, or, A Manuall of Daily Prayers and Letanies* (London, 1655), Taylor instructs his readers – in a chapter named 'The Diary', referring to daily routine – to 'spend each day religiously', laying aside time in the morning, afternoon, and evening to 'go to your usuall devotions', ibid. 47–57. Lloyd explicitly describes himself using the *Golden Grove*, and other works by Taylor, in his acts of domestic piety: see **9 February 1676**.

caled upon Mr Aynger[23] who tould us of Dr Harrisons[24] and enquireing of the Brasiers saw the outsid of the Roomes went to Dr Harrison to enquire about the Roomes who apointed me to meete at the Coffe house at 4 of the clock about 10 went to the Coffe house with Mr Smith and stayd to drinke 2 bottles of Ale came to my chamber and made this booke and writt what is in it to this place,[25] at 4 I went to the Coffe house to meet with Dr Harrison about his Roomes and went to see them and taryed till about 6 and then went to walke with Mr Smith and was to see about my things that came by the Carrier and about 7 came to my lodging about 8 I eate somthing and repayred to my chamber and about 10 went to bed.

Sunday, 22 August: Rose at 7 after I was dressed and my devotion ended I tarried in my chamber and read in Drexelious[26] till halfe an houer after 9 went downe to the house and stayd till 10 went to church to St Peters[27] parish heard Mr Tompson[28] preach on the 28 of Proverbs 14 verse[29] hap[py] [is the man who] feareth alwayes, but [he who] hardeneth [his heart shall] fall into mischief[30] came from church about 12, a little after went to diner which was the first I eate after I came to Cholchester, after diner I lay downe and slept a little while till after 1, and after my devotion and a little

---

[23] The Angiers (also spelled Aungier, Ainger, Angeir, Anger, amongst other variables) were a prominent family in Colchester. There is some suggestion, albeit unconfirmed, that they were related to the Angiers of nearby Dedham, which produced several notable nonconformists including John (1605–1677), *ODNB*. The individual referenced here cannot be definitively identified. See Charles Partridge, 'The Angier Family', *East Anglian, or, Notes and Queries*, 12 (1908), 198–201.

[24] This individual, whose Christian name is never given, has proven surprisingly difficult to trace. A Dr John Harrison ran unsuccessfully for Parliament in Colchester in 1695: *Hist. Parl. 1690–1715*, Vol. 2, 186. However, an MD of the same name, of Colchester, appears in *Cantabrigienses* in 1682: Vol. 1, pt. 2, 136.

[25] Lloyd emphasized this pause with a long dash.

[26] Hieremias Drexelius (Jeremias Drexel), 1581–1638, a Jesuit and author of devotional literature. Born in Augsburg, he was court preacher to Maximilian I of Bavaria for 23 years until his death.

[27] On North Hill to the north-west of the centre of Colchester. St Peter is of medieval origin but much of the present red-brick building dates to the mid 18th century, *TBE, Essex*, 135–136.

[28] Thomas Thompson, MA, held the living of St Peter from 1672/3 until his death in 1682, *CCEd* Person ID: 166911. He was also rector of Roydon, Suffolk, in 1672, and chaplain to Aubrey de Vere, 20th earl of Oxford: *Cantabrigienses*, Vol. 1, pt. 4, 228.

[29] Represented with an ornate 'v' symbol or versicle, ℣: this abbreviation is expanded throughout.

[30] This verse is partly rendered in an as yet unidentified shorthand; these passages are demarcated in square brackets. Translation of the shorthand was thankfully made possible by Lloyd's inclusion of chapter and verse.

stay [*illegible*][31] went to church a little after 2, and heard the same man and text and came home a little after 4 went up into my chamber and read in Drexelious and performed my devotion and stayd in my chamber till ab[out] 7 went downe and taried a little and went to my chamber and then to bed.

[fo. 3v]
Monday, 23 August: Rose at 6 of the clock after I was dressed and my devotion I stayd in my chamber till almost 10 and was studying upon decimall fractions of Dr Palmers then young Mr Smith called me and we went to Mr Wheelys[32] to see for to get me a lodging and was with him till past 11 and spoake to Mr Leete about bording with him halfe an houer after 11 I walked to the south side of the Towne and a little after 12 came back to Mr Leets to meete Mr Smith and have Mr Leets Answer which was that his wife was not willing to have any Border, Mr Smith not coming I walked cleane through the Towne to a field where I sate downe under a hay reeck[33] where I was extreamely troubled and performed my devotion and after 2 I came to the heath and soe walked home to the Three Crownes and dranke a can of beere and after 3 of the clock went to my chamber lay downe by reason of greife almost an houer afterward read about Merchants accompts[34] till about 6 afterward performed my devotion and stayd in my chamber till after 7 went downe and drunke a can of small beere and got 3 eggs for my supper which was all I eate that day after super I drunke one can of strong beere with my Landlord and talked with him till almost 9 then went up to bed.

Tuesday, 24 August: Rose at 7 after I had dressed myselfe and performed my devotion read concerning Merchants accompts till 9 then was mending a payre of linen stockings till 10 went to church and walked there halfe an houer before it began after prayers about halfe an houer after 11 I came to my Inn and went into the kitchin and drank one Can of Strong Beere and stayd below afterward halfe an houer afterward went to my chamber and after my devotion

---
[31] Edge of page torn away.
[32] This seems likely to have been John Wheely of infamous Colchester legend, an ironmonger who purchased Colchester castle in 1683 in order to demolish it and sell the raw materials to cover his debts. After causing substantial damage to the castle, the enterprise proved unprofitable and he sold it to Sir Isaac Rebow in 1705, *VCHE*, 241, 245.
[33] Archaic term for a haystack, *OED*.
[34] Here, Lloyd is referring to learning the practice of double entry bookkeeping. Lloyd did indeed become adept at this methodology: see Introduction, pp. 23, 27–28.

stayd till twas past 7 and went downe and had som eggs fryd for my supper haveing eaten nothing all day before stayd below till almost 9 went to my chamber and went to bed.

Wednesday, 25 August: Rose at 5 of the clock after I was dressed and my devotion I was in my chamber making a new lower end to the peece of writing I began at London and was about it till after 8 and then young Mr Smith came to me and we went to the Kings Head and dranke with Mr Smith there 9 cans of beere with whome we discoursed about letting the roome over the butter market but could not get it there I met with the tapster [who] knew me being at Sir William Halfords[35] with Sir John Pretyman[36] when I was with Sir William I came home to my chamber betweene 9 and 10 and stayd about a quarter of an houer and then Mr Smith came to me and I walked with him all over the commons to see for his mare but could not find her I came home a little before 11 went into my chamber and writt the writting in the first Ovall then I performed my devotion and afterward finished it all and fitted the 2 peeces of paper and then I studyed a little upon fractions in my Booke I made with Cocker a little after 5 Mr Smith came to me who went with me to Mr Cannums who promised me to see att Harlows for a roome for me and give me an account the next Morning Mr Smith called an Alderman of the towne that was neere him and we went to the Whit Lyon[37] and stayd till after 7 of the clock and drank 3 flagons of Beere and then I came to my chamber and performed my devotion and went Joyned the 2 peeces [of] paper together and went down into the house again and eate [?some] bread and butter which was all I eat that day except a [*illegible words*] all morning at the King's Head[38] I went up to [*illegible line*].

---

[35] See Lloyd's autobiographical preface above.

[36] Sir William Halford of Welham married Elizabeth Pretyman, daughter of Sir John Pretyman, 1st Bt (*c.*1612–1676), in 1663: see Cokayne, *Complete Baronetage*, Vol. 4, 195. Pretyman was MP for Leicester from 1661–1676: *Hist. Parl. 1660–1690*, Vol. 3, 284.

[37] This establishment (or another with the same name) was sold in 1700 for £300. It was in 'St Maries Street', now Church St., in the parish of St Mary-at-the-Walls, ERO, D/DU 457/10.

[38] The King's Head was one of Colchester's foremost inns in the period, though by the mid 18th century it was eclipsed by the White Hart. It was in the parish of St Mary-at-the-Walls, in Headgate Court off Head St.: D'Cruze, *Colchester People*, Vol. 3, 17–18.

[fo. 4r]

Thursday, 26 August: Rose at 6 and after I was dressed and performed my [*deleted*] devotion was in my chamber mending my black stockings and afterwards at study upon fractions where I found out the way of the rule of practice[39] another way ab a little before 11 I went downe and bespoake a neck of mutton to be fryd for my diner halfe I had got redy and eate hartily it being the 2^d diner I eate after I came to Colchester after I had dyned I went to my chamber and after my devotion lay downe on the bed but did not sleepe got up and wrote a letter to Sir William Halford to let him know I would wayt on him but did not send him as I thought a little after 1 I went to Mr Cannums but he was not within I met Mr Smith and we walked the back way to Mr Wheelys where he tould us he intended to take those chambers of Furlyes[40] I thought to have had one of and he tould me if he had them I should have one of them Mr Smith and I went to Mr Bouchers and borrowed his horse went to the field and got him up went to the meddow to catch Mr Smiths mare wher[e] we were above an houer in doeing it a little after three we caught her and went to Wivnor[41] fayer where we dranke one jug of Beere and eate 2 biskets saw the Dock and the vessells ferryed over to goe to the Oyster pitts where I saw the oysters in the pitts and how they lay to growe we had a halfe peck[42] which was more then we could eate, came home about 7 and at 8 came to towne went to my chamber within a quarter of an houer Mr Smith came to me we drank one jug of beere and he stayd till ½ an houer after 9 and a little after when I had perfor[me]d my devotion went to bed.

Friday, 27 August: Rose at 7 after I was dressed and my devotion I was in my chamber reading of Arithmaticke in my one booke[43] till almost 8 at which time young Mr Smith came to me and we went

---

[39] 'A convenient way of performing multiplication by means of aliquot parts in cases where one or both quantities are expressed in more than one unit', *OED*. Such a method would have been extremely useful in accounting (or indeed simply counting) in pre-decimal currency.

[40] This is likely to have been the merchant John Furly, a Quaker and patriarch of one of Colchester's most prosperous mercantile families. His father, John Furly (*c*.1590–1673) was a linen draper, alderman, and later mayor of Colchester in 1638 and 1650. John's brother Benjamin (1636–1714), who emigrated to Rotterdam in 1658, was an acquaintance of John Locke, Sir William Penn, John Stubbs, and Algernon Sydney, amongst others (*ODNB*).

[41] Wivenhoe, a small town and port about three miles south-east of Colchester.

[42] An archaic unit of liquid or dry measure, equal to two imperial gallons. However, measurements were not rigidly standardized in the 1670s.

[43] 'My own book'.

to Mr Wheelys to know concerning Furloes Roomes but he not having beene there we stayd halfe an houer and he not being leasure we walked into the meadow to see Mr Smiths mare and about 10 came back againe he not haveing beene there told us if we did call betweene 12 and 1 he would resolve us called at Mr Smiths shoe makers and came home to my chamber and sate downe a little while and being melencolique about 11 Layd downe on my bed and slept a little at 12 got up and performed my devotion then went to call Mr Smith to goe to Mr Wheelyes againe when we came there he had not beene at Furlyes but tould us in halfe an houer he would goe without fayle we went to the Castell and walked up and downe there and I saw where Sir Charles Lucas was shott to death[44] about 3 quarters of an houer came back and Mr Wheely was at Furlyes and about a quarter of an hou[r] came back and tould us that Furly would let noe room for a schoole because he had a tennant was a schoole Master we went to Mr Smiths and called him went to see a place at Trinity church[45] which I did not like came back to the house and saw Rose his peece which hung in the Roome and found it to be but pittiful went with Mr Smith to the Taverne and dranke a pint of white wine came back young Smith called on Mr Ayngers stayd ¼ of an houer went to walke in the east sid[e] [of] the Towne to a spring called at the King's Head to know when the Post went to London [?went] to Mr Smith about Mr [*blank*] [*deleted*] I came home it being 5 the clock went to my cham[ber] [*approximately three illegible lines*].[46]

[fo. 4v]
Saturday, 28 August: Rose a little after 6 after I had trimed and dressed myselfe and my devotion was in my chamber trying to write the ovall Itallien[47] a little before 8 Mr Smith came to me and we went to Mr Meadows[48] and seene his roomes and went to Chiles and

---

[44] Sir Charles Lucas (1613–1648) of Colchester, Essex, was a Royalist officer during the English Civil War. He was executed by firing squad following the siege of the town in 1648, and later became a Royalist martyr.

[45] Holy Trinity is in Trinity St. in the very centre of Colchester. See *TBE, Essex*, 136.

[46] The bottom of this page is badly damaged, and confident transcription of the fragments of tiny writing is impossible.

[47] A calligraphic design to showcase italic script.

[48] 'Mr Meadows', the person from whom Lloyd initially rented the premises for his school, has proven to be particularly difficult to track down. Lloyd's scattered references suggest he was renting from Robert Meadows (**22 September 1675**), and his school operated from a room above his shop (**30 August, 10 September**, and **14 October 1675**). He had a brother, probably Samuel Meadows (see **1** and **16 September 1675**). I have not been able to trace wills belonging to these individuals, nor do they appear in the

dranke our[49] mornings draught and Mr Meadows and I bargained for the 4 roomes at 18[li] per Annum about 9 Mr Smith and I walked to see my Lord Lucass his gatehouse[50] and to a mill came back to Mr Meadows and he tould me he had gott me a lodging at Mrs Strottons[51] I was in his house and shop till two then I went to the pasture to helpe Mr Smith catch his mare and walkd in the North sid of the towne and as I walked performed my devotion came round by St Maryes and came at 4 to Mr Meadows and was with the man that set up his bead[52] and in the roomes till after 6 <and performed my devotion> came downe into the house and about 7 signed with him and afterward went to Mrs Strottns and stayd a ¼ of an houer went to the Three Crownes and got my things and sent them to Mrs Strottns and came thether a little before 9 sate talking in the house till almost 10 and went to bed.

Sunday, 29 August: Rose at 7 after I was dressed and my devotion Mr Smith and Mr Meddows came to my chamber and stayd a ¼ of an houer and we went to the holy lamb[53] and dranke our mornings

Hearth Tax return for 1670. However, there is a will proved on 7 April 1718 in the Prerogative Court of Canterbury belonging to an Elizabeth Meadows, widow of Colchester. Elizabeth had six living children, Robert, Edward, Mary, Elizabeth, Ann, and Martha, and the will mentions that her late husband's name was Robert. It seems possible, therefore, that this Robert and Elizabeth Meadows were the same Mrs and Mrs Meadows referred to extensively below. See TNA, PROB 11/563/238.

[49] Here, Lloyd uses an abbreviation for the word 'our', an 'o' with a swooping line from the top, resembling an italic 'b'. Henceforth, this abbreviation will be silently expanded.

[50] Lloyd is probably referring to the gatehouse of St John's Abbey, a former Benedictine monastery founded in 1095 and dissolved in 1539. The Abbey was subsequently acquired by the Lucas family, who built a house on the property. The house and much of the rest of the Abbey was destroyed by Parliamentarian troops during the Siege of Colchester in 1648; the gatehouse, however, survives to this day, *TBE, Essex*, 137.

[51] Here again we see Lloyd attempting a phonetic spelling of an unfamiliar name: the 'Strottons' would later become the 'Strattons' or 'Strettons'. Lloyd's landlords, Mr and Mrs Stratton, appear to have been of humble social and economic status; no will can be found for either individual. Lloyd moved in as a lodger at once on this day but only arranged to 'bord', i.e. to take his meals with the Strattons later: see **31 August 1675**. Scattered references below suggest that Mr Stratton may have been a grocer of some kind. Stratton's Christian name was probably Robert (see **4 October 1677**), but this name does not appear in the Hearth Tax return for 1670. A John Stretton was assessed at two hearths in All Saints' parish, *EHT*, 296. The will of John Streaton, carpenter, was proved in March 1683, and makes no mention of a Robert Stratton or Streaton, ERO, D/ACW 20/44. Mrs Stratton appears to have been the sister of the miller Richard Orbell of St Mary-at-the-Walls: see **15 October 1675**.

[52] Lloyd probably means 'bed'. Throughout the diary, Lloyd exhibits a fascination with manual work.

[53] I can find no trace of an establishment with this exact name in Colchester, but it may have been the Lamb, on the edge of St Runwald's parish, on the north side of the High St. Also noted by Morant as the Shoulder of Mutton. D'Cruze, *Colchester People*, Vol. 3, 18,

draught and stayed ½ an houer came home and stayd ¼ of an houer went to St Peters and herd Mr Sanders[54] preach on the 6 Micah 8 He hath shewed thee o man what is good and what doth the Lord require etc. After diner and my devotion Mr Smith and I walked to see Sergant Colmans daughter went to St James[55] and herd Mr Sheldon[56] preach the Ellection sermon before the choise of the Mayor on the 29 Jeremiah 7 And seeke the peace of the City etc. After sermon walked to the Heath and drank bottle att the Swan[57] I stayd neere an houer came home at 6 and my Landlord not being at home I walked abroad into the field till neere 7 came to Mr Medems[58] and eate some cold mutton went to Mr Strotons and sate and discoursed till almost 9 then went to my chamber and after my devotion went to bed.

Monday, 30 August: Rose about 7 after I was dressed and performed my devotion went to Mr Meaddows and he tould me he could not certainely resolve me whether I could be with him or not till he had spoke with his Mrs:[59] I stayd there about ½ an houer Mr Smith came and we went to the bookesellers to buy pencills but could get none noewhere we went to the Apothecarys and I bought an ounce of gumsandrich for pounce[60] came to my chamber and pounced a sheete went to Mr Meaddows and eate some bread and cheese came to my chamber about 12 and performed my devotion then I went to write a peece in the Ovall Itallian text and was about it till almost 6 performed my devotion and

and Philip Morant, *The History and Antiquities of Colchester, in the County of Essex*, Vol. 2 (London, 1748), 9.

[54] Unidentified, not one of the regular clergy in Colchester.

[55] St James the Great is a large church on East Hill, which runs off the east end of the High St. See *TBE, Essex*, 133.

[56] Here Lloyd misspells the name of William Shelton, rector of St James from 1670 until his death in 1699. Although he is little known or researched today, Shelton was an enthusiastic controversialist and staunch defender of the Church of England against dissenters and Catholics, publishing a number of religious polemics and some Christian moralistic literature between the 1660s and the 1690s, one of which, *Moral Vertues Baptized Christian, or, The Necessity of Morality among Christians* (London, 1667), describes him as a 'late Fellow of Jesus Colledge in Cambridge'. See also *VCHE*, 318.

[57] In the parish of St Nicholas, at 110 High St., presumably giving its name to Swan Passage, which runs behind the site, D'Cruze, *Colchester People*, Vol. 3, 27.

[58] Ambiguously and untidily written, but perhaps a phonetic guess or misspelling of 'Meadows', the individual mentioned regularly below.

[59] It is unclear here whether Meadows means his wife, or a landlady from whom he was hoping to sublet the property.

[60] Gum sandarac, derived from the resin of the sictus tree, could be used for pounce; a fine powder sprinkled on a writing medium (paper) in order to prevent ink bleeding or blotting. Pounce was often made using powdered cuttlefish bone, *OED*.

went downe and stayd a little while in my Landlord Strettons shop went to Mr Meadows and stayd with Sam in the shop and eate gooseberrys and went to the parlor and playd on my violin about ¼ of an houer

[fo. 5r]
at 7 went to Mr Strattons and eate some fryd beefe for my supper and sate in the house till about 8 sent to Mr Meadows for my violin and playd ½ an houer and afterward sate and talked with the people and about 10 went to bed.

Tuesday, 31 August: Rose a little after 7 after I was up and dressed and my devotion Mr Smith came in and we went to Mr Meaddowes and was there to learne Mr Smith to make his honours and danceing[61] and sent for my violin and playd there after 10 came home and was in my chamber in doeing somthing in my Itallian peece till after 12 performed my devotion and Mr Smith and I a little after 1 went to Mr Meaddows and he let me his roomes for 5^{li} the yeare for 6 months came back and about 2 went to diner and spoke to Mr Stratton to bord with him after diner I called Mr Smith at Mr Bashers walked in Kings Meadow[62] till after 3 came back and went to Mr Edlings[63] the Joyners and he not being within came to my chamber to write and a little after [*illegible*][64] came Mr Edling to me and I went to his shop bought 3 bords to make a table and 2 for formes and bespoake a frame for my peece came to my chamber and was writing in my peece till after 6 then wrote a letter to my Brother Nicholas[65] and a note to send to London then came Mr Smith and Mr Chole and I went to my schoole roome and playd a lesson or two on my Violin and went to Crampers[66] house to speake with him and he was not wi[th]in as I came back I mett him and spoake to him came home and

---

[61] To 'make your honours' (now 'honour your partner') is to make a bow or curtsey, typically towards your partner at the beginning of a dance. Lloyd must be teaching the young Smith how to dance, *OED*.

[62] A field north of the Colne and Colchester Castle. It is now the site of a park and cricket club.

[63] Probably John Edlin(g), of the parish of St Mary-at-the-Walls, whose will was proved 19 November 1695. He also owned property in St Botolph, but was assessed at St Mary's with two hearths in 1670. ERO, D/ABW 75/109; *EHT*, 300.

[64] Ink blot.

[65] The diarist's brother, Nicholas Lloyd (*c*.1630–1680) scholar and rector of St Mary Newington: see Introduction, pp. 2–3, 21.

[66] This unusual name does not appear again but is written clearly; perhaps another example of phonetic spelling of an unfamiliar name.

sate a little while in the house with my landlady and the backers[67] daughter went to my chamber and performed my devotion and wrote a note to Mr Rooks for a bottle of Inck a little after 9 came downe into the house and eate some bread and cheese and sate talking till 10 and then went to bed.

Wednesday, 1 September: Rose at 6 after I was dressed waited for to speake with Cranfield about 7 met him and gave him my note came to my Chamber performed my devotion afterward went downe and eate some tost and cheese and drunk my mornings draught then I went to my chamber and sate to write in my peece till about 10 went over to my schoole to bied[68] the man carry his things to the iner roome stayd there halfe an houer came back to my cha[mber] to write a little after 11 Mr Smith came to me and stayd in my chamber till after 1 went downe to diner after diner Mr Smith and I went to walke and saw the fort in the east side of the towne after I had beene at my schoole and seene the table and formes sett up came to my chamber and performed my devotion and was in finishing my peece till after 6 then walked in my chamber a ¼ of an houer walked with Mr Smith and Mr Rich[69] to Lexen cross[70] came back after 8 went to Jaxsons dranke part of 3 flagons of Beere a little after 9 came to my lodgings where was Dr Elkin[71] and Mr Meadows and his brother I sent for 2 penyworth of drink and sate up talking [with] the Dr till after 10 and stayd a little below after he [?left] a little before 11 went to my Chamber performed my devotion.

[fo. 5v]
Thursday, 2 September: Up at 7 after I was a little while up performed my devotion and after dressed myselfe was in my chamber about my peece till after 1 then went to diner and after diner went to my chamber and stayd a little while Mr Meaddows being there as soone as he was gon performed my devotion and afterward

---

[67] Meaning 'baker's'.
[68] Bid.
[69] Faded and uncertain.
[70] Lexden is now a suburb of Colchester but was a separate village in the 17th century, about two and a half miles from the centre of Colchester. 'Lexen cross' may refer to one of three medieval crosses which stood in the village: 'Lamb's Cross', 'Stone Cross', or 'Peddars Cross', *VCHE*, 391–392.
[71] Perhaps Thomas Elkin of Colchester, 'practitioner in Physick', whose will dates from 1679, ERO, D/ABW 69/163. He was assessed at four hearths in the parish of Holy Trinity in 1670, *EHT*, 293.

made an end of my Peece and rubled[72] it then Mr [*sic*] Elizabeth Edlin cam to agree with me to learne her to write with whome I agreed for 20^s afterward went to my chamber stayd a little while and then went to Mr ~~Med~~ Meaddows and playd a little while Mr Smith came to me and we went to the Coffee house and drunk 3 bottles of Ale and I spoke to him to take care of my peece who promised me he would came back and went to Mr Edlins and bespoke another Table and frame, came home and stayd a little while and Mr Smith called me and we went to walke toward Lexon came home about 8 Mr Meaddows and I went to the mayor who tould me he was willing I should prooceed to keepe a schoole[73] came home and eate some bread and cheese and sate in the house and read in the history of the Clothiers of the west[74] till 10 went to my chamber and performed my devotion and to bed.

Friday, 3 September: I rose at 7 after I was dressed and performed my devotion was in my chamber till 9 went downe and drank my mornings draught and a little before 10 went over the way to the barbers to have my penknife set and stayd there till after 11 and heard Goldsbury play on the Violin about 12 dined at Mr Meaddows stayd there ½ an houer went to my chamber and performed my devotion went to walk with Mr Smith to the Drury ward[75] came back about 2 went to my chamber and stayd there writting and playing a my violin till past 5 went to Mr Smith and Mr Meaddows to walke to Lexton came back a little after 7 Mr Smith and I went to Tarboles to speak to him about his son who tould me he would send him to me on Munday came to my lodging about 8 got som stewd mutton for my super and sate up till 11 there being Mrs Cockrell[76] and Mrs King and Sam

---

[72] This usage is obscure (perhaps a slip of the pen), but it seems plausible that Lloyd was treating his parchment with pounce or similar: see n. 60, **30 August 1675**.

[73] This seems to suggest that Lloyd's school was, in some loose sense at least, a 'formal' institution for the short period of its existence. However, I have found no evidence of any official recognition of the school.

[74] Lloyd was reading Thomas Deloney, who was a silk-weaver as well as an author of ballads and prose fiction. The misremembered title given by Lloyd actually refers to *Thomas of Reading, or, The Sixe Worthy Yeomen of the West* (1599?).

[75] Whilst finding specific references to a place of this exact name is difficult, there is now a Drury Rd between Lexden and Colchester. Documents from the 16th to the 20th century at ERO relate to a 'Drury Farm' on Maldon Rd, which meets Drury Rd, D/DEI T255, D/B, D/DEI T402, D/B 6 Pb3/8291.

[76] There were many Cockerells in Colchester and surrounding locales in this period. Unfortunately, although this individual and a Mr Cockerell are mentioned regularly throughout the diary, they cannot be confidently identified.

Meaddows till after 10 went to my chamber and performed my devotion and went to bed.

Saturday, 4 September: Rose about 6 performed my devotion and was in my chamber till after 7 went to Mr Meadows and nayld my peeces of writing to the frames and hung one out at the doore of my schoole and the other at the Coffee house and stayd at the Coffy house and drank a bottle of Alle with Mr Smith and Mr Meadows and afterward went with Mr Smith to Kings Meadow to see for his mare walked about all over the pasture and could not find her came home a little before 12 was in my chamber performed my devotion a little after 12 went

[fo. 6r]
downe to diner and after diner sate in the house and read in the history of Thomas of Reading then Mr Smith came to me and we dranke a gotch[77] of Beere and stayd till past 2 went to my chamber and trimed myselfe and read about the sqaure and cube roote till neere 6 performed my devotion went downe and stayd a little came to my Chamber and gott my Linen redy to weare the next day went downe and supped about 7 and stayd below till after 8 and then went to my chamber and about 9 went to bed.

Sunday, 5 September: Rose a little before 8 after I was dressed and redy and performed my devotion was in my Chamber till after 9 reading went downe and eate a peece of toast and cheese and drank and a little before 10 went with Mr Smith to Trinity and herd his father preach on the 5 of the first to the Corinthians 7 and 8 verses Christ our passover is sacrifised for us etc he bid a sacrament after I came from Church I read till diner time after diner I went to my Chamber <performed my devotion> and read till I went to Church where I heard the same text and man after I came home I went to my Chamber and read and performed my devotion and read till almost 6 went downe and sate a little while in the house and heard my landlady read[78] and about 7 eate som cold rost beefe for supper and about 9 went to bed.

---

[77] A large pot-bellied jug, associated with East Anglia. A gotch between two people is a considerable quantity of alcohol; one 18th-century example has been found to contain 36 pints! See Charles Partridge, 'East Anglian Ringers' Gotches', *East Anglian, or, Notes and Queries*, 10 (1904), 143, 356.

[78] Although Lloyd had only known the Strattons for a matter of days, he quickly fell into a familiar routine with them, including communal Biblical readings and Psalm singing, of which more below.

Monday, 6 September: Rose a little after 5 and was a little while mending my drawers after I was redy and my devotion I stayd in my chamber and a little before 8 went to my schoole and there I mett Goodman Bell with his son to learne and I gott the schoole cleane and made him a booke and began with him and stayd till after 11 came home to my chamber and performed my devotion and stayd till after 12 went downe to diner and after 1 wen[t] to schoole and stayd till almost 4 with the boy and then mended the place goeing downe the Stayers and about 6 came away went to the barbers went my Lodging and stayd ¼ of an houer came home and was below till 7 and eat som bread and cheese and butter and stayd below till 10 went to my chamber performed my devotion and went to bed.

Tuesday, 7 September: Rose a little after 6 after I was dressd and performed my devotion went downe and eate som bread and cheese and dranke and went about 8 to my schoole and stayd there till 11 came home and performed my devotion and dined about 12 stayd within till 2 went to my schoole and stayd till after 5 and wrote 4 letters one to my Brother John[79] one to Mrs Gray[80] and one to my Landlord and one to Philoclea[81] came home and read and performed my devotion went to walke came home a little after 7 and was in the house with Sam Meaddow and Mr Gray[82] and dranck 2 gotches of drinke went to bed a little after 9.

[fo. 6v]
Wednesday, 8 September: Rose a little after 5 after I was dressed and my devotion was in my chamber till neere 8 went to my schoole and was there till after 11 and read till 12 dined at Mr Meaddows and after diner went to walke with Mr Smith to the Drury came back to my schoole a little after 1 performed my devotion and stayd there till after 5 came to my chamber and stayd there and

---

[79] See Introduction, pp. 2–3, 10.
[80] See Introduction, pp. 18–20. Note that 'Mrs' in the 17th century did not refer exclusively to married women.
[81] Here, Lloyd is being deliberately secretive; 'Philoclea' – or 'Phyloclea' – is clearly a pseudonym for another young women in whom he had some romantic interest or aspiration. In Sydney's *Arcadia* (1593), Philoclea is one of the daughters of Basilius, duke of Arcadia, secretly pursued by Pyrocles, disguised as a woman. The fictional Philoclea's sister was named Pamela and, on **30 October 1677**, we find Lloyd 'writting to Phyloclea and Pamilla'. For this reason, I speculate (though it can be no more than speculation) that Lloyd was referring to the sisters Elizabeth and Mary Lynford (or Linford), referred to regularly below. See Introduction, pp. 18–20.
[82] No relation to the aforementioned 'Mrs Gray'.

performed my devotion and about 7 went to Mr Meaddows and eate som cold beefe and came to my owne Lodgings and Sam Meaddows and Mrs Mary Bond[83] sate and talked till after 10 and had 2 gotches of Beere went to bed about 11.

Thursday, 9 September: Rose a little after 6 after I was dressed and my devotion I was in my chamber till almost 8 went to my school and taried there till after 11 came home and was below ill ½ an houer after 11 went to my chamber and performed my devotion and went downe and a little after 12 went to diner and sat in the house and playd a little while on my violin a little after 1 went to my school and stayd till after 3 came home and not being very well lay on the bed about 5 went to my chamber and read and Sam Meddows came to me and stayd till twas dark and Mr Smith came and called me to goe to Jaxons where was Phillip Eve and Robert Basher and Jo: Bond and I stayd there till almost 9 and spent 6^d and gave 6^d to the musick when I came in Sam Meddows and I eate som bread and cheese and had a gotch of beere and a little after came in Mrs Mary Bond and Phillip Eve and one man more who stayd ¾ of an houer and they went away but Mrs Bond stayd till after 10 and a little before 11 I came to my chamber and performed my devotion and was to bed.

Friday, 10 September: Rose a little after 6 and after I was dressed and performed my devotion was in my chamber till 8 went to my schoole taried there till 11 came home and was below till after 12 went to my chamber and performed my devotion and went to Mr Meddows shop and stayd there a little while and went to my schoole and stayd till after 5 came to my chamber and read and performed my devotion and was in my chamber till 7 went downe and was in the house with Sam Meaddows and Mr Gray and had one gotch of beere and sate up till past 9 and went to bed.

Saturday, 11 September: Rose at 6 and after I was dresst and performed my devotion made my humble confession to God in Dr Taylors[84] forme observing this day as a fast in order to receive the

---

[83] Mary Bond appears regularly, particularly in the first months of the diary, in Lloyd's mentions of evening socializing. He often abbreviated her name 'M: B:'.

[84] Jeremy Taylor, DD (1613–1667), was a devotional writer and bishop of Down and Connor in the Church of Ireland. Early in his career, Taylor enjoyed the patronage of Laud, becoming his chaplain and chaplain-in-ordinary to Charles I. During a period of imprisonment and exile in Wales during the Civil Wars and Interregnum, Taylor became chaplain to Richard Vaughan, 2nd earl of Carberry, and resided with him at Golden Grove, which lent its name to the devotional manual often cited by Lloyd. Taylor gained his see upon the Restoration. He was a moderate and defender of the unity of the Church

sacrament the next day, went to my schoole till 11 came home and read till after 12 performed my devotion read and stayd within all the day after 7 Mr Smith and Mr Seawell[85] and Mr Sam Meaddows and Mrs Mary Bond came in and the 2 latter stayd till almost 11 went to my chamber and stayd up a little and went to bed.

Sunday, 12 September: Rose at 6 ~~and was~~ and after I was dressed was in my chamber till church time preparing myself for the sacrament till I went to church heard Mr Smith on the 1 Corinthians 5 7:8 Christ our passover is sacrifised for us etc. Received the sacrament came to Mr Meaddows to diner after diner went to my chamber and performed my devotion and was there till church time went to church and heard Mr Smith on the 16 John last[86] came to my chamber and read [and] performed my devotion at 7 went to Mr Meadows to super and came home about 8 my Landlord and landlady cam from [*illegible*] fayre had [a] gotch of beere[87] and went to bed a little after 9.

[fo. 7r]
Monday, 13 September: Rose a little after 6 after I was ~~up~~ dressed and my devotion I went downe and stayd below till after 8 went to schoole and stayd till after 11 came home and was in my chamber till after 12 and went downe and stayd till after 1 came to my chamber and performed my devotion went downe and stayd till 2 and went to diner and afterward went to schoole and stayd till after 5 came home and was below clensing my pistalls till after 6 went to my chamber and performed my devotion and after playd on my Violin till almost 8 went downe and sate with Mrs Cockerel and my governant[88] went and read in Quarles Emblems[89] a little after 8 eate som milke and

---

of England, who earned a reputation as an advocate of religious toleration, a tendency which might also be read into Lloyd's own outlook on faith. Several of his works have also been praised for their literary qualities. *ODNB*.

[85] This was probably John or Robert Sewell, or Seawell, sons of John Sewell, grocer of St Peter's parish whose will was proved in the Prerogative Court of Canterbury in 1667. Lloyd refers to John by name on **24 January 1676**. Robert was a rower by trade; his will was proved in 1707, at which time John seems still to have been alive. See TNA, PROB 11/324/266; ERO, D/ABW 79/77. None of these individuals appear in the Hearth Tax return for 1670, but an Edward Sewell was assessed at one hearth in St Martin's parish, *EHT*, 296.

[86] John 16:33.

[87] Very faded and uncertain.

[88] An obsolete usage for housekeeper, or perhaps Lloyd's 'Landlady', *OED*.

[89] Francis Quarles (1592–1644) was a poet best known for the 1634 work *Emblemes*, read here by Lloyd. Quarles was a 'moderate protestant and royalist' – much like Lloyd

bread and cheese for my supper and had a gotch of beere and sate up till after 10 and went to my chamber and to bed.

Tuesday, 14 September: Rose a little after 6 after I was redy and performed my devotion I went to my schoole and was there till past 11 came home and sate in the house till after 12 and went to diner sate a little while after diner went to my chamber and performed my devotion and went to the schoole and stayd till after 5 came home and went to my chamber and performed my devotion went downe into the house and sate there till past 7 and then went to walke with Mr Smith and walked in the feilds came in and eate som bread and cheese and sate up till after 9 with my landlord and lady and Samuel and Mrs Bond about 10 went to bed.

Wednesday, 15 September: Rose at 6 performed my devotion and was in my chamber mending my halfe shirte after I was dressed went downe and stayd below till 8 went to schoole and about 9 Mr Foster of Rushton[90] found me at my schoole with whome I went to the Coffeehouse where was Mr Cockayne[91] Mr Ellwes[92] Mr Pollock where I stayd till 10 came to my schoole and stayd till past 11 came to my chamber and was mending a payre of stockins read and went downe to diner sate a little while and performed my devotion and went to schoole and stayd till after 3 came home and was within till after 5 then walked with Mr Smith to Kings meaddow and to the wood came home and stayd in the house a little went to my chamber performed my devotion came downe and eate some supper and sate up till 10.

Thursday, 16 September: Rose a little after 6 after I was dressed and performed my devotion stayd a little while in the house and at 8 went to schoole and stayd till after 11 came home and went to my chamber and read and performed my devotion and went dow[n] and was below till after 1 and then went to diner after diner

---

himself – and *Emblemes*, which contains illustrations by the well-known engraver William Marshall (fl. 1617–1649), 'brought to protestant England, suitably adapted, the spiritual and emotional qualities of the Catholic meditation on pictures', *ODNB*.

[90] Rushton, Northamptonshire, where Lloyd had lived and served the Cockayne family briefly before moving to Colchester.

[91] Possibly a relative of Brien Cockayne, 2nd Viscount Cullen, in whose service Lloyd had worked at Rushton and Harborough. Lloyd would have used the correct honorific had he been referring to the viscount.

[92] Possibly a relative of Sir Gervase Elwes, 1st Bt, of Woodford, Essex, whom Lloyd appears to have had some connection to and visited later in the diary: see **27 December 1675**.

I went to schoole and stayd till past 3 came home and was within all day at 6 I went to my chamber and performed my devotion and about 7 came downe was in the house Sam Meaddows being there and about 9 Mr Meadows came in and I sate up till a little after 10 and went to bed.

Friday, 17 September: Rose betweene 6 and 7 after I was dressed and performed my devotion a little after 8 went to schoole and stayd till after 11 came home and was in the house after a little while went to my chamber and performed my devotion and stayd below till past 1 went to diner and then to schoole and stayd till 5 Mr Smith came to me and went with him to the Allecoat and dranke 2 Flagons and stayd till after 6 came to my chamber and performed my devotion and was below Mr Gray Mrs Bond Sam and Mr Meadows being there and sate up till almost 10[93] went to bed.

[fo. 7v]
Saturday, 18 September: Rose at 7 after I was dressed and performed my devotion went to schoole and not being well gott som brandy burned came to my Lodging about 10 and eate a toste and went back againe to schoole and stayd till after 11 came home and went to my chamber and performed my devotion and a litte after 12 Mr Smith and I walked out toward Lexon and came home a little before 2 went to my chamber and stayd a little and went downe and payd Mr Edlin for my table and stayd below a little while and eate a little stewd mutton and was in the house all the day after and was very Ill performed my devotion about 6 and eate nothing I was soe Ill went to bed at 9 and was not well all night.

Sunday, 19 September: Rose after 7 being ill gott ready and performed my devotion and went to church and heard Mr Smith on the 3 Philippians 10 verse after sermon I came home and after diner went to my chamber and performed my devotion and read at church time I went againe and heard the same text came home and went to my chamber and read till almost 5 then went to walk with Mr Smith Mr Meaddows Mr Seawell and another young man came home about 6 went to my chamber and read and performed my devotion and went downe and sate in the house Samuel Meaddows and Mrs Bond being there a little after 10 went to bed.

---

[93] Very faded and uncertain.

Monday, 20 September: Rose at 6 and was in my chamber mending my gloves after I was dressed and performed my devotion about 8 went to schoole and stayd there till after 11 came home and was in my chamber a little while and went downe to diner sate by the fier a little while went to my chamber and performed my devotion and a little after 1 went to schoole stayd till neere 4 came to my Lodging where was the writting Master of the Heath[94] and stayd with him till near 5 went to schoole and sent my scholler home and came home and was in my chamber a little while went to Joes the Barber[95] and got him to set my penknife and Razor and stayd there till 6 came home and was below till 7 went to my chamber and performed my devotion came downe and was below and eate some supper and had a gotch of beere with Mr Gray about 9 Samuel Meaddows and Mrs Bond came in and stayd till 10 the old woman came in and smoked a pipe and then we went to bed.

Tuesday, 21 September: Rose at 8 after I was dressed and performed my devotion was in my chamber till 10 mending a cravat lace went downe and eate som tost and cheese and drunke and sate a little while below then went to St Peters church to prayers came back and went to Sam Meaddows and sett him som sumes and stayd till after 12 came to my chamber and performed my devotion and was mending my cravatt till 2 then went to diner and sate a little below then went to my chamber and was there and finished my cravat and went downe about 5 and stayd below till 6 and then went to my chamber and performed my devotion was within all the evening below Sam Meaddows being there at 10 went to my chamber and to bed.

Wednesday, 22 September: Rose a little after 6 after I was dressed and performed my devotion was below and eate a toast and dranke and after 8 went to schoole and stayd till after 11 and came home and was below till 12 went to my chamber and performed my devotion and came downe to diner after diner sate a ¼ of an houer and went to schoole and stayd till after 5 came to my chamber and playd a little on my violin and then read and

---

[94] There are several placenames in the vicinity of Colchester which contain the word 'Heath': Old Heath, Lexden Heath, Horkesley Heath, and Fordham Heath, amongst others. In the absence of further detail or a name, there is little to be done in identifying this individual.

[95] Probably Joseph Blomfield (Blumfield, Bloomfield) of St Mary-at-the-Walls: see n. 141, **15 October 1675**.

performed my devotion went and walked to Lexton warren[96] came back and sate in the house Mrs Bond being there a little after Robert Meadows and his Brother came and stayd till 9 and after 9 I eate [some] bread and cheese and about 10 I went to bed.

[fo. 8r]
Thursday, 23 September: Rose a little after 6 after I was dressed and performed my devotion was a little while in my chamber went downe and eat a tost and drank went over to my schoole and my scoller not being there by reason of the Muster, I stayd there till 10 came to my chamber and was mending a payre of stockings till after 12 performed my devotion and went to diner was within till 3 went to St Jones field[97] and saw the soldiers muster and came back and about 5 performed my devotion and was within all evening below Robert Meaddows and his Brother being there till after 10 then went to bed.

Friday, 24 September: Rose at 7 after I was dressed and performed my devotion was within till 10 went to my schoole and noe one being ther by reason of the muster I read in Iusebious[98] till 11 came home and was below till 12 went to my chamber and performed my devotion and came downe to diner stayd a little while and a little after 1 went to with my Landlord Stratton to Wivnoe and stayd there till after 5 at his sisters and came home about 7 and was below till 10 and then went to my chamber and performed my devotion and went to bed.

Saturday, 25 September: Rose a little before 7 and after I was dressed and performed my devotion was in my chamber a little while went downe and stayd a little while and went to schoole about 9 and stayd till past 11 came home and was below till after 12 went to my chamber and performed my devotion[99] and went downe to diner and stayd below a little while went to my chamber

---

[96] A piece of land enclosed for breeding game birds or rabbits. It may have been in the south-east corner of Lexden parish, where it bordered St Mary-at-the-Walls; fields named Upper Warren and Lower Warren survived here until 1838, *VCHE*, 396.

[97] The gardens and greens around the former St John's Abbey, south-east of Colchester town centre: see n. 50, **28 August 1675**.

[98] It seems likely that Lloyd was reading Eusebius of Caesarea (b.260 ×265, d.339 × 340), an early biblical scholar, historian, and Christian polemicist.

[99] The writing in this passage is larger, heavy, and erratic, and Lloyd writes 'devotion' (in its abbreviated form, 'D^t') three times, almost on top of one another. There is no explanation for this, and it does not occur again in the diary.

and was within all the afternoone about 5 performed my devotion and sat in the house till 9 and went to my chamber and about ¼ after 9 went to bed.

Sunday, 26 September: Rose a little after 7 after I was dressed and performed my devotion was in my chamber and read in the Practise of Piety[100] went downe and stayd a little before I went to church and at 10 went to Church and heard Mr Smith preach on the 3 Philippians 10 verse came home and went to my chamber and made a short prayer went downe to diner and after diner sate a little while and went to my chamber and performed my devotion and read till church and went to the same church and heard the same text came home at 4 and walked till 5 alone came to my chamber read and performed my devotion went downe and heard my landlady and Landlord read and sate till after 9 eate som bread and cheese and a little bef[ore] 10 went to my chamber and to bed.

Monday, 27 September: Rose at 7 and after I was dressed and performed my devotion went to schoole stayd till after 11 came home and sate in the house till diner after diner sat a little while below went to my chamber and performed my devotion went downe and sat a little while below and agreed with my Landlady for my bord for 12^{li} per Annum[101] sate in the house while my landlord and landlady went to Mrs Prestons abo[ut][102] the word[103] went to schoole a little before 4 stayd there till almost 5 came home and was in my chamber mending a payre of cuffes a little before 6 performed my devotion went downe and was below till 10 Mrs Mary Bond being there and then went to my chamber and to bed.

Tuesday, 28 September: Rose a little after before 7 after I was dressed and performed my devotion after [*faded word?*] went to schoole and stayd till after 11 came home and was below a little while went [to] my chamber performed my devotion and was within till 1 went to Joseph the Barber and stayd till almost 2 went [*approximately three lines faded to illegibility*].

---

[100] Lewis Bayly, *The Practice of Piety, Directing a Christian How to Walk that He May Please God* (date of 1st edn unknown; 2nd edn 1612). Bayly (*c.*1575–1631) was bishop of Bangor from 1613 until his death. *The Practice of Piety* was a 'Protestant classic' and was popular with English readers throughout the 17th century, *ODNB*.
[101] Lloyd's 'overheads' in terms of rent for both his dwelling and his business premises amounted to £22 per year, over half the average salary of a small schoolmaster.
[102] Or 'above'.
[103] Slightly unclear and ambiguous.

[fo. 8v]

Wednesday, 29 September: Rose at 8 and trimed myselfe and dressed myselfe and about 9 performed my devotion was within till 10 and then went to St Peeters to prayers came home and was within till 12 went to my chamber and performed my devotion and about 1 went to diner was within till 3 went to St Peeters to heare the sermon preacht before the swearing of the Mayor[104] in the 2 Chronicles 19 chapter 5:6 verses a little after 4 came home and walked with Mr Smith and Mr Seawell to Lexon heath came back about 6 went to Josephs the Barbers and playd on the Violin and stayd till 8 came home and was in the house till 10 Robert Meaddows being there went to my chamber and performed my devotion and went to bed.

Thursday, 30 September: Rose at 7 after I was dressed and performed my devotion went to school and stayd till after 11 came home and went to diner after diner performed my devotion and went to schoole a little after 1 and stayd till after 3 came home and sate in the house till 4 went to my chamber and mended my stockings and Mr Smith came and stayd till after 6 went to my chamber and performed my devotion came downe and was below till after 10 and then went to bed.

Friday, 1 October: Rose at 7 after I was dressed and performed my devotion went downe and eate a tost and sate below talking with Mr Meaddows about my roomes till 9 went to schoole and stayd there a little went downe and sate in Mr Meaddows house talking with him till 11 sent my Scoller home and came to him and agreed with him for 4^{li} per Annum for my roomes came home and sate a little while in the house went to my chamber and performed my devotion and went downe and read in Josephus[105] and went to diner a little before 1 and a little after went to schoole and stayd till after 2 and then went to walke with Mr Smith to see his Mare at the Royall Oake[106] came home and was in the house till almost 6 went to my chamber and performed my devotion and went downe and sate below with Mr Meaddows and Sam and Mr Smith and went to the coffie house and dranke a little mug of alle and read the sad discription of the lamantable fier in

---

[104] New mayors were chosen annually at Michaelmas (29 September), strictly speaking the halfway point of the year in the Old Style, which took Lady Day (25 March) as the first day of the year. The mayor for 1675 was one Alexander Hindmarsh.

[105] Titus Flavius Josephus (37–c.100), the Romano-Jewish historian.

[106] In East Stockwell St. in the parish of St Martin, D'Cruze, *Colchester People*, Vol. 3, 24.

Northampton[107] came home at 8 and sate in the house with Mrs Cockrill and Mrs Mary Bond till 10 went to my chamber and to bed.

Saturday, 2 October: Rose at 7 after I was dressed and performed my devotion went downe and eate som broth went to goe to schoole and mett Mr Smith and went with him to the White Lyon and drank on[e] flagon then went to schoole and stayd till 1 writting out 2 rates for a contry man[108] came home and performed my devotion and went to diner and stayd within till 4 went to walke with Mr Smith beyond the Sheaton[109] and came home a little before 6 and was below in the house with Mrs Mary Bond and about 9 came Sam and afterward his Brother I sate up till after 11 went to my chamber and performed my devotion and went to bed.

Sunday, 3 October: Rose at 11 not being well after I was dressed and performed my devotion went downe to diner at 12 sate a little while below went to my chamber and performed my devotion and went downe and sate a little while below and at 2 went to St Peeters and heard Mr Smith on the 1 Corinthians 1:4 came home and sate a little while below and read and went to my chamber [and] performed my devotion and went downe and sate below till 9 and went to my chamber [and] went to bed.

Monday, 4 October: Rose at 7 and after I was dressed performed my devotion and lay downe being not very well went to school a little before 9 stayd till after 11 [ca]me home sate in the house a little [*approximately two lines faded to illegibility*].

---

[107] The Great Fire of Northampton occurred on 20 September 1675, consuming much of the historic centre of the town, including the church of All Hallows. It was said to originate in a thatched house in St Mary St. For a contemporary account, see Anon., *A True and Faithful Relation of the Late Dreadful Fire at Northampton* (London, 1675). Ralph Josselin also wrote in his diary about the news of the fire, which apparently reached him earlier than Lloyd, on 26 September: see A. MacFarlance (ed.), *The Diary of Ralph Josselin, 1616–1683* (Oxford, 1976), 587.

[108] Lloyd's precise meaning here cannot be determined with certainty, but he seems to have been carrying out casual scrivener's work.

[109] This place name, which context seems to suggest was a river or ditch, is a mystery. I have found no reference to this term in any other sources. Below (**14 October 1675**), Lloyd mentions crossing the 'sheaton bridg' on his way home from Myland, immediately to the north of Colchester over the River Colne, crossed by North Bridge: the simplest explanation is that this was a local, colloquial name for the river and bridge there.

[fo. 9r]
downe and sate a little while in the house and went to schoole and stayd till after 4 came home and stayd a little while below went to my chamber and performed my devotion and came downe and was below till after 6 went to Mrs Cockrells where I supped with my Landlord and landlady and Mrs Mary Bond and stayd till after 9 came home and sate a little while below and about 10 went to bed.

Tuesday, 5 October: Rose at 7 after I was dressed and performed my devotion went to ~~sch~~ schoole and stayd till after 11 came home and was below till after diner and then stayd in the shop ½ an houer and went to my chamber and performed my devotion went to schoole a little after 1 and stayd till after 5 came home and went to my chamber and performed my devotion and came downe and was below mending the head of a cane eat something about 8 and sate up till after 9 Mary Bond being there went to my chamber and to bed about 10.

Wednesday, 6 October: Rose at 7 after I was dressed and performed my devotion went downe and stayd a little and went to schoole a little after 8 and stayd till past 11 came home and went to my chamber and performed my devotion and stayd in my chamber till almost 1 went downe to diner and after diner stayd a little went to schoole a little before 2 and stayd till almost 5 went to walke and gave a letter at the Kings Head[110] to my Brother John walked to Lexton warren and came home at 6 was within at 7 went to my chamber and performed my devotion and was below till 10 Sam Meaddows being there then went to my chamber and to bed.

Thursday, 7 October: Rose at 7 after I was dressed and performed my devotion after 8 went to schoole and stayd till after 11 came home and was a little while mending my chamber window performed my devotion and went to diner after diner made compast[111] and went to schoole and stayd till after 3 went with Mr Smith to Beerechurch[112] and came home by Muncks quick[113] was within and performed my devotion went downe and sate a little while and Mr

---

[110] Colchester had a purpose-made post house built in St Mary's parish in 1664/5, but there are records of the King's Head being used as a delivery and collection point by the mid 18th century, *VCHE*, 237.

[111] Compost?

[112] Berechurch, a small village about three miles south of Colchester town centre.

[113] Monkwick, an area just north of Berechurch, which now survives in the name of Monkwick Avenue.

Smith came in and we had ½ pint of brandy at 8 Samuel Meaddows and Mary Bond came in and stayd till almost 10 went to my chamber and to bed.

Friday, 8 October: Rose at 7 after I was dressed and performed my devotion went to schoole and stayd till after 11 came home and went to prayers at St Peeters came home and went to my chamber and performed my devotion went to diner and afterward scowered my belt went to schoole and about 3 went to see Richard Hawksbe[114] and stayd an houer after 4 came home and read a letter from Mrs Gray went and walked to Lexton waren and downe the little lane to the river[115] came home and went to my chamber and performed my devotion went downe and was below at 8 came Mr Gray and we had a gotch of beere and toast sate up till almost 10 went to bed.

Saturday, 9 October: Rose at 7 after I was dressed and performed my devotion was below a little came to my chamber and was confessing my sins and[116] it was my fast and before I had don Mr Smith came in and disturbd me and was forced to leave till after I came from church where I heard his father preach the fayer sermon[117] on the 55 Isaiah 1 Ho every one etc[118] came home from church about ½ houer after 12 sate a little by the fier went to my chamber and performed my devotion and finisht my confession a little after 1 went to walke and walk[ed] till past 3 toward the river by Lexton and washed my feete after came home and was within and trimed me and about ½ houer after 5 performed my devotion eate some super about 9 sate up till 10 [*illegible words*] her mother being there.

---

[114] Richard Hawksbee, of the parish St-Mary-at-the-Walls, was assessed at eight hearths in 1670, *EHT*, 300. He was the son of John Hawksby, vicar of Earls Colne from 1615 to 1640, and his wife Dionisia: Henry French and Richard Hoyle, *The Character of English Rural Society: Earls Colne, 1550–1750* (Manchester, 2007), 219–220.

[115] Probably the Colne, which flows north of Lexden into Colchester.

[116] Here the words 'sins and' are very uncertain; this passage is very ambiguous, and appears to read as a messy abbreviation 'Ss' for 'sins', and a poorly rendered ampersand. I have also speculated that this may be a fragment of the shorthand used elsewhere.

[117] A fair held on the eve and feast day in commemoration of St Denis of Paris (9 October) and six following days (reduced in 1635 to four) was granted to the burgesses of Colchester by Edward II in 1319, *VCHE*, 273. Lloyd clearly held the feast day in some reverence, fasting and making a private confession.

[118] 'Ho, every one that thirsteth, come ye to the waters, and he that hath no money; come ye, buy, and eat; yea, come, buy wine and milk without money and without price.' Isaiah 55:1.

[fo. 9v]

Sunday, 10 October: Rose a little after 7 after I was dressed and performed my devotion went downe and sate by the fier and eate som tost and dranke at 10 went to church and heard Mr Smith on the 55 Isaiah 2 verse came home after diner went to my chamber and performed my devotion but before I was quite dun was disturbed by Mr Smith went with him to walke to Mile End[119] where he tooke his mare and sent her home saw the church[120] came home and went to church before twas time ¼ houer and finished my devotion heard the same man and text came from church walkd a little with William Smith and Mr Seawell came back and met Mr Bloise went to Jaxons and stayd an houer and dranke 4 flagons came home and was below and read in Mr Doolittles booke[121] at ½ hour after 7 eate some tost and cheese a little before 9 went to my chamber and performed my devotion and about ½ hour after went to bed.

Monday, 11 October: Rose a little before 2 after I was dressed and performed my devotion went to the White Lyon to call Mr S: and J: S:[122] and taried a ½ of houer tooke horse to goe to Bury[123] went out ½ an houer before 3 called at Lanham[124] and dranke ½ pint of brandy went forward and came to Bury about 9 dranke and eate a little bread and cheese and went and walked round the towne and saw it and the Abby ruines[125] that was dedicated to St Edmond[126] which was a good one there are 2 churches Very Large and good one bulded by Edward the 6 and endowd with 200^{li} per Annum

---

[119] Myland, also known as Mile End, is a parish and formerly a village about one mile north of Colchester town centre. It is now a suburb of the town.

[120] A medieval church dedicated to St Michael.

[121] Thomas Doolittle (b.1630 × 1633, d.1707) was a nonconformist minister and devotional author born in Kidderminster, Worcestershire. Lloyd may have been reading Doolittle's very popular *A Treatise Concerning the Lord's Supper* (1667), which reappears later in the diary (n. 205, **25 December 1675**).

[122] These abbreviations have been left since they cannot be definitively expanded. However, it seems very likely that Lloyd was meeting his usual companion, William Smith, and perhaps a John Smith.

[123] Bury St Edmunds, Suffolk.

[124] Probably Lavenham, a village a little over halfway between Colchester and Bury St Edmunds.

[125] The Abbey of Bury St Edmunds was formerly one of the richest Benedictine monasteries in England until its dissolution in 1539. Its ruins are near the centre of the town, and remain a very prominent landmark.

[126] St Edmund was king of East Anglia from c.855 until his martyrdom at the hands of Viking invaders in 869. His remains were later moved to Bury St Edmunds (Beadoriceworth), attracting pilgrimages and leading to the establishment of the abbey in the 11th century.

and a schoole endowed with 22^{li} per Annum[127] saw the flying charriot and rod in it[128] and played one game at tic tac[129] with W: S: and saw him and J: S: play a game at bill cards we[nt] to our Inn to diner and had a shoulder of Mutton after diner a little after 12 set out of Towne for Schoole Inn and came there a little before 4 called and dranke one flagon and saw the finest signe post that is in Europe which cost severall 100 of pounds the bulding and paynting[130] came af[?ore] night to the Inn in Yaxeley[131] and lay there with one King[132] of Norwitch the next day and performed my devotion in the field.

Tuesday, 12 October: Rose at 6 and after I was dressed performed my devotion and at ½ houer after 7 after we had eat a toste and dranke 1 pint of brandy went forward for Ipswitch overtooke about 7 mile Mrs Merill where we dranke at her friends house came to Ipswich a little before 11 at the King's Head set up our horses and dranke and went out and saw part of the Towne next the watter and the dock and the shipyard[133] in which was a small ship about 250 Tunn redy to goe of the stocks[134] the next tide went back and went to the county[135] Goale[136] and saw Mr Merill went back to our Inn and diner not being redy went to

---

[127] Here Lloyd's information is rather muddled and misleading; Edward VI did endow a school at Bury in 1550, which remains open and still bears his name. There are two large parish churches in the town which would have existed during Lloyd's visit in 1675, neither of which was built by Edward VI. St Mary's, in particular, is an unusually grand parish church which underwent substantial renovation in the 15th and 16th centuries. The other, some 200 yards away, was formerly known as St James, but has now been rebranded as St Edmundsbury Cathedral.

[128] Probably 'rode in it', but Lloyd's precise meaning is unclear.

[129] Tick-tack is a historical 'table game', a variant on backgammon. For an overview of the rules contemporary to Lloyd, see Charles Cotton, *The Compleat Gamester* (London, 1674), 158–161.

[130] The inn at Scole, a tiny village on the Suffolk–Norfolk border, was famous in its day for its grandness and particularly the extravagance of its signpost, which elaborately arched over and across the road. The inn, a large red brick building, survives to this day, but the sign does not. A vivid description (and accompanying poem) can be found in James Brome, *Travels Over England, Scotland and Wales* (London, 1701, 2nd edn), 120–125.

[131] Yaxley, Suffolk, another small village about four miles south of Scole, on the road to Ipswich.

[132] An individual with the surname King.

[133] Ipswich, on the Orwell Estuary, is famous for its waterfront and was one of the most important ports in England.

[134] Lloyd was describing a newly constructed ship ready to be launched; the 'stocks' were the frame which supported the vessel whilst it was being built.

[135] Very unclear and faded; tight binding.

[136] This building appears no longer to exist; a former county gaol which still stands in Ipswich later served as the headquarters of East Suffolk County Council, and then Ipswich Council, until 2004. However, it was built in 1836–1837; *TBE, Suffolk*, 297.

see the other side of the Towne and went to the Coffee house and dranke a dish of Tee and saw my Lord Deavoreax his house[137] came back and dined a[?nd] had a brest of mutton went after diner to the shipyard saw the ship Launcht which went not well of the stocks came to our Inn and stayd an houer and a little after [?went] [?for]ward for Colchester and came to Towne at 8 went to [illegible] and dranke 2 flagons came home and eate som super at [?9] [s]ate up till 10 Mary Bond being there went to my chamber and performed my [devotion.]

[fo. 10r]
Wednesday, 13 October: Rose at 9 after I was dressed and performed my devotion was in my chamber till after 10 went downe with William Smith and eate a tost and dranke and stayd below till 11 went to my chamber and wrote a letter to Mrs Gray afterward a little after 1 performed my devotion and was in my chamber mending a payre of stockings and was within till 5 went to my chamber and performed my devotion and went downe and about 6 went to the post house to carry my letter and came home and stayd neere an houer about 7 went with William Smith to the Red Lyon[138] and heard the Musick and see them dance and drank a bottle of Sider which cost 1^s came home and eate some tost for my supper and sate up till ½ houer after 10 Mary Bond and Robert Meaddows being there went to bed at 11.

Thursday, 14 October: Rose at 8 and after I was dressed and performed my devotion was within till 9 went to my schoole but my boy was not there stayd till 10 with Samuel Meadows and came to Joseph the barber and was in his shop reading his pill papers and talking till 11 came to my Lodging and was below till after diner and stayd below after diner till almost 2 went to my chamber and performed my devotion and about 3 William Smith called me and I went

[137] Christchurch Mansion is a substantial Tudor house near the centre of Ipswich. It was constructed on the grounds of the dissolved Priory of the Holy Trinity by the Withypoll family. The sole heiress, Elizabeth Withypoll, married Leicester Devereux, 6th earl of Hereford, and the mansion stayed in the Devereux family until it was sold by the 10th Viscount in the 1730s. It was, at the time Lloyd visited, probably the largest house in Ipswich, with 32 hearths according to the poll tax assessment of 1702: see Michael Reed, 'Ipswich in the Seventeenth Century', PhD thesis, University of Leicester, 1973, 148.

[138] The Red Lion still exists at the same site today, as the Red Lion Hotel. Dating from about the late 15th century, it stands prominently at 42–44 High St., with beautiful exposed timber framing and projecting upper windows; it is described by Pevsner and Radcliffe as a 'remarkable building'. *TBE, Essex*, 140–141; D'Cruze, *Colchester People*, Vol. 3, 22–23.

with him and saw the Jarman woman without Armes worke with her toes and knitt and spin and play on musick and write and shoote and charge a pistall after I came thence about 4 went to walke to Mile End and met William Smith and helped him take up his mare and went home over the sheaton bridg came home and went to Robert Meadows's shop to a stranger that came to towne to keepe a schoole stayd there ½ houer went with Sam Meaddows to Rich Hawsbe stayd till after 7 came home and was in the house till after 8 Goodman Neale and his wife and Richard Orbell[139] and his wife[140] and Sam Meaddows and spent my peny amongst them after they were gon eate a butterd toste and sate up till 9 went to my chamber and performed my devotion and to bed.

Friday, 15 October: Rose at 8 after I was drest and performed my devotion was in my chamber till 7 went to schoole and stayd till past 11 came to my chamber and performed my devotion and was within till after 12 went with my Landlady to her Brother Orbells Mill to diner where was his Cousen Orbell and his wife and Goodman Golden and his wife and I stayd there till after 5 came home and was in the house below till 9 Mary Bond being there and Jo: Blumfield[141] a little while went to my chamber at 9 and performed my devotion and went to bed.

Saturday, 16 October: Rose at 7 after I was dressed and performed my devotion at 8 went to schoole and stayd till after 11 came home and eate some bread and cheese was below till after 1 mending my table book[142] went to my chamber and performed my devotion but was disturbd by William Smith before I had quite done, went to walke [to]ward Lexton warren came home and at 3 went to diner with George Smith and his wife was within till 5

---

[139] Probably Richard Orbell, a miller of St Mary-at-the-Walls. He was assessed at three hearths in 1670, and his will was proved on 26 May 1681. *EHT*, 300; ERO, D/ABW 70/61.

[140] Susan Orbell.

[141] Lloyd never gives this individual's full name, but I think it likely that this was the same individual referred to elsewhere as 'Joseph the barber'. One Joseph Blomfield, barber of St Mary-at-the-Walls, Colchester had his will proved on 13 January 1690: see ERO, D/ABW 73/95.

[142] This has two possible meanings. Firstly, as a 'notebook' or memoranda similar to a commonplace; secondly, a book, in print or manuscript, containing musical notation arranged in such a way that it might be read by people sitting round a table. For the former, see H. R. Woudhuysen, 'Writing-tables and table-books', *eBLJ*, article 3 (2004), 1–11; for the latter, Scott. A. Trudell, 'Performing women in English books of Ayres', in Leslie C. Dunn and Katherine R. Larson (eds), *Gender and Song in Early Modern England* (Abingdon, 2016), 18.

went to my chamber and performed my devotion and went to Richard Hawksbee and stayd till past 7 came home and was below and read a little while till 9 went to my chamber and after I had gott my Linen went to bed.

Sunday, 17 October: Rose at 8 after I was dresed and performed my devotion and read a little went downe and sate by the fier a little while and eat a little bread and cheese went to church at 10 to Trinity and heard Mr Smith on the 55 Isaiah 3 came home and went to diner sate a little while after diner and went to my chamber and performed my devotion and read till almost 2 went downe and sate by the fier a little while and went to church and heard the same text and ma[n] came home about 4 and could not get in went to walke toward the Sheaton came home againe and could not gett in went to [Mr] [Cock]rills and sate there a little while with him and Mrs Basher and afterward came my Landlord and landlady and Orbell [?st]ayd till ¼ houer after 7 came home and eate some super and sa[?te] be[?low] w[?ith] R: M:[143] and Mary Bond till neare[144] 9 went to my chamber and performed my devotion and [?to bed]

[fo. 10v]
Monday, 18 October: Rose at 7 after I was dressed and performed my devotion was in my chamber mending a payre of cuffes till almost 9 went downe and was below a little while at 9 went to schoole and sett Richard Orbell a copy who came to me to schoole that day stayd there till ½ houer after 10 went to St Peters to prayers came home a little after 11 eate som diner and went with my Landlord and Robert Meadows[145] to Jaxons and dranke 2 flagons of beere and a quart of Brandy came home and went to my chamber and performed my devotion and went to schoole and stayd a little while came home and go[t] my Lds Landlord to set on a lock stayd there a little while came home and too[k] my stick and the black cat[146] and carried to Orbells mill came back and went to Richard Hawksbee stayd ¼ houer came home and went to my chamber and performed my devotion went downe and sate below Mr Hast Mr Cockrell and Sam Meaddows being there and had 2

---

[143] These words very faded and obscure; abbreviation unexpanded due to uncertainty.
[144] Faded and uncertain.
[145] Originally 'R: M:'.
[146] Lloyd offers us no explanation for this passage, but his hand here is quite clear.

gotches of beere after they were gon ea[te] a tost for my super and sate up till 10 went to my chamber and to bed.

Tuesday, 19 October: Rose a little after 6 after I was dresed and performed my devotion was in my chamber mending a payre of cuffs till a little after 8 went to school and stayd till after 11 came home and made a great R[147] for Mr Hast and at 12 went to diner after diner writt the text to the Indenture and sent it home went to school a little after 1 stayd a ¼ of houer and came home and performed my devotion and went to school and stayd till after 4 came to my chamber and finished my mending my cuffs and performed my devotion and walked with my Landlord a little beyond Mile End to pasture his horse came home and was in the house at 7 came my things from Wivenoe by the Wagon and I tooke them in and uncorded them and was below with Sam Meaddows and at 10 came his Brother Robert[148] sat up till almost 11 went to my chamber and a little after 11 went to bed.

Wednesday, 20 October: Rose at 7 after I was dressed and performed my devotion stayd a little while below and went to schoole and stayd till after 11 came home and was in my chamber a little went downe to diner sate a little while after went to my chamber and performed my devotion went to school and stayd till after 4 came home and was in the house with my Landlady and Mrs Cockerill till after 5 went to my chamber and performed my devotion and was in my chamber looking amongst my things till neere 8 went downe and was below till after 10 Mr Rase and Mary Bond[149] being there went to my chamber and to bed.

Thursday, 21 October: Rose a little before 8 after I was dressed and performed my devotion went to school and stayd till after 11 came home and sate a little while by the fier and went to my chamber and performed my devotion came downe to diner and sate a little while below went to school a little after 1 stayd till a little after 3 went to the turners and goot[150] 2 handles for my ham[mer] came home at 5 and went to my chamber and performed my devotion and came do[wn] and was below getting out my old handle of my

---

[147] Lloyd attempts a kind of flourish here, albeit in his tiny and cramped hand; the result is a confusing squiggle. However, it most closely resembles his capital 'R' – perhaps the first letter of Mr Hast's Christian name – here referring to a small calligraphic showpiece.

[148] Originally 'R:'.

[149] Originally 'M: B'; Lloyd frequently uses this particular abbreviation from this point, quite clearly to refer to Mary Bond.

[150] Got.

hamer and fileing the cleekes[151] at 8 came Mr Hast and sate till 9 and gave 2 gotches of beere and brought me 2 skins of partchment to write the text at ½ hour after 9 went to my chamber and to bed.

Friday, 22 October: Rose betweene 7 and 8 after I was dressed and performed my devotion was in my chamber a little drawing the text letters of Mr Hasts Indenture went to school a little before 9 stayd till almost 12 came home and sate in the house by the fier till after diner sate a little while and went to my chamber and performed my devotion and went to schoole stayd till af[ter] 5 went to Mr Hawksbees to Richard's funeral stayd till after 6 c[ame] home and was in the house putting in a handle to my little hamer stayd up till 10 Mary Bond and Sam Meadows being here went to my chamber and performed my devotion went to bed.

[fo. 11r]
Saturday, 23 October: Rose after 7 after I was dressed and performed my devotion went to school and stayd till after 11 came home and was below till after diner at 1 went to my chamber and performed my devotion and was below in the house riveting my little hamer and cleansing my [*illegible*] hamer till after 4 and sate in the house talking with William Smith till after 5 went to my chamber and performed my devotion and was below till after 9 William Smith being there till after 8 a little before 10 went to my chamber and gott my linen redy and a little after 10 went to bed.

Sunday, 24 October: Rose at ½ hour after 8 after I was dressed and performed my devotion read in the Practice of Piety till neere church time went downe and stayd a little while after 10 went to Trinity Church and herd Mr Smith on the 55 Isaiah 3[152] came home and after diner sate a little while went to my chamber and performed my devotion and read till church time went to church and heard the same man and text came home and went to my chamber and read and performed my devotion went downe and sate in the house and read a little while at 7 came Mary Bond and I read a Sermon and afterward eat some tost and dranke sate up till after 9 went to my chamber and to bed.

---

[151] Uncertain. Lloyd may be a referring to a shim or cleat, a small wedge of wood or metal used to secure the handle in the 'head' of a tool such as a hammer.

[152] See Sunday, **17 October 1675**.

Monday, 25 October: Rose at ½ hour after 7 after I was dressed and performed my devotion went to school and stayd till after 11 came home and was below by the fyer till 12 went to my chamber and performed my devotion came downe and went to diner and sate a little while went to school and stayd till a quarter after 4 came home and was in the house with Elizabeth Edling and Jo[?seph] the Barber till 8 at 9 came Sam Meaddows and we sate up till almost 11 went to my chamber at 11 and went to bed.

Tuesday, 26 October: Rose a little after 7. After I had performed my devotion was in my chamber dressed myselfe and went to schoole at 9 stayd till after 11 came home and was by the fyer a little went to my chamber and performed my devotion went downe to diner after I had dined went to schoole and stayd till after 4 came home and warmed myselfe and cullered my belt[153] went to my chamber and performed my devotion and went to the White Lyon to Mr Smith and Mr Holland and after we had beene there a little while came Mr Rush stayd till 9 and spent a grote[154] apeece came home and was below till 10 Sam Meaddows being there, then went to my chamber and to bed.

Wednesday, 27 October: Rose at 7. After I had performed my devotion and was dressed stayd in my chamber a little while went to school and stayd till after 11 came home and was by the fier till diner after diner went to school and performed my devotion in my iner roome and stayd at school till after 4 came home and sate by the fier a little went to my chamber and performed my devotion went downe and went to Joseph the barber and stayd till neere 7 came home and sate up till 11 Mary Bond being there and Sam Meaddows till after 9.

Thursday, 28 October: Rose at ½ hour after 7 after I was dressed performed my devotion went downe and was below a little. Went to school and stayd and heard my boyes read and sent them home it being Holyday came home had som red herring went to my chamber and was there looking [*illegible words*] after performed my devotion and was in my chamber till [*two lines faded to illegibility*].

---

[153] Presumably, Lloyd altered the colour of his belt by dyeing or some other process.
[154] Four pence.

[fo. 11v]
Friday, 29 October: Rose at ½ hour after 7 after I was dressed and performed my devotion sate a little while by the fier and went to schoole and stayd till after 11 came home and sate a little by the fier went to my chamber and performed my devotion went downe to diner and sate a little while and went to school and stayd till after 4 came home and sate by the fier with Mary Bond and Mrs Cockrill till 7 went to my chamber and performed my devotion and stayd a little went downe and sate by the fier till 10 Mrs B:[155] and Mary Bond being there then went to bed.

Saturday, 30 October: Rose at ½ hour after 7 after I was dressed and performed my devotion went to school and stayd till after 11 came home and went to diner sate a little after diner and went to my chamber and performed my devotion and was within all the afternoone making a payre of sleves to my wastcoate[156] at 5 performed my devotion and was below by the fier till 10 Mr Cockerill and his wife and Mary Bond and two or 3 more being there a little whele Nathaniel[157] my Landladys Brother and one to be my scholler went to my chamber a little after 10 and went to bed.

Sunday, 31 October: Rose betweene 8 and 9 after I was dressed and performed my devotion was below by the fier a little at 10 went to Trinity and heard Mr Smith on the 55 Isaiah 3 after diner went to my chamber and performed my devotion and read till church time went to the same church and heard the same man and text came home and performed my devotion and went to my school for a copy for Mr Colemans[158] son to see and stayd at Robert Meaddows ½ an houer came home and read a sermon then eate

---

[155] Uncertain due to lack of context, but probably a relative – perhaps the mother – of Mary Bond.

[156] The decades after the Restoration saw a major shift in male fashion, in which the doublet and jerkin evolved into a long outer coat, or *justacorps*, and waistcoat or vest; a sleeveless, usually knee-length garment. Both were usually made with the same fabric. This shift reflected changing tastes on the continent and the influence of the major Catholic royal courts – namely the French and Habsburgs – over that of Charles II. Lloyd was a keen follower of fashion. See Christopher Breward, *The Culture of Fashion* (Manchester, 2015), 78–86.

[157] Originally 'Nat:'.

[158] Probably William Coleman, saymaker, whose sons William and John were admitted to Colchester Grammar School in 1672 and 1675 respectively. William Coleman junior was born in the parish of St James on 26 June 1660. A 'William Coeman' was assessed at six hearths in the parish of St James in 1670. See John Horace Round, *Register of the Scholars Admitted to Colchester School, 1637–1740* (Colchester, 1897), 64, 70; *EHT*, 285; ERO, D/P 138/1/6.

some tost for my super and after read another sermon after 9 went to my chamber and to bed.

Monday, 1 November: Rose at 7 after I was dressed and performed my devotion was in my chamber till after 9 mending the sleves and coller of my wastcoate then went to Schoole and home Orbell read and came to my Lodging and was within neere 11 then went to St Peeters to prayers came home and was below till after diner went to my chamber and performed my devotion and was within till neere 4 then walked abroad with Joseph the Barber and stayd out till almost 5 came home and was below till 7 went to my chamber and performed my devotion and was abroad in the streete walking till 10 came In and went to my chamber and to bed.

Tuesday, 2 November: Rose at 7 after I was dressed and performed my devotion went to walk till almost 9 came to school and stayd till after 11 came home and went to diner afterward sate a little while by the fier went to my chamber and performed my devotion went to school and stayd till after 4 came ho[me] and was in the house Mrs Cockerill being there at 6 went to Joseph the Barber stayd till after 7 came home and was below playing at cards with [*illegible*] [*illegible*] and his wife till 9 afterward sate drinking our winings [?Mary] Bond being there till after 10 went to my chamber and performed my devotion after [*one line faded to illegibility*].

[fo. 12r]
Wednesday, 3 November: Rose at ½ hour after 6 and went to the White Lyon to see Mr Smith take horse and stayd there till almost 8 came home and dressed myselfe and performed my devotion and cut my sleves of my riding coate shorter and put som fullers earth[159] on it and hanged it to the fier and sate by the fier after I had dun this till diner (I went not to school because Robert Meaddows had brought home his wife) after diner not being very well sate by the fier and slept a little went to my chamber and performed my devotion and came downe and sate by the fier all the Afternoone not being ~~fitt~~ fitt to doe anything not being well about 3 Mary Bond cutt of my hayre and I put on my Perriwige[160] and

---

[159] A form of fine and absorbent clay which has been used for centuries to cleanse and thicken woollen garments.

[160] This was unlikely to be Lloyd's very first time wearing a periwig, since they were already established as essential male fashion accessories by the 1670s; cf. Pepys, who

at 4 Jo:[161] and I walked out a little came in about 5 and was below all the evening about 7 Sam Meaddows came in and we had a gotch of beere and I eate a tost and butter and afterward played at cards till after 10 and sate up till 11 went to my chamber and performed my devotion and went to bed.

Thursday, 4 November: Rose a little after 7 after I was dressed and performed my devotion was below a little while and went to school and stayd till after 11 came home and was below a little and went to my chamber and performed my devotion and went downe to diner sate a little while and went to school and stayd till after 3 came home and was curling my perriwig till neere 5 write a letter for Jo: and was in the house Elizabeth Edling beeing there a little while I read a sermon and sate up till after 9 Mary Bond being there went to my chamber and performed my devotion and at 10 went to bed.

Friday, 5 November: Rose at 8 after I was dressed and performed my devotion was in my chamber a little while went downe and stayd below till after 10 went to St James and heard Mr Shelton on the 124 Psalm 6[162] verse came home at 1 went to diner Mary Bond dined with us sate after diner till 4 went and read a sermon on the 5 Judges last verse on the 5 of November[163] went to my chamber and performed my devotion and went downe and sate a little went to Jax[on's] and stayd till almost 9 came home and was in the house, William Burton and his wife being there and Mary Bond went to my chamber a little after 9 performed my devotion and went to bed.

---

first tried one in May 1663, and found he had 'no stomach' for it, despite the difficulties he had in keeping his own hair clean. He acquiesced to the new fashion by November of the same year, noting that the removal of his own hair 'went a little to my heart', *Pepys*, Vol. 4, 130, 362.

[161] Perhaps Joseph Blumfield (Bloomfield, Blomfield): see n. 141, **15 October 1675**.

[162] 'Blessed be the Lord, who hath not given us as a prey to their teeth.' Psalm 124:6.

[163] 'So let all thine enemies perish, O Lord: but let them that love him be as the sun when he goeth forth in his might. And the land had rest forty years.' Judges 5:31. The anniversary of the Gunpowder Plot on 5 November had been observed since the passage of the Observance of the 5th November Act 1605 (3 Jac. I, c. 1) in January 1606 (New Style). It was a source of occasional controversy as the political landscape changed throughout the 17th century, variously being claimed by 'puritan' champions of ongoing reformation and religious conscience, and by defenders of the divine institutions of monarchy and episcopacy. By the time of Lloyd's diary, it was 'both a divisive and unifying occasion [...] universally observed but subject to various interpretations': see David Cressy, *Bonfires and Bells: National Memory and the Protestant Calendar in Elizabethan and Stuart England* (Stroud, 2004), 171–189.

Saturday, 6 November: Rose at 6 and after I was up and performed my devotion and made my confession out of Dr Taylors Golden Guide to the Penetent[164] it being my monethiley fast, a little before 9 mad myselfe ready to goe to school but Mr Smith sent for me to the Whit Lyon I stayd there ¼ of hour and went to school and stayd till after 11 came home and sate by the fier and read a sermon and went to my chamber and performed my devotion and renewed my covenant afterward walked abroad and stayd about an houer, came back and was a little while mending my perrywig and went downe and sate by the fier and read another sermon and about 3 eate som diner and sate by the fier till after 4 went to my chamber and performed my devotion came downe and sate by the fier at 7 Jo:[165] Gray came in and Mary Bond and we had 2 Gotches of beere and I sate up till after 9 went to my chamber and gott my things redy for Sonday and went to bed.

Sunday, 7 November: Rose at 8 after I was dressed and performed my devotion went downe sate by the fier and read a sermon, eate a tost and went to church and heard Mr Smith on the 55 Isaiah 3 came home and went to my chamber and used a short prayer went downe to diner after diner sate by the fier a little and went to my chamber and performed [my devotion] sate by the fier a little and went to church and heard the

[fo. 12v]
same man and text came home and performed my devotion and went downe and sate by the fier and discoursed with my Landlord and read at 7 came Mary Bond and my Landlady in and a little after Mrs Bond and stayd a little after they went I suped and sate till after 9 discourceing and went to my chamber and to bed.

Monday, 8 November: Rose at 7 after I was dressed and performed my devotion walked to Lexton Warren and came home a little after 7 suppd a little broth and went to school and stayd till after 11 came home and was by the fier a little and comed my perriwig I curled went to diner a little after 12 and went to my chamber and performed my devotion and went to school and stayd till after 4 came home and warmed myselfe and went to my chamber and

---

[164] Here Lloyd slightly muddles the title of Taylor's *The Golden Grove, or, A Manuall of Daily Prayers and Letanies* (1655), which in later editions, included an addendum entitled *A Guide for the Penitent*. The earliest example I have found is from 1667.
[165] Unknown.

performed my devotion and went downe and made cleane my semiter and tooke the blade out of my sord[166] and after sate by the fier and read a sermon and afterward eat som tost and dranke and saste by the fier till almost 10 went to my chamber and to bed.

Tuesday, 9 November: Rose betweene 6 and 7 after I was dressed and performed my devotion was a little while in my chamber mending my shirte at 9 went to school and stayd till after 11 came home and was in my chamber a little mending my shirt went to diner and sate by the fier a little while after diner and went to my chamber and performed my devotion and went to school and stayd till after 4 came home and went to my chamber and performed my devotion and went downe and was below till after 9 Mr Terrill and Thomas Ward and Sam Meaddows and Mary Bond being there went to my chamber and went to bed about 10.

Wednesday, 10 November: Rose at ½ hour after 7 after I was dressed and performed my devotion was within a little and went to school and stayd till after 11 came home and went to my chamber and performed my devotion and went to diner and sate by the fier a little went to my chamber and mended my shirt till 1 went to school and stayd till after 4 came home and was within <performed my devotion> till after 10 Mary Bond being there till after 7 went to bed and took som oyle and suger[167] for my cold.

Thursday, 11 November: Rose at 8 after I was dressed and performed my devotion went to school and stayd till after 11 came home and after diner went to my chamber and performed my devotion after I went to school and stayd till after 3 went to Robert Meaddows and stayd till after 6 came home and was below till after 7 went to my chamber and performed my devotion and was below till after 10 Mr Hast and his wife and Mr Cockril and Mary Bond being there in the evening went to my chamber and to bed.

---

[166] A sword was an essential fashion accessory for any young man with genteel aspirations in the later 17th century; cf. Samuel Pepys, who remarked in his diary on carrying a sword 'as the manner now among gentlemen is', *Pepys*, Vol. 2, 28–29. A 'scimitar' is in fact a large, curved cavalry sword from the Middle East or North Africa – probably not what Lloyd was carrying.

[167] The precise medicinal 'oyle' chosen by Lloyd to treat his cold is a mystery, but the addition of sugar, either as a sweetener or as an ingredient with medical properties itself, was typical, Elaine Leong, 'Making medicines in the early modern household', *Bulletin of the History of Medicine*, 82 (2008), 145–168.

Friday, 12 November: Rose at 8 after I was dressed and performed my devotion went to school and brekfasted at Mr Meaddows after 11 came home and wase below till after 12 beating charcoale for pounce went to my chamber and performed my devotion and went downe to diner and went to school and stayd till after 4 came home and went to James Bond[168] and stayd till 7 came home and eate som cold meat and sate up till after 10 Mary Bond being there went to my chamber and performed my devotion and went to bed.

Saturday, 13 November: Rose at 8 after I was dressed and performed my devotion went to school and stayd till after 11 came home and sate by the fier a little and went to my chamber and performed my devotion and was mending my coate till 2 went downe to diner and stayd below till amost 4 went to my chamber and gott my Linen against Sonday and performed my devotion and went downe and helped my Landlord hang the Jack poolies[169] went to see James Bond[170] and stayed ½ hour and he had the small pox coming out, came home and eate buttered tost and sate up till after 9 went to my chamber and sowed [?on] a paire of cuffs and went to bed.

[fo. 13r]
Sunday, 14 November: Rose a little after 8 after I was dressed and performed my devotion went downe and eate some tost and dranke and at 10 went to church and heard Mr Smith on the 55 Isaiah 3[171] came home and went to my chamber and used a shorte prayer went downe to diner and sate a little while by the fier and went to my chamber and performed my devotion and went with Mr Smith to the heath to church and called at Alderman Hammonds[172] and

---

[168] Originally 'Ja: B:'.

[169] Lloyd is referring to the pulleys which helped to operate a mechanical jack, a device for lifting or suspending heavy loads. This may refer to a roasting jack, 'device for turning a spit for roasting meat over an open fire', *OED*. What Lloyd and his landlord used it for is unclear. They may have been operating a jack-operated water pump; below, he makes scattered references to 'cleansing' the jack, for instance at **9 October** and **1 November 1676**. On **21 November 1677**, Lloyd specifically mentions cleaning the 'jackhead', which the *OED* has as 'a lifting-pump used for raising large volumes of water', albeit used in the 18th century.

[170] Originally 'Ja: B:'.

[171] See Sunday, **17 October 1675**.

[172] Probably George Hammond, mentioned by Morant as an alderman who participated in a perambulation of the bounds of Colchester in 1671. A will for a George Hammond, beer brewer of St Leonard's parish, was proved on 10 February 1680, and a person of the same name and parish was assessed at four hearths in 1670. See ERO, D/ABW 69/210; *EHT*, 291.

stayd a little before church heard the same text againe after we came from church went to Stephen[173] Hebdens and stayd an houer and drank two or 3 glasses of Ale came home at 6 and stayd within till 7 went to my Mother[174] Cockrills and stayd till 9 came home and went to my chamber and performed my devotion and went to bed.

Monday, 15 November: Rose at 8 after I was dressed and performed my devotion went to school and stayd till after 11 came home and after diner went to my chamber and performed my devotion went to school and stayd till after 4 and was at Robert Meaddows's[175] making bullets till 5 came home and sate by the fier a little went to my chamber and performed my devotion and was mending my Imbroidered garters after 7 went downe and went with my Landlord to Mr Grayes and stayd till after 9 and heard Mrs Sarah play on the Dulcimur,[176] after I came home eate somthing for supper and sate up till 10 went to my chamber and to bed.

Tuesday, 16 November: Rose ½ hour after 7 after I was dressed and performed my devotion was a little while in my chamber at 9 went to school and stayd till after 11 came home and sate by the fier till after diner went to my chamber and performed my devotion and went to school and stayd till after 4 came home and sate by the fier till 5 went to my chamber and performed my devotion and was there mending my garters till 8 went to Mr Cockrills and stayd till after 9 came home and eate somthing and at 10 went to bed.

Wednesday, 17 November: Rose at 8 after I was dressed and performed my devotion went to school and stayd till after 10 came home a little before 11 to breakfast with Mr Cockrill at 12 performed my devotion and was till after 1 mending my garters and buckles went to school and stayd till after 4 came home and was steeling[177] my ribbons till after 5 and was below till almost 10 Mrs Cockrill and

---

[173] Originally 'Steph:'.

[174] Lloyd is using 'Mother' as a respectful title for an older woman unrelated to him, *OED*. This *may* have been Elizabeth Cockerell, a elderly spinster of North Hill in St Peter's parish, whose will was proved in 1686; she was apparently erroneously listed as a widow, with four hearths, in the assessment of 1670. See ERO, D/ABW 72/7; *EHT*, 287. Another 'Widow Cockerill' was assessed at nine hearths in the parish of St Mary-at-the-Walls, ibid. 299.

[175] Originally 'R: M:'.

[176] Lloyd is referring to a hammered dulcimer, a percussive stringed instrument. It consists of strings stretched across a sound board which are struck with mallets to achieve a note.

[177] Ironing.

Mary Bond being there went to my chamber and performed my devotion and went to bed.

Thursday, 18 November: Rose ½ hour after 7 after I was dressed and performed my devotion went to school and stayd till after 11 came home and was below till 12 went to my chamber and performed my devotion and was in my chamber steeleing som cloth to mend my cloth coate sleeves at 1 went to school and stayd till after 3 was below a little went to my chamber and stayd a little and performed my devotion went downe and was below all the evening and helped my Landlord make a payre of shashoones[178] at 10 went to my chamber and to bed.

Friday, 19 November: Rose ½ hour after 7 after I was dressed and performed my devotion was in my chamber till 9 then went to school and stayd till after 11 came home and sate by the fier a little and went to my chamber and was drawing two peeces of cloth till diner went to diner sate by the fier a little went to my chamber to perform my devotion and was disturbed went to school and finished it there stayd till almost 4 came home and sate by the fier Mr Jackson and his wife being there, went to my chamber and performed my devotion and stayd till 7 went downe and sate a little then went to Mrs Cakrills with Mary Bond and stayd till after 10 came home and sate a little and went to bed.

[fo. 13v]
Saturday, 20 November: Rose ½ hour after 7 after I was dressed and performed my devotion was in my chamber making up a cravat and mending the lace of a payre of cuffs at 9 went to school and stayd till after 11 came home and was in my chamber looking in my Trunck for old lynon and found some Lace and cloth to make me a payre of little cuffs after 12 performed my devotion and went downe and stayd below and made almost one cuffe went to my chamber and steeled out the ribon of my cloth sate and was about it till almost 4 went downe and made an end of my cuffe went to my chamber and performed my devotion went downe and eate some fryd beefe for supper, and after super made the other cuff and read 2 sermons and sate up till after 9 went to my chamber and sowed on a payre of cuffs and went to bed.

---

[178] Probably referring to 'sashoons', a pair of leather pads inserted into the leg of a boot to improve the fit and prevent chafing, *OED*.

Sunday, 21 November: Rose a little before 8 after I was dressed and performed my devotion went downe and eate a tost then went to church to All Saints[179] and heard Mr Hickringole[180] on the 8 of Matthew 9 verse came home and went to my chamber and made a shorte prayer to God went downe to diner and sate a little went to my chamber and performed my devotion and went downe and sate a little and went to St James and heard Mr Cufflie[181] the Minister of Lexton on the 28 Job 28 verse came home and went to my chamber and after a little meditation performed my devotion went downe and heard my Landlord and Landlady read and eate some super and read a chapter afterward and sate by the fier till 9 went to my chamber and to bed.

Monday, 22 November: Rose a little before 8 after I was dressed and performed my devotion stayd a little while in my chamber went downe and warmed myselfe and went to school and stayd till after 11 came home and sate by the fier a little and went to diner after diner went to my chamber and performed my devotion and was in my chamber riping[182] my breeches at 1 went to school and stayd till 4 and dranke a pint of burned brandy with Sam Meaddows came home and was below and Elizabeth Edlin and Sam Meaddows was at my Landlord's and we had a pinte of burned brandy and a Gotch of beere and at 8 went to my chamber and performed my devotion and went to Mr Edlins and had a pint of burned brandy and a Tanckard of beere came home at 10 went to my chamber and to bed.

Tuesday, 23 November: Rose at 7 after I was dressed and performed my devotion went to walk to Lexton Lane and stayd till almost 9 came home and eate som butterd bread and went to schoole and stayd till after 11 came home and scowred my hilt of my sword and eate a little diner not being very well by reason of the brandy I drunk over Night, <went to my chamber and performed my devotion> at 1 went to schoole and stayd till 4 came home and sate

---

[179] All Saints stands at the eastern end of the High St., facing Colchester Castle. Its tower was built in the 15th century, but the rest of the surviving building dates from the 19th. Declared redundant in 1953, it is now a natural history museum, *TBE, Essex*, 132.

[180] Edmund Hickeringill (1631–1708), rector of All Saints from 1662 until his death, was by far the most well known (or infamous) of the Colchester churchmen referred to by Lloyd. His life and career were marked by near constant legal and theological controversy which cannot be recounted here: see *ODNB*; *CCEd* Person ID: 97230.

[181] Nathaniel Cuffley was rector of Lexden from 1669 until his death in 1706, *CCEd* Person ID: 162286.

[182] Ripping.

by the fier and about 7 eate some brioled[183] Mutton and at 8 went to my chamber and performed my devotion and at 9 went to bed.

Wednesday, 24 November: Rose at 7 after I was dressed and performed my devotion was in my chamber till almost 9 mending lace for a payre of cuffs went downe and eate a tost and went to school and stayd till after 11 came home and put on the hilt of my sword and went to my chamber and performed my devotion went to diner and stayd a little and went to school and stayd till after 4 came home and was by the fier till 5 went to my chamber and performed my devotion and was drawing some cloth to mend my cloth sleeves, went downe and made a payre of little cuffs and eat som super at 9 and sate up till 10 and went to bed.

[fo. 14r]
Thursday, 25 November: Rose at 7 after I was dressed and performed my devotion went to walke to Lexton heath came back a little before 9 and was in my chamber a little and went to school and stayd till after <11 came home to diner and performed my devotion and went to school and stayd till> 3 went to Buttolfs Streete and came back and bought tredle string of the Mayor that was naught made a string of silke[184] and playd Mrs Cockerill and Mary Bond being at my Lodgings playd at cribbag[185] till 9 then my Landlord and his wife came from Stanway[186] and I eate som supper and sate up till 10 went to my chamber and performed my devotion and went to bed.

Friday, 26 November: Rose ½ hour before 8 after I was dressed and performed my devotion was in my chamber till 9 about my coate went to the school and stayd till after 11 came home and sate by the fier a little went to my chamber and performed my devotion and went to Mrs Cockrells to diner with my Landlady and sate

---

[183] Lloyd's hand is very ambiguous here, though an unusual spelling of 'broiled' is the most obvious explanation.

[184] This word is slightly obscured by tight binding, but it appears to say 'tredle'. Lloyd may be referring to a string for operating a pedal-operated (see 'treadle', *OED*) machine – probably a spinning machine, given that he then 'made a string of silk' – which, whilst unusual, is not entirely surprising given his interest in amateur tailoring. It is interesting to note, also, that Lloyd had a sufficiently good relationship with the town's mayor to receive free goods from him: 'that was Naught'.

[185] Cribbage is a 'matching' card game, usually for two players but adaptable for three or four, which involves assembling combinations of cards to score points. For an exposition of the contemporary rules, see Cotton, *Compleat Gamester*, 106–110.

[186] A small village about three miles west of Colchester.

there till I went to school and stayd till after 4 came home and sate by the fier till almost 6 went to my chamber and performed my devotion and was about my coate till 7 came downe and was below by the fier playing on my violin playd 5 or 6 games at cribbage with Mary Bond and my Landlady till after 9 sate by the fier and playd on my violin till 10 went to my chamber and to bed.

Saturday, 27 November: Rose a little before 8 after I was dressed and performed my devotion was in my chamber a little while mending my shirt wente to school and stayd till after 11 came home and was by the fier a little and after diner went to my chamber and performed my devotion and was in my chamber mending my shirt till after 2 went downe and warmd myselfe and received a letter from Philoclea and was in my chamber about my coate till 4 then got my Linen and performed my devotion and went downe and received a letter from my Brother Nicholas sate below and read an houer in the Isle of Man[187] and went to my chamber and writt a letter to Philoclea the copy[188] went downe and eate somthing and read till 10 went to my chamber and went to bed.

Sunday, 28 November: Rose after 8 after I was dressed and performed my devotion went downe and read a little and eat a peece of tost at 10 went to St Peeters and heard a stranger[189] on the 3 Lamentations 24 the first part of the verse came home and went to my chamber and made a short prayer went to diner sate by the fier and read a sermon and went to my chamber and performed my devotion and went to St Peeters againe and heard the same man and text came home and went downe and sate by the fier and discoursed with my Landlord and read a sermon or two before super and one after and sang a Psalm and discoursed a little of the duty of prayer in a family after 9 went to my chamber and to bed.

Monday, 29 November: Rose at ½ hour after 7 after I was dressed and performed my devotion was in my chamber a little mending my stockings went downe and went to school and stayd till after 11 writt a letter to Philoclea came home and went to my chamber after I had a little warmed myselfe, and performed my

---

[187] Probably the work of the puritan Richard Bernard, *The Isle of Man, or, The Legal Proceedings in Man-shire against Sin* (London, 1627), a popular 'allegory of the trial of sin' which ran to 16 edns by 1683. See *ODNB*.

[188] One of two copies: one sent to the recipient, the other kept by the sender.

[189] A visiting preacher, either by invitation for an occasion, or filling in in case of absence.

devotion and went downe to diner and sate a little after diner went to school and stayd till after 4 came home and sate by the fier a little and went to my chamber and performed my devotion and afterward cutt of my blue buttons from my camlet[190] coate and sowed some of the lyning again betweene 7 and 8 came Mr Cockrill and had a tost and 2 gotches of beere and he stayd about an houer and went aw[ay] and came againe and we played 2 games at cribbage and after they went away I went to prayers with my Landlord and his wife which was the first time we began went to my chamber and to bed betweene 10 and 11.

[fo. 14v]
Tuesday, 30 November: Rose betweene 7 and 8 after I was dressed and performed my devotion was in my chamber a little and went to prayers afterward was in my chamber (after I had eaten a red hering for brekfast) till after 10 and then went to church to St Peeters to prayers came home and wrote a Certificate for Mr Jaxkon [*sic*] and went to diner and after diner finished it and performed my devotion and when he came for it we had a gotch of beere, I went to my chamber and stayd till 4 went downe and playd on my Violin till after 5 then eate som supper and playd a tune or two and went to my chamber and performed my devotion and went downe and sate a little while and cutt of the necks of 2 halfe shirts[191] for Mary Bond to set on new ones went after 7 to Robert Meaddows and playd 5 or 6 games at Cribbage with his wife and wone 2 eat som Oysters and played 3 with him and beat him all came home and sate by the fier till 10 went to prayers and to bed.

Wednesday, 1 December: Rose a little after 8 after I was dressed and performed my devotion went to prayers and went to school and stayd till after 11 came home and sate by the fier a little and went to my chamber and performed my devotion and went downe to diner and went to school and stayd till almost 4 came home and sate by the fier and playd on my violin till after 5 went to my chamber and performed my devotion and was about my coate till almost 7 went downe and eate sum super and playd at cribbag with Mary Bond

---

[190] The term 'camlet' supposedly originally referred to a luxurious and expensive fabric from the East, but by Lloyd's time it always referred to 'a worsted fabric of plain weave. Sometimes of silk, figured or watered (camleted)', Margaret Spufford and Susan Mee, *The Clothing of the Common Sort, 1570–1750* (Oxford, 2017), 269.

[191] A shirt front – or chemisette – to 'fill in' a neckline or décolletage, popular in the 17th century: see *OED*.

till after 9 and went to prayers having read a chapter first then went to my chamber and after a little while went to bed.

Thursday, 2 December: Rose a little before 8 after I was dressed and performed my devotion went downe and we went to prayers and I went to school and stayd till after 11 came home and was in my chamber a little and performed my devotion went downe to diner and sate a little while and went to school and stayd till after 3 came home and was in my chamber about my coate a little performed my devotion and went to Joes: and stayd till after 6 came home and Mr Genkins brout home my breeches and I sate and dranke a gotch of beer and went to my chamber and was about my coate till 9 went downe and eate som supper and sate a little while read a chapter and went to prayers and went to my chamber at 10 and went to bed.

Friday, 3 December: Rose at 8 after I was dressed and performed my devotion went to prayers and sate by the fier a little went to school and stayd till after 11 came home and sate by the fier went to my chamber and was about my coate performed my devotion and went to diner sate a little and went to school and stayd till almost 4 came home and sate a little by the fier and went to my chamber and performed my devotion and was about my coate a little went downe and playd at cards with my Landlady and Mr Cockerill and his wife and had 3 gotches of beere and sate and talked and danced Mary Bond being and S: B:[192] coming till after 10 when they were gon I read a chapter and went to prayers went to my chamber and to bed.

Saturday, 4 December: Rose at 8 after I was dressed and performed my devotion went to prayers and warmed myselfe and went to school and stayd till after 11 came home and warmed myselfe and went to my chamber and performed my devotion and afterward made my confession after Dr Taylors method and renewed my covenant, and after walked abroad till 3 came in and got my Linnen redy for Sunday and went downe and sate by the fier and about 5 went to my chamber and performed my devotion and was a little while mend[ing] my shirte went downe and suppd and was a little while after mending my shirte went downe at 8 and sate by the fier Mr Cockerill being there and had one gotch of beer sate up till 10 went to prayers and went to my chamber and sowed on my cuffs and went to bed.

[192] Uncertain, though perhaps likely another Bond.

[fo. 15r]

Sunday, 5 December: Rose at 8 after I was dressed and performed my devotion went to prayers and went downe and eate somthing went to church to Trinity and heard Mr Cuffly preach on the 11 Proverbs 7 came home and made a shorte prayer went to diner sate a little went to my chamber and performed my devotion and went to the Heath and heard a stranger on the 3 Revelation 20 came home and performed my devotion and read a sermon and heard my Landlady read 2 chapters Elizabeth Edling and her sister came and sat ½ houer and after I eate som supper and read a sermon and sang a Psalm and went to prayers and anoynted my legs with brandy for a paine I had in them and at 10 went to my chamber and to bed.

Monday, 6 December: Rose at 8 after I was dressed and performed my devotion went to prayers and sate by the fier a little went to school and stayd till after 11 came home and sate a little by the fier and went to my chamber and performed my devotion and was a little about my coate went to diner and sate a little after diner and went to school and stayd till almost 4 came home and sate by the fier a little, about 5 went to my chamber performed my devotion and was about my coate till 8 went downe and eate a tost and playd at cribbag with Mary Bond till after 9 dressed my leggs and went to prayers and after 10 went to bed.

Tuesday, 7 December: Rose ½ hour after 7 after I was dressed and performed my devotion was ½ hour in my chamber mending a shirte went to prayers and sate a little by the fier a little went to my chamber and was a little about my coate, performed my devotion and went downe to diner and sate a little and went to schoole and stayd till 4 came home and was below till 5 went to my chamber and performed my devotion and was till 7 about my coate went downe and sate by the fier and read a sermon and eate somthing and went to prayers after 9 anoynted my Legs with brandy and went to bed about 10.

Wednesday, 8 December: Rose at 8 after I was dressed and performed my devotion was a little mending my shirte went to prayers and went downe and supt som potage and went to school and stayd till after 11 came home and sate a little whyle by the fier and went to my chamber and performed my devotion and was about my coate a little went downe to diner and sate a little and after 1 went to schoole and stayd till almost 4 came home and sate a little by the fier and playd two or 3 tunes at 5 went to my chamber and performed my devotion and was a little about my coate till after

6 went downe and mended my map of England and eate som super and went to my chamber and was about my coate till almost 9 went downe and read a sermon and dressed my leggs at 10 went to prayers and went to my chamber and to bed.

Thursday, 9 December: Rose at 8 after I was dressed and performed my devotion was a little mending my shirte went to prayers afterward went to school and stayd till after 11 came home and sate by the fier a little went to my chamber and was a little while about my coate performed my devotion and went to diner sate a little after diner and went to school and stayd till after 3 went to the Heath and called to see Mr Terrill and Jo:[193] and I drank 2 flagons came home and went to my chamber and performed my devotion and mended my stockings at 7 went to Mr Meaddows and playd 3 or 4 games at cribbage and came home a little after 9 eate som supper and sate up till 10 my Landlady read a chapter and we went to prayers and went to my chamber and to bed.

Friday, 10 December: Rose a little before 8 after I was dressed and performed my devotion was a little in my chamber about my drawers went to prayers and to school and stayd till after 11 after I came home sate a little by the fier went to my chamber and performed my devotion and was a little about my drawers went to diner and to school and stayd till after 4 came home and was by the fier a littl[e] went to my chamber and stayd till 7 performed my devotion and was about my drawers, went to Mrs Cockerill and playd at cards sent a letter to Mrs Gray stayd at Mrs Cock[erill's] [till] after 10 came home and sate a little my Landlady read a chapter and we went to prayers and I went to bed.

[fo. 15v]
Saturday, 11 December: Rose at 8 after I was dressed and performed my devotion went to prayers and sate by the fier a little went to school and stayd till after 11 came home and sate by the fier till diner and after a little went to my chamber and performed my devotion and was about my coat till after 3 then gott my Linnen and performed my devotion and went downe and sate by the fier till ½ hour after 5 then went to my chamber and went to bed and sweete[194] till 8 rose and dressed myselfe and sat by the fier

---

[193] Unknown.
[194] Probably an unusual spelling of sweat, 'sweated'.

till 10 and playd 3 or 4 games at cribbag with Mary Bond eate a tost and sate a little went to prayers and to bed.

Sunday, 12 December: Rose at 9 after I was dressed went to prayers and eate a little tost performed my devotion and sate by the fier till diner and heard my Landlady read after diner sate by the fier and read till 2 went to my chamber and performed my devotion and went downe and sate by the fier and heard my Landlady read at 5 went to my chamber and performed my devotion and went downe and sate by the fier Mr Cockerill and his wife being there till 9 my Landlady read a chapter and went to prayers and I went to bed not being well all day by reason of my sweete could not goe to chur[ch].

Monday, 13 December: Rose at 8 after I was dressed and performed my devotion went to prayers and to school and stayd till after 11 came home and was with Mr Ardrey[195] and promised him to learne him to write after 12 performed my devotion went to diner and to schoole and stayd till past 4 came home and went to my chamber and was a little about my coate performed my devotion and was about my coate till 7 almost was below Mr Cockerill being there till 9 after my Landlady read a chapter and we went to prayers and I went to bed.

Tuesday, 14 December: Rose a little before 8 after I had dressed and performed my devotion was in my chamber a little mending my shirte went to prayers and went to school and stayd till after 11 came home and sate by the fier a little went to my chamber and performed my devotion and was a little about my coate went to diner and sate a little by the fier and went to school and stayd till after 4 came home and was below a little went to my chamber and read my psalm and chapter and went downe bei[ng] called and stayd a little I playd 3 or 4 tunes to compose myself becau[se] my Landlord was out of humor[196] and I talked a little to him went to my chamber and after a little pause performed my devotion and was about my coate till after 7 and made an end of it went downe and sate below and eate some supper and after sate by the fier and playd on my violin till after 9 and talked till almo[st] 10 then my

---

[195] This is the first mention in the diary of the enigmatic Mr Ardrey, one of the diary's most significant 'characters': see Introduction, pp. 15–16.

[196] Christopher Marsh refers to Lloyd here in *Music and Society in Early Modern England* (Cambridge, 2010), 184.

Landlady read and we went to prayers and I went to my chamber and to bed.

Wednesday, 15 December: Rose a little before 8 after I was dressed and performed my devotion was in my chamber trying my coate, went to prayers and to school and stayd till after 11 came home and sate by the fier a little went to my chamber and performed my devotion and was a little while about my breeches went to diner and sate a little and went to school stayd till after 3 came home and sate by the fier a little went to my chamber and performed my devotion came downe a little went up and was about my bre[eches] set on som of the lace stayd above a little and went downe and read a little booke for the Instruction of young men and women Mr Delony[197] then went to my chamber againe and stayd till 8 mending my shirte went downe and eate som supper and playd till after 9 sate talking till 9 Jo: Blumfield being there my Landlady read and we went to prayers and went to my chamber and was a little mending a payre of cuffs and went to bed.

[fo. 16r]
Thursday, 16 December: Rose afore 8 after I was dressed went to prayers and performed my devotion and was a little basting[198] on the lace on one knee of my breeches went to schoole and stayd till after 11 came home and sate by the fier a little went to my chamber and performed my devotion and sowed on the lace of one knee of my breeches went to diner and afterward sate a little and went to school and stayd till after 3 went to Mr Ardrey and stayd with him till 7 and learned him to write came home and was in the house and playd a little on my Violin till after 9 went to my chamber and performed my devotion went downe and my Landlady read and we went to prayers and I went to my chamber and stayd and mended my shirt and went to bed about 11.

Friday, 17 December: Rose at ½ hour after 7 after I was dressed and performed my devotion was in my chamber sowing on som of the lace on my breeches, went to prayers and to school and stayd till after 11 came home and sate by the fier a little and eate my diner, and went to my chamber and performed my devotion and was a

---

[197] Handwriting unclear. This may not be the same author mentioned on **2 September 1675**. I have been unable to trace this book so far.

[198] A term for loose, temporary stitching, often used when altering garments or when adorning them with other fabrics, as Lloyd was doing here, *OED*.

sowing on the rest of the Lace on my breeches, went to school after 1 and stayd till after 4, came home and was in the house and playd a little went to my chamber and performed my devotion and was about my breeches altring the pockets before at 7 went to Mr Bond to see Jeames but he was asleepe stayd ½ hour cam[e] home and wrote an Answer to Mrs Grays letter I read in the evening went downe and sate by the fier and eate som supper and sate a little while and discoursed about the sckriptures my Lady read and we went to prayers.

Saturday, 18 December: Rose at 7 after I was dressed and read we went to prayers and I performed my devotion and was a little in my chamber and sowed on som ribbon to my breeches before went to school and stayd till after 11 came home and was by the fier a little went to my chamber and performed my devotion and was about the pockets of my breeches till 2 and then went to Mr Ardries and stayd till 4 called at Mr Bonds as I came home to see James and stayd ¼ of hour came home and went to my chamber and performed my devotion and was a little mending a cravat and getting my Lynen went downe and sate below till after 9 Mrs Cockerill being there then eate some super and after 11 my Landlady read and we went to prayers and I went to my chamber and mend on my cuffs and to bed.

Sunday, 19 December: Rose at 8 after I was dressed went to prayers and performed my devotion went downe and read a sermon and went to St Peeters and heard Mr Thompson on the 19 Psalm 13 came home and went to my chamber and made a shorte prayer went to diner and after sate by the fier and read a sermon and went to my chamber and performed my devotion went to St Peeters and heard the same man and text came home and went to my chamber and after a little medititation [sic] performed my devotion and went downe and sate by the fier George Rase and his wife and Mr Cockerill being there till after 6 read a sermon and sate ½ an houer Elizabeth Edlin being there eate som super my Landlady read a chapter and we sang a Psalm and went to prayers and I went to bed at 10.

Monday, 20 December: Rose a little before 8 after I was dressed and performed my devotion went to prayers and stayd in my chamber a little went to school and stayd till after 11 came home and sate a little by the fier, and went to my chamber and performed my devotion and was with Mr Ardrey teaching him to write a little eate som diner and went to schoole and stayd till after 4 and broake of for Christmas came home and sate by the fier a little performed my devotion and was about the pockets of my breeches till after 9 went downe and eate some super and sate a little and read a sermon and went to prayers and went [to] my chamber at 11 stayd up a little and went to bed.

[fo. 16v]
Tuesday, 21 December: Rose at 8 after I was dressed and performed my devotion went to prayers and was in my chamber till after 10 mending my stockings went to St Peeters to prayers and after Mr Thompson sent for to speake with me and I went to his house and he promised me his son to come to school and to doe me all the kindness he could came home and was in my chamber a little abou[t] mending my stockings went to diner and after diner made an end of my stockings and performed my devotion and after 1 went to Mr Ardries and stayd till 4 came home and was below till after 5 went to my chamber and performed my devotion and went downe and made cleane my pistolls and after I eate a tost and dranke Mr Cockerill and his wife being there after 10 my Landlady read and we went to prayers and I went to bed.

Wednesday, 22 December: Rose at 8 after I was dressed and performed my devotion went to prayers and was in my chamber a little went downe and <scowered[199] my hat and> curled my perrwig and my Landlord beeded[200] and about 1 eate som diner and was in the shop helping make up tobaco[201] till 2 went to my chamber and performed my devotion and was in my chamber till almost 4 Lyning my fringed gloves with black ribbon, and read till almost 5 then went to James Bonds funerall[202] and stayd till past 7 came home and went to my chamber and performed my devotion and read till almost 9 then was a little about my gloves and after 9 went downe and my Landlord and Landlady came home and she got som burnt brandy not being very well after 10 she read and we went to prayers and I went to bed.

Thursday, 23 December: Rose at 8 after I had performed my devotion we went to prayers and I went downe and dranke a little

---

[199] Scoured.
[200] This could mean rested, waited, or prayed, *OED*.
[201] This is the first real clue as to Lloyd's landlord Stratton's occupation: a mercer or shopkeeper.
[202] Lloyd's acquaintance, mentioned above, who was described above as developing smallpox on **13 November 1675**. It is interesting to speculate that Lloyd may have been fringing his gloves with black ribbon for the funeral.

burned brandy and stayd a little went to my chamber and made an end of my gloves and went downe and eate s[om] tost and dranke and was below and made som card matches, and performed my devotion below my Landlady being makeing cleane and washing my chamber about 1 went to diner and about 2 I went to Mr Ardries and stayd till after 4 came home at 5 and was below and read a sermon about 7 came Mary Bond and a little after my Landlord home and I sate a little and eate som super and aft[er] super I discoursed with my Landlord and his wife about the ☧[203] and persuaded then[204] to receive it neither of them ever haveing received it after 9 my Landlady read a chapter and we went to prayers and I went to my chamber and performed my devotion and went to bed.

Friday, 24 December: Rose ½ hour after 7 after I was dressed and performed my devotion went to pra[yers] and I went downe and stayd by the fier a little went to my chamber and made my confession of sins by Dr Taylors forme and renewed my covenant and stayd in [my] chamber till almost 11 went downe and sate by the fier and read a sermon and read Mr Dooleetle booke on the ☧[205] after 1 went to my chamber and performed my devotion and in the same booke againe went downe got my Lynen and clothes to were the next day and mended the heeles of my shoes and trimed myselfe and sate below a little and went into the towne to the cutlers for a fa[?re][206] scabard, came home and went to my chamber and performed my devotion and was in my chamber and read went downe and read eate som bread and dranke and read a sermon and eate a little cold meate and was bel[ow] till after 10 my Landlady read and we went to prayers and I went to my chamber and to bed.

Saturday, 25 December: Rose at 7 after I was dressed and performed my devotion, read in Mr Doolittles booke on the ☧ and then went to prayers and went to the fier and sate a little and went to my chamber and made my confession out of the Practice of Piety

---

[203] Lloyd often uses a chi rho symbol, ☧, to denote the word 'Sacrament', and does so in this case. The Greek characters chi and rho – 'X' and 'P' – form the Christogram, the first two letters of ΧΡΙΣΤΟΣ or 'Christos', used since the reign of Constantine the Great (c.306–337).
[204] Them.
[205] Doolittle, *Treatise Concerning the Lord's Supper* (1667): see n. 121, **10 October 1675**.
[206] This atypical word fades into the very tight margin.

[fo. 17r]
read and prayed till twas almost church time went downe and sate by the fier a little and went to church and stayd ½ hour before it began receved the ℞ at Peeters and the Mayor in vitted invited me to diner and I stayd with him till church time <Mr Thompson preached on the 6 John 69> came from church and church and went to my chamber and performed my devotion and sate below and Mr Gray came and we had a gotch of beere and after he was gon I read out of Mr Doolittles booke to persuade my Landlord and his wife to receive the ℞ went to super and sate a little after and then my Landlady read a chapter and we sang a Psalm and went to prayers and sate a little and I went to my chamber and performed my devotion and to bed at 8.

Sunday, 26 December: Rose at 8 after I was dressed and performed my devotion went downe and read a little went to prayers and after eate something and read went to church to Trinity and heard Mr Smith on the 8 Romans 3 came home and went to my chamber and made a shorte prayer went to diner and sate a little went to my chamber and performed my devotion and went downe and stayd till church time and went with Mr Smith and heard him at St Giles on the same text of the morning came home and caled at Mr Cockerills to know what He would send to Chambridg stayd ¼ of hour came home and sate by the fier and discoursed with my Landlord about religion about 6 I sate by the fier alone and read at 7 came Mary Bond and after ½ hour went to my chamber and performed my devotion went downe and eate som super afterward Jo: Blumfield cam and tooke a pipe and stayd till after 9 my Landlady read a chapter and we sang a Psalm and went to prayers and I went to bed.

Monday, 27 December: Rose ½ hour after 5, performed my devotion and dressed myselfe to goe to Sir Gervase Ellwes[207] but the raine in the morning hindred me till after 10 then went and about 3 gott to Stoke[208] to the Lamb extreamely wet and weary lay there all night sent to William Giffard who came and saw me and went back againe, performed my devotion in bed.

---

[207] Sir Gervase Elwes, 1st Bt (1628–1706) was a local magnate and politician with substantial influence in Suffolk and Essex. He was MP for Sudbury and Suffolk several times between 1677 and his death in 1706. He was buried in Stoke-by-Clare: *Hist. Parl. 1690–1715*, Vol. 3, 972–973. It is not clear how Lloyd knew him or why he was visiting.

[208] Stoke-by-Clare, Suffolk, a village almost halfway between Colchester and Cambridge.

THE DIARY OF GEORGE LLOYD 95

Tuesday, 28 December: Rose before 8 and performed my devotion on the bed after I was dressed, went to Sir Gervases and was there with the young gentellmen and at 11 went to prayers and wast [*sic*] up and downe there went to prayers in the parlor and to bed and lay with William Giffard and performed my devotion in bed.

Wednesday, 29 December Rose at 10 and dressed myselfe and performed my devotion and was with Andrew Giffard walking a little, and playd at Cribage an houer and lost not or wone eate some oate cake for breakefast about 12 went to walke to heare the hounds and stayd out till 3 came in and was in the parlor, about 5 went to diner the huntsmen be[?ing] coming not till after 4 after super playd at lany the looe[209] and lost a shilling after prayers about 11 went to bed and performed my devotion in bed.

Thursday, 30 December: Rose about 8 performed my devotion and got myselfe redy and about 11 went to Chambridg and got thether before 3 dressed myselfe and went to Mrs Haynes and saw her and Mrs M: L: and Mrs E: L:[210] and Mrs Crane <at 4 went to King's College Chapel> and stayd there till 10 and supped there and went to my Lodgings at the Cock in the Pease mar[ket] Hill[211] and dranke a flagon of bere as I ordenary might and performed my devotion and went to bed.

[fo. 17v]
Friday, 31 December: Rose at 6 performed my devotion and dressed myselfe and went at 7 to call Mrs Linford to goe to Whadon[212] for Mrs Kat: Harris and at 8 we went and got there by 11 stayd till 5 and came home and I stayd at Mrs Haynes till 10 went to my Lodging and performed my devotion and went to bed.

1676

Saturday, 1 January: Rose at 9 after I was dressed and performed my devotion went to St Edwards[213] to prayers but the confession and

---

[209] Lanterloo or Loo, a trick-taking game popular in the 17th century.
[210] Probably Elizabeth and Mary Lynford: see Introduction, pp. 18–20.
[211] Peas Hill and Market Hill are streets which meet at a corner in central Cambridge.
[212] Whaddon, a small village about fifteen miles south-west of Cambridge.
[213] St Edward King and Martyr is a royal peculiar in Peas Hill, Cambridge, and was founded in the 13th century.

Psalms was over before I came went to my chamber and performed my devotion and went to Mr Hunts and bought me som fidle strings and enquired for Mr Crosfield but found him not after 11 went to Mr Barrons and delivered the boxes Mrs Cockrill sent, went to Mrs Haynes to diner and stayd till 4 and went to prayers at King's College and stayd till 10 wen[t] to my Lodgings and dranke a flagon of ale and went to my chamber and performed my devotion and went to bed.

Sunday, 2 January: Rose at 8 after I was dressed and performed my devotion went to St Edwards and heard a sermon on the 2 Kings 7:9 went to walke on the fields and meditated till 12 went to Mrs Haynes to diner and stayd there till 2 went to St Marys and heard Mr Grig[214] of Penbrook Hall[215] preach on the 2 Timothy 1:13 after I came away mett with Mr Cannon and Mr Langly and walkd the back way to Peeter house[216] and went to the buttery and dr[ank] and eat som bred and cheese went to Langly's chamber and had som m-[*illegible*] and apples went to prayers to the chapell and was in the organ loft after prayers went to St Johns,[217] and heard the organs and came away to the Coffe house and dranke a dish of Coffe went to the Mitter[218] and we drank a quart of Tent[219] went bac[k] to the Coffe house and dranke a dish of tee, Mr Langly payd for all went home to my Lodgings and dranke a flagon of ale and read and performed my devotion and went to bed.

Monday, 3 January: Rose at 9 after I was dressed and performed my devotion went to Mr Herring about the Masquerade, walked in Trinity[220] walkd till almost 10 went to Mrs Haynes and stayd a little

---

[214] Perhaps Francis Grigg, BA 1660, MA 1663, and fellow of Pembroke College, Cambridge, 1665. He was ordained in 1664 and rector of Rawreth, Essex, from 1678 until his death in 1704: *Cantabrigienses*, Vol. 1, pt. 2, 268.

[215] Probably Pembroke College, Cambridge.

[216] Peterhouse, the oldest Cambridge college.

[217] Perhaps the old chapel of St John's College, Cambridge, now rebuilt.

[218] The Mitre tavern, not to be confused with the pub of the same name which still stands in Cambridge, was one of the primary alehouses of the day in the 17th and 18th centuries. It 'fell down' *c*.1634, but was rebuilt. It stood in the parish of St Edward, at the northern end of Trumpington St. (or perhaps King's Parade). The proprietor *c*.1664 was one Owen Mayfield, an alderman and mayor of Cambridge 1672–1673, d.1686. See Charles Henry Taylor, *The Annals of Cambridge*, Vol. 3 (Cambridge, 1845), 265, 515, 542, 553; John E. Foster (ed.), *The Diary of Samuel Newton, Alderman of Cambridge, 1662–1717* (Cambridge, 1890), 67, 89.

[219] A deep red Spanish wine.

[220] Trinity College, Cambridge, founded by Henry VIII in 1546. One of the largest and richest of the Cambridge colleges and famous for its grand and distinctive architecture.

THE DIARY OF GEORGE LLOYD 97

went to King's College to prayers after went to Jesus College[221] and dined with Mr Cannon and Mr Langly stayd till after 2 called and dranke ½ pint of brandy Mr Langly gave us tooke leave of them and called at William Herrings, and he told me the Masquerade held walked in Trinity walks till 4 went to Kings to prayers and afterward went to Mrs Haynes and stayd a little walked in Kings walks and went to my Lodging and pulled at [*illegible words*] and layd my [*illegible*]

[fo. 18r]
out of my pocket went againe to Mrs Haynes and after 6 we went to Mrs Curtesses and there we all dressed ourselves and a little before 9 went to the Mayors[222] in Masquerade, William Herring Meneere[223] Mr Branston and myselfe, Mrs Harris Mrs Carter Mrs Crane and Mrs Elizabeth Linford stayd there one houer before we began to dance and danced about an houer and stayd a little and went to Mrs Curtesses went Mrs Haynes and there I found Mrs Mary Linford much concerned that her sister was with us and I talked with her till after 12 went to my Lodgings and performed my devotion and went to bed.

Tuesday, 4 January: Rose at 7 after I was dressed and performed my devotion went to Kings to prayers after prayers went to Mr Haynes to take my leave and saw noebody but Mrs Haynes and Mrs Mary Linford to take my leave of and Mineere, caled at Mr Homes and went to my Lodgings and put on my bootes and got my things redy and sent to Jerebahams[224] and dranke with Mr Wise, about 11 went away and about ½ houer after 4 got to Stoke eate somthing then I went in and was in the parlor till super after super saw them play at cards a little, and Mr Andrew Giffard went to Mr Smiths to bed, ~~wenesday rose about 9~~ and performed my devotion in bed.

[221] Jesus College, Cambridge, founded in 1496.
[222] The mayor of Cambridge for 1676 was Andrew Hart, *Diary of Samuel Newton*, 75.
[223] Perhaps a phonetic attempt at spelling a foreign name. One might also speculate that Lloyd was referring to a Dutchman, without attempting to spell his name; 'Mister' (and analogues) in Dutch is 'meneer'. I am grateful to Miranda Bethell for pointing this out.
[224] Whether Lloyd is referring to a public establishment or a private individual here is uncertain; his spelling is very unusual and hard to trace to anything, but his hand is quite clear.

Wednesday, 5 January: Rose about 9 after I was dressed and performed my devotion walkd till about 11 went to Sir Gervase they being gon a hunting I met Mr Owen and we were together and walked till 1 came in and eate som cake and was in the parlor till they came from hunting about 5 we went to super and after super I playd at tables[225] with Andrew Giffard and lost 6^d at tables about 9 we went to Mrs Smiths to bed and I performed my devotion in bed.

Thursday, 6 January: Rose about 9 went to Sir Gervase and dressed myselfe and performed my devotion in Mr Owens chamber at 11 went to prayers came home and was up and downe till 2 then went to diner and after diner was in the parlor till 5, then went to dancing, Mr Cocking Mr Ellwes Mr Richard Catts Mr Andrew Giffard, and myselfe. Mrs Amy Ellwes Mrs Frances Ellwes Mrs Golden's <eldest daughter> Mrs Betty Golden, Mrs Renholds danced till 11 then eate som super after danced till 3 gave over and sate till 4 then Mr Giffard and I went to bed to Mr Smiths and I performed my devotion in bed.

Friday, 7 January: <Performed my devotion in bed and rose> at 11 after I was dressed walked a little with Mr Andrew Giffard went to Mr Catts chamber and eate some ca-[*illegible*] for breakfast and an egg about 2 Mr Owen and I walkd and saw Sir Gervase's courser[226] about 5 went to super and was in the parlor seeing them play at cards till after 9 went to bed Mr Giffard and I to Mrs Smithes and performed my devotion in bed.

[fo. 18v]
Saturday, 8 January: Rose ½ hour after 6 performed my devotion in bed, after I was dressed went to Sir Gervase and put on my boots and got my things redy <eate my breakfast> and at 8 took my leave of the young gentellmen when they went a hunting, afterward tooke my leave of Sir Gervase when he went, went into the house and dranke with the young Ladyes and tooke my leave of them and Mr Williams and Mr Owen and Mr Andrew Giffard

---

[225] Probably backgammon or a variant thereof; 'tables' are a class of historic board-games to which backgammon belongs.

[226] Whilst the meaning here is ambiguous, it is possible given Elwes's evident fondness for the hunt that Lloyd went to see his 'courser', a term which once described a medieval warhorse also used to hunt, and by the 17th century meaning a fast horse, *OED*. Otherwise, Lloyd may have been referring to a riding course.

came out at ½ hour after 10 came home ½ houer after 2 eate a tost and dranke and went to my chamber and went to prayers and went downe and sate by the fier and went to my chamber and writ all from the begining of my Journey to this place went downe to supper and sate a little went to my chamber and performed my devotion and sate up till 10 went to prayers and to bed.

Sunday, 9 January: Rose at ½ 8 <I went to prayers and> after I was dressed and performed my devotion went downe and ea[te] som bred and cheese went to Allhallows[227] and heard Mr Hickringole on <the 2 Philippians 5> came home and went to my chamber and made a shorte prayer went to diner and after diner read almost a sermon went to my chamber and performed my devotion and went [to St] Peeters and heard Mr Thompson on the 4 Hebrews 2 came home and sate by the fier a little went to my chamber and performed my devotion and went downe and my Landlady read till after 7 then Mr Lambert sent for me to his house about his son and I stayd till almost 8 came home and sate by the fier Mary Bond being there till almost 9 eate somthing and my Landlady read a chapter and we sang a psalm and went to prayers and to bed.

Monday, 10 January: Rose ½ ho at 7 after I was dressed and performed my devotion went to prayers and afterward a little after 8 I went to schoole and stayd till after 11 got som fier, there, was below till almost 12 went to my chamber and mended the lyning of my coate Dr Giffard tore went to diner and afterward sate a little went to school and stayd til aft[er] 4 went to Mr Ardrey and stayd till 6 came back and went to Mr Edlins and gott a glass desk went into his house and playd at Lany the looe and lost 6ᵈ playd afterward at cribb[age] with Mr Holisters sister and wone 3 games of her stayd till 10 came home and sate up a little my Landlady read a chapter and went to prayers and I went to my chamber and performed my devotion and went to bed befor[e] 12.

Tuesday, 11 January: Rose before 6 after I was dressed and performed my devotion went to prayers and to school and stayd till after 11 came home and was by the fier a little went to my chamber and performed my devotion and went downe and sate by the fier went to diner after 1 went to school and stayd till after 4 came home and sate by the fier a little went t[o] my chamber and performed my devotion went downe and sate by the fier and pl[ayd]

---

[227] A mistake on Lloyd's part; there has never been an Allhallows church in Colchester, but there was an All Saints: see n. 179, **21 November 1675**.

on my Violin writt a litter for Mrs White and sate by the fi[er] Mr Cockerill and his wife and Richard Orbell and his wife being there [?we] went to prayers my Landlady reading a chapter at 10 went to bed.

[fo. 19r]
Wednesday, 12 January: Rose ½ hour after 7 after I was dressed and performed my devotion went to prayers and to school and stayd till after 11 came home and sate by the fier a little went to my chamber and performed my devotion went downe and rubed[228] my bootes cleane went to diner and after diner sate a little by the fier and went to school a little after 1 and stayd till after 4 stayd at Mr Meaddows a little came home and sate by the fier a little and playd on my Violin went to my chamber and performed my devotion, after riped[229] of the lace from my breeches to alter them went downe and sate by the fier till 8 eate a tost buttred and sate up till almost 10 Mary Bond being ther went my Landlady read and we went to prayers and after my face was anointed for the swelling I went to bed ¼ hour after 10.

Thursday, 13 January: Rose before 8 after I was dressed and performed my devotion went to prayers and after to school and stayd till after 11 came home and sate by the fier a little went to my chamber and performed my devotion and sate a little below and a little before 1 went to Mr Jaxons and stayd till ½ hour after 1 went to school and heard my boyes once[230] and set them coppys and went to Mr Jaxons and a little before 3 we went to diner and I stayd a little after diner till almost 4 went to Mr Ardreys and playd a little at cards Mary Bond being there came home at 9 and my Landlord not being at home went to Mr Meaddows and tooke in my peece and stayd there till almost 10 and playd 4 games with her at cribbage and wone 2 came back and went to Mr Jaxons and stayd there till after 10 came home and my Landlady read and we went to prayers and after my face was anointed I went to my chamber and performed my devotion and after 11 went to bed.

Friday, 14 January: Rose at 8 after I was dressed and performed my devotion went to prayers and to schoole and stayd till after 11 came home and sate by the fier a little went to my chamber and

---
[228] Rubbed.
[229] Ripped.
[230] In other words, Lloyd listened to his pupils read aloud.

performed my devotion sate by the fier till diner and after diner a little went to school and stayd till after 4 came home and sate by the fier a little and went to my chamber and performed my devotion went downe and sate a little went to my chamber and my Landlady called me to goe see my coles layd up and I stayd and playd 4 or 5 games at cribbage with Mrs Meaddow came home and sate by the fier a little Mr Gray and Mary Bond being there and playd 5 games at whist[231] and lost nothing sate up till 10 Richard Orbell and his wife and Philip Eve stayd til after 9 my Landlady read and we went to prayers and went to my chamber and to bed.

Saturday, 15 January: Rose at 8 after I was dressed and read went to prayers and performed my devotion went to school stayd till after 11 came home and was by the fier a little went to my chamber and performed my devotion and riped my breeches in peeces to make them less went to diner about 12 and sate by the fier till after 2 went to Mr Ardreys and stayd but a little but went to Mrs Wheelers and agreed with her to teach her daughter for 15^s came back to Mr Ardryes and stayd till after 5 and called at Mr Sheltons who promised me his daughters in the spring, caled at Mr Richard[232] Dumells[233] and he promised to send his 2 daughters to me on mondy came home after 7 sate by the fier till after 8 went to my chamber and performed my devotion and stayd till almost 9 went downe and sate by the fier and eate a tost stayd [?up] Mary Bond being there then my Landlady read and we went to prayers and I went to my chamber [and to bed].

[fo. 19v]
Sunday, 16 January: Rose a little before 9 after I was dressed and performed my devotion went to prayers <read a letter from my Brother Nicholas and from my sister Carless[234]> and sate a little by the fier, went to All Saints and herd Mr Hickringole, on the 46 Psalm 10 went to Mr Ardreys to diner and stayd till 2 went to St James and being there before it began made a short prayer, heard Mr Shelton on the 8 Romans 33 came home and sate by the fier a little went to my chamber and performed my devotion went downe and sate a little and went over to Robert Meaddows to take

---

[231] Whist, the trick-taking card game. For an account of the rules contemporary to Lloyd, see Cotton, *Compleat Gamester*, 114–120.
[232] Originally 'Ric'.
[233] This name is very faded and a little unclear.
[234] See Introduction, p. 8.

in my peece which he carryed abroad all Satturday night and stayd a little came home and Elizabeth Edlin being there sate and talked with her till 7 then eate 2 egs for super and after super I read a Sermon and my Landlady read a chapter and we sang a Psalm and went to prayers and about 10 I went to bed.

Monday, 17 January: Rose at 7 after I had layd by my clothes dressed myself and performed my devotion and went to prayers and went to school and stayd till after 11 came home and sate by the fier and after 12 went to my chamber and performed my devotion went to diner and after eate som diner and at 1 went to school and stayd till after 4 came home and was by the fier and playd on my Violin about ½ hour after 5 went to my chamber and performed my devotion and was in my chamber till after 7 making up my cloth breeches I made less went downe and sate by the fier and talked with mother Rose[235] persuading her to leave her ill course of life and goe to church playd on my Violin till after 8 eate som bread and cheese and sate by the fier till almost 10 my Landlady read and we went to prayers and at 10 I went to my chamber and to bed.

Tuesday, 18 January: Rose after 7 after I was dressed and performed my devotion went to prayers and to school and stayd till after 11 came home and sate by the fier a little went to my chamber and performed my devotion went downe to Diner and after diner Mr Ardrey calld as he was goeing to London and I went to the King's Head and gave him 2 jugs of beere ½ hour after 1 went to school and stayd till after 4 went to Mr Leeroys and began with Mrs Susan Wheeler, called at 6 at Mr Colmans who agreed with me to learne his daughter Katherine at 7 came away and delivered a letter to the King's Head for Mrs Ardry went to Mr Smith and gave him a letter for his son playd at cards till 9 came away and sat by the fier till almost 10 Mary Bond being there went to my chamber and performed my devotion went downe and my Landlady read and we went to prayers and I went to bed after 10.

Wednesday, 19 January: Rose after 7 after I was dressed and performed my devotion went to prayers and I eate a tost and at 9 went to school and stayd till after 11 came home and was a little below and pounced my greate sheete of paper and pressed the seames of my breeches, and after performed my devotion and went downe and sate by the fier a little and went to diner a little before 1 after diner went to school and stayd till after 4 came home and sate by

---

[235] Perhaps an elderly servant?

the fier a little went to my chamber and performed my devotion and after went downe and sate below a little went to my chamber ½ hour after 5 and stayd till after 7 and was about my breeches a little before 8 went to Mr Meaddows and playd at cribbag and both with him and his wife and was beaten [by] them both after 9 came home and eate som super and sate up till [?10] my Landlady read and we went to prayers and I went to my chamber and to bed.

[fo. 20r]
Thursday, 20 January: Rose at ½ hour after 7 after I was dressed and performed my devotion went to prayers and to school and stayd till after 11 came home and sate by the fier a little went to my chamber and performed my devotion went to diner and after went to school and stayd till after 3 went to Mr Ardries and learned Mrs Wheeler and Katherine Merill stayd till 7 came home and went to Mr Edlins and mended my fiddle came home and playd at cards at cribbag with Mary Bond and after at whist with my Landlady and Philip Eve and Mary Bond sate up till after 11 my Landlady read and we went to prayers and I went to my chamber and performed my devotion and went to bed.

Friday, 21 January: Rose at 7 after I was dressed and performed my devotion went to prayers and after to school and stayd till after 11 came home and was below till after 12 mending my violin strings and puting them on eate my diner and went to my chamber and performed my devotion Learned my Landlady to make her letters went to school and stayd till after 4 came home and sate by the fier a little went to my chamber and performed my devotion and went downe Mr Edlin being there I sate a little <sent a letter to Mrs Gray> went to my chamber and was about my breeches till after 7 went downe and sate by the fier while Mr Cockrill and his wife and Richard Orbell and his wife playd at cards and after Mary Bond and I playd against Mr Cockrill and my Landlord and I lost a ½ pinte of brandy sate till after 10 my Landlady read and we went to prayers and I went to my chamber and to bed.

Saturday, 22 January: Rose at 7 after I was dressed and performed my devotion went to school and stayd till after 11 came home and was by the fier for a little went to my chamber and performed my devotion went to diner and after sate a little and playd on my violin trimed myselfe and set my Landlady a copy went to Mr Ardreys and stayd till 5 came home and went to Mr Meaddows and spoake with the old woman about her son and daughter came home and went to my chamber and performed my devotion and writt a letter to my Mother haveing this day received one from my sister went to Mr Meaddows and gave him to cary to London on Monday letters one for my Brother Nicholas one for Carless one for my Mother one to Philoclea stayd till 8 and playd at cribbage with her and beat her[236] came home and sate by the fier a little went to my chamber and got my things redy to weare went downe, eate some super and sate up till after 10 my Landlady read we went to prayers and about 11 went to bed.

Sunday, 23 January: Rose at 8 after I was dressed and performed my devotion went to prayers and sate a little went to Trinity and heard Mr Smith on the 8 Romans 33 came home and went to my chamber and made a short prayer went to diner after read a sermon went to my chamber and performed my devotion, and sate a little then went to St Giles and heard Mr Smith on the same text came home and sate by the fier and heard my Landlady read went to my chamber and performed my devotion went downe and sate by the fier a little then went to Mr Meaddows to copy a letter for Mrs Ardrey stayd there till 7 came home heard my Landlady read eate som super about 8 and sate by the fier till 9 my Landlady read a chapter and sang a Psalm went to prayers and I went to my chamber and about 10 went to bed.

[fo. 20v]
Monday, 24 January: Rose at 7 after I was dressed and performed my devotion went to prayers and to school and stayd till after 11 came home and sate by the fier and eat my diner and sate a little after diner and playd on my violin went to my chamber and performed my devotion went downe and set my Landlady a coppy and went to school and stayd till after 4 and sate at Mr Meaddows till 5 came home and sate by the fier a little and John Sewell and Philip Eve came in and stayd till after 7 and we had two gotches of beere went to my chamber and performed my devotion and went downe and sate by the fier till after 9 and eate some supper, and sate a little my Landlady read and went to prayers and I went to my chamber and to bed a little before 11.

Tuesday, 25 January: Rose at 7 after I was dressed and performed my devotion went to prayers and to school and stayd till 10 it being

---

[236] This appears to be an error; Lloyd probably played cards with a woman in the Meaddows household, not Philoclea as the syntax suggests.

Hollyday[237] came home and sate and made som penns and made me redy to goe to church to prayers to St Peeters at ½ hour after 10 went and came away ½ hour after 11 came home and sate by the fier and playd on my violin, and performed my devotion in the house and sate till after 1 and then went to diner after diner went to my chamber and basted on the lace on my breeches and at 3 went to Mr Ardreys and stayd there till 8 came home and sate a little went to my chamber and performed my devotion went downe and sate a little and supt a few potage my Landlady read and we went to prayers and I went to my chamber and to bed.

Wednesday, 26 January: Rose at 7 after I was dressed and performed my devotion went to prayers and to school and stayd till after 11 came home and sate by the fier a little went to my chamber and performed my devotion and went to diner and sate a little and went to school and stayd till after 4 came home and stayd below a little went to my chamber and performed my devotion and went downe and playd on my Violin a little went to my chamber and began to set on the lace on my breeches but was cald away to renew Richard Orbells bond, and after at 7 went to Mr Meaddows and playd at cards with her against her Brother and his wife stayd till after 9 came home and eate som supp[er] and sate up till after 10 my Landlady read we went to prayers and I went to my chamber and to bed.

Thursday, 27 January: Rose at 7 after I was dressed went to prayers and performed my devotion and went to school and stayd till after 11 went to Mr Meaddows and eate some oysters and drank som burnt Clarrett came home and performed my devotion and went thether to diner and at 1 went to school and stayd till after 3 and went to Mr Ardreys and stayd till 7 came home and was by the fier a little and went to my chamber and performed my devotion and was sowing on the lace on my breeches a little went downe at 9 and sate a little eate som supper and my Landlady read and we went to prayers and I went to my chamber and to bed.

Friday, 28 January: Rose at 7 after I was dressed and performed my devotion went to prayers and to school and stayd till after 11 came home and sate by the fier little went to my chamber and

---

[237] The Feast of the Conversion of St Paul the Apostle; not a major date on the liturgical calendar, but I can find no other explanation for Lloyd closing his school on this day. Joseph N. Tylenda, *Saints and Feasts of the Liturgical Year* (Washington, DC, 2003), 20–21.

performed my devotion and went to diner and sate a little went to see Jaxons horse my Landlady bought at 1 went to

[fo. 21r]
school and stayd till after 4 ~~came home and sate by~~ stayd at Mr Meaddows till 5 came home and sate below and playd on my Violin at 6 went to my chamber and performed my devotion and was a little sowing on the lace on my breeches, went downe and sate by the fier till after 9 eate som super and sate and talked with Goodman Cooke till almost 10 my Landlady read and we went to prayers and I went to my chamber and to bed.

Saturday, 29 January: Rose at 7 after I was dressed and performed my devotion went to prayers and to school and stayd till after 11 came home and was by the fier a little and went to my chamber and performed my devotion went to diner and sate a little while went to my chamber and trimed myselfe and was a little while sowing on the lace of my breeches, after 2 went to Mr Ardrey and stayd till 3 and walked a little on the field by Magdalen church[238] came home and sate by the fier a little went to my chamber and performed my devotion and was ~~in~~ in my chamber getting my things for Sonday went downe and sate by the fier and eate som supper and sate up till after 10 my Landlady read and we went to prayers and I went to my chamber and to bed.

Sunday, 30 January: Rose at 8 after I was dressed and performed my devotion went downe and read a little went to my chamber and prayd over the prayer I used to doe when we were together there being company below, went to church and heard Mr Smith at Trinity on the 24 of the Proverbs 22[239] came home and went to my chamber and made a shorte prayer went to diner and after read a sermon went to my chamber and performed my devotion

---

[238] South-east of the centre of Colchester in what is now Magdalen St. Possibly founded in the 12th century as the chapel of the hospital of St Mary Magdalen on the same site, it gained parochial status in 1237. The living was vacant from the Siege of Colchester in 1648 until 1721. The medieval church was demolished in 1852 and rebuilt; the replacement itself was demolished in 1994, *VCHE*, 327–328.

[239] Proverbs 24:21–22 was a particularly apt choice for a sermon on the Feast of King Charles the Martyr, the anniversary of the execution of King Charles I: 'My son, fear thou the Lord and the king: and meddle not with them that are given to change: [22] For their calamity shall rise suddenly; and who knoweth the ruin of them both?'. The Feast was abolished from the Book of Common Prayer by Act of Parliament, though it has since been partially restored in the Alternative Service Book (1980).

and was there till I went to St Giles Church and heard Mr Smith on the same text came home and went to my chamber and there meditated on what I had heard went downe and heard my Landlady read a chapter sate by the fier and after 6 my Landlady read a sermon and we went to super and had som discourse about the fast on the morrow and I found them against fasting she read a chapter and we sang a Psalm and went to prayers and at 10 I went to my chamber and to bed.

Monday, 31 January: Rose at 7 and kept it as the fast for the Kings Murder ~~after I had prayd~~ went to prayers and after I was dressed performed my devotion went downe and sate by the fier ¼ of an houer went to my chamber and made my confession out of Dr Taylors Guide to the Penitent and made my owne confession, after I had performed all this I went downe and sate by the fier and read a chapter or two describing a fast and went to church, and heard Mr Smith at St Peters on the 24 of Proverbs 21 at 1 came home and sate by the fier a little went to my chamber and performed my devotion and renewed my covenant and went downe and walked into the field by St James to heare St James bels and heareing them went to church and heard Mr Shelton on the 2 Samuel 1 last verse[240] came home after 5 stayd a little below and went to my chamber and performed my devotion and went downe and eate a tost and cheese and one linke[241] sate a little read a sermon at 8 eate a crust of bread and cheese and dranke and read the History of Francis Spira[242] my Landlady read and we went to prayers and I went to my chamber and to bed.

Tuesday, 1 February: Rose at 7 after I was dressed and performed my devotion went to school and stayd till after 11 came home and was below till diner and sate a little after diner went to my chamber and performed my devotion went to school and stayd

---

[240] 2 Samuel 1:27.
[241] A sausage.
[242] Francesco Spiera, anglicized as Francis Spira (1502–1548), was a Venetian notary whose heretical protestantism, forced recantation at the hands of the Inquisition, and subsequent psychological breakdown and death (some sources claimed suicide) was a popular (and convenient) topic in 17th-century England. Lloyd may have reading Nathaniel Bacon, *A Relation of the Fearefull Estate of Francis Spira* (London, 1638). For recent commentary on the significance of Spiera's story in early modern England, see M. Anne Overell, *Nicodemites: Faith and Concealment between Italy and Tudor England* (Leiden, 2018), 150–164; Kenneth Sheppard, 'Atheism, apostasy, and the afterlives of Francis Spira in early modern England', *The Seventeenth Century*, 27 (2012), 410–434; Michael MacDonald, 'The Fearefull Estate of Francis Spira: Narrative, identity, and emotion in early modern England', *Journal of British Studies*, 31 (1992), 32–61.

till after 4 went to Mrs Ardreys and stayd till after 7 came home and went to my chamber and performed my devotion went downe and playd 3 or 4 games at cribbage with Mary Bond and beate her 4 Lurches[243] eate some supper and playd on my violin sate up till 11 my Landlady read and we went to prayers and I went to my chamber and to bed.

[fo. 21v]
Wednesday, 2 February: Rose at 8 after I was dressed and performed my devotion went to prayers and was in my chamber makeing a caractaristic[244] for Mr Ardrey till after 10 went downe and sate by the fier and playd on my violin till 11 went to Mr Edlins and got som bords for a table came home and performed my devotion and went to diner and after sate below a little and writt my Landlady a copy went to my chamber and Ironed some ribbon and the lace on my breeches and mended a shirte and stayd till after 4 went downe and sate below and playd on my violin till 6 went to my chamber and performed my devotion and went downe and eate a tost and dranke and playd at cribbage with Mary Bond and my Landlady and beate them both stayd up till 11 my Landlady read and we went to prayers and I went to my chamber and to bed.

Thursday, 3 February: Rose at 7 after I was dressed went to prayers and performed my devotion and went to schoole and stayd till after 11 came home and sate by the fier a little and went to my chamber and performed my devotion went to diner and sate till 1 went to school and stayd till after 3 went to Mr Ardreys and stayd till 7 came home and sate by the fier a little went to my chamber and performed my devotion and was mending a payre of drawers till almost 9 went downe and playd 2 or 3 tunes and eate som super and sate up till almost 10 my Landlady read and we went to supp prayers and I went to my chamber and to bed.

Friday, 4 February: Rose after 6 after I was dressed and performed my devotion went to prayers and was in my chamber till after 8 mending a payre of drawers went downe and warmed myselfe

---

[243] Cribbage, like tennis, is a 'match' divided into games. A player 'lurches' when they score 121 points before their opponent reaches 91, thereby scoring two 'match points' instead of one for a single game. In other words, Lloyd won resoundingly.

[244] Lloyd's precise meaning is unclear here, but it seems plausible that Lloyd was creating a stylized, calligraphic letter (perhaps 'A'?) or text for Ardrey, as he did for a number of other individuals throughout the diary.

and went to school and stayd til after 11 came home and sate by the fier a little went to my chamber and performed my devotion went to diner and sate a little and went to school and stayd till after 4 came home and sate by the fier and playd on my violin and went to my chamber and performed my devotion and after read a letter I receved from Mrs Gray and writt an answer went downe and went to Mr Edlins to see my table went to Mr Meaddows and playd at cards and lost a game with her and wone one of her husband, stayd till after 9 came home and eate som super and sate up till almost 11 my Landlady read and we went to prayers and I went to my chamber and went to bed.

Saturday, 5 February: Rose after 6 after I was dressed and performed my devotion went to prayers and was in my chamber mending a payre of drawers a little went to school and stayd till after 11 came home and sate by the fier till after diner and playd a little went to my chamber and performed my devotion and trimed myselfe and after 2 went to Mr Ardreys and stayd till 5 came home and was below a little went to my chamber and performed m[y] devotion and was in my chamber till after 8 getting my things redy for Sunday and mending a payre of stockings went downe and read a sermon and sate up till 10 my Landlady read and we went to pra[yers] and I went to my chamber and to bed.

[fo. 22r]
Sunday, 6 February: Rose at 7 after I was dressed and performed my devotion went to prayers and after went downe and sate by the fier and read till after 9 went to church at 10 to Trinity and heard Mr Smith on the 8 Romans 32 came home and went to my chamber and performed my devotion made a shorte prayer went to diner and sate after diner and read went to my chamber and performed my devotion went to St Giles and heard Mr Smith on the same text came home and heard my Landlady read and after read myselfe went to my chamber and performed my devotion went downe and sate by the fier and read a sermon and sate and discoursed about the good establishment of our church read eate som super and after 9 my Landlady read a chapter and we sang a Psalm and went to prayers and went to my chamber and to bed.

Monday, 7 February: Rose at 7 after I was dressed went to prayers and performed my devotion sate a little by the fier and dranke and eate a peece of toste went to school and stayd til after 11 came home and sate by the fier a little went to my chamber and performed my devotion went downe to diner and sate a little went to school and stayd till after 4 and stayd ½ houer at Mr Meaddows and helped them make up tobaco came home and went to Josephs the barber and had my head shaved and stayd there till 7 came home went to my chamber and performed my devotion and made me a little flannell up to weare under my night cap, went downe and playd on my Violin till 9 eate some super and sate up till after 10 went to prayers my Landlady haveing read and at 11 went to my chamber and to bed.

Tuesday, 8 February: Rose after 7 after I was dressed went to prayers and performed my devotion and was in my chamber mend[ing] a shirte till 9 went downe and mended the heeles of a payre of shooes went to my chamber and Ironed som ribbon and tooke of som buttons of my cloth coate and sett them on thicker, performed my devotion and after 12 went to diner with pankakes it being shroffe Tuesday after diner set on the buttons and after 2 went to Mr Ardreys and stayd till after 8 came home and eate som super and sate up till 10 my Landlady read we went to prayers and I went to my chamber and performed my devotion and went to bed.

Wednesday, 9 February: Rose before 7 after I was dressed and performed my devotion went to prayers stayd in my chamber a little went downe after 8 and sate by the fier till 10 and read a booke called the Righteous Mans Evidence for Heaven[245] went to my chamber and made my confession out of Dr Taylors Golden Grove and after used the prayers for Ash Wedensday[246] in my chamber there being none publiclly[247] went downe halfe an houer after 11 sate by the fier and warmed me and walkd out till after 2 ofer the sheaton bridg and gathered som nettles came in and picked them and went to my chamber and performed my devotion and renewed my covenant went downe and sate by the fier and read till 4 went to my chamber and altered a cravat went downe and sate a little went to carry a letter to Esqr Ellwayes and Esqr Cockan[248] came home and stayd below a little went to my chamber and performed my devotion

---

[245] Timothy Rogers, *The Righteous Mans Evidences for Heaven* (London, 1618). Rogers (1589–1655) was a clergyman, schoolmaster, and controversialist who lived and died in Essex, *ODNB*.
[246] The wording is misleading here; Lloyd must have used a prayer for Ash Wedensday from some other source, as none is given in the *Golden Grove*.
[247] Lloyd's hand is untidy and ambiguous; his meaning is probably that there were no 'public' prayers being held at church.
[248] Presumably relatives of the above-mentioned Sir Gervase Elwes and Brien Cockayne, Viscount Cullen, since the title 'Esquire' is too junior for either of them.

and went downe and eate a buttred tost and dranke and after I sate a little read sate up till 10 my Landlady read and we went to prayers and I went to my chamber and to bed.

[fo. 22v *BLANK*]

[fo. 23r *BLANK*]

[fo. 23v]
Thursday, 10 February: Rose a little after 6 after I was dressed and performed my devotion went to prayers and dranke the juce of nettels and walked to the Sheaton and came back to school and stayd till after 11 came home and sate by the fier a little went to my chamber and performed my devotion and went to diner after diner sate a little and shewed my Landlady to write went to school and stayd till after 3 went to Mr Ardreys and stayd till 6 came home and was below a little went to my chamber and performed my devotion went downe and playd on my Violin a little playd at cribbag with Mary Bond till after 9 eate a buttred tost sate up till after 10 my Landlady read and we went to prayers and at 11 went to my chamber and went to bed.

Friday, 11 February: Rose after 6 after I was dressed and performed my devotion went to prayers dranke the Juse of nettels and walked till 8 went to school and stayd till after 11 came home and went to my chamber and was till 12 mending a shirte performed my devotion went to diner and to school and stayd till after 4 came home and went to my chamber and was till after 5 mending my shirte walked out and gathered som nettles and came in a[fter] 6 after I had picked them went to my chamber and performed my devotion and was till after 8 mending my shirte went downe and eate som super and sate up till after 10 my Landlady read we went to pray[ers] and I went to my chamber and to bed.

Saturday, 12 February: Rose after 6 after I was dressed and performed my devotion went to prayers and dranke my Juse of nettels and walked till 8 went to school and stayd till after 11 came home and sate by the fier a little went to my chamber and performed my devotion and was mending my shirte a little went to diner and after mad[e] an end of mending my shirte trimed myselfe, and after 2 went to M[r] Ardreys and stayd till 5 came home and was in my chamber a little and performed my devotion and gott my things redy after 8 went downe and eate some supper and sate up till after 11 before I could goe to prayers my Landlady read and we went to prayers and I went to my chamber and to bed.

Sunday, 13 February: Rose at 7 after I was dressed and performed my devotion went to prayers and I dranke the Juce of nettles and walked almost an houer came in and read till church time went to Trinity and heard Mr Smith on the 8 Romans 33 verse came home went to my chamber and made a short prayer went to diner sate a little and read a sermon went to my chamber and performed my devotion and read till church time went to Peters and heard Mr Tompson in the 8 Matthew 4 came home and walked and gathered som nettles came in a little before 6 read and performed my devotion and read till 7 went to super and sate after till 9 read a ser sermon and went to prayers and I went to my chamber and after 10 went to bed.

Monday, 14 February: Rose at 6 after I was dressed and performed my devotion went to prayers I dranke the Juse of nettles and walked till 8 went to school and sta[yd] till after 11 came home and sate by the fier a little went to my chamber and performed my devotion went downe to diner and sate a little went to school and stayd till after 4 came home and mended a payre of gloves and went out to walke a little gathred som nettles came home and went to my chamber and performed my devotion and playd a little on my violin went to my chamber and was a little altring my shamy[249] breeches went downe at 8 and eate som super and sate up till after 10 my Landlady read [?we] went to prayers and I went to my chamber and to bed att 11.

[fo. 24r]
Tuesday, 15 February: Rose at 6 after I was dressed and performed my devotion went to prayers after I had dranke my Juce of nettles walkd till 8 went to school and stayd till after 11 came home and sate by the fier till diner not being very well sat a little after went to my chamber and performed my devotion went to school and stayd till after 4 went to Mr Colemans to Learne Mrs Susan Wheeler and Mr I: K: stayd till after 6 went to Mrs Ardreys and stayd till 7 came home and sate by the fier and eate som rise milke[250] for my super and sat up till after 9 my Landlady read and

---

[249] Chamois.
[250] Probably rice pudding or similar made with milk, a popular dish in the 17th century.

we went to prayers and I went to my chamber and performed my devotion and read a letter I received from Philoclea and went to bed.

Wednesday, 16 February: Rose at 6 after I was dressed and performed my devotion went to prayers and dranke the Juce of nettles and walked till 8 went to school and stayd till after 11 came home and sate by the fier and eate som diner went to my chamber and performed my devotion and went to school and stayd till after 4 came home and sate a little by the fier and eate a little bred and butter and went to my chamber and was making up my pinck cullered ribon till twas after 5 went downe and sate below till after 6 went to my chamber and performed my devotion went downe and eate som tost and dranke with Mr Cockerill and his wife sate up till after 10 my Landlady read and we went to prayers and I went to my chamber and to bed after 11.

Thursday, 17 February: Rose at 6 after I was dressed and performed my devotion went to prayers and dranke the Juce of netls and walked till 8 went to school and stayd till after 11 came home and sate by the fier a little went to my chamber and performed my devotion went downe to diner and after diner was a little while ripping a payre of breeches to alter went to school and stayd till after 3 came home and was a little about my breeches and walked out and gathered som nettles and went to my chamber performed my devotion went downe and sate a little went to Mr Meaddows and playd 5 or 6 games at cribbage with her [*sic*] and lost 2 bottles of alle and came home and eate some super and sate up till after 9 went to prayers and I went to my chamber and writt a coppy of a letter to Phyloclea and went to bed.

Friday, 18 February: Rose at 6 after I was dressed and performed my devotion went to prayers and dranke the Juce of nettels and walked till 8 after went to school and stayd till after 11 came home and sate by the fier a little and put on the hilt on my semiter. went to my chamber and performed my devotion and went to diner and went to school and stayd till after 4 came home and sate by the fier a little and went to my chamber and Ironed som ribon and went to walke and gathered som nettles came in and sate a little by the fier and playd to or 3 tunes and went to my chamber and performed my devotion and was in my chamber till after 8 making up som black ribbon went downe and eate a tost and sate up till after 10 my Landlady read and we went to prayers and I went to my chamber and to bed.

Saturday, 19 February: Rose at 6 after I was dressed and performed my devotion went to prayers and dranke the Juce of nettls and walked till 8 went to school and stayd till after 11 came home and sate by the fier a little went to my chamber and performed my devotion went to diner and after washed my belt trimed myselfe and about 3 went to Mr Ardreys and stayd till after 5. Came home and sate by the fier till after 6 went to my chamber and performed my devotion and was in my chamber till almost 9 gott my things for the next day went downe and sate till 10 my Landlady read and we went to prayers and to bed.

Sunday, 20 February: Rose at 9 being ill and haveing beene soe all night after I was dressed went to prayers and performed my devotion and went downe and sate by the fier and eate a little tost and dranke and after sate by the fier and read till diner after diner sate and read and discoursed a little went to my chamber and performed my devotion and went downe and stayd a little and went to St Peeters and heard Mr Thompson on the 22 of Exodus 2 came home and sate below and read a little and discoursed till after 6 went to my chamber and performed my devotion went downe and eate som super and sate a little read a sermon sang a Psalm went to prayers and at 10 to bed.

Monday, 21 February: Rose at 6 after I was dressed and performed my devotion went to prayers and dranke my Juse of nettles and walked till almost 8 and read a letter I received from my Brother Nicholas went to school and stayd till after 11 came home and sate by the fier a little, and cullered my belt and gloves and went to my chamber and performed my devotion went to diner and to school and stayd till after 4 came home and was by the fier a little and went to my chamber and was a little mending my stuff[251] breeches and went to walke and gathered som nettles and came home and sate a little and went to my chamber and performed my devotion and was in my chamber till after 8 making a scull cap went downe and eate som super and sate up till after 10 my Landlady read and went to prayers and to bed.

---

[251] The term 'stuff' in this context refers to a woollen fabric 'made from finer, long-staple, worsted fibres, combed instead of carded, and often intermixed with other yarns such as linen, mohair, and silk'. 'Stuff' was distinct from the thicker and heavier 'cloth', which was made from carded, short-staple wool. The two terms came to be synonymous in the 19th century. Ursula Priestley, 'The marketing of Norwich stuffs, c.1660–1730', *Textile History*, 22 (1991), 193–209; Spufford and Mee, *Clothing of the Common Sort*, 108.

Tuesday, 22 February: Rose at 6 after I was dressed and performed my devotion went to prayers and dranke the Juce of nettles and walkd till after 8 went to school and stayd till after 11 came home and sate by the fier a little went to my chamber and performed my devotion went to diner and sate a little after went to school and stayd till after 4 went to Mr Ardreys and stayd till 6 came home and stayd below till 7 went to my chamber and performed my devotion and was a little about my stuff breeches went downe and sate till 9 eate som bred and cheese and sate up till after 10 my Landlady read and we went to prayers and I to my chamber and to bed.

[fo. 24v]
Wednesday, 23 February: Rose at 6 after I was dressed and performed my devotion went to prayers and dranke my Juce, and walked till almost 8 went to school and stayd till after 11 came home and sate by the fier and eate my diner went to my chamber and performed my devotion and stayd till 1 went to school and stayd till after 4 came home and sate a little below went to my chamber and was a little about my breeches went to walke and gathered my nettles came home at 6 and sate a little below went to my chamber and performed my devotion went to supper and sate up till 10 read and went to prayers and went to my chamber and to bed.

Thursday, 24 February: Rose at 7 after I was dressed and performed my devotion dranke my Juce of nettles and walked till almost 9 came in and went to prayers and was in my chamber about my breeches till after 10 went to prayers at St Peeters came home and was about my breeches till after 12 went downe to diner and after diner went to my chamber and performed my devotion and was about my breeches till almost 4 lay downe and slept a little after 4 walkd to the shacker spring[252] and came in at 6 sate a little and went to my chamber and performed my devotion and was in my chamber till 8 went downe and playd on my violin a little eate som super and sate up till almost 10 my Landlady read and we went to prayers and I went to my chamber and to bed.

Friday, 25 February: Rose at 6 after I was dressed and performed my devotion went to prayers and dranke my Juce of nettles and went to walke till almost 8 went to school and stayd till after 11 came home

---

[252] I can find no trace of a spring with this or any similar name in or around Colchester; it may have been an informal local name, or it may no longer exist.

and was a little below went to my chamber and performed my devotion and was in my chamber a little went to diner and to school and stayd till after 4 came home and was in my chamber a little went to walke and gathered som nettles came in and went to my chamber and performed my devotion went downe and sate below and playd a little on my violin went to my chamber and was there cutting out a scull cap went downe about 8 and eate some super and sate up till 10 my Landlady read and we went to prayer and I went to bed.

Saturday, 26 February: Rose at 6 after I was dressed and performed my devotion went to prayers and dranke the Juce of nettles and walked till 8 went to school and stayd till after 11 came home and was in my chamber till after 12 about my breeches went to diner and went to my chamber and performed my devotion and trimed myselfe and after 2 went to Mr Ardreys and stayd till 5 came home and was about my breeches a little went downe and sate a little and read went to my chamber and performed my devotion and was a little about my breeches and getting my things against the morrow went downe after 8 and sate below a little eate som super and sate up till after 9 my Landlady read we went to prayers and I went to my chamber and to bed at 10.

Sunday, 27 February: Rose after 6 after I was dressed and performed my devotion went to prayers and drank the Juce of nettls and walked till almost 9 came in and read a sermon and eate a peece of tost and went to St Trinity and heard Mr Smith on the 17 Acts 30 verse came home and went to my chamber and made a shorte prayer went to diner and sate a little and read a sermon, went to my chamber and performed my devotion went to church to St Giles and heard the same man and text came home and went to my chamber and read a sermon and lay downe a little performed my devotion went downe and sate a little and eate som super and after super John read we sang a Psalm and went to prayers and I went to my chamber and to bed before 10.

Monday, 28 February: Rose at 6 after I was dressed and performed my devotion went to praye[rs] and dranke the Juce of nettles and walked came to my lodging and stayd till 8 went to school and stayd till after 11 came home and dined went to my chamber and performed my ~~dev~~ devotion and was a little ripping my black breeches to alter at 1 went to school and stayd till after 4 came home and was in my chamber till after 5 about my breeches walked out and stayd till after 6 came in and was below with Thomas

Ward[253] about his boyes at 9 went to my chamber and performed my devotion went downe and eate som super and sate a little my Landlady read and we went to prayers and I went to my chamber and to bed.

[fo. 25r]
Tuesday, 29 February: Rose at 6 after I was dressed went to prayers and performed my devotion and was in my chamber till almost 8 about my breeches went to school and stayd till after 11 came home and went to my chamber and performed my devotion and was a little about my breeches went to diner and at 1 went to school and stayd till after 4 went to Mr Ardreys and stayd till 7 came home and went to my chamber and performed my devotion was a little about my breeches went downe and eate som bread and cheese and sate up till after 9 my Landlady read and we went to prayers and I went to my chamber and to bed.

Wednesday, 1 March: Rose ½ hour after 5 after I was dressed and performed my devotion went to praye[rs] and was a little about my breeches eate a tost and went to school after 8 and stayd till after 11 came home and went to my chamber and was a little about my breeches went downe to diner and after diner went to my chamber and performed my devotion went to school and stayd till after 4 came home and received a letter from Nehemiah Tompson was a little about my breeches, walked out with Jo: Blu[mfield] came in and performed my devotion and was about my breeches till after 8 went downe and eate som super and sate up till after 9 my Landlady read and we went to prayers and I went to my chamber and to bed.

Thursday, 2 March: Rose at 6 after I was dressed and performed my devotion went to prayers and was in my chamber about my breeches till almost 8 went to school and stayd till after 11 came home and sate a little went to my chamber and performed my devotion and was a little abou[t] my breeches came went to diner and to school and stayd till after 3 went to Mr Ardries and stayd till after 5 came home went to my chamber and performed my devotion and went downe and sate a little and playd on my violin and eate some super and went to my chamber and was about my breeches

---

[253] Perhaps Thomas Ward, 'Innholder' of St Mary's, Colchester, whose will was proved in November 1690. Only one son, Thomas, is mentioned in the will. See ERO, D/ACW 21/85.

till after 9 went downe and sate till 10 my Landlady read and we went to prayers and I went to my chamber and drank som physick drinke I had by Dr Elkins prescription which I drank in the morning and before 11 went to bed.

Friday, 3 March: Rose at 6 after I was dressed and performed my devotion went to prayers and was in my chamber till 8 about my breeches went to school and stayd till after 11 came home and eate my diner and stayd below till after 12 went to my chamber and performed my devotion and was a little about my breeches went to school and stayd till after 4 came home and went to my chamber and was about my breeches performed my devotion and went downe and stayd below and eate som super and there was a fier at Mrs Smiths at the King's Head but did noe harme but the stayble has burnt and puled downe sate up till 10 my Landlady read we went to prayers and I went to my church and dranke my drinke and to bed.

Saturday, 4 March: Rose at 6 after I was dressed and performed my devotion was a little about my breeches went to prayers and was a little about my breeches went to school and stayd till after 11 came home and went to my chamber and performed my devotion and was about my breeches till after 12 went to diner and after diner sate and talked with Mr Clarke about his son trimed myselfe and at 3 went to Mr Ardrey stayd till after 5 came home and went to my chamber and performed my devotion went downe and sate in the house eate som super and talked with Mr Clarke till after 10 my Landlady read we went to prayers and I went to my chamber and to bed.

Sunday, 5 March: Rose at 7 after I was dressed and performed my devotion went downe and went to prayers and sate and discoursed with Mr Clarke went to Trinity and heard Mr Smith on the 17 of the Acts 31 verse came home went to my chamber and made a shorte prayer went to diner and sate and discoursed till after 1 went to my chamber and performed my devotion and read till church time went to St Giles and heard the same man and text came home and went to my chamber and read a sermon and lay downe a little performed my devotion went downe and sate and talked and read a little went to super and sate and discoursed a little my Landlady read and we sang a Psalm went to prayers and I went to my chamber and to bed.

Monday, 6 March: Rose at 6 after I was dressed and performed my devotion was a little in my chamber went to prayers and to school stayd till after 11 came home and went to my chamber and performed my devotion and was about my breeches a little went to diner and to school and stayd till after 4 came home and was in my chamber about my breeches performed my devotion went down and clarified som rosen[254] and stayd below till 8 went to my chamber and was about my breeches till after 9 went downe and eate som bread and cheese sate up till 10 my Landlady read, we went to prayers and I went to my chamber and to bed.

[fo. 25v]
Tuesday, 7 March: Rose at 6 after I was dressed and performed my devotion went to prayers and was a little about my breeches went downe and eate som bred and cheese went to school and stayd till after 11 came home and went to my chamber and performed my devotion and was a little about my breeches went to diner sate a little went to school and stayd till after 4 went to Mr Ardreys and stayd till after 6 came home was below a little went to my chamber performed my devotion and was a little about my breeches went downe eate som tost sate up till 10 playd a little on the violin my Landlady read we went to prayers and I went to my chamber and to bed.

Wednesday, 8 March: Rose at 6 after I was dressed and performed my devotion went to prayers and to Dr Elkins and stayd till after 8, he told me I was free from the scurvy and Jaundice and dropsie[255] went to school and stayd till after 11 came home and went to my chamber and performed my devotion and was a little about my breeches went to diner and and stayd till after 4 came home and was in my chamber about my breeches, sent a letter to Phyloclea performed my devotion at 6 went downe and stayd a little went to my chamber and was a little about my breeches we[nt] downe my Landlady read we went to prayers I eate a butt of bred and cheese and dranke went to my chamber and to bed a little after 9.

Thursday, 9 March: Rose at 6 after I was dressed and performed my devotion was a little about my breeches went to prayers and was a little more about my breeches went to school and stayd till after 11 came home and was below a little went to my chamber and performed my devotion went to diner and was a little about my

---
[254] Perhaps violin rosin.
[255] 'Dropsy' is an archaic term for oedema.

breeches went to school and stayd till after 3 went to [*deleted*] Mr Ardreys stayd till after 6 came home performed my devotion was below a little went to my chamber made an end with my breeches and began to alter the sleves of my coat at 9 went downe and eate a tost sate up till after 10 my Landlady read and we went to prayers I went to my chamber and to bed.

Friday, 10 March: Rose at 6 after I was dressed and performed my devotion was a little in my chamber altring a payre of cuffs went to prayers and was till 8 about my cuffs went downe and dranke som scurvie grass alle[256] went to school and stayd till after 11 came home and was below a little went to my chamber and performed my devotion and was a little about my cuffs went to diner and to school and stayd till after 4 ca[me] home and was a little about my coate performed my devotion went downe and sate a little and playd a little on my Violin went to my chamber and was a little abo[ut] my coate went downe and eate som super playd on my Violin sate till after 10 my Landlady read we went to prayers and I went to my chamber and to bed.

Saturday, 11 March: Rose at 6 after I was dressed and performed my devotion went to prayers and after made my confession out of Dr Taylors Guide to Devotions after 8 went to school and stayd till after 11 came home and was a little below and trimed myselfe performed my devotion and walked to Mr Ardreys the field in the back side of Marlin Greene[257] stayd there till 5 came home and was in my chamber a little went downe and eate som bread and cheese and a little brasted[258] bacon sate below till 9 went to my chamber and performed my devotion and sate up till 10 my Landlady read we went to prayers and I went to my chamber and to bed.

Sunday, 12 March: Rose a little before 7 after I was dressed and performed my devotion went downe and sate by the fier and read went to prayers eate som breakfast went to church to Trinity heard Mr Smith on the 17 Acts 31 came home went to my chamber and mad a short prayer went to diner sate a little went to my chamber

---

[256] Scurvy-grass, or *cochlearia*, is a genus of herbs high in vitamin C. It has been used as a treatment for scurvy since at least antiquity; it is mentioned in Pliny the Elder's *Naturalis Historia*.

[257] This appears to be another informal or defunct place name; I can find no trace of it in other sources. On **23 March 1676**, Lloyd mentions walking by the 'back of St James's' in order to get to Ardrey's, which in this period backed onto open fields. Cf. n. 313, **27 May 1676**.

[258] This usage is unclear, but the hand is fairly legible.

and performed my devotion and lay a little on my bed went to St Giles and heard Mr Smith on the 22 Luke 19 came home and sate a little while by the fier went to my chamber and read a sermon walked into the field and meditated met Mr Meaddows and his wife walked a little with them came in and sate a little went to my chamber and performed my devotion and read a sermon went downe and eat som bread and cheese my Landlady read we sang a Psalm went to prayers and I went to my chamber and to bed.

[fo. 26r]
Monday, 13 March: Rose before 6 after I was dressed and performed my devotion went to prayers was a little about my coate went to school after 8 stayd till after 11 came home went to my chamber and stayd till after 12 performed my devotion went to diner went to school after 1 stayd till after 4 came home and was in my chamber till after 6 about a payre of cuffs performed my devotion went downe sate by the fier went to my chamber after 7 and stayd till 8 about my cuffs went downe eate som milke sat up till almost 10 my Landlady read we went to prayers and I went to my chamber and to bed.

Tuesday, 14 March: Rose at 6 after I was dressed and performed my devotion went to prayers and was about my coate till after 8 eat a tost went to school and stayd till after 11 came home went to my chamber performed my devotion and was about my coate till almost 1 went to diner and stayd till after to school and stayd till after 4 went to Mr Ardreys and stayd till after 6 came home sate by the fier a little went to my chamber and performed my devotion and was a little about my coate went downe and eate a tost sate up till after 10 my Landlady read we went to prayers and I went to bed.

Wednesday, 15 March: Rose at 6 after I was dressed and performed my devotion was a little about my coate went to prayers and was a little about it afterward went to school and stayd till after 11 came home went to my chamber and performed my devotion and was a little about my coate went to diner and to school and stayd till after 4 received a letter from Mrs Gray and came home sate a little below went to my chamber and was about my coate till 6 performed my devotion went downe sate below a little went to my chamber and was about my coate till after 8 went downe and sate till 9 my Landlady read we went to prayers and I to bed.

Thursday, 16 March: Rose at 6 after I was dressed and performed my devotion was a little about my coate went to prayers and was a little about my coate went to school and stayd till after 11 came home and went to my chamber and performed my devotion and was a little about my coate went to diner and to school and stayd till after 3 came home and got myselfe redy and rid into East Streete[259] and stayd at Mr Ardreys till 5 rid to the top of the hill beyond Grinsted[260] and came home by the heath was below a little went to my chamber and performed my devotion and was below went to my chamber and was a little about my coat went downe and sate up till 10 my Landlady read we went to prayers and I to bed.

Friday, 17 March: Rose at 6 after I was dressed and performed my devotion went to prayers and was a little about my coate went to school and stayd till after 11 came home and went to my chamber and performed my devotion and was a little about my coate went to diner and to school and stayd till after 4 came home and was in my chamber about my coate till 6 performed my devotion went downe and sate a little went to my chamber and was about my coate a little went downe and sate and eate som bred and cheese and sate up till 10 my Landlady read we went to prayers and I went to bed.

Saturday, 18 March: Rose at 6 after I was dressed and performed my devotion was a little about my coate went to prayers and to school and stayd till after 11 came home and went to my chamber and performed my devotion and was about my coate till 2 eate somthing and trimed myselfe and went to Mr Ardreys and stayd till after 6 came home performed my devotion and eate somthing sate below a little went to my chamber and was mending a shirte went downe before 9 sate up till after 10 my Landlady read and we went to prayers and I to bed.

Sunday, 19 March: Rose after 6 after I was dressed and performed my devotion went downe and went to prayers and eate a tost went to my school and read a sermon went to St Peeters and heard Mr Tomp[son] on the 1 Corinthians 11 25 verse came home and went to my chamber and mad a short prayer went to diner and

---

[259] East St. runs from the East Hill over a bridge on the Colne, and mostly outside the old walls of the town; it is a peripheral area which in the 1670s would have been surrounded by countryside.

[260] Greenstead is an ancient parish, in 1675 in the hinterlands of Colchester, but today part of the town, about two miles from the centre.

sate a little went to my chamber and performed my devotion and read parte of a sermon went to Trinity and heard Mr Smith on the 23 Luke 43 came home went to my chamber and read the other part of the sermon walked to Lexton warren came home and sate below and discoursed my Landlady read we sang a Psalm went to prayers and I went to my chamber and to bed.

[fo. 26v]
Monday, 20 March: Rose at 6 after I was dressed went to prayers and performed my devotion and was a little about my coate eate a peece of tost and went to school and stayd till after 11 came home and went to my chamber and performed my devotion and was a little about my coate went diner and to school and stayd till after 4 came home went to my chamber and was about my coate till after 5 went downe and stayd below a little went to my chamber and performed my devotion and went downe and playd on my violin a little went to my chamber and was setting on the ribbon on my stuff breeches till 9 went downe eate a little bread and cheese my Landlady read we went to prayers and I went to my chamber a little after 9 and was sowing on my ribbons till after 10 went to bed.

Tuesday, 21 March: Rose at 5 after I was dressed and performed my devotion was about Mrs Susan Wheelers peece of writing till after 6 Mr Ardrey came to my Lodgings and I sate with him till almost 8 went to prayers and to school and stayd till after 11 came home and went to my chamber and was about my coate and made an end of it went to diner and after performed my devotion and went to school and stayd till after 4 went to Mr Ardreys and stayd till almost 7 came home went to my chamber and performed my devotion went downe and sate a little went to my chamber and was about my stuff coate to make it biger went downe and eate som bred and cheese playd a little on my violin sate up till after 9 my Landlady read we went to prayers and I went to my chamber and to bed.

Wednesday, 22 March: Rose at 6 after I was dressed and performed my devotion was in my chamber mending a shirt till 8 eat som bred and cheese went to school and stayd till after 11 came home and went to prayers and performed my devotion and was about Mary Jaxons peece went to diner and to school and stayd till after 5 broak up school till after Easter came home and was about my shirt performed my devotion walkt out a little to the King's Head wash house came in and sate a little went to my chamber and mended a payre of stockings at 9 went downe eate a little bread and cheese my Landlady read we went to prayers I went to my chamber and ~~sowed on~~ <mended> the gallone[261] of my shooes and went to bed.

Thursday, 23 March: Rose a little after 5 after I was dressed and performed my devotion was about altring a cravatt went to prayers and after eate som breakfast then was about my stuff coate making it biger till after 12 went to diner and was a little about it performed my devotion and at 2 went to walke round the back side of St Jameses to Mr Ardreys and stayd there till 6 came home went to my chamber and performed my devotion went downe and eate som bread and cheese stayd a little went to my chamber and made an end of my cravat read part of a sermon went downe my Landlady read we went to prayers and I went to my chamber and to bed at 9.

Friday, 24 March: Rose after 6 after I was dressed and performed my devotion went to prayers and was below a little went to my chamber and made my confession out of Dr Taylors Golden Grove and after read till 10 went to St Peters to prayers came home read till 12 walked out till 1 came in and performed my devotion went to St James and heard Mr Shelton preach on the 26 Matthew 39 verse came home by the fields sate below a little went to my chamber and dranke a little brandy being [*deleted*] almost faint performed my devotion and eate a tost sat below till after 8 my Landlady read we went to prayers and I went to my chamber after 9 and to bed. Good Friday.

Saturday, 25 March: Rose at 7 after I was dressed and performed my devotion went to prayers and was in my chamber a little eate som brekfast and was about mending my perry wigg till 10 went to prayers to St Peters came home and was in my chamber till 1 about my stuff coate performed my devotion Trimed myselfe and washed my feete and after eat som diner about 4 went to my chamber before 5 and read in Mr Dooelittles booke on the Sacrament performed my devotion got my things redy to weare the next day and read againe about the Sacrament went downe and told John he did not well to be soe careless of celebrating the Lord's day especially Easter day my Landlady read we went to prayers and after I read to them out of the Practis of Piety what is to be performe at the ~~P~~

---

[261] Probably galloon, a strip of closely woven ribbon or braid, used for trimming garments or in this case, shoes, *OED*.

and ~~went~~ after told them how the ♃ is celebrated went to my chamber after 10 went to bed.

[fo. 27r]
Easter Sunday, 26 March: Rose after 5 after I was dressed and performed my devotion went to prayers and after was in my chamber reading in Mr Doolittles booke went downe and read to my Landlord and Landlady and after went to my chamber and we went to prayers and made our confession out of the Practis of Piety went downe and read againe went to my chamber and stayd till church time went to Trinity heard Mr Smith on the 63 of Isaiah 1:2:3:4 verse received the ♃ came home and returned God my prayers and thanks in the prayer in the Practis of Piety performed my devotion and went downe and read and after 1 went to diner after diner read part of a sermon and went to St Giles heard Mr Smith on the same text came home to my chamber read the other part of the sermon performed my devotion went downe and read sate below till 8 eat som super my Landlady read we ~~went~~ sang a Psalm went to prayers and I went to my chamber and to bed at 10.

Monday, 27 March: Rose at 7 after I was dressed and went to prayers performed my devotion was in my chamber till after 9 altring some old ribbons on my breeches went to church at St Peeters but was mistaken the bels toling to meete to choose officers[262] went to Mr Grayes and bespoake me a riding coate stayd there till ½ hour after 10 then went to prayers at St Peters came home and tooke the lace of my white hatt and <performed my devotion> at 1 went to diner and after playd on my violin an houer and was sowing the Lyening into my stuff coate, till almost 6 performed my devotion and went to Mr Ardries and helpt set up som things stayd there till after 8 came home and sate in the house and eate a bitt of bred and cheese at 10 my Landlady read we went to prayers and I went to my chamber and to bed.

Tuesday, 28 March: Rose after 6 went prayers after I was dressed performed my devotion went to Mr Ardryes and stayd till after 9 went to All Saints to prayers and stayd till after 10 went with Mr Ardrey to the heath called at the Swan drank a flagon of alle bought a chaldron of cold[263] came home at 12 went to my chamber

---

[262] Lloyd probably refers to the selection of new churchwardens or other parish officials.
[263] This is ambiguous; a 'chaldron' can be either an antiquated spelling of 'cauldron', or an archaic unit of measurement for coal and other goods (32 or 36 bushels). A chaldron is a

performed my devotion went to diner after diner made an end of doeing my stuff coate and playd on my violin and after sowed on the lace on my hat at 6 went with my Landlord and Landlady and John to Lexton heath to Mother Dies[264] stayd till 8 came home at 9 went to my chamber performed my devotion went downe my Landlady read we went to prayers and at 10 went to bed.

Wednesday, 29 March: Rose after 6 after I was dressed and performed my devotion went to prayers and performed my devotion and was in my chamber ordring my things till after 9 went downe and eate some breakfast and walked out and came in at 10 was in my chamber till 12 about maki[n]g a payre of fulle sleeves went to diner performed my devotion and was in my chamber all the afternoone about the sleeves and altring a cravatt till after 5 went downe and was below performed my devotion and went downe and made cleane my sword and sate till 8 eate somthing went to my chamber and writt a letter to Mr Jaxon and to Mrs Gray went downe my Landlady read we went to prayers and I went to my chamber and to bed.

Thursday, 30 March: Rose at 7 after I had beene at prayers and performed my devotion and was in my chamber sowing on some buttons to keepe up my riding stockings dressed myselfe and went downe and was mending my riding stockings till diner time after diner performed my devotion and was writting a letter to Mrs Gray went downe and sate below till after 3 went to Mr Ardreys and was there till almost 7 went to Mr Grayes and stayd till almost 9 came home went to my chamber and performed my devotion went downe and I read a chapter went to prayers and to my chamber and to bed.

[fo. 27v]
Friday, 31 March: Rose after 6 after I was dressed and performed my devotion went to praye[rs] and went downe and eate a tost went to my chamber and was a little about riping and cullering my shamy breeches and went downe and mended a payre of gloves after 9 went with my Landlord to Fordham[265] and saw his lane and went to his tennants and eate som backon and eggs and stayd there till after 2

---

very large quantity: compare with Pepys who in July 1664 purchased 'ten Chaldron', *Pepys*, Vol. 4, 223.

[264] Perhaps short for 'Diana' or similar.

[265] The village of Fordham about six miles north-west of Colchester.

came home about 4 went to my chamber and performed my devotion and went over at 6 to Mr Meaddows and stayd til almost 8 came home and eate som super went to my chamber and performed my devotion went downe and my Landlady read we went to prayers and I to bed.

Saturday, 1 April: Rose at 6 after I was dressed went to prayers and performed my devotion was in my chamber mending my coate put it on went downe and eate som breakefast went to my chamber and was making som little cuffs till after 12 went downe and after 1 went to diner went to my chamber performed my devotion and trimed myselfe afore 4 went to Mr Ardreys and stayd till after 6 came home went to my chamber performed my devotion went downe received a letter from my Brother Nicholas went to Mr Grayes and payd him for a coate at 8 stayd till after 9 came home sate up till after 10 my Landlady read we went to prayers and I went to my chamber and to bed.

Sunday, 2 April: Rose after 6 after I was dressed and performed my devotion went downe and heard John Clarke read eate som bred and cheese went to prayers read in Practis of Pietie concerning the Moralitie of the Sabbath went to Trinity and heard Mr Smith on the 63 Isaiah 3:4 verse came home made a short prayer went to diner and sate a little after went to my chamber performed my devotion and read part of a sermon went to St James and herd Mr Shelton on the 5 John 28:29 stayd a little at Mr Ardryes came home after 5 went to my chamber read the other part of the sermon performed my devotion went downe and sate a little John Ray:[266] read 2 or 3 chapters we sang a Psalm went to prayers and I went to my chamber and to bed.

Monday, 3 April: Rose at 5 after I was dressed and performed my devotion went to prayers and went downe and sate by the fier and eat som bread and cheese at 8 went to school and stayd till after 11 came home and went to my chamber and performed my devotion went downe to diner and after playd on my violin till 1 went to school and stayd till after 4 and taried at Mr Meaddows till 5 came to my chamber and was there about mending my shamy breeches till almost 6 went with Mr Meaddows and his wife to Grinstead to Hewets and drank bottle alle cam back at 8 stay [*sic*] at his house till almost 9 came home and sate below and eat a peece of tost

---

[266] Possible abbreviation.

after 10 my Landlady read we went to prayers and I to my chamber and performed my devotion and to bed.

Tuesday, 4 April: Rose before 6 after I was dressed and performed my devotion went to prayers and was a little mending a payre of stockings eat a tost and at 8 went to school stayd till after 11 came home went to my chamber performed my devotion went to diner and after writt to Phyloclea went to school stayd till after 4 went to Mr Ardryes stayd there till almost 7 went to George Rasses to send my letter went to Mr Coleman and he payd me for his sons quarters[267] came home at 8 went to my chamber performed my devotion and was till 9 mending a shirt went downe and pla[yd] on my Violin eat som bred and cheese sate till after 10 my Landlady read we went to prayers and I went to bed.

[fo. 28r]
Wednesday, 5 April: Rose after 6 after I was dressed and performed my devotion was a little mend[ing] a shirte went to prayers went downe and eate som bread and cheese went to school and stayd till after 11 came home went to my chamber and mended my shirt went to diner and performed my devotion at 1 went to school and stayd till after 4 came home and Mr Smith was with me ½ hour went to my chamber and was about my shamy breeches till after 8 performed my devotion went downe after 7 eate som super playd on my violin till 9 a little before 11 my Landlady read we went to prayers and I to bed.

Thursday, 6 April: Rose before 6 after I was dressed and performed my devotion was mending a payre of stockings till after 7 went to prayers and eate som breakfast went to school and stayd till after 10 came home went to <St> Peeters and heard the Archdeacon preach the visitation sermon[268] on the 35 Jeremiah 16:19 verses came home after 12 went to my chamber and performed my devotion went to diner and after sate a little and went to school and stayd till after 3 went to Mr Ardreys and stayd till after 7 went to Mr Cockerill to see him being lame and he was prety well stayd till after 9 came home went to my chamber and

---

[267] Lloyd is referring to payments due on one of the 'quarter days', on which rents were collected and salaries or debts were often paid out: Lady Day (25 March), Midsummer Day (24 June), Michaelmas (29 September), and Christmas Day.

[268] In 1676, the Archdeacon of Colchester was Charles Smith, who held the post from 1675 until his death in 1678: *Cantabrigienses*, Vol. 1, pt. 4, 95; *CCEd* Person ID: 20358.

performed my devotion playd on my violin till ~~after~~ 10 my Landlady read we went to prayers and I to bed.

Friday, 7 April: Rose at 6 after I was dressed and performed my devotion was in my chamber mending a shirte went to prayers and to school and stayd till after 11 came away went to Mr Ardreys to see about the roome for a school and measured it and Judged it big enough came home after 12 went to diner and performed my devotion went to school and after 2 gave my school a play desined by Jo: Turnill and Robert Meaddows stayd at his shop and bought me 15 yards of doules[269] cost 2^s went to my chamber and was till after 4 providing a peece for Mrs Susan Wheeler to read came home and was below a little went to my chamber and sowed on the lace on my shamy breeches performed my devotion went downe and stayd a little went to my chamber and was there till after 9 a little making som little cuffs went downe eate som super my Landlady read went to prayers and I to bed.

Saturday, 8 April: Rose after 6 after I was dressed and performed my devotion was a little in my chamber makeing som little cuffs went to prayers and eat som bread and cheese went to school and stayd till after 11 came home was in my chamber a little changing my breeches went to diner and after diner performed my devotion and was a little in my chamber sowing the ribbons on my Stuff breeches behind higher trimed myselfe and at 3 went to Mr Ardryes stayd till after 7 and after writting time helped to doe up the curtanes and Poster of a bed, came home received a letter from Phyloclea and as I was reading it one from my Brother Nicholas what brought me the Newse of my Brother Johns being extreamely ill what troubled me much went to my chamber and was a little mending my stockings went downe and eat som super went up againe and performed my devotion and writt an answer to Phylochlea went downe to prayers after my Landlady read and went to my chamber and sowed on a payre of cuffs and to bed.

Sunday, 9 April: Rose at 6 after I was dressed and performed my devotion was in my chamber reading a sermon went downe and read two or 3 Psalms eate som breakfast went to prayers and went to Mr Ardries and went to All Saints church and heard Mr Hickringgale on the 13 Hebrews 18 went to Mr Ardryes to

---

[269] Lloyd is probably referring to *dowlas*, a strong and coarse linen fabric that was used to make sails, aprons, and other practical or hardwearing applications in the 16th and 17th centuries, *OED*.

diner and walked into the garden and read a little in the Golden Grove and reade a shorte prayer standing in the wood house went to St James heard Mr Shelton on the 112 Psalm 7 went to Mr Ardryes and stayd till after 7 came home went to my chamber performed my devotion went downe my Landlady read we sang a Psalm went to prayers and I went to bed after 9.

Monday, 10 April: Rose at 6 after I was up went downe to Mr Ardryes and sate below with him till 7 dressed myselfe went to prayers and performed my devotion went to school and stayd till after 11 came home and was in my chamber a little about Katherine Merrill[270] and Susan Wheeler's peeces went to diner performed my devotion went to school stayd till after 4 went to my chamber performed my devotion sate a little ripped my cloath coate to cutt it a little less walked abroad to take the Ayer after I came in [wen]t to Mr Ardries to see where he would have my Landlords horse the next day he was at the old Taverne drunke I could not get him home went to his house and stayd till after 9 and he came in I gott him to b[?ed] and sate with Mrs Ardry[271] and Mrs Martine till 10 came home my Landlady read and we went to prayers and I to bed.

[fo. 28v]
Tuesday, 11 April: Rose at 6 after I was dressed and performed my devotion went to prayers and eat som breakfast and went to school and stayd till after 11 came home and went to my chamber and was a little flurishing Mr K: Merredales peece went to diner performed my devotion went to school and stayd till after 11 went to Mr Ardreyes stayd till 8 came home sate below till after 9 went to my chamber and performed my devotion went downe sate up till after 10 my Landlady read we went to prayers and I went to bed.

Wednesday, 12 April: Rose at 6 after I was dressed and performed my devotion was in my chamber doeing somthing to Katherine Merill[272] and Susan Wheeler's peeces went to prayers and went to school and stayd til after 9 came home and eat a little milk porrage went againe and stayd till after 11 came home went to my chamber and was about the peeces till after 12 went to diner and performed

---

[270] Originally 'K: M:'. There is some uncertainty here since Lloyd mentions a 'piece' for a 'Mr K: Merredale' in the next entry.
[271] Very tiny and obscure.
[272] Originally 'K: M:'.

my devotion went to school and stayd till after 4 was in Mr Meaddows shop till almost 5 came home and was in my chamber about the peeces till after 6 performed my devotion and playd on my Violin till after 7 went downe and stayd a little and went to Mr Ardryes and stayd till 9 came home sate in the house a little my Landlady read we went to prayers and I went to my chamber and to bed.

Thursday, 13 April: Rose at 6 after I was dressed and performed my devotion was in my chamber a little about my coate went to prayers and went to school and stayd till after 11 came home went to my chamber and writt Susan Wheeler and Katherine Merill's[273] names in them went to diner performed my devotion went to school stayd till after 3 came home and got my things and rid to Mr Ardreyes and stayd there till after 5 rid to Rowhedg[274] and sent a box of penns and Letter to Phyloclea came back and to Mr Ardryes and sent the horse home and stayd till after 9 and eat some watter gruele and Custard for super came home and performed my devotion my Landlady read we went to prayers and I to bed.

Friday, 14 April: Rose at 6 after I was dressed and performed my devotion went to pray[ers] and was a little about my coate went to school and stayd till after 11 came home and performed my devotion and went to diner and was in my chamber a little about my coate went to school and stayd till after 4 came to my chamber and lay downe and slept till 6 being troubled with my eyes performed my devotion and was playing on my Violin till 8 sate up till 10 my Landlady read we went to prayers and I to bed.

Saturday, 15 April: Rose at 6 after I was dressed and performed my devotion went to pray and was a little about my coate, went to school and stayd till after 11 came home and performed my devotion and trimed myselfe and eate som diner and went after 12 to Mr Ardreys and about 2 walked with him and his wife and Mrs Elizabeth Martine Almost to Ardley came back about 5 stayd mending pens and setting coppyes till after 6, about 7 came home and when I came home found Mr William Pagett[275] at my Landlord's he stayd till neere [?8] I performed my devotion and writt a letter to his Brother Jo: ~~before~~ eate some super and my Landlady and I

---

[273] Originally 'K: M:'.
[274] Rowhedge is a small village about three miles from the centre of Colchester. It is separated from nearby Wivenhoe by the Colne.
[275] See n. 298, **15 May 1676.**

went to the White Harte[276] to him where was Alderman Mott[277] stayd there till after 11 came home my Landlady read we went to prayers and to bed.

Sunday, 16 April: Rose at 6 after I was dressed and performed my devotion went downe and eate some breakefast and went to prayers was in my chamber reading till alm[ost] 10 went to the White Harte to Mr Pagett stayd till after 10 went to St Peeters and heard a Stranger on the 1 Peter 4:11 came home and performed my devotion went to diner Mr Pagett dineing with us sate a little after diner and went to my chamber and read a little and read [sic] went and wal[ked] round by the Chastel Lanes to St James to church and heard Mr Shelton on the 112 Psalm 7 came to the White Heart and sate a little and dranke a tankard and went with him to the Oyster pitts and gave him 1 peck of oysters came back I sate at home a little went to the White Harte and stayd an houer and tooke my leave of him came home my Landlady read we sang a Psalm went to prayers I performed my devotion and went to bed.

[fo. 29r]
Monday, 17 April: Rose at 6 after I was dressed and performed my devotion was in my chamber a little mending a pair of stockings went to prayers and to school and stayd till after 11 came home sate by the fier went to diner performed my devotion and was in my chamber mending a payre of stockings went to school and stayd till after 4 came home and went to my chamber and was mending my Lynen <threden> stockings performed my devotion playd a little on my Violin and went downe eate som super and sate till after 9 my Landlady read we went to prayers and I to bed.

Tuesday, 18 April: Rose at 6 after I was dressed and performed my devotion was in my chamber a little about my coate went to

---

[276] Now Nos 6–8 on the south side of High St. in the parish of St Peter, the White Hart was one of the primary inns in early modern Colchester, but defunct in 1816. D'Cruze, *Colchester People*, Vol. 3, 31–33.

[277] Probably Samuel Mott, prominent in Colchester politics, he was a member of the Dissenting faction. After serving as mayor in 1693–1694, he was disenfranchised for a series of misdemeanours, *VCHE*, 117; Morant, *History and Antiquities of Colchester*, Vol. 1, 97. Mott married Elizabeth Creffield, a member of one of Colchester's other prominent families, in the church of St Runwald in September 1659: St Runwald's parish register, ERO, D/P 177/1/1.

prayers eate som breakfast went to school and stayd till after 11 came home sate by the fier a little performed my devotion went to diner and sate a little was a little about my coate went to school and at 4 Mr Ardrey came to me I left of school and went to his house and stayd till 8 called at the ~~Kings~~ Queenes Head[278] stayd with Mr Smith till after 9 received 10^s:6^d for his Nephews and Neeces schooling came home eate a peece of bred and cheese went to my chamber and performed my devotion went downe my Landlady read went to prayers had my eyes dressd with Goody Linens water[279] which had beene sore 5 or 6 dayes and went to bed.

Wednesday, 19 April: Rose at 6 after I was dressed and performed my devotion was in my chamber about my coate a little went to prayers and to school after I had eaten a tost stayd till after 11 came home and was below till after diner performed my devotion and was a little about my coate went to school stayd till after 4 came home and was in my chamber till 8 about my coate walked to Lexten warren came in at 7 performed my devotion and playd on my violin till after 8 sat below till after 9 my Landlady read we went to prayers and I went to bed.

Thursday, 20 April: Rose ½ houer after 6 after I was dressed and performed my devotion went to prayers and eate a tost and went to school and stayd till after 11 came home and was mending my shooes till diner after diner performed my devotion and went to school and stayd till after 3 came home and was in my chamber till after 4 about my coate went to Mr Ardryes and stayd till 8 came home went to my chamber and performed my devotion and went downe sate below till 10 my Landlady read we went to prayers and I to bed.

Friday, 21 April: Rose at 6 after I was dressed and performed my devotion was a little about mending my camlet coate went to prayers and eate som bred and cheese went to school and stayd till after 11 came home and sate a little went to my chamber and performed my devotion went to diner and was a little about my coate went to school and stayd till after 4 came home and was in my chamber till 7 about my coate performed my devotion went downe and eate

---

[278] A substantial inn with a London coach in the High St., in St Peter's parish, near the Moot Hall. It ceased to be an inn in 1763, when it was occupied by a surgeon: D'Cruze, *Colchester People*, Vol. 3, 21–22.

[279] Lloyd is referring to a medicament of some kind; the name he gives it suggests that it was probably locally produced.

som super and playd on my violin went downe and talked with Richard the Cooper about his learning to write sate up till 10 my Landlady read we wend [*sic*] to prayers and I to bed.

Saturday, 22 April: Rose at 6 after I was dressed and performed my devotion was about my camlet coate eat some tost and drank with Mr Cockrill went to prayers and went to school and stayd till after 11 <received a letter from Phyloclea> came home and went to my chamber and performed my devotion went to diner trimed myselfe went with Mr Ardrey downe to Captaine Renholds[280] to see his roome but did not agree for it stayd till almost 5 went to Mr Ardreys and stayd till 8 made an end of Learning Mr [*sic*] Susan and Mrs Katherine came home sate below till 9 eate som bred and cheese went to my chamber and performed my devotion and got my things redy for the morrow went downe my Landlady read we went to pray and I went to my chamber and to bed.

[fo. 29v]
Sunday, 23 April: Rose at 7 after I was dressed and performed my devotion read part of a sermon and went downe and sate a little went to prayers and eat a little tost read till church time went to Trinity and heard Mr Celsie[281] on the 1 John 2:15:16 verses came home went to my chamber and made a shorte prayer went to diner sate below and read a little went to my chamber and performed my devotion and went to Mr Ardreys and stayd a little and went to St James and heard Mr Tompson on the 1 Peeter 1 Peter 2:17 verse caled at Mr Ardreys and stayd with her till after 7 came home sate below a little went to my chamber and performed my devotion went downe and eate som super and instructed J: Clarke and Antony in the principles of religion my Landlady read we sang a Psalm went to prayers and to bed at 10.

Monday, 24 April: Rose at 4 after I was dressed and performed my devotion was about my coate till almost 8 went to prayers and after 8 went to school stayd till after 11 came home received 2 letters one from my Brother Nicholas the other from Mr William Pagett was

---

[280] Samuel Reynolds (*c*.1642–1694), was a prominent and wealthy resident of Colchester. The son of Thomas Reynolds, an affluent clothier, Reynolds entered the Middle Temple in 1666. By the time Lloyd was writing, Reynolds owned one of the town's inns, was captain of the militia horse, and a JP for Essex. He was later MP for Colchester in 1681, 1689, and 1690–1694, and was a 'moderate Whig': *Hist. Parl. 1660–1690*, Vol. 3, 326.

[281] Identity unclear; not a member of the regular Colchester clergy.

a little about my cote performed my devotion went to diner went to school and stayd till after 4 came to my chamber and was till almost 7 about my coate and made an end of it performed my devotion went downe and eate som super and sate up till 10 my Landlady read we went to prayers and I to bed.

Tuesday, 25 April: Rose at 5 after I was dressed and performed my devotion went to prayers and eate something at 7 went to Mr Ardreys to goe with him and his wife to Wigborow[282] and stayd there till after 8 then went and after 10 gott there stayd there till 5 came home and stayd at Mr Ardryes till 9 came home performed my devotion my Landlady read went to prayers and I to bed.

Wednesday, 26 April: Rose at 7 after I was dressed and performed my devotion went to prayers and to school and stayd till after 11 came home went to my chamber and performed my devotion went downe to diner and sate till 1 went to school and stayd till after 4 came home went to my chamber and read a little, not being very well lay downe at 5 and lay till almost 7 walked to Richard Orbells mill and stayd a little there came home at 8 eat a tost and sate till after 9 my Landlady read we went to prayers and I went to my chamber and performed my devotion and went to bed.

Thursday, 27 April: Rose after 6 after I was dressed and performed my devotion went to prayers and was a little mending my camlet cote eate som bred and cheese and went to school and stayd till after 11 came home went to diner sate a little went to my chamber performed my devotion went to school stayd till after 3 came home was in my chamber about my coate till almost 6 playd a little went to Mr Ardryes stayd till after 8 called at Mr Bollers the shooe makers and bespoak a payre of shoos came home at 9 eate a little bread and cheese my Landlady read we went to prayers and I to my chamber and performed my devotion and to bed.

[fo. 30r]
Friday, 28 April: Rose before 6 after I was dressed and performed my devotion was in my chamber about my coate till after 7 went to prayers and eate som bread and cheese and went to school and stayd till after 11 came home and performed my devotion went to diner and was a little about my coate went to school and stayd till after

---

[282] Either Great Wigborough or Little Wigborough, a pair of tiny villages about eight miles south-west of Colchester.

4 and stayd at Robert Meaddows shop till 5 came home and was below with Mr Clarke went to my chamber and was a little while altring a payre of cuffs ~~performed m~~ went to super performed my devotion and was in my chamber till after 9 went downe my Landlady read we went to prayers and I to bed.

Saturday, 29 April: Rose after 6 after I was dressed and performed my devotion went to prayers, drank my morning draught with Mr Clarke went to school and stayd till after 11 came home and was in my chamber about a payre of cuffs went to diner performed my devotion and made an end of my cuffs trimed myselfe went to Mr Ardreys after 3 stayd till almost 9 came to my chamber performed my devotion got my things redy for the next day went downe my Landlady read we went to prayers and I to bed.

Sunday, 30 April: Rose at 7 after I was dressed and performed my devotion read a sermon went downe and eate some breakfast went to prayer and sate and discourced with Mr Clarke went to church to St Peeters and heard Mr Tompson on the 3 Titus 3 came home made a shorte prayer went to diner sate a little went to my chamber and performed my devotion lay downe a little before I went to church went to St Peeters againe and heard Mr Tompson on the 5 Galatians 21 came home to my chamber and read in Drexelious ~~performed my devotion~~ at 5 lay downe till 6 then performed my devotion and read till after 7 walkd till after 8 came in eate a piece of cake my Landlady read we sang a Psalm went to prayers and I went to bed.

Monday, 1 May: Rose at 6 after I was dressed and performed my devotion went to my school for my long ruler and cumpasses stayd with Mrs Meaddows till 8 came in and was below till almost 9 went to prayers was in my chamber till after 10 about ruling a sheete of Imperiall paper[283] and making 2 Characteristicks went to prayers at Peeters before 11 before 12 came home went to my chamber and was sowing on a small lace on my cloth breeches went to diner after performed my devotion and went at 2 with my Landlord to Wivenoe and was at his Brother's and we dranke 3 basons of pupenadoe[284] came home at 9 sate up till after 10 my

---

[283] 'Imperial' paper generically refers to a collection of pre-metric British paper sizes such as foolscap, but in this context probably refers to a very large (and perhaps expensive) sheet.

[284] Perhaps a mistaken or unusual spelling of panada or panado; a bread soup, often flavoured with nutmeg. For a recipe contemporary to Lloyd, see Robert May, *The Accomptlisht Cook* (London, 1660), 407.

Landlady read we went to prayers I went to my chamber and performed my performed my devotion and went to bed at 11.

Tuesday, 2 May: Rose at 6 after I was dressed and performed my devotion went to prayers and eate som breakfast and went to school and stayd till after 11 came home and was in my chamber pressing my coate went to diner performed my devotion Ironed som ribband went to school stayd till after 4 went to Richard the Coopers and agreed to learne him to write went to Mr Ardreys and was there setting Mrs Susan Wheeler copies till after 6 stayd there till after 8 came home eate som super performed my devotion my Landlady read we went to prayers and I to bed.

[fo. 30v]
Wednesday, 3 May: Rose at 6 after I was dressed and performed my devotion, made my confession out of Dr Taylors Golden grove, being a day I designed to fast after I had don went to prayers and to school and stayd till after 11 came home went to my chamber and performed my devotion and renewed my covenant went downe and eate som diner not being well after diner went to school and stayd till after 4 came home and read in Drexelious lay downe an houer and read againe and performed my devotion and went to Richard Fields and entred[285] him to writ walked to Lexton comon came in sate up till 10 but eate nothing that day after diner my Landlady read we went to prayers and I to bed.

Thursday, 4 May: Rose at 6 after I was dressed and performed my devotion went to prayers and was mending my belt till 10 went to St Peeters to prayers was mending my belt a little and was Ill eate noe diner performed my devotion lay downe but could not sleepe sate in the house all the afternoone after 7 performed my devotion eate a little milke sate up till after 10 Mr Kent being in the house my Landlady read we went to prayers and I to bed.

Friday, 5 May: Rose at 6 after I was dressed and performed my devotion made an end of mending my belt went to prayers and to schoole after I had eaten som breakfast, stayd till after 11 came home and sate by the fier a little went to diner and performed my devotion went to school and stayd till after 4 came home was in my chamber and was about my coate after 5 was teaching my Landlady to write and the Cooper went to my chamber and

---

[285] Perhaps 'entered' as in 'introduced' him to the art of writing.

performed my devotion and made an end of my coate ~~sate~~ eate som super and sate up till 10 my Landlady read we went to prayers and I to bed.

Saturday, 6 May: Rose at 6 after I was dressed and performed my devotion was in my chamber about my coate a little went to prayers and eate som breakfast went to school stayd till after 11 came home went to diner after diner performed my devotion made cleane and fast the hilt of my sword was in my chamber a little reading Arithmetic went to Mr Ardreys after 1 stayd till 3 came home and trimed myselfe sett my rasor and Mr Ardreys performed my devotion read a letter from my Brother Nicholas and my sister Carless eate som super and sate up till 10 my Landlady read we went to prayers and I to bed.

Sunday, 7 May: Rose before 7 after I was dressed and performed my devotion read then went to prayers and went downe and eate somthing sate till church time went to Trinity heard Mr Smith on the 63 Isaiah 3 came home made a short prayer went to diner sate a little heard John and Anthony read performed my devotion read part of a sermon went to St James herd Mr Shelton on the 112 Psalm 7 stayd at Mr Ardryes till 8 came home performed my devotion sate a little John read we went to prayers and I to bed not being very well.

[fo. 31r]
Monday, 8 May: Rose at 6 after I was dressed and performed my devotion went to prayers and walked toward Lexton came back at 8 and went to school and stayd till 11 came home and was in my chamber gettings [*sic*] my things redy to goe to London performed my devotion went to diner and to school and writt a letter to my Sister Carless stayd at school till after 4 came home and was within till 6 went to Richard the Coopers and stayd with him till 7 went to Mr Ardreys and stayd till after 9 came home eate a little bread and cheese my Landlady read we went to prayers and I to my chamber and performed my devotion and to bed.

Tuesday, 9 May: Rose at 5 after I was dressed and performed my devotion put up my things to goe to London went to prayers and to school and stayd till 11 came home went to diner performed my devotion gatt myselfe redy about 2 went to Wivenoe, at 4 tooke ship and we sayled all the evening and night till 7 the next morning came to ancor at Gravesend went ashore and stayd at

Gravesend 2 houers in an alle house and after at the bowling greene till after 12 went abord and set sayle about 1, and for want of wind went but to Blackwall that night lay at anchor till 4 the next morning and came to London Thursday about 8. In which time I had noe convenience to perform my devotion but short ejaculations[286] and when I was layd downe about 9 I went to Mrs Tilmans to enquire for Mrs Gray and her accident found her there stayed there till 11 and my Landlord came went to the Rates and saw my mother Tompson[287] dined there stayd till 5 went to London bridg and bought my Landlord a violin went back to Mrs Tompson and stayd till after 8 ~~wen~~ came to Mr Pagetts to bed at 10.

Friday, 12 May: Rose at 7 after I was dressed and performed my devotion went to find out Mr Normansill and he tould me I could not Learne Merchant's accompts under 4 weekes went to Mr Hamond who tould me the same, writt a letter and sent by the Banbry coach[288] to my Brother went to Mr Layfield and to Mrs Hafnells and after to Newington to Mr Rogers[289] and stayd an houer and called at Mr Turners went to Mrs Gray and stayd till 9 came to Mr Pagetts and went to the Red Lyon[290] and stayd till 11 went to bed and had not time to performed my devotion but in bed.

Saturday, 13 May: Rose at 6 after I was dressed and performed my devotion went out w[ith] Mr Pagett to Gildhall and stayd till 9 went to Little Brittan and bought a penknife and left my owne[291] to be ground, bought som black leat,[292] went to St James parke and walked till 12 dined in St Martaines Lane walked in Westminster Aby and performed my devotion went to Mrs Gray and stayd till after 7 about 5 [*sic*] walkd to spring gar[dens][293] dranke a bottle of wine and eate a cheese cake came home at 9 performed my devotion sate up a little and went to bed.

---

[286] Brief, spontaneous prayers or acts of religious devotion.
[287] Despite his use of 'my', Lloyd is merely using mother in its titular sense.
[288] The coach for Banbury in Oxfordshire, which would have passed through or near Aynho.
[289] This name uncertain due to a large ink blot.
[290] Here Lloyd could be referring to any number of establishments, as the Red Lion was a popular name for taverns and inns, and he provides no geographical clues.
[291] Writing ambiguous and uncertain.
[292] Perhaps an abbreviation of 'leather'.
[293] Spring Gardens is today a dead-end street in St James, Westminster, named after the gardens which once stood there.

[fo. 31v]
Sunday, 14 May: Rose at 6 after I was dressed and performed my devotion went to Mrs Gray and stayd ½ houer and walked to Newington and herd Mr Tur.[294] on the 17 John 8:9:10:11 came to Mrs Tompsons and ~~herd~~ dined and stayd till 2 walked to Lambeth and heard a stranger his text was noe man can serve 2 masters. Came to Mrs Tompsons and stayd with Mrs Gray till after 9 came home and in the way had ejaculations for my devotion went to bed at 11.

Monday, 15 May: Rose at 8 after I was dressed and performed my devotion stayd within a little went to Mr Paget to the Countess[295] and Met Charles Carter and Job: Ray:[296] went to the Red Lyon the back of the Exchange[297] and dranke my Mornings draught came to Mr Pagets and stayd till after 11 went to prayers at a church neere Leadenhall came back and performed my devotion and read in a booke of Meditations for Death[298] – after 1 went to diner at Mr Pagetts where dined his Brother and Sister and Mr Wiggens and his Brother stayd till 4 and dranke 3 or 4 bottles of wine went by watter to the spring garden and was ther till after 7 came back and went with Mr Pagett to White Chapell to Mrs Roberts and stayd till after 10 came home and eate something and went to bed.

---

[294] Lloyd's brother Nicholas was the incumbent minister at Newington by 1676. The speaker here may have been John Turton, curate in 1693 (*CCEd* Person ID: 96348), or the Mr Turner referred to on **3 June 1677**: see n. 487.

[295] Presumably Lloyd is referring to a tavern or inn, though its location is unclear.

[296] It is unclear to whom Lloyd was referring, but his hand is clear.

[297] Lloyd may here be referring to the Royal Exchange (sometimes called the 'Old Exchange', including by Lloyd) or the New Exchange (or 'Britain's Bourse'). The former stands at the corner of Cornhill and Threadneedle St. and was originally opened by Elizabeth I in 1571. The New Exchange, conceived as a competitive imitation of the Royal, was built by Robert Cecil, 1st earl of Salisbury and designed by Inigo Jones. Standing in a prominent position in the Strand, which connected the City of London to Westminster, it was opened by James I in 1609. It was demolished in 1737.

[298] Interestingly, here Lloyd was reading John Paget, *Meditations of Death* (Dort, 1638). Paget (d.1638) was a puritan and presbyterian minister, who after his ejection from the living of Nantwich in 1604 went into exile in the Netherlands. After moving to Amsterdam in 1607, he founded the English Reformed church, serving as a pastor for 30 years until 1637. Although John Paget died childless, his brother Thomas (d.1660) had a son, Nathan Paget, a noted physician who practised in London and died in 1679. Lloyd makes clear that two of the Pagets known to him were named William and 'Jo:', probably John (see **15 April 1676**). Neither Thomas's nor Nathan Paget's wills establish any link to a William, but it is interesting to speculate that there may have been some connection, since Lloyd seemingly acquired the volume whilst visiting the Pagets. See *ODNB*. For the will of Thomas Paget, see TNA, PROB 11/300/305; for the will of Nathan Paget, see TNA, PROB 11/359/74.

Tuesday, 16 May: Rose at 7 after I was dressed and performed my devotion went with Mr Pagett to Northumberland Ally and dranke my mornings draught stayd till after 9 ~~wen~~ went to Black Swan Ally and was with Dr Roberts and his son and Mr Allen and wife and Mother till 1 went to Salisbury Court to my Aunt Lettis and stayd till after 2 crossed the watter and went to Mrs Gray and stayd till after 10 came home performed my devotion and went to bed.

Wednesday, 17 May: Rose at ½ hour after 3 was writting to my Brother and Sister Carless and performed my devotion and dressed myselfe and went about 7 to Mrs Gray stayd there till after 11 walked with her to see the Monument[299] and went to top went to Mrs Tilmans stayd till almost 3 called at the Black Swan[300] in Holborn went to the Duks house[301] saw Sir Fopling Flutter[302] crossed the watter and stayd with Mrs Gray till 10 came home performed my devotion and went to bed.

Thursday, 18 May: Rose at 8 after I was dressed and performed my devotion went to Newington and dined at Mr Turners and stayd till 4 came to Mrs Gray and stayd till after 10 came home performed my devotion and went to bed.

[fo. 32r]
Friday, 19 May: Rose at 4 after I was dressed and performed my devotion went to Sabs dock[303] and spoake to the hoy[304] man went to

---

[299] The Monument to the Great Fire of London, on Fish Street Hill just to the north of London Bridge, stands on the site of St Margaret Fish Street Hill, the first church to be destroyed by the Great Fire. Designed by Christopher Wren and Robert Hooke, it was built between 1671 and 1676. *TBE, London 1*, 321–322.

[300] A coaching inn, with connections to the West Country, between Fetter Lane and Barnard's Inn, *Pepys*, Vol. 10, 418.

[301] Lloyd is almost certainly referring to the Duke's Company, which performed at Dorset Gardens, also known as the Duke's Theatre. The company was under the patronage of James, duke of York, the future King James II and VII. In 1682, the Duke's Company merged with the King's Company to form the United Company.

[302] George Etherege's *The Man of Mode, or, Sir Fopling Flutter* was first performed in 1676. A printed edition of the text of the play, dated 3 June 1676, mentions that the play was 'Acted at the Duke's Theatre'. Lloyd may have seen one of the first performances. The play is a typical Restoration comedy of manners, following the rakish Dorimant in his efforts to seduce the heiress Harriet.

[303] Sab's or Sable's Quay was one of the 20 'legal quays' established by the Act of Frauds in 1559. Along the north side of the Thames at Billingsgate between London Bridge and the Tower of London, they were the only quays in the Port of London at which goods could be unloaded, in order to protect the power and revenues of the Customs. Henry Crouch, *A Complete View of the English Customs* (London, 1725), 251.

[304] A small coasting boat or barge.

Mr Cocker and stayd till 9 went to Mrs Gray and stayd till 11 came to Mr Lardners and stayd till 12 went to Sabs dock againe and the Master told me he went not till Satterday dressed myselfe dined with Mr Paget and went to Mrs Gray and at 4 we walked to Lambeth and stayd in St George's fields drinking[305] sider and eating cake till 8 walked till almost 9 came home and sate up all night and performed noe more devotion then ejaculatio[ns] at 7 I dressed myselfe eate som Mace alle[306] and at 9 tooke my leave and came to Mr Pagetts got my things redy dined with Mr Pagett in Gratious Streete[307] after 3 went to the watterside stayd at the Bulls head till almost 5 went abord at 5 we set saile and went to Gravesend lay at anchor.

Sunday, 21 May: Set saile at 4 and sailed all day till 10 lay at anchor and sailed till 11 to the Boy[308] in the Noone lay at anchor till 3 set sayle came to Wivenoe Balast key after 7 walked to Wivenoe afore [*word cut off*] and stayd at the Falchon[309] a little came home at 10 rested myselfe performed my devotion and dressed myselfe and went to diner and after diner at 1 went to school and stayd till after 4 came home and being wery and sleepie lay downe and slept till 7 rose and performed my devotion and sate up till after 9 my Landlady read we went to prayers and I to bed.

Tuesday, 23 May: Rose at 7 after I was dressed went to prayers and performed my devotion and eate som bred and cheese and went to school and stayd till after 11 stayd at Mr Meaddows where was her mother and another kinswoman came home performed my devotion went to diner and to school and stayd till after 4 came home and was in my chamber putting up my violin and writting to London about him[310] after 5 went to Mr Ardreys and stayd till after 9 came home my Landlady read we went to prayers and I to bed.

Wednesday, 24 May: Rose at 6 after I was dressed and performed my devotion was in my chamber writing to Mrs Gray went to

---

[305] Owing to his proximity to Lambeth, Lloyd is probably referring to the former St George's Fields in Southwark, rather than the better known area in Westminster.

[306] Mace ale, as the name suggests, is ale spiced with mace, referenced a number of times in the 17th century, *OED*. Lloyd's handwriting is ambiguous here.

[307] Gracechurch St.

[308] Probably 'buoy'.

[309] The Falcon Inn, which persisted in Wivenhoe until 1975. Note that after this visit to the Falcon, Sunday just runs into Monday.

[310] Lloyd's meaning here is unclear, but the handwriting is very legible.

prayers and at 8 to school stayd till after 11 came home and was about my Letter went to diner performed my devotion and went to school and stayd till after 4 finished my letter and sent it and one to Mrs Tompson and one to Mr Pagett was in my chamber about beginning to make a peece and mended a payre of stockings performed my devotion and after 8 went downe and eate som super sate up till after 10 my Landlady read we went to prayers and I to bed.

Thursday, 25 May: Rose after 5 mended a payre of stockings after I was dressed and performed my devotion was about the great I: in my peece went to prayers and to school and stayd till after 11 came home performed my devotion and was about the I went to diner and to school and stayd till after 3 came home and was below at the dore[311] till after 4 went to my chamber and was about my I[312] a little performed my devotion eate som [su]per went at 8 to Mr Ardreys stayd till almost 10 stayd at Samuel Harlings till 12 [?came] home my Landlady read we went to prayers and I to bed.

[fo. 32v]
Friday, 26 May: Rose a little before 7 after I was dressed and performed my devotion went to prayers and to school and stayd till after 11 came home and was in my chamber about my :I: went to diner performed my devotion and was a little about him againe went to school and stayd till after 4 came home and was in my chamber about my I till after 6 went to Mrs Rayners and stayd till almost 7 and she desired me to teach 2 of her children came home and was about my I againe till 8 performed my devotion and was at Joseph the barbars till after 9 sate up till after 10 my Landlady read we went to prayers and I to bed.

Saturday, 27 May: Rose after 7 after I was dressed and performed my devotion was a little in my chamber went to prayers and to school stayd till after 11 came home and was in my chamber about my I went to diner performed my devotion and trimed myselfe finished my I walked to Mr Ardryes by St James and over Morland greene[313] after 4 stayd there till after 9 came home my Landlady read we went

---

[311] Door.
[312] A large calligraphic capital I: see n. 147, **19 October 1675**, and **16 April 1677**.
[313] Cf. n. 257, **11 March 1676**.

to prayers I went to my chamber and performed my devotion and got my things redy for the next day and went to bed.

Sunday, 28 May: Rose after 7 after I was dressed performed my devotion and read 2 sermons went downe and eate som bread and cheese stayd a little talking with Mr Clarke went to prayers and a little after went to Trinity church and heard Mr Smith on the 1 John 4:7 and 8 came home went to my chamber and mad a shorte prayer went to diner and sate after diner till after 1 talking and discourseing with Mr Clarke went to my chamber performed my devotion and went to St Peeters and heard Mr Tompson came home and was in the house with Mr Cockerill and his wife and eate som super at 6 after went to my chamber and read a sermon and performed my devotion and was in my chamber till almost 8 went downe and sate below till after 9 my Landlady read we went to prayers and I to bed.

Monday, 29 May: Rose at 7 after I was dressed and performed my devotion went to prayers and eate som tost after 9 my Landlord and I went to Wiven[oe] to babtise Geo:[314] Smiths child went to prayers there at the church was there till 1 went to diner at 3 the childrens baptised babtised Mrs Wigwood Mrs Poes and Mr [blank] and myselfe were Godfathers stayd till almost 8 came home and stayd at George Lambs[315] till ½ houer after 9 came home and I read a letter from Mrs Gray, I went to my chamber and performed my devotion my Landlady read we went to prayers and I to bed.

Tuesday, 30 May: Rose after 6 after I was dressed and performed my devotion was in my chamber a little mending a payre of stockings went to prayers and to school stayd till after 11 cam home and was in my chamber and performed my devotion went to diner and afterwards Mr Smith came and sate in my chamber till 1 went to school and stayd till after 4 came home walkd w[ith] Mr Smith to see his mare and after to Lexden and playd 2 games at bowls [*illegible words*] till after 8 came home at 9 my Landlady read we went to prayers and I went to my chamber and performed my devotion and to bed.

---

[314] Lloyd's hand is very ambiguous here, so I have left the original abbreviation; it probably stands for 'George'.
[315] One George Lambe, son of a tailor of the same name, was admitted to Colchester Grammar School in March 1647, aged seven. An individual of the same name was assessed at five hearths in St Leonard's parish in 1670. See Round, *Colchester School*, 57; *EHT*, 291.

[fo. 33r]

Wednesday, 31 May: Rose after 6 after I was dressed and performed my devotion was in my chamber a little with William Smith went to prayers and to school and stayd till after 11 came home and was in my chamber a little and performed my devotion went to diner and to school and stayd till after 4 William Smith and I walked by the Castle lanes to Mr Ardryes and stayd there till 8 came home and went to my chamber and performed my devotion after 9 my Landlady read we went to prayers and I to bed.

Thursday, 1 June: Rose at 7 after I was dressed went to prayers and before I performed my devotion William Smith came and I went to school and stayd a little and came home and performed my devotion and went againe and stayd till after 11 came home and was in my chamber a little laying up my linen went to diner and performed my devotion and went to school and stayd till after 3 came home and stayd a little went at 4 to Mr Ardrys and stayd till almost 9 went to Joseph the Barber's stayd till almost 10 came home eat a little bred and cheese went to my chamber and performed my devotion went downe and my Landlady read we went to prayers and I to bed.

Friday, 2 June: Rose at 6 after I was dressed and performed my devotion went to Joseph the Barbers and had my head shaved went to school and stayd till after 11 came home went to my chamber and performed my devotion and went to prayers we went to diner and after diner went to Joseph and fetch his violin and tryed to play a little some new tunes at 1 went to school and stayd till after 4 came home to my chamber and was pricking pounce[316] till after 6 performed my devotion and after 7 went downe and was in the house till 8 then walked till 9 with Mr Smith eate som super sate till 10 my Landlady read we went to prayers and I to bed.

Saturday, 3 June: Rose at 6 after I was dressed and performed my devotion went to prayers and made my confession out of Dr Taylors Golden Grove went to school stayd till after 11 stayd at Robert Meaddows gave him 2 letters one to Mr Lardner to pay 5^{li} and he returned it the other to Phyloclea came home performed my devotion and renewed my covenant went to diner not being well after diner Mr Smith came and we discoursed till after 3 walkd til almost 5 I went to Mr Ardryes and stayd till after 8 came home received a

---

[316] Perhaps preparing a pattern for a calligraphic design. See *OED*: 1728 … *Pounce* … Charcoal-Dust, inclosed in some open Stuff; to be pass'd over Holes prick'd in a Work, in order to mark the Lines or Designs thereof on a Paper placed underneath.

letter from my Brother and my sister Carless performed my devotion sate up till after 10 gott my things redy for the next day my Landlady read we went to prayers and I to bed.

Sunday, 4 June: Rose at 7 after I was dressed and performed my devotion went to prayers and after used the lettany out of Dr Taylors Guid to the Penitent read a sermon eate som breakfast went to Trinity and heard Mr Smith on the 1 John 3: 1 John 3:14:15 came home mad a short prayer went to diner after diner discoursd with my Landlord and Mr Smith performed my devotion went to St Giles and herd Mr Smith on the same text came home went to my chamber performed my devotion read a sermon went downe and walked with my Landlord came in eate som super sate and talked with him till after 9 he read we sang a Psalm went to prayers and I to bed.

Monday, 5 June: Rose at 6 after I was dressed went downe and talked with my Landlady who had carryed herselfe strange for a weeke and [*deleted*] [*deleted*] did reconsile her, went to prayers and performed my devotion went to school and stayd till after 11 went to Mr Edlins and bespoak a table came home and put my violin in order went to diner Mr Smith came in and I could not perform my devotion went to school and stayd till after 4 came in and performed my devotion for noone, was a little packing som things Mr Smith came and I playd on my violin went to walke went into the watter to try to swime but could not came home and went to Mr Meaddows to wh: [*word cut off*] Mr Smith and had halfe a pint of brandy burned came home sate a little my Landlady re[ad] we went to prayers and I to my chamber and performed my devotion and went to bed.

[fo. 33v]
Tuesday, 6 June: Rose after 6 after I was dressed and performed my devotion went downe and help[ed] my Landlady bottle som small beere, went to prayers and to school and stayd till after 11 came home and was a little pricking out som things went down and eate my diner and performed my devotion and went to school and stayd till after 4 came home and was within pricking som things out till after 6 went to Mr Ardryes he not within came a way caled at Mr Hutchinsons about som buttons, and at the shooemakers for to make me a payre of shooes and Coloshooes,[317] caled at Mr Aingers

---

[317] An archaic spelling of 'galoshes', *OED*.

and payd him for his Brother's mending my buckoll and buttons came home and eat som bread and cheese went to my chamber and performed my devotion and playd a little on my violin went downe after 9 my Landlady read and we went to prayers and after 10 I went to bed.

Wednesday, 7 June: Rose after 6 after I was dressed and performed my devotion went to prayers and read the lettany in Dr Taylor was in my chamber a little pricking som things went to school and stayd till after 11 came home and was in my chamber a little pricking went to diner and after performed my devotion and went to school and stayd till almost 4 let the boyes goe to see the Mountebanck was in my chamber till after 7 pricking wend [sic] downe and eate som bred and cheese went to my chamber and performed my devotion and playd on my violin till after 9 came downe and sate up till after 10 my Landlady read we went to prayers and I to bed.

Thursday, 8 June: Rose before 7 after I was dressed and performed my devotion went to prayers and was a little in my chamber a pricking went to school and stayd till after 11 came home and was below getting corks out of som bottles and getting me a Sallatt[318] went to diner and performed my devotion and went to school and stayd till after 3 was in my chamber and made an end of pricking went to Mr Ardryes and stayd till after 6 spoake with Mr Shelton was within and performed my devotion and eate som super sate up till after 10 my Landlady read we went to prayers and I to bed.

Friday, 9 June: Rose at 5 after I was dressed and performed my devotion was putting Mrs Grays letters together went to prayers and went to Mr Goldsberys and playd a tune came to school stayd till after 11 came home and performed my devotion went to diner and went to school and stayd till after 4 came home and read over some of Mrs Grayes Letters and myne to her after 6 walked and read over the rest in the field and walked till 8 came in and found Tom Elkin and sate till after 9 and playd on my violin a little went to my chamber and performed my devotion and my Landlady and I and John went to prayers in my chamber and I went to bed.

Saturday, 10 June: Rose at 6 after I was dressed and performed my devotion went to prayers and eat a little bred and butter and went to Mr Goldsberys and playd a little at 8 went to school and stayd till after 11 came home and was below till after diner playd

---

[318] Salad; for contemporary salads, see May, *Accomptlisht Cook*, 144–151.

a little and trimed myselfe performed my devotion and was in my chamber till after 4 mending a payre of drawers after 5 went to Mr Ardryes and stayd till after 8 came home and performed my devotion and eate som bread and cheese sate up till after 10 my Landlady read we went to prayers and I to bed.

[fo. 34r]
Sunday, 11 June: Rose at 7 after I was dressed and performed my devotion went to prayers and I used the Lettany in Dr Taylors went downe and eate som bread and butter and went to my chamber and performed my devotion read a sermon went to Trinity and heard Mr Smith on the 1 Peter 5:5 came home and went to my chamber and made a shorte prayer went to diner and after diner went to my chamber and performed my devotion lay a little on my bed read part of a sermon and went to St Peeters and herd Mr Thompson on the 17 Luke 10 came home and read a little and lay downe a little went downe and sate till 6 went to my chamber and read the other part of the sermon and performed my devotion went downe and sate below and examined John the catcisme and eate som super and Instructed John in the principales of religion we sang a Psalm my Landlady read we went to prayers and I to bed.

Monday, 12 June: Rose at 6 after I was dressed and performed my devotion went to prayers and eat a little bread and butter went to Mr Goldsberys and stayd till 8 and playd a little, went to school and stayd till after 11 came home went to diner performed my devotion playd a little on my violin went to school stayd till after 6 haveing Mr Sheltons son and Ashly Chayny to learne to write, came home and went to my chamber stayd a little performed my devotion sate up till 10 my Landlady read we went to pray and I to bed.

Tuesday, 13 June: Rose after 6 after I was dressed and performed my devotion went to prayers and eate som breakfast and went to school and stayd till after 11 came home and went to diner sate a little after went to my chamber and performed my devotion and playd a little and went to school and stayd till 8 was after 6 writting to Mrs Gray came home and went to Mr Ardryes and stayd till after 9 came home and eate a little super performed my devotion my Landlady read we went to prayers and I to my chamber and to bed.

Wednesday, 14 June: Rose before 6 after I was dressed and performed my devotion went to prayers and eate som breakfast went to Mr Goldsberys and stayd till 8 went to school and stayd till after 11 came home and went to my chamber and was flurishing Mall[319] Hawksbees peece went to diner and performed my devotion and went to school and stayd till after 6 came home and went to my chamber and performed my devotion and was within and playd a little on my violin at 10 my Landlady read we went to prayers and I to bed.

Thursday, 15 June: Rose at 6 after I was dressed and performed my devotion went to prayers and at 8 went to school and stayd till after 11 came home performed my devotion dined and went to Mr Goldsberry's playd till 1 went to school stayd till after 5 came home and was about a peece for William Colm[an] performed my devotion eat som super and playd a little sate up till 10 my Landlady read we went to prayers and I to bed.

Friday, 16 June: Rose before 6 after I was dressed and performed my devotion went to prayers eat som breakfast went to Mr Goldsberys stayd till 8 went to school and stayd till after 11 came home and stayd till 12 went to diner performed my devotion was in my chamber a little went to school and stayd till after 6 came in stayd a little went to Mr Ardryes at 7 stayd till almost 9 called at Mr Bollers payd for my shooes and Galloshes came home at 10 my Landlady read we went to prayers and I to my chamber performed my devotion sealed a letter to send to Mrs Gray and received one that day.

Saturday, 17 June: Rose [*shorthand*] 6 after I was dresed and performed my devotion went to prayers eat som breakfast went to Mr Goldsberry's stayd till 8 went to school stayd till after 11 came home went to diner performed my devotion trimed myselfe and was in my chamber all the afternoone fitting a peece for William Coleman performed my devotion at 8 sate up till 10 below, my Landlady read we went to prayers and I to bed.

Sunday, 18 June: Rose before 7 after I was dressed read sermon went to prayers I performed my devotion went downe and eat som breakfast and read till church time went to Trinity and heard Mr Smith on the 1 Peter 5:5 came home and made a shorte prayer and read till diner after diner performed my devotion and lay a little went to church to St Peeters and heard Mr Tompson on the 12 Romans 3 came home read a sermon lay downe a little read till after 6 performed my devotion and went into the garden and eate

[319] Perhaps short for Malcolm.

som gooseberys eate som super at 10 my Landlady read we sang a Psalm went to prayers and I to bed.

[fo. 34v]
Monday, 19 June: Rose at 5 after I was dressed and performed my devotion was bottling som beere till 7 went to prayers and eate som breakfast and went to school and stayd till 11 came home and performed my devotion and went to diner and stayd till after 1 mending a payre of stockings and went to school and stayd till after 6 came home and was in my chamber till 8 reading over Phylocleas letters performed my devotion and went downe went to Mr Bonds and playd at nine pinns till after 9 stayd there till after 10 came home my Landlady read went to prayers and I to bed.

Tuesday, 20 June: Rose at 5 after I was dressed and performed my devotion went to prayers and eat som breakfast went to Mr Goldberrys and playd a little went to school and stayd till after 11 came home performed my devotion went to diner playd a little went to school stayd till after 6 stayd a little at Mr Meaddows came home performed my devotion went to Mr Ardryes stayd till after 8 called at Mr Grays stayd till 10 came home eate som super my Landlady read we went to prayers and I to bed.

Wednesday, 21 June: Rose at 5 after I was dressed and performed my devotion went to prayers and went to Mr Goldsberys and playd a little went to school and stayd till after 11 came home performed my devotion went to diner sate a little went to school and stayd till after 6 came home and was till after 7 finishing William Colemans peece performed my devotion and went to Mr Bonds playd at nine pins till after 9 went to Jo: Blumfields and was there playing and dancing till after 11 came home my Landlady read we went to prayers and to bed.

Thursday, 22 June: Rose before 5 after I was dressed and performed my devotion went to prayers at 6 tooke horse and went to St Oseth[320] with my Landlord and Landlady came thither after 8 stayd at Goodman Trusses[321] till after 9 went to see the ground and house and went to Mr Lanes[322] after 10 went to Mr Clarks

---
[320] St Osyth, a village about twelve miles south-east of Colchester.
[321] Probably John Truss, assessed at four hearths in St Osyth in 1670; *EHT*, 326.
[322] A John Lane was assessed at three hearths in 1670, ibid.

stayd there and eate some diner after 2 went to Mr Lanes stayd there till after 3 went to see another house and stayd at Goodwife Hanes till after 7 went to Mother Trusses and stayd till neere 8 tooke horse and came home at 10 I performed my devotion went to prayers and to bed.

Friday, 23 June: Rose at 6 after I was dressed and performed my devotion went to prayers eate som breakfast went to school and stayd till after 11 came home and went to diner performed my devotion stayd till 1 went to school stayd till after 5 came home and was within performed my devotion eat som super and went to Mr Meaddows and stayd till 9 came home and sate up till after 11 Mr Clarke and his wife being at our house my Landlady read we went to prayers and I to bed.

Saturday, 24 June: Rose at 7 after I was dressed and performed my devotion went to prayers and trimed myselfe was in my chamber till 10 about drawing som lines in my peece of the text, went to St Peeters to prayers came home before 12 was within till after diner performed my devotion and lay downe till 2 Mr Ardry came to me and I sate with him till 3 was in my chamber drawing some more Lyenes till after 5 gott my things redy for the next day eate some super stood at the door till after 8 performed my devotion and after went to Mr Meaddows and stayd till after 10 came home sate up till almost 11 my Landlady read we went to prayers and I to bed.

Sunday, 25 June: Rose after 7 after I was dressed went to prayers and performed my devotion read parte of a sermon eate som breakfast went to Trinity heard Mr Smith on 1 Peter 5:5 came home made a short prayer went to diner after diner performed my devotion lay downe a little went to St Peeters and herd Mr Thompson on the 24 Acts 25 latter end, came home and red the other part of the sermon went into the garden and gatherd som goosberys lay downe, performed my devotion was within meditating at 9 my Landlord and Landlady came in she read we sang went to prayers and I to bed.

Monday, 26 June: Rose after 5 after I was dressed went to my school to see, the church text came back and performed my devotion and was about making the text all day till 6 at 9 in the morning went to prayers eat som breakfast at 10 after 12 performed my devotion at 3 went to diner at 6 went to Mr Ardrys stayd till af[ter] 8 came in performed my devotion went a little to Mr Meaddows and after to Mr Bonds stayd till 10 came h[ome] I read a chapter went to prayers and to bed.[323]

[fo. 35r]
Tuesday, 27 June: Rose at 7 after I was dressed went to prayers performed my devotion and eate som breakfast and was about my Itallian text till after 1 performed my devotion and was about the Chronogram[324] at 3 went to diner sate till after 4 went to my chamber and playd a little was about my Itallian text till 7 performed my devotion mended a payre of stockings writt a letter to my Brother playd a little eat som super my Landlady read went to prayers and to bed.

Wednesday, 28 June: Rose at 7 after I was dressed and performed my devotion went to prayers and to school and stayd till after 11 came home and was in my chamber about flurishing my peece went to diner performed my devotion went to school stayd till after 5 came home, went to Mr Ardrys stayd till 9 came home eat somthing my Landlady read we went to prayers I performed my devotion and went devotion and went to bed, sent a letter to my Brother Nicholas.

Thursday, 29 June: Rose after 6 after I was dressed went to prayers and performed my devotion was a little about flurishing my peece, went to school and stayd till almost 11 went to St Peeters to prayers came home gott a chrystall putt into my watch[325] came to diner performed my devotion and was in my chamber till after 4 about finishing my text went into the garden gathered some gooseberys and carryed som to Mrs Ardrys stayd there till 8 walke[d] through the castell lanes came home performed my devotion eate som super my Landlady read went to prayers and to bed.

Friday, 30 June: Rose after 6 after I was dressed went to prayers and performed my devotion was a little in my chamber went to school stayd till after 11 came home went to diner performed my devotion went into the garden eat som gooseberrys went to school and stayd till after 6 came home performed my devotion eat som

---

[323] The narrative structure of this entry is slightly confusing, but Lloyd seems to mean that he spent his time working on the text all day, around which he performed the rest of the actions narrated subsequently in the entry.

[324] A chronogram is an inscription wherein specific letters are indicated to denote a date; Lloyd was probably adding to his aforementioned 'Italian' (i.e. italic or chancery cursive) calligraphic piece.

[325] A crystal lens placed over the face of the watch.

super walked to Lexton warren came in at 9 went to see Mr Ardry being Just com from London stayd till almost 10 came in stayd a little my Landlady read we went to pray and I to bed.

Saturday, 1 July: Rose after 6 after I was dressed performed my devotion went to prayers and mad my confession out of Dr Taylor's Golden Grove went to school stayd till after 11 came home, performed my devotion eate a little diner, after diner went to my chamber and read and made my exam[?ination][326] and confession out of Winchester College manuall,[327] after 3 lay downe a little, then trimed myselfe, and was in my chamber and performed my devotion and renewed my covenant, was getting my things redy for the next day eate a little bred and cheese was serious in thoughts of the Lord's super at 10 my Landlady read went to prayers and I to bed.

Sunday, 2 July: Rose after 5 after I was dressed and performed my devotion was in my chamber reading went to prayers and was in my chamber read and prayed till church time went to Trinity and heard Mr Sm[ith] received the ℞ came home returned God my thanks went to diner performed my devotion and read a little went to St Giles and heard Mr S:[328] on the 1 Peter 5:5: came home and read a little not being very well lay a little went downe and stayd till after 8 and was discoursing upon the matters of religion performed my devotion my Landlady read we sang went to prayers and I to bed.

Monday, 3 July: Rose before 6 after I was dressed and performed my devotion went to prayers had my head shaved eat a little bred and butter went to school stayd till after 11 came home went to diner performed my devotion went to Mr Goldsberry at 1 went to school stayd till after 6 went to Mr Ardryes stayd till after 8 came home dranke a little burnt brandy performed my devotion my Landlady read went to prayers and I to bed.

---

[326] Lloyd was preparing himself to receive Holy Communion the following day. Thomas Ken's *A Manual of Prayers for the Use of the Scholars of Winchester Colledge* (London, 1674) instructs the reader to 'commune with your own heart' and examine one's conscience the day before receiving the Sacrament (pp. 20–28) Cf. Taylor, *The Golden Grove* (1655), pp. 58–59, which instructs the devotee to examine their conscience and 'ask pardon for what is amiss' in the evening.

[327] Ken (1637–1711), later bishop of Bath and Wells and a Nonjuror, attended Winchester College in the 1650s, leaving just as Lloyd entered, *ODNB*.

[328] This may have been Shelton or Smith.

Tuesday, 4 July: Rose at 6 after I was dressed and performed my devotion went to prayers eat som breakfast went to Mr Goldberry went to school at 8 stayd till after 11 came home performed my devotion went to diner and to school stayd till after 6 came home performed my devotion was a little about a payre of cuffs went downe and eate som milke sate up till 10 I read went to prayers and to bed.

Wednesday, 5 July: Rose at 5 after I was up in my chamber about a payre of cuffs at 6 performed my devotion went to prayers eat som breakfast went to Mr Goldsberry at 8 to school stayd till after 11 came home was a little about the cuffs went to diner performed my devotion went to school stayd till after 5 went to Mr Ardryes and went with him and his wife to Barringtons house to eat cherries and could get none stayd at Mr Vickers till 8 went to Mr Ardrey stayd till 9 came home eat som supper I read went to prayers went to my chamber and performed my devotion and went to bed.

Thursday, 6 July: Rose at 6 after I was dressed and performed my devotion was in my chamber about a paire of cuffs went to pray and eate som breakfast went to Jo: Blumfields writt out a song went to school stayd till after 11 came home was with Mr Jeffery of St Oseth went to diner sate after a little performed my devotion went to school stayd till 5 went to Mr Goldsberry playd a little came home and was a little about my cuffs performed my devotion eat som super went to Mr Bonds stayd a till 10 came home went to pray and to bed.

Friday, 7 July: Rose at 6 after I was dressed and performed my devotion went to prayers eat a bit of bred and butter went to Mr Goldsberry stayd till after 8 went to school and stayd till after 11 came home and was in my chamber a little went to diner performed my devotion went to school stayd till after 6 came home went with William Basher to Groomes at the 2 brewers[329] and agreed to learne his daughter dranke a flagon came away stayd a little at Jo: Blumfield's came in eat som bred and cheese performed my devotion was in my chamber writting an answer to Mrs Gray from whome and Philoclea I received letter this day at [*sic*] went to prayers and to bed.

---

[329] One of the less well-documented old alehouses of Colchester, the Two Brewers may have been in the parish of St Mary Magdalen, though its precise location is unknown. See Jess A. Jephcott, *The Inns, Taverns and Pubs of Colchester* (Colchester, 2015), 380–381.

Saturday, 8 July: Rose at 6 after I was dressed and performed my devotion went to prayers and was in my chamber about a paire of cuffs at 8 went to school stayd till after 11 came home went to diner performed my devotion and was till 5 altering the pockett holes of my cloth coate trimed myselfe at 6 went to Mr Ardryes stayd till 9 came home performed my devotion eate som bred and cheese my Landlady read we went to prayers and I to bed.

[fo. 35v]
Sunday, 9 July: Rose at 7 after I was dressed and performed my devotion went to prayers read till church time went to Trinity heard Mr Smith on the 6 Romans 19 came home made a short prayer went to diner read till after performed my devotion went to St Peeters heard Mr Tompson on the 4 Hebrews 13 came home read a chapter went into the garden eat som gooseberys read a sermon lay downe a little went to St Peeters heard a funerall for Jasper Watters child by a stranger 1 Job 21 performed my devotion eat som super my Landlady read went to prayers and I to bed.

Monday, 10 July: Rose at 6 after I was dressed and performed my devotion went to prayers was a little aboute my coate went to school stayd till after 11 came home went to diner performed my devotion was a little about my coate went to school stayd till 7 came home was a little about my coate performed my devotion went to Richard Orbells to eate beanes and porke stayd till after 9 came home my Landlady read we went to prayers and I to bed.

Tuesday, 11 July: Rose at 6 after I was dressed and went to prayers performed my devotion was putting up som blackscherys and branets[330] went to school at 8 stayd till after 11 came home performed my devotion playd a little, went to diner went to Mr Ardryes and stayd till after 1 went to school stayd till after 4 went with Mr Ardry and his wife to Wivenoe stayd till after came home after 10 my Landlady read went to prayers and I to my chamber performed my devotion and went to bed.

Wednesday, 12 July: Rose at 6 after I was dressed and performed my devotion went to prayers and was about a payre of cuffs till 8 went to school after I had eaten somthing stayd till after 11 came home went to diner performed my devotion and was about my

---

[330] Lloyd's hand is a little unclear here, but the word is legible. I can find no other examples of this peculiar usage; presumably it refers to a fruit of some kind.

cuffs a little at 1 went to school stayd till after 7 came home eate som bred and cheese was a little about my cuffs performed my devotion was below till 10 my Landlady read we went to prayers and I to bed.

Thursday, 13 July: Rose at 6 after I was dressed and performed my devotion was about my coate went to prayers and to school stayd till after 11 came home and was Ironing som ribon went to diner performed my devotion trimed myselfe went to school stayd till after 5 went to the dancing school[331] stayd till after 6 went to the Coffe[332] with the danc[ing] Master dranke 2 flagons went to Mr Ardrys stayd till 9 caled at the Queens Head came home performed my devotion my Landlady read went to prayers and I to bed.

Friday, 14 July: Rose at before 6 after I was dressed and performed my devotion was in my chamber a little about a payre of cuffs went to prayers and was getting my pot and things to make som Inck, went eat som breakfast went to school stayd till after 11 came home went to diner performed my devotion and was a little about my cuffs went to school stayd till after 6 came home and was about my cuffs and ended them eate som super performed my devotion playd ½ hour sate up till 10 my Landlady read we went to prayers and I to bed.

Saturday, 15 July: Rose after 6 when I was dressed and performed my devotion went to prayers and was a little about mending the lace of a cravat eat som bred and butter went to school stayd till after 11 came home went to diner performed my devotion was in my chamber till 4 mending my cravat trimed myselfe stayd below till after 6 walked to Mr Ard[rey's] by the fields stayd till almost 9 performed my devotion eat som super my Landlady read went to prayers and to bed.

Sunday, 16 July: Rose after 6 after I was dressed and performed my devotion went to prayers read a sermon eat som breakfast went to Trinity heard Mr Smith on the 6 Romans 19 came home made a short prayer went to diner sate and heard John read went to my chamber and lay downe but not long performed my devotion

---

[331] This is the first mention of the 'dancing school' which Lloyd attended for a brief period. It was probably a fairly informal, perhaps itinerant enterprise of which the 'Mr Bontall' mentioned below appears to have been the proprietor; it has left no obvious archival trace.

[332] Lloyd probably means coffee house.

went to St Peeters heard Mr Thompson on the 12 Proverbs 26 came home walked into the field with my Landlord and Landlady Mr Cockerill and his wife and Mary Bond came in at 6 sate till after 8 went to my chamber read a little performed my devotion eate som super read a chapter sang a Psalm went to prayers and to bed.

Monday, 17 July: Rose at 6 after I was dressed and performed my devotion went to prayers was a little mending a payre of stockings went to school stayd till after 11 came home went to diner performed my devotion mended my stockings went to school stayd till after 6 came home playd a little on my Violin eate som super went performed my devotion went to Mr Ardryes stayd till after 9 came home my Landlady read we went to prayers and I to bed.

[fo. 36r]
Tuesday, 18 July: Rose before 6 after I was dressed and performed my devotion went to Mr Goldsberys stayd till 8 went to school stayd till after 11 came home playd a little went to diner performed my devotion went to school stayd till after 6 went to Mr Smiths stayd till 7 went to the mill to eate backon and beanes stayd till after 9 came home my Landlady read went to prayers performed my devotion and went to bed.

Wednesday, 19 July: Rose after 5 when I was dressed and performed my devotion went to pray and went to Mr Goldsberry stayd till almost 8 went to school and stayd till after 11 came home went to diner performed my devotion went to school stayd till after 6 came to my chamber was a little about a cravat performed my devotion went to Mrs Ardrys stayd till after 9 came in my Landlady read went to prayers and to bed.

Thursday, 20 July: Rose after 5 when I was dressed and performed my devotion went to prayers and eate som bred and cheese went to Mr Goldsberry stayd till almost 8 went to school stayd till after 11 came home went to diner performed my devotion was a little about a cravat went to school stayd till after 5 came home made an end of my cravat playd on my Violin eate som super walkd to Lexton cross came in performed my devotion sate till 10 my Landlady read went to prayers and I to bed.

Friday, 21 July: Rose at 7 after I was dressed went to prayers and performed my devotion went to school stayd till after 11 came home went to diner performed my devotion playd a little on my Violin was a little about my Inck went to school stayd till after 6 came home was in my chamber riping my Shamy breeches performed my devotion eat som super my Landlady read went to prayers and to bed at 10.

Saturday, 22 July: Rose at 6 after I was dressed and performed my devotion went to prayers writt a letter to William Smith and one to my Brother went to school stayd till after 11 came home came to me a poore writting Master who I gave a shilling to went to diner performed my devotion trimed myselfe writt to[333] certificates for Mr Jackson and Mr Lamb stay within till 6 went to Mrs Ardryes stayd till 9 came home performed my devotion my Landlady read went to prayers and I to bed.

Sunday, 23 July: Rose after 6 after I was dressed and performed my devotion read and went to prayers and after read till 9 went downe and eat som breakfast at 10 went to Trinity heard Mr Smith on the 1 Corinthians 10:11:12 came home mad a short prayer went to diner performed my devotion read at 2 went to St Peeters heard Mr Tompson on 1 James 17 came home went to my chamber read and slept a little performed my devotion went downe eat somthing my Landlady read went to prayers and I to bed.

Monday, 24 July: Rose after 6 after I was dressed and performed my devotion went to school stayd till after 11 came home and was in my chamber writting a letter to Mrs Gray went to diner performed my devotion went to school stayd till after 6 sent a letter to Mrs Gray and to my Brother came home and was in my chamber playing on my Violin went to the garden to my Inck stayd a little came in performed my devotion and playd a little went downe and eat a bit of bred and cheese my Landlady read went to prayers and I to bed.

Tuesday, 25 July: Rose after 6 after I was dressed and performed my devotion went to prayers and was in my chamber altring my shamy breeches till 10 went downe and stayd below till ½ houer after went to St Peeters to prayers came home was in my chamber a little at play, went to diner performed my devotion was in my chamber till 4 received a letter from my Brother writt one to my Lord Cullen at 6 walked to Mr Ardryes stayd till 9 came home eat som bred and cheese my Landlady read went to prayers performed my devotion and to bed.

---

[333] Two.

THE DIARY OF GEORGE LLOYD 159

Wednesday, 26 July: Rose at 6 after I was dressed and performed my devotion went to prayers and went to Mr Goldsberry stayd till almost 8 went to school stayd till after 11 came home playd a little went to diner performed my devotion went to school stayd till 3 gave the boyes a play beged[334] by Mr Ainger came home stayd till 4 playd a little went to school stayd till after 6 came to my chamber playd a little my [Landlor]d and Phillip[335] Eve walked to Shakerwell[336] and drank came home eat som supper my Landlady read went to prayers I performed my devotion and went to bed.

Thursday, 27 July: Rose at 6 after I was dressed and performed my devotion was a little about my Shamy breeches went to prayers and to school stayd till after 11 came home and was a little about my breeches went to diner performed my devotion playd a little went to school and stayd till after 5 came home made an end of my breeches and was within performed my devotion after 7 eate som super stayd up till 10 my Landlady read went to prayers.

[fo. 36v]
Friday, 28 July: Rose at 6 after I was dressed and performed my devotion went to prayers eat som breakfast and went to Mr Goldsberry playd a little went to schoole stayd till after 11 came home went to diner, washed som bottles for Maligoe[337] performed my devotion playd a little went to school stayd till after 6 went to Richard Orbells mill and put up a gallon of Maligoe went to Mrs Ardryes stayd till 9 came home my Landlady read went to prayers and I to my chamber and performed my devotion and to bed.

Saturday, 29 July: Rose at 6 after I was dressed and performed my devotion went to prayers and was in my chamber a little eate a little bred and cheese went to school and stayd till after 11 came home playd a little went to diner performed my devotion trimed myselfe was Lyning my belt till after 5 at 6 walked out and went to see Mrs Ardry and received a perrywig her husband sent from London, stayd till 9 came home <performed my devotion> eat a little super my Landlady read went to prayers and I to bed.

---

[334] An unusual usage; perhaps a strange spelling of 'begot' or 'begotten'.
[335] Originally 'Phi'.
[336] This is not a street or settlement anywhere in the vicinity of Colchester; rather it is likely to mean 'Sha(c)ker well' as in 'shacker spring': see **24 February 1676**.
[337] Malaga, a sweet fortified wine from Malaga in the south of Spain, similar to port.

Sunday, 30 July: Rose at 6 after I was dressed and performed my devotion read a chapter or to[338] and went to prayers eat somthing read a little went to Trinity and herd Mr Smith on the 1 Corinthians 10:12 came home made a short prayer went to diner performed my devotion went to Mrs Ardrys read till church time she not being within went to St James herd Mr Shelton on the 22 Matthew 36 stayd at Mr Ardrys till after 5 came home read and lay a little performed my devotion and was in the house till after 8 eat som super my Landlady read sang went to prayers and to bed.

Monday, 31 July: Rose at 5 after I was dressed and performed my devotion went to prayers and eat somthing went to Mr Goldsberys and playd till almost 8 went to school and stayd till after 11 came home playd a little went to diner performed my devotion and made an end of my belt went to school stayd till after 6 came home playd a little performed my devotion and went to Mr Meaddows stayd till 9 came home sate up till 10 my Landlady read we went to prayers and I to bed.

Tuesday, 1 August: Rose at 5 after I was dressed and performed my devotion and went to prayers and was in my chamber about a payre of cuffs at 8 went to school and stayd till after 11 came home performed my devotion went to diner lay downe till after 1 not being well went to school stayd till after 6 came home performed my devotion went to Mrs Ardrys stayd till 9 sat up a little my Landlady read went to prayers and bed.

Wednesday, 2 August: Rose at 5 after I was dressed and performed my devotion went to prayers and eat som breakfast and was about a payre of cuffs at 8 went to school and stayd till after 11 came home and was below till diner after diner performed my devotion and was in my chamber till 1 went to school stayd till after 6 came home received a letter from Mrs Gray playd a little performed my devotion and walkd till almost 9 eat som supper sate up till 10 my Landlady read went to prayers and to bed.

Thursday, 3 August: Rose after 5 after I was dressed and performed my devotion went to prayers and was a little about a payre of cuffs eat som breakfast went to school and stayd till after 11 came home and playd a little went to diner performed my devotion and went to school stayd till after 5 and was in Mr Meaddow his shop till almost 6 came home was in my chamber a little walked till 8 came

---

[338] Two.

in performed my devotion and eat sum super my Landlady read went to prayers and I to bed.

Friday, 4 August: Rose at 6 after I was dressed and performed my devotion went to prayers and to Mr Goldsberys playd till 8 went to school stayd till after 11 came home playd a little went to diner performed my devotion went to school stayd till after 6 came home stayd a little in my chamber and mended a stocking went to Mrs Ardry stayd till after 9 came home my Landlady read went to prayers performed my devotion and to bed.

Saturday, 5 August: Rose at 5 after I was dressed and performed my devotion made my confession out of Dr Taylors Golden Grove went to prayers and to school and stayd till after 11 came home eate som diner performed my devotion walkd till 5 meditated came home and not being well Lay downe a little trimed myselfe performed my devotion sate up till after 9 my Landlady read went to prayers and I to bed.

Sunday, 6 August: Rose at 7 after I was dressed and performed my devotion went to prayers and eate som breakfast and was below till church went to Trinity heard Mr Tompson on the 5 Matthew 7 came home made a short prayer went to diner sate a little after performed my devotion and lay downe a little not being well went to St Peeters heard Mr Tompson on the 5 Matthew 8 came home read and was in my chamber till 6 went to the Kings to Mr Daniell to speake about his son[339] came home performed my devotion eat [deleted] some bread and cheese my Landlady read went to my chamber and to bed.[340]

[fo. 37r]
Monday, 7 August: Rose at 5 after I was dressed and performed my devotion went to prayers and eat som breakfast went to Mr Goldsberry stayd till after 8 went to school stayd till after 11 came home and went to diner performed my devotion and lay downe a little went to school stayd till after 6 came home went to see Mrs Ardrey and she was not at home walked till after 8 came in eate som super my Landlady read went to prayers and to my chamber performed my devotion and went to bed.

---

[339] Very faded and uncertain.
[340] This line very faded.

Tuesday, 8 August: Rose at 6 after I was dressed and performed my devotion went to prayers eat a bitt went to Mr Goldsberry stayd till after 8 went to school stayd till after 11 came home went to diner performed my devotion playd a little went to school stayd till after 6 came home stayd a little went to see Mrs Ardry stayd till after 9 came home eat som super my Landlady read went to prayers performed my devotion and went to bed.

Wednesday, 9 August: Rose at 6 after I was dressed and performed my devotion went to prayers and was in my chamber playing a little eat som breakfast went to school stayd till after 11 came home went to diner performed my devotion went to Mr Goldsberry playd a little went to school stayd till after 6 came home was in my chamber playing a little performed my devotion after 8 walkd eat som super read a letter from Mrs Gray my Landlady read went to prayers and I to my chamber and to bed.

Thursday, 10 August: Rose at 6 after I was dressed and performed my devotion went to prayers and eat a bit of bred and butter and was in my chamber about a paire of cuffs till 8 went to school and stayd till after 11 came home went to diner performed my devotion and went to Mr Goldsberry playd till 1 went to school stayd till after 5 came to my chamber stayd till after 6 went to [*deleted*] Mr [*sic*] Renholds and talked with her about her[341] son and man to Learne stayd at Mrs Ardrey's till 10 came home my Landlady read went to prayers performed my devotion and went to bed.

Friday, 11 August: Rose at 6 after I was dressed and performed my devotion went to prayers and eat a bitt of bred and cheese went to Mr Goldsberry playd till after 8 came to school stayd till after 11 came home went to diner performed my devotion lay downe not being very well after 1 went to school stayd till almost 6 went to Mrs Ardreys stayd till almost 9 came home eat som super performed my devotion my Landlady read went to prayers and to bed.

Saturday, 12 August: Rose at 6 after I was dressed and performed my devotion went to prayers eat som breakfast went to school stayd till after 11 came home went to diner performed my devotion

---

[341] In cases like this Lloyd assumes the wife (or sometimes servant) of the man visited is understood. (See **30 October 1676**; n. 775, **14 March 1711**; and n. 807, **3 May 1711**.) Here it seems likely that he was speaking to Judith Reynolds, wife of Samuel Reynolds; Lloyd would later act as tutor to their son Samuel. See **22 April 1676** and **9 October 1676**.

trimed myselfe washt my feete went into the field and catcht my Landlord's Mare rid out almost to Wivenoe towne field came in and went to Mrs Ardreys stayd till after 8 Mrs M: Furley[342] being there came home performed my devotion my Landlady read went to prayers and I to bed.

Sunday, 13 August: Rose after 7 not being very well after I was dressed and performed my devotion went to prayers and eat a little breakfast went to St Peeters heard Mr Thompson on the 5 Matthew 8 came home made a shorte prayer went to diner sate a little performed my devotion and went to <St> Peeters herd the same man and text came home went to my chamber and read and lay downe a little read a letter from my dr[343] Mrs Gray considered on it a while performed my devotion eat som super and discoursd with my Landlady till 9 I read sang a Psalm went to prayers and I to bed.

Monday, 14 August: Rose at 5 after I was dressed and performed my devotion was in my chamber writting to Mrs Gray went to prayers eat a little breakfast and went to school and stayd till after 11 came home and went to diner and performed my devotion playd a little and went to school stayd till after 6 went to Mrs Ardryes stayd till 9 came home performed my devotion my Landlady read went to prayers and I to bed.

Tuesday, 15 August: Rose at 6 after I was dressed and performed my devotion went to prayers eat a little break[fast] went to Mr Goldsberry playd till after 8 went to school stayd till after 11 came home went to diner performed my devotion went to school stayd till after 6 came home was in my chamber about a cravat till 7 went to Mrs Ayngers stayd a little was within and eat som super performed my devotion was at Jo Blumf[ield's] till 11 my Landlady read went to prayers and I to bed.

Wednesday, 16 August: Rose at 5 after I was dressed and performed my devotion went to prayers eat som bread and cheese went to Mr Goldsberry playd till after 8 went to school stayd till after 11 came home went to diner performed my devotion playd a little went to school stayd till after 6 came home playd till 7 went to Mrs Ardreys stayd till after 9 Mrs M. Furley being there came

---

[342] Probably Mary Furly: see **28 November 1676**.
[343] Dear?

home my Landlady read went to prayers performed my devotion and went to bed.

[fo. 37v]
Thursday, 17 August: Rose after 5 after I was dressed and performed my devotion went to prayers and went to Mr Goldsberry playd till 8 went to school stayd till after 11 came home and went to diner and performed my devotion playd a little went to school stayd till after 5 came to my chamber and playd a little walked to Mrs Ardryes stayd till 9 bought 2 slates at Mr Wheelys came home and sate up till after 10 my Landlady read went to prayers and I to my chamber and performed my devotion and to bed.

Friday, 18 August: Rose at 6 after I was dressed performed my devotion and went to prayers and eat a bitt of bread and butter went to Mr Goldsberry playd a little and went to school stayd till after 11 came home and went to diner performed my devotion lay downe a little went to school stayd till after 6 came home playd a little performed my devotion went to Mrs Ardreys stayd till after 9 came home went to prayers and to bed.

Saturday, 19 August: Rose at 6 after I was dressed and performed my devotion went to prayers eat som breakfast went to school stayd till after 11 came home went to diner performed my devotion was about a paire of drawers till 4 trimed myselfe playd till after 5 was in the shop with Mr Barker talking about his son to learne to write after 6 went to Mrs Ardryes stayd till 9 came in my Landlady read went to prayers I went to my chamber performed my devotion and went to bed.

Sunday, 20 August: Rose before 7 after I was dressed and performed my devotion went to prayers and eat som breakfast read till church time went to Sr Peeters herd a stranger on the 8 of Mark 38 came home and made a shorte prayer went to diner performed my devotion and had a dispute with my Landlord aboute schisme[344] performed my devotion and went to church and herd the same man and text came home red a little lay downe being Ill performed my devotion sate up till 9 my Landlady read went to prayers and I to bed.

---

[344] In other words, Lloyd and his landlord fell out about the issue of religious nonconformity or dissent.

Monday, 21 August: Rose at 6 after I was dressed and performed my devotion went to prayers was within till 8 went to school stayd till after 11 came home and performed my devotion went to diner went to the Queens Head to get a horse but could not went to school at 1 stayd till after 6 went to Mr Warrens and had the promise of 2 scholars[345] went to Mrs Ardrys stayd till 9 came home and eate a little bread and hyred a horse my Landlady read went to prayers performed my devotion and to bed.

Tuesday, 22 August: Rose at 6 after I was dressed and performed my devotion went to prayers and eat a little breakfast was in my chamber till 8 went to school stayd till after 11 came home performed my devotion went to diner and to Mr Goldsberry playd a little went to school stayd till almost 6 walked to meete Mr Ardry went to his house stayd till after 8 came home was in my chamber till 9 gettings [sic] my things redy to goe to London went downe my Landlady read went to prayers I to my chamber performed my devotion and went to bed.

Wednesday, 23 August: Rose at 6 after I was dressed performed my devotion and went to prayers eat a little bred and cheese went to Mr Goldsberry playd a little went to school stayd till after 11 came home went to diner performed my devotion trimed myselfe put on my botts went to school stayd till after 4 went home got myselfe redy to goe for London ½ houer after 4 set out rid to Ingerstone that night came thether before 9 went to super performed my devotion went to bed.

Thursday, 24 August: Rose after 1 got myselfe redy performed my devotion set out at 2 came to London before 6 went to the Flying Horse in Houersdich,[346] went to find my deare Mrs Gray she not being up went to Mr Sights and with him to the barbers dranke with them till after 9 then went to Mrs Gray and stayd with her all that day till 9 a clock then went to my Inn performed my devotion and went to bed.

[fo. 38r]
Friday, 25 August: Rose at 7 after I was dressed and performed my devotion went to the ear carriers and sent my basket with sirrup Mrs Gray made, bought a basket of frute and sent to Mrs Gray went to

---

[345] Originally 'prom of 2 sch:'.
[346] Houndsditch.

see Mr William Pagett he sent to his Brother Jo: we drank a mornings draught stayd till after 9 went to Mrs Gray stayd till diner after diner stayd till 3 went to Bartholomew fayer[347] and saw Jacob Hall[348] danced on the ropes walked about the fayer called at the Old Exchange bought a payre of Jessemine gloves for a fayreing[349] went to Mrs Grays she being with me stayd at her house till 10 went to my Inn performed my devotion and went to bed.

Saturday, 26 August: Rose at 5 after I was dressed and performed my devotion went to Little Brittain and bought a penknife walked round Smithfield called at Mr Fishers at the Old Exchange and agreed about paper, went to Mrs Grays stayd till 3 went to diner stayd there all that day till 10 went to my Inn and went to bed after I performed my devotion.

Sunday, 27 August: Rose at 7 after I was dressed performed my devotion went to Mr William Pagetts and called his Brother Jo: breakfasted at William went to Algate to church[350] heard a sermon on the 26 Acts 28 went to Mr William Pagett to diner after they 2 and I walked to Hackney heard a sermon on the 13 Luke 8 dranke each a Cann of beere walked home by Moorefields drank a bottle of Sider went to my Inn there we dranke a flaggon of Beere and I parted from them before 6 went to Mrs Gray stayd a ¼ of houer then walkd with her to the Sider house dranke a bottle of sider came back stayd and supt with her and suped and stayd with her till 11 then took my leave went to my Inn gott my things redy performed my devotion went to bed.

Monday, 28 August: Rose at 3 after I was dressed performed my devotion drank a draught of beere and at 4 sett out came to Chelmsford after 9 stayd till after 10 eat som bred and cheese drank a flagon of beere baited my horse set out came to Stanaway

---

[347] The famous fair, established by Royal Charter by Henry I for Rahere, founder of St Bartholomew's Hospital, was held annually on 24 August from 1133 until 1855. It was immortalized by Ben Jonson in his play of the same name (1614).

[348] Jacob Hall (fl. 1662–1681) was a famous acrobat and rope dancer, well known for his athletic prowess and dashing good looks. Pepys saw Hall perform at Bartholomew Fair in 1668, terming his act 'a thing worth seeing and mightily followed', *Pepys*, Vol. 9, 293. See also *ODNB*.

[349] Jessamine, an archaic term for jasmine. Perhaps gloves patterned with jasmine flowers. A fairing is a 'present, souvenir … from a fair', *OED*.

[350] Here Lloyd is probably referring to St Botolph-without-Aldgate, in Aldgate High St. The building attended by Lloyd was built in the early 16th century and had escaped damage during the Great Fire. The present building dates to the 18th century, *TBE, London 1*, 207–208.

dranke came home after 2 my Landlord and wife being gon I went to Mr Meaddows stayd till after 5 went to Jo: Blumfields got the key changed my cloathes performed my devotion went to Mr Ardreys suped there and lay there performed my devotion went to bed after 9.

Tuesday, 29 August: Rose at 6 after I was dressed performed my devotion stayd at Mr Ardreys till after 7 came to Jo: Blumfield got the key and fetcht som things I wanted went to school at 8 stayd till after 11 went to my chamber and performed my devotion went to Mr Ardreys to diner came to school at 1 stayd till after 6 went to Mr Ardreys and lay there supt after 8 went to bed.

Wednesday, 30 August: Rose at 6 dressed myselfe went to my owne chamber performed my devotion went to Mr Goldsberry playd till 8 went to school stayd till after 11 dined at Mr Meaddows went to my chamber performed my devotion went to school stayd till after 6 went to Mr Ardryes to lay there went to super at 9 sate up till 10 performed my devotion and went to bed.

[fo. 38v]
Thursday, 31 August: Rose at 6 after I was dressed and performed my devotion went to my owne chamber my Landlord being come tooke my violin went to Mr Goldsberry playd till 8 went to school stayd till after 11 came home went to diner performed my devotion playd a little went to school stayd till after 5 came to my chamber playd till after 6 eate som super went to Mr Shurleys stayd till 8 came home performed my devotion went to prayers and to bed.

Friday, 1 September: Rose at 6 after I was dressed and performed my devotion went to Mr Goldsberry playd till almost 8 went home went to prayers eat som breakfast went to school stayd till after 11 ~~went~~ came home went to diner performed my devotion went to school stayd till after 6 went to my chamber playd a little went to Mr Ardreys stayd till after 9 came home my Landlady read went to prayers performed my devotion and went to bed.

Saturday, 2 September: Rose at 6 after I was dressed and performed my devotion went to prayer and made my confession out of Dr Taylors Golden Grove went to school stayd till after 11 went to diner performed my devotion trimed myselfe went to Mr Ardreys and looked upon a place for a school for him and I in the back of St Nicholas church[351] stayd at his house till 7 came home got my things redy for Sonday performed my devotion eat som super my Landlady and went to prayers and bed.

Sunday, 3 September: Rose at 7 after I was dressed and performed my devotion went to prayer eat som breakfast read till church went to Trinity herd Mr Smith on 1 Corinthians 10:11:12 came home mad a shorte prayers went to diner performed my devotion read a little went to Mr Ardryes went to St James heard the elextion sermon by Mr Shelton on the 3 Proverbs 6:7 stayed at Mr Ardryes till after 5 came home performed my devotion read went downe and eat som super examined John in the Chatisme[352] gave him som Instruction my Landlord read sang a Psalm my Landlady read sang another Psalm went to prayers and I to bed.

Monday, 4 September: Rose at 5 after I was dressed and performed my devotion went to prayers went to Mr Ardryes at 7 stayd till 8 then walked with Mrs Ardrey to the farther end of Greenstead where Mr Ardrey brought a horse we rid to Frayton[353] to Mr Baythorns the ministers[354] downe there after diner walked to Mrs Berrits stayd till almost 5 eate creame and peares drank mead and Alle went back to Mr Baythorn's stayd a little came away came to Colchester about 7 where I heard the Duke of Albermale[355] was recorder and Mr Greene Mayor[356] came home received a letter from Mrs Gray such as I never had in which she termes me willing to leave my past[357] answered it in part, went

---

[351] The church of St Nicholas formerly stood in a prominent position in the High St. It was demolished in 1955.

[352] Catechism.

[353] Frating, a village eight miles east of Colchester.

[354] Thomas Baythorn, rector of Frating from 1672 until his death in 1709: *Cantabrigienses*, Vol. 1, pt. 1, 114; *CCEd* Person ID: 122533.

[355] Christopher Monck, 2nd duke of Albemarle (1653–1688), son of George Monck, 1st duke of Albemarle (1608–1670).

[356] Thomas Greene was mayor of Colchester for 1676 and 1682. Greene was a member of the pro-dissenter faction in Colchester politics, and his mayoral election alongside Albemarle as recorder marked an attempt to oust the anti-dissenter MP and erstwhile recorder Sir John Shaw (see n. 513, **10 July 1677**) and shift the balance of power in the town. Albemarle did not, in fact, successfully become recorder until the following year, as Shaw contested the election and sued the town corporation. By 1678, the dispute was resolved and Shaw became deputy recorder to Albemarle. See *VCHE*, 116; *Hist. Parl. 1660–1690*, Vol. 3, 428–429.

[357] The meaning of this message is enigmatic, but Mrs Gray may have been reproaching Lloyd for leaving her unwed in London in order to pursue his venture as a schoolmaster in Colchester.

downe my Landlord read went to prayers and I to my chamber performed my devotion and went to bed.

Tuesday, 5 September: Rose at 6 after I was dressed and performed my devotion went to prayers made an end of my letter to Mrs Gray went to school stayd till after 12 and made an end of writing to Mrs Gray went to diner performed my devotion went to school stayd till after 6 came to my chamber stayd a little went to Mr Ardreys stayd till after 9 came home my Landlady read went to prayers I to my chamber performed my devotion and went to bed.

Wednesday, 6 September: Rose at 6 after I was dressed and performed my devotion went to prayers and eat som breakfast went to school stayd till after 11 came home performed my devotion went to dine[r] went to Mr Goldsberry and there was company I came to my chamber writt 2 Letters for him went to school stayd till after 6 went with Mr Ardrey to his house stayd till 8 came home went to my chamber performed my devotion playd a little eat som

[fo. 39r]
super my Landlady read went to prayers and I to bed.

Thursday, 7 September: Rose before 6 after I was dressed and performed my devotion went to prayers and to Mr Goldsberys playd till 8 went to school at 9 came home to breakfast went againe stayd till after 11 came home playd a little went to diner performed my devotion went to school stayd till after 5 Mr Shurly came to my chamber playd a little sent for a gotch of beere, I eat som super went to Mr Ardryes stayd till 9 came home my Landlady read went to prayers I to my chamber performed my devotion went to bed.

Friday, 8 September: Rose at 6 after I was dressed and performed my devotion went to prayers went to Mr Goldsberry playd a little went to school stayd till after 11 came home playd a little went to diner performed my devotion playd a little went to school stayd till 6 received a letter from Mrs Gray answered it came home playd went to sup[er] performed my devotion my Landlady read went to prayers and I to bed.

Saturday, 9 September: Rose at 6 after I was dressed and performed my devotion went to prayers and was in my chamber a little mending a payre of stockings eat som breakfast went to Thomas

Roses to get my hat pinned[358] went to school stayd till after 11 came home went to diner writt a letter to Mrs Gray performed my devotion trimed myselfe at 3 went to Mr Ardreys stayd till 9 came home my Landlady read went to prayers I to my chamber performed my devotion and went to bed.

Sunday, 10 September: Rose a little before 8 after I was dressed ~~performed~~ went to prayers performed my devotion eat A toast went to Trinity church herd Mr Hawksbee on the 3 John 16 came home mad a short prayer went to diner performed my devotion went to Mr Ardreys stayd a little went to Greenstead heard Mr Shaw[359] on the [*deleted*] 16 Luke 8 came to Mr Ardreys stayd till after 7 came home performed my devotion eat som super sate a little my Landlady read went to prayers and to bed.

Monday, 11 September: Rose at 6 after I was dressed and performed my devotion went to prayers mended a payre of stockings eat som breakfast went to school stayd till after 10 came to my chamber where was Mr Ardrey and his wife to see the Duke of Albermarele com into towne I gave them a bottle of Maligoe and halfe a peck of Oysters went at 12 to Mr Aingers stayd till 1 went to Mr Ardreys with Mrs Ardrey stayd till after 4 performed my devotion in his chamber dined there came to my chamber and went to Mrs Aylets funerall had a payre of gloves sent herd Mr Smith preach on the 7 Ecclesiastes 4 came home stayd a little went to Mr Ardreys stayd till after 9 came home my Landlady read went to prayers I to my chamber performed my devotion and to bed.

Tuesday, 12 September: Rose after 6 after I was dressed and performed my devotion went to prayers and to school stayd till after 11 came home ~~per~~ went to diner performed my devotion sate by the fier till after 1 not being well went to school stayd till after 3 came home very Ill went to bed and was very ill till after 8 vomited and was somthing better performed my devotion in bed. Slept ~~till~~ not till 12 and not very well.

---

[358] Lloyd probably wore a wide-brimmed 'cavalier' or 'slouch' hat, the brim of which he here had 'pinned' to the side for aesthetic purposes.

[359] Thomas Shaw, MA 1675, Jesus College, Cambridge; rector of Greenstead from 1676, and Great Holland from 1678, holding both until his death in 1692. His father was the MP for Colchester, Sir John Shaw (see n. 513, **10 July 1677**): *Cantabrigienses*, Vol. 1, pt. 4, 54. *CCEd* Person ID: 166295.

Wednesday, 13 September:[360] Rose at 7 after I was up performed my devotion fearing Mr Ardrey should come before I had don he came before I was dressed stayd till after 8 and eate som tost then went to school stayd til after 11 came home performed my devotion went to diner and playd a little after I went to school stayd till 6 went to Mr Ardreys stayd till 10 came home my Landlady read went to prayers performed my devotion and went to bed.

Thursday, 14 September: Rose after 6 after I was dressed and performed my devotion went to prayers and mended a payre of stockings eat som breakfast went to school stayd till after 11 came home went to Mr Goldsberry and he was not at home playd a little performed my devotion went to diner sate a little went to school stayd till after 5 came home went to my chamber and playd a little went after 7 to Mr Ardreys stayd till 9 my Landlady read went to prayers and to bed.

[fo. 39v]
Friday, 15 September: Rose at 6 after I was dressed and performed my devotion went to Mr Goldsberry stayd till 8 came home went to prayers eat a little breakfast went to school stayd till after 11 came home went to diner playd a little performed my devotion went to school stayd till after 6 came home stayd till almost 7 went to Mr Sherleys playd a little and Isack and I tryed to dance French dances a little stayd till 9 came home eatt a little bred and cheese performed my devotion my Landlady read went to prayers and I to my chamber and read a letter Mrs Gray sent me.

Saturday, 16 September: Rose at 6 after I was dressed and performed my devotion went to prayers and writt the copy of a letter to Mrs Gray eat som breakfast went to school stayd till after 11 came home performed my devotion went to diner went with Mr Ardrey to Mr Farmans[361] and saw the rooms and tooke them for a school stayd there till 2 went to Mr Ardreys stayd till 9 came home went to Mr Meadows stayd ½ houer my Landlady read went to prayers I to my chamber performed my devotion and went to bed.

---

[360] Lloyd accidentally writes Tuesday rather than Wednesday for this entry.

[361] Lloyd writes this name inconsistently; occasionally the first letter is clearly written 'ff' or 'F'; elsewhere it is identical to 'H'. The name could also be read as 'Furman'. No wills with either name can be found from this period in Colchester. A Joseph Firman was assessed at one hearth in 1670; *EHT*, 287.

Sunday, 17 September: Rose at 7 after I was dressed and performed my devotion went to prayers and read eat som tost went to Trinity heard Mr Smith on the 4 Ephesians 1 came home went to my chamber made a short prayer went to diner performed my devotion and read went to St Giles heard Mr Smith on the same text came home went to my chamber read till neere 5 walked to Lexton warren till 6 came in <performed my devotion> eat a tost my Landlady read we sang a Psalm went to prayers and I to bed.

Monday, 18 September: Rose after 6 after I was dressed and performed my devotion went to prayers eate som breakfast went to school stayd till afte[r] 11 came home performed my devotion went to diner playd till 1 went to school stayd till 6 came home performed my devotion went to Mr Ardreys stayd till after 11 he came in drunck and mad threat to kill and murder his wife and maid I had a great deale of doe to keepe him from hurting her and at last after 12 he lay on the bed and fell asleepe and at 2 I went to bed but she sat up with her maid all night.

Tuesday, 19 September: Rose at 6 dressed myselfe and performed my devotion dranke a glace[362] of maligoe and sirrup of cloves came to my Lodging at 7 writt to Mr Ardrey to lett him know his condition he was in went to school stayd till after 11 came home performed my devotion went to diner went to Mr Goldsberry but he was not within came to my chamber and playd a little went to school stayd till 6 came home went to my chamber performed my devotion playd a little went to Mr Ardreys stayd till 9 my Landlady read went to prayers and I to bed.

Wednesday, 20 September: Rose after 6 after I was dressed and performed my devotion went to prayers eat som tost went to the new school and saw the men begin there[363] worke came to school stayd till after 11 came home performed my devotion Goldsberry's[364] boy came and we playd a little went to diner and to school stayd till after 6 came to my chamber performed my devotion playd went to Mr Ardreys stayd till 9 came home my Landlady read went to prayers and to bed.

---

[362] Glass.
[363] Their.
[364] Originally 'Golds:'.

[fo. 40r]
Thursday, 21 September: Rose after 6 after I was dressed and performed my devotion went to prayers eat som breakfast went to my school and got som things to alter my peece for to put in (English to be taught) was about it till after 10 went to see the carpenters stayd a little went to Peeters to prayers went to Mr Grays and stayd diner and till almost 1 came to my chamber performed my devotion and made an end of the writting mended a payre of stockings playd a little went to Mr Ardreys and stayd till 9 came home eate som super my Landlady read went to prayers and to my chamber performed my devotion and to bed.

Friday, 22 September: Rose before 7 after I was dressed and performed my devotion went to prayers eat som breakfast went to school stayd till 11 came home playd went to diner performed my devotion went to my new school and the men not there came back mended a payre of stockings went to school stayd till 5 went to the Kings Head drank a flagon with Mr Bontall[365] went to Mr Ardreys and with him to Mrs Wheler at Mr Renholds house came back at 8 went to the Queens Head drank a jug with Mr Smith went to Mr Edlins stayd a little came home eat som supper performed my devotion my Landlady read went to bed.

Saturday, 23 September: Rose at 5 after I was dressed and performed my devotion went to the carpenters to my school and gott them som deale bords[366] and stayd till 8 came to my Lodgings and went to prayers eat som breakfast went to school stayd till 11 went to Mr Ardrey made a bond eat som diner came home performed my devotion trimed myselfe mended a payre of stockings went to the carpenters stayd till after 5 went to Mr Ardreys stayd till 8 came in eate som super performed my devotion sat up till 10 my Landlady read went to prayers and to bed.

Sunday, 24 September: Rose at 7 after I was dressed and performed my devotion went to prayers and went downe and eate som tost sate a little and read went to Mr Brasiers to see John being sent for he haveing the smallpox stayd till after 10 went to Trin[ity] heard Mr Smith on the 1 Corinthians[367] 1:4 came home

---

[365] Unfortunately, 'Mr Bontall', master of Lloyd's dancing school, has not been identified outside the diary.

[366] A deal is 'a slice sawn from a log of timber [...] and usually understood to be more than seven inches wide, and not more than three thick', *OED*.

[367] Very unclear.

mad a short prayer went to di[nner] sate a little performed my devotion read went to church to St Giles heard the same man and sermon came home read and performed my devotion was sent for to Mr Ardreys the child not being well stayd there and supt came home my Landlady read sang a Psalm ~~my~~ went to prayers and I to my chamber and to bed.

Monday, 25 September: Rose at 6 after I was dressed and performed my devotion went out to the Coffe house for my peece went to my new school to see the Carpenters stayd till 8 called to see John Brasier stayd a little he was Cherefull came home supt a little warmed milk went to school and stayd till after 11 came home and playd went to diner did not goe to prayers forgetting it at noone performed my devotion went to Sherecrofts to aske the prise of my stand and to talke about the boy Thompson called at Goldsberys but he was not at home went to my new school to see the worke and beat downe the pins that was to high made him set them lower went to school stayd till 6 went to the school agane to see the worke and to Mr Ardreys stayd till 8 came home and ea[t] some tost and read in Parismus[368] till 10 my Landlady read went to prayers I to my chamber performed my devotion and to bed.

Tuesday, 26 September: Rose at 6 after I was dressed and performed my devotion was in my chamber went to prayers eat a tost went to school stayd till after 11 came home performed my devotion went to diner went to Mr Grays to see som patterns went to my chamber to choose one went to school stayd till after 5 went to Mr Grays to tell him which camlet I would have went to Mr Ardreys stayd till after 7 went to Mr Brasier stayd till 11 Mr Legg being there came home performed my devotion went to bed.

Wednesday, 27 September: Rose after 6 after I was dressed and performed my devotion went to pray eat som breakfast went to school stayd till after 11 came home performed my devotion went to diner and to Mr Goldsberry playd till 1 went to school stayd till 6 came to my chamber performed my devotion playd a little went to Mr Ardreys stayd till after 10 came home my Landlady read went to prayers and to bed.

---

[368] Emanuel Ford, *Parismus, the Renowned Prince of Bohemia* (London, 1598–1599). This very popular Elizabethan romance was reprinted several times throughout the 17th century.

[fo. 40v]
Thursday, 28 September: Rose after 6 after I was dressed and performed my devotion went to prayers playd a little eate a tost went to school stayd till after 11 came home playd a little performed my devotion went to diner went to Mr Brasiers to see John he was very sored[369] stayd till after 1 went to school stayd till after 5 went to Thomas Wards drank a flagon and he payd me for his sons schooling[370] went to Mr Ardreys he lent me 10^{li} stayd till 8 came home eat som supper my Landlady read went to prayers performed my devotion and to bed.

Friday, 29 September: Rose after 5 after I was dressed and performed my devotion got some of my things put up to remove to Mr Ardreys, before 7 went to my school to remove my things was there till after 8 payd Mr Meaddows for ½ a yeare gave him warning before Mr Ardrey at which he was very huffing[371] and told me he would not take it for a warning[372] went to my Landlords and my Landlady was more angry because I told her not before got my things sent away told her I would come the next day and pay her husband went to St Peeters to prayers went to Mr Ardreys performed my devotion was a little seting my things in order went to diner sate and wound a little went to the school and set the tables where I would have them stand went to here the sermon preached before the mayor at Allhallows [sic] by Mr Hickringole on the 3 Proverbs 31 came home stayd a little went againe to the school stayd a little expecting the carpenter but he came not stayd talking a little with Mr Farman, came home sate below Mrs M: Farman[373] being there went to super sate a little and playd with the child, went to my chamber performed my devotion and to bed.

Saturday, 30 September: Rose after 5 after I was dressed and performed my devotion was within in my chamber till 8 went to Mr Colemans he payd me for his child's schooling went to the Whit Lyon to Mr Smith got him to goe to Mr Strattons, to be wittness I payd him, he threatnd to Sue me for his horse,[374] I went to my

---

[369] An unconventional usage, but presumably here Lloyd means afflicted with smallpox lesions, or 'sores'.

[370] Originally 'sch:'.

[371] Lloyd's hand is untidy here, but similar 17th-century usages, meaning blustering, angry, puffed up, and so on can be found in the *OED*.

[372] In other words, he would not accept Lloyd's notice payment for quitting the premises.

[373] Originally 'F:'.

[374] Stratton's precise reason for suing Lloyd over a horse cannot be confidently inferred from the diary. It seems that Stratton sought redress after being incensed by Lloyd's sudden

school stayd till after 10 went to the White Horse with Mr Ardrey and Mr Smith our neighbour[375] stayd a little went home to diner performed my devotion went to the school stayd there till neere 6 and saw it finished came home performed my devotion trimed myselfe went to super sate a little while Ashley read Mr Ardrey went to prayers and I to bed.

Sunday, 1 October: Rose at 7 after I was dressed and performed my devotion was in my chamber a little not being well went downe and sate by the fier till after 9 went with Mr Ardrey to the heath herd Mr Hickringole on the 1 Corinthians 10:6 being a ℞ came home went to my chamber made a short prayer went to diner performed my devotion went to St James herd Mr Shelton on the 1 Romans 18 came home was very ill sate by the fier till after 7 eate a little panado[376] sate up till 9 Mr Ardrey went to prayers performed my devotion and to bed.

Monday, 2 October: Rose at 6 after I was dressed and performed my devotion eat som breakfast went to my new school with Mr Ardrey stayd till after 11 went to Mr Brasiers to see John who was then at the hight with the smallpox went to Mr Goldsberys but he was not at home came home performed my devotion went to diner and to school stayd till after 5 came home sate by the fier and playd a little went to super sat and talked a little went to prayers I to my chamber performed my devotion and to bed.

Tuesday, 3 October: Rose at 6 after I was dressed and performed my devotion went to Mr Goldsberry stayd a little and gave him his bunch of strings I sent for called at Mr Brasiers and saw John went to school stayd till after 11 went to Mr Brasiers for a bar of Iron went home to diner performed my devotion went to school stayd till almost 6 went to Mr Smith with Mr Ardrey stayd there with Alderman Mot and Mr Turman till 8 came home went to super performed my devotion sate up till 10 went to prayers and to bed.

---

move to Ardrey's, and the horse was a pretext. As we can see below, it appears either that Lloyd and Ardrey had lost or sold Stratton's horse, or that a deal had fallen through as a result of the falling out. Lloyd and Ardrey went to search for the horse on **12 October 1676**. Lloyd did not 'confess' what had happened in the diary, but possibly the events of 4 September 1676 were related. Cf. entries for **10 April** and **12 August 1676**.

[375] Unclear if this is the William Smith referred to above, or a new acquaintance.
[376] See n. 284, **1 May 1676**.

[fo. 41r]

Wednesday, 4 October: Rose at 6 after I was dressed and performed my devotion was within till 8 eat som tost went to school stayd till after 11 went to Mr Goldsberry he was not within came home performed my devotion went to diner mended my peece of writting mended a box went to school stayd till 6 stayd at Mr Smiths till 7 then was with the brick layer till after 8 came home eat som super went to prayers and to my chamber performed my devotion and went to bed.

Thursday, 5 October: Rose at 6 after I was dressed and performed my devotion eat som breakfast went to Mr Goldsberry playd a little came ~~home~~ to school stayd till after 11 came home to diner playd a little after diner performed my devotion went to school stayd till after 5 went to Mr Brasiers stayd till after 6 went to Mr Halls to see paper[377] and to Mr Whelys went to the school to see the men doe the chimny came home at 9 eat went to prayers to my chamber performed my devotion and to bed.

Friday, 6 October: Rose at 6 after I was dressed and performed my devotion went to Mr Goldsberry he was not within went to school stayd till after 11 went to the Red Lyon with Mr Ardrey and Mr Farman to see Roses peece went home to diner performed my devotion went to school stayd till after 5 went to the Queens Head stayd till 7 went home sate winding till 9 eate som super went to prayers went to my chamber performed my devotion and went to bed.

Saturday, 7 October: Rose at 6 after I was dressed and performed my devotion was in the house expecting Dr Thompson[378] to come and give me a vomit[379] which I tooke at 9 it worked 6 times and gave me 3 stooles after 12 performed my devotion was below till 6 performed my devotion at 7 eat a mess of panadoe sat up till 9 went to pray and to bed.

Sunday, 8 October: Rose at 7 after I was dressed and performed my devotion and eate som breakfast we[nt] to Allsaints herd Mr Hickeringill on the 1 Peter 3:8 came home and made a short

---

[377] This may have been William Hall, a bookseller of St Runwald's parish, whose will was proved on 28 July 1697, ERO D/ACW 22/131. He was assessed in the same parish at two hearths in 1670, *EHT*, 302.

[378] Probably the Colchester physician Richard Thompson, of Holy Trinity parish, whose will was proved on 22 April 1691, ERO, D/ABW 73/253.

[379] An emetic.

prayer went to diner performed my devotion read a little went to St James heard Mr Shelton ~~on the 1 Romans~~ on the 1 Romans 8 came home sate a little by the fier performed my devotion read 2 sermons went to super sate till 9 went to prayers and I to bed.

Monday, 9 October: Rose at 7 after I was up cleansed the Jack and set it up dressed mysefe and performed my devotion and was within till 10 went into towne and dranke my mornings draught with Dr Tompson and Mr Farman at the Queens Head went to St Peeters and heard the fayre sermon Mr Shelton preached on the 3 Philippians 19 came home performed my devotion playd a little at 1 went to diner was within learning Mrs Ardrey and Peg and Sam Renholds[380] to write till 5 went to Mrs Vickers stayd till 7 came home sate up to 10 went to prayers performed my devotion and went to bed.

Tuesday, 10 October: Rose at 6 after I was dressed and performed my devotion was within helping Mrs Ardrey make sugar cakes was within till diner after diner playd a little performed my devotion was writting the afternoone a little and a little in the morning for my great peece at 6 performed my devotion after 6 went into the towne to the carriers and sent som old things to my sister caled at Mr Brasiers to see John stayd till 9 came home sate a little went to prayers and to bed.

Wednesday, 11 October: Rose at 6 after I was dressed and performed my devotion went to Mr Goldsberry playd a little eat my breakfast with 2 of debnham musick:[381] sent for a flagon of alle stayd till after 9 called at Dr Thompsons came home was within learning [S]am Renholds at 12 went to diner Mr Chapell and his wife being there performed my devotion was within till after 4 went with Mr Chapell his wife Mr Ardrey his wife to see the Ellephant came home performed my devotion went with Mr Ardrey to Captaine Renholds stayd and supt there came home at 10 went to prayers and I to bed.

---

[380] This seems very likely to have been the Samuel Reynolds, eldest son of Captain Samuel Reynolds, later MP for Colchester (see n. 280, **22 April 1676**). He was born in July 1666, and was admitted to Colchester Grammar in 1677, and went on, like his father, to pursue the law, entering Gray's Inn in 1683, Round, *Colchester School*, 72.

[381] Lloyd's meaning is ambiguous but his hand is clear; he may be referring to musicians from Debenham, a village in Suffolk about thirty miles from Colchester.

Thursday, 12 October: Rose at 5 performed my devotion went with Mr Ardrey to Layre[382] to enqire about Strattons horse could here nothing there called at Mr Parkers and we went to a house and dranke ¾ of a pinte of burnt brandy went to Aberton[383] greene to enquire found a farrier who promised to enquire drank 2 flagons of beere came home by 12 went to diner performed my devotion was within all day at 5 performed my devotion about 10 went to bed.

Friday, 13 October: Rose after 6 tooke a purge worked 6 times at 2 eat som diner performed my devotion trimed one glove aft at 6 performed my devotion went to bed about 10 Mrs Baythorne lay in my chamber and I below.

[fo. 41v]
Saturday, 14 October: Rose after 6 after I was dressed performed my devotion was all the morning till 10 making a hen coope went to diner sate a little performed my devotion was within at 4 trimed myselfe was below Mr Far[?man] and Mrs Bety being there at 8 eate som super performed my devotion[384] went to prayers and to bed.

Sunday, 15 October: Rose after 7 after I was dressed and performed my devotion eat som breakfast went to Trinity herd Mr Smith on the 6 Ephesians 10:11:12 came home went to my chamber made a short prayer sate below a little went to diner performed my devotion went to St James herd Mr Shelton on the 12 Luke 4 came home went to my chamber read a sermon performed my devotion went downe and sate below at 8 eate som super went to prayers and to bed about 10.

Monday, 16 October: Rose at 5 after I was dressed and performed my devotion was within eat som breakfast went to school stayd till after 11 went to Alderman Motts bought a payre of bellows went home playd traced my glove I lost on Satterday went to diner set Samuel Renholds som Copys performed my devotion went to school stayd till almost 6 went to Mr Lamberts called for a pint of wine stayd till after 7 came home playd a little went to super went to my chamber and writt out the prayer for the evening went downe I read a

---

[382] Layer de la Haye, a village almost five miles south-west of Colchester.
[383] Lloyd may mean Abberton, a village three miles east of Layer de la Haye.
[384] Here Lloyd wrote merely 'per:'.

chapter went to prayers went to my chamber performed my devotion and went to bed.

Tuesday, 17 October: Rose at 6 after I was dressed and performed my devotion sate by the fier and eat som breakfast went to school stayd till after 11 came home playd a little went to diner sate a little performed my devotion went to school stayd till after 6 went to speake with the carrier called at Mr Halls came home sate and wound till 9 performed my devotion went to super sate up till 11 read went to prayers and I to bed.

Wednesday, 18 October: Rose at 6 after I had performed my devotion sate by the fier after 8 put on my boots to goe to Mr Chapells was below till after I dressed myselfe after 10 went away carried Mrs Ardrey came thether at 12 dined there stayd till 4 came away came home about 6 I pulled of my boots performed my devotion eat som super sate up till 9 I read went to prayers and to bed.

Thursday, 19 October: Rose after 6 after I was dressed and performed my devotion eate som breakfast went to school stayd till after 11 came home was below making copy books went to diner performed my devotion went to school stayd till after 5 came home sate below Mrs M: Far[?man] being there at 10 went home with her eat som super went to prayers and to my chamber performed my devotion and went to bed.

Friday, 20 October: Rose at 6 after I was dressed and performed my devotion was in my chamber powdring my perywigg went downe eate some breakfast after 8 went to school came home after 11 made cleane my watch went to diner performed my devotion went to school stayd till after 6 came home was below till 8 performed my devotion went to super sat up till after 9 went to prayers Mr Ardrey [sic] I went to my chamber and to bed.

Saturday, 21 October: Rose after 6 after I was dressed and performed my devotion sate a little below eat a little bred and butter went to school stayd till after 12 Simpson being there came home to diner performed my devotion went to school stayd till after 3 came home was mending chaires till 5 was below till 7 went to super sate up till after 9 Mr Ardrey went to prayers I to my chamber performed my devotion and to bed.

[fo. 42r]

Sunday, 22 October: Rose at 7 after I was up performed my devotion went downe and sate by the fier till 9 <and read> then came Mr Person[385] and let me blud sate by the fier <and read a sermon> till after 11 dressed myselfe eat som broth after 12 went to diner read a sermon performed my devotion went to St James herd Mr Shelton on the 6 Genesis 8 came home read 2 sermon performed my devotion went downe sate by the fier till after 8 Ashly read Mr Ardrey went to prayers and I to bed.

Monday, 23 October: Rose at 6 after I was dressed and performed my devotion sate by the fier a little eat a little broth went to see James Lamb he was asleepe went to school stayd till 1+1 11 went to Robert Goldsberry stayd not came home playd a little went to diner performed my devotion went to school stayd till after 6, came home wound till after 7 went to super sate a little performed my devotion went downe and we went to prayers and I to my chamber and to bed.

Tuesday, 24 October: Rose at 7 after I was dressed and performed my devotion eat som bred and cheese went to school stayd till after 11 came home playd a little went to diner performed my devotion went to school stayd till after 6 came home was winding till 8 went to super sate a little performed my devotion went to prayers and to bed.

Wednesday, 25 October: Rose at 7 after I was dressed and performed my devotion eat som tost went to school stayd till after 11 came home was a little riping the cloake I had of Mr Ardrey performed my devotion went to diner and to school stayd till after 6 went to Mr Grays and had my measure taken came home and was winding till after 8 went to super received a letter from Mrs Gray which told we had[386] miscarried went to super wound till after 10 went to prayers I to my chamber performed my devotion and went to bed.

Thursday, 26 October: Rose after 6 after I was dressed and performed my devotion went to school stayd till after 11 came home playd a little went to my chamber and was a little about riping the cloake performed my devotion went to diner and to school stayd till after 5 came home and was within playd a little and was papering

---

[385] Or perhaps 'Parson'?
[386] The words 'we had' are ambiguous and uncertain here.

up my periwigg went to super and made an end of my perrywigg went to prayers and I to my chamber performed my devotion and went to bed.

Friday, 27 October: Rose after 6 after I was dressed and performed my devotion eate som breakfast went to school stayd till after 11 came home performed my devotion went to diner and to school stayd till after 6 came home went to my chamber performed my devotion went to Mrs Vickers to fetch home Mrs Ardrey came home at 8 sate up till after 9 eat som super and went to bed.

Saturday, 28 October: Rose after 9 not being well after I was dressed and performed my devotion eate som breakfast went to St Petters to prayers came home a little before 12 sate by the fier a little Mr Bontall came to me and was with him in the Hall neere an houer sate by the fier a little went to diner, performed my devotion was within all the afternoone and was takeing my plate buttons of my cloth coate and boiled them about 7 performed my devotion after 8 eate som super sate up till 10 went to prayers and I to my chamber and to bed.

Sunday, 29 October: Rose at 8 after I was dressed and performed my devotion eat som breakfast went to St James herd Mr Shelton on the 6 of Genesis 8 came home went to my chamber made a short prayer went to diner sate a little went to my chamber performed my devotion went to church to St James heard the same man and text came home sate by the f[ier] a little performed my devotion read 2 sermons went to super sate till 10 went to prayers and to bed.

[fo. 42v]
Monday, 30 October: Rose before 7 after I was dressed and performed my devotion eat som breakfast went to school stayd till after 11 went to Mr Goldsberry playd a little came home to diner performed my devotion went to school stayd till after 6 went to Mr Brasiers payd her [*sic*] for Coales stayd till after 8 came home playd till 9 went to super sate up till after 10 went to prayers and to ~~bed~~ my chamber performed my devotion and to bed.

Tuesday, 31 October: Rose before 7 after I was dressed and performed my devotion eat som breakfast went to school stayd till ~~after~~ 11 went to Mr Goldsberrys playd a little came home performed my devotion went to diner sate a little went to school stayd till after 6 came home, <performed my devotion> playd a little sate by the fier till after 8 went to super sate till after 9 went to prayers and to bed.

Wednesday, 1 November: Rose at 5 after I was dressed and performed my devotion eat some breakfast stayd below till almost 7 then Mrs Bety and Ashly and I went out for Frayton stayd at Mr Aylets a little there Mr Ardrey and his wife ~~then~~ Came then Mrs Bety and I got on horsback I rid but a little way and the boy got up I walkd with Mrs Ardrey and him almost to Frayton then I and Mrs Ardrey got up and rid to Mr Baythons we eat som tost and drank and stayd an houer then Mr Baython and I walked to the wood to see if I could kill a rabbet but it rayned soe we were forst to come back and I made cleane the Jack we went to diner and after diner we stayd till neere 4 I brought Mrs Bety behind me upon Mr Baythons horse to the Black Boy at Greensted then I rid before Mrs Ardrey home came home about 6 sate by the fier a little not being very well performed my devotion eate a little tost went to pray and to bed.

Thursday, 2 November: Rose before 7 after I was dressed and performed my devotion went downe eat a little bred and butter went to school stayd till after 11 came home sate by the fier went to diner performed my devotion sate a little went to school stayd till after 5 then came home sate and wound till almost 8 then performed my devotion went downe to super sate up till after 9 went to prayers and to bed.

Friday, 3 November: Rose before 7 after I was dressed and performed my devotion eat a little breakfast went to school stayd till after 11 went to Mr Goldsberys playd a little dined there came home performed my devotion went school stayd till after 6 came home performed my devotion playd a little went to super playd a little read in Mr Featlys[387] Devotions, went to prayers I to my chamber and read a little and to bed.

Saturday, 4 November: Rose after 6 after I was dressed and performed my devotion read in Mr Featlys Devotions till after 8 went to school stayd till after 11 came home warmed myselfe went to my chamber and performed my devotion walked into the garden and walked and clipt myselfe came in after 1 went to my chamber and was there till almost 3 making my confession out of Dr Taylors Golden Grove and renewing my covenant went downe sate below

---

[387] Featley, Daniel, *Ancilla pietatis, or, The Handmaid to Private Devotion* (London, 1626).

warmed myselfe read a sermon sate till 5 dranke a little brandy and performed my devotion went downe and sate a little eate som super sate till 9 went to prayers and to bed.

Sunday, 5 November: Rose before 8 after I was dressed and performed my devotion went downe and eate some brekfast went to St Nicholas heard Mr Shelton on the 45 Genesis 5 came home made a short prayer went to diner read a little performed my devotion went to St James herd Mr Shelton on the 6 Genesis 8 came home sate a little performed my devotion read 2 sermons went to super sate up till 9 went to prayers and to bed.

[fo. 43r]
Monday, 6 November: Rose before 7 after I was dressed and performed my devotion eat som breakfast went to school stayd till after 11 came home stayd below till after diner playd till 1 went to my chamber read and before I had performed my devotion Mrs Bety came in I writt her a letter went downe to Mr Chapell stayd neere an houer performed my devotion sate below winding till 8 went to super read till after 10 went to prayers to my chamber performed my devotion and to bed.

Tuesday, 7 November: Rose before 7 after I was dressed and performed my devotion eat som breakfast went to school stayd til after 11 came home performed my devotion eat som diner went to school stayd till after 6 came home sat by the fier a little went to super sate by the fier and cutt out a payre of shamy sleeves of my stockings performed my devotion sate up a little went to prayers and went to my chamber and was a little getting som Lyning for my sleves after 10 went to bed.

Wednesday, 8 November: Rose at 7 after I was dressed and performed my devotion eat somthing went to school stayd till after 11 came home was below till after diner performed my devotion went to school stayd till after 5 went to Mr Aingers with Mr Ardrey and his wife and Mrs Bety stayd ¼ of houer went to Mr Wheelys payd for 3 slates called on Mr Sherly, went to Mr Grays and bought button[s] went to Mr Halls payd for things went to Mr Aingers stayd till after 9 came back performed my devotion eat som bred and cheese sate a little I went to prayers and to bed.

Thursday, 9 November: Rose at 7 after I was dressed and performed my devotion eat a little breakfast went to school stayd till after 11 came home was ill sate by the fier till after diner performed my devotion went to school stayd till 5 came home was ill sate by the fier till after 7 performed my devotion eat som milke went to prayers sat up till 11 went to bed.

Friday, 10 November: Rose at 7 after I was dressed and performed my devotion eat som breakfast went to school stayd till 11 went to Mr Goldsberry stayd till after 12 came home performed my devotion went to diner went to school stayd till after 6 and received a letter from Mrs Gray in which she declared her affection for me writ one back by the post to her [*deleted*] went to Mr Smiths with Mr Ardrey and his wife and Mrs Bety stayd till after 10 playd at cards and eat cakes and drinke a botle of wine and sider came home sate a little went to prayers I to my chamber performed my devotion and to bed.

Saturday, 11 November: Rose after 6 after I was dressed and performed my devotion was within till after 8 eat som brekfast went to school stayd till 11 came home and dressed myself to goe to Mr Chappells performed my devotion went to diner at 12 I tooke horse came thether at 2 stayd till 4 got a direction for the pay[n?]e in my head came home at 6 was below till super playd a little trimed myselfe sate up till after 9 went to prayers and I to my chamber performed my devotion and to bed.

Sunday, 12 November: Rose at 8 after I was dressed and performed my devotion sate by the fier till church time went to Trinity herd Mr Smith on the 23 of Jeremiah 5 came home made a short prayer went to diner sate a little performed my devotion went to St James herd Mr[388] on the 6 Genesis 8 came home sate by the fier a little read a sermon performed my devotion sate by the fier and playd with the child till after 8 then Mr Ardrey and his wife came in sate up till after 9 went to prayers and I to my chamber and to bed.

Monday, 13 November: Rose after 6 after I was dressed and performed my devotion was in my chamber powdring a perrywigg eat som breakfast went to school stayd till after 11 came home tyd up a perrywigg went downe to diner performed my devotion sate by the fier a little went to school stayd till 6 came home sate by the fier and playd till 8 Mrs M. Furly being there performed my devotion eat som super was a little making my shamy sleves sate up till after 10

---

[388] Cramped against the edge of the page, there is no name.

Mr Smith and his Brother clearke[389] being there went to prayers and to bed.

[fo. 43v]
Tuesday, 14 November: Rose at 7 after I was dressed and performed my devotion eat som breakfast went to school stayd till after 11 came home was by the fier a little mending a payre of shamy sleeves went to diner performed my devotion went to school stayd till after 6 went to Mr Grayes supt there stayd till after 9 came home sat a little went to prayers to my chamber performed my devotion and went to bed.

Wednesday, 15 November: Rose at 7 after I was dressed and performed my devotion went downe sate by the fier a little went to school not being very well stayd till after 11 came home sate by the fier and was a little about my sleeves went to diner performed my devotion went to school stayd till after 6 came home was about my sleves a little went to super after super Mr Smith came sate up till almost 11 went to prayers I to my chamber and performed my devotion and went to bed.

Thursday, 16 November: Rose at 7 after I was dressed and performed my devotion sate by the fier and warmed myselfe went to school stayd till after 11 went to Mr Grays to speak about my coate came home sate by the fier a little went to diner performed my devotion went to school stayd till after 5 came home sat by the fier and was about my sleeves till after 7 went to super and sate by the fier a little was a little about my sleeves performed my devotion sate up till after 10 went to prayers and to bed.

Friday, 17 November: Rose at 7 after I was dressed and performed my devotion eat som breakfast performed my devotion went to school stayd till after 11 went to Mr Goldsberry stayd till after 12 came home went to diner performed my devotion went to school stayd till after 6 went to Mr Smiths supt there stayd till after 10 Mr Ardrey and his wife and Mrs Bety being there came home performed my devotion in my schoole sate up till 12 and was a little about my shamy sleeves. Went to bed.

Saturday, 18 November: Rose at 7 after I was dressed and performed my devotion eat som breakfast went to school stayd till

---

[389] Probably not his brother, but rather a fellow clergyman.

after 12 and was putting up bords over my closset came home went to diner after diner made an end of my shamy sleves performed my devotion was above setting buttons on my Cloth coate from 2 till after 5 went to Mr Vickers stayd till 7 came home went to super made an end of setting on the buttons performed my devotion sate up till 11 went to bed.

Sunday, 19 November: Rose at 8 after I was dressed and performed my devotion sate by the fier went to Trinity herd Mr Smith on the 23 Jeremiah 5 came home made a short prayer went to diner sate a little by the fier performed my devotion sate a little by the fier went to St James herd Mr Shelton on the 6 Genesis 8 came home sate a little by the fier went to Mr Smiths with Mr Ardrey and his wife stayd till 6 came home went to super sate by the fier performed my devotion read a sermon sat up till after 9 went to prayers and to b[ed.]

Monday, 20 November: Rose at 7 after I was ~~dress~~ washt eat som tost dress[ed] myselfe and performed my devotion went to school stayd till after 11 went to Mr Grays he being not within came home tyd up my perrywigg went to diner performed my devotion playd a little went to school stayd till 4 was writting the secretary[390] for my peece the boys playd from 2 of the clock came home was about my coate setting downe the lyning sat up til 12 Mr Ardrey being abroad and fuddled[391] I performed my devotion at 9 I eat a little tost for my super went to bed after 12.

Tuesday, 21 November: Rose at 7 after I was dressed <and performed my devotion> eat som breakfast went to school stayd till after 11 went to Mr Grays and he tooke a true measure came home went to diner playd a little performed my devotion went to school stayd till after 6 and was a little writting for my peece came home playd a little performed my devotion sate up till after 9 went to prayers and to bed.

[fo. 44r]
Wednesday, 22 November: Rose at 7 after I was dressed and performed my devotion went to school stayd till after 11 ~~came~~ went to Mr Goldsberys playd a little came home went to my chamber

---

[390] Secretary hand; Lloyd's piece was probably intended to demonstrate his breadth of calligraphic skills.
[391] Drunk.

performed my devotion went to diner and to school stayd till after 7 and was writting for my peece went to Mr Smiths and supt there Mr Richardson being there and Mr Smith fetcht Mrs Ardrey and Mrs Bety stayd till 9 came home sate up till after 10 went to prayers and I to my chamber and performed my devotion and to bed.

Thursday, 23 November: Rose at 7 after I was dressed and performed my devotion eat som breakfast went to school stayd till after 12 and was writing about my peece came home went to diner performed my devotion went to school stayd till after 5 came home and was below mending a payre of drawers and stockings till 9 went to super performed my devotion went to prayers and I to my chamber and to bed.

Friday, 24 November: Rose at 7 after I was dressed and performed my devotion eat som breakfast went to school stayd till after 12 came home playd a little performed my devotion went to diner and to school stayd till after 6 came to Benjamin Bakers and cast up his bill stayd till after 7 came home sate by the fier playd till 8 went to super playd a little performed my devotion sate up till 10 went to prayers and to bed.

Saturday, 25 November: Rose at 7 after I was dressed and performed my devotion eat som brekfast went to school stayd till after 1 after I was writting for my peece came home performed my devotion went to diner went to my school stayd till 4 and was writting a little and cleaning my closet came home sate by the fier trimed myselfe performed my devotion mended my breeches eat som super sate a little while went to prayers and after 9 to bed.

Sunday, 26 November: Rose at 8 after I was dressed and performed my devotion sate by the fier and was troubled with the griping[392] drank hot beere and ginger went to St Peters herd Mr Ayers on the 6 Ma: 33[393] came home made a short prayer went to diner sate by the fier performed my devotion went to St James herd Mr Shelton on the 6 Genesis 9 came home sate by the fier a little performed the devotion sate by the fier talking with Mr Ardrey who came from London went to super went home with Mrs Vickers came home sate by the fier till after 9 went to prayers and to bed.

[392] Pain in the bowels, diarrhoea.
[393] Lloyd could be referring here to the gospels of Matthew or of Mark.

Monday, 27 November: Rose at 6 after I was dressed and performed my devotion sate by the fier and read Mrs Grays Leter Mr Ardrey brought from London eat som breakfast went to school stayd till after 12 came home went to diner playd a little performed the devotion after at 2 went with Mr Ardrey to the Kings Head to see a prise stayd till after 3 before it was began stayd till after 4 the sport was little worth came home stayd a little wound a bobin went to super performed the devotion went to prayers and at 10 to bed.

Tuesday, 28 November: Rose at 7 after I was dressed and performed the devotion eat som breakfast went to school stayd till after 12 was writing for my peece went to diner performed the devotion and to school stayd till after 6 came home playd a little went to cards playd till 11 with Mrs Mary Furly[394] and Mr Smith and Mrs Bety lost 6^d eat cake went with Mrs Mary Furley home went to prayers and to my chamber performed the devotion and to bed.

[fo. 44v]
Wednesday, 29 November: Rose at 7 after I was dressed and performed my devotion eat som breakfast went to school stayd till after 12 came home to diner performed my devotion went to school stayd till after 4 came home was at home a little went to Mr Smiths with Mr Ardrey and his wife and Mrs B supt there put up Malligoe each of us a gallon and halfe came home performed my devotion sat up till 10 went to prayers and to bed.

Thursday, 30 November: Rose at 7 after I was dressed and made a shorte prayer went to Richard Fields to see for a horse but could not get one came home performed my devotion eat som breakfast went to my school and was writting for my peece till after 10 went to St Peeters to prayers went to Robert Goldsberry playd a little dined there went to the Goate to see a watch stayd ¾ of an houer dranke part of 2 flagons went to my school performed my devotion was there till 4 writting came home sate a little and playd performed my devotion and was mending som cuffs till 9 went to super sate

---

[394] Definitive identification is difficult, but this seems likely to have been Mary (bap. 14 June 1658), daughter of Stephen Furly (bap. 3 December, 1630) and his wife Elizabeth, née Reynolds. Stephen was the brother of the better-known John and Benjamin (see n. 40, **26 August 1675**), and there is some suggestion he was not a Quaker. Mary's baptism took place in the parish of St Leonard, though Stephen does not appear in the Hearth Tax return of 1670 in Colchester, nor can any will be found, See ERO, D/P 245/1/1; Henry J. Cadbury, 'A Quaker before the Privy Council, 1663', *Bulletin of Friends Historical Association*, 49 (1960), 37–38.

talking till after 10 Mr Smith being with us went to prayers I sate up ½ an houer talking with Mrs Bety went to bed.

Friday, 1 December: Rose at 7 after I was dressed and performed my devotion eat a little breakfast went to school stayd till after 12 and was writing for my peece went to diner performed my devotion went to school stayd till after 4 came home was mending a payre of stockings playd a little went to my school and had my frets[395] made performed my devotion there went downe to Mr Smiths supt there after super we had a sak posset[396] pakt plums stayd till after 10 came home went to prayers and I to bed.

Saturday, 2 December: Rose at 7 after I was dressed and performed my devotion went to school stayd till after 11 came home brought a goose was sent by Goodwife Ryboe[397] was below reading Mrs Baython and Mr Ardrey and his wife and Mrs Bety being in my chamber John Clarke brought me a [*illegible*][398] gate I went to Mr Goldsberys to see about the Carrier came home walked in the garden went to my chamber performed my devotion and made my confession out of Dr Taylors Golden Grove about 3 eat a little diner trimed myselfe and was within at 7 performed my devotion and renewed my covenent sate up till 12 because Mr Ardrey was out but came home Prety sober[399] went to bed.

Sunday, 3 December: Rose after 5 performed my devotion put on my bootes called Mr Smith gott myselfe redy to goe to Mr Chappels at 9 we went Mr Ardrey his wife Mr Smith Mrs Bety and myselfe came thether after 10 I went to Church it being just begun heard Mr Chappel[400] on the 31 Jeremiah 33 dined

---

[395] 'Frets' here probably refers to a decorative design of some sort, whether written or drawn, or added to a piece of furniture, *OED*.

[396] Posset is a dessert or sweet beverage made with curdled milk or cream; in this case it was curdled with sack, a fortified wine, perhaps the same 'Malligoe' referred to in the entry for Wednesday this same week.

[397] Perhaps a member of the prominent and wealthy Rebow family. John Rebow (d.1699) was a clothier and merchant, and one of Colchester's principle citizens. His son Sir Isaac Rebow (1655–1726) was MP for the town on several occasions between 1689 and 1722, amongst other offices, and was a consistent Whig, *Hist. Parl. 1690–1715*, Vol. 5, 262–265.

[398] This word is sloppily squeezed into the inner margin: possibly 'pitt'.

[399] 'Prety sober' is very untidy and ambiguous; this transcription is speculative.

[400] Originally 'Mr Chaps'. This and other references to 'Mr Chappel' are likely referring to John Chappel (d.1681?), BA 1658/9 and MA 1662, Emmanuel College, Cambridge; rector of Inworth 1662/3–1678 and rector of Great Wigborough 1669–1681. He married Ariana Bland, daughter of Robert, from whom he inherited the latter

about 1 stayd there till after 7 came home after 9 performed my devotion went to prayers and I to bed.

Monday, 4 December: Rose at 7 after I was dressed and performed my devotion went to school stayd till after 11 came home sate by the fier put up a barrell of Oysters for Mr Gray[401] performed my devotion went to diner and to school stayd till after 6 came home put up a goose to send to Mrs Gray carried them to Mr Goldsberry got him to carry them to the carriers stayd at his house till 8 caled for my hilits[402] came home sate below till 9 performed my devotion boyled the hilit of my sword after 11 went to bed.

[fo. 45r]
Tuesday, 5 December: Rose at 7 after I was dressed and performed my devotion eat som breakfast went to school stayd till after 12 came home went to diner performed my devotion went to school stayd till after 6 came home sate by the fier a little performed my devotion sate by the fier mending a lace at 11 went to bed.

Wednesday, 6 December: Rose at 7 after I was dressed and performed my devotion eat som breakfast went to school stayd till after 12 came home went to diner performed my devotion went to school stayd till 5 came home sate by the fier and altered a cravatt performed my devotion eat som tost washt my feete and after 10 went to bed.

Thursday, 7 December: Rose at 7 after I was dressed and performed my devotion eat somthing went to school stayd till almost 12 went to Mr Grays stayd till almost 1 eat som turky[403] py came home went to diner performed my devotion went to school stayd till after 6 and gott the chimny mended came home performed my devotion playd a little and was a little Altring a cravat sate up till 10 Mr Ardrey his wife and Mr Smith and Mr Mott came from Frayton sate while they smoakt a pipe went to prayers and I to bed.

---

living. *CCEd* Person ID: 161805. See Nicholas Carlisle, *Collections for a History of the Ancient Family of Bland* (London, 1826), 148; *Cantabrigienses*, Vol. 1, pt. 1, 324. Cf. **27 February 1677**.
   [401] It seems likely that Lloyd meant to write 'Mrs Gray'.
   [402] Hilts?
   [403] Turkey had only recently been introduced to English tables in the 17th century, and would have been something of a novelty; May's *Accomplisht Cook* contains several elaborate recipes for 'turky', 444.

Friday, 8 December: Rose a little after 4 being mistaken by the moone made a fier dresst myselfe performed my devotion sate by the fier till almost 7 eat a tost walkt to Bourne ponds[404] came back to school stayd till almost 12 came to diner performed my devotion went to school stayd till after 4 came home sate by the fier and made a cravatt went to super performed my devotion went to prayers and I to bed.

Saturday, 9 December: Rose after 7 after I was drest and performed my devotion eat som breakfast went to school stayd till after 12 came home performed my devotion went to diner sate a little at 2 went to school and was about my peece stayd till after 3 came home sate by the fier playd at 6 performed my devotion sate up till 9 eat somthing at 10 went to prayers and sate up till after 12 with Mr [sic] Bety went to bed.

Sunday, 10 December: Rose at 8 after I had washt sate by the fier and read a sermon dressed myselfe performed my devotion went to St James heard Mr Shelton on the 1 Cor 1 Corinthians 16 last save one if any man love not the Lord Jesus Christ came home made a short prayer sate and warmed myselfe went to diner read a sermon performed devotion sate by the fier a little, went to St James herd the same man and text came home sate by the fier a little performed my devotion went to super sate a little went to prayers and to bed.

Monday, 11 December: Rose after 7 after I was dressed and performed my devotion eat som breakfast went to school stayd till after 12 came home went to diner performed my devotion went to bed school stayd till after 5 performed my devotion there came home wound a littl[e] washt my gloves and belt at 9 came in Mr Ardrey fuddled had much adoe to keepe him quiet playd to him till 11 went to bed.

Tuesday, 12 December: Rose at 7 after I was dressed went to school stayd till after 11 came home cullered my belt and gloves went to diner performed my devotion went to school stayd till after 6 went to Mr Grayes stayd till 9 eat som minst py came home performed my devotion sate up till after 10 went to bed.

---

[404] Bourne Mill and its pond still exist today, about one mile to the south of Colchester Castle (see National Trust).

[fo. 45v]
Wednesday, 13 December: Rose at 7 after I was dressed and performed my devotion eat som breakfast went to school stayd till after 11 came home playd went to diner performed my devotion stayd till after 5 came home mended a payre of stockings performed my devotion went to super and to prayers and to bed.

Thursday, 14 December: Rose after 7 after I was dressed and performed my devotion eat som breakfast went to school stayd till after 11 went to Mr Goldsberry to see about my horse called at Mr Shewcross he payd me for his Grandsons schooling came home per went to diner performed my devotion went to school stayd till 5 came home playd a little mended my baggs performed my devotion eat som super went to prayers and after to bed.

Friday, 15 December: Rose after 7 after I was dressed performed my devotion eat som breakfast went to school stayd till after 11 came home was a little about cutting of the sleeves of my stuffe coate went to diner performed my devotion went to school stayd till after 5 came home was a little about making my sleeves less performed my devotion eat som super went to prayers and to bed.

Saturday, 16 December: Rose after 7 after I was drest and performed my devotion went to breakfast went to school stayd till after 11 came home and was below till 12 making an end of my coate Mr Ardrey was mad and out of humor with all the house and with me I went to my chamber made an end of my coat performed my devotion walked round by Marlin Greene came home went to my chamber was about geting my cloathes in redyness for my Journey went downe sate by the fier t[ill] after 5 wound a little went to my chamber performed my devotion went dow[n] sate til[405]

Sunday, 17 December: Rose at 8 after I was dressed and performed my devotion eat som breakfast went to St James heard Mr Shelton on the 1 Corinthians 16 last save one came home made a short prayer went to diner sate by the fier performed my devotion warmed myselfe went to church and herd the same man and text came home sate by the fier performed my devotion read in Josephes[406] went to super sate a little went to prayers and to bed.

---

[405] This entry abruptly ends without explanation. Perhaps Lloyd was interrupted by Ardrey.
[406] Lloyd probably means Josephus: see n. 105, **1 October, 1675.**

Monday, 18 December: Rose after 7 after I was dresd and performed my devotion went to school stayd till after 11 came home sate by the fier tyd up my perrywig went to diner performed my devotion went to school stayd till after 4 came went to Mr Smith he was not within went to Mr Goldsberry saw my mare drank 2 flagons of Alle at the Maydonhead came home playd a little performed my devotion went to super to prayers and to bed.

Tuesday, 19 December: Rose after 7 after I was dressed and performed my devotion eat som breakfast went to school stayd till almost 12 broiding[407] sate by the fier a little went to diner performed my devotion trimed myselfe got my things redy to goe to Aynehoe[408] after 6 performed my devotion eat som super went to prayers and to bed.

[fo. 46r]
Here, the narrative of the diary pauses, and Lloyd copies out a loosely paraphrased extract from the middle of 'An Evening Prayer for a Family' from Lewis Bayly's The Practice of Piety – perhaps because he was travelling to visit relatives in Aynho, Northamptonshire. Note the insertion of the Lord's Prayer in the middle does not occur in Bayly's original: there, it appears at the end.[409]

Beseeching thee to pardon and forgive all our crying and abominable Sins, bless O Lord we besseech thee our gratious sovereigne Lord the King and all the royall family, all our majestrates and ministers all that love thee or call up on thy name, all our Christian brethren or sisters that are in affliction especially those that suffer for the testimony of a good conscience grant them patience in al[l] their sufferings and a hapy issie out of all their afflictions, which way may seeme best to thy divine wisdome, Christ[410] these and all other mercyes which thou seest to be needfull for us and thy whole church we beg of thee concluding these our weake and imperfict prayers in that most holy forme of prayer Christ himselfe hath taught us Our Father. Who art in Heaven Hallowed be thy name thy Kingdom

---

[407] This word is very ambiguously written and this transcription is speculative. 'Broiding' is an antiquated variant of 'braiding', and 'broidering' is an alternative form of 'embroidering', *OED*. Both could make sense here, given Lloyd's proclivity for making and altering garments. He could even be braiding the silk strings he had 'wound' on his machine. See n. 184, **25 November 1675.**)

[408] Aynho, a small village in Northamptonshire; for Lloyd, a long journey of some 130 miles.

[409] For the original prayer, see Bayly, *Practice of Piety*, 468–480, esp. 477–479. Cf. the 1675 edn (printed by Philip Chetwinde), 225–230.

[410] Originally a stylized 'X'.

Come thy will be don in earth as it is in heaven give us this day our daily bred and forgive us our trespasses as we forgive them that trespass against us and lead us not into temptation but deliver us from evell for thine is the kingdom the Power and glory for ever and ever amen, thy grace o Lord Jesus Christ thy love our Heavenly father thy comfort and consolation o holy and blessed spirit be with us and remane with us this night and forever more, amen.

And lord never suffer us to forget our last <end and those> reckoning that them we must make unto thee in health and prosperity make us mindfull of sickness and the evill day that is behind that those things may never over take us as a snare but that we may in sum measure be fitted for the coming of Christ the sweete bridgroome of our soules.

[fo. 46v]
Wednesday, 20 December: Rose at 4 after I was dressed and performed my devotion got myself redy to goe for Aynhoe eat som milk about 6 went to Goldsberys for my horse at 7 tooke horse rid to Ashton[411] <performed my devotion> in Cambridgshire 26 mils came there about 1 stayd and bayted my horse and selfe after 2 set out went to Wixleford bridg[412] which is about 7 miles from Ashton lay there came in about 4 got a fier in my chamber was Ill could eat nothing performed my devotion and went to bed.

Thursday, 21 December: Rose after 7 performed my devotion got myselfe redy eat som breakfast tooke horse before 9 rid to Royston[413] that is 8 miles called at the post house to be informed the way drank a tankard of ale went to Gosfield[414] bayted there stayd till after 1 went to Oburne[415] came in about 5 lay there per eat som super performed my devotion and went to bed. frid:

---

[411] This seems likely to be the village of Ashdon, about four miles north-east of Saffron Walden, near the Cambridgeshire border.
[412] Probably Whittlesford, a village about seven miles south of Cambridge.
[413] Royston, Hertfordshire.
[414] This is a puzzling reference, and perhaps a mistake. Gosfield is a small village in the Braintree district of Essex, two miles west of Halstead. Lloyd would, in fact, likely have passed near or through Gosfield on his initial journey from Colchester to Ashdon. It seems plausible that Lloyd wrote the account of his journey in retrospect, and simply wrote Gosfield in error.
[415] Perhaps Woburn, Bedfordshire, between Royston and Aynho. There is no 'Oburne' in the vicinity. Lloyd would, however, have needed to make speedy progress in order to make the journey described in the following morning; it is some thirty miles from Woburn to Aynho.

Friday, 22 December: Rose at 7 after I had performed my devotion got myselfe redy came away did not eat or drinke came to Aynhoe before 1 called and set up my horse at the Bell went to the Doctor's came when they were at diner eat som diner after diner playd 3 or 4 games at 4 handed Cribbage[416] lost a bottle of Sider walked in the garden an houer till 4 came in and got som poltice for my horse, sate by the fier talking with Mrs Margaret went to super sate up till 11 went to my chamber performed my devotion and went to bed.

Saturday, 23 December: Rose at 8 after I was dresst and trimed performed my devotion and was below till 11 went to my Brother in the Gallery and read my Brother Johns letters discourst till after 12 I performed my devotion went to diner and was below till after 6 performed my devotion went downe and to super and read a sermon of Dr Duns[417] sate up till after 10 was in the Kitchinn with Mrs Margarett.

Sunday, 24 December: Rose at 8 after I was dressed and performed my devotion went downe and eat som breakfast read a sermon of Dr Dunns went to church heard Mr Ellin on the [*blank*] Isaiah [*blank*] to Us a child is given[418] came home made a short prayer went to diner sate by the fier a little performed my devotion went to Church to prayers stayd a little with Mrs Mary[419] and my sister Mary walked above an houer alone and had serious thoughts about the Lord's super came in and walkd in the gallery ½ an houer went downe and sate till super and after a little performed my devotion and sate up till 10 went to bed.

Christmas Day: Rose at 7 after I was dressed and went to the back garden shut myselfe in performed my devotion and made my confession out of Dr Taylor was there meditating till church time went to Church my Brother preacht on the 7 Isaiah behold a Virgin shall conceive and beare[420] and receved the sacrament came home made a short prayer went to diner performed my devotion read a little went to prayer walked toward Souldren[421] cam[e] in sat below and

---

[416] In other words, Cribbage adapted for four players instead of the traditional two.
[417] Lloyd may be referring to the sermons of John Donne, the metaphysical poet (1572–1631).
[418] Isaiah 9:6.
[419] Possibly Margaret; obscured by tight binding.
[420] Isaiah 7:14.
[421] Souldern, a small village some two miles south of Aynho.

read went to super performed my devotion sat up till 10 went to [bed.]

Tuesday, 26 December: Rose after 8 after I was dressed and performed my devotion was within eat som break[fast] after 11 went to prayer came back was below till after 12 went to diner per performed my devotion was within all the afternoone playd a little at cards went to super at 7 playd a little at cards performed my devotion sate up till after 10.

[fo. 47r]
Wednesday, 27 December: Rose at 8 after I was dressed and performed my devotion went with my Brother to Dedington[422] to Mr Langstons called at Mr Lawleys stayd ½ an houer came to Mr Langstons before 11 stayd in the parlor a little went to the New Allehouse my Brother and Mr Langston Mrs Langst[on] and I dranke 3 Flagons came back sate and talked till after 12 went to diner there dined som of the Neigbours after diner I playd at cards 2 games at Whish[423] with a woman against Mrs Langston and another woman playd at Cribbage with Mr Appletrees won 6^d gave it to the maid stayd till 5 came home was below went to supper after went to my sisters chamber where she was troubled for what the Dr sayd to her I brought her to the kitchin stayd and warmed her and we dranke a little burnt brandy I had her into the hall where was Mr Lawly and Mr Gabell and Mr Longman and Mr Berry[424] at Cards. Sate up till after 11 went to bed.

Thursday, 28 December: Rose at 7 was in my sisters chamber till 8 dressed myselfe and performed my devotion eat som breakfast was writting Letters till after 11 I washt som bottles and drew out som of the Doctor's Sack went to diner drew out the rest performed my devotion sent for the fidler he came before 3 we danced about 4 with som of the towne girles till 8 went to super danced till after 11 went to bed performed my devotion in bed.

Friday, 29 December: Rose at 9 after I was dressed and performed my devotion eat som breakfast was in my sisters chamber

---

[422] Deddington, Oxfordshire, just under four miles west of Aynho.
[423] 'Whist'.
[424] This seems likely to have been Richard Berry, who became vicar of Bicker, Lincolnshire, in 1680, in part thanks to the endorsement of Nicholas Lloyd. See Introduction, pp. 21. *CCEd* Person ID: 86274.

and cutt her corne[425] was below till diner after diner performed my devotion and walked in the garden was below till after super playd 2 games at 4 handed Cribbage lost both after super sate with my sister in my lap whislt [sic] they playd at cards at 10 performed my devotion sate up till after 11 went to bed.

Saturday, 30 December: Rose after 8 after I had trimed myselfe and was redy went to Mr Lawleys with my Brother he not being at home we called on Mr Hanslop[426] stayd till 11 came back performed my devotion was below walked with my sister into the field came back to diner after diner performed my devotion was below and saw them play at cards went to super after 7 I performed my devotion and sate by the fier with my sister while they playd at cards after 10 went to bed.

Sunday, 31 December: Rose after 8 after I was dresst performed my devotion in the gallery my Brother being in the chamber helpt dress my sister eat som tost went to Church herd Mr Thornton on the 2 Hebrews [blank] he tooke not on him the Nature of Angells[427] and came home made a shorte prayer went to diner sat by the fier and read the life of St Jude and St John[428] performed my devotion went to Church to prayers came home sate by the fier till after 5 performed my devotion and tyd up my perrywig and got my things together went downe sate by the fier till super time went to super sate up till after 9 went to bed.

[fo. 47v]

1677

Monday, 1 January: Rose at 7 got my things redy and myselfe to goe for London performed my devotion in the gallery was with my Brother in our[429] chamber received 5^{li} to returne into Hampshire talked and resolved to settle at Newington[430] I was below till 12

---

[425] Probably a corn on the foot.
[426] Writing messy and obscure here.
[427] Hebrews 2:16.
[428] I can find no single publication with this title or similar. Lloyd may have been reading any number of hagiographical or quasi-historical texts, or indeed the gospels themselves (though they are particularly patchy on the 'life' of St Jude).
[429] 'Our' symbol.
[430] Nicholas Lloyd's living at St Mary, Newington Butts. According to Nicholas's own autobiography, he only 'settled' at Newington in 1677: BODL MS Rawl. D. 32/1.

then tooke my leave of my Brother and sister and Mr Burry and Mr Thornton who went to Mrs Cartrets I stayd and dined with the Dr and his Neighbours at 2 I tooke horse and went for Alisbury[431] came thither after 5 met Mr Turner at the Whit Hart we went to the Crowne had a pullet for super sat up till 10 performed my devotion and went to bed.

Tuesday, 2 January: Rose after 5 got myselfe redy and performed my devotion set out of Alisbury after 7 walkd a mile rid with the Coach 2 miles mett a Oxfordshire Man had his Company overtooke Alisbury men before we came to Chafant[432] called and drank into Acton and called and dranke came to London about 3 I went with much dificulty to the Flying Horse set up my horse about 5 I went to Mrs Gray where I was received with much Joy I supt there went and ordered my horse came and lay in her bed sate up till after 1 performed my devotion in bed.

Wednesday, 3 January: Rose at 8 after I was dressed and performed my devotion was within till 3 it being a wett day I went to Mr Breminghams was trimed and got a perrywig I went to Mrs Hughnagts[433] came back about 5 sat up till 1 went to bed and performed my devotion in bed.

Thursday, 4 January: Rose at 7 after I was dressed and performed my devotion eat som brekfast went out to Dr Roberts stayd an houer went to Mr Jefferyes stayd an houer saw his Lady delivered her case for a diamond ring went to the Windmill in Shoe Lane[434] payd 5^{li}, went to Mr Smith, writt a letter to Aynhoe went to Smithfield delivered a letter to Mrs Whitfield we went to the Wheatsheafe at Holborne bridg[435] and dined I went to the Watchmakers called Mr Smith we came to my Ine drank a tankard of alle went to a Coffy house stayd to drink one dish of coffe went to Mr Canham I

---

[431] Aylesbury, the county town of Buckinghamshire, on the route from Aynho to London, where Lloyd was heading.

[432] Potentially one of three villages in south-east Buckinghamshire collectively called the Chalfonts: Chalfont St Peter, Chalfont St Giles, and Little Chalfont.

[433] Partly obscured by tight binding.

[434] It was at the Windmill Inn in Shoe Lane that John Felton resolved, after reading the Parliamentary Remonstrance, to assassinate the duke of Buckingham in 1628: Ben Weinreb, Christopher Hibbert, Julia Keay, and John Keay, *The London Encyclopedia, 3rd edn* (London, 2008), 835.

[435] A bridge across the Fleet Ditch, at the eastern end of Holborn St., close to the present Holborn Viaduct.

went with him to Moregate came back and came to Mrs Gray went to super and sate up till after 12 performed my devotion in bed.

Friday, 5 January: Rose after 9 after I was dressed and performed my devotion was within Mrs Grays chamber till diner went to diner and went out to meete Mr Smith but not finding I walked to Temple Bar bought some Card and ribband came back found him stayd till 4 went to Mr Bremingham left his perrywig came back to Mrs Gray sate within till 8 went to super Mr Halford being ther[e] playd at Cards 3 games I lost 2 sate up till after 2 and after I was abed she sate by me till 3 I performed my devotion and went to sleepe.

[fo. 48r]
Saturday, 6 January: Rose at 7 performed my devotion it being a wett morning I did not dress myselfe till after 8 but sate with my deare till Mr Halford came I put on my boots and got myselfe redy went to breakfast dranke a pot of sack went to the Flying Horse after I had tooke my leave tooke horse at 10; overtooke some travelers that went almost to Chelmsford I stayd there above an houer came there after 4 came to home before 8 stayd at Mr Goldsberys payd him for my horse delivered a letter to Mr Smith came to my Lodgings where I found Mr Ardrey very Ill but asleepe I sate up till after 10 performed my devotion and went to bed.

Sunday, 7 January: Rose after 8 after I was dressed and performed my devotion eat som breakfast went to Allsaints herd Mr Hickringole on the 1 Peter 2:10 came home made a short prayer went to diner sate with Mr Ardrey I performed my devotion and went to St James herd Mr Shelton on the 1 Corinthians 16 last but one came home sate in Mr Ardreys chamber till after 8 performed my devotion eat somthing sate up till after 10 performed my devotion went to prayers and to bed.

Monday, 8 January: Rose after 7 after I was dressed and performed my devotion went to school stayd till after 12 was making up knotts for my coate came home performed my devotion went to diner went to school stayd till after 6 went to Mr Grays stayd till 8 came home sate up with Mr Ardrey and eat som super in his chamber went to prayers performed my devotion and went to bed.

Tuesday, 9 January: Rose at 7 after I was dressed and performed my devotion eat som breakfast went to school stayd till after 11

~~came home was~~ performed my devotion at school came home ~~went to~~ was in Mr Ardreys chamber till diner after diner sate with Mr Ardrey till after 1 went to school stayd till after 6 came home was with Mr Ardrey eat som super sate up till after 9 went to prayers and to bed.

Wednesday, 10 January: Rose after 7 after I was dressed and performed my devotion eat somthing went to school stayd till after 11 performed my devotion came home went to diner sat with Mr Ardrey went to school stayd till after 4 came home was with Mr Ardrey till after 9 went downe went to prayers sat up till after 10 went to my chamber performed my devotion and went to bed.

Thursday, 11 January: Rose after 7 after I was dressed and performed my devotion eat somthing went to school stayd till after 11 <performed my devotion> went to Childs to Mr Salter dranke 3 Flagons of alle talked about his son at 12 came home went to diner and was with Mr Ardrey till 1 went to school stayd till after 5 came home was with Mr Ardrey till after 9 supt in his chamber went to prayers sate up till 12 and talkd with Mrs Ardrey about her concernes when she was a mad[436] and marrid at 12 went to my chamber performed my devotion and went to bed.

Friday, 12 January: Rose at 7 after I was dressed and performed my devotion eat somthing went to school stayd till after 11 <performed my devotion> went to Mr Goldsberry he was goeing out I came home went to diner sate a little went to school stayd till after 6 came home was below eat som super with Mrs Vickers went with her home went to Mr Grays stayd till 9 came home went to prayers sate up till after 11 performed my devotion and went to bed.

Saturday, 13 January: Rose at 7 after I was dressed and performed my devotion eat somthing went to school stayd till after 11 performed my devotion came home was a little mending my coate went to diner after 1 was till 5 about my coate trimed myselfe went to Mr Smiths drew out his Maligoe came home received 2 letters one from Phyloclea the other from Policrity writt an answer to the last performed my devotion went to bed.

---

[436] Maid.

[fo. 48v]

Sunday, 14 January: Rose at 8 after I was dressed and performed my devotion eat somthing went to All Saints heard Mr Hickeringole on the 2 Peter 1:10 came home made a short prayer went to diner sate a little performed my devotion went to St James heard Mr Shelton on the 2 Timothy 4:8 came home was below till after 5 went to my chamber was serious and read in the Practice of Piety about the state of the death of the wicked and the godly performed my devotion went downe eat noe super went to prayers after 9 and to bed.

Monday, 15 January: Rose after 7 after I was dressed and performed my devotion went to school stayd till after 11 went to Mr Goldsberys playd a little came home performed my devotion went to diner and to school stayd till after 6 went to Mr Hitchonsons to get my buckle mended came home playd a little eat som super sate up till after 10 went to prayers and to my chamber performed my devotion and went to bed.

Tuesday, 16 January: Rose after 7 after I was dressed and performed my devotion went to brekfast and to school stayd till after 11 performed my devotion came home was altring a cravatt went to diner sate a little went to school stayd till after 6 went to Hitchsons for my buckle came home was below about my cravat till after 8 eat som thing after 9 went to prayers went to my chamber performed my devotion and went to bed.

Wednesday, 17 January: Rose at 7 after I was dressed and performed my devotion went to Mr Gray to get my coate altred in the sleefe stayd and dranke my morning draught went to school stayd till after 11 <performed my devotion> came home was mending a payre of stockings went to diner mended a payre of gloves went to school stayd till after 6 came home was getting my things to goe the next day to Mrs Betys weding sate up till after 10 went to prayers performed my devotion and went to bed.

Thursday, 18 January: Rose after 5, to goe to Mrs Bettys weding[437] got myselfe redy performed my devotion stayd till 9 then tooke horse and carryed Mrs Ardrey to Frayton came there after 10 dressed myselfe and was with the company till neere 12 went to Church and helped lead Mrs Bride to church they were married I

---

[437] The marriage of William Smith and Elizabeth Martin is recorded in the Frating parish register on 18 January 1676/7; ERO, D/P 349/1/1.

got a garter came home we went to diner but the Bridgroome and we Bridmen waited and dined afterward and the Brid and Brid maids waited on us stayd there till 5 then came home I went to the Bride's house and we eate cake and dranke wine after 10 put them to bed I threw the stocking and hit the Brid eat som sack poset came home after 11 Mrs Baython and the Bridmaids lay in my bed I performed my devotion and went to bed.

Friday, 19 January: Rose at 6 after I was dressed I went to my school and performed my devotion went first to see the brid and Bridgroome after I had performed my devotion went downe againe was afterward in my school till after 11 < performed my devotion> went downe to Mr Smiths stayd there and dined after diner his Brother and Sir Thomas Smith[438] went away I to my school and stayd till 2 then Mrs Brid and her company came and begane a play stayd a little at their house came to Mr Ardreys stayd till after super I playd to them after super went with Mr Ardrey to leave them home and put them to bed came home went to prayers performed my devotion and went to bed.

Saturday, 20 January: Rose at 7 after I was dressed and performed my devotion went to school stayd till after 11 went to Mr Smiths eat oysters and cake stayd there till after 3 Mr Bontall was with me there came home performed my devotion sent a letter to Mr Chappell stayd within and was not well eat som panada for super performed my devotion went to prayers and to bed.

Sunday, 21 January: Was ill and got som burnt maligoe and got a little sweate rose after 11 after diner I dressed myselfe performed my devotion went to St Giles with Mrs Ardrey and Mr Bridg:[439] and his wife heard Mr Smith on the 12 John 16 came home was below till 7 went to super after super sate till 9 went to prayers and I to my chamber performed my devotion and went to bed.

---

[438] A puzzling reference; there are no prominent residents of Essex with this name at this period. It may be Sir Thomas Smith, 2nd Bt of Hatherton, Cheshire, who had inherited the title from his uncle, Sir Thomas Smith, 1st Bt, in 1675. He was the son of Laurance Smith, of Bow, Middlesex, now part of London. John Burke and John Bernard Burke, *A Genealogical and Heraldic History of the Extinct and Dormant Baronetcies of England* (Baltimore, 1985), 492.

[439] Lloyd is referring to the bridegroom. Cf. 'Mrs Brid' above.

[fo. 49r]

Monday, 22 January: Rose at 7 after I was dressed and performed my devotion went to school and went into Mr Smiths and eate som tost and dranke at 9 went into school stayd til after 11 performed my devotion came home was below, went to my chamber and papered up my perrywig went to diner sate a little went to school stayd till after 6 went to Mr Grays payd him for my coate stayed till after 8 came home went to super sate up till after 10 went to prayers went to my chamber performed my devotion and went to bed.

Tuesday, 23 January: Rose at 7 after I was dressed and performed my devotion went to breakfast and to schoole stayd at Childs till neere 9 went to school stayd till after 11 came home performed my devotion was in my chamber about my perrywigg went to diner and to school stayd till after 6 <performed my devotion> went to Mr Smiths stayd till 7 came home was below in the house after 8 went to super sate up till after 10 went to prayers and to bed after 11.

Wednesday, 24 January: Rose at 7 after I was dressed <and performed my devotion> went to school made a fier stayd till after 12 performed my devotion and was writing for my peece came home helped Mr[s] Ardrey pull out clothes went to diner helpt her pull out clothes till almost 2 went to school stayd till after 6 performed my devotion came home held the child and helped pull out clothes at 8 went to super sate till after 9 went to prayers and to my chamber and to bed.

Thursday, 25 January: Rose after 8 after I was dressed and performed my devotion eat som breakfast went to Mr Goldsberrys playd till 12 came home performed my devotion was in my chamber till after 1 went to diner was within till 6 went to the dancing schoole and danced 7 or 8 cuntry dances went home at 9 with Mrs Sarah Gray stayd there till 11 came home performed my devotion received a letter from Policritie[440] and read it and went to bed.

Friday, 26 January: Rose before 7 after I was dressed and performed my devotion went to the King's Head to see for Mr Bontall he was not there went to Mr Goldsberrys and spoke to him to mend my Violin went to school stayd till after 11 went to

---

[440] See n. 81, **7 September 1675**. 'Policritie' or 'Policrity' seems likely to be another pseudonym used by Lloyd to obliquely refer to a woman in whom he had some romantic interest, perhaps one of the Lynford sisters, or 'Mrs Gray'.

the dancing school stayd till 12 and saw them practise came home performed my devotion went to diner sate a little went to school stayd till 6 went to the Queen's Head to Mr Bontall stayd till 8 came home went to supper and to prayers to my chamber performed my devotion and to bed.

Saturday, 27 January: Rose at 7 after I was dressed and performed my devotion went to the Queen's Head to Mr Bontall stayd till almost 9 went to school stayd till after 11 performed my devotion came home was in my chamber mending a payre of stockings went to diner and was in my chamber till after 2 went downe and trimed Mr Ardrey and myselfe was below till 7 went to my chamber performed my devotion went downe to super sate up till 10 went to prayers and to my chamber and to bed.

Sunday, 28 January: Rose after 7 after I was dressed and performed my devotion eat som breakfast and went to All Saints herd Mr Hickringole on the 5 Romans 5 came home mad a short prayer sate by the fier a little went to diner sate a little performed my devotion walked in the gard[en] a little went to St James herd Mr Shelton on the ~~16~~ 1 Corinthians 16 last verse came home sate and warmed myselfe went to my chamber performed my devotion walked and meditated in the garden sate by fier a little read 3 sermons eat som super went to prayers and to bed after 10.

Monday, 29 January: Rose before 7 after I was dressed and performed my devotion eat som breakfast went to school stayd till after 11 performed my devotion came home mended my gloves went to diner after 1 I went to school stayd till almost 6 came home stayd till after 6 went to the dancing school to meete the schollers there being but four and one women went to Mr Grays to see for his daughter he was not at home came back and danced a little stayd till almost 9 came home eat som bred and cheese went to my chamber and performed my devotion and went to bed.

[fo. 49v]
Tuesday, 30 January: Rose after 7 after I was dressed and performed my devotion warmed myselfe went to my chamber and prayd the Lettany[441] out of Dr Taylor, went downe and sate by the fier till after 10 went to Trinity heard Mr Smith on the 1 Jonah 14 came home made a short prayer went downe sate and warmed

---
[441] Litany.

myselfe performed my devotion went to St Giles heard Mr Smith on the same text came home and sate by the fier renewed the Bond for Richard Orbell eat som super performed my devotion made my confession out of Dr Taylor sate a little went to prayers and to bed.

Wednesday, 31 January: Rose after 6 after I was dressed and performed my devotion eat som breakfast after 8 went to school stayd till after 11 came home got my shamy breeches and sleeves washt went to diner performed my devotion sate a little went to school stayd till almost 6 went to Mr Smiths stayd ½ an houer, went to the dancing school stayd till 9 we lerned to dance contry dances and I to walke a Corant[442] a little went with Mr Bontall to the Queen's Head dranke a flagon of beere and payd Mr Bontall my entrance came home cullered Mr Ardryes belt eat som super sate a little went to prayers went to my chamber performed my devotion and went to bed.

Thursday, 1 February: Rose at 6 after I was dressed and performed my devotion went to the Queen's Head to Mr Bontall dranke my morning draught with him and Abraham Daniell and Mr Sherly went to the school danced a little went to my school before 9 stayd till after 12 came home trimed myselfe and Mr Ardrey went to diner performed my devotion went to school stayd till after 5 came home dressed myselfe went to the dancing school danced contry dances till almost 9 came home and went home with Mrs Mary Furley came back went to super and to prayers to my chamber performed my devotion and went to bed.

Friday, 2 February: Rose after 6 after I was dressed and put on my boots I eat somthing stayd til after 8 tooke horse for Mr Chappells came thether after 10 stayd till 5 came home at 7 I performed my devotion eat a tost went to my chamber and to bed.

Saturday, 3 February: Rose after 7 after I was dressed and performed my devotion went to school stayd till almost 12 came home sate by the fier a little went to diner mended a payre of stockings performed my devotion afterward Cullered my shamy breeches, was within all the afternoone playd a little was below playd againe about 6 went downe and sate below after 8 eat som super sate up

---

[442] The courante was a style of dance of French and Italian origin, in triple metre, which was extremely popular throughout Europe from the 16th to the 18th centuries: Louis Horst, *Pre-Classic Dance Morms* (Princeton, NJ, 1987), 34–43.

till after 9 went to prayers and washed my feete went to my chamber performed my devotion and to bed.

Sunday, 4 February: Rose after 7 after I was dressed and performed my devotion sate by the fier and eat som breakfast went to All Saints heard Mr Hickringole on the 21 Jeremiah 12 part came home made a short prayer sate by the fier went to diner sate and read a sermon walked in the garden a little performed my devotion went to St James heard Mr Shel[ton] on the 2 Corinthians 5:8 came home and playd with the child walked into the garden read a sermon performed my devotion went downe eat som super sat till after 8 went to prayers and to my chamber and to bed.

Monday, 5 February: Rose at 7 after I was dressed and performed my devotion went to school stayd till after 12 performed my devotion came home sate by the fier a little went to diner Cullered my shamy breeches went to school stayd till almost 6 <performed my devotion> went to Mr Greats stayd till 7 went to Mr Sherlyes stayd till after 8 came home was below and eat som super sate up till after 10 went to prayers and to bed.

[fo. 50r]
Tuesday, 6 February: Rose at 7 after I was dressed and performed my devotion went to school stayd till after 11 came home cut of the sleeves of my coate for the taylor to mend sate by the fier went to diner performed my devotion went to school stayd till after 6 came home playd with the child a little playd on my Violin went to super sate up till after 10 went to prayers went to my chamber performed my devotion and went to bed.

Wednesday, 7 February: Rose after 6 after I was dressed and performed my devotion was in my chamber a little went downe eat a little bred and cheese went to school stayd till after 12 came home went to diner performed my devotion Trimed myselfe went to school stayd till after 6 went to the dancing danced cuntry dances to learne the young scholars stayd till 8 came home was below went to super performed my devotion sate up till after 10 went to prayers and I to my chamber and to bed.

Thursday, 8 February: Rose after 6 after I was dressed and performed my devotion eat somthing went to the Dancing school stayd till ½ houer after 8 went to my school stayd till after 11 came home <performed my devotion> went to Diner cut my shamy breeches less went to school stayd till after 6 came home and sate by the fier and sewed up my breeches eat som super after 9 went to prayers went to my chamber performed my devotion and went to bed.

Friday, 9 February: Rose at 6 after I was dressed and performed my devotion went to the dancing school and noebody there stayd a little went in and stayd ½ houer and Mr Bontall came not in went to my owne school stayd till almost 11 went with Mr Bontall to the school Learned a little came home was below till after diner performed my devotion went to school stayd till 7 went to Mr Vickers stayd till 8 came home performed my devotion sate up till 10 went to prayers and to bed.

Saturday, 10 February: Rose at 7 after I was dressed and performed my devotion went to school stayd till after 12 performed my devotion went home to diner after 1 went to my school and was there till almost 4 about my peece came home sate by the fier not being well after 7 performed my devotion eat a tost and butter received a letter and a box with a shade for Mr Ardrey from my dear Polycrity and a small Almanack she sent me went to prayers and I to bed.

Sunday, 11 February: Rose at 8 after I was dressed and performed my devotion eate som tost went to St James heard Mr Shelton on the 8 John 36 came home made a short prayer went to diner sate by the fier read a sermon performed my devotion went to St James herd Mr Shelton on the 2 Corinthians 5:8 came home sate by the fier read a sermon went to my chamber performed my devotion went downe sate by the fier eat som super sate up till 9 went to prayers and I to my chamber and to bed.

Monday, 12 February: Rose at 7 after I was dressed and performed my devotion eat somthing went to school stayd till 11 went to Mr Goldsberys playd till after 12 came home performed my devotion went to diner sate a little went to school stayd till after 7 writting a letter to ~~Phy~~ Policritie came home was mending my shamy breeches till 9 then Mr Ardrey came in drunke I sate with him a litttle performed my devotion went downe sate till after 11 before I could get him to bed and was quiet after he went to bed before 12 I went to bed.

Tuesday, 13 February: Rose at 6 after I was dressed and performed my devotion was in my chamber till after 7 went downe and eat a tost went to school stayd till after 11 performed my devotion came home went to diner playd a little went to school stayd till after 6 came home was about sewing the lace onto my shamy breeches sate up till after 9 went to super to prayers to my chamber performed my devotion to bed [*deleted*]

Wednesday, 14 February: Rose after 6 after I was dressed and performed my devotion went to school stayd till after 11 went to Mr Goldsberry dined there playd a little went to school stayd till after 6 came home dressed myselfe went to Mr Earels[443] danced till after 9 came home at 10 went to prayers eat a little bred and cheese went to my chamber and performed my devotion and went to bed.

[fo. 50v]
Thursday, 15 February: Rose at 6 after I was dressed and performed my devotion went to dancing school stayd till after 8 went to school stayd till after 12 came home performed my devotion went to diner mended my gloves went to school stayd till after 5 came home was below Mrs Vickers being there playd a little at 8 went home with her eat som super sate up till 10 went to prayers to my chamber performed my devotion and went to bed.

Friday, 16 February: Rose at 6 after I was dressed and performed my devotion went to the dancing school stayd til after 8 went to my school stayd till after 11 went to the dancing school and learned a little came home went to diner performed my devotion went to the school stayd till after 6 went to Mr Vickers stayd till after 8 came home performed my devotion eat som super sat up till after 10 went to prayers and to bed.

Saturday, 17 February: Rose at 7 after I was dressed and performed my devotion went to school after I had eat som breakfast stayd till after 12 <performed my devotion> came home was about mixing my gold to write with, went to diner after 2 went to my chamber and was there till after 4 writing in gold went downe stayd till after 5 went to Captain Wheelers with Mrs M: Furley came home trimed myselfe performed my devotion got my things redy for Sunday eat som super went to prayers to my chamber and to bed.

Sunday, 18 February: Rose at 7 after I was dressed and performed my devotion eat somthing read part of a sermon went to

---

[443] 'Earl's'? Lloyd's hand is unclear here.

St James herd Mr Shelton on the 8 John 36 came home made a short prayer went to diner sate below a little performed my devotion made an end of the sermon went to St James herd Mr Shelton on the 2 Corinthians 5:8 came home was below a little went to my chamber read 2 sermons and meditated a little performed my devotion went downe sate below till super after sate till after 8 the boy read went to prayers and at 9 to bed.

Monday, 19 February: Rose after 6 after I was dressed and performed my devotion eat som breakfast went to school stayd till after 11 went to Mr Goldsberry playd a little came home went to diner performed my devotion went to school stayd till after 6 came home playd till after 8 sate in the house till after 10 went to my chamber performed my devotion went downe and then Mr Ardrey and his wife came in eat som tost went to prayers I to my chamber and to bed.

Tuesday, 20 February: Rose at 6 after I was dressed and performed my devotion was below till 8 eat somthing went to school stayd till after 11 performed my devotion came home playd a little went to diner sate a little went to school stayd till after 6 went to Voales sent a small parcell to Policrity went to Mr Sherleys stayd till after 7 came home playd a little mended a payre of drawers eat som super sat up till after 10 went to prayers performed my devotion and to bed.

Wednesday, 21 February: Rose at 6 after I was dressed and performed my devotion eat som tost went to school stayd till after 11 went to Mr Goldsberys playd till after 12 came home went to diner performed my devotion went to school stayd till 6 stayd at Mr Smiths a little went to the dancing school stayd till 8 went to the King's Head drunk 2 Juggs came to Mr Greats paid him for my Electuarys[444] went to Mr Braisiers danced till after 10 playd 3 games at cribbage with Mr Great won all came home after 11 eat a little bred and cheese performed my devotion and went to bed.

Thursday, 22 February: Rose at 6 after I was dressed and trimed myselfe performed my devotion went to school stayd til after 11 went to dancing learned a little came home went to diner performed my devotion went to school stayd till after 4 came home dressed myselfe went to dancing school danced French dances and contry dances till

---

[444] A non-specific medicine mixed with honey or other sweetening agent, *OED*.

9 came home eat som super performed my devotion went to prayers and bathed my knees with brandy and went to bed.

[fo. 51r]
Friday, 23 February: Rose before 6 after I performed my devotion drest myselfe went to Mr Bontalls chamber and stayd till after 7 and was learning the Antick[445] went to school after 8 stayd till 11 went to Goldsberys dined there came home eat a few old beanes and porke performed my devotion went to school after 2 went and lay upon Mr Smiths bed not being well till after 4 went to my school stayd till 6 came home was very Ill performed my devotion eat som panada went to prayers and to bed.

Saturday, 24 February: Rose at 7 after I was dressed and performed my devotion went to school stayd till 1 came home went to diner performed my devotion was in my chamber till 4 about my peece in Gold went downe sate by the fier eat som broth performed my devotion sate up till after 9 went to prayers and to bed.

Sunday, 25 February: Rose before 8 not being very well dressed myselfe performed my devotion went to St James heard Mr Shelton on the 8 John 36 came home mad a short prayer went to diner performed my devotion read a little in Drexelious went to church to St James heard Mr Shelton on the 2 Corinthians 5:8 came home sate and warmed myselfe went to my chamber read 2 sermons performed my devotion walked a little in the garden sate by the fier till after 7 sate up till 9 went to prayers and to bed.

Monday, 26 February: Rose at 6 after I was dressed and performed my devotion eat a little bred and cheese went to schoole stayd till after 12 came home went to diner performed my devotion was a little about polishing my gold walked to the field came home was setting on buttons on my coate and playd a little went downe after went to Mr Vickers stayd till 9 came home went to prayers performed my devotion and went to bed.

Tuesday, 27 February: Rose at 6 after I had performed my devotion trimed myselfe dressed myselfe to goe to Mr Chappells went to Mr Renholds to see Mr Ardreys horse he bought that was soe poore

---

[445] Lloyd's phrasing implies that the 'Antick' was a clearly defined dance with particular steps; cf. *OED*, under 'antic', a slightly later use by Defoe 'The Gentleman … led me only a Courant, and then ask'd me, if I had a-mind to dance an Antick'.

he could scarce goe tooke horse at 8 came to Inworth[446] with Mr Ardrey and his wife and Ashley at 10 stayd there till after 5 had a most stately diner came home at 8 sate till 9 went to prayers performed my devotion went to bed.

Wednesday, 28 February: Rose at 7 after I was dressed and performed my devotion walked in the garden a little sate below after 9 went to my chamber made my confession out of Dr Taylor went with Mr Ardrey to see a horse at Appellbys came home stayd below a little went to my chamber and used the prayers for the day being Ash Wednesday there being none at any church walkd into the fields and meditated till almost 2 came to my chamber performed my devotion and used the Letany in Dr Taylor went downe and went to my school and fetcht my papers for my peece and was about them till after 5 performed my devotion went downe sate till after 7 eat som tost and a little cold beefe sate up till after 9 went to prayers washed my feete and went to bed.

Thursday, 1 March: Rose at 7 not being very well dressed myselfe performed my devotion went to school stayd till after 11 came home was very ill of my head performed my devotion eat a little diner sate by the fier till after 1, went to school stayd till 5 came home was about putting the canvas to my frame playd till 7 eat som super was below till 9 went to prayers performed my devotion and went to bed.

Friday, 2 March: Rose after 5 after I was dressed and performed my devotion eat som broth went to the Queen's Head to Mr Bontall he was not up came back to Faine brothers gott 2 plates for my frame carried them home nayled them on stayd till after 8 went to school stayd till after 11 went to the dancing school stayd till after 12 came home performed my devotion went to diner and to school stayd till after 6 came home was below mended stockings at 8 eat som super went to prayers at 10 to my chamber performed my devotion and went to bed.

[fo. 51v]
Saturday, 3 March: Rose before 6 after I was dressed and performed my devotion eat somthing went to the Queen's Head met Mr Bontall learned a little of the Antick called at Clemtrees saw

---

[446] A village ten miles south-west of Colchester.

Tom Peaks[447] peece saw Delight saw Ladukes peece went to school stayd till after 11 came home went to diner pasted on som of my peece performed my devotion was in my chamber a little mending a paire of stockings walked a little the wind being very high was within till 7 performed my devotion eat som super sate up till after 9 Mr Ardrey came home drunke I went to bed.

Sunday, 4 March: Rose at 8 after I was dressed and performed my devotion eate som breakfast and sate by the fier went to All Saints heard Mr Hickrin[gole] on the 23 Matthew 27 came home made a short prayer went to diner sate by the fier read 2 sermons went to St James heard Mr Shelton on the 2 Corinthians 5:8 came home sate by the fier till 5 went to Mr Ardrey being ill came home sate a little performed my devotion eate som super sate a little went to prayers and to bed.

Monday, 5 March: Rose at 6 after I was dressed and performed my devotion eat som breakfast went to school stayd till after 11 went to Mr Goldsberry stayd till 12 came home performed my devotion went to diner and to school stayd till after 6 came home playd a little went to Mr Grayes at 7 stayd till 10 came home went to prayers performed my devotion went to bed.

Tuesday, 6 March: Rose after 6 after I was dressed and performed my devotion was puting on som paper on my peece playd ½ an houer, eat som bred and cheese went to school stayd till after 11 came home mad some past[?e] sate by the fier went to diner performed my devotion went to school stayd till after 6 almost came home performed my devotion was by the fier a little clensing my semiter[448] and pistoll went to Mr Greats he was busie I stayd not went to Mr Smiths stayd ¼ of an houer came home eat som super sat below till after 9 went to prayers and to my chamber and after a little to bed.

Wednesday, 7 March: Rose after 6 after I was dressed and performed my devotion was pasting on my writing on my peece eat a little bred and cheese went to school stayd till after 11 went to Mr Goldsberry playd a little came home performed my devotion went to diner went to school stayd till after 6 went to Dancing school stayd till after 8 went to the Allcoate stayd till 9 came home eat som super went to prayers performed my devotion writt to Mrs

---
[447] Or perhaps 'Packs'.
[448] Scimitar.

Chappell and presented her as my Valintin[449] with ½ duz:[450] gloves 2 payre whit buttons went to bed.

Thursday, 8 March: Rose at 6 after I was dressed and performed my devotion went to Mr Bontall and practised the Antick till 7 went to school and learned part of the boree vasell[451] went to school stayd till after 11 came home trimed myselfe went to diner performed my devotion went to school stayd till after 5 was below with Mrs Smith and shewed her my nakedness, for which I am sory[452] came home dressed myselfe went to dancing school stayd till 9 came home eat som super performed my devotion sate up till 11 expecting Mr Ardrey and his wife but they came not went to prayers and to bed.

Friday, 9 March: Rose at 6 after I was dressed and performed my devotion went to school stayd till after 11 came home <went to dancing school> went to diner performed my devotion went to school stayd till 8 came home being very Ill went to bed.

Saturday, 10 March: Rose at 6 after I was dressed and performed my devotion went to Mr B[?ontall] he being not very well I walked in the Castell lanes till 8 went to school stayd till after 11 went to the

---

[449] The idea of choosing a 'Valentine' on 14 February did exist in the 17th century, though not necessarily with the romantic implications it carries now. Here Lloyd had selected a (probably) married woman, Ariana, wife of John Chappel, the rector of Wigborough (see n. 400, **3 December 1676**). Valentines in this period were often selected by lottery amongst a group of friends, or by chance – the first person of the opposite sex you saw that day – so Lloyd did not necessarily make a deliberate choice. That his Valentine was a friend's wife was not unusual; cf. *Pepys*, Vol. 1, 55, where Pepys's wife Elizabeth 'challenged' his friend Mr Moore to be her Valentine, as he was the first man she saw that day. Lloyd's gifts were typical of the period, as was the practice of writing a Valentine's note. The association of Saint Valentine's Day with unambiguous romantic love, and its slow commercialization through the development of the practice of sending greetings cards, began to emerge later in the 18th century: see Sally Holloway, 'Love, custom and consumption: Valentine's Day in England *c.*1660–1830', *Cultural and Social History*, 17 (2020), 295–314; *Pepys*, Vol. 10, 377–378. Why Lloyd waited until 7 March to declare his intention, though, is a mystery!

[450] This abbreviation almost certainly represents the word 'dozen', but here Lloyd is probably referring to the coarse woollen or kersey fabric, originating in Devonshire, by this name, i.e. gloves made half of dozen cloth, rather than six gloves! Spufford and Mee, *Clothing of the Common Sort*, 270.

[451] 'Boree' refers to the *bourrée*, a French dance in double time similar to a gavotte; it would have been newly fashionable in the 1670s. 'Vasell' is unclear, though Lloyd's hand is quite legible. See Horst, *Pre-Classic Dance Forms*, 78–84.

[452] Lloyd wrote this line in an extraordinarily tiny hand, evincing his evident guilt. 'Mrs Smith' probably refers to Elizabeth Smith, whose wedding to his friend William Smith Lloyd had attended on 18 January 1677.

Queen's Head to Mr Bontall and practised a little the Antick came home performed my devotion went to diner was within my chamber mending som linen till 5 went to walke a little was ill performed my devotion eat som super sate up till 10 went to prayers and to bed.

Sunday, 11 March: Rose at 8 not being very well after I was dressed and performed my devotion eat som bred and butter went to All Saints herd Mr Hickringhole on the 23 Matthew 27 came home made a short prayer went to diner performed my devotion read a sermon went to St James heard Mr Shelton on the 2 Corinthians 5:8 came home sate by the fier read 2 sermons performed my devotion went downe sate below read eat som super sate up till 10 went to prayers and to bed.

[fo. 52r]
Monday, 12 March: Rose at 6 after I was dressed and performed my devotion eat somthing went to school stayd till after 11 came home performed my devotion went to diner and to school stayd till after 6 came home playd a little was below eat som super sate up till 10 went to prayers went to my chamber performed my devotion went to bed.

Tuesday, 13 March: Rose at 6 after I was dressed and performed my devotion eat somthing went to school stayd till after 11 came home performed my devotion went to diner trimed myselfe went to school stayd till after 6 came home performed my devotion men [ded] stockings eat som super sate up till after 10 went to prayers and to bed.

Wednesday, 14 March: Rose at 7 after I was dressed and performed my devotion went to school stayd till after 11 came home ruled som of my peece went to diner performed my devotion went to school stayd till after 6 stayd in Mr Smiths shop till 7 went home went to see for Mr Stilliman he was not within came home mended a stocking sate up till 10 eat som super went to prayers performed my devotion went to bed.

Thursday, 15 March: Rose at 6 after I was dressed and performed my devotion eat a little bred and butter went to school stayd till after 11 came home made an end of ruling my peece went to diner performed my devotion went to school stayd till after 5 came home trimed myselfe walked into the Castell Lanes mett Mr Stilliman and Mr Sevile walked to Saywards[453] and he not being at home I came home sate till after 8 eat som super went to prayers went to my chamber performed my devotion and went to bed.

Friday, 16 March: Rose after 6 after I was dressed and performed my devotion eat som breakfast went to school stayd till after 11 came home went to diner performed my devotion went to Fane brothers made cleane my pistoll went to school stayd till after 6 came home walkd to the Castell Lanes came in playd sate up till 9 eat a little bred and butter after 10 went to prayers and to my chamber performed my devotion and went to bed.

Saturday, 17 March: Rose at 6 after I was dressed and performed my devotion eat som breakfast went to school stayd till after 11 came home was a little about my drawers went to diner sate a little by the fier and did som of my drawers performed my devotion and was mending the sleeves of my new camlet coate made an end of my drawers before I went to St James heard Mr Shelton preach a funerall upon the 25 Psalm 18 came home sate a little below performed my devotion sate up till after 9 went to super and to bed Mr Ardrey not being com home from the taverne.

Sunday, 18 March: Rose at 7 after I was dressed and performed my devotion eat som breakfast read 2 sermon went to St James heard Mr Shelton on the 8 John 36 came home made a short prayer went to diner sate a little read a sermon performed my devotion went to St James herd Mr Shelton on the 2 Corinthians 5:8 came home red 2 sermons went downe war[med] myselfe performed my devotion walked in my chamber till super where suped Mr Smith his wife Mrs Baythorne Mrs Vickers sate up till after 9 went to prayers and to bed.

Monday, 19 March: Rose at 6 after I was dressed and performed my devotion was below helping Mr Ardrey get his horse redy to goe to the North eat a bitt of bred and butter went to school stayd till after 11 went to Mr Goldsberry playd till after 12 came home eat my diner performed my devotion went to school stayd till after 6 came home playd till 8 eat som super went to prayers at 9 to my chamber performed my devotion and to bed.

Tuesday, 20 March: Rose at 6 after I was dressed and performed my devotion eat som breakfast powdred my perrywigg went to school

---

[453] Lloyd's hand is untidy and ambiguous here.

stayd till after 11 came home was by the fier till after diner performed my devotion went to Fane brothers clensed the lock of my pistoll went to school stayd till 6 went to the dancing school stayd till after 7 went to Mr Smiths shop stayd a little went back to school and began a figure[454] with Mrs Robertson and Mr Bontall stayd till after 9 came home eat som super went to prayers performed my devotion and went to bed.

[fo. 52v]
Wednesday, 21 March: Rose before 6 after I was dressed and performed my devotion went to the Queen's Head to Mr Bontall practist the Antick went to my school stayd till after 11 went to the dancing school stayd till after 12 went to Mr Smiths to diner performed my devotion in my school stayd till 6 came home playd a little walked in St Johns fields went to dancing school stayd till after 8 came home eat som supper performed my devotion went to prayers and bed.

Thursday, 22 March: Rose at 6 after I was dressed and performed my devotion eat som milke went to the dancing school stayd till after 7 went with Mr Bontall to Childs dranke a flagon went to school stayd till after 11 went to dancing school stayd till after 12 came home went to diner performed my devotion went to school stayd till 5 came home was very ill with my head sate by the fier till after 8 went to prayers and to bed performed my devotion in bed.

Friday, 23 March: Rose before 6 after I was dressed and performed my devotion went to dancing school stayd till 8 noebody being there went to my school stayd till after 11 went to dancing school stayd till after 12 came home to diner performed my devotion went to school stayd till after 6 came home performed my devotion playd a little was below eat som super date up till after 9 went to prayers and to bed.

Saturday, 24 March: Rose after 7 after I was dressed and performed my devotion went to school stayd till after 11 came home trimed myselfe performed my devotion went to diner was within part below talking with Mrs Vickers and Mrs Ardrey and somtime in my chamber making redy the sheete of paper for another peece

---

[454] In other words, a basic step or series of steps essential for learning a given dance or style, such as a dosado.

performed my devotion after 7 eate som super sate up till 10 went to prayers and to my chamber and to bed.

Sunday, 25 March: Rose after 7 after I was dressed and performed my devotion read a sermon, eat som breakfast went to St James heard Mr Shelton on the 8 John 36 came home mad a short prayer went to diner read a sermon performed my devotion went to St James heard Mr Shelton on the 2 Corinthians 5:8 came home walked a little in the garden read 2 sermons performed my devotion was a little in my chamber went downe was below eat som super sate up till after 9 went to prayers and bed.

Monday, 26 March: Rose at 6 after I was dressed and performed my devotion eat a little breakfast went to school stayd till after 11 came home went to diner performed my devotion went to school stayd till after 6 came home playd a little was below till after 8 eat som super stayd up till 10 went to prayers and to my chamber performed my devotion and to bed.

Tuesday, 27 March: Rose at 6 after I was dressed and performed my devotion eat somthing went to school stayd till after 11 came home went to diner performed my and to school and performed my devotion at my school stayd till after 6 walked till afor 7 came home performed my devotion was below went to super sate up till 10 went to prayers and to bed.

Wednesday, 28 March: Rose at 6 after I was dressed and performed my devotion eat som thing went to school stayd till after 11 came home went to diner performed my devotion went to school stayd till after 6 went to dancing stayd till 8 came home eat som super sate up till after 9 went to prayers went to my chamber performed my devotion went to bed.

Thursday, 29 March: Rose before 6 after I was dressed and performed my devotion went to the dancing school stayd till 8 went to school stayd till 11 went to dancing school stayd till after 12 came home went to diner performed my devotion trimed myselfe at 3 I went to my school giveing the boys a play stayd till 5 came home dressed myselfe went to the dancing stayd till 9 came home eat som super went to prayers performed my devotion and to bed.

[fo. 53r]

Friday, 30 March: Rose at 5 after I was dressed and performed my devotion went to the Queen's Head called Mr Bontall went to the school stayd till 8 went to my school stayd till after 11 went to the dancing school stayd till after 12 came to diner performed my devotion went to school stayd till 6 went to the dancing school stayd till afor 7 went to Mr Greats stayd at play at cribadg till 11 came home performed my devotion went to bed.

Saturday, 31 March: Rose after 6 after I was dressed and performed my devotion walked till 8 went to school stayd till after 11 went to Mr Lamberts received money for school came home performed my devotion was below puking violent eat a little unusually by myselfe was within all the afternoon not being well at 6 went to super performed my devotion sate up till after 9 went to prayers and to bed.

Sunday, 1 April: Rose at 8 after I was dressed and performed my devotion eat som breakfast went to Church to Trinity heard Mr Powell[455] on the 15 Luke 7 came home mad a short prayer went to diner performed my devotion read a sermon went to St Giles heard the same man and text came home read a sermon went downe stayd below till after 6 read a sermon and performed my devotion eat som super sate up till 10 went to prayers and to bed.

Monday, 2 April: Rose at 6 after I was dressed and performed my devotion eat som breakfast went to school stayd till after 11 went to Mr Goldsberry playd a little came home to diner performed my devotion went to school stayd till after 6 came home was within till after 7 walked till 8 came in eat som super went to prayers performed my devotion and to bed.

Tuesday, 3 April: Rose at 6 after I was dressed and performed my devotion eat som breakfast went to school stayd till after 11 came home went to diner performed my devotion and to school stayd till after 6 came home was a little about making a shirt performed my devotion eat som super sat up till after 10 went to prayers and to bed.

---

[455] Joseph Powell succeeded John Smith as rector of St Mary-at-the-Walls in February 1677 and held the living until his death in 1698. He was also rector of Halstead, Essex (1670–1676), Aldham, Essex (1671–1692), and Balsham, Cambridgeshire (1693–1698). His will was proved in the Prerogative Court of Canterbury on 9 April 1698, TNA, PROB 11/445/96. See *Cantabrigienses*, Vol. 1, pt. 3, 387; *CCEd* Person ID: 18772.

Wednesday, 4 April: Rose at 6 after I was dressed and performed my devotion was a little about making a shirt went to school stayd till after 11 came home was about my shirt went to diner performed my devotion went to school stayd till after 6 went to dancing school stayd till 7 walkd till 8 came home was below till 9 eat som super performed my devotion sate up till 12 about my shirt Mrs Ardrey being at Captane Renholds she being in Labour went to bed.

Thursday, 5 April: Rose at 5 after I was dressed and performed my devotion went to dancing school stayd till 8 went to Childs dranke a glas went to to school stayd till 11 went to dancing school stayd till 12 came home went to diner made an end of my shirt performed my devotion went to school stayd till 5 dressed myselfe went to dancing school stayd till after 9 performed my devotion eat a tost went to bed.

Friday, 6 April: Rose after 5 after I was dressed and performed my devotion went to dancing school stayd till after 7 went to the Alecoate stayd till 8 went to school stayd till after 11 went to dancing school stayd till almost 12 came home to diner performed my devotion went to school stayd till after 6 came home very ill went to bed performed noe other devotion but Ejaculation.

Saturday, 7 April: Rose before 6 after I was dressed went to dancing school stayd a little went to school stayd till after 11 went to dancing school stayd not but went to Mr Goldsberry got him to goe to the dancing playd over the Antick twise and we danced it went home to diner performed my devotion was within till after 5 walked till 6 was within eat som super sate up till after 9 went to prayers performed my devotion went to bed.

[fo. 53v]
Sunday, 8 April: Rose at 8 being ill dressed myselfe performed my devotion eat a little breakfast went to St James heard Mr Shelton on the 8 J 3 8 John 36 came home made a short prayer eat som diner being ill lay downe till church time went to St James heard Mr Shelton on 1 Corinthians 5:8 came home being very ill sate by the fier performed my devotion after 8 eat som milke went to prayers and to bed after 9.

Monday, 9 April: Rose at 5 after I was dressed and performed my devotion was by the fier writting to Mrs Gray eat som breakfast went to school stayd till 12 came home went to diner performed my devotion went to school stayd till 6 came home was within performed my devotion sate up till 10 went to super and to prayers and to bed.

Tuesday, 10 April: Rose at 5 after I was dressed and performed my devotion eat a little B[read] and C[heese] went to dancing school stayd till after 7 went to my school stayd till after 11 came home was in my chamber till diner performed my devotion went to school stayd till almost 6 went to dancing school stayd till after 7 came home performed my devotion eat som super sate up till after 10 went to prayers and to bed.

Wednesday, 11 April: Rose at 5 after I was dressed and performed my devotion went to dancing school stayd till almost 8 went to my school stayd till after 11 came home performed my devotion went to diner went to school stayd till after 6 went to the King's Head to see for Mr Bontall but not finding him came home was within eat som till 8 went with Mrs Vickers home eat som super performed my devotion went to prayers and to bed.

Thursday, 12 April: Rose at 5 after I was dressed and trimed myself and p went to and performed my devotion went to see for Mr Bontall but cold nat[456] find him went to my school stayd till after 11 broak up came home went to diner performed my devotion went into the bead[457] lay an houer put on cleane Linen dressed myself at 3 went to the Ball stayd till 6 at Goodwife Baytie to dance an Antick but noe company coming did it not went into the school Danced till after 10 came home performed my devotion eat a tost went to bed.

Friday, 13 April: Rose at 7 after I was dressed and performed my devotion walked came home and went to prayers at All Saints came home and was not very well lay downe a little performed my devotion went to St James heard Mr Shelton on the 15 John 13 came home was within performed my devotion eat som super went to prayers and to bed.

Saturday, 14 April: Rose after 6 after I was dressed and performed my devotion walkd till 10 came in made my confession out of Dr Taylor and was within performed my devotion and at 3 eat somthing after 4 went to the King's Head to Mr Pagget stayd a little went

---

[456] Could not.
[457] Bed.

to the White Hart stayd a little walked to the Castell bayly with him came home read and performed my devotion went downe eat som super went to prayers and to bed.

[fo. 54r]
Easter Sunday, 15 April: Rose at 5 walked into the Castel Baylie to see the Son danced which to ones seeming did move,[458] came in performed my devotion read and meditated till after 8 dressed myselfe read and prayd till 10 went to All Saints heard Mr Hickringall on the 1 Revelation 10 received the ℞ came home and returned thanks to God went to diner performed my devotion went to St James herd Mr Shelton on the 27 Matthew 62 came home read went to my devotion eat som super went to prayers and to bed before 10.

Monday, 16 April: Rose after 5 after I was dressed and performed my devotion was within till after 8 went to Mr Goldsberry playd till after 10 went to Mr Sherleys stayd ¼ of an houer went to St Peters to prayers went to Mr Thompsons stayd ½ an houer came home to diner performed my devotion was within all the afternoone and playd a little and was about making an (I) for a peece after 8 eat som super went to prayers went to my chamber performed my devotion and went to bed.

Tuesday, 17 April: Rose at 5 after I was dressed and performed my devotion was within my chamber till almost 10 went to All Saints to prayers went to Mr Goldsberys playd till after 11 dined there came home after 12 walked to overtake[459] Mrs Ardry and Mrs Thompson found them a little beyound Greensteed cald at Mr Beakons stayd ½ an houer he and his wife walked with us to Aylots stayd an houer and ½ came back to Mr Beakons stayd till after 7 supt there the Doctor sent a horse for his wife I carried her and Aylot Mrs Ardry came home before 9 stayd ½ houer at Mrs Tompsons came home went to prayers to my chamber performed my devotion went to bed.

---

[458] This enigmatic passage, the interpretation of which is not aided by untidy and cramped writing ('danced' may be 'dawnd') may be a strangely worded reference to a sighting of comet observed in the northern hemisphere in April 1677, and documented in Robert Hooke, *Cometa* (London, 1678).

[459] Lloyd's hand is cramped here; this word uncertain.

Wednesday, 18 April: Rose after 5 after I was dressed and performed my devotion was within my chamber till diner about my (I) after diner was till 1 performing my devotion trimed myselfe dressed myselfe went to find Mr Paget but could not came home was in my chamber till after 4, went to the funerall of Mr Samuel Shaw[460] to Trinity saw him buryed came home performed my devotion was within eat som milke went to prayers and to bed.

Thursday, 19 April: Rose at 7 after I was dressed and performed my devotion eat som breakfast was in my chamber about my great peece till after (10) went to Mr Goldsburys stayd till after 12 came home went to diner performed my devotion was in my chamber all the afternoone about my peece the most part playd a little before 8 performed my devotion eat som super went to prayers and to my chamber and to bed.

Friday, 20 April: Rose at 7 after I was dressed and performed my devotion eat som bred and butter was in my chamber till after 9 went to Mr Goldsburys but he was goeing out came back was in my chamber till diner performed my devotion was in my chamber and slept a little was a little about my Peece at 6 walked till 8 came in was below eat som super went to prayers performed my devotion and to bed.

Saturday, 21 April: Rose at 6 after I was dressed and performed my devotion went to my school but stayd not but for somthing I wanted went to Mr Goldsberry playd till 10 came home was below till diner performed my devotion was in my chamber all the afternoone abo[ut] my peece after 7 performed my devotion went downe eat som super went to prayers and to my chamber and to bed.

[fo. 54v]
Sunday, 22 April: Rose after 6 after I was dressed and up read 2 sermons and performed my devotion went downe and eat som tost dressed myselfe and made use of the lettany in Dr Taylor went to St James herd Mr Shelton on the 8 John 36 came home made a short prayer went to diner performed my devotion went to St James heard the same man and text came home read 2 sermons

---

[460] Samuel Shaw was the son of Sir John Shaw, MP for Colchester (see n. 513, **10 July 1677**). He was a lawyer, having studied at Jesus College, Cambridge, before entering Lincoln's Inn in 1669. See *Cantabrigienses*, Vol. 1, pt. 4, 53.

was below read another sermon performed my devotion eat som super went to prayers and to bed.

Monday, 23 April: Rose afer[461] 5 after I was dressed and performed my devotion eat somthing went to school and writt a letter to Policrity kept not school because twas the Coronation of the King[462] came home was within till afer 10 went to All Saints herd Mr Hickringhole on the 92 Psalm 10[463] preach before the Mayor and Aldermen came home went to diner playd a little Mr Crockshall came stayd an houer, performed my devotion, was within about the Italian text of my peece afer 7 went to the Kings Head delivered a letter walked till 8 came in eat som super went to prayers performed my devotion and to bed.

Tuesday, 24 April: Rose at 6 after I was dressed and performed my devotion eat somthing went to school stayd till after 11 came home washed my belt went to diner performed my devotion did a little of the Italian text went to school stayd till after 6 came home mad an end of filling up my Pallumtext[464] playd afor 8 Mr Ardrey came home I delivred a letter to the Carrier went to super performed my devotion went to prayers and to bed.

Wednesday, 25 April: Rose at 6 after I was dressed and performed my devotion eat som breakfast went to school stayd till after 11 came home was below and playd went to diner sat a little performed my devotion went not to school it being St Marks day[465] was in my chamber till 6 making flurishes in it walked till 8 came home eat somthing sate up till 10 went to prayers performed my devotion and to bed.

Thursday, 26 April: Rose at 6 after I was dressed and performed my devotion eat som thing went to school stayd till after 11 came home went to diner performed my devotion went to school stayd till after 5 and after 3 read the sermon preached on the funerall of

---

[461] 'After' or 'afore'. Lloyd had a peculiar, and at times frustrating, habit of changing his habitual spellings and abbreviations as the diary went on.

[462] Charles II was officially crowned king of England and Ireland on 23 April 1661; he had already been crowned king of Scotland at Scone on 1 January 1651.

[463] The choice of sermon reflected the day of national celebration: 'But my horn shalt thou exalt like the horn of an unicorn: I shall be anointed with fresh oil.' Psalms 92:10.

[464] Lloyd means *palimpsest*, a paper or parchment which can be reused when a previous inscription has been erased. The term can also refer to a manuscript in which one text has been overwritten with another, but Lloyd intends the former usage.

[465] The Feast of St Mark the Evangelist, ascribed author of the Gospel of Mark.

the Countis of Pembrooke[466] came home and was a little Flurishing my P:[467] performed my devotion went downe sate below eat som super and after Ironed som of my Cravats and hankerchifes went to prayers and to bed.

Friday, 27 April: Rose at 6 after I was dressed and performed my devotion eat a little bred and butter went to school stayd till after 11 came home trimed myselfe went to diner was in my chamber mending and doing up a cravat performed my devotion went to school stayd till after 6 came home was mending som linnen performed my devotion playd went to super playd a little went to prayers and to bed.

Saturday, 28 April: Rose at 5 after I was dressed and performed my devotion was on eat som bred and cheese went to the dancing school but the Master came not stayd till 7 and did over all my dances went to school stayd till after 11 came home was a little about mending a cravat went to diner performed my devotion was in my chamber mending linen till 4 walked till 5 cam in was within playd a little performed my devotion eat som super went prayers and to bed.

[fo. 55r]
Sunday, 29 April: Rose at 7 after I had washt I read 2 sermons performed my devotion went downe and dressed myselfe eat som breakfast dressed myselfe went to church to St James heard Mr Shelton on the 3 Lamentations 39 came home mad a short prayer went to diner sate a little read a sermon performed my devotion went to St James heard the same man and text came home read a sermon and made use of the Letany in Dr Taylor, went downe and sate below a little went to my chamber read a sermon performed my devotion went to super walkd in the hall ½ houer went to prayers and to bed.

Monday, 30 April: Rose at 5 after I was dressed and performed my devotion was in my chamber a little putting my things in order, eat

---

[466] Edward Rainbowe, *A Sermon Preached at the Funeral of the Right Honorable Anne Countess of Pembroke, Dorset, and Montgomery* (London, 1677). Anne, countess of Pembroke etc., is better known as Lady Anne Clifford (d. 22 March 1676). She was the author of an important series of diaries and memoirs: see Jessica L. Malay, *Anne Clifford's Autobiographical Writing, 1590–1676* (Manchester, 2018).

[467] Lloyd may have meant 'my piece' or a flourished letter 'P'.

som breakfast set Alice a coppy went to school stayd till after 11 went to Mr Goldsberry playd till after 12 came home went to diner performed my devotion went to school stayd till after 6 came home playd a little performed my devotion went to super Alice read went to prayers and to bed.

Tuesday, 1 May: Rose after 6 went downe, greased my boots washt dressed myselfe performed my devotion, was in my chamber about making a coller to my cloth coate, after 10 went to St Peeters to prayers stayd a little at Mr Sherleys came home, set my chamber to rights put all my things into my closset, performed my devotion after 2 went to diner, was in my chamber mending stockings set Peg and Allice a Copy after 7 went downe was below a little went to Mr Smith stayd a little carried a letter to the Carrier for my deere Policrity came home after 9 Mr Ardrey was not com in <performed my devotion> stayd up till after 10 went to prayers and to bed.

Wednesday, 2 May: Rose at 6 after I was dressed and performed my devotion eat som bred and butter went to school stayd till after 11 came home was Ill eat som diner performed my devotion, was so bad I was forst to ly downe and could not go to school at 3 went to bed was very bad about 9 sent to Dr Tompson who came and gave me somthing to make me sweat but did not, I performed no devotion but ejaculations.

Thursday, 3 May: Rose at 6 after I was dressed and performed my devotion went to school not being very well stayd till after 11 came home sate by the fier and playd a little went to diner performed my devotion went to school stayd till after 5 came home playd a litte went to Trinity to Mrs Robertsons funerall sermon which was preacht by Mr Powell on the 1 Corinthians 15 last[468] came home performed my devotion eat som supper went to prayers and to bed at 10.

Friday, 4 May: Rose after 5 after I was dressed and performed my devotion eat somthing went to the dancing school stayd almost an houer nobody came, I came away to my school stayd till after 11 came home, performed my devotion sate by the fier went to diner and to school stayd till after 6 came home was within performed my devotion was troubled to know how to get 3^{li} to pay Peak for the school Mrs Ardrey promised it eat som super went to prayers and to bed.

---

[468] 1 Corinthians 15:58.

Saturday, 5 May: Rose at 6 after I was drest and performed my devotion eat som tost went to school stayd till after 11 payd Mr Farman Peaks[469] rent which I borrowed of Mrs Ardrey came home mended a payre of stockings performed my devotion went to diner was in my chamber till after 3 about taking of[470] the lace from my cloth breeches playd a little after 6 performed my devotion was in my chamber till 8 went to super walked in the chamber[471] till 10 went to prayers and to bed.

[fo. 55v]
Sunday, 6 May: Rose before 7 after I was up washt myselfe read a sermon where I found a greate deale of comfort performed my devotion went downe not being very well sate by the fier eat a little broth drest myselfe went to church to All Saints herd Mr Hickringill on the 5 Ma: 24[472] came home made a short prayer went to diner read a sermon performed my devotion went to St Giles herd Mr Powell on rose againe for our Justification[473] came home not being well lay downe till after 6 walked a little in the garden read a sermon performed my devotion after 8 eat som super herd the children[474] read went to prayers and to bed.

Monday, 7 May: Rose at 6 after I had putt up my things I Irond the day before went downe and washt, drest myselfe performed my devotion eat somthing went to school stayd till after 11 went to Mr Goldsberry playd till after 12 came home performed my devotion went to diner to school stayd till after 6 came home stayd a little, went to St James heard a funerall sermon preacht by Mr Bridges[475] on the 1 Philippians 23:24 came home eat som super performed my devotion I went to prayers and to bed.

---

[469] Lloyd's sense is confusing here; he is referring to two individuals, and Farman was an intermediary of some kind for the landlord, Peak.
[470] 'Off'.
[471] This word is obscured by ink.
[472] This could mean Matthew or Mark.
[473] 'But for us also, to whom it shall be imputed, if we believe on him that raised up Jesus our Lord from the dead; [25] Who was delivered for our offences, and was raised again for our justification.' Romans 4:24–25.
[474] Originally 'child:'.
[475] There is no 'Bridges' amongst the Colchester clergy in the 1670s, but rather curiously the nearby villages of Wivenhoe and Alresford (which lie two miles apart) both had rectors named Samuel Bridge at this time; one of them seems the most likely candidate here. See *Cantabrigienses*, Vol. 1, pt. 1, 214, for details of both; *CCEd* Person ID: 4998 (Alresford); and 86489 (Wivenhoe).

Tuesday, 8 May: Rose after 5 after I was dressed and performed my devotion went to Mr Goldsberys playd till neere 8 went to school stayd till after 11 came to Fane brothers and made an end of a haft for a penknife came home went to diner performed my devotion put up the ends of my perrywig went to school stayd till after 6 came home was in my chamber cutting of the silver thred from som old buttons walked a little came in performed my devotion eat som super I went to prayers and to bed.

Wednesday, 9 May: Rose after 5 after I was dressed and performed my devotion eat som[thing] went to William Balls got my knife blade put in and my pen knife mad a tang[476] went to school stayd till after 11 went to Mr Goldsberys playd a little dined there, came home performed my devotion went to school stayd till after 6 came home playd a little fitted my pen knife eat som super sat up till after 10 went to prayers and to bed.

Thursday, 10 May: Rose at 5 Mr Ardrey went for London I trimed myselfe and dressed myselfe performed my devotion eat som breakfast went to Mr Goldsberry playd a little came to my school at 8 stayd till after 11 went to the dancing school stayd an houer and did over my dances came to dine performed my devotion went to school stayd till after 5 went to the dancing school stayd till almost 8 came home walked into the Baily came in eat som super performed my devotion I went to prayers and to bed.

Friday, 11 May: Rose after 6 when I was dressed and performed my devotion eat somthing went to school stayd till after 11 came home was in my chamber and performed my devotion went to diner and to school stayd till after 7 came home playd a little performed my devotion eat som super sate up till after 10 went to prayers and to bed.

Saturday, 12 May: Rose after 5 after I was dressed and performed my devotion eat somthing went to Mr Goldsberry he was not within I went to William Balls and got my penkife don went to school stayd till after 11 came home went to diner performed my devotion went to Mr Chapells stayd an houer came home at 7 was in my chamber performed my devotion sate up till after 10 I went to prayers and to bed.

---

[476] The tang of a blade; the metal of the blade forms the core of the handle, strengthening the knife, *OED*.

Sunday, 13 May: Rose at 5 and tooke som powder to purge walked in my chamber at 7 performed my devotion, kept within all day at 12 went to diner and performed my devotion at 4 read 2 sermons performed my devotion at 7 eat a little super and went to bed at 10.

[fo. 56r]
Monday, 14 May: Rose at 5 and tooke a powder dressed myselfe performed my devotion stayd within till 8 went to school stayd till after 11 went to Mr Goldsberry playd a little, came home performed my devotion went to diner and to school stayd till after 6 came home was within at 8 performed my devotion playd a little eate som super went to prayers and to bed after 10.

Tuesday, 15 May: Rose at 6 after I was dressed and performed my devotion eat somthing went to school stayd till after 11 came home performed my devotion went to diner and to school stayd till after 6 came home was about my Chronagram went to the Kings Head to Mrs Linford stayd till after 9 hyred a horse to carry her to Dedham[477] eat somthing went to prayers, performed my devotion and to bed.

Wednesday, 16 May: Rose after 5 after I was dressed and performed my devotion went to the Kings Head stayd for Mrs Linford till after 8 carried her to Dedham came thether before 10 stayd till 7 came home performed my devotion and went to bed.

Thursday, 17 May: Rose after 5 tooke my powder dressed myselfe performed my devotion was a little about my Chronogram went to school stayd till after 11 came home was a little about it again went to diner performed my devotion went to school stayd till after 5 came home was a little againe about it performed my devotion playd a little, sate up till afor 9 not being very well I went to bed.

Friday, 18 May: Rose after 5 tooke my powder dressed myselfe was very ill walked and sate till after 8 went to school stayd till after 11 came home lay downe was very Iill [*sic*] eat an egg lay downe till almost 2 performed my devotion went to school stayd till after 6 came home, was ill I eat a little super performed my devotion playd a little sate up till after 10 went to prayers and to bed.

---

[477] A village about nine miles north-east of Colchester.

Saturday, 19 May: Rose at 5 after I was dressed and performed my devotion eat som breakfast went to Mr Goldsberry he was not within walked a little went to school at 7 stayd till after 11 came home, performed my devotion went to diner was in my chamber sewing the lace on my hat and I was about my chronagram playd a little walked a little in the evening eat som super performed my devotion sate up till 10.

Sunday, 20 May: Rose at 6 after I was ~~dress~~ washt, read a sermon used the Lettany in Dr Taylors went downe stayd a little read 2 sermons more performed my devotion went downe eat som breakfast dressed myselfe went to Church heard Mr Shelton on 3 Lamentations 39 came home made a short prayer went to diner read a sermon performed my devotion went to St James heard the same man and text came home lay downe a little walked in the garden a little read a sermon performed my devotion walked in the chamber eate a little bred and butter sate up till after 9 went to prayers and bed.

Monday, 21 May: Rose after 5 tooke my powder was Ill after it performed my devotion at 8 went to school stayd till after 11 went to Mr Goldsberry playd a little came home performed my devotion went to diner to school stayd till after 6 came home was not very well playd a little eat a little bred and butter performed my devotion went to bed.

Tuesday, 22 May: Rose after 6 not being very well eat a little bred and butter walkd a little at 8 went to school stayd till after 11 came home was not well walked in the garden performed my devotion went to diner lay ½ an houer went to school stayd till after 6 went to Goodman Orbells and walked till 8 came in performed my devotion playd a little sate up till 10 went prayers and to bed.

[fo. 56v]
Wednesday, 23 May: Rose after 5 after I was dressed and performed my devotion eat ~~som~~ somthing ~~walked~~ writt a letter to Mrs Gray walked a little went to school stayd till after 11 came home was below went to diner performed my devotion went to school stayd till after 6 came home playd a little performed my devotion eat a little super sate up till after 9 went to prayers and to bed.

Thursday, 24 May: Rose after 7 after I was dressed and performed my devotion was within till 10 went to Mr Colemans stayd not came in was in my chamber about finishing my Itallian text performed my devotion and used the Collect[478] and Psalm and chapter for the day haveing no prayer it being assention day[479] was in my chamber all the afternoone about my text and setting coppyes for Peg and casting up Ardreys rates, performed my devotion playd a little eate a little super went to prayers and to bed.

Friday, 25 May: Rose at 6 after I was dressed and performed my devotion eat som bred and butter went to Faine brothers stayd a little went to school stayd till after 11 came home was getting som cakes and wine for Mrs Linford that was to com to my chamber went performed my devotion went to the White Harte to diner stayd there till after 3 with Mr Mills and his wife and Mrs Alston caried them to my chamber stayd till 6 went to the White Harte stayd till after 7 I walked came to my chamber performed my devotion playd a little walked in the back side went to prayers and to bed.

Saturday, 26 May: Rose after I was dressed and performed my devotion went to Mr Goldsberry playd a little went to school stayd till after 11 performed my devotion at my school came home dressed myselfe to goe to Mr Chappells went to diner at 12 tooke horse stayd there till 6 came home at 8 performed my devotion eat som super I went to prayers and to my chamber and to bed.

Sunday, 27 May: Rose at 7 after I had read a sermon used the Lettany in Dr Taylor went downe and washt stayd a little went up read another sermon performed my devotion dressed myselfe eat som breakfast went to St Jame[s] herd Mr Shelton on the 3 Lamentations 39 and 40 came home mad a short prayer went to diner performed my devotion lay a little went to St James heard the same man and text came home stayd till 5 went agane to St James heard Mr Shelton Chatichis[480] the Children[481] came home performed my devotion walked in the Castle Lanes with Mr Ardrey and

---

[478] 'A name given to "a comparatively short prayer, more or less condensed in form, and aiming at a single point, or at two points closely connected with each other" [...] Applied particularly to the prayer, which varies with the day, week, or octave, said before the Epistle in the Mass or Eucharistic service, and in the Anglican service also in Morning and Evening Prayer', *OED*.

[479] The Feast of the Ascension, which celebrates the bodily ascension of Jesus to Heaven. It is held on a Thursday, on the fortieth day of Easter.

[480] Catechize.

[481] Originally 'Child:'. It is unclear whether Lloyd meant 'children' or was using a colon as punctuation; I have chosen the former.

his wife went to super went home with Mr Smith walked in the Castle bayly came in went to prayers and to bed.

Monday, 28 May: Rose at 4 after I was dressed and performed my devotion put up my perrywiggs went to Mr Goldsberry he was goeing out came home put up my cloathes to send to London eat som bred and butter went to school stayd till after 11 came home was below till after diner performed my devotion went to school stayd till after 3 came home performed my devotion walkd a little sate up till after 9 went to prayers and bed.

Tuesday, 29 May: Rose after 3 dressed myselfe performed my devotion set out for Dedham after 4 got thether after 6 stayd there till after 7 was with Mrs Linford went to church heard Mr Lander[482] on the 41 Isaiah 16 dined at Mr Mills came in after 9 performed my devotion eat som super went to prayers and bed.

Wednesday, 30 May: Rose before 6 sent my things to London performed my devotion went to Mr Goldsberry he was not within came back stayd till 8 went to school stayd till after 11 came home went to diner performed my devotion went to school stayd till after 6 came home was providing for my Journey performed my devotion eat somthing went to bed.

[fo. 57r]
Thursday, 31 May: Rose ½ houer after 12 got my horse redy dressed myselfe performed my devotion tooke horse for London ¼ before 2 got to Ingerstone at 6 eat som Rost beefe stayd till 7 met Mr Warden of Wadham[483] Mr Thorneton Mr Freake Mr Potts went with them to Ilford[484] there left them came to the Cross Keys in Gracechurch Streete at 11 went to Mrs Elizabeth Lynford delivered her a letter stayd ¼ of an houer went to Mrs K: Harriss delivered her a letter stayd ½ houer went to Mrs Gray stayd till after 4 took horse at the Cross keys came

---

[482] John Launder, vicar of St Mary Dedham from 1672 until his death in 1678: see *Cantabrigienses*, Vol. 1, pt. 3, 51.

[483] If Lloyd meant 'Master Warden of Wadham', as opposed to a person named 'Mr Warden' or similar, he met Gilbert Ironside the Younger (1632–1701), who was warden of Wadham College, Oxford, from 1665 until 1689. Lloyd's brother, Nicholas, was an alumnus of Wadham and had been chaplain to the previous warden, Walter Blandford, so George may have had some previous familiarity with Ironside.

[484] Ilford, formerly a town in its own right, is now part of east London.

to Newington after 5 was there till after 7 eat som super to prayers I performed my devotion and went to bed at 9.

Friday, 1 June: Rose at 9 after I was dressed and performed my devotion walked to the dining roome and read in the Manuell for Winton College after 11 I went to diner <performed my devotion> at 12 went with Mr Turner over the watter to Old Pallace yard[485] I went to Mr Cratches and bespoake a violin for Mr Goldsbury went to Mr Smiths chamber but could not find him went to Mr Cloughs to see about a watch, sold my old silver for 17^s went to Mrs ~~Huff~~ Huffnells delivered her a letter, went to Mr Sicks delivered him a letter went to Mrs Gray stayd till almost 9 came home performed my devotion and went to bed after 10.

[*The rest of this folio and the following has been rather roughly cut out.*]

[fo. 57v *BLANK*]

[fo. 58r]
Sunday, 3 June: Whitsunday[486] Rose after 7 after I was dresst and performed my devotion walked in the dining roome went to church heard Mr Turner[487] on 5 Galatians 22 came home was with Mr William Smith and Mr Turner a Lawer[488] till Mr Turner came from the Sacrament went to diner sate a little I performed my devotion went to church heard a strainger on 8 Romans 9:10 came in stayd a little walked over the bridg to Mrs Gray stayd till 9 performed my devotion went to bed.

---

[485] Part of the grounds of Westminster Palace, between the Houses of Parliament and Westminster Abbey.
[486] The seventh Sunday after Easter, Whitsunday or Pentecost celebrates the descent of the Holy Spirit upon the Apostles during the Feast of Weeks.
[487] This individual – the same 'Mr Turner' mentioned several times above and below – is likely to have been Bryan Turner, rector of St Faith under St Paul's, London, *c.*1662, and of Souldern, Oxfordshire *c.*1665 (a mile and a half south of Aynho; note that in the next entry Lloyd and Turner travel together to Souldern). He was later made prebend of Hereford, but died before he could be installed, in 1698. Note his reference to Galatians 5:22; the same chapter and verse was cited in Bryan Turner, *A Sermon Preached before the Right Honourable the Lord Mayor, and Aldermen of London at the Guild-Hall Chappel, Octob. the 28th 1677* (London, 1678), 8. It seems plausible that this was the same sermon being read, in pre-published form, by Lloyd on **6 December 1677**. See *Cantabrigienses*, Vol. 1, pt. 4, 273; *CCEd* Person ID: 167031.
[488] A second 'Mr Turner'.

Monday, 4 June: Rose at 4 dressed myselfe made a short prayer Mr Turner being redy to goe for Souldren tooke horse ½ houer after 4 came to Alisbury ½ houer after 12 dined at the Crowne stayd till almost 7 I got to Aynhoe after 8 eat som super after 10 went to my chamber performed my devotion and to bed.

Tuesday, 5 June: Rose after 8 after I was dressed and performed my devotion eat som breakfast my Brother and I walked till after 10 at 11 went to prayers to Church went to diner I performed my devotion and we went to Dr Bews[489] to Aderbury[490] stayd till 8 came home eat som super performed my devotion and went to bed.

Wednesday, 6 June: Rose afor 7 after I was dressed and performed my devotion my Brother and I went to Mr Turners stayd till 11 came home went to diner performed my devotion playd at Ninepins with my sister went in and sate with Mr Hanslope and my Brother about 3 came in strangers with Mr Lawley and his wife and Mrs Briese and Mrs Ellis stayd till after 7 went to Mr Lawleys with them stayd till after 8 called at Mrs Cartwrights stayd till after 9 cam in performed my devotion and to bed.

Thursday, 7 June: Rose after 7 after I was dressed and performed my devotion eat som breakfast was within till diner performed my devotion stayd within till [?3] went to Mr Hanslops stayd till 4 went to Mr Turner and Mr Friend they stayd till after 5 my Brother and I walked and after my sister and I eat som super performed my devotion and to bed.

Friday, 8 June: Rose at 6 it being a wett morning I dressed myselfe and performed my devotion and got myselfe redy to goe for London but being wett could not till after diner, I performed my devotion and after 2 tooke horse went to Misenden[491] came thether after 8 had a brest of mutton and sallaett there being a

---

[489] William Beaw, DD (1616–1706), bishop of Llandaff (1679). At the time of the diary, Beaw was rector of Adderbury, a living which he held from 1661 until his death. An alumnus of Winchester College and New College, Oxford, and an active Royalist during the Civil Wars, Beaw would have shared much in common with Lloyd and his brother Nicholas. See *ODNB*; *CCEd* Person ID: 7575.

[490] Adderbury, an Oxfordshire village some three and a half miles north-west of Aynho.

[491] Great Missenden, a village in the Chiltern Hills in Buckinghamshire, on the route from Aynho to London.

Wostershiere glassman[492] with me, went to bed and performed my devotion in bed.

Saturday, 9 June: Rose after 2 dressed myselfe performed short devotion dranke a little burnt brandy before 4 tooke horse with 2 men of Misenden and Mr Rogers came to London at 9 came to Newington before 10 dressed myselfe and trimed myselfe eat som diner went into London called on Mrs Elizabeth Linford stayd a little delivered a letter to Dr Roberts and one to Mr Langerman bought 2 penknifes after 4 came to Mrs Gray stayd all day Lay there that night she being with me [*shorthand*] till 12 performed short ejaculations in bed.

Sunday, 10 June: Rose at 9 dressed myselfe and performed my devotion went to Allgate church[493] herd the Minister on the 25 Matthew 6 came to Mrs Gray dined there we went to Allgate Church heard the Lecturer on 1 John 5:7 went to her house stayd there all day Lay there she being on the [*shorthand*] till 12.

[fo. 58v]
Monday, 11 June: Rose after 5 dressed myselfe performed my devotion went out to carry a letter to send to my Brother called on Mr Smith dranke my morning draught went to Mr[?s] K Harris stayd an houer Mrs Linford came in I went with her to the top of the monument went home with her went to my Barbers and to Mrs Gray. Was in her chamber till she came I eat som diner performed my devotion and after diner we lay up [*shorthand*] she [*shorthand*] but would not let me feele [*shorthand*] through [*shorthand*] Coat we were very tird[494] after 6 I tooke my leave went to Newington and Mr Smith being there went to Mr Rogers dranke 2 bottles came in went to super I put up my thing[s] and went to bed.

Tuesday, 12 June: Rose after 3 dressed myselfe performed my devotion tooke horse at 4 went to the Kings Armes set up my horse went to call Mrs Linford went with her to the Coach at 6 set out after 11 came to ~~Ingers~~ Ingerstone dined Mr Cullever a French boy Mrs Linford and Mr Powells sister came to Colchester

---

[492] A dealer in glassware or glazier; in the 17th century, the former occupation was sometimes used as a pretext for begging, so Lloyd may have been engaging in an act of charitable generosity: see *OED*.
[493] Probably St Botolph Aldgate: see n. 350, **27 August 1676**.
[494] Lloyd's hand is ambiguous.

after 6 I was up and down to get a horse to carry Mrs Linford to Dedham at last her Cousen came I went to my chamber performed my devotion eat som super went to prayers and to bed.

Wednesday, 13 June: Rose after 6 dressed myselfe performed my devotion was within till almost 8 went to school stayd till ~~after 11 came home~~ almost 11 went to prayers to Trinity came home went to diner performed my devotion went to school stayd till after 6 came home mended the handle of my sword eat som bred and butter <performed my devotion> went to prayers and to bed.

Thursday, 14 June: Rose at 6 after I was dressed and performed my devotion went to Mr Goldsberry he was not within came to my chamber strung my violin at 8 went to school stayd till after 11 went to Mr Lamberts stayd till almost 12 came home to diner performed my devotion playd a little went to school stayd till after 5 came home playd till after 6 went to dancing school stayd till after 9 walked in the Castle Lanes with Mr Je.[495] Shaw and Mr Seavill came home went to prayers I eat a little bred and cheese performed my devotion and went to bed.

Friday, 15 June: Rose before 6 after I was dressed and performed my devotion was in my chamber mending stockings eat som breakfast went to school stayd till after 11 came home was within went to diner performed my devotion lay on the bed ½ of an houer went to school stayd till after 6 came home playd a little performed my devotion playd a little eat som bred and cheese went to prayers and to bed.

Saturday, 16 June: Rose after 5 after I was dressed and performed my devotion went to Mr Giles stayd a little came to school stayd till after 11 came home eat som diner performed my devotion went to Dedham stayd at Mr Mills till almost 8 came home at 10 performed my devotion eat som super went to prayers and to bed.

Sunday, 17 June: Rose at 7 after I was dressed and performed my devotion eat somthing went to St James herd Mr Shelton on 3 Lamentations 40 came home mad a short prayer went to diner performed my devotion lay a little went to church heard the same man

---

[495] Perhaps Jeremy Shaw, son of Sir John Shaw, MP for Colchester (see n. 513, **10 July 1677**). Born on 10 January 1656, he was admitted to Colchester Grammar School in 1672, and was later a JP for Essex, Round, *Colchester School*, 64–65.

and text came home slept till after 6 performed my devotion eat som super sat up till 10 went to prayers and to bed.

[fo. 59r]
Monday, 18 June: Rose after 4 after I was dressed went to the 3 Crownes to carry Mrs Linfords gowne to send to London came home performed my devotion was puting my Linnen and things in order eat som breakfast went to school stayd till after 11 went to Mr Goldsberry playd a little came home performed my devotion went to diner and to school stayd till after 6 came home playd a litte performed my devotion eat som super stayd up till after 10 Mr Ardrey came not in I went to bed.

Tuesday, 19 June: Rose after 6 after I was dressed and performed my devotion eat a little brekfast went to Balls to bespeake a blad, and to Bollers to pay for sowling[496] my shooes went to the castle and walkd went to school stayd till after 11 came home liquored[497] my boots went to my chamber performed my devotion went to school stayd till after 6 went to Mr Grays stayd till 7 came home playd a little eat somthing performed my devotion sate up till almost 11 went to prayers and to bed.

Wednesday, 20 June: Rose after 5 after I was dressed and performed my devotion went to Mr Goldsberys playd a little went to the Kingshead pasture came back and playd a little went to school stayd till after 11 came home was in my chamber performed my devotion went to diner and to school stayd till after 6 came home playd a little performed my devotion went to Thomas Wards stayd an houer came home eat som bred and butter sate up till 11 went to prayers and to bed.

Thursday, 21 June: Rose after 5 after I was dressed and performed my devotion eat som breakfast went to Balls to get my semiter[498] goe into the scabard caled at Mr Fordhams for Mrs Lynfords watch went to school stayd till after 12 came home put on the hilt of my sword went to diner performed my devotion went to school stayd till after 5 went to Goodwife Tibbals eat creame and strawberries and sullybub[499]

---

[496] Soling.
[497] Oiled.
[498] Scimitar.
[499] Syllabub, dessert, popular in the 17th century, made by curdling sweetened cream or milk with alcohol and fruit juice.

stayd till 8 gave her a shilling came home playd a little performed my devotion went to prayers and bed.

Friday, 22 June: Rose after 5 after I was dressed and performed my devotion went to Mr Goldsberry playd a little went to school stayd till after 11 came home playd a little performed my devotion went to diner lay downe a little went to school stayd till after 6 came home playd a little performed my devotion walked a little came in sate up till after 9 went to bed.

Saturday, 23 June: Rose after 5 trimed myselfe dressed myselfe performed my devotion went to Mr Fordhams to see for my watch went to school stayd till after 11 performed my devotion in the school went to the 3 Crownes to speake with Mr Carrs Brother about his daughters Learning to rite went to diner and at 1 I went to Dedham came thether a little after 2 stayd ther till after 6 went with the 2 Mrs Linfords to Mrs Alstons stayd ¾ of an houer went back to Mr Mills's stayd till after 7 came home put my mare to pasture came home went to my chamber performed my devotion went to bed.

Sunday, 24 June: Rose at 6 after I had washed myselfe read in Judg Hales first booke[500] went downe eate som bred and butter dressed myselfe went to St James heard Mr Shelton on the 3 Lamentations 40 came home made a short prayer went to diner Lay dowe downe a little performed my devotion went to Church heard the same man and text came home lay a little then read in Judg Hales his booke, and performed my devotion and was in my chamber till 8 eat som super after 9 went to bed.

[fo. 59v]
Monday, 25 June: Rose before 6 after I had put up my cloathes dressed myselfe and performed my devotion and used the lettenay in Dr Taylor went to school it being a fayre[501] had but 4 boys stayd there and read in Judg Halles his book till 11 went to St Nicholas Church heard Mr Shelton preach the fayre sermon on

---

[500] Matthew Hale, *Contemplations Moral and Divine by a Person of Great Learning and Judgement* (London, 1676). *Contemplations Moral and Divine: The Second Part* was published the same year. Both were anonymous, but an edition from 1677 can be found with a frontispiece depicting Hale (1609–1676).

[501] Colchester celebrated a four-day fair for the Feast of St John the Baptist (24 June). It was granted to St John's Abbey at its foundation, and was confirmed by Henry I in *c.*1104. *VCHE*, 269–274.

the 8 Luke 37 came home performed my devotion eat som diner lay upon my bed and slept a little after 2 I read in Judge Hale's booke about the consideration of Christ and I made my confession out of Dr Taylor and renewed my Covenant walked in the chamber next the streete till 7 went to St James herd Mr Shelton preach Mrs Lawrences[502] funerall sermon on the 14 Romans 12 came home performed my devotion read 2 letters one from Mrs Gray and one from Mr Turner walked till 9 came in eat a little bred and cheese sate till 10 went to prayers and to bed.

Tuesday, 26 June: Rose after 4 was in my chamber mending stockings till almost 6 went downe washt myselfe and dressed myselfe performed my devotion went to Mr Goldsburys playd a little went to school writt a letter to Mrs Lynford and Coppy of one to Mrs Gray stayd till after 11 having by 11 5 or 6 boys gave them leave to play by reason of the fayer came to Fayne brothers and was a little mending Mr Mills box went home to diner performed my devotion was mending stockings till after 4 playd a little at 7 went to Fayne brothers agane to mend the box but cold not do it I performed my devotion and eat som super and playd a little sat up til after 10 went to prayers and to bed.

Wednesday, 27 June: Rose at 6 after I was dressed and performed my devotion went to Hitchersons to cary Mrs Lynfords box caled at Mr Fordhams he was not within I walked in the castle lanes a little went to school stayd till after 11 went to Mr Goldsberry he was not within came home went to diner performed my devotion set Mrs Ardrey a coppy went to school stayd till after 6 went to Mr Carrs stayd till 7 came home performed my devotion playd a little eat som super playd a little went to prayers and at 10 to bed.

Thursday, 28 June: Rose at 6 after I was dressed and performed my devotion went to Mr Goldsberry but playd not came back to Mr Fordhams stayd till after 8 went to school stayd till after 11 came home went performed my devotion went to <diner and> to school stayd till after 5 came home went to Fayne brothers and put on the hilt of my simiter performed my devotion walked a little came in eat som bred and butter sate up till 10 went to prayers and to bed.

---

[502] Entered in the parish register as Martha, wife of Nathaniel Lawrence, a prominent figure in Colchester, and son of Thomas Lawrence who had been mayor in 1643–1644. Nathaniel was mayor of the town four times (1672, 1679, 1683, 1709) and was elected to represent Colchester in Parliament in 1685. He was a dissenter or 'occasional conformist'. ERO, D/P 138/1/7; *Hist. Parl. 1660–1690*, Vol. 2, 714.

Friday, 29 June: Rose at 2 dressed myselfe and performed my devotion and before 3 set out with Ashley for Dedham came thether at 5 stayd there till 9 walked with Mrs Lynford to Barfield[503] to prayers met an old Gentellman which carried us into his house and very civily treated us and we saw his grandchild a pretty undrest[504] young genttellwoman with whome Mrs Lynford made a greate friendship went to prayers came back to the house stayd till after 12 and the minister came to us and gave us a bottle of Cowslip wine[505] we went to Dedham and went to diner after diner I was with the 2 sisters in the house till 4 then

[fo. 60r]
came in Mr Lander and his wife and Mrs Alston we sate in the parlour till after 5 playd at Ninepins till after 7 about 8 set forth the 2 Ladys and Mr Mills goeing part of the way with us.

Saturday, 30 June: Rose after 6 not being very well dressed myselfe performed my devotion eat a little bred and butter went to Hitchisons to cary Mrs Mills her box went to school stayd till after 11 I read one sermon and part of another of Mr Ardreys Fathers[506] came home went to diner performed my devotion lay downe after 1 slept till after 2 was within till after 4 went to Mr Goldsberry he was not within stayd a little at Mr Smiths shop a little at Mr Farmans went to Mr Fordhams stayd a little came home got my things redy to weare the next day performed my devotion trimed myselfe eat som bred and butter walked in the field called at Mr Goldsberry he was not com in I came to Puckels and hyred his horse to go to de Dedham the Next day came home and went to bed Mr Ardrey being out and all gon to bed had no prayers.

Sunday, 1 July: Rose after 3 dres: performed my devotion went to Puckels and called the man to get my horse to goe to Dedham came home dressed myselfe tooke horse a little before 5 got there after 6

---

[503] This seems to be an error on Lloyd's part; there is no 'Barfield' in the vicinity, and the Essex villages of Great Bardfield and Little Bardfield lie some thirty miles to the west of Dedham. He may, however, have been referring to a private property of which I can find no trace.

[504] Unkempt or ill-groomed, *OED*; a rare example of Lloyd being explicitly disparaging.

[505] A wine made from the common perennial, cowslip. The well-known diarist John Evelyn included a recipe for cowslip wine in his *Acetaria: A Discourse of Sallets* (London, 1699), unpaginated.

[506] John Ardrey, at the time rector of Great Musgrave, Westmorland (1671–1684). See Introduction, n. 63.

went in and nobody was there stayd a little went into the garden found Phyloclea[507] stayd ½ houer went in dressed myselfe read a little eat som bred and butter at 10 went to Church heard Mr Lander on the 4 James 7 came home went to diner sate a little went into the garden with Phyloclea stayd till Church time heard the same man and text came home sate a little within walked into the garden and Mrs Betty came to us gathered som Currance[508] for them went in to super I stayd till after 8 came away came home after 9 went to prayers and to my chamber performed my devotion and to bed.

Monday, 2 July: Rose at 6 after I was dressed and performed my devotion was within till 8 eat som bred and butter went to school stayd till 11 came home to Mr Mills dranke 2 bottles of Ale he went home I sent a letter to Mrs Lynford and had one from her went to diner performed my devotion lay a little after 1 went to school stayd till after 6 came home playd a little performed my devotion eat som super playd a little went to prayers and after 9 to bed.

Tuesday, 3 July: Rose after 5 after I was dressed and performed my devotion went to Mr Goldsberry playd a little went to school stayd till after 11 came home was in my chamber playd a little went to diner performed my devotion went to school stayd till after 6 came home playd a little mended a hole or two in my shamy breeches performed my devotion eat som super stayd a little sat up till 10 went to prayers and to bed.

Wednesday, 4 July: Rose after 5 after I was dressed read in Judg Halles 2^d book performed my devotion mend a payre of stockings at 7 went to Balls and seene a blade forged went to Hitchesons for Mrs Mills her box went to school stayd till after 11 went home was below lay downe a little performed my devotion went to diner and to school stayd till after 6 walked with Mr Sewell meett[509] Mr Sherley stayd till after 7 came in playd a little performed my devotion eat som super sat up till after 9 went to prayers and to bed.

[fo. 60v]
Thursday, 5 July: Rose after 5 after I was dressed and performed my devotion went to Mr Goldsberry playd a little went to school

---

[507] Perhaps one of the Lynford sisters; cf. entry and note (n. 81) for **7 September 1675**.
[508] Currants?
[509] Handwriting obscure here; uncertain.

stayd till after 11 came home trimed myselfe performed my devotion went to diner and to school stayd till after 5 came home put on my boots got redy to goe to Dedham performed my devotion before I went at 6 I went out of towne came thether about 7 was within till 8 went into the garden see [*sic*] them play at ninepins went in eat som super playd till after 10 and was about to com home but I stayd all night after 12 went to our chamber the young Ladys went in with us I Kisst them both upon my bed I went to bed had but little or no sleepe at 4 I rose went into Mrs Lynfords chamber and stayd till almost 7 sate by her beds side and Kist her several times more than I ever did dressed myselfe performed my devotion eat som breakfast stayd till after 8 came home after 9 went to school stayd till after 11 came in lay downe till 12 went to diner performed my devotion lay a little after 1 went to school stayd till after 6 came to my chamber playd a little performed my devotion went to Fayne brothers and cleaned the old forke that lay in the window for myselfe came in eat a little bred and butter playd a little I went to prayers Mr Ardrey being drunke at Mr Smiths I went to <bed.>

Saturday, 7 July: Rose at 7 after I was dressed and performed my devotion went to school stayd till after 11 came home was not very well lay downe a little about 12 Mr Flack of Hadley[510] came and agreed with me to teach his son to write went to diner performed my devotion was within till 5 walked till 6 then made short cakes performed my devotion went to prayers and to bed.

Sunday, 8 July: Rose before 7 after I was dress up washt myselfe and read in Judg Hales booke 2^d part performed my devotion went downe and eat somthing was not very well stayd below till after 9 dressed myselfe went to St James heard Mr Shelton on the 13 Hebrews 5 came home mad a short prayer went to diner lay a little performed my devotion went to St James herd the same man and text came home read in Judg Halls at 5 went to St James heard Mr Shelton Chatichise and expound came hoe home read in Judge Hale and performed my devotion went downe eat a little bred and buter at 9 went to prayers and to bed.

Monday, 9 July: Rose before 6 after I was drest and performed my devotion eat som bred breakfast went to Mr Goldsberry playd a little went to school stayd till after 11 came home playd went to diner

---

[510] Seemingly Hadleigh, Suffolk, a town some fifteen miles north of Colchester – a strange choice for a prospective pupil, but Lloyd's hand is quite clear.

performed my devotion received a letter from Mrs Gray went to school stayd till after 6 and wrote a letter to M[?rs]: G[?ray] at 5 John Basher came and told me Stratton had an action against me Mr Smith was my pledg[511] I gave him ½ a crowne for his fees after I came home I read in Judg Halles about the bearing of affliction[512] performed my devotion and eat a little milke told Mr Ardrey about my busines and desired his ayd in it went to prayers and to my chamber and stated my matter for him to aske advise about it.

Tuesday, 10 July: Rose at 5 read in Judg Hales after I was dressed and then performed my devotion at 6 eat somthing and gave Mr Ardrey my [*deleted*] paper to aske Captane Renholds advise I went to Mr Goldsberys playd a little came to school stayd till after 11 came home playd a little went to diner performed my devotion

[fo. 61r]
called at Sir John Shaws[513] to speake with Mr Smith went to school stayd till after 6 performed my devotion in my school went to Mr Smith at Charles Miles he was busie walked till after 7 came to him sent for R: Stratton he was so high[514] that there could be no composition he refused to give a receipt for what he had received of me he went away in a passion and I free from one I came home received a letter from Phyloclea playd a little eat somthing went to prayers and to bed.

Wednesday, 11 July: Rose at 6 after I was dressed and performed my devotion calld at Mr Fordhams but stayd not stayd a little at Balls and called at Mr Hitchinson went to Mr Smiths he was not up called at Mr Balls to chaing a whip called at Goldsberys to see for his mare he was to goe out, came to Mr Smiths and advised what Attorney to go to and his oppinion was Mr Earle, I met Jo: Blumfield and went to

---

[511] 'A person who becomes surety for another; a bail; a surety; a member of a frankpledge or frithborh', *OED*. It is unclear, however, whether Lloyd was using this term strictly accurately, or in what capacity Smith acted.
[512] See Hale, *Contemplations*, 53–102.
[513] Sir John Shaw (1617–1690) was one of Colchester's most prominent and powerful citizens. Educated at Cambridge and Lincoln's Inn, he followed his father into town and county politics during the Civil War and Interregnum, in spite of his Royalist sympathies. Shaw was recorder for the town in 1655, 1658–1677, and 1688. He was elected to represent Colchester in Richard Cromwell's Parliament in 1659, re-elected in 1660, and again to the Cavalier Parliament in 1661, where he was a moderately active member. Aligned with the 'Court' party, Shaw was active in persecuting dissenters, and was described as 'thrice vile' by Shaftesbury; *Hist. Parl. 1660–1690*, Vol. 3, 428–429.
[514] Angry, *OED*.

the Alecoate and stayd ½ an houer talked about R: Stratton I went to Mr Earle he was not com from London, went to school stayd till after 11 went home playd a little went to diner performed my devotion went to school stayd till after 6 came home playd a little went to Kings Meddow to see Mr Ardreys mare came home performed my devotion eat som super playd a little while went to prayers and to bed.

Thursday, 12 July: Rose at 6 after I was dressed and performed my devotion was within till 7 eat som bred and butter went to Balls and stayd till 8 fitting my forke and knife went to school stayd till after 11 went to Balls and finished my knife stayd till 12 came home per performed my devotion went to diner, went to Mr Barnwell at William Halls retained him for my Atturney against Stratton went to school stayd till after 5 came in was in my chamber playd a little read in Judg Hales performed my devotion walked till after 8 came in and was stamping hearbs till after 9 eat som super after 10 went to prayers and washt my feete went a bed at 11 dranke the Juse of herbs Liverwort[515] Sorrill[516] etc.

Friday, 13 July: Rose before 6 after I was dressed and performed my devotion was in my chamber drawing out som letters with the pencill eat a little broth at 8 went to school stayd till after 11 came home sowed on a black ribbon on my black coate went to diner performed my devotion went to school stayd till after 6 came home playd a little read in Judg Halles performed my devotion walked into the Castell lanes mett Mr Shaw walked with him till after 9 came in eat som codlings[517] and milke went to prayers and to bed.

Saturday, 14 July: Rose after 5 after I was up was mending a payre of stockings till after 7 dressed myselfe performed my devotion went to school stayd till after 11 came home trimed myselfe went to diner performed my devotion playd a little dressed myselfe to goe to Dedham after 3 I went came thether 6 it rayning I stayd a little by the way I wase there talking with the young women Mr Mills being gon to Chambridg went to super sate up till after 12

---

[515] There are thousands of species of liverworts, or *Marchantiophyta*, so it is impossible to say which precise 'herb' Lloyd was consuming. Historically, as the name suggests, these small non-vascular plants were considered to have beneficial medical effects for liver complaints.
[516] Sorrel is a very common herbaceous plant, occasionally used in cookery today, but very popular in the 17th century.
[517] An unripe or green cooking apple, *OED*.

Mrs Mary being with me in my chamber alone performed my devotion and went to bed.

[fo. 61v]
Sunday, 15 July: Rose after 7[518] after I was dressed and performed my devotion read in a boo[k] of Bishop Halls went to Church at 10 heard a stranger on the 2 Romans 10 came home made a short prayer went to diner performed my devotion went to church heard the same man and text came home was below till super walked in the garden gathered som gooseberrys walked after super I read and Mrs Mary a chapter I went to prayers we went up at 10 Mrs Mary and I sate up till almost 4 I performed my devotion and went to bed.

Monday, 16 July: Rose before 6 performed my devotion dressed myselfe and before 7 came for Colchester was here about 9 went to school stayd till after 11 came home lay on the bed and slept a little went to diner performed my devotion went to school stayd till after 6 came home playd a little performed my devotion eat a little bred and cheese went to bed not being very well.

Tuesday, 17 July: Rose after 7 dressed myselfe performed my devotion went to school stayd till after 11 went to Mr Goldsberry playd a little came home went to diner performed my devotion went to school stayd till after 6 came home playd a little walked ½ an houer performed my devotion eat a little bred and butter sat up till almost 10 went to prayers and to bed.

Wednesday, 18 July: Rose at 6 after I was dressed and performed my devotion eat som breakfast went into Towne to Mr Fordham stayd till almost 8 went to school stayd till after 11 came home was in my chamber a little dressed a sallet[519] performed my devotion went to diner and to school stayd till after 5 came home to Mr Mills stayd with him ½ houer drank one flagon of Alle went back to school stayd till after 6 came home playd a little performed my devotion was within till 8 then walked with Mr Shaw and Mr Sewell till almost 9 went to the Angell[520] to see for a horse but could get none came home went to prayers and to bed.

---

[518] Lloyd overwrote '6' here.
[519] See n. 318, **8 June 1676**.
[520] This tavern was at the corner of Angel Lane and High St., in the parish of St Runwald, D'Cruze, *Colchester People*, Vol. 3, p. 3.

Thursday, 19 July: Rose at 5 performed my devotion trimed myselfe drest myselfe went to Applebees to get a horse but could not got one at Puckles came home at 7 eat a little bred and cheese went to school stayd till 11 came home dressed myselfe performed my devotion went ½ houer after 11 with Mr Savill to Dedham came thether a little after 12 dined at Mr Mills about 2 set out for the Cherry garden came thether after 3 sate under a walnutt tree eat over 10 pound of cherrys had the Musick and we danced 5 or 6 Cuntry dances came away after 7 came to Dedham after 8 stayd till after 9 came to Colchester at 10 I had home my horse came home performed my devotion went to bed.

Friday, 20 July: Rose after 6 dressed myselfe performed my devotion was not very well at 8 I went to school stayd till after 11 came home lay downe till after 12 went to diner performed my devotion went to school stayd till after 6 came home playd a little performed my devotion eat som super playd a little went to prayers after 9 to bed.

Saturday, 21 July: Rose at 6 after I was dressed and performed my devotion eat som breakfast went to Mr Barnwells to see whether Stratton had declared he told me no I went to school stayd till after 11 came home was in my chamber read a little went to diner performed my devotion was within playd a little at 3 went to Mr Fordhams for Mrs Linfords watch came in trimed myselfe helpt wash the Celler at 7 read and performed my devotion sate up till 10 went to prayers and to bed.

[fo. 62r]
Sunday, 22 July: Rose at 7 after I was dres had washt myselfe read in Judg Hales 2^d booke performed my devotion dressed myselfe and read agane till 10 went to St James at the 2^d leason was called out of the Church came home received a letter from Phyloclea to goe into Suffolke with her the next day sent back an answer stayd at home and read 2 sermons and used the lettany in Dr Taylors Golden Grove went to diner read and performed my devotion went to St James heard Mr Shelton on the 13 Hebrews 5 came home went to see for my horse writt a letter to Mrs Gray read eat som sullybub with Mr Roofe of Harwich[521] and Mr Smith and his wife performed my

---

[521] Harwich and Harwich Haven, with its several ports, are 20 miles east of Colchester, at the mouth of the Stour and Orwell estuaries.

devotion and read in Judg Hales mad an end of it eat a little bred and butter sate up till 10 went to prayers and to bed.

Monday, 23 July: Rose at 3 got me redy to goe to Dedham performed my devotion before 4 I tooke horse got there before 5 stayd there till after 7 set forth I carried Mrs Elizabeth Mrs Mary[522] rode single and a man she hyred carryed our things we got to Woodbridg[523] before 11 stayd till almost (1) got to Redlingham[524] about 4 after we had rested a little walked and see the ground and wood came in eat Sulybub at 9 went to super after 10 went to bed I performed my devotion.

Tuesday, 24 July: Rose after 6 after I was dressed had som ejaculation not haveing a place to performed my devotion we weare in the barne an houer went in and treated about the Land[525] first with John Ravence he offered 920^l, afterward Mr Whitman he offered 5^l more[526] we went to diner after (1) set out came to Mr Lomaxes about 4 stayd till 5 went to Schole Inn came thether about 8 stayd there all night, I performed my devotion went to bed, we had milk and butter and cheese for supper.

Wednesday, 25 July: Rose at 3 performed my devotion dressed myselfe dranke and eat one mouthfull of bred and butter tooke horse about ½ houer after 4 came to Ipswitch at 9 at 10 Mr Mills and wife came my horse was so fant[527] and hot he would not eat and wee[528] weare forsed to leave Mrs Elizabeth behind at Mr Golds[529] we walked in the towne after 1 went to diner after walkd into the fayre[530] saw the porcupine walked to the key and to our Inn got redy to come away at 7 tooke horse at 10 came to

---

[522] Cf. n. 81, **7 September 1675**.
[523] Woodbridge is a market town in Suffolk, some 20 miles north-east of Dedham.
[524] This seems likely to mean Rendlesham, six miles north-east of Woodbridge, known for its forests.
[525] Possibly 'Lane'.
[526] Lloyd's lack of exposition is frustrating here, but we can infer from the circumstances of his life that he did not own did not own land of such considerable value himself; it may have belonged to one of the Lynford sisters.
[527] Possibly faint.
[528] Slightly unclear.
[529] Presumably not Mr Goldsberry of Colchester, though Lloyd often abbreviated his name in this way.
[530] A fair was granted to Ipswich on St James's Day (25 July) early in the reign of King John (c.1199) for the benefit of the town's lepers; 'some small Remains' of the tradition were still upheld by the mid 18th century: see John Kirby et al., *The Suffolk Traveller* (London, 1764), 34.

Dedham I was not well went to bed and performed no devotion but only som ejaculations.

Thursday, 26 July: Rose not till 12 being very Ill with a griping and looseness, eat a little mutton stayd there till 8 performed no devotion but ejaculations came home at 9 performed my devotion eat som super went to prayers and to bed.

Friday, 27 July: Rose after 6 dressed myselfe performed my devotion eat somthing went and payd 7^s for my horse went to school stayd till after 11 came home went to diner performed my devotion went to school stayd till after 6 came home playd a little performed my devotion eat som super went to prayers and to bed.

[fo. 62v]
Saturday, 28 July: Rose after 6 after I was dressed performed my devotion eat somthing walked a little in the Castle Lanes went to school stayd till after 11 came home went to diner performed my devotion was within all the afternone playd a little received a letter from Mrs Gray but an odd one writt an Answer, put som cheryes up in brandy eat som super went to prayers and to my chamber performed my devotion went to bed.

Sunday, 29 July: Rose after 5 washt myselfe read and performed my devotion went downe stayd below till after 8 read a sermon dressed myselfe eat somthing went to Trinity herd a Stranger on the 1 Peter 2:7 came home made a short prayer performed my devotion very late before I dined because Peg went to church after diner walked to Greensted with Mr Shaw and Mr ~~Fre~~ Freaman herd Mr Shaw on the 6 Romans 1 and part 2^d verse went with the pa[r]son to his house drunke 2 or 3 bottles of Alle saw his garden came home went into the Castell bayly and into the Castle came in read a sermon performed my devotion eat som super walked into the castle bayly with Mr Shaw and Mr Freeman stayd a little it raned came in made the boy read went to prayers and to bed.

Monday, 30 July: Rose at 7 after I was dressed and performed my devotion went to school stayd till after 11 came home was in my chamber coming[531] my perrywig and making cleane my shoes performed my devotion went to diner eat a few gooseberries went to school stayd till after 6 came home playd a little walkd till 8 came

---
[531] Combing.

in eat som super, sate up till 9 went to prayers performed my devotion and went to bed.

Tuesday, 31 July: Rose after 6 after I was dressed and performed my devotion eat som breakfast went to school stayd till after 11 came home performed my devotion went to diner went into the garden eat som Gooseberrys went to school stayd till after 6 came home playd a little walked in the Castell Lanes came in performed my devotion eat som bred and cheese walked with Mr William Smith to his mothers house came back went to prayers and to bed.

Wednesday, 1 August: Rose after 7 after I was dressed and performed my devotion eat somthing went to school stayd till after 11 came home received a letter from Phyloclea[532] that her sister was not well sent her an answer went to diner performed my devotion went to school stayd till 6 came home went to Dedham to see Mrs Bety when I came they were gon out I walked in the garden after ¾ of an houer Mrs M[?ary] came we walked ¼ of an houer went in and they came in I eat somthing with Mr Mills went out saw him make candles Mrs Mary and I walked into the garden I gave her a greene gowne walked till 11 went into Mrs Betys chamber sate till 12 then I came away came home at 1 performed my devotion went to bed.

Thursday, 2 August: Rose after 5 called Ashley sent home my horse I went to bed againe but could not sleepe lay till almost 8 rose dressed myselfe performed my devotion went to school stayd till after 11 came home performed my devotion went to diner went to school stayd till after 5 came home was not well sate below performed my devotion eat som super went to prayers and to bed.

Friday, 3 August: Rose after 7 dressed myselfe performed my devotion eat somthing went to school stayd till 11 went to Goldsberry stayd a little came home was a little a mending a payre of stockings went to diner performed my devotion went to school stayd till after 6 came home playd a little mended a payre of stockings went to super sate up till 9 went to prayers performed my devotion and went to bed.

---

[532] This strongly suggests that 'Philoclea' or 'Phyloclea' is Mary Lynford: see n. 81, **7 September 1675**.

[fo. 63r]

Saturday, 4 August: Rose after 6 after I was dressed and performed my devotion eat somth[ing] went to school stayd till after 11 stayd at Mr Smiths shop till 12 came home performed my devotion went to diner trimed myselfe wound a bobin a ½ playd a little was within received a letter from Mrs Gray in which she tould me she understood all things were at an end betweene us, I writt an answer, but did not send it, I performed my devotion and playd a little sate up till 9 eat a little tost went to bed had no prayers because Mr Ardrey was fuddled.

Sunday, 5 August: Rose before 7 after I had washt read a sermon performed my devotion went downe eat som breakfast dressed myselfe went to church to All Saints herd Mr Hickeringill on the 20 Exodus 3 came home mad a short prayer went to diner went into the garden eat a few gooseberyes and read a sermon performed my devotion went to St James heard Mr Shelton on the 6 Hebrews 4 2^{d}[533] came home walked in my chamber and meditated read a sermon sat and slept not being very well performed my devotion walked in the Castell Lanes, came in eat som super went to prayers and to bed.

Monday, 6 August: Rose after 5 after I was dressed and performed my devotion supt a few broth, went to Mr Goldsberry playd till 8 went to school stayd till after 11 came home was not well lay downe eat no diner performed my devotion went to school and made a shift to stay till almost 6 came home went to bed being very ill, eat nothing dranke a little burnt wine at 9 Mr Ardrey went to prayers. About 11 I slept.

Tuesday, 7 August: Rose after 7 after I was dressed and performed my devotion went to school stayd till after 11 came home made a little tost and eate performed my devotion went to diner and to school stayd till after 6 came home playd a little walked into the Castle lanes came in eat som super sat up till after 9 went to prayers and to my chamber performed my devotion and to bed.

Wednesday, 8 August: Rose at 6 after I was dressed and performed my devotion went to Mr Goldsberry playd till 8 went to school came home performed my devotion went to diner after

---

[533] 'For it is impossible for those who were once enlightened, and have tasted of the heavenly gift, and were made partakers of the Holy Ghost...' Hebrews 6:4. Presumably Lloyd meant that the sermon focused on the latter half of this verse.

diner came Mrs Mills and Mrs Linfords they stayd at my chamber till almost 2 drank a glass or 2 of sack eat som short cakes walked to Mr Aingers to buy som ribbon went into the Castell Bayly came to my chamber went to Mr Tospoites[534] garden gathered som Goosbery [s] they eat som bred and butter, stayd till after 4 went to Mr ~~Hich~~ Hitchensons Mrs Mary gave me a silver taster[535] cost her 9^s went to the White Hart had a tankard stayd till after 6 I walkd in St John's field came in before 8 performed my devotion eat som broth ~~pr~~ sat up till after 9 went to prayers and to bed.

Thursday, 9 August: Rose after 6 after I was dressed and performed my devotion went to Mr Fordham for my watch dranke a flagon of alle at the Swan went to school stayd till after 11 went to see Mr Bontall but could not find him came home performed my devotion went to diner and to school stayd till after 5 came home playd a little went to bed to sweate and swat[536] frely at 8 rose agane sat up till 10 performed my devotion went to prayers and to bed.

Friday, 10 August: Rose after 6 after I was dressed and performed my devotion got som milke went to school stayd till after 11 came home performed my devotion and went to diner gathered som goosberys in Mr Toispotes garden went to school stayd till after 6 came home performed my devotion playd a little went to super sate up till after 9 went to prayers and to bed.

[fo. 63v]
Saturday, 11 August: Rose after 6 after I was dressed and performed my devotion went to school stayd till after 11 came home was about my watch but could not do it went to diner performed my devotion tryd my watch but could not do it was within playd a little trimed myselfe performed my devotion after 9 went to prayers and to bed. Put somthing to my <eyes>[537]

Sunday, 12 August: Rose after 7 after I had washed eat som tost performed my devotion drest myselfe went to St James heard Mr Shelton on 13 Hebrews 5 came home made a short prayer, went to diner performed my devotion went downe heard the boys read went to Church heard the same man and text came home read 2

---

[534] Handwriting slightly unclear; an unusual name or spelling.
[535] A small silver cup for 'tasting' wine, *OED*.
[536] Cramped against the edge of the page; sweat.
[537] Very cramped in a tight margin.

sermon walked till 6 came in read a sermon and performed my devotion.

Monday, 13 August: Rose after 6 after I was dressed and performed my devotion went to Mr Goldsberry playd a little went to school stayd till after 11 came home was pounding Cherys went to diner performed my devotion went to school stayd till after 6 came home playd a little went downe eat som super sate up till after 9 went to prayers and to my chamber performed my devotion and went to bed.

Tuesday, 14 August: Rose after 6 after I was dressed and performed my devotion went to se school writt a letter to Phyoclea but could not send it stayd till after 11 got som mulberrys and sent a messenger with them and the letter went to diner performed my devotion went to school stayd till after 6 came home to Fayne brothers put on the handle of a hamer came home, received a letter from Phyloclea was ill supt som broth. Performed my devotion went to prayers and to bed.

Wednesday, 15 August: Rose after 6 after I dressed and performed my devotion went to school stayd till after 11 came home performed my devotion went to diner and to school stayd till after 6 stayd at Mr Smiths till 7 with him and Alderman Mott walked into the Castell lanes came in stayd a little walked with Mr Shaw and Bontall and Freeman till 10 came in eat som super performed my devotion and went to bed.

Thursday, 16 August: Rose after 6 cul[?oured] my hat trimed myselfe dressed myselfe performed my devotion eat som breakfast went to school stayd till after 11 came home performed my devotion went to diner and to school stayd till after 5 came home set on the lace to my hatt went to the dancing school stayd till after 8 walked with Mr Shaw till afor almost 9 came in performed my devotion eat som super sate up talking with Pegg till after 10 went to bed.

Friday, 17 August: Rose after 6 after I was up mended a payre of stockings dressed myselfe performed my devotion went to school stayd till after 11 came home went to diner performed my devotion went to school stayd till after 6 came home walked with Mr Shaw till 8 came in eat som super performed my devotion.

Saturday, 18 August: Rose before 6 dressed myselfe and trimed myselfe performed my devotion went <Mr Smith>

~~to school stayd till after 11 came~~ to Mr Smiths went to the Whit Lyon sent for Mr Stratton we agreed to choose 2 men I went to school after 9 stayd till after 11 came home performed my devotion dressed myselfe for Dedham eat som diner after 12 went came thether at 3 stayd there lay at Mr Shermans performed my devotion in bed.

[fo. 64r]

Sunday, 19 August: Rose after 6 and read in a booke I found in the window being the Arte of Weaving Spiritualised[538] performed my devotion after 7 went to Mr Mills dressed myselfe went to church herd a stranger preach on the 73 Psalm 25 came home went to diner sat in the house walked with Phyloclea into the garden went to Church heard the same man and sermon came home put on my shooes and things to com home eat som super after 6 I went Mr Mills and the 2 Ladys walked to the heath I persuaded Mrs Elizabeth to come home we came in before 10 got her bed made she went to bed I performed my devotion and went to bed.

Monday, 20 August: Rose after 6 after I was dressed and performed my devotion went to Mrs Lynford and got her such things as she needed stayd within with her till after 9 went to school stayd till after 11 called on Mr Phylips came home playd a little went downe went to diner performed my devotion stayd till after 1 went to school stayd till after 5 came home was within till after 7 went to Mr Gray he was not within came home eat som super sate up till 10 went to prayers performed my devotion went to bed.

Tuesday, 21 August: Rose after 6 I was dressed and performed my devotion went to Mr Grays came home eat som breakfast went to school stayd till after 11 came home was below went to diner after diner performed my devotion went to Furleys and Mr Ayngers with Mrs Lynford came back after 2 went to school stayd till after 6 came home was within at 8 went to super sat at 9 to prayers I went into Mrs Lynfords chamber stayd till after 10 went to my owne performed my devotion went to bed.

Wednesday, 22 August: Rose after 7 after I was dressed and performed my devotion went to school stayd till after 11 went to Mr Phillips and gave him an account of my busniss came home went

---

[538] Probably *The Weavers Pocket-Book, or, Weaving Spiritualised* (London, 1675) by John Collinges (1623/4–1691), a presbyterian and erstwhile rector of St Stephen's Norwich; he was ejected for nonconformity in 1662.

to diner performed my devotion went to school stayd till after 5 went to Mrs Jacksons where I had Mr Phillips and Mr Stratton had Mr King to end our difference after 9 they brought in their award I was to pay 20^l [539] for hors Joyrney[540] and 7^s and 6^d for other things and a bill to Mr Cockrill came home was a ¼ of an houer in Mrs Lynfords chamber performed my devotion went to bed.

Thursday, 23 August: Rose after 5 trimed myselfe dressed and performed my devotion eat som breakfast went to school stayd till after 11 went to see for Mr Barnwell but could not find him bought a duzen of Apricocks for Mrs Lynford I gave Mrs Ardrey 4 and Peg 1 went to diner performed my devotion went to school stayd till after 5 came home was within playd a little went to supper sate up till after 9 went to prayers went to my chamber performed my devotion and[541]

Friday, 24 August: Rose after 5 dressed myselfe performed my devotion got redy to goe to Dedham before 7 tooke horse carried Mrs Elizabeth stayd ½ houer went to Wivenhoe came thether before 11 eat Oysters dyned stayd an houer saw the shipyard and key tooke a boate went to the Balast key stayd an houer dranke bottell ale came back went up and downe the fayer about 6 came away went to Dedham stayd ½ an houer they were all out of humor I came home performed my devotion I went to prayers and to bed Mr Ardrey came not home.

[fo. 64v]
Saturday, 25 August: Rose after 6 dressed myselfe performed my devotion went to ~~seh~~ Mr Barnwells but could not find him went to school stayd till after 11 went to Mr Barnwell's but could not find him walked till 12 called agane but he was not within, came home went to diner performed my devotion was within and was not well about 4 Mrs Ardrey was taken very ill swonded[542] severall times I was with the Child in the garden till almost 7 I walked till almost 8 came in was within, about 8 I found Mr Ardrey at Isaac Mitchells got him home he was out of humor because Mrs

---

[539] Lloyd's superscript 'l' is messy and could also be read as 'd': this seems very unlikely, since it would hardly have been worth Stratton's time or effort to bring legal proceedings over twenty pence.

[540] Frustratingly, this transcription is uncertain. Lloyd writes this word very ambiguously, but the most likely conclusion that the word is an unusual spelling of 'journey', presumably one during which Stratton's horse was injured or lost.

[541] Entry cuts off here.

[542] Probably 'swooned'.

Reynold[s] spoke to him got him to bed I performed my devotion and went to bed.

Sunday, 26 August: Rose after 6 after I was up washt myselfe and not being very well eat som breakfast dressed myselfe performed my devotion went to St James herd Mr Shelton on 13 Hebrews 5 came home, went to diner performed my devotion lay a little [*deleted*] went to St James herd the same man and text came home was within and in the garden Mrs Ardrey being Ill and company with her could not goe to my chamber I read a little in Mr Smiths booke[543] about 7 went with Mrs Reynolds home, stayd there and suped after 9 came home performed my devotion and went to bed.

Monday, 27 August: Rose after 6 after I was dressed and performed my devotion eat som breakfast went to school stayd till after 11 came home performed my devotion went to diner gathered som plumbs went to school stayd till after 8 walked in St Johns fields called at Mr Cockrills but he was not within came home was within eat som super sat up till 10 performed my devotion and went to bed.

Tuesday, 28 August: Rose before 6 after I was dressed and performed my devotion went to Mr Cock[erill's] paid him dranke a flagon at the King's Head came home eat som breakfast went to school stayd till after 11 went to Mr Goldsberry playd a little, came home performed my devotion went to diner and to school stayd till after 6 went to Mrs Jacksons sent for Mr Stratton dranke a flagon went to his house paid him gave each other releases came home went to super after 9 to prayers performed my devotion writt to Phyloclea and to bed.

Wednesday, 29 August: Rose after 6 after I was dressed and performed my devotion eat som[thing] went to school stayd till after 11 came home performed my devotion went to diner and to school staydt [*sic*] till after 6 tooke horse went to Dedham stayd there all night performed my devotion went to bed.

Thursday, 30 August: Rose after 4 performed my devotion drest myselfe after at 7 tooke horse came for Colchester brought Mrs Betty behind me Mrs Mary rode single after 8 came home went to school stayd till after 11 came home went to din[er] performed no devotion because I could get no place but in my school standing at the window stayd till after 5 came home drest myselfe went with the 2 Ladys to

[543] See n. 14, **20 August 1675.**

dancing school stayd till after 9 came home eat somthing went to bed performed my devotion in bed. Went to prayers first.

[fo. 65r]
Friday, 31 August: Rose at 6 after I was dresst shew Mrs Mary to make pens after 8 went to school <performed my devotion> stayd till after 11 came ho performed my devotion came home stayd to eat to diner after 1 went to school stayd till 6 came home walkd with the 2 Ladys and Mr Sherley saw the Castle came in Mr Sherley and Mrs Mary playd at draughts and I and Mrs Betty at cards till after 9 eat somthing went to prayers and performed my devotion and to bed.

Saturday, 1 September: Rose at 6 after I was drest went to Mr Goldsberry he was not within went to Mr Fordhams for Mrs Lynfords watch went to school performed my devotion stayd till after 11 performed my devotion came home trimed myselfe drest myselfe to meete the Bishop with Captain Reynolds at 2 went mett him at the windmill[544] came in went to the Beare[545] with Mr Bontall drunk 2 bottels of Ale came home was within till 5 walked with the 2 Ladys to St Johns And old Aingers[546] gott some fruite came in sate up till 9 went to prayers sat in Mrs Lynford's chamber till 11 went to bed performed my devotion by ejaculations.

Sunday, 2 September: Rose at 7 dressed myselfe performed no devotion but Ejacul[ations] because I had no place at 9 went to St Peeters to heare the Bishop he preached on the 22 Matthew 22 came home went to diner performed no devotion but Ejaculations went to St Peeters heard Mr Sill[547] 6 John 66 came home was within performed my devotion standing at the window sat up till 9 went to prayers sat up till 11 in Mrs Lynfords chamber went to bed.

Monday, 3 September: Rose at 7 drest myselfe and performed my devotion was within till almost 10 went to St Peters heard

---

[544] Probably a windmill as a meeting point; no tavern or inn by this name is recorded in Colchester.

[545] A small inn, with links to the carrying trade, at the corner of Bear Lane and the High St., *Colchester People*, Vol. 3, p. 3.

[546] Handwriting slightly unclear here.

[547] Christopher Sill, rector of East Donyland, some four miles south of Colchester, from 1664 until his death in 1687. *CCEd* Person ID: 166358.

Mr Pooly[548] on the 2 Can[ticles][549] 5 came home went to diner performed som ejaculations, was within all the afternoone at 9 went to prayers performed some ejaculations went to bed.

Tuesday, 4 September: Rose after 5 went to Mr Langsdales but he was not up came to school performed my devotion writt a letter, went againe received 5^{li} came back to school stayd till almost 10 went home drest myselfe went to St Peters heard Mr Shelton on the 1 Corinthians 4 last[550] came home performed my devotion went to diner stayed within playd at tables with Mrs Lynford at 6 walked a little came in at 9 went to super and to prayers performed my devotion went to bed.

Wednesday, 5 September: Rose after 6 dressed myselfe performed m eat somthing went to school performed my devotion stayd till after 11 <performed my devotion> went home, washed my gloves went to diner and to school stayd till after 6 went home, playd at tables with Mrs Lynford till 8 Mr Sherley and Mrs Betty playd at Cribbag Mr Bond was there after 9 I went to prayers performed my devotion and went to bed.

Thursday, 6 September: Rose after 6 dressed myselfe went to Mr Fordhams stayd till 8 went to school stayd till 11 <performed my devotion> went hom went to diner after 1 went to school stayd till after 5 went home playd a little went to super playd at cards with Mrs Bety Lynford went to prayers performed my devotion and went to bed.

[fo. 65v]
Friday, 7 September: Rose at 6 after I was dressed went to Fields to see for a horse, he was not within went to Mr Goldsberry playd a little went to school performed my devotion stayd till after 11 went home performed my devotion was a little mending my breeches went to diner went to school stayd till almost 6 came home to walk with Mrs Lynfords they were gon out I went into the Castle Baylie came back found them, they told me that I did not wayt on

---

[548] Not a member of the usual Colchester clergy, and difficult to identify with certainty in the absence of other information. One possible candidate could be Robert Pooley, vicar of Stow Bedon and Rockland St Peter until his death in 1690: *Cantabrigienses*, Vol. 1, pt. 3, 380; *CCEd* Person ID: 126802.

[549] Now more commonly referred to as the Song of Solomon.

[550] 1 Corinthians 4:21.

them as I should in a kind of Irony which troubled me at which Mrs Mary was concerned playd at tables went to super playd a little at tables went to prayers stayd in their Chamber a little but were very dull I went to my chamber and performed my devotion and went to bed.

Saturday, 8 September: Rose at 6 after I was dressed and performed my devotion went to see for a horse gott Sillitoes the Smithes went to school stayd till after 11 came home gave Mrs Lynford a peck of Oysters got the Horses redy performed my devotion went to diner got redy to cary them home at 2 went came thether after 3 stayd there till 8 playd at tables and cards eat som super came home went to prayers I performed my devotion and went to bed.

Sunday, 9 September: Rose at 7 after I was drest and performed my devotion went to St James herd Mr Shelton on the 13 Hebrews 5 came home made a short prayer, went to diner sat and talked with Mr Broome performed my devotion went to church to St James herd the same man and text came home read a sermon walked read another sermon performed my devotion read in a booke being a pacquet against Shaftesbury men[551] went to super went to prayers and to bed.

Monday, 10 September: Rose at 6 after I was dressed and performed my devotion eat som broth went to Mr Goldsberry playd a little after 8 went to school stayd till after 11 went home Cullered my gloves and breeches went to diner performed my devotion went to school stayd till after 6 came home playd performed my devotion eat som super after 9 went to prayers and to bed.

Tuesday, 11 September: Rose after 6 dressed myselfe performed my devotion eat somthing went to school stayd till after 11 came home performed my devotion put on the handle of my symiter went to diner performed my devotion went to school stayd till after 6 went to Mr Hitchinsons sould him som old silver payd him for Mrs Bety Lynfords box came home playd till 8 then Ashley

---

[551] Anonymous, though attributed to Marchamont Nedham, *A Pacquet of Advices and Animadversions Sent from London to the Men of Shaftsbury* (London, 1676). This was a hostile response to Shaftesbury's famous pamplet, *A Letter from a Person of Quality to his Friend in the Country* (1675), in which he had accused Danby's ministry of attempting to introduce 'absolute and Arbitrary government' and episcopacy by divine right, amongst other charges. See Tim Harris, *Politics under the Later Stuarts: Party Conflict in a Divided Society 1660–1715* (London, 1993), esp. ch. 3.

brought me a letter from Dedham and Mrs Mary came with him and knocked at doore to speake with me as a stranger, I sate with her in my chamber ½ houer went down she eate a little milke dranke sate in the hall till almost 10 then Mr Ardrey and his wife came in we sate up till after 11 performed my devotion went to prayers and to bed I lay with Isaac Bloome.

Wednesday, 12 September: Rose at 6 after I was dressed and performed my devotion was within till after 8 with Mrs Lynford eat somthing went to school stayd till after 11 came home performed my devotion after 12 went to diner was Peggis birthday had a little of Reynish[552] I went to school stayd till 2 Mr Bloome begged a play[553] came home I performed my devotion was within till after 4 Mrs Lynford being most part in the towne[554] with Mrs Ardrey eat reasons[555] and nutts dranke a glass of sack after 5 set out for Dedham on foot came thether about 8 at 12 went to bed performed my devotion lay with Mr Mills his wife lying with the young Ladyes.

[fo. 66r]
Thursday, 13 September: Rose after 5 performed som ejaculations ½ houer after 5 set out from Dedham came home at 7 dressed myselfe performed my devotion eat som breakfast went to school stayd till after 11 went with Mr Bontall to Childs dranke a flagon brought him to diner walked into the Castell baylie after 12 went to diner I received a letter from Phyloclea I writt another sent her a quart of brandy 3 Leamons[556] and a letter before 2 went to school stayd till after 5 came home lay downe slept a little playd till after 7 went to super after 8 sat up till after 9 went to prayers talked a little with Mr Blome went to my chamber performed my devotion went to bed.

Friday, 14 September: Rose at 6 after I was dressed and performed my devotion went to Mr Goldsberry he was not within came home was a little mending a payre of stockings went to school stayd till after 11 came home was mending my stockings till 12 performed my devotion went to diner and to school stayd till after 6 came into the castle lanes walked a little came in and performed

---

[552] Rhenish wine.
[553] See n. 334, **26 July 1676**.
[554] Handwriting slightly unclear.
[555] Raisins.
[556] Uncertain; Lloyd's hand is very ambiguous here.

my devotion eat som broth washt my feete after 9 went to prayers and to my chamber and to bed.

Saturday, 15 September: Rose after 6 after I was dressed and performed my devotion tould Mr Ardrey I intended to leave my school went to school stayd till after 11 came home went to diner afterward performed my devotion was with Mr Bloome raysing a paper ruler lyne walked into the Castle bayly was within after 7 performed my devotion sate up till after 9 eat som super went to prayers and to bed.

Sunday, 16 September: Rose after 8 dressed myselfe performed my devotion read a sermon went to St James heard Mr Shelton on the 11 Hebrews 5 came home made a short prayer went to diner performed my devotion ~~read a sermon~~ went to church to St James heard the same man and text came home went to my chamber read a sermon went downe eat som Aple py with Mr Smith and his wife dranke som sullybub read a sermon performed my devotion went downe heard the boyes read went to super Mrs Allis read I went to prayers and to my chamber and to bed.

Monday, 17 September: Rose at 6 performed my devotion drest myselfe went to Rose about taking my school stayd till 8 went to school stayd till after 12 for him but he came not came home performed my devotion went to him shewed him the roome went to puck:[557] and talked but they would not serve him promised to see him on Satterday and give him an answer went to school stayd till after 6 came home, was not very well sate up till 9 eat som super went to prayers and to my chamber performed my devotion and went to bed.

Tuesday, 18 September: Rose after 5 dressed myselfe performed my devotion went to Goldsberry playd till 8 went to school stayd till after 11 came home playd went to diner performed my devotion went to school stayd till after 6 came home playd a little sate by the fier eat som super after 9 went to prayers performed my devotion and went to bed.

Wednesday, 19 September: Rose at 7 dressed myselfe performed my devotion went to school stayd till after 11 came home was mending my shamy breeches went to diner performed my devotion went to school stayd till after 6 came home performed my devotion

---

[557] Possibly 'Puckle' or 'Puckel', mentioned above and below.

went into towne stayd at Mr Grayes till after 8 came in eat s[558] went to prayers went to my chamber and to bed.

[fo. 66v]
Thursday, 20 September: Rose after 6 after I was dressed and performed my devotion trimed myselfe talked with Mr Bloome about learning him to writt eat som tost went to school stayd till after 11 came home was a little sowing on the lace on my breeches went to diner performed my devotion went to school stayd till after 5 came home was within not being well playd a little was below before 8 eat som super sat till after 9 went to prayers went to my chamber performed my devotion went to bed.

Friday, 21 September: Rose at 6 drest myselfe performed my devotion, sent the boy for a horse at last got Benjamin Bakers at 8 went for Nayling[559] to speake with Mr Right[560] he was gon out, eat som beefe at the Inn. Set up my horse with Russells at the [deleted] Maidenhead of Colchester I went to Church being the Lecture day and fayre, heard Mr Ashwell of Easton[561] on the 13 Jo: 17[562] tooke my horse went for Dedham came thether before 2 after 4 went to church heard a funerall sermon by Mr Lander on the 1 Peter 5:8 stayd and suped afor 7 came away came home after 8 had a letter William Smith brought me from Newington from my Brother went to see him he was abed came home went to prayers and to my chamber performed my devotion and went to bed.

Saturday, 22 September: Rose before 6 after I was dressed and performed my devotion went to Mr Roses he not being up went to Mr Goldsberry playd a little called at Roses he told me he had no occation for any things, went to Fordhams for my watch he tould me twas not com home went to school stayd till after 11 went to Mr Smiths saw William came home performed my devotion mended a napkin went to diner sowed on the lace of my breeches was in my chamber writt a letter to my Brother Smith came we walked into the Castle Lanes came in stayd till after 6 went to Mr Colemans stayd till

---
[558] Torn away here; 'something' or 'supper'.
[559] Probably Nayland, a Suffolk village nearly seven miles north of Colchester.
[560] Or 'Kight'.
[561] This could be Great Easton, an Essex village some 25 miles west of Colchester, or Little Easton, one mile to the south of Great Easton. However, neither parish had an incumbent named Ashwell, *CCEd*.
[562] This could mean Job 13:17 or John 13:17.

after 7 came in eat som super sate up till almost 9 went to prayers performed my devotion went to bed.

Sunday, 23 September: Rose after 8 after I was dressed and performed my devotion went to St James herd Mr ~~Shel~~ Cuffley on the 1 Corinthians 7:31 came home made a short prayer went to diner performed my devotion went to Greenesteed with Mr Ardrey and his wife herd Mr Bond[563] on the 11 Ecclesiastes 9 came home read a sermon performed my devotion was below till super after Mrs Alice and Ashley read went to prayers I to my chamber and to bed.

Monday, 24 September: Rose after 5 after I was dressed and performed my devotion stayd a little within payd Benjamin Baker for his mare went to Mr Fordhams he had not got my watch went to Balls got 4^s went to school stayd till after 11 went home performed my devotion playd a little went to diner lay downe a little went to school stayd till almost 6 went to Richard Orbells stayd till 7 came back called at Voales he was not within came home eat som broth performed my devotion sat up till after 9 went to prayers and to bed.

[fo. 67r]
Tuesday, 25 September: Rose before 6 after I was dressed and performed my devotion went to Mr Delights and told him I was to leave the towne saw his school he went and saw mine I stayd at school till after 11 came home shewed Isaac Bloome the way to make Church text[564] and Itallian text[565] went to diner performed my devotion went to school stayd till after 6 came home playd a little Mr Delight came to call me we went to Isaac Mitchells dranke a Flagon talked an houer came home eate som broth performed my devotion went to prayers and to bed.

---

[563] The rector of Greenstead at this time was Thomas Shaw (see n. 359, **10 September 1676**). This seems most likely to have been Robert Bond, rector of Layer Breton, about seven miles south-west of Colchester, from 1677 until his death in 1688/9. See *Cantabrigienses*, Vol. 1, pt. 1, 177; *CCEd* Person ID: 122986.

[564] 'Church text' is not a standard name for any early modern writing hand; Lloyd may have been referring to the non-cursive chancery hand, or perhaps the ubiquitous secretary hand. For a good summary of early modern writing hands, see Grace Ioppolo, 'Early modern handwriting', in Michael Hattaway (ed.), *A New Companion to English Renaissance Literature and Culture*, Vol. 1 (Oxford, 2010), 177–189.

[565] Chancery cursive, a writing hand based on humanist minuscule, also known as italic or Italian script owing to its origins in 15th-century Italy. Lloyd's brother, Nicholas, habitually wrote in this clear and readable hand.

Wednesday, 26 September: Rose before 5 Called Mr Ardrey to goe to London I dressed myselfe performed my devotion trimed myselfe went to Mr Edlin stayd 1/3 an houer to find him I bid him send me a bill and told him I would sell him my things I bought of him had his son to school I stayd till after 11 went to Fordhams to see for my watch and could not find him, but suspected he had cheated me of my watch went home performed my devotion got a horse to goe to Layre[566] to find Mr Smith he told me he had none of him I went to Captain Hall Mr Prestine payd me for his son I came home went to Mr Lyns[567] and ordered him to arest Fordham went after 4 to my school stayd till almost 6 stayd a little with Mr Smith came home went to super performed my devotion went to prayers and to bed.

Thursday, 27 September: Rose after 5 dressed myselfe performed my devotion went to Mr Fordhams to enquire I heard he was within I called Mr Lyns ordred him to goe to him went home went to prayers and to schoole about 9 Mr Lyns sent to me to come to the George[568] he had taken Mr Fordham I stayd till 10 and could do nothing for Mr Richardson had my watch in pawne I went to school stayd till after 11 came to the George and stayd till 12 I got my watch went home to diner performed my devotion went to school stayd till after 5 came home dressed myselfe went to the dancing school stayd till 9 came home eat som super performed my devotion went to prayers and to bed.

Friday, 28 September: Rose at 6 performed my devotion after I was dresst and made my confession out of Dr Taylor before 8 I went to school stayd till after 11 went home tooke my watch in peec[?es][569] went to diner performed my devotion went to school stayd till after 5 I broke of schoole and told my boyes I should never keepe schoole any more went to Puckles and set of for my horse hiyre for [*illegible*] went to Dr Tompson paid him for my physick he would take no fee stayd till 10 came home eat somthing went to prayers and to my chamber performed my devotion and went to bed.

---

[566] Probably Layer de la Haye.

[567] Probably John Lynnes, of St Peter's parish, assessed at one hearth in 1670, *EHT*, 291.

[568] A coaching inn, of lower reputation and importance than the Red Lion or White Hart. Of medieval origin, it stood in the parish of St Nicholas on the corner of the High St. and George Lane. *Colchester People*, Vol. 3, p. 12.

[569] Edge of page torn away.

Saturday, 29 September: Rose afor 6 after I was dressed and performed my devotion went to ~~Field~~ Richard Fields to see for his horse went to school at 7 tooke downe all my things before 10 went home trimed myselfe and drest myselfe went to prayers to St Peters came home writt som coppys went to diner performed my devotion was within till almost 2 went to Hitchensons for my buttons went to St Nicholas heard Mr Shelton on the 1 Kings 3:8:9 came home was in my chamber preparing for the ℞ performed my devotion eat som super went to prayers and to bed after 9.

[fo. 67v]
Sunday, 30 September: Rose at 6 after I was dressed and performed my devotion made my examination and confession out of Winchester Manuell and was reading and praying till church time went to St James herd Mr Shelton on the 81 Psalm 10 received the ℞ came home mad a prayer and thanks went to diner performed my devotion went to St James herd the same man on the 13 Hebrews 5 came home Mr Ardrey was com home and was not sober I walked in the garden cam in performed my devotion eat som super, went to prayers and to bed.

Monday, 1 October: Rose at 6 after I was dressed went to Mr Goldsberry he was not within called at Mr Edlins went to ~~To~~ Mr Tomlinsons had a cristall[570] put in my watch came home was within setting coppies and making penns went to diner performed my devotion was within writing and shewing Mr Bloome to make Church text playd a little walked with Mr Shaw went to the Carrier payd her went to Jo Blumfields came home, performed my devotion sate up till after 9 eat som super went to bed.

Tuesday, 2 October: Rose after 4 dressed myselfe performed my devotion after 6 tooke horse went to 3 Ashes[571] to Burrowes who promis[ed] to send me my money went to Pedmash[572] to Tompsons could get but 2^s went through Buers[573] and Nayling to Dedham got thether by 12 stayd till after 5 came home was very Ill performed my devotion went to bed.

---

[570] See n. 325, **29 June 1676**.

[571] Perhaps the Three Ashes, a very ancient pub on Ashes Rd, Cressing, just outside Braintree, some fifteen miles west of Colchester.

[572] Pebmarsh, a tiny village near Halstead, Essex, some thirteen miles north-west of Colchester and about eight miles from Cressing.

[573] Bures, another village, four miles east of Pebmarsh, on the way to Dedham.

Wednesday, 3 October: Rose after 6 dressed myselfe performed my devotion was within till after 8 went to speake with our Landlord Peake payd him his rent came home was setting coppys till diner after diner performed my devotion was within till 4 went to see a mare of Mr Hitchensons which Mr Ardrey bought but returned not long after came home playd a little after 5 performed my devotion went to Mr Grays stayd till ater 9 came home eat som milke potage went to prayers at 11 went to bed.

Thursday, 4 October: Rose at 6 after I was dressed and performed my devotion went to Mr Delights he was not within went to Richard Orbells for som money which I had called at Robert Strattons to see his mare but did not take her stayd till 10 saw Mr Mahucks pictures came home was making pens playd a little went to diner at 1 was shewing Beck: to substract performed my devotion was within till 4 walked till 5 came in performed my devotion, sate up till 9 went to prayers and to bed.

[*line bisects page*]

* a little eat som super went to pray performed my devotion went to bed.

[fo. 68r]
Friday, 5 October: Rose after 6 after I was dressed and performed my devotion went to Mr Delight he was not within went to Goldsberys there came Mr Delight I playd went home was within Lerninge Mr Bloome after 11 went to Mr Delight got the Jerman text saw his peece shewed him my way to take out my things he came to my chamber I playd a little gave him som chery brandy he went away I to diner performed my devotion received a letter from Mrs Lynford that Mrs Harris was come got a horse at 3 I went to Dedham set my horse at the Son[574] went to Mr Mills supt stayd till 10 went to the Son to bed performed my devotion went to bed.

Saturday, 6 October: Rose at 6 after I performed my devotion drest myselfe went to Mr Mills stayd there till 9 made cleane the Jack; went with Mr Bloome to Harwitch came there before 12 eat som bred and butter and dranke went to Captaine Taylor[575] spoake

---

[574] The Sun Inn is still standing and operational in Dedham.

[575] Probably Captain Silas Taylor (1624–1678), a former parliamentary officer, antiquary, and, at this time, commissioner of the King's storehouse at Harwich (appointed 1664). He was known to Pepys, who mentioned him several times in his diary, describing

to him he promised him he would send to him, went to the key saw the Duke of Albermale land met Charles Smith dranke at the Royall Oake went to our Inn gave the horses in eate dranke after 2 tooke horse I went to Dedham overtooke Mr Newton who was goeing to his place neere Sudberry[576] I lost Mr Bloome he was taken with a payne in his side was forst to Ly by the way stayd at Dedham till 8 came home at 9 wet to prayers performed my devotion went to bed.

Sunday, 7 October: Rose after 8 after I was dressed and performed my devotion went to All Saints herd Mr Hickringhole on the 20 Exodus 15 came home made a short prayer went to diner sate a little performed my devotion went to St James heard Mr Shelton on the 13 Hebrews 5 came home read a sermon performed my devotion asked Tom the Catechisme Instructed them in the principalls of religion went to Mr Smiths stayd till 9 came home went to prayers and to bed.

Monday, 8 October: Rose at 6 after I was dressed and performed my devotion writt a letter to Tom Ware, went to Mr Colemans, and to Mr Edlin spoke to him to come to see the things he would at 3 went to Mr Ayngers paid him and dranke my mornings draught after 10 came home was within till after 12 went with Petter to see my things came home went to diner was within till 4 went to find Mr Edlin but could not stay till after 5 went to Mr Hast and John Daniells received their money came home playd <a little eat som super went to prayers performed my devotion went to bed.>[577]

[fo. 68v]
Tuesday, 9 October: Rose at 6 after I was dressed and performed my devotion, went to Mr Edlins he promised to com see the things went to Goldsberry but did not stay, walked to the Sheaton grounds called on Mr Carr went to Fayre[578] Brothers came home drest myselfe stayd within till 11 went to All Saints heard Mr Hickringall preach on the fayre sermon [blank] com let us fill ourselves with strong drinke and tomorrow shall be as this day and much more Abundant[579] came home went to diner performed my

---

him as 'a good understanding man [...] a good Scholler – and among other things, a great antiquary', *Pepys*, Vol. 6, 81. See *ODNB*.
[576] Sudbury, Suffolk, 15 miles north of Colchester.
[577] Inserted at base of page facing.
[578] Lloyd usually spells this name 'Fayne': see **14 August 1677**.
[579] Isaiah 56:12.

devotion got me redy went to Dedham brought Mrs Harris behind me and my deare Phyloclea single came home at 7 sate up till 9 went to prayers to their chamber and after to mine and stayd ¼ of an houer sate up with them in their chamber till 2 performed my devotion went to bed.

Wednesday, 10 October: Rose after 5 drest myselfe performed my devotion went to Dedham fetcht Mrs Bety came home before 10 trimed myselfe and drest myselfe stayd within till after diner performed my devotion went into the fayer and was up and downe till after 3 buying things for them went to see Punchenello[580] Mrs Bety bought me a cravat and ruffels Laced with good[581] twills and presented me and Phyloclea a ring and put her owne hayre in it but gave it me not till the next day came in stayd till 7 went to the dancing school stayd till after 9 came home eat som super sate up till 11 performed my devotion went to bed.

Thursday, 11 October: Rose at 6 after I was dressed and performed my devotion went to Mr Edlin and reckoned with him called at Balls; went to Mrs Laduckes and see the peece came home was within looking out som of my things and Phyloclea was in my chamber writting at 11 I gave them som Oysters and a bottle of wine went to diner performed my devotion got myselfe and the horses redy they went into the fayer after 4 tooke horse went with them I carried Mrs Bety Ashley Mrs Mary and Mrs Haris in singles got thether after 5 I stayd there all night it rayning Mrs Mary gave me the ring in a letter I answered it performed my devotion at 12 went to bed at the Sun.

Friday, 12 October: Rose at 6 got the horses redy but could not send them because the boy could not lead them, dressed myselfe performed my devotion went to Mr Mills after 9 sent the horses away after dinner playd at 9 pins ti after 11 went to church heard Mr Lander preach a preparation sermon for the ₽ performed my devotion in the garden went to diner after diner playd at 9 pins till 4 I lost a bottle of wine walked toward Lawford[582] called at Mr Alstons stayd an houer went home playd at there was Mr Steele and wife

---

[580] A marionette show of Italian origin, popular in Restoration England, and an ancestor of Punch and Judy; cf. *Pepys*, Vol. 7, 257.
[581] Possibly 'gold'.
[582] A village almost ten miles north-east of Colchester.

[fo. 69r]
Mr Fanes[583] his daughters and Mr [sic] Pricilla Sherman, after they went away we had the wine and lamswooll[584] in it at 11 I went to my Inn performed my devotion went to bed.

Saturday, 13 October: Rose after 7 performed my devotion dressed myselfe dranke 3 flagons of Alle had a tost went to Mr Mills after I had been there a little went to play at 9 pins lost 2 bottles of wine to Phyloclea playd with Mrs Bety and Mrs Harris went to diner playd at 3 handed Cribage afterward at tick tack with Mrs Haris went to super after 9 I went to my Inn dranke 2 potts of alle per had my bed warmed performed my devotion in bed.

Sunday, 14 October: Rose after 7 performed my devotion dressed myselfe payd what I had at my Inn went to Mr Mills read a little after 9 ¾ went to Stratford[585] heard the minister on the 33 Ezekiel 11 came home performed my devotion in the garden read till 1 they came from the P went to diner I stayd at home having no cloathes fitt to go out in I read stayd ½ an houer after they came home and then tooke my Leave for good and came home before 7 eat som milke porrage performed my devotion went to prayers I to my chamber and writt what I had don from Monday went to bed.

Monday, 15 October: Rose at 6 after I was dressed and performed my devotion was putting up my things till 10 went to Wivenoe came home at 1 went to diner performed my devotion was a little in my chamber Mr Meliux came I sate a little with him went to the Ale Coate dranke 2 potts came home put up the rest of my things performed my devotion eat som super mended a payre of stockings went to prayers and to bed.

Tuesday, 16 October: Rose after 6 dressed myselfe performed my devotion went to Mr Langsdale returned my money came back sent away my things to Wivenhoe made even with Mr Ardrey went to diner performed my devotion cleansed the Jack at 3 tooke my leave went to Wivenhoe to take boate, when I came there it was not com from London lay at Colchester eat som super went to prayers performed my devotion went to bed.

[583] Lloyd's hand is ambiguous here, as is the spelling.
[584] Lambswool is an antiquated term for wassail, a mulled wine or ale beverage now associated with Christmas.
[585] Stratford St Mary, a village lying one and a half miles north of Dedham. The village rector, Richard Shaw, MA 1673, Emmanuel College, Cambridge, had been appointed that year (1677): *Cantabrigienses*, Vol. 1, pt. 4, 53; *CCEd* Person ID: 102758.

Wednesday, 17 October: Rose after 5 dressed myselfe performed my devotion at 7 tooke horse went to Halsted to Mr Richardsons, stayd at Coggeshall[586] with Isaack Bloome till after 12 called at Inworth[587] stayd an houer and halfe she gave me a payre of garters and buckells came home stayd below eat som super performed my devotion went to prayers and to bed.

Thursday, 18 October: Rose at 6 dressed myselfe performed my devotion was within setting Mrs Ardrey Coppyes after 11 went to diner performed my devotion went to Wivenhoe the paquet[588] did not go I stayd with Mr Ardree till after 3 he tould me his sad condition

[fo. 69v]
I hyred a horse went to Dedham set up my horse went to Mr Mills his house there was company went to my Inn got a fyer dryed myselfe stayd with my Landlady[589] till 7 Mr Mills came I went with him supt there sate up till after 11 went to my Inn performed my devotion went to bed.

Friday, 19 October: Rose at 6 dressed myselfe performed my devotion went to Stratford called for a letter I sent brought it to Phyloclea stayd there till 10 eat a breakfast ~~called~~ tooke my last leave called at Colchester for a letter she sent had it went to Wivenhoe got my things put all up and shipt went to diner after (1) set fast sayle to the send[590] of the bar[591] came to an anchor performed my devotion as well as I could for want of conveniencie I sate in the masters cabin about 6 set sayle sayled that day but within 2 myles of the boy[592] in the Nore[593] I performed my devotion that day 3 times as I did before I lay in the bayes.

---

[586] A town ten miles west of Colchester.

[587] A village four miles south of Coggeshall.

[588] In other words, a packet-boat, or a small coasting ship travelling regularly between two points, usually for the transport of mail, *OED*.

[589] The landlady of the Sun Inn, where Lloyd usually stayed when he went to Dedham. See Friday, **5 October 1677**, and **11–14 October 1677** above.

[590] The 's' in 'send' is very faint: this word probably means 'sand', but may have been used in the nautical sense as a noun, the 'carrying or driving impulse of the sea', *OED*.

[591] In other words, the bar, or bank, at the mouth of the Blackwater Estuary.

[592] Buoy.

[593] Probably the Nore, especially after the reference to the buoy, later (1732) the position of the first lightship in the world.

Sunday, 21 October: Set sayle about 6 went that day to Woolligh[594] came to an Anchor there I performed my devotion as I used to doe read 3 chapters and the Psalms for the day and had severall ejaculations.

Monday, 22 October: Set sayle at 2 came to the key after 6 dranke with the company went to Mr Lardner received 40^s at the Coffee house dranke 2 dishes of Chocolet went to the vessell got my things carryed over the watter and a burden brought to Newington eat som diner performed my devotion after 12 went to Long Lane[595] bought me a Brusells Camlet Coate[596] bought a ring of Canalion[597] went to Mrs Gray stayd till 5 gave it her eat a barrell of Oysters came home performed my devotion at 9 went to super my Brother coming in not before sate up till 12 went to bed.

Here, Lloyd leaves a large gap at the bottom of the page. His normal custom was to fill every page as much as possible. Perhaps this was intended to signify a 'break' in his life, and the end of his adventure in Colchester.

[fo. 70r]
Tuesday, 23 October: Rose after 6 after I was dressed and performed my devotion was placing my things till 12 performed my devotion went to diner at 2 went over the watter with my Brother to Dr Roberts stayd an houer went to Holborne tooke 2 places in the Alisbury coach to goe on Thursday to Aynhoe writt a letter at the Bishop's Head[598] to goe to my Brother John caryed it and Mrs Lynfords to the Post Office went home performed my devotion at 9 went to super at 10 to bed.

Wednesday, 24 October: Rose after 6 dressed myselfe performed my devotion writt a letter to Phyloclea went to Mrs Herrings delivered her letter then to Mr Mansurs delivered his went to Mrs Grays dined went to Covent Garden to Mr Locklys he was not at home bought a payre of silke stocking[s] went to Mrs Grays stayd till 4 my Landlord went to Newington with me called at the Rates

---

[594] Probably Woolwich.
[595] A prominent east–west road in Southwark, one mile north-east of Newington Butts.
[596] Camlet from Brussels was the finest available at the time; an extravagant purchase for a man who had recently lost his livelihood.
[597] Carnelian, a red mineral used as a gemstone, *OED*.
[598] There was a Bishop's Head in Chancery Lane, Holborn, mentioned as early as 1636 by John Taylor in his *Travels and Circular Perambulation* (London, 1636).

to see the Toll man⁵⁹⁹ and his wife he lay a dying we dranke 6ᵈ apeece went home he tooke his coate I went back to St George's Church⁶⁰⁰ came back performed my devotion went to super and to bed.

Thursday, 25 October: Rose after 5 performed my devotion in bed not having time dressed myselfe made a short prayer before 7 we went for the Black Swan⁶⁰¹ tooke watter at the Kings barge house⁶⁰² stayd at the Swan till 9 tooke Coach there was Captain Styles Mr Harris his kinsman Mr Siexes Mrs Saunders we 2 called at the Kings head in Acton drunke 2 tankerds of Strong Ale came to Uxbridg after 12 stayd till 2 had a dish of staks⁶⁰³ came to Alisbury at ½ hour after 7 lay at the Crowne performed my devotion only by ejaculations and in bed.

Friday, 26 October: Rose after 6 got a man sent him to Aynehoe to bring back the horses hyred 2 horses for 6ˢ at 9 tooke horse came at ½ houer after 1 had som staks for diner I walked in the garden an hour and was up till after 10 supt at 9 performed my devotion in bed.

[fo. 70v]
Saturday, 27 October: Rose after 9 dressed myselfe performed my devotion was within till after diner performed my devotion went at 2 with my Brother to Norrisis⁶⁰⁴ to Mr Fayrfax stayd till after 5 came in sate below a little opened my box tooke out my things got them redy for Sonday performed my devotion sate up till after 10 went to bed.

Sunday, 28 October: Rose after 7 drest myselfe performed my devotion <read a little> went to Church herd Mr Ellis⁶⁰⁵ on the

---

⁵⁹⁹ There was no specific place called 'the Rates' in Newington. It seems likely, from the context, that Lloyd was visiting the operator of the turnpike which stood to the north of Newington at the entrance to the town.

⁶⁰⁰ The church of St George the Martyr, Southwark, which dates back to the 12th century but was rebuilt in 1734–1736 by John Price; *TBE, London 2: South*, 576.

⁶⁰¹ See n. 300, **17 May 1676**.

⁶⁰² On the south bank of the Thames, about halfway between the Tower of London and Westminster.

⁶⁰³ Steaks.

⁶⁰⁴ Norris's?

⁶⁰⁵ The identity of this individual is uncertain; he was not the minister at Aynho or nearby Souldern. It seems possible that it was George Ellis, who had been ordained a deacon in June 1677, and later became rector of Over Worton, about eight miles west of Aynho, in 1683, *CCEd* Person ID: 14059.

[*blank*] came home made a short prayer went to diner performed my devotion went to church to prayers came home there was company I stayd a little I went to my chamber performed my devotion came downe stayd below went to super sate up till after 10 went <to bed.>

Monday, 29 October: Rose after 9 dressed myselfe performed my devotion writ to[606] letter to Mr Davine[607] was within till 12 went after the Carrier and gave it him came back went to diner performed my devotion after 2 went to Souldren stayd till after 4 came home was within went to super performed my devotion sate up till after 10 went to bed.

Tuesday, 30 October: Rose after 7 dressed myselfe performed my devotion was writting to Phyloclea and Pamilla[608] went to diner performed my devotion was a little in my sisters chamber sate below and read som verses walked till after 4 came in sate below till after super performed my devotion at cards till 10 went to bed.

Wednesday, 31 October: Rose after 7 trimed myselfe dressed myselfe performed my devotion went to Mr Lanleys to borow a horse with my Brother called at Mr Hanslops stayd till after 10 came in was in my chamber till after 11 went at 12 to diner to Mr Lanleys my Brother Mr Ellis Mrs Morgan[609] Mrs Mary Mrs Ellis Mrs Miers Mrs Breese stayd till after 8 all they but playd at cards we stayed there after 9 my sister and I came away not being well either of us had som burnt wine sat up till 11 went to bed performed my devotion in bed.

Thursday, 1 November: Rose after 6 dressed myselfe performed my devotion put up the things was within till almost 11 went to diner performed at 12 tooke horse to come for Alisbury my Brother Mrs Mary Roberts and I called at Stoake[610] dranke ½ pint of brandy came to Alisbury after 5 had som burnt wine at 8 went to super sate up till 10 performed my devotion went to bed.

---

[606] Two.

[607] Handwriting ambiguous.

[608] In Sidney's *Arcadia*, Pamela is the sister of Arcadia, adding further credence to the possibility that Lloyd is referring obliquely to the Lynford sisters.

[609] Ambiguous; untidily cramped in margin.

[610] Probably Stoke Mandeville, three miles south of Aylesbury, though this would mean they took a circuitous route.

[fo. 71r]
Friday, 2 November: Rose before 6 dressed myselfe performed my devotion had som burnt wine after 7 tooke Coach came to Woxbridg[611] after 1 stayd till after 2 came to the Swan after 5 went to Dr Roberts stayd till 6 called at the Post Office came home after 7 performed my devotion went to bed after 9.

Saturday, 3 November: Rose after 9 dressed myselfe performed my devotion was below a little, and went to my chamber ript my brusels camlet coat made it redy to be layd in went downe there was Mr Berry went to diner sate below till after 2 went to my closet and did my coate after 5 was below a little performed my devotion sate up till after 9 went to prayers and to bed.

Sunday, 4 November: Rose after 7 dressed myselfe performed my devotion read a little after 9 went to church heard Mr Berry on 4 Ephesians 30 came home made a short prayer was a little below went to diner performed my devotion after 2 went to church herd Mr Sparks[612] on the 6 Matthew 9 came home was in my chamber a little went downe and read a little performed my devotion went to bed super went up went to prayers and to bed.

Monday, 5 November: Rose at 7 dressed myselfe performed my devotion was within till after 10 went to prayers at church came home went to diner performed my devotion was writting Letters was below with Mr Sparke was above a writting performed my devotion went to super went up went to prayers and to bed.

Tuesday, 6 November: Rose at 7 dressed myselfe performed my devotion my Brother and I went to London called at the Joyners and at Mr Sissons went to Mr Lardners we drunke our mornings draught went to Dr Roberts stayd and dined called at Henery Bloomes went to Mr Worlyes dranke a quart of sack went to Mr Carrters stayd ½

---

[611] Perhaps Uxbridge, now in suburban west London.

[612] Robert Sparke, a lecturer of uncertain office, published *A Sermon Preached in S. George's Church Southwark, at the Funeral of that Pious and Worthy Gentlewoman, Mrs. Frances Fenn* (London, 1679). The title page describes him as 'R. Sparke of Newington M.A.' The burial of Elizabeth, the wife of a 'Robert Sparke Lecturer', is recorded in the parish register for St Mary Newington on 13 December 1677: see LMA, P92/MRY/007. Lloyd mentions his brother reading the funeral service on this day in the diary. A Robert Sparke, MA, of St Mary, Newington was also granted a licence to practice medicine in the province of Canterbury in 1682; LPL, VX 1A/10/186. A possible *CCEd* Person Record may be found with ID 166586. See *Cantabrigienses*, Vol. 1, pt. 4, 127–128; John Venn, *Biographical History of Gonville and Caius College, 1349–1897*, Vol. 1 (Cambridge, 1897), 228.

houer went to Whithall Chappell[613] to prayers saw Mr Alford stayd a little at Mr Jefferys chamber crossed the watter came home performed my devotion writt a letter went to super sate up till 9 went up and to prayers and to bed.

Wednesday, 7 November: Rose before 7 dressed myselfe performed my devotion went to London bought a violin of Mr Sisson called at Mr Herrings went to Mrs Cheneys went to Mrs Grays dined went to Smithfield to Jorden and after to Mr Lockleys delivered the letter came back to Mrs Grays stayd a little bought a payre of shooes came home performed my devotion went to super and up to prayers and to bed.

[fo. 71v]
Thursday, 8 November: Rose at 9 drest myselfe and trimed me performed my devotion was within till diner performed my devotion went to diner at 2 went to London went to Mr Lardner we dranke a dish of Coffee I received my money went to Mr Totenhams to see Mrs Lynford Mrs Mary was abrod I stayd till 5 she came stayd ½ houer went to Mr Herrings stayd till after 7 had the them home came home at 8 went to super performed my devotion went up to prayers and to bed.

Friday, 9 November: Rose after 7 dressed myselfe performed my devotion was within helping my Brother sett his books till after 11 Mr Tompson came I was with him after 12 went to diner went into the boate and I land[ed] and longe walke[d] playd a little before 11 he went I walked to the end of St George's Fields[614] came back performed my devotion we set up the books before 9 went to super performed my devotion sate up till after 10 went to prayers and to bed.

Saturday, 10 November: Rose after 7 dressed myselfe performed my devotion writ helped saw wood till after 10 writt a letter to Mr Griffin was about shelves for my closset performed my devotion after 1 went to diner went into the boate with my Brother was till after 4 fitting shelves and things in my closset performed my devotion was below went to super to prayers and to bed.

---

[613] Probably the old Chapel Royal at Whitehall, which, like much of the complex which existed in Lloyd's day, was destroyed by a fire in 1698.

[614] A former area of open fields in Southwark, immediately to the north-west of Newington Butts, where the Imperial War Museum and St George's Cathedral now are.

Sunday, 11 November: Rose after 7 dressed myselfe performed my devotion read a little in the Whole Duty of Man[615] went to church herd my Brother on [*blank*] came home made a short prayer read in the Whole Duty of Man went to diner sate a little performed my devotion went to church herd Mr Sparke on the 6 Matthew 9 came home walked in the gleabe lane[616] read and performed my devotion went into the parlor read in Sparks his Booke after super read in the Whole Duty of Man went to prayers and to bed.

Monday, 12 November: Rose after 7 dressed myselfe performed my devotion was till after 10 about my coate Mr Roberts children came was with them went to diner performed my devotion was ~~abo~~ above playd a little and danced a little playd att cards till super after sate till 9 went to prayers and to bed.

[fo. 72r]
Tuesday, 13 November: Rose after 7 performed my devotion trimed myselfe was within till after 11 performed my devotion went to diner and after we went over the watter with Dr Roberts child[?ren] landed at the Black Swan went to Mrs Allens stayd ½ houer I went to Leadenhall Streete to Mrs Lynford stayd till 5 called upon Mr Jarot and told him my payne he gave me som Oyntment we dranke a pott at the Bull[617] I came home performed my devotion went to super to prayers and to bed.

Wednesday, 14 November: Rose after 7 dressed myselfe performed my devotion went to Mr Griffins he was not at his house I walked in St James Parke met Mr Pratt talked a little with him met the King[618] walked a little called to see Mr Sparrow but he was not within went to Smithfield and to Mrs Grays dined there and stayd till 5 came home performed my devotion went to super sat up till after 9 went to prayers and to bed.

---

[615] The anonymous *Whole Duty of Man* (1658) was a classic foundational text of Anglicanism. The most likely author is usually considered to be the Royalist clergyman and provost of Eton, Richard Allestree (1621/2–1681). Lloyd represented 'of' here with a symbol resembling the number '4', perhaps slipping into the shorthand used elsewhere in the diary.

[616] Possibly Camberwell Glebe, about two miles south of Newington Butts, but Lloyd's meaning is uncertain.

[617] We can only speculate, but one of London's largest inns at the time was the Bull in Bishopsgate, just to the north of the former site of Gresham College. It was demolished in 1866. *Pepys*, Vol. 10, 419.

[618] Lloyd's hand is quite clear here; this would appear to be one of the more extreme examples of his frustratingly taciturn understatement.

Thursday, 15 November: Rose after 7 dressed myselfe performed my devotion went over to Whit Hall to Mr Griffin and just spoake to him walked in the stone walke[619] till after 10 went to the Chappell to prayers stayd to speake with Mr Alford we went to the Harpe and Ball[620] dranke 2 potts of Alle and beere went back to Whitehall and went into the Gallry saw the King Prince of Orange[621] and all the Court in their splendour it being the Queen's birthday[622] the King and Queen dined privately I went with Mr Alford and saw them and the Queen's bed Chamber, went to St Martains Lane to diner at Cooks walked in St James Parke till 4 went to the Chappell after prayers Mr Alford carryd me into the grand chamber intending to get me in to see the ball we stayd till 7 but could not get in I went to the water and tooke boate landed at Lambeth got a linke and lighted myselfe home[623] went to super performed my devotion went to prayers and to bed.

Friday, 16 November: Rose after 7 dressed myselfe performed my devotion was within it being a wett day was about making my breeches longer till diner after I put a string to my watch performed my devotion went to Mr Buyzards carryed my watch stayd ¾ of an houer came home received a letter from Mrs Roberts was within playd a little performed my devotion went to super and to prayers and to bed.

Saturday, 17 November: Rose after 7 dressed myselfe performed my devotion was within doeing my breeches went to diner performed my devotion made an end of my breeches trimed myselfe put up the hanging shelfe and maps in my clossett was within mended a cravatt went to super performed my devotion went to bed prayers and to bed.

Sunday, 18 November: Rose after 7 dressed myselfe performed my devotion went to church herd my Brother on the 6 Romans 23

---

[619] Here Lloyd is probably referring to the Stone Gallery at Whitehall, which ran along the southern edge of the Privy Garden. Lloyd's access is not as exclusive as it might seem; by the Restoration, the area appears to have become something of a 'through-passage', and Pepys fell into a ditch passing through it at night. See *Pepys*, Vol. 1, 26; Vol. 10, 479–483.

[620] The Harp and Ball was a large tavern on the 'river side' of Charing Cross, approximately on the site of No. 25, Whitehall. The proprietor at about this time, Hugh Roberts, was described as a gentleman and his will; the premises had 20 hearths in 1666, *Pepys*, Vol. 10, 422.

[621] The future William III. William had married Mary, the daughter of Charles II – the future Mary II – at St James's Palace on 4 November 1677.

[622] Catherine of Braganza (1638–1705); her birthday was in fact on 25 November.

[623] A link was a flaming torch used by pedestrians to light their night-time journeys.

came home made a short prayer read a little went to diner performed my devotion read a little went to church herd Mr Sparks on the 6 Matthew 9 came home sate below till after super talking with Mr Smith and my Brother performed my devotion read a little went to prayers and to bed.

[fo. 72v]
Monday, 19 November: Rose after 7 drest myselfe performed my devotion eat som breakfast went to Mrs Lynford went to the Tower to know why the quay went of[624] and twas because the Prince of Orange went for Holand I went back stayd till they were redy and then we eat a little beefe tooke Coach I carryed them and Mrs Rebecha to Westmester shewed them the Tames and the Parliament Houses both and Westmester Hall[625] went into St James his Parke saw the birds and walked round the Parke went up the privy stayers[626] and throw the prayer garden and went into the Kings Presence chamber[627] and the gallery and the roome where the King dines publickly went to the Taverne called at the New Exchang walked through it tooke Coach came to the Royall Exchang and called for a gowne carryed them home stayd an houer it cost me 10^s and 4^d came home went to super performed my devotion went to prayers and to bed.

Tuesday, 20 November: Rose after 7 went downe helpt George Rich cut downe an old tree performed my devotion helpt him cut another my Landlord came we eat som breakfast I drest myselfe went with him and dined there stayd all day and night at 6 we went into the musick house in Morefields[628] dranke 2 muggs went back went to super sat up till 11 went to bed talked with my Landlord till after 4 performed no devotion but Ejaculations.

Wednesday, 21 November: Rose after 9 made cleane the Jackhead performed no devotion but ejaculations drest myselfe sate

---

[624] 'Off'? Perhaps meaning closed.

[625] The oldest part of the Palace of Westminster, constructed in the 11th century by William II.

[626] A strange reference; the Privy Stairs were the King's river stairs down on the Thames, but Lloyd writes as if they were part of their journey around the grounds; perhaps he was mistaken. *Pepys*, Vol. 10, 483.

[627] A room in the Palace of Whitehall in which presentations were made, apparently 'open to anyone who was entitled to appear at court'. How Lloyd and his companions gained this privileged access is something of a mystery. *Pepys*, Vol. 10, 482.

[628] Moorfields, a former open area near Moorgate, just north of the Wall.

by the fier till diner went to diner playd and sate by the fier till 3 made Beck a booke set her a coppy after 4 came away called at Mrs Lynford they were not within received a letter at Mr Lardners from Mrs Ardrey that her Husband had abused her and left her and accused her of me[629] I performed my devotion went to super and to prayers and to bed.

Thursday, 22 November: Rose after 7 dressed myselfe performed my devotion was within nayled on som laths[630] in the garden wen[t] to diner mended the parlor doores performed my devotion was nayling on laths and choping wood till after 4 was within mending a payre of drawers performed my devotion sate up till after 9 went to prayers and to bed.

[fo. 73r]
Friday, 23 November: Rose after 7 drest myselfe performed my devotion eat som tost went with my Brother into London called at Mr Fosters at Tower Hill, at Dr Clutterbucks[631] and Dr Pittis[632] about my Brother Johns tenths, went to Mr Masters there came in Mr Harts[633] we stayd till after 12 went to the Phenix in Newgate Streete to diner went thence to the Old Dogg Taverne dranke 2 bottles of Clarrett called at Dr Roberts stayd till after 6 came home performed my devotion sate up till after 9 went to bed.

Saturday, 24 November: Rose after 7 dressed myselfe performed my devotion was putting on stufe to the knees of my breeches was setting on locks till diner performed my devotion bottled som beere trimed myselfe was below a little performed my devotion went to super sate up after 9 went to prayers and to bed.

---

[629] In other words, accused her of committing adultery with Lloyd.

[630] Thin, flat strips of wood used in trelliswork, or as a base for applying plaster or tiles, *OED*.

[631] Thomas Clutterbuck, DD (d.1700), was rector of St Mary Southampton and prebendary of Leckford, Hampshire. He later held the Middleton Prebend at Chichester Cathedral (1678–1682) and became archdeacon of Winchester in 1684. See *Oxonienses*, Vol. 1, 294; *CCEd* Person ID: 62992.

[632] Thomas Pittis, DD (bap. 1636, d.1687), held a number of livings; Gatcombe, Isle of Wight (1662), a lectureship at Christ Church Newgate (1670), Lutterworth, Leicestershire (1678), and St Botolph without Bishopsgate (1678). He was also a royal chaplain. He was the immediate predecessor of Lloyd's brother, John, in the living of Holyrood, Southampton, from 1666–1675. There must have been some dispute or discussion to be had, as Lloyd notes in this entry, with regard to the tithes or 'tenths' owing to this living, which had only recently passed to John Lloyd. See *ODNB*; *CCEd* Person ID: 95105.

[633] 'S' very faint.

Sunday, 25 November: Rose after 8 dressed myselfe performed short devotion went to church it was Just begun herd my Brother on the 6 Romans 23 came home warmed myselfe made a short prayer went to diner read and performed my devotion went to church herd Mr Sparke on 6 Matthew 9 came home warmed myselfe read performed my devotion went to super to prayers and to bed.

Monday, 26 November: Rose after 7 dressed myselfe performed my devotion eat somth[ing] went to London called upon Mrs Lynford went to Mr Sykes stayd till after diner went to see Francis Docker and after to Mrs Grays stayd till 5 called at Mrs Lynfords they were not within came home performed my devotion went to super to prayers and to bed.

Tuesday, 27 November: Rose after 8 dressed myselfe performed my devotion, was within writting letters went to diner performed my devotion was putting my things in order and made an end writting Letters performed my devotion went to super to prayers and to bed.

Wednesday, 28 November: Rose after 7 dressed myselfe performed my devotion went to London caled on Mrs Lynford she was not within went to Whithall saw Mr Alford spoake to him went to Mr Griffins but Mr Sparrow not being within did not stay called at Dr Roberts and Smithfield sent to Aynhoe to Mr Roberts dined in Bishopsgate Street at a Cooks at 2 went to Mrs Grays stayd all night was very Ill performed my devotion went to bed.

[fo. 73v]
Thursday, 29 November: Rose before 9 dressed myselfe performed short devotion went to St Michaels Cornhill[634] herd the Bishop of Oxford[635] preach before the ministers sons on the 3 Acts 25 went to Mrs Grays to diner where was Mr Boner he stayd a little after diner I till after 3 went to Mrs Lynford stayd a little came home received a letter from Mr Ardree he writt att Rogers went to super performed my devotion answered him left it for him to be left for him at Rogers his house went to prayers and to bed.

---

[634] Originally a possession of Evesham Abbey from 1133 until 1503, St Michael Cornhill subsequently became the property of the Drapers' Company. The church was destroyed in the Great Fire but the tower survived; the body was rebuilt in 1669–1672. The tower was rebuilt by Hawksmoor in 1718–1722; *TBE, London 1*, 249–251.

[635] Henry Compton (1632–1713) became bishop of Oxford in 1676 and held the office until his death. He was liberal on matters of Protestant dissent, but was vehemently anti-Catholic, *ODNB*.

Friday, 30 November: Rose after 8 drest myselfe performed my devotion Mr Ardrey came stayd with him till after diner at 12 came Mr Ellis dined performed my devotion went with Mr Ardrey to Mile End went to the post office to Smithfield came home Mr Ellis stayd went to super at 10 performed my devotion at 10 to bed.

Saturday, 1 December: Rose after 9 drest myselfe performed my devotion went to diner performed my devotion went with Mr Ellis to Fish Street Hill[636] payd 50^s at Bloomfields for Southton[637] went to the Post Office called upon Mrs Lynford stayd till after 5 came home performed my devotion got my things redy went to super to prayers and to bed.

Sunday, 2 December: Rose after 7 drest myselfe read performed my devotion went to church herd my Brother on the 1 Peter 2:11 came home mad a short prayer went to diner read performed my devotion went to church herd Mr Sparke on 6 Matthew 9 came walked a little in the garden came in read till 7 went to super performed my devotion sat up till after 9 went to prayers and to bed.

Monday, 3 December: Rose at 7 dressed myselfe performed my devotion was within my closet till after 9 mended som trenchers and the parlor latch and the court gate went to diner performed my devotion was in my closet writing till after 3 playd till after 4 read in the History of England[638] till after 6 performed my devotion after 7 went to super read the life of Mahomet[639] after 7 went to prayers and to bed.

Tuesday, 4 December: Rose after 7 dressed myselfe performed my devotion was in my closet writing till 12 went to diner performed my devotion was to see for gravell in the Pingle[640] and in the garden

---

[636] Fish Street Hill still exists today, connecting Monument St. to Lower Thames St. During Lloyd's lifetime, however, it was the main road connecting to the old London Bridge.

[637] Lloyd's brother John lived in Southampton, and so this payment may have related to him.

[638] This may have been John Milton, *The History of Britain, That Part Especially Now Called England* (London, 1670). Lloyd's brother Nicholas, with whom he appeared to be cohabiting during this phase of the diary, owned a copy: see John Dunmore, *Catalogus librorum bibliothecæ Reverendi Nicolai Lloydii* (London, 1681), 30.

[639] Probably Sir Walter Raleigh, *The Life and Death of Mahomet* (London, 1637), a copy of which was also owned by Nicholas Lloyd. Dunmore, *Catalogus*, 42.

[640] 'A small enclosed piece of land; a paddock, a close', *OED*.

choping downe and swaeing[641] a tree till 3 made an end of my writing was below read a little in Sams his Britta:[642] performed my devotion went to super mended a payre of stockings went to prayers and to bed.

[fo. 74r]
Wednesday, 5 December: Rose at 7 drest myselfe performed my devotion was a little in my closet preparing to write the Jerman Text at 10 I went with my Brother to London tooke watter at Strand gate landed at Yorke House[643] I went to Westmester and St James to see for Lodgings for Mrs Lynford came to Mr Bradburys stayd a little went and stayd a little with Mr Winsloe stayd till almost 1 at Mr Bradburys shop we went to the Golden Lyon[644] had an Ill diner stayd till almost 5 my Brother came I came away landed at Stand [*sic*] gate came home I received a letter from my sister Carless answred it performed my devotion went to super to prayers and to bed.

Thursday, 6 December: Rose at 7 drest myselfe performed my devotion went to London called at Mrs Lynfords stayd a little went to Smithfield to cary my letter and to see for the butter saw som Lodgings in Holborne for Mrs Lynford, went to Henery Broome writt a letter to Mr Ardrey went to Mr Sickes stayd till after diner went to Mrs Grays she was not within stayd till 4 set Beck som coppys went to Mrs Lynfords stayd till after 7 came home went to super read Mr Turners Sermon[645] performed my devotion went to prayers and to bed.

Friday, 7 December: Rose after 7 dressed myselfe performed my devotion was in my closet making a S: for the peece and setting the Jerman text till after 12 after 1 went to diner performed my devotion

---

[641] Ambiguous, probably meaning 'sawing'.

[642] This abbreviation has been left unexpanded since absolute certainty is impossible, but this seems very likely to have been Aylett Sammes, *Britannia antiqua illustrata, or, The Antiquities of Ancient Britain derived from the Phœnicians* (London, 1676). This volume was owned by Nicholas Lloyd: Dunmore, *Catalogus*, 24.

[643] This is a curious route description, since York House, a large mansion which once stood on the banks of the Thames, was the location of the principle watergate giving access to the Strand. Presumably Lloyd meant that he took to the water *opposite* the Strand, and landed at York House watergate.

[644] Since Lloyd was in the vicinity of St James, this may have been either of the taverns of this name mentioned by Pepys; one at Charing Cross (*Pepys*, Vol. 1, 19) and another in the Strand (Vol. 7, 424): see also Vol. 10, 421.

[645] See n. 487, **3 June 1677**.

was washing and Oyling of pictures till after 6 performed my devotion went to super sat up till after 9 went to prayers and to bed.

Saturday, 8 December: Rose at 9 dressed myselfe performed my devotion was in my closet till after 12 about the Jerman text went to diner performed my devotion was a little more about drawing the lynes trimed myselfe playd after 5 performed my devotion writt to Mr Ardrey went to super was below till after 9 went to prayers and to bed.

Sunday, 9 December: Rose after 8 dressed myselfe performed my devotion read went to church herd my Brother on the 1 Peter 2:11 came home made a short prayer went to diner sate a little performed my devotion read went to church herd Mr Sparke on the 6 Matthew 9 came home read till super after 6 performed my devotion went to super read till 9 went to prayers and to bed after 10.

Monday, 10 December: Rose after 7 dressed myselfe performed my devotion eat som breakfast went to London called to have 2 penknives ground in the [*illegible*] called at Mr Sissons lost my stich[646] went to Mrs Lynfords they were Just goeing out went after 9 to Mrs Grays stayd till after 4 called at Mrs Lynfords stayd till after 7 came home went to super performed my devotion went to prayers and to bed.

[fo. 74v]
Tuesday, 11 December: Rose at 7 drest myselfe performed my devotion was looking on Lambert a little was filling up the Jerman text till diner performed my devotion made an end after 2 was till 5 looking upon Lambert and Goodheart performed my devotion went to super at 7 read in Bishop Hall[647] till 9 went to prayers and to bed.

Wednesday, 12 December: Rose after 8 Mr Tompson came I drest myselfe made short prayers was within all day somtimes teaching him multiplication somtimes playd on the violin together

---

[646] Stick?
[647] Joseph Hall (1574–1656), bishop of Norwich from 1641 until he was deprived of his office by Parliament in 1646 and episcopacy was abolished. A prolific writer, satirist, and occasional controversialist, he was sometimes called the 'English Seneca'. The catalogue of Nicholas Lloyd's library shows that he owned several of his works. *ODNB*.

performed short devotion after diner the evening being wet he lay with me I made short prayers and after super we lay together.

Thursday, 13 December: Rose after 8 drest myselfe got Mr Thompson som breakfast went into St George's Fields with him came in performed my devotion was looking on the masons till after 1 went to diner performed my devotion was with them till 4 got myselfe redy to go to Church read stayd till after 6 herd my Brother preach Mrs Sparks Funerall sermon upon the 12 Ecclesiastes 7 came home eat som super sat up till after 9 made short prayers went to bed.

Friday, 14 December: Rose before 10 not being well drest myselfe performed my devotion after 11 I went to London with my Brother and Mr Masters who came to see him landed at Blackfryers went to Mr Masters stayd and dranke a bottle of alle called at Henery Broomes stayd till after 1 went to Dr Roberts stayd till after 4 came home performed my devotion eat som super went to prayers and to bed.

Saturday, 15 December: Rose at 8 ~~drest myselfe~~ performed my devotion trimed myselfe drest myselfe eat som breakfast before 11 went to London called on Mrs Lynford stayd till after 1 went to Mrs Grays dined stayd till after 4 went to Holborne bridg to see for Southton Coach it not being com went to Mr Smith stayd in the court walking while he wend to Mr Ardrey stayd with him in the chamber till 7 went to the Swan to see for the coach but could find nothing callled [sic] upon Mrs Lynford but stayd not came home went to super performed my devotion went to prayers and to bed.

Sunday, 16 December: Rose after 7 drest myselfe read in Dr Taylors Rule of Holy Living[648] performed my devotion went to church heard my Brother on the 1 Peter 2:11 came home made a short prayer went to diner read performed my devotion went to church heard a stranger on the 30 Job 23 came home sat below talking till 5 read and performed my devotion to super read went to prayers and to bed.

Monday, 17 December: Rose after 7 drest myselfe performed my devotion made a place for the little dogg digged in the garden till 12 went to diner performed my devotion was below in the parlor till 2

---

[648] *The Rule and Exercises of Holy Living* (London, 1650), followed by *Holy Dying* (1651).

playd a little walked in the garden till 5 sate below my Brother being abrod at 7 eat som super performed my devotion sate up till 9 went to prayers and to bed.

Tuesday, 18 December: Rose before 9 not being very well drest myselfe performed my devotion then came my Aunt Lettis and the company to be married about 11 went with them and my Brother to my grandmo[?ther][649] to diner stayd till after 5 came home my Brother Henery[650] was com performed my devotion eat somthing.

[fo. 75r]
Wednesday, 19 December: Rose after 7 drest myselfe performed my devotion was within with my Brother Henery after 12 went to diner performed my devotion playd the afternoone being within all alone performed my devotion went to super after 9 to bed.

Thursday, 20 December: Rose after 9 not being very well Ashley and Thomas Cheney came to see me got them som breakfast drest myselfe performed my devotion was within the parlor with them till diner performed my devotion, Chopt som wood and carryed in after 2 my Land Lord came I stayd with him till 4 walked into St George's Fields with him came home went into the Burrough bought som gloves to send to my Mother and sister and the Children, came home performed my devotion went to super and to prayers and to bed.

Friday, 21 December: Rose after 7 drest myselfe got Hary his breakfast performed my devotion he went away I to London called on Mrs Lynford at Tower Streete stayd till after 10 went to prayers with her at St Dunstons[651] after I went with her to Whitehall to Sir Herbert Prise[652] after to her aunts and through St James Parke

---

[649] This word is very cramped into a margin with very tight binding, and therefore uncertain.

[650] This must have been a brother-in-law or even the husband of a more distant female relative (such as the unidentified 'Aunt Lettis'): Lloyd did not have a brother named Henry.

[651] St Dunstan-in-the-East, just off Tower St., now Great Tower St. Perhaps of pre-Conquest origin, but the building was substantially enlarged in 1382. The church was damaged, but not destroyed, during the Great Fire. Repairs were carried out 1668–1671, and the tower was rebuilt by Wren 1695–1701. Unfortunately, the body of the church was badly damaged in the Blitz in 1941, and it was not repaired. The site of the ruin is now a public garden. See *TBE, London 1*, 213–214.

[652] Sir Herbert Price, 1st Bt (*c*.1608–1678) of the Priory, Brecon, was MP for Brecon in 1640, 1641–1643, and 1661–1678. A lieutenant-colonel in the Royalist army during the Civil War, he fought at Naseby and went into exile following the Parliamentarian victory.

back againe by watter we shott[653] the bridg I went to Mrs Grays stayd till after 5 called at Mr Lardners stayd ½ houer came home performed my devotion went to super to prayers and to bed.

Saturday, 22 December: Rose after 8 drest myselfe performed my devotion was within helping Nell put up lyns[654] in the citchin and cutting meat till after diner performed my devotion was cutting suett for pyes mended a towell trimed myselfe performed my devotion went to super to prayers and to bed.

Sunday, 23 December: Rose after 7 drest myselfe read and performed my devotion went to Church herd my Brother on the 9 Isaiah 6 came home mad a short prayer went to diner performed my devotion read went to church heard Mr Sparke on the 6 Matthew 9 came home was below till after 5 read performed my devotion went to supper read till after 9 went to prayers and to bed.

Monday, 24 December: Rose at 7 drest myselfe performed my devotion went to see the trees that were cut downe was in my closset writting in my Comon Prayer Booke Ejaculations and praying for the ℞ till 11 then made my confession out of Dr Taylors Golden Grove and performed my devotion after 12 went downe was below by the fier then went up and renewed my covenant and prayed went downe and picked som fruits and pared som apples went up and performed my devotion went downe and made a pye went to super made 2 pyes went to prayers and to bed, this was a fast day with me.

Tuesday, 25 December: Rose before 7 drest myselfe performed my devotion was in my closset reading and praying went to church herd my Brother on the 9 Isaiah 6 received the ℞ came home mad a short prayer and thanksgiving went to diner read performed my devotion went to church to prayers came home was belo[w] till after 5 read went to super performed my devotion went to prayers and to bed.

Wednesday, 26 December: Rose before 7 drest myselfe performed my devotion went to Mrs Lynford brought them over to diner after 10 they stayd till after 11 I went back stayd with them

---

He was an inactive member on the 'Court' side during the Cavalier Parliament, and was marked 'thrice vile' in Shaftesbury's list of 1677; *Hist. Parl. 1660–1690*, Vol. 3, 285–286.

[653] Passed quickly under London Bridge, always dangerous when the tide was running high: see *OED*.

[654] Handwriting unclear: lines?

till 9 ~~came home~~ playd 3 games at Whist they Mrs Hunt and I came home performed my devotion went to prayers and to bed.

[fo. 75v]
Thursday, 27 December: Rose after 7 drest myselfe performed my devotion was within mending the sleeves of my camblet great coate after 10 went to prayers at Church made an end of my coate went to diner alone my Brother dining at Mitchells performed my devotion went after one to London to Mrs Allens funerall stayd till almost 4 came away in a Coatch to Newington where she was buried I helpt hold up the pall came in read performed my devotion after 7 went to super after 9 to prayers and bed.

Friday, 28 December: Rose after 7 drest myselfe performed my devotion eat somthing was within with Bowers and Goodheart and ~~La~~ Lambert till 12 went to London called at Mr Lardners went to Mrs Grayes stayd a little called at Mrs Lynfords but they were gon out, went to the Swan at Holborne bridg and brought the Coppy of my Brother's booke[655] went to Mrs Grays stayd super and till almost 9 came home performed my devotion went to prayers and to bed.

Saturday, 29 December: Rose after 8 drest myselfe performed my devotion eat somthing went to London to Mr Mullins for my Brother John and spoake about his businis sent him an account saw Mr Smith stayd an houer went to Mrs Lynford they were gon out went to see for the Carrier at the Rose went to turnstile[656] to see for it went back by Fleete Streete at Mr Lambs met Mrs Gray stayd ½ houer went by the Rose caled but there was nothing came home performed my devotion went to super made 4 pyess went to prayers and to bed.

---

[655] Certainty is impossible, but I consider it likely that Lloyd was referring to a manuscript copy of his brother John Lloyd's *Shir ha shirim, or, The Song of Songs being a paraphrase upon the most excellent canticles of Solomon in a pindarick poem* (London, 1682). The preface to this edition alleges that a previous printing (1681), which appeared anonymously and without dedications or epistles, had been plagiarized after being 'Committed privately to a Friend in *London* (and not intending to trouble the Press) [it] was, under pretence of being borrow'd (as the Gentleman who lent it sends me word) Wrote out by a Stranger'. Lloyd's diary may contain references to the sharing around London of this manuscript. George Lloyd also contributed a dedicatory poem to the introductory matter, as did Thomas Lardner (mentioned here) who addresses John as his 'Worthy Friend'.

[656] Here, Lloyd may have been referring to an actual turnstile, or Great Turnstile, an alleyway connecting High Holborn to Lincoln's Inn Fields.

Sunday, 30 December: Rose after 7 drest myselfe performed my devotion went to church herd my Brother on the 1 Timothy 3:16 came home brought Mr Syks and his wife to diner and Rogers and wife Lane[657] and his wife and Goody Boorne dined after diner I performed short devotion went to Church after the text was just named I came home with Mrs Syks who was very ill and continued very Ill all day I stayd with her till 8 I eat som super performed my devotion and went to bed.

Monday, 31 December: Roose [*sic*] at 7 drest myselfe performed my devotion eat som thing saw Mrs Syks who was very ill all night at 9 went to London called on Mrs Lynford tould her I would com in the evening to play at Cards called on Mr Lardner tould him of it went to Mrs Grays stayd till 11 then I brought them to diner after diner I performed shord [*sic*] devotion shewed Mrs Gray the garden and house they stayd till after 4 went home with them then called Mr Lardner wee went to Mrs Lynfo[rd] playd at Cards had [*deleted*] som oysters and 2 bottles of wine stayd till 11 went to the Bulls Head Taverne stayd till 12 came to Mr Lardners talked a little performed short devotion went to bed.

1678

Tuesday, 1 January: Rose after 9 drest myselfe performed my devotion after 10 went to the Coffe house dranke som tea called at Mrs Lynfords not home I came home Mrs Smith came after super I performed my devotion he stayd till 5 I performed my devotion eat som super went to prayers and to bed.

[fo. 76r]
Wednesday, 2 January: Rose after 7 drest myselfe performed my devotion was below with Mr Jacob after 11 came Mr Ellis went to diner I was with Mrs Syks till after 2 performed my devotion was with her till 7 performed my devotion sate with her till super and after till 9 10 made pyes till after 1 went to bed.

Thursday, 3 January: Rose after 8 drest myselfe performed my devotion was within with Mr Syks and his wife till after 10 writt som of my Brother's booke till 1 went to diner performed my devotion at 3 began to write till after 4 playd a little writt a little till super performed my Devotion writt till after 9 went to prayers and to bed.

---
[657] Very cramped in margin; ambiguous.

Friday, 4 January: Rose after 8 drest myselfe performed my devotion writt till after 10 then helpt Nell gett diner was up and downe after ~~diner~~ 12 went to diner Dr Roberts and wife son and daughter dined, after diner I performed my devotion after 3 came my Landlord Tompson to take his leave stayd till after 5 I went to my closset writt performed my devotion writt till after 7 went to super sat till after 9 went to Prayers and to bed.

Saturday, 5 January: Rose before 7 drest myselfe performed my devotion went to London calld on Mr Jacob who promised me to go to Southton for 5^{li} and his Charges I went to Mrs Lynford stayd till after 10 went to Mr Mullins house but he was not within went to Temple Bar bought som loops for my coate called againe at the Mermayd for Mr Mullins discourst with him dranke a bottle of wine he tould me he would not goe under 50^{li} I came home set on my loopes performed my devotion writt a little in the booke for my Brother John went to super trimed myselfe writt a little, went to prayers and to bed.

Sunday, 6 January: Rose after 7 drest myselfe read performed my devotion went to church herd my Brother on 3 Ephesians 5:6 came home made a short prayer read a little went to diner read a little slumbred walked in the garden read and performed my devotion went to church herd Mr Sparke on the 6 Canticles 3 came home with Mr Lardner he stayd ¾ of an houer I walked as far as the Kings Bench[658] came home read performed my devotion went to super read a little went to prayers and bed.

Monday, 7 January: Rose at 7 drest myselfe performed my devotion went to London to Mrs Grays stayd there till 12 then she her Mother and Brother and I and the Liuetenat[659] went to Dedford[660] went abord the Ann yott[661] stayd not went ashore and saw the yard and shipps went abord the Queens Frigget[662] and eate beefe and

---

[658] Here Lloyd referred not to the law court but to the King's Bench Prison, in Southwark not far from Newington. The Court of King's Bench was based at Westminster Hall.

[659] Perhaps the guide for Lloyd and his companions on their tour of ships which ensues in this entry. Cramped at the edge of the page; ambiguous and with a possible tilde.

[660] Deptford.

[661] The *Anne* (1661) was a royal yacht, or a 'pleasure boat' officially designated for the use of the monarch. J. D. Davies, *Pepys's Navy: Ships, Men and Warfare, 1649–1689* (Barnsley, 2008), 63.

[662] The term 'frigate' was ambiguous in the 17th century, with several contradictory definitions (*Pepys*, Vol. 10, 585). There was no ship with this precise name, but Lloyd may have been referring to the HMS *Royal Katherine* (1664), built by Christopher Pett

Bisket and Cheese and drank stayd ¾ of an houer I gave the man 1ˢ went to the Globe⁶⁶³ drunke 3 bottles of Clarett and pint of sack I payd 5ˢ tooke boate came home to Mrs Grays after 5 I stayd all night she lay on the bed till 1 and held me by and all⁶⁶⁴ but no ill thoughts or acctions performed no devotion but Ejaculations.

Tuesday, 8 January: Rose after 8 drest myselfe performed som short Ejaculations went to Mr Humpherys brought him to Mrs Grays to diner at 1 went to diner I stayd till 2 then went to Mrs Syks stayd till almost 4 went to Mrs Lynford stayd and playd at Cards till after 8 came home sate up till 10 went to prayers performed my devotion went to bed.

Wednesday, 9 January: Rose at 8 drest myselfe performed my devotion was within all day and most part writting my Brother's booke⁶⁶⁵ after 1 went to diner performed my devotion writt till after 4 was below till after super then mended a payre of stockings performed my devotion sate up till 10 went to prayers and to bed.

[fo. 76v]
Thursday, 10 January: Rose at 7 drest myselfe performed my devotion writ ½ houer was in the garden helping Wagstafe till 11 then being wet we gave over Mr Lardner caled in stayd ¾ of an houer I was below looking after diner Nell being abroad went to diner playd a little performed my devotion writt till after 4 was below till 6 playd a little went to super performed my devotion writt a little went to prayers and to bed.

Friday, 11 January: Rose at 7 drest myselfe performed my devotion was till after 9 cleansing the Coach house and stable, was helping the man cut wood till after 12 went to diner performed my devotion was till 5 helping him came in sate by the fier till after 6 performed my devotion was below mending a payre of stockings went to super to prayers and bed.

---

and named after the wife of Charles II, Catherine of Braganza. The launch of the ship was attended by Pepys, *Pepys*, Vol. 5, 305.

⁶⁶³ This may have been the same establishment visited by Pepys on visits to Deptford on Admiralty business. In September 1660, after visiting Deptford to disburse pay on the ship *Success*, Pepys, Sir George Carteret, and Sir William Penn 'had a very good dinner' at the Globe: see *Pepys*, Vol. 1, 253–254.

⁶⁶⁴ Lloyd's hand here is imprecise and ambiguous, but this seems very likely to have been his meaning.

⁶⁶⁵ See n. 655, **28 December 1677.**

Saturday, 12 January: Rose at 7 drest myselfe performed my devotion was writing a letter to Mrs Syks to send my lace to mend writ a little of the booke went to diner performed my devotion trimed myselfe was below and got my linen redy for the next day went to super after was cutting and paring apples for a pye went to prayers and to bed.

Sunday, 13 January: Rose after 7 drest myselfe performed my devotion went to church herd my Brother on the 12 Romans 1 came home made a short prayer went to diner Mr Sparke dined sate till 1 performed my devotion went to Church herd Mr Sparke on the 6 Canticles 3 came home walked and sate by the fier till 6 read till almost 7 performed my devotion went to super read went to prayers and to bed.

Monday, 14 January: Rose at 7 drest myselfe performed my devotion went to London called at Mr Moores about the hangings dranke an houer with him and som of his acquaintances called at Mrs Lynfords stayd till 11 went to Dr Galles[666] from thence to Mrs Grayes she was not within stayd and writ a letter to Mrs Ardrey went to see Pegg and herd som nuse from Colchester went back stayd till Mrs Gray came in then was with her in her chamber where we were very famillar and kind came away at 5 called Mr Lardner at the 3 Tunns Taverne[667] stayd and dranke 4 bottles of wine with Mr Wild and his 2 sons we went to Mrs Lynford stayd till after 11 I Lay at Mr Lardner's performed my devotion went to bed.

Tuesday, 15 January: Rose after 6 was not very well performed my devotion went downe and sate by the fier drest myselfe after 8 went to Mrs Lynford and stayd till almost 10 Mr Lardner came we went to Newington at 1 went to diner after diner we sate and talked <performed my devotion> at 8 we went to church where I read the

---

[666] Perhaps Thomas Gale (1635/6–1702), antiquary and clergyman. A good friend of Samuel Pepys, Gale became high-master of St Paul's School, London, and DD at Cambridge in 1675, before being made a prebendary of St Paul's Cathedral the following year. He became dean of York Minster in 1697. *ODNB*; *CCEd* Person ID: 35534.

[667] A common name for taverns in the period, but two possible locations are: the Three Tuns at Charing Cross south of the Strand (now Whitehall), valued at 16 hearths in 1664, which continued into the 19th century under the name Rummer; and the Three Tuns on the north side of Hart St. or Crutched Friars, kept by John Kent until his death in 1689, which had previously existed in Lombard St. but was destroyed in the Great Fire. *Pepys*, Vol. 10, 427.

Marriage servis to Mr Lardner and Mrs Bety[668] they both answring came home were very mery and danced 3 or 4 dances after 4 went to London to Mr Lardners he gave us som Oysters and a cuple of Rabets for super stayd till after 9 wayted on the ladys home called at a strong watter[669] man[670] stayd ¾ of an houer went to Mr Lardners and sate up a little performed my devotion went to bed.

Wednesday, 16 January: Rose at 8 drest myselfe performed my devotion at 9 came away with Mr Lardner he walked to the Lady Williams[671] we called but did not stay he went to Moreclack[672] stayd at Braburns I came in Mr Turner was in was within all day writting letters and som in the booke after 12 went to diner, mended performed my devotion mended the dogs coller was within went to super <performed my devotion> sate up till 10 went to prayers and to bed.

[fo. 77r]
Thursday, 17 January: Rose at 8 drest myselfe performed my devotion was in my closset mending my black cloathes went to diner performed my devotion made an end, mended a payre of drawers, playd a little mended a payre of stockings, writt out a table of the religeous [*illegible*] in England, performed my devotion went to super, to prayers and to bed.

Friday, 18 January: Rose at 8 drest myselfe performed my devotion was within all day mending my coate at 1 went to diner playd a little performed my devotion writt till after 4 playd was below a little mending a shirt Mr Turner came in I was with him went to super sate with him till after 8 then my Brother came in I performed my devotion sate up till 10 went to prayers and to bed.

Saturday, 19 January: Rose at 9 not being well having a cold drest myselfe performed my devotion went out and was till 12 of the clock

---

[668] This was probably an informal betrothal ceremony of some kind; it was certainly not an official or binding wedding, since Lloyd was not ordained. The 'official' marriage, between Elizabeth Lynford and Thomas Lardner, a London apothecary, was granted by licence and took place on 21 February 1678, at the church of All Hallows the Great (see Register of baptisms, marriages and burials, All Hallows the Great, 1666–1720, LMA, P69/ALH7/A/001/MS05159).
[669] Strong alcoholic spirits, *OED*.
[670] Handwriting unclear; ambiguous.
[671] Unfortunately this is not a sufficient basis on which to identify this individual.
[672] Probably Mortlake, now in the London Borough of Richmond.

helping carry the faggotts came in dryed myselfe went to diner after 2 performed my devotion was writing till after 4 was below performed my devotion got my things redy to were, went to super sate up till 10 went to prayers and to bed.

Sunday, 20 January: Rose aft at 9 being ill with a cold drest myselfe performed my devotion went to church after the Confession was begun, herd my Brother on the 12 Romans 1 came home made a short prayer was by the fier a little went to diner sate till 1 read performed my devotion went to church heard Mr Sparks on the 6 Canticles 3 came home walked in the dining roome and read a little went downe and lookt after Mr Turners horse read a little went to super performed my devotion went downe and sate by the fier till 9 went to prayers and to bed.

Monday, 21 January: Rose at 8 drest myselfe performed my devotion looked after Mr Turners horse set on buttons on my Brother's Doublet till 10 then was with Goodhert in the chamber till after 12 went to diner performed my devotion was in the chamber till after 3 then below in the parlor and stable till after 5 looked after Mr Turners horse was in my closet blacking the heads of som letters in Johns booke performed my devotion went to super sate in the parlor till 10 went to prayers and to bed.

Tuesday, 22 January: Rose after 7 drest myselfe to go to London performed my devotion then the upholster came I stayd and helpt him after 12 went to diner performed my devotion left after 5 was in my closet till after 7 performed my devotion writt a little of the booke went to super sate up till 10 went to prayers and to bed.

Wednesday, 23 January: Rose after 7 helpt Mr Turner looke after his horse drew up the boate mad him cleane drest myselfe performed my devotion eat som beefe from the spitt after 10 went to London called at Mr Moores the upholster went to Dr Roberts then to Mrs Bartons and to Mr Sykes after to Mrs Grays stayd till after 4 called at Mr Lardners apointed to meete him at Mrs Lynfords went to the post office went to Mrs Lynfords they were not within after I went to Mr Herrings stayd a little then went back Mrs Bety and I playd at Cribage then Mrs Mary and I and Mr Challener and Mall[673] Hunt playd at whist lost a bottle of wine Mr Lardner came we had it and Challener brought 2 lobsters we

---

[673] Abbreviation for 'Malcolm'?

stayd till after 11 went to Mr Lardners sat and talked a little of the concerne[674] performed my devotion went to bed.

Thursday, 24 January: Rose after 8 performed my devotion drest myselfe eat a tost went to Mrs Lynfords stayd till 10 Mr Lardner came at 11 we went to the Dog Taverne in Thames Streete[675] stayd till after 5 had oysters and a pullet and wine went to their lodging stayd till after 8 came home performed my devotion went to prayers and to bed.

[fo. 77v]
Friday, 25 January: Rose at 12 not being well drest myselfe performed my devotion went to diner performed my devotion writt in the booke performed my devotion went to super sate up till 10 went to prayers and to bed.

Saturday, 26 January: Rose after 7 drest myselfe performed my devotion mended a payre of stockings writt till diner performed my devotion writt till 5 trimed myselfe got my things redy to were the next day went to super sate up till almost 10 went to prayers and to bed.

Sunday, 27 January: Rose after 7 drest myselfe performed my devotion went to church herd my Brother on the 12 Romans 2 came home made a short prayer went to diner read performed my devotion went to church heard a stranger Mr Stone on the 1 Peter 4:7 came home read walked in the garden read another sermon went to super sate up till 10 went to prayers and to bed.

Monday, 28 January: Rose after 7 drest myselfe performed my devotion was till after 11 in the greene chamber finishing the hangings, writt till after 12 went to diner performed my devotion writt till after 4 cutt downe som of the older trees lookt after Mr Turners horse writt a little performed my devotion was seting buttons on a coate went to super sate up till 10 went to prayers and to bed.

Tuesday, 29 January: Rose after 6 drest myselfe performed my devotion was writing and mending my coate went to diner performed my devotion got me redy and Mr Turners horse went to

---

[674] Perhaps the effort to publish John Lloyd's book.
[675] The Dog Tavern Yard can be found on Rocque's 1746 map on the corner of Thames St. and St Dunstan's Hill.

Hampstead to enquire after the Minister who I heard was dead 3 dayes before came back looked after the horse performed my devotion went to supper to prayers and bed.

Wednesday, 30 January: Rose after 9 not being well drest myselfe performed my devotion went to church herd prayers came home sate by the fier and read a sermon used the confession out of Dr Taylors Golden Grove after 1 went with my Brother to meete my Brother and sister after 3 she came we stayd till 5 went all 3 and dranke a bottle of wine came home went to super performed my devotion went to prayers and to bed.

Thursday, 31 January: Rose after 6 drest myselfe performed my devotion after 7 went with my Brother and Mr Turner to meete Mr Whitfield Mr Maynard and Mr Dixon at Billingsgate we tooke boate ½ houer after 8 we came to Erit[676] at 12 stayd till after 3 for the tide then went to Jarsey Frigget[677] the Captaine made us very welcome stayd till almost 12 came away after 3 came home I performed short devotion not being well having drunke a little wine and punch went to bed.

Friday, 1 February: Rose at 11 not being well I performed shorte devotion after 12 went to diner Mr Berry dineing with us I performed short devotion after 2 my Brother and I went to see my Brother and sister stayd till 4 then we went to the Kings Head Taverne against the Temple[678] met Mr Fiffild dranke 2 bottles of wine we came home I performed my devotion went to super to prayers and to bed.

---

[676] Erith, on the south bank of the Thames, a small port in Kent in the 17th century, now part of Greater London.

[677] The HMS *Jersey* (1654) was a 4th-rate frigate; much to his amusement, Pepys was made captain of the vessel for one day in 1669 in order that he could sit as an 'expert assessor' for a naval court martial relating to the loss of the *Defiance*, a 3rd-rate ship lost to fire the year before: see *Pepys*, Vol. 9, 481.

[678] This 'old and notable tavern' stood in Chancery Lane near the junction with Fleet St., 'against the Temple' as Lloyd suggests. It was known as a meeting place of the Green Ribbon Club (originally known as the King's Head Club, such was its association with the venue), radical members of the 'country party' during the Popish Plot and the Exclusion Crisis, *Pepys*, Vol. 10, 423.

[London Diary]

[fo. 81r]

1711

Monday, 1 January: Performed my devotion within doeing things till after 11 at prayers at Lothbury[679] within performed my devotion within puting things in order, till neare 5 went to Bowe[680] and there was no prayers there having beene a Sermon the afternoone went to see for my wife at Champnyes and mett her just come out nobody being at home, came home at prayers performed my devotion etc.

Tuesday, 2 January: Performed my devotion. Within till after 10 went to Mrs Luckis[681] and left word sh[e] should come to her Daughter not being well bought a littl[e] spitt and racks for Chopps came in and left them went to a Coo[k] by London Wall and bought a shoulder Mutton within performed my devotion at 4 at prayers at St Peters[682] bought a ~~skine~~ scaine of flurishing thread at Mr Kettles and left a letter at post house for Sir Edward Barkam on Mrs Bowyers business within at prayers performed my devotion.

Wednesday, 3 January: Performed my devotion. At 8 went to the Peacock brewhouse[683] for Ale but could get none within my wife

---

[679] St Margaret Lothbury, destroyed during the Great Fire, the church was rebuilt by Christopher Wren 1683–1692 (and tower, 1698–1700). *TBE, London 1*, 233–235.

[680] Probably the church of St-Mary-le-Bow in Cheapside. One of the City's most historic and significant churches, it is famous for its bells. It was destroyed in the Great Fire, and was rebuilt by Wren 1670–1680. *TBE, London 1*, 242–245.

[681] Probably meaning 'Mrs Luckey's'; the same individual mentioned on **6 January** below.

[682] St Peter upon Cornhill. An ancient and prominent church standing at the corner of Gracechurch St. and Cornhill. The present building was built by Wren, with the likely assistance of Hooke, in 1677–1684, *TBE, London 1*, 256–258.

[683] One of the major breweries in early 18th-century London, the Peacock was in White Cross St. in Cripplegate, and was owned by the Calvert family: see Alan Pryor, 'The industrialisation of the London brewing trade: Part I', *Brewery History*, 161 (2015), 73.

being very ill with the Rhumatisme performed my devotion with all day at prayers performed my devotion.

Thursday, 4 January: Performed my devotion. Within till after 11 at prayers at Walbrook[684] performed my devotion at 2 went [?to] Harrison and received 4^{li} for half year due at Michaelmas at Mr Field [?ing] with Mr Stanford and received a quarter's Rent due at Michaelmas and talkt with Mr Stanford about severall things at Mrs Powells and bought pint of brandy and shewed her how much there wanted to be measure of the brandy she sent and she gave more to make it up within at prayers performed my devotion etc.

Friday, 5 January: Performed my devotion within all morning performed my devotion within my wife being very ill at p[?rayers]

Saturday, 6 January: Performed my devotion went to Speake to Mrs Luckey but she was not within bought sweetebread and Liver at Spittle[fields] Market within till 11 called at the Cooks at the Beare[685] at London Wall and spoke to him to rost me a joynt of Meate on Sunday at prayers at All Hallows Wood Streete[686] bought sugar at Mr Keyes within performed my devotion within till 4 bought Loyne of veale at Hony Lane Market carried it to the Cooks at prayers at St Mary Woollnorth[687] [*large ink blot*].

Sunday, 7 January: Performed my devotion etc. Heard a stranger at St Laurance[688] 15 Psalm the whole Psalm ☧.[689] Performed my

---

[684] St Stephen Walbrook, in the heart of the City next to Mansion House. Dating to at least the 11th century, the previous 15th-century church was destroyed by the Great Fire and rebuilt by Wren 1672–1680, *TBE, London 1*, 260–264.

[685] Perhaps the Bear Inn on the eastern side of Basinghall St., very near London Wall, also called the White Bear in Strype's Survey and on Rocque's 1746 map; Henry Harben, *A Dictionary of London* (London, 1918).

[686] There is no All Hallows Wood St. Lloyd was probably referring to All Hallows, Bread St., a road that virtually continues Wood St. to the south. Destroyed by the Great Fire, it was partially rebuilt by Wren *c*.1677–1684. It was demolished in 1878 after the parish was merged with St Mary-le-Bow, Elizabeth Young and Wayland Young, *Old London Churches* (London, 1956), 46–47.

[687] St Mary Woolnoth stands at the corner of Lombard St. and King William St. in the City. The current building, designed by Hawksmoor, was funded by the Commission for Building Fifty New Churches, and was completed in 1727, *TBE, London 1*, 247–249.

[688] St Lawrence Jewry, in Gresham St. adjacent to London Guildhall. The original 12th-century church was destroyed in the Great Fire and rebuilt by Wren in 1671–1680, *TBE, London 1*, 229–230.

[689] In the Colchester Diary, Lloyd's use of the chi rho symbol, ☧, always indicated the Sacrament. This seems likely to have remained the case, but Lloyd's even more laconic style of writing here makes it difficult to be certain.

devotion heard Mr Mooree[690] 13 Hebrews 1 within Mrs Cousey being her[e] read at prayers performed my devotion.

Monday, 8 January: Performed my devotion went to Mr Higgs[691] and had an account of the whole proceedings sin[?ce][692] a generall Meeting received the last ticket mony of the 100000 Lotery[693] called at Lord Powers[694] but he was not at home within performed my devotion within till[695]

---

[690] One of Lloyd's favourite preachers in his later years; he seems likely to have been Thomas Morer (c.1651/2–1716), rector of St Anne and St Agnes with St Zachary, in Gresham St. just south of the Barbican where Lloyd worked collecting rents. Lloyd evidently had difficulty with the spelling of this name, though he occasionally got it right: see **20 April 1712**. *Oxonienses*, Vol. 3, 1027; *CCEd* Person ID: 165104.

[691] William Higgs was the founder of and later secretary to the Charitable Corporation for the Relief of the Industrious Poor, founded by royal charter in his name in 1707, C. T. Carr (ed.), *Select Charters of Trading Companies, 1530–1707* (London, 1913), 256–263. The Charitable Corporation is known to history as the source of a major financial and political scandal in the 1720s and 1730s, by which time it was controlled by a committee of MPs and financiers. For an excellent summary, see P. Brealey, 'The Charitable Corporation for the Relief of Industrious Poor: Philanthropy, profit and sleaze in London, 1707–1733', *History*, 98 (2013), 708–729. The Corporation was essentially a pawn broker which claimed rather grandiose philanthropic intentions; for an early statement of its purpose, see Anon., *The New Lombard Houses* (London, 1708), GHL, 7.99. Lloyd's diary offers further insight into the apparently crooked nature of the enterprise from its inception: see n. 858, **3 August 1711**.

[692] Edge of page torn away.

[693] Lotteries were a recent innovation embraced by the state as a way of raising revenue through the sale of tickets. The first state lottery, conceived by Thomas Neale, was known as the 'Million Adventure', and was held in 1694 to raise funds for the Nine Years' War. The model was designed to be generous and raise encourage sales of tickets; 100,000 tickets (hence Lloyd's description) were sold for £10 each. There were 2,500 prizes to be won – the highest being £1000 – which would be paid in annuities over 16 years. Non-winning tickets, or 'blanks', were effectively government bonds worth £1 per annum for 16 years. The lottery of 1710, held by the Godolphin-Marlborough ministry, was slightly different, with an annuity period of 32 years. Lloyd's precise meaning here is a little uncertain; perhaps Lloyd was involved in collecting revenues for the sale of tickets in 1710, or, perhaps more likely, he may have been collecting his final return from participation in the lottery of 1694. See Anne Murphy, 'Lotteries in the 1690s: Investment or gamble?', *Financial History Review*, 12 (2005), 227–246, and Bob Harris, 'Lottery adventuring in Britain, c.1710–1760', *English Historical Review*, 133 (2018), 284–322.

[694] This was almost certainly John Power (or sometimes Poore), the attainted 9th Baron Power. A Jacobite, he served James II in Ireland as a Lieutenant Colonel. Despite his attainder, by 1715 he was in receipt of a pension and styled 'Lord Power'. He died in Paris, supposedly murdered by his servant, in 1725: see *Complete Peerage*, Vol. 6, 287. Power was a tenant of Lady Mathews (for whom Lloyd worked collecting rents) in a tenement between Charing Cross and Spring Gardens. Lloyd appears to have carried out certain duties and favours for Power also. See G. H. Gater and E. P. Wheeler (eds), *Survey of London: St Martin-in-the-Fields I: Charing Cross* (London, 1935), 111–113. For some examples of Lloyd's dealings with Power, see **8 May** and **2 October 1711**.

[695] The line breaks off here.

[fo. 81v]
Tuesday, 9 January: Performed my devotion within all Morning performed my devotion within till 4 bespoke small beere at the 3 Mariners called on Mr Page and told him he had made a Mistake about 20^s he had Charged young Mr Stanford and he promised if my Lady[696] would send the account and if it was so he would set it to rights called on young Sandford to com and Mend the Chimny paid the Cooke for dressing the loyne of Veale at prayers at Bow within at prayers performed my devotion.

Wednesday, 10 January: Performed my devotion after 8 went amongst the Tenants and received 2^s for a quarter's Rent of Mr Gamball for Michaelmas last past and after and allowd [*illegible*][697] for Watch and 3^d to drinke was at Mr Sawyers and see the ground where he was to build a House within and was busy all the afternoone with Roger Sandford about mending [t]he Chimny and could perform my devotion but by Ejaculations within at prayers performed my devotion.

Thursday, 11 January: Performed my devotion within all Morning performed my devotion within till 4 at Plow Coffee House[698] at [?W]arners and bought severall things at Star Coffee House[699] at prayers at Bow within at prayers performed my devotion etc.

Friday, 12 January: Performed my devotion went amongst the Tenants and received a quarter rent of Mrs James [d]ue at Ladyday 1709 went to enquire for Kenton at the smith and [fo]und him <his House> at St Brids Lane[700] called on Mr Rowlandson [?f]or Higgs's papers called on Mr Wade to know if he could let me have 30^{li} but he could not went to Mrs Lukey to see if she could come and she promisd she would in the evning within performed my devotion within 5 went to Roger Sandford and bid him get me 2 tyles for my stove within at prayers performed my devotion.

---

[696] See Introduction, pp. 25–30.
[697] Edge of page torn away.
[698] The Plough Coffee House, Coleman St., *c.*1702–1714, *LCH*, 449.
[699] Lillywhite lists five coffee houses with this name in London during Lloyd's time; at Mitre Court off Fleet St., at the Mint, at Crutched Friars, at the Royal Exchange, and finally at Exchange Alley. Lillywhite gives all of these establishments the same years of operation, *c.*1702–1714, *LCH*, 547.
[700] Bride Lane, just off Fleet St., next to the church of St Bride.

Saturday, 13 January: Performed my devotion within till 11 at prayers at St Bartholomew[701] called on Mr Standford and some others but got no money bought Porke at Cooks performed my devotion within till Neare 5 called at Rabys for my Stockings but they were not don at prayers at Bow bought Cheese at prayers performed my devotion.

Sunday, 14 January: Performed my devotion heard Mr Baker[702] at St Michael's Cornwell[703] 7 John 38.39 performed my devotion heard the Lecturer at Lothbury[704] left my wife at Mr Finches walkt to St Paules and heard the latter end of the prayres [*sic*] called my wife at Mr Finches within read at prayers performed my devotion etc.

[fo. 82r]
Monday, 15 January: Performed my devotion went to Mr Sandford and we went to Mr Stones[705] and spoke to him about his back yard and his Lease and he promised me I should see it on Friday called on other Tenants and talked with Mrs Bunker within a little went to M[r] Lambe and received a yeares rent 5¹ and allowed 20ˢ received Goodsons quarter's rent of Mr Payne for Christmas quarters and 5ˢ for part of Ann Darby Christmas rent,[706] at prayers at St Laurance. Performed my devotion within Mrs Hall and Mr[?s] Hunt being her at prayers performed my devotion and within till [*blank*].

---

[701] Probably St Bartholomew the Great, Smithfield, very near to the Barbican where Lloyd spent much of his time during this later diary. Originally an Augustinian priory founded in the 12th century by the courtier and monk Rahere, after he purportedly saw a vision of St Bartholomew after falling ill on a pilgrimage to Rome. The hospital, of course, survives today. The church was made a parochial church following the Dissolution. During Lloyd's time, the site was in poor repair and had been encroached upon by various other parties, with parts of the church being rented by people for secular purposes, namely physicians, but it was still a functioning church, and the incumbent at the time was John Pountney (1707–1719). *TBE, London 1*, 196–203; Young and Young, *Old London Churches*, 68–70.

[702] Samuel Baker (1670–1749), rector of St Michael Cornhill from 1705 until his death in 1749. He was also reader at St Michael Bassishaw, 1708–15. See *Oxonienses*, Vol. 1, 58; *CCEd* Person ID: 160824. See nn. 856, **26 July 1711**, and 900, **10 October 1711**.

[703] St Michael Cornhill: see **29 November 1677**.

[704] Samuel Hilliard, who, amongst several other offices, held the lectureship at St Margaret Lothbury from 1698 until 1712: *Oxonienses*, Vol. 2, 715; *CCEd* Person ID: 81990.

[705] Thomas Stone, in conflict with Lady Mathews, claimed to hold a 99-year lease for buildings and a yard on Barbican Street. This resulted in a Chancery case: Mathewes v. Stone, 1712, TNA C 8/654/26.

[706] Ann Darby was evidently a poor tenant; here Lloyd was probably collecting parish relief in payment of her rent.

Tuesday, 16 January: Performed my devotion within till 11 went to Mr Rowlandsons and left a Noate for him to meete me Friday Evening at Wrights Coffee House[707] called on Mr Davis to know if he had any Money by him but he had not within performed my devotion within till 6 left a letter at Post House fo[r] Lady Mathews heard part of a sermon at St Swithins[708] at Mr Cocks and heard Mr Goodgroome Mr Cocke and Sister play on 3 base viols[709] till after 9 stayd till 11 supt there at prayers performed my devotion.

Wednesday, 17 January: Went to see for Dayley[710] to bid him bring in Ale on Thursday Morning performed my devotion within performed my devotion after within till 5 went to Mr Rowlansons for my wife supt stayd till 9 at prayers performed my devotion.

Thursday, 18 January: Performed my devotion went to Mr Moore[711] gave him 10ˢ and desired him to speak to Mr Mayben[712] to looke after the business above bridge[713] bought rusks of the

---

[707] Lillywhite lists two establishments by this name; in Aldersgate St., and in Artillery Lane, both *c.*1702–1714, *LCH*, 664.

[708] St Swithin London Stone stood on the northern side of Cannon St. It was damaged in the Blitz and demolished in 1962. The eponymous London Stone now stands on display on a plinth in Cannon St.

[709] Viols are fretted, stringed, bowed instruments, played upright like a cello. They come in a variety of sizes and tunings, including the bass.

[710] Possibly 'Dagley'.

[711] Samuel Moore, Surveyor of the Coast Waiters, was also a noted draughtsman and engraver. He created the plates in Francis Sandford's *History of the Coronation of James II ... and of ... Queen Mary* (1687), *ODNB*. He is mentioned in the correspondences of a number of print and ballad collectors of the period, including John Bagford, Samuel Pepys, and Humfrey Wanley. See Bagford to Wanley, BL, Harley MS 3777, fo. 146; Pepys to Bagford, BL, Harley MS 4966, fo. 129, Wanley to Bagford, 25 June 1701, BL, Harley MS 4966, fo. 127. The last of these suggests that he was not 'major player' in these circles; it opens 'I intreat you to go speedily to Mr More (I think that's his name) and procure of him the Receipt of his Ink [...]'. I am very grateful to Tim Somers for providing me with these references.

[712] Peter Maybin or Mabin was another Coast Waiter: see Assessment book, Land Tax, Farringdon Without, Walbrook, 1711–1712, LMA, CLC/525/ MS11316/038.

[713] London Bridge, still the only bridge in 1711. Lloyd is probably referring to some duties upstream or *west* of the bridge, beyond the legal quays; the phrase is used in Richard Hayes, *Rules for the Port of London, Or, The Water-Side Practice* (London, 1722), 117. The watermen, mentioned in the same entry below, were hired to transport assessed goods onward up the Thames, often 'above the Bridge'. For Lloyd and London Bridge, see also n. 979, **30 April 1712**.

Duch baker at St Catherine's[714] at Custom House[715] paid Mr Mabyn 10^s for Gravesend and he promised to looke after the watermen, at prayers at St Edmond[716] performed my devotion within till 5 at prayers at Bow bought Oatecakes within at prayers performed my devotion etc.

Friday, 19 January: Performed my devotion tooke Coach at Cheapeside went to St Martins Coffee House in St Martins Streete[717] to Mr Dawson paid him 42:10^s per Lady Mathews Order and tooke his Receipt at Mr Higgs and talkt with him about selling his afaire stayd till after 12 came home bought meate at the Bear for diner performed my devotion within till 6 met Mr Dawson and Mr Rowlanson at Wrights Coffee House to goe to Stones to see his Lease but he was not to be found within at prayers performed my devotion etc.

[fo. 82v]
Saturday, 20 January: Performed my devotion went to Mr Stone and he was gon out amongst the Tenants but got no money bought a Loyne Mutton and staks of Mrs Denis received 9^{li} in p[ar]t[718] of Mrs Harris called on Veares and told him I would pay him in the afternoone within performed my devotion called at Stones and he was at Diner, at prayers at Charterhouse[719] called at Stones and received 13^{li}

---

[714] Originally 'St Cath'. Probably St Katharine Cree, an ancient church in Leadenhall St. which had existed since at least 1108. The present church was rebuilt in 1628–1631, and is the only surviving City church dating from the first half of the 17th century. It was consecrated by Laud in 1631, and the vestments and service used during the ceremony were later used against him during his trial. See *TBE, London 1*, 228–229; Young and Young, *Old London Churches*, 92–94.

[715] Originally 'C. H.' Frustratingly, Lloyd used the same abbreviation to represent 'Coffee House' and 'Custom House', and visits to both were frequent. It is usually possible to infer Lloyd's intention, but it is sometimes not immediately obvious. Ambiguity will be noted. Cf. n. 935, **12 January 1712**.

[716] St Edmund, King and Martyr. Standing in Lombard St., the church is of medieval origin but was destroyed by the Great Fire and rebuilt, probably by Hooke, in 1670–1674; *TBE, London 1*, 217–218.

[717] Lillywhite's list does not include a coffee house with this exact name, but it may be Martin's Street Coffee House, probably at Northumberland House in Aldersgate Ward, 'on the west side of St Martin's Lane', which may in the late 17th century have been occasionally referred to as St Martin's St. (though there is in fact a street nearby with this name, dating to the 1690s). This establishment was active c.1702–1714, *LCH*, 362.

[718] Alternatively 'payment'.

[719] A complex of buildings which 'conveys a vivid impression of the type of large rambling 16th-century mansion that once existed all round London'. Originally founded as a Carthusian Priory by Sir Walter de Manny in 1370, it became a private residence in the 1540s after the Dissolution. In the early 17th century it came into the ownership of

for ½ yeares Rent due at Christmas within payd Veares his Bill 3^{li} within paid Sanfords bill which remained and 7^s 6[720] for empt[y]ing the Vault at prayers performed my devotion etc.

Sunday, 21 January: Performed my devotion heard a stranger 3 John 5 performed my devotion heard a stranger againe at St Laurance 6 Luke 36 within read at prayers performed my devotion etc.

Monday, 22 January: Within till after 11 at prayers at St Laurance bought Turpentine pills[721] at Mr Warners within at prayers performed my devotion within till 5 at prayers at Bow bought oatecakes and Cheese within at prayers performed my devotion.

Tuesday, 23 January: Performed my devotion within till after 11 went to the Cooks and bought 6^d veale after bought Nayles at Plow Coffee house performed my devotion within till 5 at prayers at Bow within at prayers performed my devotion etc.

Wednesday, 24 January: Performed my devotion after 8 amongst the Tenants received 10^s of Mrs Cooley for a [q]uarter's rent due at Michaelmas after received of Jon Harding 6^s for a quarter's rent due at Christmass after received of Mr Higham 5:5 for a quarter's rent due at Christmas for his House and 7^{li} was Mrs Bickerstafes; bought shoulder Mutton of Mrs Denis at prayers at St Alphage[722] within at prayers performed my devotion.

Thursday, 25 January: Performed my devotion after 7 went to Mr Higgs but the money was not paid in as I expected at Westminister Abby heard a Sermon 32 Deuteronomy 29 called at

---

Thomas Sutton, who endowed an almshouse, hospital, and school on the site when he died in 1611. It was still functioning in this capacity during Lloyd's lifetime. Lloyd was attending the chapel on the site, which is also still in operation today. See *TBE, London 4: North*, 614–620.

[720] This is scribbled untidily; it looks like 76^s, but this seems an unlikely sum.

[721] In spite of its toxicity, turpentine has long been used as a medicament; Pepys had it recommended to him by his physician, Dr Alexander Burnet, for the treatment of kidney stones, a malady with which Pepys had a long and troubled history. The turpentine pills were recommended to him in January 1664, and by December of that year, Pepys was attributing his unusually good health to them, *Pepys*, Vol. 5, 1–2, 359.

[722] The original parish church of St Alphage London Wall was abandoned following the Dissolution in favour of the former buildings of Elsing Spital Priory. Destroyed during the First World War, the ruins stand at the corner of London Wall and Wood St., *TBE, London 1*, 190.

Mr Higgs and heard part of a Sermon at his Chappell[723] 1 Timothy 1.15 then he told me he had seene the Man that Managed the affayre betweene him and the New Subscribers and that they were to meete this Evening came home at 1 within performed my devotion within till after 4 left my wife at Mrs Wades at Starr Coffee House at prayers at Bow at Mr Wades[724] supt there stayd till after 9 at prayers performed my devotion.

Friday, 26 January: Performed my devotion within till after 11 at prayers at St Alpage amongst the Tenants but received no money within performed my devotion within till after 5 at prayers at Bow within at prayers performed my devotion.

[fo. 83r]
Saturday, 27 January: Performed my devotion within till 11 at prayers at St Laur[ence] with Mr Page and shewed him my Lady Mathews accounts and he desired a little time to looke after his accounts amongst the Tenants but could receive no mony I lett Goodsons Roome to Creeke Junior for 30^s per Annum and he is to leave his roome in the little yard performed my devotion within till after 4 at prayers at St Dionis[725] and after bespoke part of a loyne of Veale of Baynes the Cooke at prayers performed my devotion.

Sunday, 28 January: Performed my devotion heard a stranger at St Michael Cornhill <5 Matthew 8> performed my devotion heard Mr Moore[726] at St Laurance 4 Genesis 6.7 within read at prayers performed my devotion.

---

[723] The precise location of Higgs's 'chapel' is uncertain, but it was referenced in a letter from William Quarles to Archbishop Tenison as one of the locations at which the Nonjuror Thomas Brett preached a controversial sermon which evinced a sacerdotal view of absolution, on 18 November 1711. For the most part, however, the febrile atmosphere of early 18th-century religious controversy rarely makes an impression in Lloyd's diary. See LPL, MS 941 fo. 30.

[724] See Introduction, p. 30.

[725] St Dionis, Backchurch was a small and wealthy City parish which played a comparatively significant role in the events of Lloyd's diary, as we shall see below. In Langbourne ward, it roughly encompassed the area where Gracechurch St. bisected Fenchurch St. and Lombard St. It was dissolved in 1878. For more on this parish, and a study which influenced my own efforts to piece together the life of Lloyd, see Jeremy Boulton, 'Microhistory in early modern London: John Bedford (1601–1667)', *Continuity and Change*, 22 (2007), 113–141. See also Young and Young, *Old London Churches*, 79.

[726] Possibly Thomas Morer, a Reader or Lecturer for St Lawrence Jewry in 1700 (see n. 690, **7 January 1711**): see *CCEd* Person ID: 165104. The incumbent for St Lawrence Jewry in 1711 was John Mapletoft: see n. 727.

Monday, 29 January: Performed my devotion within till 11 at prayers at St Bartholomew amongst the Tenants received 23ˢ.5ᵈ from Mrs Denis and 9ˢ.6ᵈ of Mrs Ladyman within performed my devotion within till 5 bought Sugar Cur[?ran]ts and barly at Mr Keyes and stakes at Mrs Denis within within [*sic*] at prayers performed my devotion etc.

Tuesday, 30 January: Performed my devotion etc. Heard Dr Mapletoft[727] at St Laurance 51 Psalm 14 performed my devotion etc within till 3 went with my Wife as far as Mrs Wards left her there called at Lawrence Hollker[728] to see how he did and wrote a letter to his father in answer to his I received this day from him that his young son was dead went to St Dunstants [*sic*][729] heard Mr Haley[730] 26 Jeremiah 15 within at <prayers>

Wednesday, 31 January: Performed my devotion at 10 went amongst the Tenants received 10ˢ for a quarter's Rent <~~due at Christmas~~> of Mrs Creeke <due at Christmas 1709> and let young Creeks roome to Ann Ladyman, received a quarter's Rent due at Christmas last after paid 4ˡⁱ 17 9 to Mr Cornwall for Mr Dawson within performed my devotion after 2 went to Mrs Halls stayd till 7 within at prayers performed my devotion etc <at prayers at the Temple Church[731] that day>

---

[727] John Mapletoft, MD, DD (1631–1721), was vicar of the united parishes of St Lawrence Jewry and St Mary Magdalen, Milk St. from 1686 until his death. Mapletoft was a Fellow of the Royal Society, president of Sion College, Gresham professor of physic, and a friend of Locke, Hooke, and Tillotson. Like many of the clergy favoured by Lloyd in his London years, Mapletoft had low church, latitudinarian leanings and was an early member of both the Society for Promoting Christian Knowledge and the Society for the Propagation of the Gospel in Foreign Parts. *ODNB*; *CCEd* Person ID: 126258.

[728] The Holkers were a prominent family of Gravesend, Kent, who owned a series of breweries, inns, and, it seems, wharfs in the town. It is therefore unsurprising that Lloyd knew them, since his Customs work occasionally took him to Gravesend (see below). The Lawrence Holker mentioned here would have been a young man; he would commence his studies at Pembroke College, Cambridge, the following year, before pursuing a career as a physician. His father, Thomas Holker, son of Lawrence Holker (d.1708) is the 'Mr Holker' referred to regularly below. See *Cantabrigienses*, Vol. 1, pt. 2, 392; Will of Lawrence Holker, Gentleman of Gravesend, Kent, 1708, TNA, PROB 11/504/196, and Will of Lawrence Holker, Doctor in Physic of Milton next Gravesend, Kent, 1738, PROB 11/690/263. No will for Thomas Holker survives.

[729] Whether this was St Dunstan-in-the-East on St Dunstan's Hill near the Tower of London, or St Dunstan-in-the-West in Fleet St. is unclear; elsewhere, Lloyd sometimes specifies.

[730] Probably William Haley, rector of St Giles-in-the-Fields from 1695 until his death in 1715.

[731] Temple Church is a royal peculiar off Fleet St., consecrated in 1185 as the headquarters of the Knights Templar in England, *TBE, London 1*, 266–270.

Thursday, 1 February: Performed my devotion within till 11 at prayers at St Edmond called to see Mrs Ward within performed my devotion within till 5 at prayers at St Mary Woollworth at Mrs Cocks for my wife till 7 within at prayers performed my devotion.

Friday, 2 February: Performed my devotion within till 8 called on Mr Page but he was not within a[t] Major Lacuse[732] received 1^{li} 10^s for a quarter rent due at Christmas last call[ed] at Mrs Lukyes and she very ill and did not know when she could come bought a piece of porke at the Cooks at the White Beare[733] at prayers at St Alphage within performed my devotion and my wife and I had many words for her passio[?n] within till 3 at prayers at St Laurance but very drousee within till 5 made the bed and received of Mrs Bunker 1^{li} for Midsummer at prayers at Bow within at prayers performed my devotion etc.

[fo. 83v]
Saturday, 3 February: Performed my devotion went <to Bi[?ggs] to speake with Mayh[?ew]> to the Tenants received 12^s.6^d of Hawgood for Christmas rent afterward at Mr Maddox's and promised Mrs Linett she should have their hous at Mr Sherwoods and received 2^l:10^s for Michaelmas rent afterward at Mrs Bristows and received ½ a yeares due at Christmas 6^{li} called at home and told her my wife I would goe to see for Margaret and stayd at the Spread Eagle[734] till she came and she told me her Mistress would not ly in[735] till middle March within performed my devotion and Mrs Ladyman came for her daughters Earnest[736] and I gave it her after enquired of Mrs Creeke what kind of woman and her

---

[732] Peter Lekeux (1648–1723) master weaver and, by his death, a colonel in the Tower Hamlets trained bands. The Lekeux family, of Huguenot origin, was one of England's most important silk-weaving families, and Lekeux himself was one of the founders of the Royal Lustring Company in 1692, *ODNB*.

[733] Probably the same establishment as the 'Bear', mentioned above: see n. 685, **6 January 1711**; see also **19 January** and **21 July 1711**.

[734] Perhaps the Spread Eagle in Gracechurch St., a prominent coaching inn which dates back at least to the 17th century, John Camden Hotten (ed.), *The Little London Directory of 1677* (London, 1863). See p. 313, **3 March 1711**.

[735] Postpartum confinement, usually for about a month; for a useful introduction to the cultural practices surrounding childbirth in early modern England, see Adrian Wilson, 'The ceremony of childbirth and its interpretation', in Valerie Fildes (ed.), *Women as Mothers in Pre-Industrial England: Essays in Memory of Dorothy McLaren* (London, 1990), 68–107.

[736] In other words, a kind of security or deposit to finalize an agreement or transaction. In this case, it appears that Lloyd may have been securing the employment of Mrs Ladyman's daughter, either in his own service or that of another individual – perhaps Lady Mathews.

Husband were Kitchinman at prayers at St Bartholomew within at prayers performed my devotion.

Sunday, 4 February: Performed my devotion etc heard the Bishop of the Ile of Man[737] at St Laurance 1 Timothy 1.15 Christ[738] and had his blessing performed my devotion heard a stranger at St Laurance called at Mrs Cowsies left my wife there walked round St Pauls and caled my wife at Mrs Cowseys and stayed till 6 within read at prayers performed my devotion.

Monday, 5 February: Performed my devotion went Within all day my wife being very ill performed my devotion as usualy at prayers.

Tuesday, 6 February: Performed my devotion within till 10 heard Dr Moss[739] at St Lawrance 4 Ephesians 25 performed my devotion within all the afternoone at prayers performed my devotion.

Wednesday, 7 February: Performed my devotion within till 11 at prayers at <All> Hallows the wall called at Mrs Lukyes who was very ill went to Mrs Cousies to desire the mayd should not come till Friday performed my devotion within till 3 called at Mr Bunkers and he gave me a Bond to pay a yeares rent which would be due at ~~Midsomer~~ <Lady Day> at Mr Sandfords and talkt about severall things came in at 5 within at prayers performed my devotion.

---

[737] Thomas Wilson (1663–1755), bishop of Sodor and Man from 1697 until his death. Popular for his personal piety, integrity, and charitable disposition, Wilson appears to have been held in particular esteem by Lloyd. Like many of Lloyd's favourite churchmen, he was a proponent of the Society for the Propagation of the Gospel in Foreign Parts. Wilson was a noted advocate of religious toleration; one biographer has suggested that the 'mutual respect Wilson shared with non-Anglican Christians suggests some degree of proleptic ecumenism', *ODNB*. A 'life' of Wilson printed in an 18th-century edition of his works claims that 'he was so great a friend to toleration, that the Papists who resided in the island [...] not unfrequently attended his sermons and his prayers. The Dissenters too attended even the Communion-Service, as he had allowed them a liberty to sit or stand; which, however, they did not make use of, but behaved in the same manner with those of the established Church.' C. Cruttwell (ed.), *The Works of the Right Reverend Father in God Thomas Wilson, D.D.* (London, 1782), 57.

[738] Originally 'X^t'; perhaps denotes the Sacrament.

[739] Robert Moss, DD (*c.*1666–1729), held the Tuesday Lectureship at St Lawrence Jewry, from 1708 until 1727. He was made chaplain to William III in 1701, and also served Anne and George I. He became dean of Ely in 1713 and rector of Gilston, Hertfordshire, the following year. Moss was a skilled and popular preacher. A vocal high churchman and Tory, he publicly supported Sacheverell throughout the controversies of 1710. *ODNB*; *CCEd* Person ID: 17976.

Thursday, 8 February: Performed my devotion within till after 10 at the Cooks bought a piece of beefe at prayers at St Bartholomew within performed my devotion within all afternoone my Wife and I had many bitter words for nothing but her peevish temper. At prayers performed my devotion.

Friday, 9 February: Performed my devotion within all morning it rayning hard performed my devotion within till after 3 Mr Williams being here from Cherriton[740] at Mr Bunkers got him to signe a Noate for a quarter's rent more than the Bond was for at Mr Standfords and sent for Mrs Kitchinman and told her I would let her the roome that young Creeke went out of and bid her bring me in 4 gallons of Ale after at Mr Smiths and received a quarter's Rent for Christmass Allowed 12^s 6^d for the poore 3^d [f]or over rate 1^s.2^d for the watch 4 to drink within at prayers performed my devotion etc.

[fo. 84r]
Saturday, 10 February: Performed my devotion within till past 11 went to the Rose at Holourne [*sic*] bridg and carried a letter for Cousin Nicholas[741] to Mr William and he gave me a pint of wine within performed my devotion within till after 3 went to see Mrs Lucky and carried her a Cordiall[742] went to Market and bought a Shoulder Veall within went to the Cooks and told her I should not have anything drest tho I had before told her as I came from prayers I thought I should within at prayers performed my devotion etc.

Sunday, 11 February: Performed my devotion heard the Reader of St Laurance[743] 13 Luke 3 performed my devotion heard Mr ~~Moory~~ Moory 3 Romans [*deleted*] 1[744] walkt a little within read at prayers performed my devotion etc.

---

[740] Cheriton, a tiny Hampshire village some fifteen miles from Wonston, Lloyd's birthplace.
[741] See Introduction, p. 31. Perhaps a coach for Wiltshire left from the Rose with the mail. See also two references to a carrier at the Rose, **29 December 1677.**
[742] Medicine.
[743] Perhaps George Stanhope, DD (1660–1728), who had been Tuesday Lecturer at St Lawrence Jewry until 1708, and a reader at the same church until 1711. He was also rector of St Nicholas, Deptford, and dean of Canterbury (1704). Like Robert Moss, who preceded him as Lecturer at St Lawrence (see n. 739, **6 February 1711**), Stanhope was a noted Tory and high churchman. *ODNB*; *CCEd* Person ID: 3379.
[744] This citation is ambiguous; originally 'Ron:', followed by a messy deletion. 'What advantage then hath the Jew? or what profit is there of circumcision?' Romans 3:1, which seems like an unusual choice of sermon.

Monday, 12 February: Performed my devotion went to Mr Pages and he promised to meete me at Coffee house in Jewin Streete[745] at severall of the Tenants Received a quarter Rent due at Midsummer of Mr Rogers <1:10: allowed to drinke 3> and a quarter Rent of Mrs Blackden 1:10^s and allowed her 2½ to drinke after mett Mr Page and he gave me 20^s for a quarter Rent due from Mr Sandford for Michaelmas 1708 which he had Mistaken and placed it to my Lady as a debt to her, but I shewing him the receipt he gave Mr Sandford he was sattisfied and I gave him a receipt for it went to C[?ustom] H[?ouse] and stayd a little but saw very few people but Mr Lewis[746] promised to pay me the end of the weeke performed my devotion within till 5 at prayers at Bow within at prayers <performed my devotion.>

Tuesday, 13 February: Performed my devotion at 8 went to Mr Higgs and after he had acquainted me t[?o] what had beene done he made and signed a Bond to put 30^{li} for me into the Corporation at 11 came away heard part of a sermon by Dr Mosse within performed my devotion within till after 3 with my Wife to Mrs Sykes but she was not within went to Mr Sandford and left word I would come to Mr Maddox on Thursday Morning called at Mrs the ca went to St Donstons heard Mr Haly 3 Proverbs [blank] within at prayers performed my devotion etc.

Thursday, 15 February: Performed my devotion. Went to Mr Maddox and he sent for Mr Linnett and I let him Mr Maddoxs house and went to the Bunch of Grapes above the barrs[747] and Mr Linnett gave us a pinte of wine received of Mr Dallaway 10^s for a quarter's Rent due at Christmass allowed 3^d ½ to drinke at prayers at Charter house received of Mr Howard 10^s for a quarter's Rent due at Christmas called at Mrs Powells and had a quarte of brandy within performed my devotion all afternoone Mrs Sykes being here at prayers performed my devotion.
the 14 is on the other side*

[fo. 84v]
Wednesday, 14 February: Performed my devotion etc within till 10 went to severall churches and no sermons at prayers at St

---

[745] Possibly Wither's Coffee House, listed by Lillywhite as existing in Jewin St. during c.1702–1714, *LCH*, 661.

[746] Perhaps Thomas Lewis, who was a Jerquer in the Customs House in 1711: see Assessment book, Land Tax, Farringdon Without, Walbrook, 1711–1712, LMA, CLC/525/ MS11316/038.

[747] 'Above the bars' suggests a premises in that part of the parish St Andrew Holborn which sat outside the jurisdiction of the City.

Hellens[748] called to see Mrs Lucky who was better within performed my devotion within <till> 5 bought 2 wiggs at the uper end of Gracechurch Streete heard a stranger at St Clements[749] 2 Joell 12.13. within at prayers performed my devotion etc.

Friday, 16 February: Performed my devotion within till 9 went to meete the Woman about the Celler next the 3 Cupps and we could doe Nothing till I spoke to Kenton to know where the key was and whether he was content to have me let it at Wrights Coffee House and left word if any letter came there for me to take care of it went to Mr Keyes and bought ¼ pound Nuttmegg 1 ounce Cloves ½ mace 1 ounce of Cinamon at the Cooks and bought a piece of porke within a little at prayers at Coleman Streete[750] within performed my devotion after 2 went with my wife to Mrs Sykes left her there I went to Kentons to know where the Key and he sayd the woman had it and told me I might let it called at Mr Rowansons[751] and asked him what he must have for Mrs Bowyers business and he said 15^s.8^d stayd a little at prayers at St Dunstons West[752] at Mr Byfields and left my old perrywig to be made a Ribon ends. called my wife at Mrs Powells stayd a little came home and after went to Honny Lane Market[753] to buy beefe but there was none within at <prayers performed my devotion.>

Saturday, 17 February: Performed my devotion within till 10 at prayers at Charter House went and carried dropps to Mrs Lukey went to the Spread Eagle Inn and spoke to Margaret at C.H[754] but could not get any money within performed my devotion after 3

---

[748] St Helen's, Bishopsgate; a large medieval church which survived the Great Fire, it was Shakespeare's parish church in the 1590s. *TBE, London 1*, 221–226.

[749] St Clement Eastcheap, in Clement's Lane off what is now King William St. It was destroyed in the Great Fire and was rebuilt by Wren in 1683–1687, *TBE, London 1*, 212–213.

[750] St Stephen Coleman St. was originally a chapel of ease for St Olave Old Jewry before being made a parish in 1456. It was burned in the Great Fire and rebuilt by Wren in the late 1670s. Sadly, it was destroyed during the Blitz in 1940 and not rebuilt; Young and Young, *Old London Churches*, 128–129.

[751] Probably 'Mr Rowlandson', mentioned frequently throughout. I have not identified this individual, but context would suggest that he was a lawyer; **24 April 1711**.

[752] St Dunstan-in-the-West in Fleet St. has medieval origins, being first mentioned *c*.1170. The medieval church was demolished in the 19th century to facilitate the widening of Fleet St., and the present building was constructed to the design of John Shaw in 1830–1833, *TBE, London 1*, 214–217.

[753] A grocery market constructed after the Great Fire off the northern end of Wood St., partially on the site of All Hallows' Church, which was burned but not rebuilt. It was closed in 1835 and subsequently was the site of the City of London School. See *Cripplegate*, 127–128.

[754] Uncertain; this may mean 'Custom House' or 'Coffee House'.

went to Mr Sandfords and carried the Key of the Celler to wher Kenting was at prayers at Bow went to Market but could Not buy Meat it was to deare went to Mrs Dennis and she had none small enough at severall places but could get none under 4^d a pound either beefe or Mutton within at prayers performed my devotion etc.

Sunday, 18 February: Performed my devotion heard Dr Mapletoft 6 Matthew 24 performed my devotion heard Mr Moore 116 Psalm 1 within read at prayers performed my devotion.

Monday, 19 February: Performed my devotion within all day Roger Sandford being mending the Chimny and Mrs Sykes helping my Wife makeing her Muff and Mrs Hammond and her daughter being here performed my devotion and at prayers.

[fo. 85r]
Tuesday, 20 February: Performed my devotion within till 10 at prayers at Charterhouse [?and] amongst the Tenants received $1^l:10^s$ of Rice and Allowed 1½ to drinke received quarter's Rent also of Hancock within performed my devotion within till 5 at St Donstons heard Mr Haley 11 Ecclesiastes 8 left a letter for Mr Lewis at the Queens Armes Coffee House[755] called at Mr Wards but not within at home performed my devotion at prayers.

Wednesday, 21 February: Performed my devotion within till 10 at severall of the Tenants but got no Money at St Bartholomew heard Dr Stubbs[756] 16 Luke 11 performed my devotion within till Neare 5 at Tom's Coffeehouse[757] heard Mr

---

[755] Originally 'Queens Arms C.H'. This seems very likely to have been the Queen's Arms Coffee House at the Custom House, *c.*1702–1714, as listed by Lillywhite. It may also have been the better-documented Queen's Arms Tavern, sometimes described as a coffee house, on Ludgate Hill *c.*1706–1833, *LCH*, 461–464.

[756] Probably Philip Stubbs (1665–1738), though Lloyd was mistaken in his attribution of 'Doctor'. Stubbs was a renowned preacher and, again, an early proponent of the SPG. He was rector of Woolwich (1694–1699) and subsequently St Alphage London Wall (1699) and St James Garlickhythe (1705). Stubbs vacated these livings when he became archdeacon of St Albans, though in 1719 he became rector of Launton, Oxfordshire. *ODNB*; *CCEd* Person ID: 3485.

[757] 'Tom's Coffee House' was an extremely popular name for such establishments in the early 18th century, and several existed in London during Lloyd's time. They included: premises in Birchin Lane, *c.*1702–1749, which was also known as 'Old Tom's' to distinguish it from the establishments: on Cornhill, at No. 3, possibly established in 1714; at Fulwood's Rents, Holborn, 1702–1714; at Ludgate, or Half Moon Court, Ludgate Hill, *c.*1699–1715; in Wood St., Cheapside, *c.*1714–1741; in Spring Garden, Charing Cross, *c.*1711–1725; a

Pullen[758] at St Clement's 5 Ephesians 15:16 within performed my devotion at prayers etc.

Thursday, 22 February: Performed my devotion within till 11 at prayers at Coleman Streete performed my devotion within till after 3 heard Dr Gatford[759] 22 Matthew 39 within at prayers performed my devotion.

Friday, 23 February: Performed my devotion amongst the Tenants received 3^{li} 15^s of Mr Jones and allowed him 3^d to drinke bought beafe at the Cooks at prayers at St Peters at Custom House received my salery for Christmas within performed my devotion after 3 went to Mr Higgs and he told me the reason of signing to what wee had paid in was appointed and gave me an account of the whole afaire, stayd till neare 6 came home at 7 within at prayers performed my devotion.

Saturday, 24 February: Performed my devotion within till 10 amongst the Tenants but got no mony but of Widow Tompson 7^s. 6^d for a quarter's Rent due at Christmas at Mrs Powells and fetch Mrs Holkers Hood she carryed to be changed at prayres at St Bartholomew bought Loyne of V̶e̶ Mutton of Mrs Dennis within performed my devotion within till 4 carried the box to Billingsgate delivered it to Lomas the Waterman in which was 4^{li} grounds powder cost $1^s{:}4^d$ $\frac{1}{4}^{li}$ Nutmegg 3^s ounce Cloves 10 ounce Cinamon 10½ ounce Mace Sarsnet Hood 5:6 all $11{:}2^d$ at Starr Coffee House dranke a Single Mugg Ale at prayers at Bow. Within at prayers performed my devotion etc.

Sunday, 25 February: Performed my devotion heard Dr Mapletoft 6 Matthew 26 performed my devotion heard Mr Moore 116 Psalm 1:2 went with my Wife to see Mrs Herne in St Laurance Lane within read at prayers performed my devotion.

---

prominent and oft-referenced Tom's in St Martin's Lane, c.1695–1761; in Russell St., Covent Garden, c.1700–1814; one reference to an establishment in Maiden Lane, Covent Garden, c.1711; and finally in Devereux Court, near Temple Bar, again a notable coffee house with many famous patrons, c.1702–1775. See *LCH*, 580–596.

[758] John Pullen or Pulleyn (c.1683/4–1713), appointed rector of St Clement's Eastcheap in 1707, he held the living until his death. He was also made rector of Warcham St Michael, Dorset, in 1713. *Oxonienses*, Vol. 3, p. 1219; *CCEd* Person ID: 165932.

[759] Lionel Gatford (1665–1715). Amongst several other appointments, Gatford was rector of St Dionis Backchurch from 1684 until his death. He was also made archdeacon of St Albans in 1713 and precantor and treasurer of St Paul's Cathedral in 1714. *Cantabrigienses*, Vol. 1, pt. 2, 200; *CCEd* Person ID: 88733.

Monday, 26 February: Performed my devotion after 9 at severall of the Tenants but received nothing at Mr Sandfords and Received a bill for worke for Lord Powers House 3:11:1 and one for worke for my Lady till No:[760] 16:50:3:11½ at prayers at Bishopsgate went to see Mrs Lucky within performed my devotion within till after 4 at Sta[?r] Coffee House at prayers at Bow at Sun Coffee House[761] at Mrs Champnys till 11 supt there at p[?rayers].

[fo. 85v]
Tuesday, 27 February: Within all Morning the Man being Mending the topps of the Chimny next ours performed my devotion within till 3 at Mr Sandfords paid him $3^l:11^s$ for my Lord Powers House and 20^{li} in part of his other Bill at Wrights Coffee House called at home at St Dunstons heard Mr Haley 5 Deuteronomy 28:29 within.

Wednesday, 28 February: Performed my devotion within all the Morning doeing things and setting down the Cloths for washing performed my devotion within till Neare 3 went with my Wife to Mrs Hamons in Bishopsgate Streete stayd till 5 left my wife there went to St Clement's heard Mr Pullen 14 Luke 18 called my Wife at Mrs Hamonds stayd till 8 within at prayers performed my devotion etc.

Thursday, 1 March: Performed my devotion within till 9 went to Mrs Harris received 2^l to Make up 3^{li} I had received before for a quarter's rent due at Midsomer at Mr Sandfords stayd till Neare 11 went to Mrs Powells for a flask of Brandy stayd till 12 it rayning hard within performed my devotion within all the afternoone waiting for Mr Holker that did not come at prayers <performed my devotion>.

Friday, 2 March: Performed my devotion within till 10 went to Lyme Streete to Mr Briscoes for Hedges[762] Rent but he would pay None went to his House and told his wife so and Mr Sandford

---

[760] November?

[761] Again, there are a number of candidates for this location: at York Buildings, Buckingham St. (*c.*1681–1714); in Queen St., Cheapside (*c.*1702–1714); The Sun, Sunn, or Sunne Tavern, 'behind the Royal Exchange (well documented, referenced from 1651 until 1734 at least); in Chancery Lane (*c.*1702–1714); and at 'Holbourne Conduit' (*c.*1702–1736?). Since Lloyd mentions visiting 'Bow' – probably meaning St Mary-le-Bow in Cheapside – immediately afterward, we might suggest that the most likely location is that in Queen St., Cheapside; *LCH*, 556–558.

[762] See Introduction, pp. 28–30.

who told me the Woman would come to see the Coach house stables at prayers at St Alphages bought Meate at Cooks at prayers within all afternoone expecting Mr Holker and Wife but they came not at prayers performed my devotion etc.

Saturday, 3 March: Performed my devotion within till after 9 <called at Mr Frutrells to call Mr Holker> amongst the Tenants but got no Mony at prayers at Charter House called at home went to the Spread Eagle in Gracechurch Streete to Speake to Margaret to get ½ pound butter but could get none within Mr Higgs came to Me and we went to the Starr and drank ½ pinte wine and he told me more of the concerne and gave me a Noate on Trev Treviso[763] and I promised to get him 5^{li} and meete him at Starr Coffee House at 5 within performed my devotion at 3 went to Mr Peales and received 7^l.10^s for a quarter's rent due at Christmas and allowed 6^d to drinke within till about 5 went to Starr Coffee House and paid Mr Higgs 5^{li} within Mr Holker and his Wife being here they stayd till 7. Within at prayers performed my devotion etc.

[fo. 86r]
Sunday, 4 March: Performed my devotion etc heard the Reader at Coleman Streete 4 Matthew 1 ⅌ performed my devotion heard Mr Moore at St Laurance 116 Psalm 2 stayd in the Church and heard the Bishope of the Ile of Man 4 Mark 26 within read at prayers performed my devotion.

Monday, 5 March: Performed my devotion amongst the Tenants but received no Money at prayers at St Bartholomew at Mr Rowlandsons performed my devotion him 10^s. for Mrs Bowyers business and he allowed me 5^s and gave me 2 bottles wine performed my devotion within till 5 at prayer at St Mary Woollnorth at Star Coffee House called my Wife at Mrs Couseys at prayers againe with her at Foster Lane within at prayers performed my devotion.

Tuesday, 6 March: Performed my devotion after 9 amongst the Tenants Received 9^s for a quarter's Rent of Mr Berrill due at Michaelmas 1709 <allowed 1½> and a quarter's Rent of Mr Watkinson due at Christmas 1^l:15^s Allowed 1^s for poor 1^s for Watch 2^s Over rate, went to Custom House heard Mr Johnson dyed this Morning received of

---

[763] An unusual name: I have not been able to identify this individual. Note that this is not a reference to the Italian city of Treviso.

Mr Mayben 1^l: 1^s: 6^d for midle station[764] at prayers at St Edmond within performed my devotion within till after 4 heard Mr Haley at St Donstons 15 Luke 18 <19> within at prayers performed my devotion.

Wednesday, 7 March: Performed my devotion within till after 11 at prayers at Lothbury performed my devotion within till Neare 3 left my Wife at Mrs Cowseys called on Mrs Windsors and told her Fielding would give but 50^s for her things the she left in her House called to see Mrs Coggill who was very lame with a fall downe stayrs went to Mr Johnsons but Nobody was came heard part of prayers and Catichizing at St Austins[765] walkt about St Pauls till 5 went againe and nobody was come but Mr Mayben and Mr Pinder stayd till after 7 before we went to Church <he was buried in vault> called my Wife at Mrs Cowseys for my wife stayd till 9 at prayers performed my devotion etc.

[fo. 86v *BLANK*]
[fo. 87r *BLANK*]

[fo. 87v]
Thursday, 8 March: Performed my devotion within till after 10 at St Laurance and heard Dr Mapletoph 13 Romans 4 called at Mrs Cowseys and had ½ pound butter and a sugar dish performed my devotion within till after 3 heard Mr Lassenby[766] at Bow Charrity seeketh not her owne[767] at Mrs Johnsons till Neare 7 within at prayers performed my devotion etc.

Friday, 9 March: Performed my devotion went to Mr Sandfords but he not within there came one Smith a Quaker that lives at the Legg and Starr in Barbican to take Bunkers house I went with him and he see it and after I called at his House and his sun in Law

---

[764] Probably referring to taking in ships on the 'middle' quays in the Port of London.

[765] Lloyd was probably referring to St Augustine, Watling St., owing it its proximity to St Paul's. First mentioned *c*.1148, it was destroyed in the Great Fire and rebuilt by Wren in 1680–1684, with the tower completed in 1695–1696. The church was destroyed during the Blitz, and though the body was not rebuilt, the tower was restored and incorporated into St Paul's Cathedral Choir School, *TBE, London 1*, 336–337.

[766] The identity of this preacher is unclear; he was not rector at St Mary-le-Bow (or St Mary Bow, Stratford). No one with appropriate dates appears in *Oxonienses* or *Cantabrigienses*, nor are any contemporary sermons printed under this name or similar (Lazenby, Lassenby, Lasenby). Lloyd's hand here is quite clear.

[767] Perhaps 1 Corinthians 13:4–5: 'Charity suffereth long, and is kind; charity envieth not; charity vaunteth not itself, is not puffed up, [5] Doth not behave itself unseemly, seeketh not her own, is not easily provoked, thinketh no evil ...'

tooke the House at 12^{li} per Annum gave a Shilling Earnest for a yeare Certaine and ½ yeares Warning Wittness James Adams, John Adams is the Tenant called at home and my Wife went with me to Cousin Amyes[768] and I went to Mr Chumleys to speake to him about Mr Sawyers building a House on my Ladys piece of Ground but he was not at home called at Cousin Amyes and stayd a little went to St Mary overs[769] heard Dr Tipping[770] wo to them by whome the Offence cometh[771] dined at Cousin Oddys[772] crossed the Water went to Mr Sandford and we went to Feilding but he would give no more than 50^s for the goods and we made no end I came home performed my devotion and at 5 went for my Wife to cousin Oddyes and stayd till Neare 6 crossed the water and went to prayers to Foster Lane[773] within at prayers performed my devotion.

Saturday, 10 March: Performed my devotion at 9 went amongst the Tenants Received of Mrs Gambal 2^{li} for Christmas rent Allowd 3^d received of Mrs Garret 2^{li} for Michaelmas rent at prayers at Charter House received of Mrs Hill 1.7.6 for Christmas rent within performed my devotion within till 5 at prayers at Bow bought sugar and raysons of Mr Keyes within at prayers performed my devotion.

---

[768] The will of Elizabeth Lloyd makes reference to a 'Mr Amy of Camberwell and his Wife' but provides no further detail. It seems most likely that they were distant relations of hers, and they are completely omitted from George Lloyd's will.

[769] Originally the Augustinian priory of St Mary Overie, it became a parish church after the Dissolution with a new dedication to St Saviour. In 1905, it became Southwark Cathedral, *TBE, London 2: South*, 564–572.

[770] Probably Ichabod Tipping, DD, a rather obscure figure, rector of St Giles Camberwell from 1691 until his death in 1727; *CCEd* Person ID 96287: see also Douglas Allport, *Collections Illustrative of the Geology, History, Antiquities, and Associations, of Camberwell, and the Neighbourhood* (London, 1841), 109. Interestingly, Tipping was a founding subscriber to the joint stock of the Charitable Corporation, mentioned in its 1708 charter: see Carr, *Select Charters*, 257.

[771] 'Woe unto the world because of offences! for it must needs be that offences come; but woe to that man by whom the offence cometh!' Matthew 18:7.

[772] This seems likely to have been Philip Oddy, gentleman of Islington, whose will states that he also owned property in Bermondsey, south of the Thames, as well as in Saffron Walden and Ashdon in Essex: see will, TNA, PROB 11/694/304. Oddy witnessed the wills of both George and Elizabeth Lloyd, though he appears to have been a relative of the latter. He was an uncle of Philip Oddy, DD (d.1731), rector of Clifton, Bedfordshire. The family may have been of Yorkshire origin: *Cantabrigienses*, Vol. 1, pt. 3, 274.

[773] St Vedast Foster Lane is of very ancient origin, perhaps pre-dating the Norman Conquest. It was severely damaged, though not completely destroyed, by the Great Fire, and the ruins were restored 'by parochial initiative' in 1669–1672. The church was again rebuilt, by Wren, in 1695–1701, and a new spire added in 1709–1712, *TBE, London 1*, 265–266.

[fo. 88r]
Sunday, 11 March: Performed my devotion heard Dr Mapeltoph at St Lau[rence] 6 Matthew 4 last verses performed my devotion heard a Stranger at St Laurence and afterward Mr Rowlandson and spouse was with us till 7 read at prayers performed my devotion tooke Dr Hunter's dropps[774] etc.

Monday, 12 March: Performed my devotion in bed rose after 12 being in a gentle Sweate all Morning performed my devotion within all day at prayers performed my devotion and tooke more of Hunter's Dropps.

Tuesday, 13 March: Performed my devotion in bed rose after 11 performed my devotion within all day at prayers performed my devotion.

Wednesday, 14 March: Performed my devotion within till after 10 called at Mr Snells and bid her[775] come to my wife at prayers at St Alphage within performed my devotion Within till after 3 amongst the Tenants Received $7^{li}.10^s$ of Mr Buttler for ½ yeares Rent Allowed 1.10 for the Taxes and 6^d to drinke within at prayers at Foster Lane at prayers <performed my devotion.>

Thursday, 15 March: Within till after 8 called at Mr Stones to know where to meete him and his Lawyer he agreed to meete at Purcells at 3 Next day Received of Mrs Stiff 10^s for Christmass rent and allowed 2^s for Two latches and other things he put up when he came in called on Mr Moon and desired him to take away the dung and mend the wall and he promised he would doe it quickly caled at Wrights Coffe house and received a letter from Cousin Nicholas and called on Mr Wad and askt him if he could let me have 30^l but he could Not within after at prayers at Wallbrooke performed my devotion within till after 1 and then caled at Mr Stones who agreed to Meete at 3 at Purcells went to tell Mr Rowlandson of it and he was not within left a Noate for him called at Mr Byfield to tell him I would have my perrywigg

---

[774] Various quack 'medicines' were available in 18th-century London; this one is rather obscure. Lloyd sometimes refers to it has 'Hunter's Elixir'; a substance of the same name (alongside 'Hunter's Restorative') is included in Richard Burn, *The Justice of the Peace, and Parish Officer* (London, 1788), 129, in a 'Schedule of Medicines subject to the Duties', though this may have referred to a later cure-all.

[775] Perhaps Mr Snell's wife or servant.

don as soon as he could called my wife at Madam Halls stayd till 5 called at Mrs Couseuys and she was at Starr Coffee House we went thether and drank a Mugg of Alle and stayd till after 6 at prayers at Foster Lane. Within at prayers performed my devotion etc.

[fo. 88v]
Friday, 16 March: Performed my devotion within till 10 at prayers at Charter house amongst the Tenants met Mr Stone and he refused to let Mr Rowlandson see his Lease and went to let Mr Rowlandson know it within performed my devotion within till 6 at prayers at Foster Lane at prayers performed my devotion.

Saturday, 17 March: Performed my devotion within till after 9 went to Samuel Moore and talked about my goeing to Gravesend and he approved of it I Spake to him about William Johnson[776] called on Mrs Bunker and told her I had let the House and gave her the Noate for 3^{li} at prayers at Roode Lane[777] left my hat with the Hatter in Thames Streete to be cleaned and bespoke a new one within performed my devotion went to Mr Sandfords but he not at home within till 6 at prayers at Foster Lane at prayers <performed my devotion.>

Sunday, 18 March: Performed my devotion heard Mr Pullen 17 Acts 30 performed my devotion heard Mr Morre 3 Matthew 8 called to Speake with Mr Sandford within read at prayers performed my devotion etc.

Monday, 19 March: Performed my devotion amongs the Tenants but received no money at prayers at Charter House with Mr Sandford at the Crooked Billet[778] and sold the things of Mrs Windsor to Mrs Fielding for 50^s Mr Sandford Wittness afterward he went with me and called Mr Williams to see the Wall and he told us it was beteene my Lady and him within performed my devotion within till 6 at prayers at Foster Lane and at Mrs Cocks and heard Musick till after 10 within at prayers performed my devotion.

---

[776] William Johnson was one of Lloyd's fellow Coast Waiters in 1711, LMA, CLC/525/MS11316/038.

[777] Probably St Margaret Pattens, which stands in Rood Lane. Dating to at least the 18th century, the church was rebuilt once *c.*1538 and again, by Wren, after its destruction in the Great Fire, in 1684–1687, *TBE, London 1*, 235–236.

[778] John Rocque's 1746 map of London has a Crooked Billet standing in Long Alley, near the former Moorfields area, in what is now Finsbury and very close to Charterhouse, where Lloyd had just been praying.

Tuesday, 20 March: Performed my devotion amongst the Tenants Made up Mrs Lickrish accounts and paid her bill received 3^{li}:12^s received besids 18^s for ¾ Rent due at Christmass received 4^{li} of Mr Richards for a quarter's Rent due at Christmass allowed 3^d to drinke within a little brought home a flask of brandy from Mrs Powells and called at Mr Lloyds to have a Cask of beere changed at prayers at Coleman Street performed my devotion within all afternoone Mrs Martin being here and stayd till 7 and told us all her concerns at prayers performed my devotion.

[fo. 89r]
March ye 21st. 1710/11 Thursday Performed my devotion went to Mr Higgs he Spake to me that some of the first contributers would Transfer Their shares to me and I Transfer them and mine

Wednesday, 21 March: Performed my devotion amongst the Tenants but got no Money went to Mr Taners bespoke shoes etc at Toms Coffee House at prayers at St Edmond performed my devotion within till 5 at St Clement's heard a Stranger 1 Corinthians 11.26 within at prayers performed my devotion.

Thursday, 22 March: Performed my devotion went to Higgs and talked about Transfering severall of their subscriptions to me and I to Mr Bromfield and Mr Oneby[779] and I went to them both and Mr Rowlandson who told me it could be no damage called at home at prayers at St Edmond within performed my devotion at 3 at Bow heard Dr Bradford[780] 26 Matthew 43 went to Mrs Creeke but cold get no Money called at home and writ a letter to Mr Higgs caled my Wife at Couseys within at prayers performed my devotion etc.

Friday, 23 March: Performed my devotion within till after 10 went to St Clement's Church and enquired of the sexton woman for my

---

[779] Thomas Bromfield and John Oneby, 'gentlemen', are listed as subscribers of the joint stock of the Charitable Corporation in its original charter of 1708, Carr, *Select Charters*, 257.

[780] Samuel Bradford (1652–1731). Bradford was lecturer at St Mary-le-Bow before being made rector there in 1693. In 1697, he also became reader at All Hallows Bread St. Created DD by Queen Anne in 1705, he became prebend of Westminster. In 1716 he became master of Corpus Christi College, Cambridge. He subsequently was appointed bishop of Carlisle in 1718 and then bishop of Rochester, replacing the high churchman, Tory, and Jacobite Francis Atterbury in 1723. A low churchman and Whig, he was a member of the Society for the Propagation of the Gospel, of which Lloyd was a patron. *ODNB*; *CCEd* Person ID: 92213.

hanch.[781] I left in the pew and she gave it me at prayers at St Olive Jury[782] within performed my devotion within till 4 at Mr Hattons and viewed the glasiers worke and the brick layers bills it rayning hard went to Coffee house and had a letter and stayd till after 6 it rayning hard within at prayers performed my devotion etc.

Saturday, 24 March: Performed my devotion within till after 11 at prayers at St Edmond within performed my devotion within till 4 at prayers at St Peters heard Dr Waugh[783] 1 Corinthians 11.29 went to Mr Breamers to enquire about Candles bought Cheese and Mustard within at prayers performed my devotion.

Sunday, 25 March: Performed my devotion heard Dr Mapletoff 6 Matthew 33 performed my devotion heard the Bishop of Norwich[784] at Alhalows Lumbard Streete 5 Galatians 6 at Mrs Wards a little heard a stranger at St Edmonds 6 Matthew 19 20:21 within read at prayers performed my devotion etc.

[fo. 89v]
Monday, 26 March: Performed my devotion went amongst the Tenants but could get no money, at Market bought brest Veale and came home with it went to Mr Keyes and bought a suger lofe for Mr Holker and sugar for myselfe and Bohee Tea[785] at prayers

---

[781] Probably 'handkerchief'.

[782] St Olave, Old Jewry. It was rebuilt by Wren in 1671–1679 following its destruction in the Great Fire, and subsequently demolished in 1892. Only the tower now remains, which was converted into a rectory for St Margaret Lothbury, *TBE, London 1*, 256.

[783] John Waugh (1661–1734) was a fellow at his *alma mater*, Queen's College, Oxford, from 1688 until 1691, during which time he tutored Thomas Hearne, who praised his teaching but criticized his whiggish sympathies. BD and DD in 1691, he lectured at St Bride's and at a chapel of ease at St-Martin-in-the-Fields until he was made rector of St Peter Cornhill in 1704. He became bishop of Carlisle in 1723, replacing Samuel Bradford (mentioned above), but was allowed to keep his living at St Peter Cornhill because his new bishopric was considered too poor to support him. *ODNB*; *CCEd* Person ID: 167228.

[784] Charles Trimnell (1663–1723) was made bishop of Norwich in 1708. Like the other churchmen referenced in this section of the diary, Trimnell was an ardent whig, and condemned Sacheverell in the House of Lords during his impeachment, an event Lloyd would have been very aware of, as the most pressing matter of the day. Thus we can tentatively build up an impression of Lloyd as a man of whiggish sympathies. *ODNB*; *CCEd* Person ID: 128213.

[785] The English name for Wuyi teas, a category of black teas including oolong and lapsang souchong. In the early 18th century, it appears to have been regarded as having medicinal qualities; an advertisement from 1710 describes it as 'the most absolute Cure for Consumptions, inward Wastings, and all other Decays of Nature whatsoever'. The advertisement also claims that the tea could only be obtained at Batson's Coffee House

at Bow, afterward at Custom House and received 10^s for the Quarterly Dividend within performed my devotion and Cousins Clark[786] and Oddy came to see us and stayd till 5 at prayers at St Mary Woollnorth and after went to Mrs Allens stayd till 8 within at prayers performed my devotion etc.

Tuesday, 27 March: Performed my devotion within till after 10 at prayers at St Laurance heard the Bishop of the Ile of Man 1 Peter 4.16 performed my devotion within till after 3 went to Mr Kenting and ordered him not to pay the Money to Mrs Bunker, and afterward to Mr Howard and ordered him Not to pay his to her, within till 6 at prayers at Foster Lane within at prayers performed my devotion.

Wednesday, 28 March: Performed my devotion etc heard Mr Ibbot[787] at Foster Lane 5 Isaiah 4.5.6 performed my devotion then eate som cold meate after at prayers in my Closset within till 4 at prayers at St Peters afterward at Mr Bunkers and got a Noate from him for 3^{li} upon Kenting called my wife at Mrs Champneys stayd till 7 within at prayers performed my devotion. This day I paid 10^{li} for my Lady Mathews to Thomas Edwards the Windsor Coachman.

Thursday, 29 March: Performed my devotion within till Neare 10 went to Mr Barley and he Not within at prayers at St Mary Hill[788] and heard Mr Browne[789] 22 Luke 46 within and had many words with my Wife for Nothing to both our great griefe performed my devotion called at Mr Bawlers and had Elixir and Lozenges at Wrights Coffee House received a unwelcome letter from Nicholas[790] being not please[d] I did not lend him Mony answred it there aranged the Bohee Tea I bought of Mr Keyes for sugar carried

---

by the Royal Exchange: perhaps this is where Lloyd purchased his goods from Mr Keyes? See Anon., *The Volatile Spirit of Bohee-Tea* (London, 1710).

[786] 'Mrs Clarke of Islington' is mentioned in the will of Elizabeth Lloyd, as the mother-in-law of Philip Oddy: see nn. 768 and 772 at **9 March 1711**.

[787] Benjamin Ibbot (1680–1725), was a favourite of Thomas Tenison, whiggish latitudinarian, and archbishop of Canterbury from 1694 until 1715. Tenison made Ibbot treasurer of Wells Cathedral in 1707, and also conferred him the living of St Vedast-alias-Foster and St Michael-le-Querne. An ardent supporter of the Hanoverian succession, he became chaplain-ordinary to George I in 1716 and DD in 1717. *ODNB*; *CCEd* Person ID: 36204.

[788] Off Eastcheap very near to St Dunstan-in-the-East, St Mary-at-Hill was founded in the 12th century, destroyed in the Great Fire, and rebuilt by Wren in 1670–1674, *TBE*, *London 1*, 245–247.

[789] Very cramped and unclear in margin.

[790] His nephew 'Cousin Nicholas'.

the sugar loafe to Laurence Holker for his Father carried the bottle of Elixir to Mr Bunker and gave it her for him

[fo. 90r]
at prayers at Foster lane and after eate some cold Meate in Fore Street haveing made a bad diner by reason of our falling out at prayers performed my devotion.

Friday, 30 March: Performed my devotion etc heard the Reader at St Laurance 1 Peter 2:21 performed my devotion and prayd heard Dr Bradford at Bow 1 Peter 3:13 called at Mrs Cowseys and stayd a little within at prayers performed my devotion.

Saturday, 31 March: Performed my devotion went amongst the Tenants but got no money but of Mrs Allen 4^l for a quarter's Rent due at Christmas alllowed her 4^d to drinke caled at Mrs Cowseys and told her my wife would call on her after diner went to the Hatters in Thames Streete but my hat was not done at Griffiths Coffee House[791] in Tower street at prayers at St Donstons at the Hatters and bought a hat within prayers within till after 5 went to Mrs Dennis's and bought a Loyne Mutton and sent home called at Mr Beechcrafts and left word I would paye 42:10 the latter end of the Next weeke at prayers at Foster Lane within at prayers performed my devotion.

Easter Sunday, 1 April: Performed my devotion etc heard the Bishop of the Ile of Man 11 Hebrews 8 ₤ which was the greatest I ever see and not done till Neare 2 performed my devotion heard Mr Moore 1 Corinthians 15:58 within read at prayers performed my devotion.

Monday, 2 April: Performed my devotion within till 11 at prayers at Lothbury performed my devotion within till 2 called on Moone for his Rent but it was not ready called my Wife after 3 went to Mrs Cleaves left my Wife there went to Mr Byfields and bid him get my wigg made called my wife at Mrs Cleaves stayd till Neare 7 called to see Mrs Hall but she was not at home stayd till Neare 8 at prayers at St Laurence at prayers performed my devotion.

Tuesday, 3 April: Performed my devotion within till after 10 at St Laurence heard a Stranger 6 Matthew 33 performed my devotion

---

[791] Not listed by Lillywhite, and I can find no record of such an establishment.

within till 5 heard Mr Haley 1 Corinthians 15.12 at Market with my wife bought shoulder Veale at prayers performed my devotion.

Wednesday, 4 April: Performed my devotion within till 11 at prayers at our Church[792] performed my devotion within till 3 left my wife at Mrs Cocks at Starr Coffee House walkt a little at prayers at Bow at Mrs Cocks till 8 within at prayers performed my devotion etc.

[fo. 90v]
Thursday, 5 April: Performed my devotion went to the Tenants Received of Mrs Creeke 10^s for a quarter's Rent due at Ladyday 1710 after of Mrs Durton[793] 7^s for a quarter's Rent due at Christmas and of Mr Rogers 1^l:10^s for a quarter's Rent due at Michaelmas and of Robert Cocker 7^s.6^d for a quarter Rent and paid him 7^s for pumping the pond. Received of Mr Moone 10^{li} for a quarter's Rent due at Christmass within a little called to see Mrs Sykes and Mrs Cowsey at prayers at St Laurance performed my devotion within till after 9 paid Mr Beechcraft 42:10 for Mrs Mary Tempest at Starr Coffee House within at prayers at St Bartholomew Lane[794] within at prayers performed my devotion etc.

Friday, 6 April: Performed my devotion within till 11 at prayers at St Alphage bought butter and Cheese at Cripplegate Church[795] within performed my devotion after 3 called on Kenton and told him I had orders from Bunker to receive his Money went to Mr Higgs and talkt with him who told me the business was Neare finished called at Kentons and he accepted Bunkers Noate and signed it at prayers at Foster Lane within at prayers performed my devotion.

Saturday, 7 April: Performed my devotion within till 11 at prayers at St Edmond performed my devotion within till 5 left a letter at Post

---

[792] Presumably Lloyd is referring to the church closest to his home, or perhaps closest to the Custom House, which would have been St Dunstan-in-the-East: see n. 651, **21 December 1677**.

[793] Or 'Purton'.

[794] St Bartholomew-by-the-Exchange stood at the corner of Bartholomew Lane and Threadneedle St. Destroyed in the Great Fire, it was rebuilt by Wren in the late 1670s, before being demolished in 1841: Young and Young, *Old London Churches*, 67–68; *Cripplegate*, 133.

[795] St Giles-without-Cripplegate, a rare example of a medieval church in London, having survived the Great Fire and damage during the Blitz, *TBE, London 1*, 219–220.

house for my Lady at prayers at Bow within at prayers performed my devotion etc.

Sunday, 8 April: Performed my devotion heard Dr Bradford at Bow 24 Luke 45.46 performed my devotion heard Mr Moore 12 Daniel 2 went with my Wife to Mrs ~~Mar~~ Martins stayd and supt there at prayers performed my devotion etc.

Monday, 9 April: Performed my devotion within till 11 at prayers at St Bartholomew amongst the Tenants and received a quarter's Rent of Mr Hunter 1.5^s allowed 2^s for 2 locks within performed my devotion within till 5 went to Mr Sandford and talkt to him about the piece of ground but he had not Neede of it at prayers at Foster Lane called at Mrs Couseys and had 2^{li} Cheese within at prayers performed my devotion etc.

Tuesday, 10 April: Performed my devotion within till 9 called on Mr Wyat at Christian Coffee House[796] to tell him I could not pay him till Next weeke at Mr Sherwoods and received 2^{li}.10^s for a quarter's Rent allowed 6^d to drinke at prayers at Coleman Streete performed my devotion within all the afternoone Mrs Hall and Mrs Cock being here went home with Mrs Cock at prayers performed my devotion etc.

Wednesday, 11 April: Performed my devotion went to Major Lekeux received 1:10^s for a quarter's Rent for Ladyday allowed 12^s for Taxes called at Mr Moores but he was not within at Starr Coffee House at prayers at Coleman Streete performed my devotion within till 6 at prayers at Foster Lane called at Mrs Cowseys we stayd and supt with Mr Wade at prayers performed my devotion etc.

[fo. 91r]
Thursday, 12 April: Performed my devotion within till after 10 heard young Mr Lamb at St Mary Hill 3 John 5 called at Mrs Cocks and stayd ½ houer at the Temple to speake to Mr Rowlanson within performed my devotion within till 5 at Star Coffee House at prayers at Foster Lane within at prayers performed my devotion.

---

[796] Most likely in St John St., West Smithfield Bars, references to this establishment range between 1702 and 1744, *LCH*, 158.

Friday, 13 April: Performed my devotion within till 7 amongst the Tenants received of Mrs Holybrooke 12^s 6^d for Ladydays Rent, with Mr Starkey and received his Rent for Christmas and Allowed each 1½ within performed my devotion after 2 went with my wife to Mrs Halls and I went to Mr Higgs but the busines was not finished called my wife at Mrs Halls at prayers at Ludgate[797] in the Morning I heard the Lecturer of St Laurance 1 Thessalonians 5.15 at prayers performed my devotion.

Saturday, 14 April: Performed my devotion within till 10 went to Tower to speake to Brother Walker[798] but he was not there mett him in Mincing Lane and went to the C[?offee] Hous[799] and drank 2 dishes Coffee at prayrs at St Edmond within performed my devotion went to Mrs Dennis and told her my wife had bought Meate and desired her to sell what I had bought of her within till 4 at prayers at St Peters within at prayers performed my devotion.

Sunday, 15 April: Performed my devotion heard Dr Bradford 24 Luke 45:46 performed my devotion heard Mr Moore 1 Colossians 9.10 within at prayers performed my devotion etc.

Monday, 16 April: Performed my devotion within till 9 went to the back side St Clement's bought old gold buttons Cloth to face sleves shalloon[800] to line Skirts of a Wastcoate at prayers at St Clement's within performed my devotion within till 6 at prayers at Lom St Edmond within at prayers performed my devotion etc.

Tuesday, 17 April: Performed my devotion within till 11 at prayers at Coleman Streete within performed my devotion within till 3 went to St Clement's and bought more cloth at Starr Coffee House at St

---

[797] St Martin Ludgate on Ludgate Hill probably dates to the 12th century, though legend holds that it was founded by Cadwallader in 677. The present building, however, was constructed by Wren, 1677–1684, following its destruction in the Great Fire, *TBE, London 1*, 237–238.

[798] Richard Walker, brother of Lloyd's wife Elizabeth. His will, which was proved in the Prerogative Court of Canterbury on 17 October 1730, styles him a 'gentleman'. It directs that he should be buried at Camberwell, alongside his 'sister Dell' (see **28 July 1712**) and an unmentioned Elizabeth and George, TNA, PROB 11/640/212. We cannot be certain of his occupation, but there was a Tide Surveyor named Richard Walker employed by the Customs in 1711, LMA, CLC/525/ MS11316/038.

[799] I can find no references to a coffee house in Mincing Lane in 1711.

[800] 'A woollen stuff, twilled on both sides', Spufford and Mee, *Clothing of the Common Sort*, 272.

Donstons heard a stranger 2 Thessalonians 2:11 within at prayers performed my devotion.

Wednesday, 18 April: Performed my devotion within till after 8 went to Mundayes and could get no Money Went to the Christian Coffee House and told him I was disapointed of Money and he told me he would stay longer I received in part 4^{li} from Mr Harrington went to Mr Moore and he paid me told him I hoped to be able to goe to Gravesend went to Mr Walker and made up the account for Ladyday last and allowed him 7.5.6 within at prayers within all the till 6 at prayers at Foster Lane called at Mrs Cowseys at prayers performed my devotion.

[fo. 91v]
Thursday, 19 April: Performed my devotion after 9 went to my Lady Mathews paid her 9^{li} after called at Mrs Bonelass to bid her bring home my Wives gowne within performed my devotion within all afternoone Mrs Ward being here at prayers performed my devotion.

Friday, 20 April: Performed my devotion within till 9 went amongst the Tenants received of Mr Fielding 20^s in part for Mrs Windsors goods received of Mrs Ladyman 9^s 6^d for a quarter's Rent due at Ladyday last allowed for a lock 1^s Received of Mrs Creeke 1^{li} for Rent for ½ yeare due at Christmas Received of Mrs Dennis in part Received of Mrs Olive 6^{li}.10^s for a quarter's Rent due at Christmass allowed to drinke 6 went to Higgs at prayers at his Chappell and talkt with him within at prayers within till 6 at prayers at Foster Lane within at prayers performed my devotion tooke Elixir.

Saturday, 21 April: Rose not till 10 performed my devotion in bed performed my devotion within all day performed my devotion as usualy at prayers.

Sunday, 22 April: <Performed my devotion in bed> rose not till after 11 being in a sweate performed my devotion dined performed my devotion heard Mr Morre 1 Colossians 23.24 called to see Mrs Cowsey left my wife there went to St Anns Church[801] heard a stranger

---

[801] Probably St Anne and St Agnes in Gresham St., rebuilt after the Great Fire by Wren in 1677–1687, *TBE, London 1*, 95–96.

16 Luke 25 called my wife at Mr Cowseys within read at prayers performed my devotion.

Monday, 23 April: Performed my devotion within till after 9 amongst the Tenants received 5.^{1}15^s of Mr Higham for a quarter's Rent due at Ladyday Allowed 2^{li} for tax and 1^{li}.5^s for Repayres and 6^d to drinke at my Ladys and payd her that Money within performed my devotion within till 5 at prayers at Bow with Mr Sandford and talkt with him and he is willing to allow 5^s per Annum for the garden at Cousin Bennetts[802] for my Wife stayd till neare 8 within at prayers performed my devotion.

Tuesday, 24 April: Performed my devotion went to Munday but could got no money went to the Temple to speake to Rowlanson but he was not come to Towne at prayers at St Brids within performed my devotion after 2 went to the Temple and Mett Mr Rowlandson and talked about my Ladys business at my Ladys and gave her the account at Mr Byfields and paid him 14^s for a perry wigg New made at prayers at Foster Lane at Mrs Cowseys with my wife a little within at prayers performed my devotion etc.

Wednesday, 25 April: Performed my devotion within till 8 went to the Temple and spoke to Mr Rowlandson at Mr Wades but he could pay me no money at prayers at St Alphage performed my devotion within till 6 at prayers at Foster Lane at Couseys a little at prayers performed my devotion.

[fo. 92r]
Thursday, 26 April: Performed my devotion within till 10 amongst the Tenants Received of Mrs Harding 6^s for a quarter's Rent at Ladyday and of Mrs Lucas 6^s.3 for a quarter's due at Michaelmas received of Mrs Cooley 10^s for a quarter's due at Michaelmas Received of Mr Maddox 4:5^s for a quarter's due at Ladyday Allowed 1^s Watch 2 poor overrate 4^s Received of Mrs Blackden 1^1.10^s for a quarter due at Ladyday, payd Mr Pope 7^{li}.6^s for the Tax due for the 3 yards for Ladyday within performed my devotion within all the afternoone till 6 at prayers at Foster Lane called to see Cowsey at prayers performed my devotion.

---

[802] Identity unclear, though the will of Philip Oddy (see n. 772, **9 March 1711**) mentions a 'Brother and Sister Bennett', a 'Nephew Philip Bennett', and was witnessed by a Thomas Bennett. Neither George nor Elizabeth Lloyd included any Bennetts in their respective wills.

Friday, 27 April: Performed my devotion within till after 9 went to the East India House[803] and received 6^{li} for Interest for Ladyday 1711 at Mr Moores and he told me Mr Hagley would goe to Gravesend went to Custom House with him and gave him a pint of sack at prayers at St Edmond called to see Mrs Ward performed my devotion within till 5 at Hattons Received 3 quarters' Rent due at Michaelmas last 13:10^s Allowed him for taxes and repayres 13:0:0 and 3^d to drinke at prayers at Foster Lane at Honylane and Leadenhall but could get No meate within at prayers performed my devotion etc.

Saturday, 28 April: Performed my devotion within till 9 went amongst the Tenants Received 20^s of Fielding for Mrs Windors goods Received 3^s.15 of Monday in part for Michaelmas rent received of Mrs Halsey 11^s.3^d for a quarter Rent due at Michaelmas last allowd 1½ carried Mrs Windsor a receipt allowed 2^d at prayers at Ludgate performed my devotion within till 5 at prayers at Bow within at prayers performed my devotion etc.

Sunday, 29 April: Performed my devotion heard Mr Moore <at St Ann> 2 Kings 4.28 performed my devotion heard Mr Buttler at Clement's Lane[804] 1 Kings 18.21 if God be God follow him if Ball follow him walked a little heard Dr Moss at St Edmond is Not the Cupp we bless the Comunion of the bloud of Christ etc[805] within at 7 read at prayers performed my devotion etc.

Monday, 30 April: Performed my devotion within till 11 at prayers at St Laurance and met the Bishop of Ile of Man and had his blessing and desired I might have the Honour to waite on him and he kindly told me at any time called at Mrs Sycks and desired she would come to us on Wednesday bought butter at Cripplegate performed my devotion within till 6 at prayers at Foster Lane within at prayers performed my devotion tooke Elixir.

---

[803] The headquarters of the East India Company, then at Craven House, neighbouring the previous premises, the former house of Sir Christopher Clitherow (1578–1641) in Leadenhall St. The Company occupied 'Old' East India House from 1648 until 1726, when it was rebuilt and reopened in 1729. See William Foster, *The East India House* (London, 1924).

[804] St Clement's, Eastcheap.

[805] 1 Corinthians 10:16.

Tuesday, 1 May: Performed my devotion in bed being in a sweate rose at 12 performed my devotion within all day <at prayers performed my devotion etc.>

Wednesday, 2 May: Performed my devotion after 9 went to Christian Coffee House but Mr Wyatt was gon amongst the Tenants Received of Mr Monday 15^s to Make up Michaelmas quarter and 40^s of Mr Harrison for a quarter Rent for Christmas and allowd 3^d of Mr Heyward 10^s for a quarter's at Ladyday at prayers at St Anns and called at the Temple to see Mr Wyat but he was not within at my Ladys paid her 7^{li} and tooke a receipt stayd till aft[er] 3 went to Mr Wyatt and desired him to stay a little longer

[fo. 92v]
for his Money came home performed my devotion within till 8 at prayers at St Laurence called to see Mrs Cowsey within at prayers performed my devotion etc.

Thursday, 3 May: Performed my devotion within 9 went to Christian[806] Coffee House but Mr Wyatt was gon at Mrs Harriss's and received <5 7> a quarter's Rent due at Michaelmas last allowed her 7^s.6 in her Rent and 3^d to drinke received of Mr Jones 3:15 Allowed 2^s for the Tax and 3^d to drinke bought a pound of butter of her[807] and Legg Lamb of Mrs Dennis it rayning hard Roger Sanford borrowed a Coate[808] [?me][809] came home and brought the Lamb and butter after at prayers at Coleman [S]treete performed my devotion within till 6 at prayers at Foster Lane within at prayers performed my devotion.

Friday, 4 May: Performed my devotion ~~amongst the tenants~~ at Christian Coffee House paid Mr Wyat 4.16.4 for ½ a years Water[810] received of Mr Harrington 1.7.6 more that made up a

---

[806] Originally 'Can'; this expansion is a little speculative and could also be interpreted as 'Cannon', the name of at least one establishment listed by Lillywhite, but first mentioned in 1729. It stood in Cockspur St., *LCH*, 146. However, Lloyd makes clear references to similar appointments at the Christian Coffee House above and below.

[807] Likely Mr Jones's wife or servant.

[808] Or 'Coach'. Very tight binding.

[809] This word torn away.

[810] 'Clean' water was a valuable commodity in 18th-century London, and those who wished to access it had to purchase it through private companies such as the New River Company. For an account of the commercialization of water in early modern London, see Mark S. R. Jenner, 'From conduit community to water network? Water in London,

quarter's Rent for Christmas called at Mr Bawlers bought 2 bottles of Elixir called at Mr Wades and left my 2 blank Tickets with him Received a Noate for them at Custom House[811] received 45^s of Mr Elliott for Porters Key[812] and River, and after at prayers at St Mary Hill then at Queen's Arms Coffee House[813] and Mr Sandall promised to be security for me Received my Sallery for Ladyday left left a bottle of Elixir for Mrs Martain within performed my devotion within till 4 called at Mr Rowlansons Chamber to see his wife but she was not within went to my Lady Mathews and paid 20^{li} for Mrs Hall to take up the Judgment on her goods stayd till 7 at prayers at St Laurance within at prayers performed my devotion.

Saturday, 5 May: Performed my devotion after 9 went to Mrs Kents to bid her send home my Wives Scarfe went to Houndsdich and after to Billiter Lane to buy black silke and met with some there at Mr Garretts and received 2^{li} for a quarter Rent due at Christmass at prayers at St Bartholomew at Hony Lane Market bought piece beefe within performed my devotion within till 5 at prayers at Bow within at prayers performed my devotion etc.

Sunday, 6 May: Performed my devotion etc heard Mr Ibbott at Foster Lane 14 Revelation 13 ℟ performed my devotion heard Mr Moorree 6 Ephesians 18 within Read at prayers performed my devotion etc.

Monday, 7 May: Performed my devotion within at prayers at Coleman Streete performed my devotion within till 7 at prayers at St Edmond at prayers performed my devotion.

Tuesday, 8 May: Performed my devotion tooke Water Pauls Wharfe went to Higgs and he promised to bring the 5^{li} to me the Next Evening to Starr Coffee House called at my Lord Powers and see what he wanted and he gave me a dram of Usquebaugh[814] at my Lady Mathews at prayers at St Brids within performed my devotion within till 7 at prayers at St Edmond at prayers performed my devotion etc.

1500–1725', in Paul Griffiths and Mark S. R. Jenner (eds), *Londinopolis: Essays in the Cultural and Social History of Early Modern London* (Manchester, 2000), 250–272.

[811] Ambiguous: originally 'C.H'.
[812] Porter's Quay, one of the 'legal quays' at the Port of London: see n. 303, **19 May 1676**.
[813] Originally 'Q. A. C. H.'
[814] From the Irish *uisce beatha*, meaning 'water of life', in other words, whiskey.

[fo. 93r]
Wednesday, 9 May: Performed my devotion was amongst the Tenants Received of Mrs Lucas 6:3^d for a quarter Rent due at Christmas allowd 1½ Received of Mr Rogers for a quarter's Rent 1:10^s for Christmas allowed 1½ within a little at Custom House and got Captain Jarvis to promise to be one of my security at prayers at Roode Lane within performed my devotion within till 7 at Starr Coffee House to meete Higgs but he came Not at prayers at St Laurance at prayers performed my devotion etc.

Thursday, 10 May: Performed my devotion within all day my Wife being Very ill performed my devotion as usualy performed my devotion at prayers.

Friday, 11 May: Performed my devotion went to carry a letter from the Lady Mathews to Mr Andrews but could not meet with him at prayers at St Dionis within performed my devotion within till 4 went to the Temple and paid Mr Wyatt 9^r.10^s for my Lady Mathews, at her Lodgings till after 7 called my wife at Mrs Cowseys at prayers at St Laurance performed my devotion at prayers etc.

Saturday, 12 May: Performed my devotion went amongst the Tenants to see the paveing and called on Veares to come to me at prayers at [*blank*] performed my devotion within till 4 at prayers at St Dionis within at prayers performed my devotion etc.

Sunday, 13 May: Performed my devotion heard a stranger at St Lawrance Jury 5 Matthew 44 performed my devotion heard Mr Moore 8 John 7 went to see Mrs Martine stayd till 7 within read at prayers performed my devotion etc.

Monday, 14 May: Performed my devotion went ~~to St Dionis to prayers after~~ to a man in Rose Ally to overlooke my Lady accounts went to Mr Moore and talkt to him at Custom House to ask about giving New Security and spoke to Mr Matthew Jarvice and Mr Thomas Sandall who promised to be ready When I should desire them. Called on the Man for my papers and stayd till after 1 within performed my devotion within till 6 called my Wife at Mr Cowseys stayd till 8 at prayers at St Laurance at prayers performed my devotion.

Tuesday, 15 May: Performed my devotion went to my Lady and shewed her the account and receipts which she was pleased with but Not being very Well my Lady told me I should take them back and after Midsommer she would be in Towne I lent her 5 Guines and tooke a receipt stayd till Neare 6 at prayers at Foster Lane within at prayers performed my devotion etc.

Wednesday, 16 May: Performed my devotion within till 11 at prayers at Coleman Streete and went to Mr Andrews for my Lady Mathews to receive 10^l but could not find him performed my devotion within till after 7 at Guildhall Coffee House[815] at prayers at St Laurence at prayers performed my devotion.

Thursday, 17 May: Performed my devotion in bed haveing taken Hunter's stuff rose at 11 performed my devotion within all day performed my devotion at prayers etc.

[fo. 93v]
Friday, 18 May: Performed my devotion among the Tenants received 3^l 5^s of Mr Smith, allowed 10^s for pumping the Pond watch 1^s.2 poore 1:6 over rate 3^d to drinke 3 of Mrs Stiff 10^s Received of Mr Deall 7^{li}.10^s Allowd to drink 6 Received of Mr Dallaway allowed 1^d ½ at prayers at St Bartholomew performed my devotion within till 5 at Lyme Streete to speake with Dr Gatford but could not at Mr James[816] and paid for a p[?air]e shooes and ordred them to be sent home within till after 7 at prayers at St Laurance at prayers performed my devotion.

Saturday, 19 May: Performed my devotion went to Mrs Garrett and told her I thought to have her daughter to live with us and see for Meate but got none at prayers at Coleman Streete went throug [*sic*] the Market but cou[ld] Not buy within performed my devotion within till 5 at prayers at Bow bought piece beefe Asparagrass and butter within at prayers performed my devotion.

Sunday, 20 May: Performed my devotion etc heard Dr Bradford at Bow 4 Ephesians 8 ℟ performed my devotion heard Mr Mooree at St Laurence 2 Joell 27:28 within read at prayers performed my devotion.

---

[815] In King St., Cheapside. Referenced between 1685 and 1878, *LCH*, 252–254.
[816] Obscure owing to very tight binding.

Monday, 21 May: Performed my devotion within till 11 at prayers at St Alphage called on Mr Bawler and had his Noate on Mr Richard Streete for $4^l.14^s$ to receive at Rochester[817] within performed my devotion within till 4 at prayers at St Peters came home and tooke a Vomit of the Indian Roote[818] which workt very well I bless God at prayers performed my devotion.

Tuesday, 22 May: Performed my devotion within till 11 at prayers at Aldermanbury[819] performed my devotion within till Neare 8 at prayers at St Laurance at prayers performed my devotion.

Wednesday, 23 May: Performed my devotion within till 10 amongst the Tenants but got no Money at prayers at Charter House performed my devotion within till after 7 walkt round St Pauls called my wife at Mrs Johnsons at prayers at St Laurance at prayers performed my devotion etc.

Thursday, 24 May: Performed my devotion at 7 called on Kenton but he had no money went to Higgs but he was Not to be found called at Mr Lloyds at the Black Boy to know how far the business was carried on by the Earle of Clarendon[820] but he could give me

---

[817] In other words, fees accruing for Customs work (probably 'receiving' ships) at Rochester, Kent, on the River Medway.

[818] The rather vague medical lexicon of early 18th-century England makes absolute certainty of identification impossible, but the 1708 edn of Steven Blankaart's *Physical Dictionary* describes turmeric as 'an Indian Root', which 'is reckoned the best of all Medicines for opening Obstructions' (p. 93). Other authorities from the 17th and 18th centuries seem to use the term to refer to various 'rhubarb' roots. One example is Mechoacan (Mexican) or 'White Rhubarb' (also described as 'Bryony', actually a member of the gourd family and not a rhubarb), which 'purgeth *Fleam* and *watry humours* without griping', Alexander Read, *Most Excellent and Approved Medicines and Remedies* (London, 1651), 4. By 1710, William Salmon (an archetypal 18th-century quack) writes approvingly of 'True Indian or China Rheubarb', or 'True Indian Root' (perhaps *Rheum palmatum*, still sometimes called Chinese rhubarb or East Indian Rhubarb, a folk medicine) claiming that 'divers of our Physicians have oftentimes used them, with many other Persons, to very good purpose', *Botanologia: The English Herbal* (London, 1710), 939.

[819] The church of St Mary Aldermanbury stood at the junction of Aldermanbury and Love Lane. It was destroyed in the Great Fire and rebuilt by Wren in 1671–1675. It was gutted during the Blitz, and its remains were transported to Westminster College Fulton, Missouri, where it was rebuilt in 1965–1969, *TBE, London 1*, 413–414.

[820] Edward Hyde, 3rd earl of Clarendon (1661–1723), also known as Lord Cornbury, had inherited the earldom in 1709. A Tory, Clarendon had in 1711 recently returned from the North America after a controversial tenure as governor of New York and New Jersey, which was mired by scurrilous accusations of financial impropriety and transvestitism. Upon his return, he was elevated to the privy council, and played an active role in the House of Lords, *ODNB*. Lloyd's diary seems to suggest that he was somehow involved in the affairs of the Charitable Corporation, perhaps as a contact 'inside' the corridors of

No account called at Mr Byfields to bid him call on Brother Walker called at Mrs Halls at prayers at Coleman Streete within performed my devotion within till 5 at prayers at Bow stayd at Mr Wades 2 houers it rayning hard at prayers performed my devotion etc.

[fo. 94r]
Friday, 25 May: Performed my devotion within till after 8 went to St Dionis to speake to the Churchwardens but could not find eith either at Mr Moores and told him I intended by Gods blessing to goe to Gravesend on Wednesday at Custom House spoke to Mr Evans about giving Bond who told me after I came from Gravesend would doe at prayers at St Dunstons left my hat at the hatter's to be drest within performed my devotion within all the Afternoone it rayning hard at prayers performed my devotion.

Saturday, 26 May: Performed my devotion within till Neare 10 paid Mr Lloyd for 3 ferkins[821] beere and bought a flask of brandy of Mrs Powell amongst the Tenants but got no Money at prayers at St Laurance performed my devotion within till 6 at prayers at Foster Lane bought quarter's Lamb in the Market called to see Mrs Cowsey within at prayers performed my devotion.

Sunday, 27 May: Performed my devotion heard Dr Bradford 28 Matthew 19.20 performed my devotion heard Mr Castle[822] at Allhallows Lumbard Streete 36 Job 26 called to see Mrs Ward stayd till 7 called at Mrs Martins supt stayd till after 9 at prayers performed my devotion etc.

Monday, 28 May: Performed my devotion within till 8 went to speake to the Churchwar<dens> of St Dionis and to Custom House and got paper etc came back after Went to Higgs but could Not see him or Treviso called and spoke to the Lady Swan[823]

---

official power, though I have found no corroborating evidence of this: see **4 December 1711**.

[821] A firkin is a historic unit of measurement or barrel size for beer and ale, amongst other commodities. A firkin of beer contained nine gallons.

[822] Perhaps Philip Castell (*c*.1675–1718), rector of St Bartholomew-the-Less from 1701 to 1715, and later rector of Christ Church Newgate from 1715 until his death in 1718: *Cantabrigienses*, Vol. 1, pt. 1, 305; *CCEd* Person ID: 161763.

[823] I have not been able to identify 'Lady Swan' with any certainty; however, an authority of the same name is mentioned amongst the collection of medical recipes assembled by Elizabeth Freke, Lloyd's contemporary and fellow 'life-writer'. Freke copied a recipe

about my Eyes Who advised me against Milk bought Grounds and Raysons within performed my devotion within till 4 Went with my Wife to se Mrs Sandford called to see Sykes but she was Not within at Mrs Couseys a little at prayers at St Laurence at prayers performed my devotion etc.

[fo. 94v]
Tuesday, 29 May: Performed my devotion amongst the Tenants Received of Mr Blunt 2^{li}:5^{s824} for ½ a yeares Rent due at Ladyday of Mr Moone 10^{li} for a quarter Rent due at Ladyday allowd 4^{li} for Taxes Received of Mr Richards 4^{li} for a quarter's Rent due at Lady day at St Laurances heard a stranger 22 Matthew 37 performed my devotion within till 4 called at Mr Fletchers and tooke my Cane and left my tuck[825] received a Noate from the Churchwardens of St Dionis for Hedges to order him to remove at Midsommer called on the Hatter but my hat was not done called on Mr Miller but he was not within at St Dunstons heard a Stranger 30 Proverbs 8 we called to see Mrs Rigbour but she was not within stayd a little at Mr Carlesses called at Mrs Champnys but she not at home called at Mrs Allens stayd till after 8 at prayers performed my devotion.

Wednesday, 30 May: Performed my devotion at Bow gave Dr Bradford ½ a guinie for the use of the Society of the propogacon of Religion[826] calld on Mr Wade but could not receive any Money at Prues and told her if they did not goe away I would pull downe the House and told Hedges Wife the order of the Churchwardens called on Fordham[827] for My Watches after at Mr Fletchers for my

---

entitled 'To prevent miscarrying proved. Lady Swan.' See D. Oren-Magidor, 'Literate laywomen, male medical practitioners and the treatment of fertility problems in early modern England', *Social History of Medicine*, 29 (2016), 308.

[824] Very untidy and unclear.

[825] Possibly referring to a small, thin sword carried as a fashion accessory, *OED*.

[826] This was either the Society for Promoting Christian Knowledge (established 1698) or the Society for the Propagation of the Gospel in Foreign Parts (established 1701), both founded by Thomas Bray, rector at St Botolph's, Aldgate, *ODNB*. Whilst Bray was doctrinally pragmatic in his efforts to establish his Societies, his biographer notes that he was 'no non-juror', and that he supported the Hanoverian Succession. For a recent account of the history and historiography of the SPCK and the SPG, see D. Manning, 'Anglican religious societies, organisations, and missions', in J. Gregory (ed.), *The Oxford History of Anglicanism*, Vol. 2: *Establishment and Empire, 1662–1829* (Oxford, 2017), 429–451.

[827] Cf. **21 and 23 June 1677, 21 July 1677, 9 August 1677**, and **1, 22, 24, 26, and 27 September 1677**. It may have been more than a coincidence that Lloyd's clockmaker of choice was named Fordham in the 1670s and in 1711, since such trades were often passed down through families. A John Fordham of Dunmow, Essex, manufactured

tuck and at the Hatter's for my Hat and called at Millers to bid her tell him he should come the Next day met Sam Moore and gave him a pint of sack came home performed my devotion within till after 5 at prayers at St Bartholomues within at prayers performed my devotion.

Thursday, 31 May: Performed my devotion was puting up my things for Gravesend after 8 Carried my box of plate and writings to Mr Wades and bought little cakes at 10 got a porter and sent by him and the Waterman to Custom House and we went to Tower Wharfe and met Mr Richards and dranke Rum at 11 tooke boate and when we came past Blackwall[828] the water was very rough and my wife frightned and were forst to put in at Woolwich and went to the Anchor and Crowne[829] and dranke brandy and beere and hired two horses and a boy to fetch them back and paid 9^s and 2^d and spent 3^d tooke horse before 3 stayd at Mrs Wagstaffs till after 6 came to New Taverne[830] after 8 very weary and ill both of us haveing delivered the Horses to the boy at the Angell at prayers performed my devotion etc.

[fo. 95r]
Friday, 1 June: Rose at 6 being ill and weary with the Journey and my Wife worse performed my devotion within and eate bread and butter and put things in order at 11 went with Mr Johnson to Gravesend bought shoulder Lamb cost 1^s:2^d at prayers at Church[831] and met Mr Holker there came home and dined performed my devotion within Mr Holker and his wife came after 3

---

surviving clocks dating from 1680. There was a Joseph Fordham, of Bocking, Essex, trading c.1700. A Thomas Fordham was admitted to the Company of Clockmakers in London in 1687, and a surviving clock dating from 1730 was made by a man of the same name trading in Braintree. C. Clutton, G. H. Baillie, and C. A. Ilbert (eds), *Britten's Old Clocks and Watches and their Makers* (London, 1975), 394.

[828] Blackwall Point is opposite Poplar (the north-east corner of the Isle of Dogs), on the south bank of a distinctive bend in the Thames.

[829] The Crown and Anchor – Lloyd mixed up its name – stood in Woolwich High St. from the 17th century until its demolition in 1974, Peter Guillery (ed.), *Survey of London*, Vol. 48: *Woolwich* (London, 2012), 52.

[830] Now the site of New Tavern Fort, which stands on the south bank of the Thames between Gravesend and Milton. The fort was built to shore up perceived weaknesses in defences of the Thames and London following the American War of Independence; the New Tavern Inn, then owned by one Mr Houghton, was purchased by act of Parliament, such was the site's strategic significance. Robert Pierce Cruden, *The History of the Town of Gravesend* (London, 1843), 438.

[831] Probably St George's Church, Gravesend.

stayd till 7 walkt a little with them at prayers performed my devotion etc.

Saturday, 2 June: Performed my devotion within being ill and my Wife worse performed my devotion after 3 went to prayers to Church within all day at prayers performed my devotion.

Sunday, 3 June: Performed my devotion within all day my wife being Very ill of the Rhumitisme and not able to stir read at prayers and performed my devotion as usualy.

Monday, 4 June: Performed my devotion within all day read at prayers performed my devotion as usualy my Wife being still very <bad>.

Tuesday, 5 June: Performed my devotion within all Morning performed my devotion within till after 5 went to Gravesend to Mr Curtis and bought a drachm[832] of Gascoin powder[833] at the Flushing[834] and dranke a pott of their beere came home within at prayers performed my devotion.

Wednesday, 6 June: Performed my devotion within till 9 went to Gravesend bought Mint water and a loafe came home stayd till neare 11 at the Flushing and sent home 2 bottle small beere at Coffee house at prayers performed my devotion within till 4 at Mr Curtis about a plaster but he had none he being with Me at the Flushing thought it to Rott and came to see my Wife and would have given her things but she thought it Not fitt to take them gave him a pott here and one at the Flushing within at prayers performed my devotion.

Thursday, 7 June: Performed my devotion within all day my Wife being very ill read at prayers performed my devotion as usuall.

---

[832] A unit of weight; prior to standardization in the 19th century, this could mean an avoirdupois drachm (1/16 of an ounce) or an apothecary's drachm (1/8 of an ounce); the latter is perhaps more likely in this context.

[833] Gascon or Gascoigne Powder was a popular cure-all in early modern England. The recipe, which includes ingredients such as powdered pearl, crab's eyes, and white amber, features in the Countess of Kent's *Choice Manual* (London, 1653), 172–173.

[834] I have found references to 'The Flushing' particularly difficult to trace; it seems to have stood in the High St. since at least the late 16th century, being mentioned in a couple of Recognizances from West Kent Quarter Sessions: see KRO, QM/RLv/31/6; QM/RLv/32/2. It may also have been known as The George, KRO, Gr/A1120/7.

Friday, 8 June: Performed my devotion within all Morning my Wife being Very bad performed my devotion within till 4 at Towne at C.H[835] with Mr Johnson called at Mr Holkers but they were both abroad within at prayers performed my devotion.

Saturday, 9 June: Performed my devotion within all Morning performed my devotion within till 3 at Gravesend at prayers at the Flushing with Mr Johnson and Mr Curtis till 5 within with Mr Hunt and Thomas Rutton in the greate roome at prayers performed my devotion.

Sunday, 10 June: Performed my devotion at prayers at Gravesend within and was drinking with Mr Rutton and Mr Tretaine[836] etc at prayers performed my devotion etc.

Monday, 11 June: Performed my devotion within all Morning performed my devotion within till 5 and as I was going to Gravesend Mett Mr Holker came back stayd till Neare 9 walkt to the camp stile within at prayers performed my devotion.

[fo. 95v]
Tuesday, 12 June: Performed my devotion within till 11 went to Gravesend bought pease within performed my devotion within till 5 walkt at the Flushing with Mr Johnson dranke 2 tankards within at prayers performed my devotion.

Wednesday, 13 June: Performed my devotion within till 11 at Church heard the Minister of Northfleet Swanscome[837] 11 Romans 22 within performed my devotion within till 5 at Gravesend and spoke to the Master that delivered his Coales to give an account[838]

---

[835] There was no official Custom House in Gravesend until 1782; prior to this, Customs officers used various local inns as their headquarters, as Lloyd describes. Hence, Lloyd is probably referring to a coffee house, or perhaps an informal 'Customs House'.

[836] Perhaps Matthew Tretane, a Tide Surveyor in the Customs in 1711, LMA, CLC/525/ MS11316/038.

[837] Originally 'Northfle'. Unclear if Lloyd means the minister of Northfleet or Swanscombe, both of which are west of Gravesend, some two miles apart. Either Robert Barry, installed at Northfleet 1708: *Oxoniensis*, Vol. 1, 79; Cecil Fielding, *The Records of Rochester* (Dartford, 1910), 199–201; *CCEd* Person ID: 382. Or Henry Bosse, rector of Swanscombe 1705–1737: Cantabrigienses, Vol. 1, pt. 4, 183; *CCEd* Person ID: 616.

[838] In other words, Lloyd was going about his official Customs business, taking account of the cargoes of a ship bearing coal towards London.

when he was out at the bowling greene a little at the Flushing and drank a tankard within at prayers performed my devotion etc.

Thursday, 14 June: Rose after 3 performed my devotion went to Northfleete in the boate with Mr Johnson to speake to the Collier delivering her Coales there landed at Mr Chiffins's Key walkt to the fields beyond the stone bridge to see for straberys stayd till 7 called at the Custom House bought a p[?acket]t of Goosberys within till 10 at Gravesend to buy beanes within performed my devotion within all day at prayers performed my devotion.

Friday, 15 June: Performed my devotion within all day my wife being ill performed my devotion as usualy at prayers.

Saturday, 16 June: Performed my devotion within till neare 10 went to Market bought straberys called to see Mr Holker and borrowed his horse to goe to Rochester[839] on Monday within performed my devotion afore 3 went to Gravesend to prayers at Church bought a loafe came home read at prayers performed my devotion.

Sunday, 17 June: Performed my devotion read etc. Heard Mr Siddell[840] 19 Psalm 13 performed my devotion heard Mr [*blank*] 2 Mark 17 <at Milton[841]> 17 read at prayers performed my devotion.

Monday, 18 June: Performed my devotion within till 9 went to Mr Holkers to tell him I should not use his Horse stayd till 10 within performed my devotion within at prayers performed my devotion.

Tuesday, 19 June: Performed my devotion within all Morning performed my devotion till 9 went with Mr Johnson by water to Northfleete to see Mr Chiffins stayd there til 11 was on the water till 1 takeing shipps performed my devotion within till 3 walkt to

---

[839] Rochester, some eight miles south-east of Gravesend, famous for its beautiful and ancient cathedral.

[840] I have not been able to trace this preacher; it may have been a curate. The rector at Gravesend at this time was William Savage (*c*.1670–1736), later master of Emmanuel College, Cambridge; *Alumni Cantabrigienses*, Vol. 1, pt. 4, 22; *CCEd* Person ID: 2955.

[841] Milton-next-Gravesend, then a semi-rural ecclesiastical parish, served by the church of St Peter and Paul. The rector at this time was William Wall (1647–1728). His primary living was Shoreham, Kent, which he held from 1674 until his death, only taking on Milton in 1708. In this case, Lloyd probably heard either Wall himself or his curate, one Mr Thomas. Wall also published a number of theological writings, the most well known of which was *A History of Infant Baptism* (London, 1705). *ODNB*; *CCEd* Person ID: 3593.

the Windmill hill and downe by Mrs Cousens's to the Ale House in that lane Mett Mr Hodges and another Gentleman stayd till after 5 within at prayers performed my devotion etc.

Wednesday, 20 June: Performed my devotion within till Neare 11 at prayers at Gravesend performed my devotion within till 7 at the Flushing till 8 at prayers performed my devotion.

Thursday, 21 June: Performed my devotion within all Morning performed my devotion within till 6 walked to Gravesend with my Wife and Mr Johnson to the Flushing dranke 2 tankards came back at prayers performed my devotion.

Friday, 22 June: Performed my devotion within till 11 at prayers at Church dined at Mr Holkers I went out in the Schear[842] with him stayd till 9 at prayers performed my devotion etc.

[fo. 96r]
Saturday, 23 June: Performed my devotion within performed my devotion within till 3 at prayers at Church within at prayers performed my devotion etc.

Sunday, 24 June: Performed my devotion heard Mr Siddell 13 Mark 32:33 performed my devotion at prayers at Gravesend at Mr Holkers till 7 within at prayers performed my devotion etc.

Monday, 25 June: Within till 8 at Mr Holkers and tooke my leave and brought my Ham[843] within puting up my things performed my devotion within till after 2 on the water till 5 and tooke severall shipps walkt at prayers performed my devotion.

Tuesday, 26 June: Performed my devotion within Nobody came to relieve me performed my devotion within walkt a little with my wife and after to the garden for Cur[?ran]ts but there was None went to towne and bought som at prayers performed my devotion etc.

Wednesday, 27 June: Performed my devotion was puting my things in a readyness went to speake to Mr Holker to carry my

---

[842] Perhaps a boat.
[843] Tight binding: possibly 'Fam' as in 'Family', but 'H' looks more likely.

Wife to Dartford but he was not within at Custom House within performed my devotion at 2 oClock came away Landed at Tower wharfe after 7 had a bad Tyde and my wife frightned tooke a Coach and brought home our things got some ale and Cheese at prayers performed my devotion.

Thursday, 28 June: Performed my devotion within till 7 went to see for Mrs Parnell but she was Not within called att Mr Couseys who told me his Wife was dead within till after 10 at Custom House received of Mr Pinder for the quarterly dividend 1:8:6 and for Gravesend Money 1:19.6 came home at 1 within all the afternoone Mrs Ward being here at prayers performed my devotion.

Friday, 29 June: Performed my devotion within till after 8 went to Mr Wade for my box and had it within a little went to Millers and paid his wife $1^l:4^s$ for the Gravesend Money within till 11 at prayers at St Bartholomew at Mr Sandfords to enquire about the Noates I left but he had received none within performed my devotion within till 8 at prayers at St Laurance at prayers performed my devotion.

Saturday, 30 June: Tooke Elixir performed my devotion in bed rose after 11 performed my devotion within till after 7 at prayers at St Laurance bought shoulder Lamb at Market within at prayers performed my devotion.

Sunday, 1 July: Performed my devotion in bed haveing taken Elixir rose at 9 performed my devotion within all Morning performed my devotion heard Mr Moore 1 Ecclesiastes 17 went to Mrs Hall within at prayers performed my devotion.

Monday, 2 July: Performed my devotion within all day my wife being very ill performed my devotion as usuall at prayers.

Tuesday, 3 July: Performed my devotion within till after 8 bought a loafe and paid for Flouer called at Mr Garretts and told his daughter I had hyred a Mayd and She should not come received of Mr Hunter 1.5^s for a quarter Rent for Midsummer at Mr Bawlers to ask advice about my Rupture[844] and went to a Man about it in Bartholomew Close[845] but did nothing at Goodmans Fields[846] to

---

[844] At this time Lloyd appears to have been plagued with a boil, wound, or sore that would not heal. This may have been the same malady alluded to on **6 June 1711**.

[845] Near the Barbican, London.

[846] An open field which lay just north of Prescot St., Whitechapel.

enquire the price of a truss[847] left a Noate at Millers hous to be sent to Mrs Baker within performed my devotion bought Cheese

[fo. 96v]
performed my devotion within till 7 at prayers at St Edmond at prayers performed my devotion.

Wednesday, 4 July: Performed my devotion within till 8 went to Mr Jarvice to Speake to him to be bound for me but he was gon into the Country told Mr Evans of it and he sayd twas well enough bought beanes at Stocks Market[848] within went to Mr Powells and spoke for 5 quarts brandy at prayers at St Alphage performed my devotion within till 6 at prayers at St Bartholomew Lane within at prayers performed my devotion.

Thursday, 5 July: Performed my devotion at 8 went amongst the tenants Received 2^l of Mr ~~Garret~~ <Gamball> for a quarter's Rent due at Lady day allowd 3^d to drinke received of Mrs Hanckock $1^l.5^s$ for ½ yeares rent due at Lady day called on severall more but got no money bought sugar at Mr Keyes and beanes within at Moorefields to see for a Joynstoole[849] but could find None performed my devotion within all afternoone Mrs Hall being here at prayers performed my devotion.

Friday, 6 July: Performed my devotion at 8 went to Mr Rigburgs and he was not up at prayers at Berkin[850] then found Mr Rigburg and he came to me at Mr Sandalls at 10 they went with me and was bound for Me I went with them and gave them a quart of wine at the Rose and Dolphin bought Loyne Mutton within performed my

---

[847] Lloyd was probably enquiring about a 'truss' in a medical context; that is, a strap or bandage to apply pressure to his 'rupture'.

[848] Standing just south of the junction of Cornhill, Threadneedle St., and Poultry, the Stocks market took its name from the disciplinary stocks which once stood at the site. The market building, which was home to butchers and fishmongers, had first been erected in the time of Edward I, but was destroyed during the Great Fire and rebuilt. It was eventually demolished in 1739 during the construction of Mansion House. See *Pepys*, Vol. 10, 404.

[849] A joint stool was a very common piece of domestic furniture, a small rectangular piece of seating.

[850] All Hallows Barking, also known as All Hallows-by-the-Tower. An ancient church, it was first mentioned in 1086 as a possession of Barking Abbey in Essex, and is the only London church with standing Anglo-Saxon elements, *TBE, London 1*, 184–186.

devotion within till 6 called to see Mr Cowsey bought 6^l sugar at Mr Keyes paid Mr Harrison 9^s for Powell plaisterer[851] and had his Receipt at prayers at St Laurance at prayers performed my devotion.

Saturday, 7 July: Performed my devotion at prayers at Bow called on Mr Wade but he was Not at home within performed my devotion within till neare 5 at Market but could buy Nothing Meate was so deare at prayers at Bow bought Legg Lamb of the Woman in Bell Ally within at prayers performed my devotion.

Sunday, 8 July: Performed my devotion heard Mr Stoonestreete at Walbrooke 1 Corinthians 13:7 performed my devotion heard Mr ~~Moore~~ Mooree 77 Pslam 10:11 we went to see Mrs Johnson playd till after 6 eate some Lamb read at prayers performed my devotion.

Monday, 9 July: Rose at 12 haveing taken Dr Hunter's Licquor and Sweating very Much performed my devotion in bed performed my devotion eate at 2 a Clock within all day performed my devotion at prayers.

Tuesday, 10 July: Rose at 12 haveing taken Dr Hunter's Liquor performed my devotion in bed within all day performed my devotion as usualy at prayers.

Wednesday, 11 July: Performed my devotion within till 11 at prayers at St Alphage at Wrights Coffee House bought beanes within performed my devotion within till 4 bought balme water[852] went with Mr Johnson to Mrs Powells and spoke for 6 quarts of brandy at prayers at Bartholomew Lane at Starr Coffee House within at prayers performed my devotion etc.

---

[851] 'Plaisterer' is an antiquated spelling of the word 'plasterer', the ancient building occupation, which survives today in the name of the London livery company of the Worshipful Company of Plaisterers. Why Lloyd was paying for plastering for or by Powell, from whom he usually bought brandy, is unclear; perhaps he was carrying out a favour, or dealing with a different Powell.

[852] A distillation of 'balm' or mint leaves, to relieve digestive discomfort. According to William Salmon, the recipe for 'Water of Balm' is as follows: 'Take of Spirits ten gallons, Water five gallons, Aniseeds one pound, Balm-Leaves eight handfuls; mix and distill them, draw nine gallons of Water, and sweeten it with Sugar', *The Family-Dictionary, or, Houshold Companion* (London, 1705), 364.

[fo. 97r]
Thursday, 12 July: Performed my devotion amongst the Tenants Received of Mr Monday 3^{li} in part for Christmas rent and 1^l:15^s of Mr Watkinson for Ladyday rent allowd 4^s for Watch poore and overrate at prayers at St ~~Alphage~~ performed my devotion within till 5 at prayers Bow. At home at prayers performed my devotion etc.

Friday, 13 July: Amongst the Tenants but received nothing at prayers at St Alphage performed my devotion within till 7 at prayers at Lumbard Streete within performed my devotion at prayers etc.

Saturday, 14 July: Performed my devotion went to the Tenants but got no money at [*blank*] performed my devotion within till 5 at prayers at St Dionis within till 8 at the Cooks and bespoke a shoulder Lamb for Sunday at prayers performed my devotion.

Sunday, 15 July: Performed my devotion heard a Stranger at Old Jury 4 Philippians 12 performed my devotion heard Mr Moorer 17 Luke 37 went with my Wife to see Mrs Rowlandson but they were not in Towne stayd a little and dranke 2 glasses of Ale called at Mrs Halls and stayd till after 8 at prayers performed my devotion.

Monday, 16 July: Performed my devotion within till 10 went to Custom House stayd till 11 at prayers at St Edmond within performed my devotion within till 4 went with my Wife to bridgfoot[853] at Custom House and spoke to Mr Evans to looke out my former bond at King's Arms Coffee House[854] at the Hat[t]ers and had my hat he was to cleane and at Mr Townlys who askt me to drinke a dram of brandy at prayers at St Dionis met my wife there she went to Mr Tretaynes and I to Mr Costins and tooke the Noat I gave him on Kenton and enquired at the Cross Keyes what time Camberwell Coach went called my Wife at Mr Tretaynes stayd till 8 at prayers performed my devotion etc.

Tuesday, 17 July: Performed my devotion within till neare 10 went to the White Horse Inn and received a Receipt from my Lady

---

[853] The area around the point at which Old London Bridge met Southwark on the south bank of the Thames.

[854] Lillywhite finds several examples of this name: one 'behind the Exchange' at 'Sweeting's Rents' or Sweeting's Alley', first referred to by Pepys in 1663, and references continue until 1749; at West Smithfield (probably a tavern in its early days) *c.*1700–1834; opposite Tower Gate on Tower St., first mentioned in 1720 but potentially extant in 1711; finally at Ludgate Hill, 'near the bridge', *c.*1705–1732, *LCH*, 314–315 and 708.

Mathews and gave up the Noate I had from Thomas Edwards called at Mr Wades but he was not within went to Mrs Bristows and received halfe a yeares rent due at Midsomer and allowd 3^d at prayers at Christ Church received of Mrs Harris 4^{li} in part for Christmas Rent, afterward afterward [*sic*] received of Mr Higham 5^{li}.15^s for a quarter Rent due at Midsomer and allowd 1^l.5^s for repayres and 6^d to drink within performed my devotion within till after 7 left a letter at post house at prayers at St Laurence at prayers performed my devotion.

Wednesday, 18 July: Performed my devotion went to Mr Garratts to see if his daughter was gon to service and she was trimed and drest myselfe and went to Camberwell called at Mrs Bowyers at Church at prayers and went to Cousin Amyes but stayd not met my wife in the Coach and went to Mrs Bowyers to diner at 5 went to see Mrs Cooke and the Coach caled us and we came to prayers at St Edmonds at prayers performed my devotion etc.

[fo. 97v]
Thursday, 19 July: Performed my devotion within till after 9 amongst the tenants but got no money bought beanes at prayers at Walbrooke performed my devotion within till after 7 at prayers at St Laurence at prayers performed my devotion.

Friday, 20 July: Performed my devotion called on Mr Stone who promised to pay me Next Friday went to Coll. Lekeux received 1^{li}.10^s for a quarter Rent for Midsomer allowed 6^s for a part quarter's Tax called and left ¼ pound Creame of Tarter at Mr Tretayne within a little bought piece of beefe at Cooks at prayers at St Alphage. Performed my devotion went with my wife to Mr Rowlandsons stayd till Neare 5 at prayers at Lincolne Chapell[855] called to see Mrs Cleave went to Mr Rowlandsons stayd till 8 within at prayers performed my devotion.

Saturday, 21 July: Performed my devotion within till 10 went to Mrs Martins to see the bed she sent us and told her Kinswoman I thought to send for it on Monday at prayers at St Peters within performed my devotion within Mrs Hall being here at prayers at

---

[855] Built to serve the lawyers of Lincoln's Inn, the old medieval chapel was demolished in 1618 and rebuilt by John Clarke in *c.*1620–1623. The chapel is often mistakenly attributed to Inigo Jones, who was in fact merely the first choice of architect for the job. The foundation stone was laid by John Donne, Young and Young, *Old London Churches*, 219–220.

Bow within all afternoone else Mrs Hall being there after 8 bespoke som Veale of the Cook at the White Beare at prayers performed my devotion.

Sunday, 22 July: Performed my devotion heard a Stranger at Bow 2 Peter 3:3.4 performed my devotion heard Mr Mooree 10 Proverbs 22 within Read at prayers performed my devotion etc.

Monday, 23 July: Performed my devotion went amongst the Tenants Received $7^s.6^d$ of Mrs James for a quarter Rent ten shillings of Mr Darby for part of ½ a yeares Rent Allowed her 1½ Received of Mrs Thomas $7^s.6^d$ for a quarter Rent of Mr Gr allowd 1½ of Mr Greene 3^l in part for Christmas Rent bought beanes within till 11 at prayers at Coleman Streete performed my devotion within in all day it rayning at prayers performed my devotion.

Tuesday, 24 July: Performed my devotion within till after 8 bought Shoulder Mutton of the woman in Bell Ally went to Mrs Martains and tooke in p[?iece]s the press bed and left it to be brought by the Porter within at prayers at C and could not goe to prayers Staying for the Porter performed my devotion within till 5 at prayers at Bow at Starr Coffee House till 7 called at home but did not stay at prayers at St Laurence at prayers performed my devotion etc.

Wednesday, 25 July: Performed my devotion after 8 amongst the Tenants but could get no money except $2^l.10^s$ from Mr Crisp and Allowd $1^s.4^d$ for Trophee Money and $3:6^d$ for paveing the doore and 2^d to drinke at prayers at Cripplegate within performed my devotion within till Neare 8 at prayers at St Laurance at prayers performed my devotion etc.

Thursday, 26 July: Performed my devotion within till after 10 heard Mr Browne at St Mary Hill 9 Hebrews 27 at Custom House performed my devotion within till 5 at Basinghall Church[856] within at prayers performed my devotion etc.

Friday, 27 July: Performed my devotion within till after 7 went to Mr Stones but could not have any Money Received 7.10^s of Mrs

---

[856] The church of St Michael Bassishaw, which stood in Basinghall Street immediately to the north of the Guildhall. Originally dating from the 12th century, it was destroyed in the Great Fire and rebuilt by Wren in 1679. Structural weaknesses were discovered in its foundations in 1892; thereafter it was closed (and the parish merged with St Lawrence Jewry), before its demolition at the turn of the 20th century. Young and Young, *Old London Churches*, 114–115.

Peale within at prayers at St Alphag performed my devotion within at Mr Sherwoods Received 2^l.10^s for a quarter Rent due at Lady day at 4 went to Mrs Halls at prayers at Lincolns Chappell at Mrs Hals til after 7 within at prayers performed my devotion etc.

[fo. 98r]
Saturday, 28 July: Performed my devotion at Custom House received my salery at prayers at performed my devotion ~~within performed my devotion within~~ received ½ a yeares rent of Mr Buttler allowd 1^{li}:10^s for the Tax and 6^d to drink performed my devotion within till Neare 5 at prayers at Christ Church went to the White Horse to enquire for Edwards the Windsor Coach Man but he did not come to Towne called at Mr Buttlers and left word I had allowd 2^s too Much for the Tax within at prayers performed my devotion.

Sunday, 29 July: Performed my devotion heard Dr Bradford at Bow 4 Philippians 6.7 performed my devotion heard Mr Castle at Alhallows Lombard Streete 2 Corinthians 3.5 went to see Brother Richard but he was not within heard Mr Shephard within read at prayers performed my devotion etc.

Monday, 30 July: Performed my devotion went to Higgs but could not find him nor Treviso at Mrs Callis's a little at prayers at Higgs his Chappell within performed my devotion within till 5 at prayers at Basinghad [*sic*] Church bought Codlings within at prayers performed my devotion.

Tuesday, 31 July: Performed my devotion within till 10 went to see for Edwards the Windsor Coach man but he was not in Towne came back at 11 went with my wife to Cousin Browns, dined there went to Cousin Oddys but they were gon to Camberwell stayd at Cousin Browns till 6 at Cousin Birds[857] till 7 came home performed my devotion etc.

Wednesday, 1 August: Performed my devotion went to Mrs Champnys to see how she did after to the Tower to see Brother Richard, within performed my devotion within till 8 at prayers at St Laurence at prayers performed my devotion.

---

[857] See Introduction, p. 27.

Thursday, 2 August: Performed my devotion went to Mr Stones but could get no money received 12^s.6^d for a quarter at Midsomer of Mrs Holyoake and 10^s of Mrs Kitchinman for a quarter's Rent due at Ladyday and a quarter's Rent of Mr Fielding for Ladyday and allowd the tax etc at prayers at Walbrook and after received 12^s.6 of Hawgood within performed my devotion within till 5 at Mr Beachcrofts and gave Mrs Tempest 5 Counterparts of Leases and paid her 42^l:10^s, at prayers at Foster Lane called my wife at Mrs Johnsons at prayers performed my devotion etc.

Friday, 3 August: Performed my devotion within till called on Windsor Coachman to know how far twas from Slow to Wexham who told me a mile and ⅓ went to Mr Oneby and talked with him Whoe told me Higgs was in Custody[858] and that they should have a Comity on Tuesday at prayers at St Andrews[859] performed my devotion within till 8 at prayers performed my devotion etc.

---

[858] William Higgs was a con-artist of sorts, and it is interesting to speculate how much Lloyd knew of his true character. In this case, he was arrested for masquerading as the servant of one or more foreign diplomats while 'not being Registered according to the late Act of Parliament' (Diplomatic Privileges Act; 7 Anne c. 12); Sir Edward Northey, to unknown, 29 August 1711, TNA, SP 34/37/48, fos 91–92. He did this in order to try to gain diplomatic immunity from his unhappy creditors. The diplomats themselves seem also to have fallen prey to his deception; Friedrich Bonet, Prussian Resident in London and Higgs's unsuspecting employer, initially protested against the arrest and demanded Higgs's release, claiming he was 'detained Prisoner to my detriment and his own' in violation of 'the Law of Nations'; Friedrich Bonet to unknown, 22 August 1711, TNA, SP 34/37/37, fo. 72. Later, Bonet's opinion appears to have swayed: he wrote that 'Mr Fortescue the Chief Plaintiff against My Servant William Higgs and the Under Sheriff attended on me, and gave him a very bad character, desiring that I should withdraw my protection from him, in order that the said Plaintiff may gett his own.' He promised that 'should the said Higgs prove such a knave as represented by the Plaintiff, I will turn him out of My Service', but maintained that 'should he prove an honest man, as I was assured by other hands he is, I would protect him.' However, the aforementioned Act of Parliament ensured that Bonet did not, in fact, have the power to protect Higgs, since it provided that 'no merchant or other trader whatsoever […] shall put himself into the service of any such ambassador or publick minister', presumably in order to prevent this very situation. The man responsible for Higgs's arrest, John Fortescue (or someone with the same name) was an investor named in the original charter of the Charitable Corporation; Carr, *Select Charters*, 257; Memorandum, possibly in connection with the case of W[illia]m Higgs, 1711?, TNA, SP 34/37/39, fo. 74. The case against Higgs appears to have gone no further; Northey suggested (in the same letter) that there was no judge available to hear it.

[859] This could be St Andrew Holborn (Holborn Viaduct), St Andrew Undershaft (Leadenhall St. and St Mary Axe), or St-Andrew-by-the-Wardrobe (then at Puddle Dock Hill; now in Queen Victoria St.), *TBE, London 1*, 190–195.

[fo. 98v]

Saturday, 4 August: Performed my devotion within till 11 at prayers at Coleman Streete dined at 1 went to Mr Stones and he had not dined at Wrights Coffee House and received a letter from Cousin Nicholas then Received 13^{li} from Mr Stone walked in the Charter House garden a little but prayer was not till 5 called at Mr Bawlers and paid him for a bottle of Elixir within till 4 at prayers at St Peters performed my devotion within performed my devotion very disturbedly the man that has the Coppy of Stones Lease coming after 9 and I told him I could not talke with him at prayers.

Sunday, 5 August: Performed my devotion etc heard a stranger at Bow 32 Psalm 5 performed my devotion heard Mr Moore at St Laurance 3 Colossians 13 within read walkt in Moorefields and called to see Mr Snell at prayers performed my devotion.

Monday, 6 August: Performed my devotion called on Mr Stone to desire him to Speake to Mr Ling if he should see him to send me word when he would come to me called at the White Horse Inn to know when Edwards the Windsor Coachman would be in Towne at prayers at Bow within at 10 went with my Wife to Islington to Cousin Oddyes stayd there till 7 performed my devotion by Ejaculations came home aft at 8 at prayers performed my devotion.

Tuesday, 7 August: Performed my devotion within till 10 called at the White Horse to enquire for Edwards the Windsor Coachman but he was not in Towne at prayers at Charterhouse within performed my devotion within till 8 at prayers at St Laurence prayed <performed my devotion.>

Wednesday, 8 August: Performed my devotion at Custom House till 11 at prayers at St Peters performed my devotion within 3 at Custom House at King's Arms Coffee House with at Starr Coffee House at prayers at Bow within at Warner's for pills for Mary at prayers performed my devotion.

Thursday, 9 August: Performed my devotion within till 9 amongst the Tenants Received 3^{l} 5^{s} of Mr Smith <for Midsomer> allowd him for pumping the pond, etc received of Mr Dallaway 10^{s} for a quarter's rent due at Midsomer paid Mr Standford[860] for

---

[860] Unclear: cramped and untidy due to tight binding.

seawage[861] and turncock for ½ yeare at Midsomer within performed my devotion within till 5 at prayers at Bow at Mrs Randalls daughter a little at prayers performed my devotion etc.

Friday, 10 August: Performed my devotion within till 9 went to Mr Oneby and talkt about the business who told me the Next Tuesday my Lord[862] had promised to meete and if they were ready would enter on it came back at prayers at Coleman streete performed my devotion within till after 4 and haveing received a letter from my Lady went to speake to Edwards the Coachman at prayers at Bow and came in and writ a letter to my Lady and put up 2 sheetes and carried them to the White Horse and delivered them to the Porter and tooke 2 places for Tuesday in the Windsor Coach at prayers performed my devotion.

Saturday, 11 August: Performed my devotion within till neare 11 at prayers at St Peters at Custom House to speake to Chamberlaine but could not find him performed my devotion within till 4 at prayers at St Peters within at prayers performed my devotion.

[fo. 99r]
Sunday, 12 August: Performed my devotion heard Dr Green[863] at the Old Jury 19 Psalm 10 performed my devotion 9 Psalm 10 performed my devotion herd Mr Mooree 119 Psalm 83 went to see Mr Nall[864] stayd till 7 within read at prayers performed my devotion etc.

Monday, 13 August: Performed my devotion went to tell Mr Moore I was goeing into the Country for 3 or 4 dayes - went to Custom House and met Mr Chamberlaine and we went to the Harpe in Harpe Lane and drank a pot of beere at the Coffee House in St Peters Alley[865] at prayers at St Peters was to see for Mr Dansey in Chang Ally but could not find him called at the

---

[861] 'Sewage'?
[862] Perhaps the 3rd earl of Clarendon, mentioned at Thursday, **24 May 1711**.
[863] Thomas Green (*c.* 647/8–1720). Fellow (1673–1679) and DD (1684), Peterhouse, Cambridge. Rector of St Olave Old Jewry 1768–1720; also prebend of Norwich and rector of St Martin Pomeroy. *Cantabrigienses*, Vol. 1, pt. 2, 258; *CCEd* Person ID: 163576.
[864] Untidy: perhaps 'Hall'.
[865] Perhaps the 'Smyrna', near 'the west end of of the church and churchyard in St Peter's Alley' in Cornhill, *c.*1693–1714, *LCH*, 532. Subsequent references by Lloyd to a coffee house at 'Peters Alley' (as oppose to St Peter's) probably refer to the same establishment.

bank to ask Mr Collier about a Lottery Ticket but there was none that were single[866] within performed my devotion within till [*blank*]

Tuesday, 14 August: Performed my devotion after 10 tooke coach with my Wife to the White Horse in Fleete Streete for Wexham[867] baited at Hounsloe came to the Crowne at Slow[868] stayd and rested walkt to Wexham to my Lady Mathews Mr Dawson[869] being gon that Morning and Wife etc to his House at Windsor my Lady Received us very kindly and we see the garden etc at prayers performed my devotion etc.

Wednesday, 15 August: Performed my devotion was all day settling the last accounts of Gooding performed my devotion as usuall performed my devotion.

Thursday, 16 August: Performed my devotion and in the Morning settled my accounts and we both signed them and my Wife and Mrs Woodier were Wittness performed my devotion by Ejaculations after 3 I was goeing for Windsor and Mr Dawson sent his Chaise for us I went back and tooke up my wife and got to Windsor after 4 and went to Mr Dawsons and after to the Cathedral[870] and heard part of the prayers and met Mrs Dawson he shewed us the Lodgings and we mett Dr Snape[871] and Mr Browne in the private Chappell but could not see the Queene Mr Browne envited me to diner at the Chaplins table the Next day and tho I had taken 2 places for the Next Morning put them off till Saterday in hopes to see the Queene the Next day eat some salmon etc at Mr Dawsons and he sent his Man and Chaise home to his house and let them tarry all night at prayers performed my devotion.

---

[866] See n. 693, **8 January 1711**. Lottery tickets in the early 18th century were expensive financial investments, and could be purchased collectively alongside fellow 'adventurers'; it seems Lloyd wanted a ticket of his own.

[867] A civil parish immediately north and east of Slough.

[868] Slough.

[869] Thomas Dawson (d.1740), DD Cantab. (1714), rector of New Windsor (1703) and Wexham (1708), was married to Lady Mathews's daughter Elizabeth, TNA, C 8/654/26 (Mathews v. Stone). See also *Cantabrigienses*, Vol. 1, pt. 2, 22; *CCEd* Person ID: 24236.

[870] There is no cathedral in Windsor, but Lloyd was probably referring to the Royal Peculiar of St George's Chapel at Windsor Castle, which is very large and cathedral-like in appearance.

[871] Andrew Snape, DD (1675–1742), then headmaster of the nearby Eton College, *ODNB*.

Friday, 17 August: Performed my devotion at 9 went to Windsor to Mr Dawsons and we expected to see the Queene to goe out that Morning but the guards and Chaise etc were sent back and the Queene did not goe out. Mr Dawson and I went and dined with the Chaplaines and stayd till Neare 3 and we Walkt on the Tarris[872] Walkt till Mrs Dawson and my Wife came to us and after 4 at prayers at the Cathedrall and we could not heare that the Queene went out and she did not stayd at Mr Dawsons til 7 and went to Wexham in the Callash[873] and it stayd all night at prayers performed my devotion.

[fo. 99v]
Saturday, 18 August: Rose at 5 performed my devotion got myselfe ready and after 7 we went in the Chaise to the Pyd Horse and stayd ½ an houer then tooke Coach came to Bell Savage Inn[874] after 1 came home got som bread drinke and Meate and eate performed my devotion within till 5 at prayers at Bow at prayers performed my devotion.

Sunday, 19 August: Performed my devotion heard a stranger at St Laurence 1 Thessalonians 5:19 performed my devotion heard a stranger at St Laurence 1 Corinthians 7.29 at Mrs Halls at prayers performed my devotion.

Monday, 20 August: Performed my devotion within till 7 amongst the Tenants Received of Mr Sawer 2^l of Mr Jones in part 3 allowd to drink 3 of Berrill 9^s: ½ to drink Mr Walkinson 1.15 to drink 3^d Mrs Allen 4^l to drink 3^d of Mrs Ladyman 9^s.6 to drink 1½ Mrs Cooley $10^s.1½^d$ to drink Mr Rice 1:10 for the tax 10^s to drink 1:½ Mr Harrison 2^l for the tax 16^s to drink 1½ Mr Walker 4^l:10^s to drink 3^d within performed my devotion within all a till 6 at prayers at St Bartholomew lane at prayers performed my devotion.

Tuesday, 21 August: Performed my devotion at prayers at Bow left the whipp at Mrs Coopers she left behind her in the Coach

---

[872] Terrace?
[873] Another term for a chaise, or small, light carriage with a folding 'calash' roof, *OED*.
[874] A historic tavern and playhouse of great note, on the north side of Ludgate Hill in the City of London, from the early 15th century until 1873. See Herbert Berry, 'The Bell Savage Inn and Playhouse in London', *Medieval & Renaissance Drama in England*, 19 (2006), 121–143.

when we came from Windsor bought beanes in Newgate Market at Custom House till after 12 performed my devotion within till 5 at prayers at Basinghall Church at Mr Powells and had a flask of brandy called at Mr Greenes and recd 15^s to make up the quarter at Christmass at Mr Stanfords and talkt about severall things within at prayers performed my devotion etc.

Wednesday, 22 August: Performed my devotion at Mr Mounts bought a booke and pag[875] at Custom House at prayers at St Dunstons at Custom House till neare 1 performed my devotion within till 5 at prayers at Basinghall at Mrs Olives received a quarter Rent for Ladyday last allowed for the Tax 2:12 to drink 6^d paid Mr Sandford 10^l in part for his bill at prayers performed my devotion.

Thursday, 23 August: Performed my devotion within till 9 called at Mr Onbys but nothing was done at Mrs Halls and paid her 5^s more for my Lady at prayers at St Mary Hill at Custom House performed my devotion within till 5 at prayers at Basinghall Church called my wife at Mrs Hamonds at prayers performed my devotion etc.

Friday, 24 August: Performed my devotion within till after 10 heard a Stranger at St Laurance ₽ performed my devotion within till 4 at prayers at St Peters walkt in Moorefields called to see Mrs Hancock and she was dead dr dranke a pint of Ale at the First Farthing pye house[876] called to see old Mrs Halford at prayers performed my devotion

Saturday, 25 August: Performed my devotion at prayers at Bow at the Tenants but Received no Mony at Custom House till 1 performed my devotion within till 6 at prayers at St Bartholomew within at prayers performed my devotion etc.

Sunday, 26 August: Performed my devotion heard a Stranger at the Old Jury 18 Revelation 4 performed my devotion heard a stranger at Alhallows Lumbard Streete [*deleted*] 8 Romans 6 at Mrs Wards a little heard a stranger at St Edmond 6 Galatians 9 within at prayers performed my devotion etc.

---

[875] Or 'pay'.

[876] Probably the Farthing Pie House in Marylebone, on Euston Rd. It was subsequently the Green and now Greene Man, and is still trading. See H. B. Wheatley, *London, Past and Present*, Vol. 2 (London, 1891), 33.

[fo. 100r]
Monday, 27 August: Performed my devotion at prayers at Bow at Custom House performed my devotion within till 7 at prayers at St Edmond at prayers performed my devotion etc.

Tuesday, 28 August: Amongst the tenants received of Mr Monday $1^l.5^s$ to make up Christmass quarter's <and 3^l toward Ladyday> and allowd $1:6^d$ for the poore 3^d overrate $1^s.2^d$ Watch 3^d to drinke at prayers at Bow within a little at Custom House performed my devotion within till 6 at prayers at St Bartholomus at prayers performed my devotion.

Wednesday, 29 August: Performed my devotion at Custom House at prayers at St Edmond performed my devotion within till 6 at prayers at St Bartholomew at prayers performed my devotion.

Thursday, 30 August: Performed my devotion within till 11 at Custom House performed my devotion within till 5 at prayers at Basinghall Church at Mr Sandfords and talkt with him at Mrs Martins to see for my Wife but she was not there at prayers performed my devotion.

Friday, 31 August: Performed my devotion amongst the Tenants to give order to the workmen Received of Mr Blackden $1^l.16^s$ for a quarter's Rent allowd to drinke 3^d received of Margaret King 6^s for a quarter Rent due Midsummer 1709 at prayers at Bow within performed my devotion againe that I had not time to doe before at Custom House till 1 performed my devotion within till 5 at prayers at Bow walkt round St Pauls with my Wife called to see Mrs Freeman at prayers performed my devotion.

Saturday, 1 September: Performed my devotion at prayers at Bow. Within performed my devotion that I had not finished at Custom House performed my devotion within till 6 at prayers at Foster Lane at prayers performed my devotion.

Sunday, 2 September: Performed my devotion heard a stranger at Bow 1 John 3: 11 ₽ performed my devotion heard Mr Moree at St Laurence 4:11[877] performed my devotion walk't round St Pauls within reade at prayers performed my devotion.

---

[877] Lloyd omitted the book here.

Monday, 3 September: Performed my devotion heard a Stranger 4 Amos 11 at the Poltry[878] performed my devotion heard a Stranger at Bow 111:2[879] went to see Mr Allen stayd till after 7 at home at prayers performed my devotion.

Tuesday, 4 September: Performed my devotion at prayers at Bow went with Mr Johnson to see theire New Lodgings after bought piece beefe at Cooks and called on Mr Overton to know when the Money would be due for use for the Money My Lady Mathews had on Mortgage within performed my devotion at 1 went to see Cousin Oddy and I.[880] at Islington stayd there till 5 and after at Cousin Birds till 6 at prayers performed my devotion.

Wednesday, 5 September: Performed my devotion within till after 9 at Custom House at prayers at St Donstons performed my devotion within till 6 at prayers at Bartholomew Lane at prayers performed my devotion etc. Was with Mr Ingham and eate somthing.

Thursday, 6 September: Performed my devotion within till 7 called at Mr Stones and he promised me to give me the sight of the Lease at Mr Linets and received 3^s.15 for Midsomer Rent and allowd 2^s.6^d he gave for earnest at Custom House went to Cousin Bird to her house and stayd till Neare 6 at prayers at Bartholomew Lane performed my devotion in the church within at prayers performed my devotion.

[fo. 100v]
Friday, 7 September: Performed my devotion within till Neare 10 bespoke 8 sacks Coales to come in at 3 at prayers at St Donstons at Custom House till 1 left a bill to let Mrs Birds House at Mr Blagues paid and tooke in my Coales paid 19^s.4^d for them and 3^d shooting[881] and 2^d for opneing [*sic*] the bord and puting it in; went with Mr Ingkam to Mr Lloyds to bespeake beere of him we drank a pint of Alle at the 3 Marriners stayd at Mr Lloyds till after 6 we went to

---

[878] Poultry, a short street contiguous with Cheapside, at its east end, connecting the latter to the junction with Threadneedle St., etc.

[879] Again, Lloyd omitted the book cited, but it seems likely to have been Psalm 111:2: 'The works of the Lord are great, sought out of all them that have pleasure therein.'

[880] Meaning unclear; could also read 'J'.

[881] Perhaps this is a reference to work done to Lloyd's chimney *chute*, albeit spelled phonetically.

Jacks Coffe House[882] and after to prayers at St Edmond at prayers performed my devotion.

Saturday, 8 September: Performed my devotion amongst the Tenants Received 4¹ of Mr Richards for a quarter's Rent due at Midsomer last at Custom House till after 1 performed my devotion within till 5 at prayers at Basinghall Church walkt a little within at prayers performed my devotion.

Sunday, 9 September: Performed my devotion heard a Stranger at Bow 5 Deuteronomy 19 performed my devotion heard Mr Castle 16 Luke 24:25:26 at Mrs Wards a little within read at prayers performed my devotion.

Monday, 10 September: Performed my devotion at prayers at Bow but was so ill came home and grew worse tooke som surfiet watter[883] and that brought away by Vomit tooke Cardus Pea[884] and Vomited more and was better within performed my devotion Cousin Newington came and stayd till 6 was within all day at prayers performed my devotion.

Tuesday, 11 September: Performed my devotion at prayers at Bow. Within and bottled a little drink, at Custom House till after 11 called on Mr Sanford, and at Mr Reynolds performed my devotion within till 6 at prayers at Bartholomew Lane at prayers performed my devotion.

Wednesday, 12 September: Performed my devotion at prayers at Bow at Custom House performed my devotion within till 5 at prayers at Basinghall Strete within at prayers performed my devotion etc.

Thursday, 13 September: Performed my devotion within till 9 called at Mr Reynolds for a Noate to his father and carried it to

---

[882] Lillywhite lists five establishments of this name, but only two can be found referenced during Lloyd's time; one at Sweeting's Alley 'by the Exchange', and one in Birchin Lane, both mentioned c.1702–1714.

[883] 'Surfeit water' was a common treatment for indigestion dating to at least the 17th century; for an exemplar recipe containing mint, thistle, and wormwood, amongst other ingredients, see Hannah Woolley, *The Accomplisht Ladys Delight, in Preserving, Physick, Beautifying and Cookery* (London, 1675), 93.

[884] *Carduus* is the genus to which thistles belong; it seems Lloyd was suffering badly with indigestion!

him but he would not pay me No Money at prayers at St Mary Hill at Custom House performed my devotion within till 6 at prayers at Bartholomew Lane at prayers performed my devotion etc.

Friday, 14 September: Performed my devotion within till 7 amongst the Tenants and received 1^l:5^s of Mr Monday to make up Ladydays rent Allowd for poore 1^s:6^d over rate 3^s Watch 1^s.2^d called at Mr Sandfords and paid for sending to Mr Liquorish about the bill at prayers at Bow at home a little at Custom House performed my devotion within till after 4 at Wrights Coffee House and received a letter from Cousin Nicholas at prayers at Bow walkt with my Wife in St Pauls Churchyard at prayers performed my devotion.

Saturday, 15 September: Performed my devotion within till after 8 at prayers at Bow at Custom House till Neare 1 within performed my devotion within till 4 at prayers at St Peters within performed my devotion at prayers.

Sunday, 16 September: Performed my devotion heard a Stranger at Old Jury 26 Matthew 41 performed my devotion heard a stranger at St Laurance 1 Corinthians 2:2 within read at prayers performed my devotion.

[fo. 101r]
Monday, 17 September: Performed my devotion etc paid Mr Overton Stationer without Newgate[885] 9^{li} for a yeares Interest for 150^{li} for the Lady Mathews called at Mrs Halls but she was not up went to Lord Powers but he was out of Towne went to Higgs but could not find him Nor Treviso calle[d] on Mr Lloyd in the Pallace Yard[886] but he was not within called to see Mr Prin but stayd Not went to see for Mr Sanders Mrs Wards Rent gatherer but he was not within at an Alehouse and drank and eate bread and Cheese at prayers at Higgs's Chappell and left word with the Watchman I would be at Kingstreete Coffee house[887] dined at the

---

[885] Henry Overton (1675/6–1751), second son of John Overton (1639/40–1713), who took over his father's printing and publishing business in 1707. It operated from the 'White Horse without Newgate'. For a good summary of the Overton family and its operations, see *ODNB*.

[886] Either Old Palace Yard or New Palace Yard: grounds around the Palace of Westminster.

[887] Lillywhite lists one establishment from Lloyd's time as 'King Street Coffee House', at King St., Westminster, referred to in the fifth edn of Izaak Walton's *Compleat Angler* (1676): *LCH*, 317. There are, however, several King Sts in London (in Cheapside, Covent Garden,

Crowne called on Mr Oneby and he told me the business would goe forwards when Higgs was at liberty at Mr Rowlandsons and Met My Wife there and Mrs Ward stayd till after 6 within at prayers performed my devotion.

Tuesday, 18 September: Performed my devotion at Custom House at prayers at St Dionis performed my devotion within till 6 Mr Cleave and daughter being here at prayers at St Bartholomew within at prayers performed my devotion.

Wednesday, 19 September: Performed my devotion at Custom House at prayers at St Dunstons at the Shipp Taverne[888] with Mr Moore within performed my devotion within till Neare 5 at White Horse Yard[889] lett Mr Stiffs roomes to Susan Andrews at prayers at Bartholomew Lane within at prayers performed my devotion.

Thursday, 20 September: Performed my devotion within till after 9 went to speake to Veares the Paviour and called at Mr Fordhams, and he did mend the click of the striking watch[890] at Custom House at prayers at St Mary Hill performed my devotion within till 5 at prayers at Bow at Starr Coffee House at prayers againe at Bartholomew Lane. Met my Wife and Mrs Bierd and went with her to Mrs Martins stayd till 9 at prayers performed my devotion.

Friday, 21 September: Performed my devotion etc at prayers at Bow ₤ went to Mr Overton to speke for Mr Herne for his voate for Clark of Embroiderers Company amongst the Tenants but could get no money within performed my devotion within till after 2 we stayd a little at Mr Wades went to see Mrs Hall at prayers at Lincoln's Inn Chapell at Mrs Halls till after 6 within and in Mr Ingshams Roome till after 10 at prayers performed my devotion.

Bloomsbury, Soho, West Smithfield, etc.), each of which were home to more than one coffee house; too many, in fact, to be worth listing here. Ibid. 789.

[888] See n. 962, **15 March 1712.**

[889] There are numerous White Horse Yards on Rocque's 1746 map of London, but the most likely candidate here is that off Goswell Rd, just north of the Barbican where it becomes Aldersgate St. Lady Mathews owned property in the adjacent Vine Yard, mentioned frequently below.

[890] Lloyd was probably referring to a 'repeater', a watch which would 'strike' hours, or sometimes smaller intervals within the hour, though minute repeaters were not invented until 1767. In 1711, such devices would have been unreliable and inaccurate, but were expensive novelties and status symbols; Samuel Macey, *Clocks and the Cosmos: Time in Western Life and Thought* (Hamden, 1980), 30.

Saturday, 22 September: Performed my devotion amongst the Tenants but gott no money at Custom House with Brother Richard and drank with him with performed my devotion at prayers at St Peters within at prayers performed my devotion etc.

Sunday, 23 September: Performed my devotion heard the reader at St Laurance 2 Timothy 2:19 performed my devotion heard Mr Castle at Alhallows Lumbard Streete 1 Samuel 2:19[891] at Mrs Allens a little read at prayers performed my devotion etc.

[fo. 101v]
Monday, 24 September: Performed my devotion amongst the Tenants Received of Michael Corker 11^s.6^d for a quarter's Rent due at Midsummer 1710 of Mr Harrington 5:7 for a quarter Rent due at Ladyday 1711 Allowd for Poore 2^s over rate 4^s watch 1:6 to drink 6^d, received of Mrs Dennis 20^s in part for a quarter's Rent due at Midsomer 1710 allowed 1^s Trophee Money within a little at Custom House at prayers at St Catherine performed my devotion within till Neare 5 at prayers at St Mary Woollnorth within at prayers performed my devotion.

Tuesday, 25 September: Performed my devotion at prayers at Bow, at Custom House till after 11 at Mr Sandfords to speake to him and the Paviour, performed my devotion within till 6 at prayers at St Bartholomew at prayers performed my devotion.

Wednesday, 26 September: Performed my devotion within till 10 at prayers at St Donstons at Custom House at the Ship[892] with Mr Moore till after 12 within till performed my devotion within till 4 at St Pauls and heard the Anthem and the later end of the Prayers and Spoke to Dr Standly[893] about the Charitable

---

[891] 'Moreover his mother made him a little coat, and brought it to him from year to year, when she came up with her husband to offer the yearly sacrifice', 1 Samuel 2:19. It seems possible that Lloyd cited the wrong chapter and verse here, since it is identical to that of the earlier sermon, and also seems an unlikely passage on which to preach.

[892] The Ship Tavern.

[893] This seems likely to have been William Stanley (1647–1731), who was prebendary of Codington Major and later canon residentiary at St Paul's. Stanley was created DD by Archbishop Sancroft in 1685. He was appointed master of Corpus Christi College, Cambridge, 1693–1698, and later became dean of St Asaph, Wales, in 1706. Stanley was a leading Fellow of the Royal Society, and also (like many of the clergymen whom Lloyd appears to have favoured or associated with) preached in support of the Society for Propagating the Gospel in Foreign Parts. *ODNB*.

Corporation but there was nothing done in it; at Starr Coffee House at prayers at St Pauls met my wife and we walked round St Pauls at prayers performed my devotion.

Thursday, 27 September: Performed my devotion within till after 8 at Dr Bradfords to enquire when a Confirmation would be and he told me on Tuesday the 2^d October and promised Mary should be confirmed and gave me a paper for her to use at Mr Rowlandsons and talked with him about Stones Leace etc at prayers at St Mary Hill at Custom House performed my devotion within till 5 at prayers at Bow within at prayers performed my devotion.

Friday, 28 September: Performed my devotion within till 8 at prayers at Bow and had Mary to Dr Bradford to be examined within a little at Custom House performed my devotion walking dined at the Ship with our Officers within till 5 at prayers at Bow at prayers performed my devotion.

Saturday, 29 September: Performed my devotion amongst the Tenants Received a quarter's Rent of Mr Hunter for Michaelmas and 1^1.5 and received of Mr Stiff for 2 quarters due at Michaelmas gave warning to Ann Darby and to Mrs Boucher at prayers at Cripelgate performed my devotion paid Mr Partridg[894] a quarter Rent at prayers at St Peters within at prayers performed my devotion.

Sunday, 30 September: Performed my devotion after 9 went with my Wife to Islington Church heard a Stranger 13 Hebrews 5 dined at Cousin Oddyes performed my devotion by Ejaculations heard a stranger Matthew[895] at Cousin Oddyes a little called at Cousin Birds and at Cousin Browns came home after 6 read at prayers performed my devotion.

Monday, 1 October: Amongst the Tenants but got no Money at Custom House at prayers at St Catherine within performed my devotion within till after 3 went to see Darts House and Hedges to see how padlocks might be put on paid[896] Mr Lloyd for 7 fer[?kins] beere at prayers at Bartholomew Lane at prayers performed my devotion etc.

---

[894] Lloyd's own landlord or rent-gatherer cannot be identified.
[895] No chapter or verse.
[896] Very unclear in bottom corner: originally 'pd' (uncertain).

[fo. 102r]
~~Monday~~
~~Tuesday Octob^r.~~
~~2st 1711 performed my devotion amongst the Tenants~~

Tuesday, 2 October: Performed my devotion after I carryed Mary to Bow to Dr Bradfords to be Confirmed heard Mr Ibbott 8 Acts 17 at Starr Coffee House within performed my devotion within till 5 heard Mr Haley at St Donstons 119 Psalm 153 within at prayers performed my devotion etc.

Wednesday, 3 October: Performed my devotion amongst the Tenants but got no money at Custom House at prayers at St Donstons at Custom House performed my devotion Brother Walker dined here at home till 5 called at Mr Sandfords to bid them send the poore Duch Man to the Change to see for some of his Countrymen at prayers at Bartholomew Lane at prayers performed my devotion.

Thursday, 4 October: Performed my devotion went to Lord Powers and Spoke to him about his paying ground Rent and he said twas Taxes talked with Higgs and he told me he had Hopes he should effect his business shortly at prayers at his Chappell dined at Mr Callis's called againe to see My Lord Powers House called at Mrs Wiblins and she told me that my Lord said twas ground Rent called at Mrs Halls at prayers at Basing Lane[897] within at prayers performed my devotion.

~~5 Performed my devotion at the Tenants and received 10^{li} of Mr Moone for Midsomer at 5 performed my devotion amongst the Tenants but received no money at Custom House at prayers at St Donstons at Custom House within performed my devotion~~

Friday, 5 October: Performed my devotion amongst the Tenants but got no money at Mr Jones's in Bartholomew Close and had a Truss fitted and put on at Custom House at prayers at St Donstons at Custom House performed my devotion within till after 3 received 10^{li} of Mr Moone for a quarter Rent at Midsomer Allow'd 6^d to drink called my Wife at Mrs Sandfords stayd till

---

[897] Basing Lane connected Bow Lane to Bread St.; it lay roughly in line with part of what is now Cannon St.

after 5 at prayers at Foster Lane within at prayers performed my devotion.

Saturday, 6 October: Performed my devotion at prayers at Bow after paid Mr Beachcroft 42^l:10^s for a quarter's Us[ance] money[898] for Mrs Tempest due at ~~Michaelmas~~ September 15th 1710 at Custom House performed my devotion after 1 went to see for Roger Sandfords and left word he should come to me in the Evening at prayers at Charter House within at prayers performed my devotion etc.

Sunday, 7 October: Performed my devotion etc heard Dr Mapletoft 7 Matthew 14 ₽ performed my devotion heard Mr Moore 6 Matthew 33 walkt to St Pauls within read at prayers <performed my devotion.>

Monday, 8 October: Performed my devotion went to Mr Rowlandson to talke with him at Custom House at prayers at St Edmond within. Performed my devotion within till 6 at prayers at St Bartholomew at prayers performed my devotion read Dr Uptons funerall sermon[899] etc.

Tuesday, 9 October: Performed my devotion at Custom House at prayers at St Edmond performed my devotion within till 6 at prayers at Foster Lane at prayers performed my devotion etc.

[fo. 102v]
Wednesday, 10 October: Performed my devotion went amongst the Tenants but could get no money went to Mr Nash and talked about the Mortgage at prayers at Charter House at Custom House performed my devotion within till 5 at prayers at Basing Hall Church heard the Reader[900] 18 Psalm 1 within at prayers performed my devotion etc.

---

[898] In other words, for money borrowed or lent, often at interest, *OED*.

[899] Samuel Wright, *A Funeral Sermon, upon the Sudden and Much Lamented Death of Dr. Francis Upton; who Died September 4th, 1711. Preached at Black-Fryars* (1711). Samuel Wright (1683–1746) was a noted presbyterian and dissenter, whose meeting house was wrecked by the mob during the Sacheverell riots in 1710, *ODNB*. Upton appears to have been a rather obscure figure, but the contents of the sermon suggests that he was a fellow nonconformist of some kind, and Lloyd's interest in him again hints at a whiggish, Low Church, and even latitudinarian sensibility.

[900] For Samuel Baker, the reader at St Michael Bassishaw in Basinghall St., see n. 702, **14 January 1711.**

Thursday, 11 October: Performed my devotion amongst the Tenants and to see about how to Seize Darts and Hedges goods within it rayning hard at prayers at Coleman Streete performed my devotion within till 6 at prayers at Bartholomew Lane at prayers performed my devotion etc.

Friday, 12 October: Performed my devotion went to the Constable about seizing Hedges and Darts goods have but could not find him at prayers at Bow at Custom House performed my devotion went to the Cunstables so to desire him to doe with me Next Morning called on Dallaway to order him to be in the Way Next Morning called at Mr Stones and Mrs Peales at Bluecoat Coffee House[901] called at Mr Bawlers and he not within at home till 6 at prayers at St Bartholomew Lane at home at Cards with Mr Ingsham at prayers performed my devotion.

Saturday, 13 October: Performed my devotion called at Mr Greene the Cunstables and went to Whipp and Topp[902] and stayd till he came went to Hedges and he was ill in bed and we could not take away his goods went to Darts and seized his and he promised to get Mony by Tuesday and promised not to stir the goods at Mr Bawlers and was Let bloud at prayers at St Peter at Custom House performed my devotion within at prayers at Bartholomew Lane at prayers performed my devotion at Custom House called on [blank] 4 at prayers at Charter House called on Dallaway and ordered him to looke after Darts goods within at prayers performed my devotion.

Sunday, 14 October: Performed my devotion tooke phisick being very ill performed my devotion as usually at prayers etc.

Monday, 15 October: Tooke phisick performed my devotion as usually at prayers etc.

Tuesday, 16 October: Performed my devotion at prayers at Charter House to see that Darts goods were not removed at

---

[901] In St Swithin's Lane, or 'Swithin's Alley': possibly two separate establishments, or perhaps the same. Sweeting's Alley was sometimes referred to as 'Swithin's'. The former found referenced c.1681–1714, the latter 1708–1738, *LCH*, 126, 684–685.

[902] I can find little reference to such an establishment, except that a tavern by the same name still existed in Aldersgate St. in 1731, *London Journal*, 19 June 1731, BL, *Burney Collection*. This seems likely to have been the same premises visited by Lloyd, since Vine Yard is just off Aldersgate St.

Custom House performed my devotion at Mr Sandfords to watch Darts house open and at last put Mr Sandfords man in possession stayd till after 4 at prayers at Bartholomew Lane at Mrs Martins for my wife within at prayers.

Wednesday, 17 October: Performed my devotion after 9 at Darts to see the goods were not gone at Custom House performed my devotion after 2 at Darts house tooke an Inventory of his goods and had them praysed and the Constable to give an oath and left them in his possession and tooke 2 Noates of him one for 3^l 10^s at a Moneths end the other for 5^{li} on sight at C[?offee] H[?ouse] drank a dish Coffee my head being Very bad and giddy within and very bad at prayers performed my devotion in bed and tooke Squirs Elixir.

Thursday, 18 October: Performed my devotion in bed rose after 12 performed my devotion dined performed my devotion within at prayers performed my devotion etc.

Friday, 19 October: Performed my devotion at prayers at Charter House received $1^l.10^s$ for a quarter's Rent due at Christmas of Richard Creeke and $7^l.10^s$ of Mrs Peale for a quarter's Rent due at Michaelmas at Mr Bawlers and bespake a blister plaster performed my devotion within till 6 at prayers at Bartholomew Lane at prayers performed my devotion went with Mr Jones and had a new plaster to my bely[903] put on the blister.

[fo. 103r]
Saturday, 20 October: Performed my devotion in bed and lay in bed till after 12 and my blister did not rise and it was not taken off rose at 1 performed my devotion within and about 5 Mr Bawler came and tooke off the plaster but there was hardly any blister performed my devotion at prayers.

Sunday, 21 October: Performed my devotion in bed and had a fresh Mellilott[904] plaster layd on but it did hardly run at all after 10 rose performed my devotion dined performed my devotion read at prayers performed my devotion.

---

[903] Belly.
[904] Melilot, or sweet clover, is a variety of plant which was formerly used – amongst other things – in plasters and dressings to reduce swelling, *OED*.

Monday, 22 October: Performed my devotion in bed rose after 9 performed my devotion dined performed my devotion within all day at prayers performed my devotion.

Tuesday, 23 October: Performed my devotion within till 10 at East India House received 6^{li} for ½ yeares Interest at prayers at St Peters at Custom House performed my devotion within till 4 at Custom House received my salery at St Donstons heard Mr Haley 6 Matthew 33 within at prayers performed my devotion.

Wednesday, 24 October: Performed my devotion went to Mr Nash to aske him about the Money my Lady had of him but could not find him called at Mr Sherwoods but he had no money at the White Horse in Fleete to enquire after Edwards but he was not in Towne called to see Mrs Hall called on Poole but he was not in ~~Towne~~ at home at prayers at St Donstons at prayers at Custom House called at Mr Renoylds [*sic*] at broken Wharfe but he had No Money called at Mrs Coggills and she got some black wooll out of my Ears and I gave her a shilling within performed my devotion amongst the Tenants and Received of Mr Higham a quarter's Rent for Michaelmas and ½ a yeares Rent of Mrs Harding and a quarter of Mr Heywood and 5^s for Ann Darby and a quarter Rent of Greene for Ladyday and a Quarter's Rent of Mrs Harris for Ladyday and a quarter of Mr Crisp for Michaelmas at Basing Hall Church heard a sermon 25 Matthew 13 at home at prayers performed my devotion.

Thursday, 25 October: Performed my devotion within till after 10 <~~called at~~> at St Mary Hill heard Mr Browne 12 Hebrews 6 at Custom House at the Shipp with Mr Moore and Elliot till 1 within performed my devotion within till after 5 at Plow Coffee house at prayers at Bartholomew Lane within at prayers performed my devotion tooke Mrs Martins powder of snuff[905] and it worked well with me.

Friday, 26 October: Performed my devotion in bed rose after 8 my Nose runing much performed my devotion within all day performed my devotion as usualy at prayers.

Saturday, 27 October: Amongst the Tenants but got no Money at prayers at Charter House eat a Mess of pottage at Christ Church

---

[905] This was presumably a medicament of some kind rather than tobacco snuff, though I have not been able to trace it.

Passage at Custom House performed my devotion within till 6 at prayers at Bartholomew within at prayers performed my devotion etc.

Sunday, 28 October: Performed my devotion heard Dr Mapletoph 7 Matthew 15 performed my devotion heard Mr Mooree at St Laurance 2:3 verses of St Jude heard a stranger at St Edmond 13 John 31 within heard the Maid read at prayers performed my devotion tooke the herbe snuff, and it workt well with me.

[fo. 103v]
Monday, 29 October: In bed haveing taken the Snuff rose after 10 performed my devotion within all day performed my devotion as usually at prayers.

Tuesday, 30 October: Performed my devotion at Peeles and Bell the shoemakers at prayers at St Lawrance at Custom House at the Shipp with Mr Moore etc performed my devotion within till Neare 5 at St Donstons heard Mr Haley 12 Ecclesiastes 1 called at Mr Cocks for my wife stayd till 11 supt there performed my devotion etc.

Wednesday, 31 October: Performed my devotion called at Mr Stones but he was not within went to Nurs Hatch but she was not at home went to Madam Gomark and she directed me to Mrs Lacy and I had 3 papers of her Snuff at Higgs's and talkt about the affaire and he told me it would goe forward tooke water at White Hall at Custom House performed my devotion at 3 went with my wife to Mrs Halls and left her there called on Nurs Hatch and she told me she would call and see us at Mr Onebys and talkt with him about the Lombard office[906] called my Wife and at prayers at Foster Lane at prayers performed my devotion took sneecing snuff.[907]

---

[906] Several early pamphlets issued by the Charitable Corporations place its offices at 'New Lombard House', Duke St., Westminster, at the site of the former Admiralty Office. See Anon., *Advertisement: From the Charitable Corporation for Relief of Industrious Poor* (London, 1709?), GHL, 7.105; Anon., *From the Lombard house in Duke-street, Westminster: Abstract of the settlement for insurance of goods against loss by fire, inrolled in the high court of Chancery, by the Charitable corporation* (London, 1708?), GHL, 7.101; Anon., *From the new Lombard-house in Dukes-street, Westminster: The method of securing the fund of the Charitable corporation* (London, 1708?), GHL, 7.100; Anon., *An account of the office now setting up by the Charitable Corporation*, BL, Add MS 61619, fo. 213.
[907] 'Sneezing' snuff, a 'powder or preparation for inducing sneezing', *OED*.

Thursday, 1 November: Performed my devotion within all day performed my devotion as usualy at prayers etc.

Saturday, 3 November:[908] Performed my devotion within till after 9 went to Mr Bell shoemaker and had a pair of shoes and paid for them called at the White Hart and Star[909] in Paternoster Row and bespake a sett of Loops for a Coate at prayers at St Peters at Custom House at prayers at Charter House at Mr Jones's and had a new plaster for my Rupture within at prayers performed my devotion etc.

Friday, 2 November: Performed my devotion within till 11 at prayer at Lothberry at Custom House performed my devotion within till 5 at prayers at Bow within at prayers performed my devotion.

Sunday, 4 November: Performed my devotion heard a stranger at St Laurance 2 Hebrews 13 ℙ performed my devotion heard a Stranger at St Laurance 13 Mark 37 within read a little at prayers performed my devotion.

Monday, 5 November: Performed my devotion heard a the reader at St Laurance 10 Matthew 16 performed my devotion heard a sermon at Bow Mr Boyles[910] Lecture 111 Psalm 29 within at prayers performed my devotion.

Tuesday, 6 November: Performed my devotion amongst the Tenantts received 6^{li} 10^s of Mrs Olive for a quarter's Rent due at Midsomer allowd 6^d received of Mr Starky 16:6 for a quarter's Rent due at Midsummer received of Mrs Thomas 7:6^d for a quarter's Rent due at Michaelmas received of Mrs [*blank*] 11^s.3^d for a quarter's rent due at Ladyday at the Christian Coffee House paid Mr Wiat 4:16.4 for River w[?ater][911] at prayers at Charter House called for my Loops at the White Hart in Paternoster Row at Custom House performed my devotion within till Neare 5 heard Mr Hally 119 Psalm 92 within performed my devotion at prayers etc tooke Snuff.

---

[908] The entries for 2 and 3 November are in reverse order.

[909] Still a 'well-accustomed button shop' in Paternoster Row by 1744, *LTR*, Vol. 3, 161.

[910] The Boyle Lecture for 1711–1712 was delivered by William Derham (1657–1735), a clergyman and natural philosopher. His lectures were published as *Physico-Theology, or, A Demonstration of the Being and Attributes of God* (London, 1713).

[911] Untidy and unclear.

Wednesday, 7 November: Performed my devotion within all day performed my devotion as usualy at prayers etc.

Thursday, 8 November: Performed my devotion within till after 10 at St Mary Hill heard Mr Browne 39 Psalm 5:6 at Custom House performed my devotion within all the afternoone Mr Hall being here at prayers performed my devotion etc.

[fo. 104r]
Friday, 9 November: Performed my devotion went to see Mr Moore and he was very ill at prayers at Aldgate at the Cooks at the Pye in Fenchurch Streete[912] and enquired of the Cooke about the people at the Apothecary within performed my devotion after 3 went with my wife called at Mr Sherwod but got no money at Mrs Sandfords with my wife till 6 at prayers at Foster Lane within at prayers performed my devotion.

Saturday, 10 November: Performed my devotion amongst the Tenants received a quarter's Rent of Mrs Holyoake due at Michaelmas received a quarter Rent of Mrs Hill due at at Lady day Received of Jone Harding 2 quarters' Rent due at Midsomer within a little at Custom House performed my devotion at prayers at Charter House within.

Sunday, 11 November: Performed my devotion heard a Stranger at St Laurance 7 Matthew 12 performed my devotion heard Mr Moore [*blank*] at Laurence Holker's to see how he did at prayers at St Swithins called my Wife at Mrs Cocks within read at prayers performed my devotion.

Monday, 12 November: Performed my devotion at prayers at Bow at Custom House above bridg to see for the Watermen but could find None at Mrs Coggells and had some silke she bought for me received 4^{li} from Mrs Reynolds father for his rent called on Mr Sherwood but he could not pay me within performed my devotion within till 5 at prayers at St Mary Woollnorth at prayers performed my devotion.

---

[912] Probably the Pye Tavern, actually at Aldgate (which joins Fenchurch St.), which stood from at least the 17th century and was the venue for occasional plays; *London, Past and Present*, Vol. 1, 28. It still stood in 1720, Anon., *Tryals for High-Treason, and Other Crimes*, pt. 5 (London, 1720), 642.

Tuesday, 13 November: Performed my devotion went to Mr Moore to enquire about the Watermen above bridge and but one man was there at prayers at St Peters went toward the Custom House and mett Mr Smith and he told me he would looke after the business above bridg within performed my devotion within at prayers within till 5 at prayers and heard Dr Haly at prayers performed my devotion.

Wednesday, 14 November: Performed my devotion within all day haveing taken snuff. Performed my devotion as usualy performed my devotion.

Thursday, 15 November: Performed my devotion amongst the Tenants received 4^{li} of Mrs Allen for Midsomer Rent $3^{li}.5^s$ of Mr Smith 10^s of Dallaway for Michaelmas each 10^s of Mrs Cooley for Midsomer $7:6^d$ from young Creeke for Midsomer within Tom Holker and his wife being here at Custom House with Mr Moore within performed my devotion within till 6 at prayers at Bartholomew at Cousin Amyes for my wife within at prayers performed my devotion.

Friday, 16 November: Performed my devotion Received $2^{li}:10^s$ of Mr Sherwood and bought 3 yards blew Cloth of Mr Hart and had it carried to Mr Pooles at prayers at St Peters at Custom House at Mr Sandfords and received 10^s of Kitchinman and $4:10^s$ of Mr Walker within performed my devotion within till 6 at prayers at Foster Lane at prayers performed my devotion.

Saturday, 17 November: Performed my devotion fetch the loops and buttons for my blew coate from Pater Noster Row and carried them to Pooles at prayers at St Edmond at Custom House performed my devotion within till [ink blot] at prayers at Bartholomew Lane at prayers performed my devotion.

[fo. 104v]
Sunday, 18 November: Performed my devotion heard a stranger at St Laurance 23 Matthew 23 performed my devotion heard Mr Moore.

Monday, 19 November: Performed my devotion at prayers at St Peter at Custom House performed my devotion within till 5 at prayers at Posthouse[913] within at prayers performed my devotion tooke the Snuff.

Tuesday, 20 November: Within all day haveing taken Snuff performed my devotion as Usually at prayers.

Wednesday, 21 November: Performed my devotion with the Tenantts Received of Mr Linnett 3:15^d for a quarter's Rent due at Michaelmas and 2^{li} of Garrett for a quarter's Rent due at Ladyday at prayers at Custom House at [*sic*]Custom House at prayers at St Magnes[914] performed my devotion within till 4 at Mrs Halls stayd with my Wife till Neare 3 at prayers at St Laurence at prayers performed my devotion.

Thursday, 22 November: Tooke pills within all day performed my devotion as Usualy at prayers etc.

Friday, 23 November: Performed my devotion at the Temple with Mr Rowlandson till 10 called on Mr Oneby to know what he heard about the Lumbard Office but he had Nothing at prayers at St Peters at Custom House performed my devotion within till 4 at Mr Sandfords but he not within at prayers at St Swithins at Mr Sandford and talkt with him at Mrs Cocks for my Wife till Neare 9 at prayers performed my devotion.

Saturday, 24 November: Performed my devotion at prayers at St Peters at Custom House performed my devotion within till 7 at prayers at St Edmond performed my devotion at prayers etc.

Sunday, 25 November: Performed my devotion heard Dr Mapletoff 7 Matthew 21:22 performed my devotion heard Mr New <ton> at St Laurence 4 Proverbs 23 within at prayers read performed my devotion tooke Hunter's drops.

Monday, 26 November: Performed my devotion in bed rose at 2 performed my devotion within all day and Mr Sandford was with me

---

[913] Ambiguous; rendered unclear by tight binding.

[914] A large and magnificent church in the heart of the City, St Magnus the Martyr has a long and storied history. Standing prominently in (Lower) Thames St., the church probably dates to the 11th century, predating St Magnus of Orkney, to whom it is dedicated. The present building, however, was built by Wren in *c.*1671–1684 after initial work begun by the parish in 1668. See *TBE, London 1*, 231–233; Young and Young, *Old London Churches*, 96–98.

and we adjusted the Accounts betweene my Lady and him my Lady allowing him 13^l.11^s for repayres he allowd 1 yeare and ½ Rent and paid 4^{li}.10^s for Mr Harris for a yeares Rent and I gave him a Noate for 6.10^s and he gave me a Receipt in full for his Bill of 50^l.3^s:11½^d there being 30^{li} paid before, and he gave me a Receipt for 13:11 for Repayres at prayers performed my devotion etc.

Tuesday, 27 November: Performed my devotion after 10 at Custom House at Queen's Arms Coffee House at prayers at St Edmonds within performed my devotion within till 6 at [*sic*] day at prayers performed my devotion.

Wednesday, 28 November: Performed my devotion amongst the Tenants Received 2^l:5^s of Mr Blunt for ½ a quarter Rent due at Michaelmas of Gamball 2^{li} for a quarter Rent due at Midsomer of Mrs Ladyman for a quarter Rent due at Michaelmas at prayers at St Dunstons at Custom House performed my devotion within till 2 at Mrs Halls and she and I went and bought Velvit at backside of St Clement's went to my Ladys Lodgings and after I went to enquire at the Cheq[?ue]r Inn and met the Coachman and he told me my Lady would not come till Saterday called my wife at Mrs Cleves stayd till after 7 at prayers at St Laurance within at prayers performed my devotion.

[fo. 105r]
Thursday, 29 November: Performed my devotion within till after 11 at Custom House at Mr Moores at Mrs Wards to know when she would be at home within performed my devotion at St Mary Wool North within at prayers performed my devotion.

Friday, 30 November: Performed my devotion within till 9 amongst the Tenants received of Mr Monday 4^l:9^s:5[915] for a quarter's Rent due at Midsomer last received of Mr Jones 3.15^s for a quarter Rent due at Michaelmas at prayers at St Peters within performed my devotion within till 4 at Mr Sandfords with my Wife till after 7 came home with my Wife after at prayers at St Laurance at prayers performed my devotion.

---

[915] Crammed into the edge of the page: very untidy and unclear.

Saturday, 1 December: Amongst the Tenants and received 4^{li} of Mr Richards for a quarter's Rent due at Michaelmas at prayers at Charterhouse at Custom House called at Mrs Wards to know if she would be within performed my devotion within till 7 at prayers at St Edmond within at prayers performed my devotion.

Sunday, 2 December: Performed my devotion etc heard Dr Mapletoff 7 Matthew 21:22 ℞ heard Mr Mooree 19 Matthew 17 went to St Pauls churchyard bought 2 bunns called at the Widows Coffee house[916] <and had a loose stoole> in ½ Moone Court within read at prayers performed my devotion.

Monday, 3 December: Performed my devotion amongst the Tenants received of Mrs James 7^s:6^d for a quarter Rent due at Michaelmas 1709 at prayers at Charterhouse at Custom House performed my devotion at Mr Moons received a quarter's Rent due at Michaelmas at prayers at Basinghall Church within at prayers performed my devotion.

Tuesday, 4 December: Performed my devotion at 8 went to Higgs's and he gave me hopes my Lord Clarendon would shortly appoint a generall meeting at prayers at St Laurance at Custom House at the Shipp with Mr Moore within performed my devotion within till 5 at St Donstons heard Mr Haley 119 Psalm 106 within at prayers performed my devotion etc.

Wednesday, 5 December: Performed my devotion at prayers at St Donstons at Custom House performed my devotion within till 4 at prayers at St Peters went to see for Mr Stanford but he was not within at home performed my devotion at prayers.

Thursday, 6 December: Performed my devotion within till after 9 at Custom House a little heard Mr Browne at St Mary Hill 9 John 4 within performed my devotion within till 5 at prayers at St Mary Wooll North within at prayers performed my devotion.

Friday, 7 December: Performed my devotion at 8 tooke water and went to my Lord Powers but he had Not a Tax bill for

---

[916] Lillywhite lists three potential establishments by this name: at Half Moon Alley, Cheapside, at Bedford Court – both *c.*1702–1714 – and, less probably, at Devereux Court, first referenced in 1734. *LCH*, 646 and 746. Lillywhite also lists several coffee houses with 'Widow' and a surname, such as 'Widow Nixon's' – too many, in fact, to list here, ibid. 65.

Michaelmas rent but told me Mr Halsey would give him one went to Higgs but No time set for a Meeting went to St James's to enquire for Mr Halsey and found him and my Lord had not payd Michaelmas Tax called to see Mr Lloyd at the Queens Celler[917] at prayers at St James's see the Queen goe in Parliament House and called and told my Lord what Mr Halsey said dined at a Cooks received Mr Searles Rent for Michaelmas called at Mrs Halls came home performed my devotion at prayers.

[fo. 105v]
Saturday, 8 December: Performed my devotion within till neare 9 amongst the Tenants Received of Mr Rogers 1^{li}.10 for a quarter Rent due at Lady day last at Mr Jones's and had a new plaister at prayers at Charterhouse at Custom House at the Shipp with Mr Moore Smith and Chamberlaine performed my devotion within till 4 at prayers at St Peters within at prayers performed my devotion.

Sunday, 9 December: Performed my devotion heard Dr Mapletoff 7 Matthew 24 etc performed my devotion heard Mr Moore 4 Malachi 5 was to see Mrs Ward a little within read at prayers performed my devotion.

Monday, 10 December: Performed my devotion at prayers at St Dionis at Custom House till after 12 performed my devotion before 3 went to Speake with the Plaisterer but Met Mr Dawson and was up and downe the yards till 4 at Wrights Coffeehouse till after 5 at prayers at Foster Lane within at prayers performed my devotion.

Tuesday, 11 December: Performed my devotion at prayers at Bow called on Poole to mend my Coate left a pair of old stockings for Mrs Coggill called on old Mr Reynolds and desired him to send his son the yeares Tax which he promised me to doe at Custom House performed my devotion etc within, Mr Hall being here at prayers performed my devotion.

Wednesday, 12 December: Performed my devotion within till after 10 at prayers at St Donstons at Custom House performed my

---

[917] This may have been the cellar at one of the royal residences in London at the time: Kensington Palace, Whitehall, or St James's; perhaps the rest of the entry indicates the latter.

devotion within till 5 at prayers at St Mary Woollnorth within at prayers performed my devotion.

Thursday, 13 December: Performed my devotion amongst the Tenants received of Elizabeth Rives 6^s for a quarter's Rent for Margaret King due 5th Instant at prayers at St Mary Hill at Custom House at the Dolphin with Samuel Moore to drink with Mr Good about a Coppy of a Minute from the Commissioners[918] about an Office at Willies Coffee House[919] with Mr Danes about it at the Vine[920] with Mr More[921] and Moore who gave us his foy[922] for Gravesend within performed my devotion after 4 went with my Wife to Mr Sandfords and I walkt and in Charterhouse yard at Mr Sandfords a little at prayers at Foster Lane within at prayers performed my devotion.

Friday, 14 December: Performed my devotion at prayers at St Dionis at Custom House till neare 11 within performed my devotion dined about 12 tooke up Oares at Queene Streete and went to Lord Powers but could get no money called at Mrs Halls at prayers at St Donstons within at prayers performed my devotion.

Saturday, 15 December: Performed my devotion at home till 11 at prayers at St Peters at Custom House performed my devotion within till 5 at prayers at St Mary Woollnorth at prayers performed my devotion.

Sunday, 16 December: Performed my devotion heard Dr Mapletoff at St Laurence 1 John 4:7.8 performed my devotion heard a stranger 13 Romans 4 at St Laurence within at prayers performed my devotion.

Monday, 17 December: At prayers at Bow amongst the Tenants Received a quarter rent of Mr Berrill and a quarter rent of Mr

---

[918] Originally 'Com~'. Lloyd and his colleagues were discussing a minute from the Commissioners of the Customs.

[919] Lillywhite lists no establishments as 'Willies', but has 'Willey's' or 'Willet's' as standing 'near the Custom House' – this seems the likely candidate. References date from *c.*1702–1714, *LCH*, 659. Lillywhite lists far too many establishments by the name 'Will's' to cover here.

[920] 'The Vine' was a popular name for taverns or inns, but this may have been the Vine coffee house, which stood on the western side of Bishopsgate Street Within from 1677 until perhaps the 1830s, *LCH*, 743–744. It can be seen on Rocque's 1746 map.

[921] Possibly 'Mord'.

[922] Possibly a parting gift or drink, *OED*.

Harrison at Custom House performed my devotion within till 5 at prayers at Foster Lane within at prayers performed my devotion etc tooke Hunter's Stuff.

[fo. 106r]
Monday, 17 December: Performed my devotion in bed rose after 1 being in a sweat performed my devotion and prayed etc.[923]

Tuesday, 18 December: Performed my devotion at prayers at Bow got my Spectacles Mended at Custom House performed my devotion within till 5 at prayers at St Mary Woollnorth within at prayers performed my devotion.

Wednesday, 19 December: Performed my devotion went to speake to Mr Sandford about the Com[?mittee][924] it had spoken about the building the Church[925] called to see Mr Dawson and told him all I could learne he told me my Lady was come to Towne I waited on her and paid her 10^{li} and called on Mr Rowlandson to let him know my Lady was com to Towne and he was Not within at Custom House at the Shipp with Mr Moore and Chamberlaine etc within performed my devotion within till 3 at prayers at home at prayers performed my devotion.

20 Performed my devotion went to Mr Dawson and told him all I could hear about building the Church

Thursday, 20 December: Performed my devotion.

[*blank*]

Friday, 21 December: Performed my devotion went to Mr Rowlandson and talkt with him at Lord Powers and he appointed me to call againe called on Higgs but Nothing was done at prayers at St James at Mrs Jacke's and had a bottle of Hunters water at Lord Powers and my Lady [was] paid Michaelmas quarter's Rent

---

[923] Here things become confused; Lloyd appears to have written two incompatible entries for Monday 17 December, but in the second the '17' is written over a deleted 18, in the next entry '18' replaces '19', and the ensuring '19' is written over 20, before an entry dated '20' is deleted. Which precise day is represented by which entry is not entirely clear.

[924] Lloyd uses an abbreviation here which is unclear as the ink has blotched; alternatively 'commission'.

[925] See Introduction pp. 29–30.

and I carried it to my Lady and paid it to her eate a legg of a fowl called my wife at Mr Rowlandsons stayd a little and went to Mrs Hall and paid for a loyne of porke and after at Mr Rowlandsons and stayd till neare 6 at prayers at Foster Lane and had my sword stolen from me at the corner of the Lane within at prayers performed my devotion etc.

Saturday, 22 December: Performed my devotion at Mr Hatfields and told him I thought it Not proper to goe to Stone with him at prayers at Bow after called at severally sword Cuttlers to leave word I had lost my Sword and desired if such an one was offerd to stopp the person and left word at one Done's at the Duke of Graftons Head in Old Bayley[926] about the sword at Custom House performed my devotion within till 5 at prayers at post house at prayers performed my devotion.

Sunday, 23 December: Performed my devotion heard the Bishop of Salisbury[927] at St Laurance 4 Philippians 4 performed my devotion heard Mr Moore 1 Peter 5.5 called at Mr Sandfords to heare Stones Name read at prayers performed my devotion.

[fo. 106v]
Monday, 24 December: Performed my devotion called on Mr Hatfield and he gave me a a Noate to get my Ladys hand to it at prayers at Bow and carried the Noate to my Lady but she was not up and Mrs Woodier was gone to Mrs Halls I leaft the Noate with her went to the Tenants and received a quarter Rent from Mr Watkinson at Custom House at the Vine with Mr Moore and Job within at prayers within till 4 at prayers at St Peters within read at prayers performed my devotion.

Tuesday, 25 December: Performed my devotion etc heard Dr Mapletofe 1 John 4.7.8 ₽ performed my devotion at prayers at St Peters within at prayers performed my devotion.

---

[926] The sign of the Duke of Grafton's Head in Old Bailey appears to have been used at this time as a base of operations for thief-takers. By 1715, the infamous 'Thief-taker General' Jonathan Wilde (1682/3–1725) was advertising his services from this location, *Post Man and Historical Account*, 28–30 June 1715, issue 11150, BL, *Burney Collection*.

[927] Gilbert Burnet (1643–1715), a Scottish philosopher and historian, bishop of Salisbury from 1689 until his death. For his long and significant career, in which he displayed whiggish and 'low church' leanings, cannot be summarized here, see *ODNB*.

Wednesday, 26 December: Performed my devotion within till after 10 went to Mr Mooree the Minister and talked with him about severall things at prayers at St Laurence called at Mr Hatfields to know what he had done and he had given him Warning that is Stone called at the Graftons Head in Old Bayley but could heare Nothing of my Sword within performed my devotion at prayers at St Peters at Mr Inghams chamber and eate playd at Cards at prayers performed my devotion.

Thursday, 27 December: Performed my devotion within till neare 11 at St Peters heard Mr Lassenby[928] 1 John 3:8 performed my devotion within till 3 called at the Brewers but they were busy I could not pay them called at Mrs Lodges to send the woman that doth Mrs Ingshams business to send her to her Mother on Saterday morning at Mr Sandfords till 4 at home a little at prayers at Bow at Mrs Cocks till 8 within at prayers performed my devotion etc.

Friday, 28 December: Performed my devotion within till 11 at prayers at Lothbury performed my devotion within till 4 at prayers at St Peters within at prayers performed my devotion.

Saturday, 29 December: Performed my devotion within till 9 at Darks but could get no Money called on Mrs Sandford to tell her of Mrs Ingsham if her daughter had not beene provided with a Mid Wife at prayers at Post house at Custom House found out Mr Job and went with him to Mr Banes and they agreed to settle the Matter about an office for us[929] performed my devotion after 2 went to Lady Mathews and adjusted the account till Midsomer last and paid her the Ballance 13^{li} at prayers at Foster Lane at prayers performed my devotion.

Sunday, 30 December: Performed my devotion heard the Reader at St Laurence 5 Hebrews 9 performed my devotion heard Mr Mooree 4 Galatians 10:11 within read at prayers performed my devotion etc.

Monday, 31 December: Performed my devotion at Custom House and gott Mr Banes and Mr Moore and the Wharfinger[930]

---

[928] Identity unclear. See n. 766, **8 March 1711**.
[929] 'Us' referring to the Coast Waiters of the Customs.
[930] A custodian of a wharf, today more commonly known as a harbourmaster.

together and came to agreement about an office for the Coastwaiters at prayers at St Edmond performed my devotion within till 4 at prayers at Basinghall Church within playd a little at Cards with Mr Ingsham at prayers performed my devotion.

[fo. 107r]

1712

Tuesday, 1 January: Performed my devotion at prayers at Bow P at St Laurence heard a Stranger 3 John 17 performed my devotion within till 5 at St Peters at prayers at St Donstons heard Mr Haley 23 Matthew 26 with called my Wife at Sir Stephen Evances[931] and she told me he was broak at prayers performed my devotion.

Wednesday, 2 January: Performed my devotion at Mr Hunter's and received a quarter's Rent for Christmas paid old Corker for pumping the pond and abated for a quarter's Rent at prayers at St Donstons at Custom House called to see Mr Tretaine within performed my devotion at prayers at Bow within at prayers performed my devotion took the Elixir.

Thursday, 3 January: Performed my devotion in bed. Rose after 12 performed my devotion dined performed my devotion went to Lady Mathews and left my Wife at Mrs Halls called her at 5 and stayd till 7 came home called at Mr Sandfords to know about Dark at prayers performed my devotion.

Friday, 4 January: Performed my devotion within till neare 11 at prayers at St Michael Cornhill at Custom House at the Shipp Taverne with Mr Moore and Smith within performed my devotion within till 7 at prayers at St Edmond met my wife within at prayers performed my devotion.

---

[931] Sir Stephen Evance (1654/5–1712) was a merchant, financier, goldsmith, and MP for Bridport, 1690–1698. Amongst various other entrepreneurial activities, Evance was twice a governor of the Hudson's Bay Company (1692–1696; 1700–1711), and in 1691 founded the Hollow Sword Blades Company, which went on to play a central role in the South Sea Bubble. Evance also lent very substantial sums to the crown, being one of its biggest financiers in the 1690s. By the end of 1711, however, his business prospects were less favourable, and an attempt to establish an enterprise insuring merchants led to his downfall and bankruptcy. He hanged himself on 5 March 1712, at the house of Sir Caesar Child, a fact reported by Lloyd on **6 March 1712**. Lloyd appears to have also known the Childs: see **6 January 1712**. See also *ODNB*; *Hist. Parl. 1690–1715*, Vol. 3, 993–995.

Saturday, 5 January: Performed my devotion within till after 10 at prayers at St Peters called to see Mr Wade who had beene ill called to enquire about my Sword but heard nothing within performed my devotion amongst the Tenants Received of Mrs Hill ½ a yeares Rent due at Michaelmas received of Mr Bayley a quarter Rent due at Michaelmas at prayers at Foster Lane within at prayers performed my devotion.

Sunday, 6 January: Performed my devotion etc heard Dr Mapletoft 1 John 4:7:8[932] performed my devotion heard Mr Castle [*blank*] and at Sir Stephen Evances with My Lady Child[933] and Mrs Ward condoleing Sir Stephen's misfortune af after 8 came home read at prayers performed my devotion.

Monday, 7 January: Performed my devotion within till 11 at prayers at ~~St Peters~~ <Walbrook> performed my devotion within till neare 7 at prayers at St Edmond at Mrs Champnys for my Wife supt there stayd till 1 at prayers performed my devotion.

Tuesday, 8 January: Performed my devotion amongst the Tenants but got no money at prayers at Charter House at Mrs Powels and had a flask of brandy at Custom House at Queen's Arms Coffee House within performed my devotion within till 4 called at Mr Whites about a sword at prayers at St Peters within at prayers performed my devotion.

Wednesday, 9 January: Performed my devotion at prayers at St Donstons at Custom House performed my devotion within till 5 at prayers at St Swithins at a Coffeehouse in Fenchurch Streete[934] at

---

[932] See Sunday, **16 December 1711**.

[933] Probably Dame Hester Child, née Evance (*c.*1682/3–1733), who married Sir Caesar Child, 2nd Baronet (*c.*1678–1725) in November 1698. Hester was probably the daughter of John Evance, brother or some other relation of Sir Stephen Evance mentioned above, who may have been a 'waiter in the Custom House', potentially explaining Lloyd's connection to them. However, this source is unreliable, erroneously giving the year of the aforementioned marriage as 1718: see George Marshall (ed.), *Le Neve's Pedigrees of the Knights* (London, 1873), 435. Sir Stephen and Hester Goodyer, mother of Hester Child, gave consent to the marriage: see Joseph Foster (ed.), *London Marriage Licences, 1521–1869* (London, 1887), 276. For the wills of Sir Caesar Child and Dame Hester Child, the latter of which notes that she inherited the remaining estate of Sir Stephen Evance, see TNA, PROB 11/602/127 and PROB 11/657/264, respectively. For the will of one John Evance, merchant of Southwark (d.1661), probably the father of Sir Stephen Evance and another John Evance, see TNA, PROB 11/304/133.

[934] Establishments at Fenchurch St. dating from Lloyd's time listed by Lillywhite include 'Brown's', 'Frampton's', and 'Kimpton's', *LCH*, 780.

Cousin Amyes to enquire how she did within at prayers performed my devotion.

[fo. 107v]
Thursday, 10 January: Performed my devotion after went to Coll: Lekeux and receive ½ a yeares Rent due at Christmass went to Mr Lamb and received a year[s] Rent at Custom House a little heard Mr Browne at St Mary Hill the 6 Luke 46 at Custom House a little within performed my devotion went to my Lady and paid her 18^{li}:16^s:6^d stayd till called for my Wife at Mr Rowlandson's but he was gon home at prayers at Bow within at prayers performed my devotion.

Friday, 11 January: Performed my devotion within till neare 10 at Custom House at prayers at St Donstons at Custom House performed my devotion within till 3 amongst the Tenants received at quarter's Rent of Mrs Blackden at Mr Sandfords and ordered Roger to get into Darks House at prayers at Basinghall Church within at prayers performed my devotion.

Saturday, 12 January: Performed my devotion went to Mr Sandfords and gott the possession of Darks house and goods and lockt it up with a padlock at prayers at C[?harter] H[?ouse] went to C[?ustom] H[?ouse][935] at the Vine with Mr Moore within performed my devotion within till neare 5 at prayers at St Denis within at prayers performed my devotion etc.

Sunday, 13 January: Performed my devotion heard Dr Mapletoft 1 Peter 1:17 performed my devotion heard a Stranger at Alhallows Lombard Streete 22 Job 21 at Mrs Wards till Neare 8 read at prayers performed my devotion etc.

Monday, 14 January: Performed my devotion at prayers at St Dionis at Custom House at Dr Bradfords and talked with him about several things within performed my devotion within till after 4 at prayers at Basinghall Church at Mr Sandfords within Mr Bellamy being here at prayers performed my devotion.

---

[935] Here we see the difficulty of interpreting Lloyd's abbreviations: 'Charter House' and 'Custom House' were both rendered 'C.H'. However, Lloyd only ever went to prayers at Charterhouse, and Moore was a fellow Customs official. Lloyd also occasionally used the same abbreviation for 'Coffee House'. See n. 715, **18 January 1711**.

Tuesday, 15 January: Performed my devotion at prayers at St Dionis at Custom House at St Laurance heard Dr Moss 10 Acts 34:35 within performed my devotion within till after 4 at prayers at St Laurance at 4 went to Mr Rowlandsons for my wife stayd till after 6 within at prayers performed my devotion.

Wednesday, 16 January: Performed my devotion etc heard Dr Mapletoft 37 Psalm [*blank*] performed my devotion etc within till 5 heard the reader of Basinghall Church 1 [*blank*] 4:15 within at prayers performed my devotion this was a publick fast.

Thursday, 17 January: Performed my devotion at prayers at St Dionis at Dr Gatfords at Custom House called to see Mr Wade and went to enquire about my Sword bought sugar at Mr Keyes within performed my devotion went to Stones but he not within at Phillips received a yeares Rent and paid a bill of 16^s at Mrs Olives and received a quarter for Michaelmas in Vine Yard called on the brewer at prayers at Basinghalll Church within at prayers performed my devotion.

Friday, 18 January: Performed my devotion within till after 10 at prayers at St Peters at Custom House within performed my devotion within till 6 at prayers at St Bartholomew Lane within at prayers performed my devotion.

Saturday, 19 January: Performed my devotion within till 11 at prayers at St Peters at Custom House performed my devotion walkt to Acks[936] Hospitall at prayers there came back to Bow to prayers within at prayers performed my devotion.

Sunday, 20 January: Performed my devotion heard a stranger at Bow 12 Romans 19 performed my devotion heard Mr Moore 6 Galatians 15 at Mrs Wards till after 7 within at prayers performed my devotion etc.

[fo. 108r]
Monday, 21 January: Performed my devotion amongst the Tenants Received of Mr Fielding in part for a quarter's Rent due

---

[936] 'Acks' is likely an unusual spelling of 'Axe'. Whilst there was no hospital in London with this name, Ax or Axe Yard, off Little Britain in Aldersgate, was immediately adjacent to (and now subsumed within) the premises of St Bartholomew's hospital, Harben, *Dictionary of London*.

at Midsomer last etc[937] 1^l.19^s received of Mrs Bristow 6^l for 2 quarter's Rent due at Christmas last at prayers at St Edmond at Custom House performed my devotion within till 6 at prayers at Bartholomew Lane at prayers performed my devotion.

Tuesday, 22 January: Performed my devotion within till neare 10 at Custom House till 11 at prayers at St Edmond at Custom House a little within performed my devotion at 3 went to my Lady paid her 12^{li} called at Mr Rowlandsons to see how shee did which was better called at Mrs Halls to heare how they did and the Doctor was gon at Kentons but got no Money at prayers at Bow within at prayers performed my devotion.

Wednesday, 23 January: Performed my devotion within till neare 10 at Custom House at prayers at St Peters at Custom House performed my devotion within till 3 amongst the Tenants Received of Mr Starky for a quarter Rent due at Michaelmas last and of Mr Howard for a quarter's Rent due at Christmass and of him 5^s for part of a quarter Rent due at Christmass and of Mr Higham for a quarter's Rent due at Christmass 5:15^s allowed Trophee Money 3^s.6 and for the plasterer for mending the House after the House of Office[938] was taken away 3^s at severall places to see for a Hilt for a Sword came in about 6 not well at prayers performed my devotion.

Thursday, 24 January: Performed my devotion amongst the Tenants to see the Houses pulled downe behind Rogers's House and stable and bespoke some old boards to make up the Walls thereof Received of Jone Harding 6^d for a quarter's Rent due at Christmass at Custom House at St Mary Hill heard a stranger at St Mary Hill 19 Matthew 16 at Custom House till 1 at Queen's Arms Coffee House within performed my devotion within till 4 amongst the Tenants Received 20^s of Mrs Boucher in part and 10^s of Mrs Cooley for a quarter's Rent due at Michaelmas allowd 1^s:3^d to her at Mr Sandfords a little at prayers at Bartholomew Lane within at prayers performed my devotion.

Friday, 25 January: Performed my devotion at 8 went to see the Houses pulled downe that Rogers joyned to and see the faults in the wall after went to Higgs's but nothing was done at prayers at his

---

[937] Very ambiguous and unclear due to ink blotching.
[938] A domestic building or outhouse; a pantry, storehouse, or, euphemistically, a toilet, *OED*. See **12 June 1712**.

Chappell performed my devotion there at my Ladys paid her 8^{li} and told her what must be done to secure Rogers's house dined at Mr Rawlinsons stayd till after 4 within till 6 ~~at prayers at Bartholomew lane~~ at prayers performed my devotion.

Saturday, 26 January: Performed my devotion within till 9 was at Mr Barfoots for Tent for my Wife[939] but could get None at Mrs Martins and she sent me to ~~Wat~~ one Glasbrooks in St Mary Axe and there I had a pinte brought it home at prayers at St Peters at Custom House within till 5 at prayers at St Mary Woolnorth at prayers performed my devotion.

Sunday, 27 January: Performed my devotion heard Mr East[940] at St Laurance 19 Matthew 17 performed my devotion heard a Stranger at St Laurance 55 Isaiah 7 within at prayers performed my devotion etc.

[fo. 108v]
Monday, 28 January: Performed my devotion amongst the Tenants and to see the Wall made up against Rogers House, at Mr Jones's and had a new plaster for my Rupture at prayers at Charter House at Custom House at the Shipp with Mr Moore received my Salery within performed my devotion within till 5 at prayers at Bow at Mr Wades and Eate stayd till 10 at prayers performed my devotion.

Tuesday, 29 January: Performed my devotion within till after 8 amongst the Tenants and see the mending the Houses at ~~p[?rayers]~~ the Brewers for drink at prayers at St Peters at Custom House performed my devotion within till 5 at St Dunstons heard Mr Haley [*blank*] called my Wife at Cousin Amyes within at prayers performed my devotion etc.

Wednesday, 30 January: Performed my devotion etc heard a stranger at Bow 27 Matthew 25 performed my devotion eate went with my Wife to Mr Rowlandsons but they were out of Towne went to my Lady Mathews stayd till Neare 8 within at prayers performed my devotion etc.

---

[939] Very unclear: cramped at edge of page.

[940] This name, though partly obscured by another word, can be read with some confidence. However, I have not been able to identify this preacher.

Thursday, 31 January: Performed my devotion within till after 8 went to Mr Motts and he gave me a bag of Raysons and 6 Nutmeggs brought them home at Custom House heard Mr Browne at St Mary Hill 3 John 19 called on old Mr Reynolds but he was not at home at prayers at 2 went to Mr Stone and amongst the Tenants at Wrigts [*sic*] Coffee house with Mr Sandford within a little at 5 at prayers at St Mary Woollnorth bought orring[941] Chipps and Venis Treakle[942] within at prayers performed my devotion and at Mr Inghams Chamber etc.

Friday, 1 February: Performed my devotion within till after 10 at Custom House at prayers at St Dunstons at Custom House at the Ship with Sam Moore at Custom House till after 1 being appointed to attend the Commissioners but they sent word we must stay till another day within performed my devotion was at Vine Yard till 5 at prayers at Bow called my Wife at Mrs Cocks stayd till 8 within at prayers performed my devotion.

Saturday, 2 February: Performed my devotion within till 10 at Vine Yard a little received a quarter's Rent of Mr Crisp and Allowd the quarter's Tax at prayers at Bow bought Cheese at Cripplegate within performed my devotion within till 5 at prayers at St Mary Woollnorth within at prayers performed my devotion.

Sunday, 3 February: Performed my devotion etc heard a Stranger at St Laurance 2 Philippians 12 ₽ performed my devotion heard Mr Shepherd 101 Psalm 7 called to see Mrs Ward but stayd not she being to goe to her sons at Mrs Allens stayd till after 7 within heard the Mayd reade at prayers performed my devotion.

Monday, 4 February: Performed my devotion at 9 at prayers at St Dionis at Custom House till after 12 performed my devotion within till 4 at Vine Yard to see how the Worke of the houses went on at Mr Powells and had a flask brandy at prayers at Bartholomew Lane at

---

[941] Probably 'orange'.

[942] Theriac, popularly known in early modern England as 'Venetian treacle', was an ancient and well-known panacea which had its origins in classical antiquity. Its name in English owes to its production in Venice during the medieval period; the word 'treacle' is a corruption of theriac. Doubts about its efficacy were raised in a treatise by William Heberden (1710–1801), and it declined in popularity thereafter. For an excellent summary of the history of theriac, see J. P. Griffin, 'Venetian treacle and the foundation of medicines regulation', *British Journal of Clinical Pharmacology*, 58 (2004), 317–325.

Mrs Cocks for my wife stayd till 8 within at prayers performed my devotion.

Tuesday, 5 February: Performed my devotion at prayers at Bow amongst the Tenants received 7^s.6^d from Mr Thomas for a quarter Rent due at Christmas and of Mr Harrington 5.7.6 for a quarter Rent due at Midsomer last at Custom House performed my devotion within till 3 at Vine Yard at St Dunstons heard Mr Haley 6 Matthew 21 at prayers performed my devotion.

[fo. 109r]
Wednesday, 6 February:[943] Performed my devotion amongst the Tenants Received of Mr Sawyer for 2 quarters Rent due at Christmas in Vine Yard to see the Wall goe up called at Sherwoods but got no money at prayers at St Pulchers[944] at the Cooks to order the 9 fowles Mr Ingsham bought to be ready before 1 within performed my devotion dined with Mr Ingsham and Wife son and daughter with the fowles he and I lost at Cards and had a bottle of Wine and dranke the Queens Health it being her birthday at Vine Yard but got no money at St Dunstons heard Mr [?H] at Basing home and went with my Wife to Mrs Hamonds and left her there at a Coffee House till after 5 at Basinghall Church heard a Stranger 3 Proverbs 17 went for my Wife to Mrs Hamonds stayd till after 8 within at prayers performed my devotion.

Thursday, 7 February: Performed my devotion called on Stone but he was not within Received of Dalloway for a quarter's Rent for Christmass 10^s allowed 1½ received of Mr Ladyman 9^s:6^d for Christ mass in Vine Yard at Mr Reynolds at Broaken Wharfe but got no money at Custom House a little at St Mary Hill heard Mr Ramsey 119 Psalm 80 at Custom House till 1 within performed my devotion within till 3 amongst the Tenants but got no money in Vine Yard and at the building the Wall at Mr Sandfords at Darks house and let have som of her Linen at prayers at Bow within playd at Cribage with Mr Ingsham lost 5 games wone 4 at prayers performed my devotion etc.

---

[943] Here, Lloyd erroneously records this entry as a Tuesday.

[944] St Sepulchre-without-Newgate, just north of Holborn Viaduct, is of medieval origin. It was originally dedicated to St Edmund, and was a possession of the Priory of St Bartholomew. Rebuilt in the 15th century, it was damaged, but not destroyed, in the Great Fire; the present building is mostly a restoration of the same structure, *TBE, London 1*, 258–260.

Friday, 8 February: Performed my devotion within till neare 12 my wife being Very ill at Custom House within performed my devotion within till after 3 at Yine Yard and at Mr Sandfords at prayers at Basinghall Church at prayers at Bow within at prayers performed my devotion.

Saturday, 9 February: Performed my devotion amongst the Tenants and in Vine Yard to see the wall and etc goe on Received of Mr Rogers <1.10> for a quarter's Rent due at Midsomer last Received of Mrs Allen for a quarter Rent due at Michaelmas last at prayers at Charter House at Custom House within performed my devotion within till 4 at prayers at St Peters within at prayers performed my devotion.

Sunday, 10 February: Performed my devotion heard a Stranger at St Laurance 1 Corinthians 2:6 performed my devotion heard Mr Mooree 3 Psalm last verse within read at prayers performed my devotion etc.

Monday, 11 February: Performed my devotion at Vine Yard to see how the wall went on at Custom House performed my devotion as I walked met Mr Stone at the Plow Coffe house he paid me ½ a yeares Rent went to the Magpye in Aldersgate Streete[945] and received of Mr Hartley 1:17.6 for a quarter's Rent for the Stable Coach house and Roome 1 quarter for Stable etc due at Ladyday 1711 and for the roome a quarter's for Michaelmas received of William Lee 10^s for a quarter's due at Lady day last called at home at prayers at Bartholomew Lane playd at Cards with Mr Ingsham at prayers performed my devotion etc.

[fo. 109v]
Tuesday, 12 February: Performed my devotion at Vine Yard till after 9 at Custom House a little called at home at prayers at St Laurence went to Lady Mathews dined there stayd till after 4 and Mr Reynolds came and my Lady would not abate anything came away after 5 at prayers at Bartholomew Lane within till after 7 called my wife at Mrs Cocks at prayers performed my devotion.

---

[945] A 'Magpye Alley' off Aldersgate St. is recorded in William Stow, *Remarks on London: Being an Exact Survey* (London, 1722), 50; Rocque's 1746 map shows it on the western side of the street where it meets St Martin's Le Grand, immediately south of St Botolph's churchyard.

Wednesday, 13 February: Performed my devotion within till after 10 at Custom House at Tower Wharfe with Mr Johnson who was takeing up Wine[946] at Custom House till after 12 performed my devotion within till 5 at Basinghall Church heard a sermon 119 Psalm 111 within at prayers performed my devotion.

Thursday, 14 February: Performed my devotion amongst the Tenants received a quarter's Rent of Mr Garret for Midsomer last at Custom House performed my devotion within till 3 with Roger Sandford about buying old bricks at prayers at Bow within playd at Cards wth with Mr Ingsham at prayers performed my devotion.

Friday, 15 February: Performed my devotion within till after 10 at Custom House at prayers at Pudding Lane Church[947] at Custom House performed my devotion within till Neare 5 Mrs Hunt being here at prayers at Bow within at prayers performed my devotion.

Saturday, 16 February: Performed my devotion at prayers at St Dionis at Custom House at Queen's Arms Coffee House performed my devotion within till 4 at Vine Yard at prayers at Basinghall Church within at prayers performed my devotion.

Sunday, 17 February: Performed my devotion heard Dr Mapletoffe 24 Joshua 15 performed my devotion heard Mr Moore 52 Isaiah 3 at Mrs Wards a little within at prayers performed my devotion.

Monday, 18 February: Performed my devotion caled on Stone and Roger Sandford and left Muslin for two turnovers[948] with Mrs Holyoak went to Mr Nash and desired him to goe to my Lady and after to Mr Hatfielde to goe to her received a quarter Rent of Mrs Holyoak at Christmas at prayers at St Dionis at Custom House at Queen's Arms Coffee House performed my devotion went with my Wife to Mrs Halls and afterward to

---

[946] In other words, taking account of wine being unloaded from a ship at the wharf for the purposes of taxation.

[947] Strictly speaking, no church stood or stands in Pudding Lane. There are several churches nearby, including the famous St Magnus-the-Martyr, but the most likely candidate is the now demolished St George, Botolph Lane, which, as Rocque's 1746 map shows, stood in George Lane connecting Pudding Lane and Botolph Lane, its rear overlooking the former. Destroyed in the Great Fire, it was rebuilt by Wren, in c.1671–1674. It was demolished in 1904. Young and Young, *Old London Churches*, 85.

[948] Lloyd's meaning here is not entirely clear; the term 'turnover' may denote a type of shawl or collar, *OED*.

my Ladys called my wife and came home at prayers performed my devotion.

Tuesday, 19 February: Performed my devotion at prayers at St Dionis at Custom House performed my devotion within till 5 at St Donston heard Mr Haley 119 Psalm 9 within at prayers performed my devotion.

Wednesday, 20 February: Performed my devotion called on Mr Stone and he told me he could not be at my Ladys till the next day left word at Mr Hatfields at prayers at St Donstons at Custom House at Shipp Taverne with Mr Moore within performed my devotion within till 4 at Shaws Coffeehouse[949] at Basinghall Church heard a stranger 6 Matthew 33 within at prayers performed my devotion received of Mrs Harris a quarter's Rent for Midsomer 5.7.6 Allowd 7.6.

Thursday, 21 February: Performed my devotion amongst the Tenants Received of Mr Sherwood a quarter Rent for Michaelmas at prayers at St Mary Hill at Custom House performed my devotion at Lady Mathews and Mett Mr Stone stayd till neare 6 at prayers at St Donstons within playd at Cards with Mr Ingham at prayers performed my devotion etc.

[fo. 110r]
Friday, 22 February: Performed my devotion amongst the Tenants Received of Mrs Gamball a quarter's Rent due at Michaelmas last part at prayers at Charter House at Custom House performed my devotion within till 5 at prayers at Bow within performed my devotion at prayers.

Sunday, 24 February:[950] Performed my devotion heard a Stranger at St Laurence 1 John 14 performed my devotion heard Mr Mooree 21 Job 7 heard Mr Stonestreete[951] at St Edmond 26 Psalm 6 called

---

[949] The only 'Shaw's' found by Lillywhite stood at Tower Royal, Watling St., in the 1660s, and was presumably destroyed by the Great Fire in 1666; *LCH*, 527.

[950] Lloyd wrote '24' over '23'; unusually, there is no entry for Saturday 23, and no explanation for its omission.

[951] This was probably William Stonestreet (d.1716), rector of St Stephen Walbrook from 1689–1716, president of Sion College in 1710, prebend of Chichester in 1712–1716. See *Cantabrigienses*, Vol. 1, pt. 4, 169; *CCEd* Person ID: 20436.

my Wife at Mrs Cocks within reade at prayers performed my devotion.

Monday, 25 February: Performed my devotion amongst the Tenants within after 10 went with my Wife to Islington called at Cousin Birds went to Cousin Browns drank Bohee Tea went with him and Mr Wicket to a garden to buy trees dined and stayd till after 4 went to Mr Wickets stayd till after 3 came home performed my devotion at prayers at St Laurence at prayers performed my devotion etc.

Tuesday, 26 February: Performed my devotion within till neare 10 at Custom House performed my devotion called on Old Reynolds but got no money went to see Mr Williams and found him at his Inn amongs the Tenants Received of Mr Buttler ½ a yeares Rent for Michaelmas last and a quarter's Rent from Mr Linnet due at Christmass and 5^s of Mrs Bunker. At St Dunstons and heard Mr Haley [*blank*] Luke [*blank*] within at prayers performed my devotion.

Wednesday, 27 February: Performed my devotion amongst the Tenants but received no Money at prayers at St Donstons at Custom House at the Ship with Mr Moore performed my devotion Mr Daws[on] calle[d] and after I called him at Sion College liberary[952] and he Went and see the Wall Makeing in Moons stable and those in Vine Yard I went to Mr Browns and left a letter for Mr Williams to Cary to Cousin Nicholas at Basinghall Strete and heard a stranger within at prayers performed my devotion etc.

Thursday, 28 February: Performed my devotion amongst the Tenants but received no Money at St Mary Hill heard a Stranger 22 Luke 19 within performed my devotion amongst the Tenants received a quarter's Rent from Mr Richards for Christmas and a quarter's Rent of Mr Hatton for Ladyday last at Bow and heard a sermon 20 Exodus 15 within at prayers performed my devotion.

Friday, 29 February: Performed my devotion paid Mr Beachcraft for Mr Tempest 42^{li} ~~for~~ 10^s for a quarter Interest due 15 December 1710 at Higgs's a little at prayers at St Margaret's Westminster at

---

[952] Established in 1631 under the will of Thomas White, former rector of St Dunstan-in-the-West, as a clerical guildhall and library, Sion College was on the same site as St Alphage London Wall. The present building, constructed in the 1880s, is some distance away in Tufton St., Victoria Embankment, *TBE, London 1*, 337–338.

prayers at Higgs's Chappell at the Crown in Charles Streete[953] and dined at my Lady Mathews till 4 but she had not made an end of the booke at prayers at Basinghall Strete at prayers performed my devotion.

[fo. 110v]
Saturday, 1 March: Performed my devotion amongst the Tenants at prayers at Charter House at Custom House at the Shipp with Mr Moore performed my devotion amongst the Tenants but gott no Money at prayers at St Mary Woollnoth within at prayers performed my devotion.

Sunday, 2 March: Performed my devotion heard a stranger at St Laurence 1 James 22 ℞ performed my devotion heard a stranger at St Edmond 24 Luke 16 at Mrs Wards till after 6 read at prayers performed my devotion etc.

Monday, 3 March: Performed my devotion amongst the Tenants but received no money at Bridge House[954] at Custom House and spoke to Mr Johnson to send his sister to my wife about a place at prayers at St Edmond performed my devotion at Bridg house till after 6 at prayers performed my devotion.

Tuesday, 4 March: Performed my devotion at Bridge House till after 10 at prayers at St Peters performed my devotion at Bridge House till 5 herd Mr Haley at St Donstons 58 Isaiah 6 within at prayers performed my devotion.

Wednesday, 5 March: Performed my devotion and at etc heard a stranger at Bartholomew Lane 4 Matthew 4 performed my devotion at my Lady Mathews left my Wife at Mrs Cleaves till 7 called her at prayers at St Laurence at prayers performed my devotion.

---

[953] Perhaps the Crown Coffee House listed by Lillywhite as operating in 1767 in the no-longer extant Charles St. in Covent Garden, *LCH*, 691.

[954] Originally 'B. House'. Bridge House was the headquarters of Bridge House Estates, the charitable trust established by royal charter in 1282 to maintain London Bridge. It was on the south side of the Thames, near St Olave's Church (now Southwark Cathedral). Lloyd regularly attended Bridge House in the transaction of his Customs duties, though he never gives the specific purposes of his visits. Thereafter, Lloyd subsequently writes 'Bridg house' in the same entry. He always renders Bridge House 'B.H', which I have silently expanded.

Thursday, 6 March: Performed my devotion at the Cooks and spoke for a piece of Beefe at Bridge House at Custom House and askt Mr Metcalfe about seizing 2 pipes of Wine in Baker[955] for the London duty but he told me it could not be done but stopt heard a stranger 4 James 8 at St Mary Hill went to see Mrs Ward after the Newse Sir Steven[956] had hanged himselfe. Performed my devotion at Bridge House till neare 6 at prayers at Bartolomew Lane within at prayers performed my devotion etc.

Friday, 7 March: Performed my devotion relieved at Bridge House stayd till 9 carried suffrances[957] for Fellows and a Pryn[O958] man to cleare at King's Arms Coffee House at prayers at St Peters at Mr Sandfords and ordered the goods of Darts to be agred againe performed my devotion after 2 went to Bridge House stayd till neare 6 at Mr Warners bought Venis Trea[cle] at prayers at Bartholomew Lane within at prayers performed my devotion.

Saturday, 8 March: Performed my devotion within till 9 at Mr Sandfords and at Darts and left a woman to looke after them at prayers at St Bartholomew called to see Liquorishs Chimney and ordered it to be Mended received of Mr Harrison for a quarter Rent due at Michaelmas last Allowed for the Tax 1 and 2 1711 within performed my devotion within till 5 at prayers at St Mary Woolnorth got a porter and brought a bed of Darks[959] within at prayers performed my devotion.

Sunday, 9 March: Performed my devotion heard part of a sermon of the Bishop of Salsbury at St Magnes but was forct to come out of the Church before twas done it was so late performed my devotion heard Mr Castle at St Alhalows Lombard Streete 95 Psalm 7:8 at Mrs Wards within read at prayers performed my devotion.

---

[955] The pipe, also known as a butt or cask, was a unit of measurement for wine equal to half a tun or or 252 old wine-gallons (1008 pints). Meaning of 'in Baker' unclear. Perhaps Bakers Hall, headquarters of the Bakers' Company, then located on Harp Lane off Thames Street, near the Custom House. Why Lloyd wished to seize two pipes of wine, and for which 'London duty', is also unclear in the absence of further information.

[956] See n. 931, **1 January 1712**.

[957] A suffrance was a licence to ship or discharge cargoes at a port; Hayes seems to apply the term with particular reference to the shipping of corn, *Rules for the Port of London*, 42–43.

[958] The meaning of this abbreviation is unclear. It does not bear any obvious resemblance to the titles of any of the offices of the Customs. Lloyd's handwriting is untidy, but legible.

[959] Here we see that 'Dart' and 'Dark' almost certainly refer to the same individual.

Monday, 10 March: Performed my devotion at 10 went to Lady Mathews to settle her accounts dined there stayd till 7 within at prayers performed my devotion etc.

Tuesday, 11 March: Performed my devotion within till after 8 mett Mr Sandford and Clack and they paid 5^{li} for Darks goods and a Noate of his for $3^{li}.1^{s}$ within till 11 at prayers at St Edmond called at Mrs Wards within at prayers called on Mr Sandfords and told him what Clack and I had don at Bridge House a little at a Coffee House heard Mr Haley at St Donstans 3 Acts 19 within at prayers performed my devotion etc.

[fo. 111r]
Wednesday, 12 March: Within till 9 went to Clack and Darks House and delivered the Key and Inventory to Clack at home till 11 at prayers at the little Church[960] at the wall received a quarter's Rent of Mr Jones performed my devotion within till after 4 and went with my wife to Mr Sandfords received at Basinghall Church heard the Curat 3 Matthew called my wife at Mr Sandfords within at prayers performed my devotion tooke Elixir.

Thursday, 13 March: Performed my devotion in bed rose after 12 performed my devotion dined performed my devotion within all day at prayers performed my devotion etc.

Friday, 14 March: Performed my devotion within till 11 carried my little pistoll to the gunsmiths at the end of Old Jury and had the lock taken off and Oyled at prayers at the Old Jury called at Roger Sanfords and left word for him to come to me in the evening performed my devotion within till 4 at prayers at St Peters within at prayers performed my devotion etc.

Saturday, 15 March: Performed my devotion after 9 went to Lady Mathews and Roger Sandford within called at Mr Overtons and told him I would pay him the ½ yeare for the use Money he had lent my

---

[960] This reference is slightly mysterious; Lloyd referred to St Alphege London Wall regularly and so this seems an unlikely candidate. The church of All Hallows-on-the-Wall is the most likely; the present (rather large) building dates from 1765–1767 and is the work of George Dance the Younger, but the previous building dated to the 12th century, *TBE, London 1*, 186–188.

Lady. Roger went home and My Lady was not ready at prayers at Covent Garden[961] performed my devotion in the Church. At my Ladys dined there and was Makeing up the accounts till after 4 but could not Finish it my Lady had so confounded them came home after 5 within till Neare 6 at a Coffee House in Shipp Yard[962] at prayers at St Bartholomew within at prayers performed my devotion.

Sunday, 16 March: Performed my devotion heard a Stranger at St Laurence 1 Samuel 3:18 performed my devotion heard a Stranger at St Laurence 6 Romans 21 at Mr Finches and he had beene dead 6 weeke stayd till after 7 within read at prayers performed my devotion.

Monday, 17 March: Performed my devotion within amongst the Tenants left word for Roger Stanford to come to me called at Mrs Powells for a flask of brandy to be sent called at the Brewers at prayers at St Peters at Custom House at the Ship with Mr Moore and Mr ~~Reev~~ Reeve and agreed for him to goe to Gravesend and I to doe his business above stayres, performed my devotion within at prayers at Bartholomew Lane at prayers performed my devotion.

Tuesday, 18 March: Performed my devotion within till after 9 paid Mr Overton $4^{li}:10^s$ for ½ a yeares use for 150^{li} for my Lady Mathews went to her and Made up the accounts dined there stayd till after 2 performed my devotion as I walkt within till after 4 walked with my wife to St Pauls at Starr Coffee house with her till 6 at prayers at Foster Lane within at prayers performed my devotion etc.

Wednesday, 19 March: Performed my devotion amongst the Tenants Received of Mrs Rives 6^s for a quarter's Rent for Margaret King due at 6 present and of Mrs Boucher 5^s More bought severall things at Warners etc at prayers at Lothbury performed my devotion at Bridge House and gave Mr Chamberlaine and Bayley

---

[961] St Paul's, Covent Garden. Sometimes known as the 'actors' church' due to its associations with the theatre, it was designed by Inigo Jones in 1631.

[962] There was more than one 'Ship Yard' – that is, yards with this name, not actual shipyards – in 18th-century London, but Rocque's map shows one just off Glass House Yard, across Goswell Rd from Lloyd's frequent haunt of Vine Yard. However, Lillywhite has a 'Ship Tavern' at Ship Yard, Temple Bar, first mentioned in 1571, and later referenced throughout the 18th century until 1799. Alternatively, it may have been the 'Ship Tavern' off Bartholomew Lane (n. 794, **5 April 1678**), at 'Ship Court', also known as 'Black Swan Yard, formerly Ship Yard', found referenced between 1656 and 1724, *LCH*, 736–737.

10^s each for theire trouble at prayers at St Dionis at Valentines and talkt about John Benet met my wife at St Edmond within at prayers performed my devotion tooke Hunters Elixir etc.

[fo. 111v]
Thursday, 20 March: Performed my devotion in bed haveing taken Hunter's stuff rose after 12 performed my devotion within all day performed my devotion as usualy at prayers etc.

Friday, 21 March: Performed my devotion went to Vine Yard seized Creeks Horses and Hartley came and pretended to bring a repleven[963] and by persuasion I consented to take 40^s a Moneth after for which he gave me a noate and Mr Biggs engaged he should pay it and he promised to pay the quarter's Rent after Ladyday and Mrs Creeke promised her Husband should give me his noate for the rest bought Lozenges at Bawlers at prayers at Mr Warne St Laurance heard a stranger Exodus 34:7 verse performed my devotion within till 5 at prayers at Basinghall Church went for my watch at Fordhams Bought Gascoin powder at Warner's at prayers performed my devotion.

Saturday, 22 March: Performed my devotion in bed haveing taken Hunter's Stuff rose at 12 performed my devotion within all day performed my devotion as usualy at prayers etc.

Sunday, 23 March: Performed my devotion heard a Stranger at St Laurance 2 Corinthians 1:12 performed my devotion heard a stranger Mr Moore 35 Psalm 13 went with my Wife to Mrs Halls eate a Tart at the Cooks in St Pauls Church Yard stayd at Mrs Halls till 7 within read at prayers performed my devotion etc had many words about being at Mrs Hall to my great trouble and sorrowe.

Monday, 24 March: Performed my devotion amongs the Tenants Received of Mr Hancock ½ a yeares Rent due at Michaelmas and of Mr Berrill a quarter's Rent at Midsomer 1710 and of Mrs Halsey a quarter's Rent due at Michaelmas 1710 went to Mrs Hall and talkt with her about Mr Walker the brasier and about our goeing to board

---

[963] Replevin is a legal remedy which allows a party to recover property which has been seized, subject to the reasons for its seizure being tried in a court of law.

with her bought sugar at Custom House and at Sandalls Coffee House[964] within performed my devotion within till after 5 gott a bottle Mount[?ain] Mallaga[965] at Mr Viberts and sugar at Fenchurch Streete at prayers at St Dionis bought syropps and red rose water at Warners within at prayers performed my devotion.

Tuesday, 25 March: Performed my devotion amongst the Tenants at prayers at St Bartholomew the Lesser received 20^s of Mrs Dennis in part for a quarter's due at Michaelmas 1710 performed my devotion within till after 4 went to Leadenhall to buy beefe but could get none at St Donstons heard Mr Haley 22 Matthew 39 within at prayers performed my devotion.

Wednesday, 26 March: Performed my devotion amongst the Tenants at Custom House at prayers at St Edmond performed my devotion within till 3 at Bridge House and at Rams Head with Chamberlayne at prayers at Bartholomew Lane at prayers performed my devotion.

Thursday, 27 March: Performed my devotion in bed rose at 10 being very ill all Night <at prayers at Bartholomew the Lesser> performed my devotion within till 4 walkt at prayers at St Mary Woollnorth within at prayers performed my devotion etc.

Friday, 28 March: Rose after 10 haveing taken Elixir performed my devotion in bed performed my devotion dined performed my devotion within all day performed my devotion at prayers etc tooke Elixir.

Saturday, 29 March: Performed my devotion in bed rose at 12 performed my devotion dined performed my devotion within all day performed my devotion etc performed my devotion at prayers etc.

Sunday, 30 March: Performed my devotion heard Dr Mapletof 24 Joshua 15 performed my devotion heard Mr Moore 14 Psalm 4 within read at prayers performed my devotion.

---

[964] In Thames St. 'over against the Custom House', mentioned in an advertisement from 1711 proposing a 'Joynt Adventure' in the £1,500,000 Lottery, *LCH*, 516–517.

[965] See n. 337, **28 July 1676**. In this case, Lloyd is probably referring to a wine from the Sierras de Málaga region, today a protected DOP in Spain. An advertisement in the *Daily Courant* of 18 March 1712 prices it at 6^s per gallon and 16^d per quart; issue 3253, BL, *Burney Collection*.

Monday, 31 March: Performed my devotion at prayers at Bow amongst the Tenants but got no money at Custom House performed my devotion within till after 3 at prayers at St Peters bought things at Warners and Pauls churchyard came home within at prayers performed my devotion.

[fo. 112r]
Tuesday, 1 April: Performed my devotion within till after 8 at prayers at Bow came in to see how things went at Custom House performed my devotion within till 4 bought 2 bushels Coales very deare at St Dunstons heard Mr Haley 12 Ecclesiastes 13 within at prayers performed my devotion.

Wednesday, 2 April: Performed my devotion within till after 9 at Custom House at prayers at St Dunstons at Custom House till 1 performed my devotion within till 6 at prayers at Bartholomew Lane at Warners and bought things at prayers performed my devotion.

Thursday, 3 April: Performed my devotion performed my devotion [*sic*] within till after 9 went amongst the Tenants but could get no money at Custom House and entered some Transires[966] I left the day before at prayers at St Mary Hill at Custom House till after 12 called at Mr Reynolds but he could pay me no money within performed my devotion within till after 9 at Bow heard a Stranger 23 Luke 43 within at Mrs Sykes but she was not at home my wife went to Mr Powells and I walkt in the Cloysters at Christ Church called my Wife and stayd at Mr Powels till after 7 within at prayers performed my devotion.

Friday, 4 April: Performed my devotion within till neare 8 at Mr Wades and left my blank Ticket N°.[967] 223 in the 1500000 Lottery[968] for him to get Exchanged with his at prayers at Bow at Custom House till neare 1 within performed my devotion within

---

[966] A 'transire', from the Latin for 'go across', was a type of permit issued to merchants moving goods coastwise which were not subject to duty on export, or were subject to export duties under 20 (later 40) shillings, and therefore did not require a 'cocket' or Coast Bonds to be issued. It was, therefore, a 'free pass' for certain types of coastwise cargo. Hoon, *Organization*, 265–266; Carson, *Ancient and Rightful Customs*, 322.

[967] Ambiguous: rendered slightly unclear by binding.

[968] See n. 693, **8 January 1711**. The lotteries of 1711 and 1712 functioned slightly differently to previous adventures, with much more generous terms. The ratio of prizes to 'blanks' (which Lloyd, sadly, seems to have ended up with) was nearly ten times higher than in 1710, the rate of interest on prizes and blacks was 6 per cent, and repayment of the

till 3 at prayers at St Pulchers amongst the Tenants Received a quarter's Rent of Fielding and one of Garnet and Hunter within at prayers performed my devotion.

Saturday, 5 April: Performed my devotion at prayers at Bow at Custom House at Queen's Arms Coffee House performed my devotion within till 4 at prayers at St Peters within at prayers performed my devotion etc.

Sunday, 6 April: Performed my devotion etc heard Dr Mappletoff 24 Joshua 15 ₽ performed my devotion heard Mr ~~Moore~~ Mooree 34 Psalm 8.9 at the Cake house in St Pauls Churchyard eat a tart with my Wife at prayers at St Edmond caled my Wife at Mr Wards within read at prayers performed my devotion etc.

Monday, 7 April: Performed my devotion within till after 8 amongst the Tenants received 20^s of Mr Harrington and a quarter's Rent of Mr Watkinson paid Mrs Standford 2.^{s}5 at prayers at Charter House at Custom House performed my devotion within till after 2 went with my Wife to walke but twas too Cold went to see Mrs Champnys but she was not within went to Mrs Allens stayd till after 6 at prayers at St Edmond within at prayers performed my devotion tooke Elixir.

Tuesday, 8 April: Performed my devotion in bed rose after performed my devotion at Custom House till 1 performed my devotion within till 4 at Custom House at St Donstons heard Mr Haley 4 Philippians 11 within at prayers performed my devotion.

Wednesday, 9 April: Performed my devotion within till 8 at prayers at Bow went to Mr Reynolds and received ¾ rent for his son and alowd a yeares Tax for 1711 at Custom House performed my devotion within till 6 at prayers at Bartholomew Lane met Brother Richard and he my wife and I went to the Ship Taverne in that Lane and drank a quart Wine within at prayers performed my devotion.

[fo. 112v]
Thursday, 10 April: Performed my devotion amongst the Tenants Received in part of Mr Moone 8^{li} for Christmas quarter

---

principal was *guaranteed* within 32 years. See Bob Harris, 'Lottery adventuring in Britain', 289.

and of Mrs Orbell for a quarter due at Lady day left my Mony at Custom House at prayers at St Mary Hill at Custom House performed my devotion within till 3 heard Mr Ibbott at Bow 13 Mark 37 walkt to Mrs Cocks but she was not within at home at prayers performed my devotion.

Friday, 11 April: Performed my devotion at prayers at Bow called on Mr Smith at Grigbys Coffee House[969] and told him I would send Squires Elixir to him at Custom House performed my devotion after 2 went with my Wife to Mrs Halls I went to prayers at St Donstons and afterward at the Temple at prayers called my wife stayd at Mrs Halls and talkt about our coming thether. At prayers performed my devotion.

Saturday, 12 April: Performed my devotion within till after 8 called Mr Bawler and went with him to Grigbys Coffee House to sell his Elixer at Custom House at prayers at St Peters at Custom House till 1 performed my devotion within till 6 at prayers at Bartholomew Lane at prayers performed my devotion etc.

Sunday, 13 April: Performed my devotion heard a stranger at St Laurence 10 Jeremiah 25 performed my devotion heard Mr Moree 27 Matthew 46 within read at prayers performed my devotion etc.

Monday, 14 April: Performed my devotion amongst the Tenants Received a quarter's Rent of Mr Higham for Ladyday 1712 a quarter's Rent of Susan Andrews for Ladyday a quarter's Rent of Rogers for Michaelmas ul^t.[970] at prayers at Charter House at Custom House performed my devotion within till 5 at prayers at Bow we walked round St Pauls eat a tart at that Cooks called on Mrs Freeman within at prayers performed my devotion etc.

Tuesday, 15 April: Performed my devotion at prayers at Bow amongst the Tenants Received of Hartly a quarter Rent for Creeks C.H[971] and stable due at Lady day of Bayley for a quarter's Rent

---

[969] Lillywhite finds many references to Grigsby's Coffee House 'near the Royal Exchange on the Threadneedle Street side' (though it appears to have moved location and perhaps changed its name a number of times), *c.*1702–1833, though the precise establishment visited by Lloyd may have closed or moved by 1732, *LCH*, 247–250.

[970] i.e. *ultimo*, last Michaelmas. Cf. last Ladyday: **25 April**, **12 May**, **15 July 1712**.

[971] This seems likely to stand for 'coach house' rather than 'coffee house', owing to Lloyd's mention of seizing Creek's horses at Vine Yard on **21 March 1711**. The plan drawn up of Vine Yard for the consideration of the Commission for Building Fifty New Churches notes the presence of 'Stables, Coach Houses and Tenements in the said

due at Christmass and 1^l of Mr Howard toward Lady days rent at Custom House performed my devotion within till neare 5 heard Mr ~~Haley~~ Haly at St Donstan's 1 Peter 2.24 went to Mr Hunts supt there at prayers performed my devotion.

Wednesday, 16 April: Performed my devotion at prayers at Bow at Custom House performed my devotion went to the Rose at Holborn Bridge for a Chine[972] at prayers at St Pulcher's amongst the Tenants Received of Mrs Cooley a quarter's Rent due at Christmas last and a quarter of Widow Harding for a quarter due at Lady day last and of Mr Greene in part 1^{li} for a quarter's due at [*blank*] of Mrs Allen 1^{li} for a quarter's due at Christmas last of Mr Heywood for a quarter due at Lady day last and 5^s for part of Ann Darby for a quarter due at Lady day and of Mrs Harris for a quarter's Rent due at Michaelmas within at prayers performed my devotion.

Thursday, 17 April: Performed my devotion at prayers at Bow at East Indie House Received ½ a yeares Interest due at Ladyday 6^{li} at Custom House performed my devotion went with my wife to Mrs Halfords for [*illegible*] paid a quarter Interest for Mr Tempest at prayers at St Laurence at prayers performed my devotion.

[fo. 113r]
Friday, 18 April: Performed my devotion etc heard a Stranger at St Laurence 55 Isaiah 5 ℟ performed my devotion heard Dr Bradford at Bow 13 Hebrews 18 within read at prayers performed my devotion.

Saturday, 19 April: Performed my devotion at prayers at Bow at Custom House till after 2 performed my devotion at prayers at Bow within at prayers performed my devotion.

Sunday, 20 April: Performed my devotion etc heard Dr Mapletoff 2 Corinthians 5.15 ℟ performed my devotion heard Mr Morer 2 Corinthians 5:15 within read at prayers performed my devotion.

---

yard': Valuation of land and houses adjoining Cripplegate belonging to Lady Mathews, widow of Sir Philip Mathews, Bt, 20 December 1712, LPL, MS 2714, fo. 239.

[972] Lloyd's meaning is uncertain here. This may be an unusual spelling of 'China' earthenware, or perhaps in the sense of a joint of meat, particularly of pork, 'chine' being an archaic term for back or spine, *OED*.

Monday, 21 April: Performed my devotion within till 11 at prayers at St Peters at Custom House but did not stay at Queen's Arms Coffee House went to Frys but nobody at home performed my devotion after 2 went with my Wife to Hoxton to sister Dells[973] but she not within at Mr Proughtons to see Mrs Laurance in the garden till after 5 within and eate cold rost beefe and Mrs Prowton was with us till after 7 came back to St Laurence to prayers at prayers performed my devotion.

Tuesday, 22 April: Performed my devotion within till 10 heard Dr Moss at St Laurence 1 Corinthians 15:55:56:57 Within performed my devotion within till after 2 went with my Wife to Mrs Champny left her there at Custom House and lookt after my Transires and the suffranes[974] and found them to agree at St Donstans heard Mr Haley [*blank*] within at prayers performed my devotion.

Wednesday, 23 April: Performed my devotion went with my wife to Islington to Cousin Oddy at prayers there dined at Cousin Oddys stayd till neare 8 within at prayers performed my devotion.

Thursday, 24 April: Performed my devotion at prayers at Bow at Custom House at the Shipp with Mr Moore within performed my devotion after 2 called at Mr Wades to see Silk for my Wife and stuff for me walked about St Pauls and eate a tart at prayers at Foster Lane within at prayers performed my devotion.

Friday, 25 April: Performed my devotion amongst the Tenants received a quarter's Rent of Mrs Olive for a quarter's Rent due at Christmas paid Mr Pope 7^l.6^s for the Taxes and Mr Wiatt 4.16:4 for the water Due at Ladyday ul^t.[975] called on Mr Byfield to take Measure to make me a perrywigg called at Mrs Halls after to see Mr Rowlandson at prayers at St Brids within performed my devotion within till 3 at Custom House to see my Cubbord made etc till 6 walkt at prayers at St Edmond within at prayers performed my devotion.

---

[973] Mary Dell, the sister of Lloyd's wife Elizabeth, married to a Samuel Dell, both of whom are mentioned in Elizabeth's will: see also n. 798, **14 April 1711**.

[974] Very faint: could also be 'suffrancs'. Probably 'suffrances' was intended: see n. 957, **7 March 1712**.

[975] Unclear: cramped at edge of page.

Saturday, 26 April: Performed my devotion at Custom House and see my cubbard finished at prayers at Barkin[976] at Custom House at King's Arms Coffee House performed my devotion within till 4 at prayers at St Peters at prayers performed my devotion.

Sunday, 27 April: Performed my devotion heard Dr Mappletoff 24 Joshua 15 performed my devotion heard Mr Moore 6 Romans 9 called to see Mrs Ward and she was at Mr Valintines stayd till after 6 walked with Mrs Ward being ill on Tower Hill and coming back met Mr Orton and wife and they carried us to their Lodgings and we stayd till 8 and Mrs Ward very ill went to Mr Valintanes and she was worse and Mr Valintine seeing her fell into fitts we stayd and supt there at 10 came home haveing left Mrs Ward at her lodgings at prayers performed my devotion.

[fo. 113v]
Monday, 28 April: Performed my devotion at Custom House till 10 called to see Mr Valintine and Mrs Ward and they were both better at prayers at Edmond at the Coffee House in Peters Ally performed my devotion within till 3 received of Mrs Blackden for a quarter's Rent due at Christmas of Hawgood for Raby for a quarter due at of [sic] Hatton of Mr Moone 2^{li} to make up his Christmass rent for a quarter's at Midsomer last of Crisp for a quarter for Ladylady last within a little at prayers at St Laurance at prayers performed my devotion.

Tuesday, 29 April: Performed my devotion within till 9 at Custom House entered what Transires[977] was left of Saterday at Ship with Aubery paid Mr Reeve and Johnson their Money for the Moneth above Stayres performed my devotion within till 5 heard Mr Haley at St Dunstons 1 Corinthians 15.53 within at prayers performed my devotion.

Wednesday, 30 April: Performed my devotion within till 9 went with Mr Holker who came to see us to Mr Wades to buy things and he carried us to 3 Ton Taverne[978] and gave us a quart of

---

[976] All Hallows-by-the-Tower: see n. 850, **6 July 1711**.
[977] See n. 966, **3 April 1712**.
[978] This may have been the Three Tuns, still in operation and now at 36 Jewry St., near the corner of Aldgate High St. It can be seen on Rocque's 1746 map at the corner of the High St. and what was then Jewry Lane, a mere ten minutes' walk from the Custom House. Other establishment with this name existed in London at a time, in Holborn,

Wine, and it was too late to goe to prayers within performed my devotion at Vine Yard to see Roger Sandford mend Hunter's stable etc above bridg till 5 but no boate[979] at prayers at Bow. At Starr Coffee House at prayers againe at Foster Lane missing it in the Morning within at prayers performed my devotion.

Thursday, 1 May: Performed my devotion within till 10 at St Mary Hill heard a Stranger within performed my devotion within till after 7 Mrs Holker and Mr Fruterells daughter being here went into Aldersgate Streete to enquire about Mr Webb the surgeon but Mr Richardson was very ill abed and I could know nothing at prayers at St Laurance at prayers performed my devotion.

Friday, 2 May: Performed my devotion after 5 above bridg till neare 8 but no watermen within till 9 went with Mr Holker to Mr Byfields and he bespoke a wigg crosed the water with him and went to Mr Wood the Surgeon and to a Taverne where he and Mr Holker agreed for 40^{li} to take his son for 4 yeares as a Turnover[980] and to Make him Free at Mr Hatches on the bridge left him there at Custom House met Mr Holker on the Change and went with him to Stiles to by Stockings and to the White Beare to buy gloves and he gave me a p[?air]e within performed my devotion within till 4 at prayers at St Peters above bridg and met the watermen and gave them leave to lanch a new boate at prayers at Bow within at prayers performed my devotion.

Sunday, 4 May:[981] Performed my devotion etc heard Dr Mapletoff 24 Joshua 15 ₽ performed my devotion heard Mr Morer at St Laurence 10 Acts 25:26:27 we went to see Mr Holker and Wife at Mr Frutrills stayd till 7 read at prayers performed my devotion.

Saturday, 3 May: Performed my devotion amongst the Tenants Received a quarter's Rent of Dallaway for Lady day and of Mrs Allen for a quarter at Ladyday and ½ a yeare for Ladyday of Mrs Hill talkt with Monday about goeing into the Country with Mr

---

and in Smithfield: see *Daily Courant*, 897 (1 March 1705) and 1667 (17 June 1707), BL, *Burney Collection*. Lloyd also mentions 'the 3 Tons in Wood Streete', **23 May 1712**.

[979] Customs business. Lloyd was stationed above London Bridge, either watching ships arriving along the Wharfs by the Custom House, or supervising the transport of goods onward by watermen. See n. 713, **18 January 1711**.

[980] 'An apprentice whose indentures are transferred to another master on the retirement or failure of his original one', *OED*.

[981] Lloyd writes the entries for Saturday 3 and Sunday 4 in reverse order.

Valintine and told him I believed I should agree with him at prayers at St Edmond performed my devotion within till neare 4 at Mr Bawlers till after 5 to have my Wife let blood but he could not be found at prayers at Bartholomew Lane at prayers performed my devotion.

[fo. 114r]
Monday, 5 May:[982] Performed my devotion amongst the Tenants Received a quarter's Ren[t] of Starky <for Christmas> ½ a yeares Rent of Jone Lucas, a quarter for Ladyday and a quarter's Rent of Mrs Holyoake for Ladyday a quarter Rent for Ladyman caled at home at Custom House till after 11 with Mr Owen and talked with him and told him he should as often as I could supply my place at prayers at St Edmond performed my devotion within till 5 at Mr Wades till 8 with my wife and I bought a piece of sagathy[983] at prayers at St Laurence at prayers performed my devotion etc.

Tuesday, 6 May: Performed my devotion above bridg and went to Higgs and he was gone from his House to Lodg at Mr Pims but could not find him called at Mr Byfields but he was not within called at Mrs Halls to see her at prayers at St Andrews at Mr Sandfords performed my devotion within till 5 heard Mr Haley at St Donstons 133 Psalm 1 within after above bridg till neare 10 at prayers <performed my devotion.>

Wednesday, 7 May: Performed my devotion within till 11 at prayers at St Peters at Custom House performed my devotion within till 7 at prayers at St Edmond at prayers performed my devotion.

Thursday, 8 May: Performed my devotion within till 10 above bridg at Custom House at prayers at St Edmond above bridge performed my devotion within till 3 at Mr Lloyds the Brewers within at prayers at Bartholomew Lane within at prayers performed my devotion.

Friday, 9 May: Performed my devotion after 6 went to Mr Slater the Translater[984] at Chayring Cross[985] and changed my shoes. At

---

[982] Lloyd mislabels this entry as Tuesday instead of Monday.
[983] A light woollen stuff, similar to serge, sometimes containing silk, *OED*.
[984] An archaic occupation; one who mends, alters, or refashions old clothing or shoes, *OED*. In this case, Lloyd was having his shoes altered, or perhaps replaced altogether.
[985] Here abbreviated with a cross symbol.

Higgs's but he was not within called at Mrs Halls and gave her 20^s per my Ladys Order called at Mrs Powells to send Mrs Hall 5 gallons brandy for my Lady called at home at prayers at St Donstons at King's Arms Coffee House at Custom House performed my devotion within till 7 at prayers at St Edmond at prayers performed my devotion.

Saturday, 10 May: Performed my devotion within till 9 at Custom House received my sallery for Ladyday at prayers at Charter House at Custom House at the Ship with Mr Moore above bridg a little within performed my devotion above bridg till after 4 at the Coffee House in Peters Ally at prayers at St Dionis within at prayers performed my devotion etc.

Sunday, 11 May: Performed my devotion heard a Stranger at St Laurence 1 Corinthians 15.26 performed my devotion heard a Stranger at St Laurence 19 Matthew 16.17 went with my wife to see Mrs Hall stayd till neare 8 at prayers performed my devotion.

Monday, 12 May: Performed my devotion amongst the Tenants Received of Mrs James a quarter's Rent for Christmas 1709 of Mrs Thomas for a quarter's for Ladyday ul^t. at prayers at St Peters at Custom House performed my devotion within till after 3 above bridg and went to the Temple in my boat bought Callamanko[986] for breeches behind St Clement's at Mr Hartlys and received 2^{li} on Richard Creeks account within and cousin Newington and daughters and Mrs Ward was here I stayd with them till after 8 at prayers performed my devotion.

[fo. 114v]
Tuesday, 13 May: Performed my devotion within till 11 at prayers at St Peters went to Mr Merryweatthers about my hat but found him not bought shamy skins of Mr Hatch at Custom House performed my devotion within till 5 heard Mr Haly at St Donstons 1 John 5:4 within at prayers performed my devotion.

Wednesday, 14 May: Performed my devotion within till 11 at prayers at St ~~Peters~~ <Michael Cornhill> at Custom House performed my devotion within till 4 above bridg till neare 7 at prayers at St Edmond within at prayers performed my devotion.

---

[986] 'A woollen stuff of Flanders, glossy on the surface, and woven with a satin twill and chequered in the warp, so that the checks are seen on one side only', *OED*.

Thursday, 15 May: Performed short devotion above bridg went cross to Southwark to Merryweathers about my hat but he was not at home went into my boate to Westminster to Higgs and he told me the business was concluded with my Lord Clarindon and soone be finished called at Byfields about my perriwig bespoke buttons at Mr Smiths and called on Poole to come to me next Morning within a little heard a stranger at St Peters 10 Proverbs 27 performed my devotion within till 7 at prayers at St Edmond at prayers performed my devotion.

Friday, 16 May: Performed my devotion within till 11 at prayers at St Alphage performed my devotion went with my wife to Mr Rowlandsons stayd till 5 above bridg till 7 at prayers at St Edmond within at prayers performed my devotion.

Saturday, 17 May: Performed my devotion within till 11 at prayers at St Peters at Custom House performed my devotion within till 4 at prayers at St Peters at Queen's Arms Coffee House to see for a letter within at prayers performed my devotion.

Sunday, 18 May: Performed my devotion heard a sermon at St Magness 19 Acts 6 dined at Mr Berklyes in the Burrow.[987] Heard Dr Lynford at St Clement's 119 Psalm 60 within read at prayers performed my devotion.

Monday, 19 May: Performed my devotion went to Coll. Lekeux to enquire about buying silke in Spittlefields above bridg went to Higgs but no newse of a generall Meeting at prayers at St Peters at Custom House at Shipp Taverne with Mr Moore within performed my devotion after 4 walked a little caled at Mrs Sykes and left my wife there and bought a pidigeon py at Mr Adames the Cook called my Wife and at prayers at Foster Lane at prayers performed my devotion.

Tuesday, 20 May: Performed my devotion after 6 amongst the Tenants received in part 20 of Mrs Bouchers at Mr Nashes and gave him a guinea at Byfields about my ~~perr~~ perrywigg at Mrs Halls at prayers at Coleman Streete performed my devotion within till 5 heard Mr Haley at St Donstons 6 Micah 8 within supt at the

---

[987] Probably an antiquated spelling of 'borough', *OED*, but Lloyd's precise meaning is not clear.

button Makers and carryed the buttons to Pooles within at prayers performed my devotion.

Wednesday, 21 May: Performed my devotion within till 10 above bridg went to finde Dr Agar[988] but he was not within at prayers at Aldermanbury bought Meat at the Cook performed my devotion within all afternoone being very ill at prayers performed my devotion.

[fo. 115r]
[*Half of line blotted out*] **Thursday, 22 May:** Performed my devotion within till 11 at prayers at Walbrook at Custom House a little at Mr Wades received 8^{li} to make up the Interest besids stuff I had of him performed my devotion within till 3 walkt with my wife a little left her at Mr Herrabys while I went to Spittlefields to see at Mr Stevens for silks called her and I went home and Mrs Hall was here within all the afternoone at prayers performed my devotion.

Friday, 23 May: Performed my devotion within till 11 at prayers at Walbrook at Custom House performed my devotion within till 5 at prayers at Bow at Starr Coffee House within after gott a pint of Mountain Malligoe at the 3 Tons in Wood Streete at prayers performed my devotion.

Saturday, 24 May: Performed my devotion within till 11 at prayers at St Mary Woollnorth performed my devotion within till 3 went to Mrs Halls to meete my Wife at Ludgate Hill I went to Custom House at Ludgate went to them to severall shopps they bought a gown and new coate at Mr Thatchers went with them to Horne Tavern[989] at prayers at St Laurence at prayers performed my devotion.

Sunday, 25 May: Performed my devotion heard Dr Mapletoft 4 Matthew 17 performed my devotion heard Mr Moore 9 Matthew 2.2[990] went to see Mrs Ward heard Dr Lynford at St Edmond 8

---

[988] The title of doctor should make this individual identifiable, but I can find no trace of any person whose name and dates correspond to the diary.

[989] Perhaps the Horn on the north side of Fleet St., a 'well-known tavern' according to Latham and Matthews, mentioned in *Pepys*, Vol. 4, 102: see also Vol. 10, 423. It can be found in advertisements in the *Daily Courant*, 6 May 1712, BL, *Burney Collection*. It can still be seen on Rocque's 1746 map.

[990] This is an error; there is no such verse.

John 22 called my Wife at Mrs Wards stayd till 9 at prayers performed my devotion.

Monday, 26 May: Performed my devotion within all Morning haveing taken a pill for the Rhume performed my devotion within till 6 at prayers at Bartholomew Lane at prayers at St Edmond within at prayers performed my devotion.

Tuesday, 27 May: Performed my devotion amongst the Tenants Received for a quarter's Rent from Mr Harrington due at Michaelmas went to Mr Thatchers and he promised to change the silk and he promised to doe it at Mr Rowlandsons and gave him a guinea from my Lady and talkt about our Landlady who told me he would take care she should performe her bargaine at prayers at St Peters at Custom House at the Ship with Mr Moore within performed my devotion within till 4 at Hartlys at the Magpye and paid him for the pot I owd him at St Donstsons heard Mr Haley 10 Ezekiel 27.28[991] at prayers performed my devotion etc.

Wednesday, 28 May: Performed my devotion within till after 10 at prayers at St Donstons at Custom House called at the Tun Ale House to enquire for Mr Clarke bought pomatum[992] within performed my devotion after 3 went with my wife to Mr Rowlandsons left her went to Mr Byfields about the wiggs at prayers at Christ Church at Mr Wades and gave him a receipt on his Bond for the Use Money the last yeare ending 7th Aprill paid him 3^s to make up the Money for the piece of Sagathy and see the booke Crossed. Within and Roger Sandford helpt me take downe the bed teaster[993] and I paid him 7^s.6^d all is due to him at prayers performed my devotion.

Thursday, 29 May: Performed my devotion within till 11 at prayers at Coleman Streete went to Mrs Jones's for a plaster for my Rupture performed my devotion within till after 5 walked with my wife on the Change at prayers at Bartholomew Lane at Mrs Allens at prayers performed my devotion.

Friday, 30 May: Performed my devotion within till 9 went to Spittlefields to find Mr Clarke and bid him get Kenton at Custom

---

[991] Again, Lloyd must have been mistaken, as these verses do not exist.
[992] Pomade.
[993] 'A canopy over a bed, supported on the posts of the bedstead or suspended from the ceiling', *OED*.

House at Byfields to order him to get the Wiggs called at Mrs Halls at prayers at St Donstons performed my devotion within till 6 at prayers at Bartholomew amongst the Tenants Received ½ a yeares Rent of Mr Rice at prayers performed my devotion.

[fo. 115v]
Saturday, 31 May: Performed my devotion within till 9 amongst the Tenants but got no money at Custom House at the Ship Taverne with Aubery at prayers at St Edmond performed my devotion within till neare 5 at prayers at St Dionis at the Cooks and bespoke [*deleted*] beefe within at prayers performed my devotion.

Sunday, 1 June: Performed my devotion etc heard Dr Mapletof 4 Matthew 17 ₽ performed my devotion heard Mr Mooree 16 Mark 16 within read at prayers performed my devotion.

Monday, 2 June: Performed my devotion within till 9 bought sparragrass[994] in Stocks Market at Custom House at prayers at St Peters at the Hoy with Mr Moore etc at the Shipp with him within performed my devotion within till 4 called on severall of the Tenants but got no money at Mrs Halls at prayers at St [*sic*] Foster Lane met my wife and we went to the 3 Ton Taverne in Wood Streete and drank a pint of wine within at prayers performed my devotion.

Tuesday, 3 June: Performed my devotion within till 9 at Mrs Dennis and received 15^s and 2 Tax bills 1^l:4^s went to Kentons and ordered him to come to me on Thursday Morning at Mr Rowandsons [*sic*] and talkt with him about my business and my Ladys at Byfields and Mr Holkers perrywigg was not done at prayers at Walbrook at Custom House performed my devotion within till 5 heard Mr Haley 30 Proverbs 7:8 within at prayers performed my devotion.

Wednesday, 4 June: Performed my devotion went to Higgs but could not find him called at Mr Byfields to see Mr Holkers perrywigg called at Mr Halls and Mr Rowlandsons within a little at prayers at St Alphage paid the Cook for piece beefe bought horsradish at Mr Gees and gave him a receipt for the Dropsy performed my devotion within till 3 at Custom House and had my cubbord mended and went with Mr Byfield to the Bell at Billingsgate and we left his

---

[994] Asparagus.

wigg and after I hard Mr Holker was come to Towne and he carried it ~~thethe~~ to his sons within a little and we went to prayers at Bartholomew Lane walkt to St Pauls called at Mrs Bellamies and stayd till after 8 at prayers performed my devotion.

Thursday, 5 June: Performed my devotion within till after 10 heard Mr Browne at St Mary Hill 3 Colossians 1 at Custom House at Queen's Arms Coffee House performed my devotion within till neare 7 at prayers at St Edmond within at prayers performed my devotion.

Friday, 6 June: Performed my devotion within till 9 amongst the Tenants but got no money changed my socks at ~~Holbor~~ Fleete bridg bought sal. Volat.[995] and Elixer proprietatis[996] at Moults at Custom House at prayers at St Mary Hill went with Mr Ramsey to see Mr Harper at his House in Coleman Church[997] performed my devotion within till 8 at prayers at St Laurence at prayers performed my devotion.

Saturday, 7 June: Performed my devotion amongst the Tenants Received a quarter's Rent of Mr Walker for Christmas a quarter of Mr Watkinson for Ladyday a quarter's of Rogers for Christmas within a little at prayers at St Mary Hill but very drowsy and not well at Coffee House in Peters Ally at prayers againe at St Peters within prayers performed my devotion.

[fo. 116r]
Sunday, 8 June: Performed my devotion etc heard Dr Mapletof 8 Romans 13:14 ₽ performed my devotion heard stranger at St Laurence [*blank*] at Mr Valintines till 7 at Mrs Cooks[998] till 10 supt there at prayers performed my devotion.

---

[995] Probably *sal volatile*, another term for smelling salts, usually based on ammonium carbonate.

[996] *Elixir Proprietatis* was a supposed panacea which dubious classical origins, which was regularly advertised in England in the 17th and 18th centuries. According to one pamphlet, penned by 'J. H. a Lover of Truth', it was composed of 'Myrrh, Alloes, and Saffron'. The author outlined its efficacy in treating maladies such as 'dropsie and scurvey', 'headach', 'consumption and coughs', 'green-sickness', and even the plague. *The excellent virtues and uses of the great antidote of Van Helmon, Paracelsus, and Crollius; by them called the Elixir Proprietatis* (London, 1674).

[997] Perhaps Lloyd meant to write 'Coleman Street'?

[998] Ink blotchy.

Monday, 9 June: Performed my devotion within till after 9 went to Islington with my wife drank at Prince Eugens Head[999] at prayers at the Church[1000] and heard the Charity Child[1001] make severall speeches to the Governors and Catichized dined at Cousin Brownes stayd till 6 at Cousin ~~Brownes~~ Birds till 7 at Cousin Oddys till after 8 at prayers performed my devotion.

Tuesday, 10 June: Performed my devotion within till 8 gott a tubb to wash in called on Poole to come to me within a little went to the Water House[1002] to turn in the Water at Guild Hall Coffee House[1003] to hasten the turning the Cock at St Laurence heard Mr Bell <16 John 19> ~~16 John 17:18~~ performed my devotion within till 5 heard Mr Haley 16 John 17:18 within at prayers performed my devotion.

Wednesday, 11 June: Performed my devotion within till after 8 went to enquire for Lodgings came in a little went to Madam Halls to know when Mr Thornly would leave the Lodgings and she sayd by Midsomer at prayers at St Brids within performed my devotion within till after 7 at prayers at St Laurence at prayers performed my devotion.

Thursday, 12 June: Performed my devotion after 8 amongst the Tenants and gave Mr Fielding a Receipt for Christmass and allowd

---

[999] I can find no record of an establishment with this name in Islington. Several others existed in London proper, including one in Leadenhall St. (*Daily Courant*, 22 February, 1712), Charing Cross (*Post Boy*, 3–5 May 1712, BL, *Burney Collection*), and a coffee house or tavern listed by Lillywhite, which stood in St Alban's St., *LCH*, 681.

[1000] If Lloyd and Elizabeth were still in Islington, this was likely the church of St Mary.

[1001] A child, probably an orphan, supported by the parish as an act of charity. A public exhibition of the child's religious education and piety would have functioned to demonstrate that the parishioners' philanthropy was worthwhile.

[1002] This was probably the London Bridge Waterworks, on the western side of the bridge on the north bank. Established in 1581, it was one of the major companies supplying water to both the City and, after 1761, Southwark. On Rocque's 1746 map, it is labelled 'Water H[ouse]'. See Leslie Tomory, 'Water technology in eighteenth-century London', *Urban History*, 42 (2015), 381–404. Alternatively, a building called Water House stood at New River Head, a reservoir just south of Sadler's Wells, which collected water from the New River, an artificial waterway constructed to supply London with water from Hertfordshire in the early 17th century. It was the headquarters of the New River Company, another of the private enterprises set up to profit from the capital's demand for water, Tomory, *The History of the London Water Industry, 1580–1820* (Baltimore, MD, 2017), 55.

[1003] Abbreviated 'C.H'. Established in 1685, the Guildhall Coffee House stood in King St., Cheapside, only a few minutes' walk from the London Guildhall after which it was named. It operated until at least the 1870s, *LCH*, 252–254.

him 40^s for repayres and 1^s 4^d for for [*sic*] the House of Office,[1004] received of Mr Harrison for a quarter Rent for Christmass within at prayers at Walbrook at Custom House within till 6 at prayers at Bartholomew Lane at prayers performed my devotion etc.

Friday, 13 June: Performed my devotion within till 7 went to Islington to Cousin Oddys and gott some of Mrs Ingrams searcloth[1005] within a little at prayers at ~~Walbrook~~ Charterhouse at prayers at St Donstons at Custom House at Queen's Arms Coffee House performed my devotion within till after 5 carried my Ring to out of which I lost the middle stone 3 dayes and found it in my basket amongs my nayles and ordered it to be new sett at prayers at Foster Lane at prayers performed my devotion.

Saturday, 14 June: Performed my devotion amongst the Tenants Received of Mrs Linett for a quarter's Rent due at Ladyday etc allowed Watch 1:6 over rate 4^s at prayers at St Peters at Custom House at Queen's Arms Coffee House performed my devotion within till 6 at prayers at Bartholomew Lane at prayers performed my devotion.

Sunday, 15 June: Performed my devotion heard Dr Snape at St Mary Hill 3 John 16 performed my devotion heard Mr Lamb at Berkin 12 Ecclesiastes 1 at Mr Hunts supt there at Mrs Wards till Neare 10 at prayers performed my devotion.

Monday, 16 June: Performed my devotion within till 7 at Mr Powells and had a flask of brandy within till 10 at Custom House at prayers at St Peters performed my devotion within all afternoone at prayers performed my devotion.

Tuesday, 17 June: Performed my devotion amongst the Tenants Received a quarter's Rent of Mr Jones for Ladyday and a quarter's Rent from Mr Richards at Mrs Halls to know when we should come thether at prayers at St Peters performed my devotion within till 5 at St Donstons heard Mr Haley 1 Timothy 3.16 within at prayers performed my devotion.

[1004] See **23 January 1712** and n. 938.
[1005] Probably cerecloth, a textile impregnated with wax or a similar substance, used for bandaging wounds and wrapping the dead, *OED*.

[fo. 116v]
Wednesday, 18 June: Performed my devotion within 10 bought Shoulder Mutton at Custom House at prayers at St Clement's Lane went to Mr Rice to order him to come to me in the Evening performed my devotion within till 5 at prayers at Bow within at prayers performed my devotion.

Thursday, 19 June: Within till 8 went to Brother Walker and talked with him about my Ladys business at Custom House at St Mary Hill heard Dr Browne at St Mary Hill 1 Corinthians 11:19 at the Shipp with Mr Moore performed my devotion within till 5 at prayers at Bow within at prayers performed my devotion.

Friday, 20 June: Performed my devotion within till 8 amongst the Tenants Received of Mr Greene in part for Midsummer 1711 1:18.6 <at prayers at Bow> went to Mrs Halls but could know nothing w[?he]n Thornly would goe out at Custom House [deleted] [deleted] performed my devotion within all the afternoone Mr Sandford and Wife and Mrs Westbrooke being here performed my devotion etc.

Saturday, 21 June: Performed my devotion amongst the Tenants received a quarter's Rent of Mrs Ollive for Lady day Allowed the Tax 2:12:2[1006] at prayers at St Bartholomew performed my devotion within till near[e] 3 at prayers at St Pulkers at Mr Planks and had my Diamond ring he new sett within at prayers performed my devotion etc.

Sunday, 22 June: Performed my devotion heard a stranger at St Laurence 130 Psalm 4 performed my devotion heard Mr Moore 16 Mark 16 at Mrs Halls within at prayers performed my devotion.

Monday, 23 June: Performed my devotion amongst the Tenants received of Mrs Corker Jan^r.[1007] 11^s.6^d for a quarter's Rent due at Michaelmas 1710 at Custom House called to see Mrs Ward at prayers at St Edmond performed my devotion within all the afternoone putting up things at prayers performed my devotion.

Tuesday, 24 June: Performed my devotion was putting up the rest of the things gott a Carte and after 11 Carried the things in the Cart and went to Mrs Halls and see them delivered went back and stayd

---

[1006] Final digit extremely faint and uncertain.
[1007] Meaning unclear: January or Junior?

till the Porter carried all the things paid Patridge and after 6 went to Mrs Halls very weary at prayers performed my devotion.

Wednesday, 25 June: Performed my devotion within setings a little to rights till 11 at prayers at St Swithins at Custom House received 1^{li}:10^s for the quarter's Dividend and 1^{li}:14^s.6^d of Mr Owen for the Middle Keys at Custom House with him within till 9 at prayers at St Donstons at prayers performed my devotion.

Thursday, 26 June: Within all day haveing taken purging Snuff doeing things in order performed my devotion as usualy at prayers etc.

Friday, 27 June: Performed my devotion within till after 10 at prayers at St Dunstons at Custom House met Mr Vise and talked about his acting for me at King's Arms Coffee House performed my devotion within till 5 at prayers at Lincolns Inn within all Evening at prayers performed my devotion.

Saturday, 28 June: Performed my devotion within till 8 amongst the Tenants received of Mr Monday in part for a quarter Rent due at Midsomer 1711 received a quarter's Rent of Mr Gamball for Christmas at Custom House performed my devotion within till 4 at prayers at the Temple within at prayers performed my devotion.

Sunday, 29 June: Performed my devotion heard Mr Sherlock[1008] at the Temple 1 Corinthians 10:19 performed my devotion heard Mr Buttler at St Clement's 7 Math 35:36[1009] at Mrs Wards till 8 within at prayers performed my devotion.

Monday, 30 June: Performed my devotion within till 9 at Custom House at prayers at St Edmond performed my devotion within till 6 at prayers at Ludgat[e] at prayers performed my devotion etc.

[fo. 117r]
Tuesday, 1 July: At prayers at St Dionis at Custom House got a Coppy of a Minute for Samuel Brooks and selfe etc amongst the

---

[1008] Thomas Sherlock (1677–1761), who succeeded his father William Sherlock (1639/40–1707) as master of Temple Church in 1705. In 1711, he became chaplain to Queen Anne, and in 1713, prebend of St Paul's. He subsequently became bishop of Bangor (1728), Salisbury (1734), and finally London (1748): *ODNB*; *CCEd* Person ID: 20305.

[1009] Lloyd's hand is quite clear, but there are no such verses in Matthew, or similar.

Tenants but got no money performed my devotion within till 6 at prayers at Ludgate performed my devotion at prayers.

Wednesday, 2 July: Performed my devotion within all morning at prayers at Lincolns Inn performed my devotion within till 5 at prayers at Lincolns Inn at Kentons to get the Irons ~~Pulled~~ putted out of the topps of my bed at prayers performed my devotion.

Thursday, 3 July: Performed my devotion within till 11 at prayers at Woollnorth at Custom House performed my devotion within till 3 at prayers at St Donstan met Mr Vize at Nixsons and I showed him my Case and the Minute and a Coppy of the Bond he was to give to me at prayers at ~~Lincolns Inn~~ <St Donstons> within at prayers performed my devotion.

Friday, 4 July: Performed my devotion within till 11 at prayers at Lincolns Inn within performed my devotion within <all afternoone setting up the bed> ~~till 5 at prayers at St~~ all afternoone being ill at prayers performed my devotion tooke Elixir.

Sunday, 6 July:[1010] Performed my devotion in bed rose at 10 performed my devotion dined performed my devotion within all Morning performed my devotion after 4 went to St Laurence heard Mr Newton 13 Hebrews 16 came home at prayers performed my devotion.

Monday, 7 July: Performed my devotion amongst the Tenants Received of Mr Hunter for a quarter's Rent due at Midsomer and a quarter's Rent of old Corker <due at Midsomer> at prayers at Charter House received a quarter's Rent of Mr Moone at Custom House at Mr Hunts to see about his haveing a perrywig performed my devotion within till 5 at prayers at Lincolns Inn within at prayers performed my devotion.

Tuesday, 8 July: Performed my devotion went to Mr Byfields to order him to come to me on Thursday Morning to goe to Mr Hunts went to Higgs and he told me he was in a faire way to bring his business to beare at prayers at St Peters a[t] Custom House at Queen's Arms Coffee House within performed my devotion at prayers at St Donstons within.

[1010] There is no entry for Saturday 5 July.

Wednesday, 9 July: Performed my devotion within till 11 at prayers at Lincolns Inn called at Mr Rowlandsons but he was not within performed my devotion within till 5 at prayers at ~~Lincolns Inn wi~~ St Dunstons at home performed my devotion at prayers etc.

Thursday, 10 July: Performed my devotion within till 8 went with Mr Byfield to Mr Hunts but he was not within at prayers at Berkin at Custom House at Queen's Arms Coffee House at Mr Sandfords and settled his account within performed my devotion at prayers at St Donstons at Starr Coffee House to meete Mr Vize but he had done nothing within at prayers performed my devotion.

Friday, 11 July: Performed my devotion went to the Strand and changed a pair of Shoos at prayers at St Peters at Custom House at the Dolphin with Mr Moore performed my devotion within till 3 at prayers at St Donstons at Mr Rowlandsons within at prayers performed my devotion.

Saturday, 12 July: Performed my devotion within till neare 10 at prayers at Charter House amongst the Tenants at Custom House at Queen's Arms Coffee House performed my devotion within till 5 at prayers at Lincolns Inn within at prayers performed my devotion.

Sunday, 13 July: Performed my devotion heard a stranger at Ludgate 6 Matthew 19.20.21 performed my devotion heard Mr Buttler at St Clement's at Mrs Wards came home after 7 performed my devotion at prayers etc.

Monday 14 July: Performed my devotion within till 10 went to see Mr Moore and left my penknife at Mr Rabys[1011] at prayers at St Edmond performed my devotion within till 5 at prayers at Lin[?coln's Inn] at Mrs Cloves with my Wife at prayers performed my devotion.

[fo. 117v]

Tuesday, 15 July:[1012] Performed my devotion called on Mr Collier in St Johns Lane about [?a] truss amongst the Tenants received a quarter's Rent of Mr Fielding Ladyday ul^t. and ten shillings of Lee[1013] for a

---

[1011] Very cramped at the edge of the page.
[1012] The binding is so tight at fos 117v–118r that the margins are completely unreadable in places.
[1013] Unclear.

quarter Rent due at Midsomer 1711 at Wrights Coffee House at prayers at Ludgate performed my devotion a[t] prayers at the Temple within at prayers performed my devotion.

Wednesday, 16 July: Performed my devotion called at Mrs Wards at prayers at St Donstons in the East at Custom House within till 4 went to Picadilly for large Whipcord at prayers at Covent g[ar]den within at prayers performed my devotion.

Thursday, 17 July: Performed my devotion went to Charring Cross changed a pair of shoes amongst the T[enants] Received 3^{li} in part of Mr Harrington for Christmass quarters and 10^s for a quarter's Ren[t] of Mr Kitchinson[1014] for Christmas called at Mr Pace's to know how M[?rs] Monk gott w:[1015] Oxon and she did at prayers at Lincoln's Inn performed my devotion within till 4 met [?Mr] Vise at Starr Coffee House and he told me he had spoken to Mr Ewers and he had given the papers to Captain Gibbon at prayers at Bow within performed my devotion at prayers.

Friday, 18 July: Performed my devotion amongst the Tenants Received of Mr Smith ½ a yeares rent due at [*illegible*] and a quarter's Rent of Mr Burgen for Midsomer at Mr Colliers and had a st [*illegible*][1016] tts put on at ~~Custom House~~ prayers at St Donstons East at Custom House at Mr Moores performed my devotion a[?t prayers] at Ludgate with my Lady Mathews paid her 10^{li} within at prayers performed my devotion to[?ok] Hunter's Liquor and greene snuff.

Saturday, 19 July: Performed my devotion in bed rose after 12 performed my devotion dined performed my devotion within all day performed my devotion at prayers.

Sunday, 20 July: Performed my devotion read within all Morning it being very wet and not well performed my devotion he[?ard] a stranger at Ludgate 1 James 26 within and Wat Gaff[1017] was with me [*illegible*] write the names of the Tenants and their arrears etc performed my devotion at prayers etc.

[1014] Ambiguous: may be 'Hitchinson'.

[1015] Ambiguous: perhaps 'with'. Could also be interpreted as 'to'; colon very faint.

[1016] Obscured by tight binding.

[1017] Presumably an abbreviation, though to whom it refers to is unclear. Hand untidy and ambiguous: may read 'Wat GH'.

Monday, 21 July: Performed my devotion at prayers at Bow received ½ a yeares Rent of Coll Lekeux a[?t] Custom House at Queen's Arms Coffee House called at Mr Hatfields to remember him to meete me at the Black Horse on Tuesday 3 a Clock at Mr Sandfords and received 1^{li}.10^s for Mr Evans Ladyday quarter ~~performed my devotion~~ dined [?at] prayers at St Donstons West performed my devotion within all the afternoone performed my devotion at prayers.

Tuesday, 22 July: Performed my devotion went to Mr Stone and received ½ a years Rent due at Midsomer at prayers at St Dionis at Custom House ~~till~~ at Mr Moores within at prayers performed my devotion etc at prayers at Lincoln's In[?n] with my wife a little in the garden there within at prayers performed my devotion.

Wednesday, 23 July: Performed my devotion within till 9 amongst the Tenants Received of Jone Hardin[g] a quarter's Rent due at Midsomer last and a quarter's Rent of Mrs Thom[?pson] for a quarter's Rent due at Midsomer last and a quarter's Rent of M[r] Starky due at Ladyday last at prayers at Coleman Streete at Custom House [?and] the Dolphin and drank a pint of sider within performed my devotion after 3 called on Byfield and went to my Lady and paid her 10^{li} at prayers at Covent gard[en] went to Coventry Streete to a seller for shoes but could find [?none] at prayers performed my devotion etc.

Thursday, 24 July: Performed my devotion within all Morning performed my devotion after 2 at Nixons Coffee House[1018] went with [?Mr] Hatfield and Mr Sandford to view my Ladys Houses at Chairin[g] Cross called on my Lady at Mr Rowlandsons till 11 at prayers performed my devotion etc.

[fo. 118r]
Friday, 25 July: Performed my devotion within till 10 Received of Mrs Bristow ½ a yeares Rent at prayers at St Bartholomew the Greate, within performed my devotion within till 6 at prayers at Ludgate at prayers performed my devotion etc.

[1018] In Fleet St. 'at Fetter Lane End'. This establishment is well documented in our period; Lillywhite notes that the proprietor, Nixon, probably died in 1713–1714, and that the business was carried on by his widow, and one 'Mr Peele' – interesting, since these names are both mentioned more than once by Lloyd himself; could they have been the same individuals? *LCH*, 410.

Saturday, 26 July: Performed my devotion within till neare 10 at prayers at Charter House amongst [th]e Tenants but received no Money at Custom House performed my devotion within till after 3 at prayers [?at] St Clement Danes within at prayers performed my devotion.

Sunday, 27 July: Performed my devotion heard a stranger at Ludgate 3 Matthew 2 performed my devotion heard a Stranger [?at] Ludgate 71 Psalm last within read at prayers performed my devotion.

Monday, 28 July: Performed my devotion after 7 amongst the Tenants received a quarter's Rent of Hatton [?due at] Michaelmas last and a quarter's Rent of Mr Higham for Midsomer [*illegible*] at Custom House at the Tower with Brother Walker and Sister Dell performed my devotion within till 5 at prayers at Lincoln's Inn amongst the Tenants Received a quarter's Rent [?of] Mrs Allen for Ladyday at prayers performed my devotion tooke Hunter being very ill. At prayers.

Tuesday, 29 July: Performed my devotion in bed rose at 12 performed my devotion within all day at prayers performed my devotion was very ill performed my devotion within being very ill performed my devotion as usualy at prayers.

Wednesday, 30 July: [Performed my] devotion not well at 10 went out to Custom House at Queen's Arms Coffee House received my salery [with]in performed my devotion within till after 4 at Golden Lyon Taverne with Brother [?Wal]ker and Sister Dell to take our leave of her goeing to Wales to her [?dau]ghter came home after 6 not well performed my devotion at prayers tooke Elixir etc.

[?Friday, 1] August:[1019] Performed my devotion in bed being very ill lay in bed till 5 performed my devotion eate after 6 at prayers performed my devotion.

[1019] The entry for either Thursday, 31 July or – less likely – Friday, 1 August is missing, perhaps as a result of the severe bouts of illness Lloyd was experiencing at this time. By this stage in the diary, Lloyd labelled his entry only with the numerical day, so, '30' would stand for 'Wednesday, 30 July'. In this case, the binding is so tight that the number cannot be seen at all for any of the entries, resulting in a speculative dating for this week of the diary.

[?**Saturday, 2**] **August:** Within till 11 at prayers at Lincolns Inn performed my devotion at prayers at St Dunstons [wit]hin at prayers performed my devotion.

Sunday, 3 August: [?Performed my devotion] etc heard a stranger at Ludgate 2 Philippians 14 ₤ performed my devotion heard a stranger [?J]ob 14:15 within a little walkt with my wife to Grays Inn [wa]lks read at prayers performed my devotion etc.

Monday, 4 August: Within till 10 amongst the Tenants received of Mrs Blackden a quarter Rent [?due at] Ladyday at prayers at Lincolns Inn at Mr Rowlandsons performed my devotion with my [*illegible*] till 7[1020] at ~~the Insurance~~ within at prayers performed my devotion.

Tuesday, 5 August: Within all Morning settling the accounts performed my devotion at prayers at St Donstons with [my] Lady till 6 at the Insurances office[1021] to know about the terms of it [?dine]ed at my Ladys and stayd a little within at prayers performed my devotion.

Wednesday, 6 August: [?Performed my devotion] at prayers at Charter House at Custom House at the Queen's Arms Coffee House performed my devotion called Mr Rowland[?son] and went to my Ladys I stayd till after 7 at prayers performed my devotion paid Mr Bell 5[li].

Thursday, 7 August: [?Performed my devotion] at prayers at Charter House at Queen's Arms Coffee House performed my devotion called Mr Rowlandson we went to my Ladys stayd till 7 not well at prayers performed my devotion etc.

Friday, 8 August: [?Performed my devotion] very ill performed my devotion in bed rose after 12 performed my devotion within at prayers performed my devotion.

[1020] '6' overwritten with '7'.

[1021] Lloyd wrote his diary during the genesis of the insurance business in London. Surviving policies from the famous Sun Fire Office (established 1708) now constitute a treasure-trove of information about 18th-century London and Londoners: see Lance Whitehead and Jenny Nex, 'The insurance of musical London and the Sun Fire Office, 1710–1779', *The Galpin Society Journal*, 67 (2014), 181–216, and 'Wealth, occupations, in insurance in the late eighteenth century: The policy registers of the Sun Fire Office', *The Economic History Review*, 36 (1983), 365–373.

Saturday, 9 August: [?Performed my devotion] [ve]ry ill performed my devotion in bed rose at 12 was very ill within all day at prayers performed my devotion.

Sunday, 10 August: [?Performed my devotion] in bed being very ill all day performed my devotion at 5 went into the Citty to [?he]are a Sermon but could find none called at Mr Bawlers but he not withi[?n] called at Mr Powells and she not well met Mrs Fruitrill there and she told me [?tha]t Mr Holker was brought a [*illegible*] read at prayers performed my devotion.

[fo. 118v]
Monday, 11 August: Performed my devotion in bed being very ill performed my devotion at 3 Mr Moore sent to see me I made a hard shift to see to him who was extreame weake at prayers at Bartholomew Lane caled my wife at Mrs Hamonds at prayers performed my devotion etc.

Tuesday, 12 August: Performed my devotion tooke Dulwich waters[1022] performed my devotion at prayers at Christchurch called to see Mrs Powell who was very bad at prayers performed my devotion.

Wednesday, 13 August: Performed my devotion drank Dulwich Water performed my devotion at 3 at prayers at St Donstons left my wife at the end of Paternoster Row and went amongst the Tenants but got but 10^s of Mrs Darby within at prayers performed my devotion.

Thursday, 14 August: Performed my devotion within till 10 called at the Tower to see Brother Richard but he was not there at Custom House performed my devotion at prayers at St Donstons called on Mr Rowlandson met Mr Vize at Nixons within till 6 went with my Wife and Mrs Ward to Mr Rowlandsons stayd there till 11 and supt at prayers performed my devotion.

Friday, 15 August: Performed my devotion within till after 8 called on Mrs Guild[?e]rs and told her I had beene with Mr Tortane amongst the Tenants received a quarter's Rent for Ladyday of Mrs

---

[1022] Dulwich Water was a purgative mineral water from Dulwich, then a small village outside London. Its efficacy was doubted in the 18th century. Leigh Waley, *Women and the Practice of Medical Care in Early Modern Europe, 1400–1800* (London, 2011), 80.

Cooley and a quarter's Rent of Mr Creeke for his roome for Ladyday and a quarter's Rent of Mr Linnet and a quarter's Rent of Mr Watkinson for Midsomer each at prayers at Christ Church performed my devotion at prayers at St Donstons with my Wife left her in Cheapeside and I paid Mr Beachcroft 42^l 10^s for Mr[1023] Tempest at Starr Coffee house at prayers againe at Bow called my Wife at Mrs Cocks stayd till after 7 within performed my devotion.

Saturday, 16 August: Performed my devotion within performed my devotion.

Sunday, 17 August: Performed my devotion heard a stranger at Ludgate 17 Luke 10 performed my devotion heard a stran[ger] 8 John 34 called to see Mr Rowlandson performed my devotion at prayers.

Monday, 18 August: Performed my devotion went to Higgs and after to Mr Searles and received 11^l.5^s and allowd 14^s.6^d bought pair shoes at Coventry Streete at prayers at St Mary Woo[l] North at Custom House called to see Mr Rowlandson performed my devotion within till neare 5 at prayers at Charter House received a quarter's Rent of Rice for Ladyday called at Mr Burtons and ordered 1^l Raysons to be sent in at prayers performed my devotion.

Tuesday, 19 August: Performed my devotion after 9 tooke the sheas[1024] with my wife to goe to Mrs Tempest came there ½ houer after 10 and drank 2 glasses Wine and she let me have the Marriag settlement went across the Thames in the Ferry at Lambeth to Mrs Bowyers dined there and stayd till neare 3 at Cousin Newingtons till neare 5 took sheas and came to Hunters stayd a little at Mr Sandfords within performed my devotion at prayers in the parler and after at prayers etc.

20. Performed my devotion within till 10 at Mr Rowlands and left the Marriage Deede at Custom House at prayers at St Mary Woollnorth performed my devotion at prayers at St Donston at Nix[?on's] to meete Higgs and he sent word he could not come within at prayers performed my devotion.

[1023] Unclear and blemished: possibly 'Mrs'.
[1024] Probably a 'chaise', a small carriage.

21 Performed my devotion within till after 10 at Mr Rowlandsons and helpt to examine the Deede within performed my devotion.

[fo. 119r]
Wednesday, 20 August: Performed my devotion carried the Marriage deede to Mr Rowlandsons; went to Custom House mett Mr Vize and went to the Mitre and he signed a Bond performed my devotion at prayers at St Donstons Met H at Nixons to meete Higgs but he came not within at prayers performed my devotion etc.

Thursday, 21 August: Performed my devotion at 12 went to Mr Rowlandsons and helpt examine the Marriage deede performed my devotion after 9 carried the deede to Mr Beachcraft and left it there for Madam Tempest, called and spoke to Mr Nash abo about Mr Overtons Money at prayers at Lincolns Inn within at prayers performed my devotion.

Friday, 22 August: Performed my devotion after 8 amongst the Tenants and received of the overseer of the poore 5^s for Ann Darby for Midsomer Rent and 6^s for Margaret King for a quarter's Rent within and sent away the Reasons[1025] bought for my Lady and paid Thomas Edwards 10^s the remaining Money of Searles 2 quarters at prayers at St Donstons w[e] met Mr Rowlandson and went to a Coffee House Received a quarter's Rent of Mr Walker for Ladyday and allowed 3 and 4 tax for 1711 called at Mr Nashes but he had not seene Mr Overton within performed my devotion within till 5 at prayers at Lincoln's Inn walkt in the garden and after to my perrywigg maker within at prayers performed my devotion.

Saturday, 23 August: Performed my devotion amongst the Tenants Received ½ a yeares rent of Mr Sawyer went to Mr Powells for a flask of brandy within a little changed a pair stockings at Mr Stills's at Mr Bearfotts and left a flask for wine at Custom House at Mrs Hunts and left her receipt for a Cough called for my flask within performed my devotion at prayers at St Dunstons within at prayers performed my devotion.

Sunday, 24 August: Performed my devotion heard a stranger at Ludgate performed my devotion heard a stranger at St Clement's

---

[1025] Raisins.

PROB 11/567/206 – Will of George Lloyd, Gentleman of St Dunstan in the East, City of London, Prerogative Court of Canterbury, proved 29 January 1719.
PROB 11/569/85 – Will of Elizabeth Lloyd, widow of St Dunstan in the East, City of London, Prerogative Court of Canterbury, proved 11 June 1719.
PROB 11/594/278 – Will of Elizabeth Lardner, Widow of Peter Street in the Bowling Alley, Westminster, Prerogative Court of Canterbury, proved 7 December 1723.
PROB 11/599/126 – Will of Thomas Lynford, Rector of St Edmund the King Lombard Street, Prerogative Court of Canterbury, proved 22 August 1724.
PROB 11/602/127 – Will of Sir Caesar Child of Woodford, Essex, Prerogative Court of Canterbury, proved 8 March, 1725.
PROB 11/640/212 – Will of Richard Walker, Gentleman of London, Prerogative Court of Canterbury, proved 17 October 1730.
PROB 11/676/196 – Will of Dame Anne Mathews, widow of St Andrew Holborn, Middlesex, Prerogative Court of Canterbury, proved 24 March, 1736.
PROB 11/690/263 – Will of Lawrence or Laurence Holker, Doctor in Physic of Milton next Gravesend, Kent, Prerogative Court of Canterbury, proved 30 June 1738.
PROB 11/694/304 – Will of Philip Oddy, Gentleman of Islington, Middlesex, Prerogative Court of Canterbury, proved 10 February 1739.
SP 34/37/37 – Friedrich Bonet to unknown recipient, 22 August, 1711.
SP 34/37/38 – Friedrich Bonet to unknown recipient, 26 August, 1711.
SP 34/37/39 – Memorandum, possibly in connection with the case of W[illia]m Higgs, 1711?
SP 34/37/48 – Sir Edward Northey, to unknown, 29 August, 1711.
SP 100/67 – Foreign Ministers in England, miscellaneous, 1718–23.
T 1/219 – Treasury Board papers and in-letters, 1718.
T 4/1 – Treasury Reference Book of Applications, 1680–82.
T 11/8 – Treasury book of out-letters to the Board of Customs and Excise, 1681–84.

Printed Primary Sources

Anon., *Advertisement: From the Charitable Corporation for relief of industrious poor* (London, 1709?), GHL, 7.105.
Anon., *From the Lombard house in Duke-street, Westminster: Abstract of the settlement for insurance of goods against loss by fire, inrolled in the high court of Chancery, by the Charitable corporation* (London, 1708?), GHL, 7.101.
Anon., *From the new Lombard-house in Dukes-street, Westminster: The method of securing the fund of the Charitable corporation* (London, 1708?), GHL, 7.100.
Anon., *Rules of the Water-Side, or, The General Practice of the Customs* (London, 1715), BL, C.194.a.962.
Anon., *The New Lombard Houses* (London, 1708), GHL, 7.99.
Anon., *The Whole Duty of Man* (London, 1658).
Aubrey, John, *The Natural History and Antiquities of the County of Surrey*, Vol. 5 (London, 1719).
Bacon, Nathaniel, *A Relation of the Fearefull Estate of Francis Spira* (London, 1638).
Bayly, Lewis, *The Practice of Piety, Directing a Christian How to Walk that He May Please God* (London, 1612, 1613, 1675).

SELECT BIBLIOGRAPHY

Bernard, Richard, *The Isle of Man, or, The Legal Proceedings in Man-shire against Sin* (London, 1627).
Collinges, John, *The Weavers Pocket-book, or, Weaving Spiritualised* (London, 1675).
Cotton, Charles, *The Compleat Gamester* (London, 1674).
Crouch, Henry, *A Complete Guide to the Officers of His Majesty's Customs* (London, 1732).
Daniel, Thomas, *Ductor Mercatorius, or, The Young Merchant's Instructor with respect to the Customs* (Newcastle, 1750).
Deloney, Thomas, *Thomas of Reading, or, The Sixe Worthy Yeomen of the West* (1599?).
Doolittle, Thomas, *A Treatise concerning the Lord's Supper* (London, 1667).
Dunmore, John, *Catalogus librorum bibliothecæ Reverendi Nicolai Lloydii* (London, 1681).
Etherege, George, *The Man of Mode, or, Sir Fopling Flutter* (London, 1676).
Featley, Daniel, *Ancilla pietatis, or, The Handmaid to Private Devotion* (London, 1626).
Ford, Emmanuel, *Parismus, the Renowned Prince of Bohemia* (London, 1598–1599).
Hale, Matthew, *Contemplations Moral and Divine by a Person of Great Learning and Judgment* (London, 1676).
Hooke, Robert, *Cometa* (London, 1678).
Hoole, Charles, *A New Discovery of the Old Art of Teaching Schoole* (London, 1661).
Ken, Thomas, *A Manual of Prayers for the Use of the Scholars of Winchester Colledge* (London, 1674).
Lloyd, John, *Shir ha shirim, or, The Song of Songs being a Paraphrase upon the Most Excellent Canticles of Solomon in a Pindarick Poem* (London, 1682).
May, Robert, *The Accomptlisht Cook* (London, 1660).
Milton, John, *The History of Britain, That Part Especially Now Called England* (London, 1670).
Nedham, Marchamont, *A Pacquet of Advices and Animadversions Sent from London to the Men of Shaftsbury* (London, 1676).
Paget, John, *Meditations of Death* (Dort, 1639).
Quarles, Francis, *Emblemes* (London, 1634).
Rainbowe, Edward, *A Sermon Preached at the Funeral of the Right Honorable Anne, Countess of Pembroke, Dorset, and Montgomery* (London, 1677).
Raleigh, Sir Walter, *The Life and Death of Mahomet* (London, 1637).
Rogers, Timothy, *The Righteous Mans Evidences for Heaven* (London, 1618).
Sammes, Aylett, *Britannia antiqua illustrata, or, The Antiquities of Ancient Britain Derived from the Phœnicians* (London, 1676).
Shelton, William, *Moral Vertues Baptized Christian, or, The Necessity of Morality among Christians* (London, 1667).
Shelton, William, *Some Account from Colchester of the Quakers Errors against the Very Foundation of the Christian Religion* (London, 1699).
Smith, John, *Christian Religion's Appeal from the Groundless Prejudices of the Sceptick to the Bar of Common Reason* (London, 1675).
Smith, John [?], *The Doctrine of the Church of England, concerning the Lord's Day* (London, 1683).
Sparke, Robert, *A Sermon Preached in S. George's Church Southwark, at the Funeral of that Pious and Worthy Gentlewoman, Mrs. Frances Fenn* (London, 1679).
Stow, John, and John Strype, *A Survey of the Cities of London and Westminster*, Book III (London, 1720).
Stow, William, *Remarks on London: Being an Exact Survey* (London, 1722).
Taylor, Jeremy *A Discourse on the Liberty of Prophesying* (London, 1647).

Taylor, Jeremy, *The Rule and Exercises of Holy Dying* (London, 1651).
Taylor, Jeremy, *The Golden Grove, or, A Manuall of Daily Prayers and Letanies* (London, 1655; 1667).
Taylor, John, *Travels and Circular Perambulation* (London, 1636).
Turner, Bryan, *A Sermon Preached before the Right Honourable the Lord Mayor, and Aldermen of London at the Guild-Hall Chappel, Octob. the 28th 1677* (October, 1678).

Edited Primary Sources

Carr, Cecil T. (ed.), *Select Charters of Trading Companies, 1530–1707* (London, 1913).
Cruttwell, Clement (ed.), *The Works of the Right Reverend Father in God Thomas Wilson, D.D.* (London, 1782).
Ferguson, Catherine, Christopher Thornton, and Andrew Wareham (eds), *Essex Hearth Tax Return Michaelmas 1670* (London, 2012).
Fielding, John (ed.), *The Diary of Robert Woodford, 1637–1641*, Royal Historical Society, Camden 5th ser., 42 (Cambridge, 2012).
Foster, John E. (ed.), *The Diary of Samuel Newton, Alderman of Cambridge, 1662–1717* (Cambridge, 1890).
Latham, Robert C., and William Matthews (eds), *The Diary of Samuel Pepys*, 11 vols (London, 1995).
Macfarlane, Alan (ed.), *The Diary of Ralph Josselin, 1616–1683* (Oxford, 1991).
Malay, Jessica L., *Anne Clifford's Autobiographical Writing, 1590–1676* (Manchester, 2018).
Money, John (ed.), *The Chronicles of John Cannon, Excise Officer and Writing Master*, 2 vols (Oxford, 2010).
Port, Michael H. (ed.), *The Commission for Building Fifty New Churches: The Minute Books, 1711–27, a Calendar* (London, 1986).
Redington, Joseph (ed.), *Calendar of Treasury Papers, 1557–1728*, 6 vols (London, 1868–1889).
Round, John Horace, *Register of the Scholars Admitted to Colchester School, 1637–1740* (Colchester, 1897).
Sachse, William L. (ed.), *The Diary of Roger Lowe of Ashton-in-Makerfield, Lancashire, 1663–74* (London, 1938).
Shaw, William A., and F. H. Slingsby (eds), *Calendar of Treasury Books, 1660–1718*, 32 vols (London, 1904–1962).

Secondary Sources

Alsop, James, 'Religious preambles in early modern English wills as formulae', *Journal of Ecclesiastical History*, 40 (1989), 19–27.
Baer, William C., 'Landlords and tenants in London, 1550–1700', *Urban History*, 38 (2011), 234–255.
Betham, William, *The Baronetage of England, or, The History of the English Baronets* (London, 1802).
Bradley, Simon, and Nikolaus Pevsner, *The Buildings of England: London 1: The City of London* (New Haven, CT, 2002).

SELECT BIBLIOGRAPHY

Brealey, Peter, 'The Charitable Corporation for the Relief of Industrious Poor: Philanthropy, profit and sleaze in London, 1707–1733', *History*, 98 (2013), 708–729.

Breward, Christopher, *The Culture of Fashion* (Manchester, 2015).

Brewer, John, 'Servants of the public – servants of the Crown: Officialdom of eighteenth- century English central government', in J. Brewer and E. Hellmuth (eds), *Rethinking Leviathan: The Eighteenth-Century State in Britain and Germany* (Oxford, 1999), 127–147.

Burke, John, and John Bernard Burke, *A Genealogical and Heraldic History of the Extinct and Dormant Baronetcies of England* (Baltimore, MD, 1985).

Carson, Edward, *The Ancient and Rightful Customs: A History of the English Customs Service* (London, 1972).

Cherry, Bridget, and Nikolaus Pevsner, *The Buildings of England: London 2: South* (New Haven, CT, 2002).

Cherry, Bridget, and Nikolaus Pevsner, *The Buildings of England: London 4: North* (New Haven, CT, 2002).

Cokayne, George E. (ed.), *The Complete Baronetage*, Vol. 4 (Exeter, 1904).

Cooper, Janet (ed.), *The Victoria History of the County of Essex*, Vol. 9: *The Borough of Colchester* (Oxford, 1994).

Cressy, David, *Literacy and the Social Order: Reading and Writing in Tudor and Stuart England* (Cambridge, 1980).

Cressy, David, 'The drudgery of schoolmasters: The teaching profession in Elizabethan and Stuart England', in Wilfred Prest (ed.), *The Professions in Early Modern England* (London, 1987), 129–153.

D'Cruze, Shani (ed.), *Colchester People*, Vol. 3 (Morrisville, NC, 2010).

Dickens, Arthur G., *Lollards and Protestants in the Diocese of York* (Oxford, 1959).

Earle, Peter, *The Making of the English Middle Class: Business, Society and Family Life in London, 1660–1730* (London, 1989).

Everitt, Alan, 'Social mobility in early modern England', *Past and Present*, 33 (1966), 56–73.

Farooq, Jennifer, *Preaching in Eighteenth-Century London* (Woodbridge, 2013).

Foster, Joseph (ed.), *Alumni Oxonienses: The members of the University of Oxford, 1500–1714, their parentage, birthplace, and year of birth, with a record of their degrees, being the matriculation register of the university*, 4 vols (London, 1891).

Grassby, Richard, *Kinship and Capitalism: Marriage, Family, and Business in the English-Speaking world, 1580–1740* (Cambridge, 2001).

Greyerz, Kaspar von, 'Spuren eines vormodernen Individualismus in englischen Selbstzeugnissen des 16. und 17. Jahrhunderts', in W. Schulze (ed.), *Ego-Dokumente: Annäherung an den Menschen in der Geschichte* (Berlin, 1996), 273–282.

Griffiths, Paul, and Mark S. R. Jenner (eds), *Londinopolis: Essays in the Cultural and Social History of Early Modern London* (Manchester, 2000).

Harben, Henry, *A Dictionary of London* (London, 1918).

Hayton, David, and Eveline Cruickshanks, *The History of Parliament: The House of Commons, 1690–1715*, 5 vols (London, 2001).

Henning, Basil Duke, *The History of Parliament: The House of Commons, 1660–1690*, 3 vols (London, 1983).

Hitchcock, Tim, and Robert Shoemaker, *London Lives: Poverty, Crime and the Making of a Modern City, 1690–1800* (Cambridge, 2015).

Hoon, Elizabeth, *The Organization of the English Customs System, 1696–1786* (New York, 1938).
Horst, Louis, *Pre-Classic Dance Forms* (Princeton, NJ, 1987).
Jephcott, Jess A., *The Inns, Taverns and Pubs of Colchester* (Colchester, 2015).
Lillywhite, Bryant, *London Coffee Houses: A Reference Book of Coffee Houses of the Seventeenth, Eighteenth and Nineteenth Centuries* (London, 1963).
McKay, Elaine, 'The diary network in sixteenth- and seventeenth-century England', *Eras*, 2 (2001), unpaginated.
Marsh, Christopher, *Music and Society in Early Modern England* (Cambridge, 2010).
Martin, Geoffrey 'The history of Colchester Royal Grammar School', *The Colcestrian*, NS 131 (1947), 1–38.
Matthews, William, *British Diaries: An Annotated Bibliography of British Diaries Written between 1442 and 1942* (London, 1950).
Morant, Philip, *The History and Antiquities of Colchester, in the County of Essex*, 3 vols (London, 1748).
O'Day, Rosemary, 'Church records and the history of education in early modern England 1558–1642: A problem in methodology', *The History of Education*, 2 (1973), 115–132.
Patterson, Daniel, 'Writing time: Charting the history of clock time in seventeenth-century diaries', *Huntington Library Quarterly*, 82:2 (2020), 305–329.
Pevsner, Nikolaus, and Enid Radcliffe, *The Buildings of England: Essex* (London, 1965).
Pevsner, Nikolaus, and Enid Radcliffe, *The Buildings of England: Suffolk* (London, 1974).
Spufford, Margaret, and Susan Mee, *The Clothing of the Common Sort, 1570–1750* (Oxford, 2017).
Tomlinson, David, ' "Young gentlemen are at a reasonable rate to be boarded": An account of the Free Grammar School, Colchester *c*.1690–*c*.1820', *The Transactions of the Essex Society for Archaeology and History*, 4th ser., 4 (2013), 158–176.
Venn, John, and John A. Venn, *Alumni Cantabrigienses: A biographical list of all known students, graduates, and holders of office at the University of Cambridge, from the earliest times to 1900*, Vol. 1: *From the earliest times to 1751*, 4 parts (Cambridge, 1922–1954; 2011)
Weinreb, Ben, Christopher Hibbert, Julia Keay, and John Keay, *The London Encyclopedia*, 3rd edn (London, 2008).
Young, Elizabeth, and Wayland Young, *Old London Churches* (London, 1956).

INDEX

Contemporary names and titles used.

accounts and bookkeeping 23, 27, 28, 44, 46, 139, 298, 303, 318, 325, 330, 331, 350, 370, 376, 391, 392, 414, 418
Angier family 43, 47, 146, 159, 163, 170, 184, 251, 253, 256, 266
Anne, Queen 318n, 350–351, 372, 384, 412n
Ardrey, Mr (William?) 15–16, 89, 90, 91, 99, 100, 101, 102, 103, 105, 106, 108, 109, 110, 111, 112, 114, 115, 116, 117, 118, 119, 120, 121, 122, 123, 124, 125, 126, 127, 128, 129, 130, 131, 133, 134, 135, 136, 137, 138, 142, 143, 145, 146, 147, 148, 149, 150, 152, 151, 153, 154, 155, 156, 157, 158, 160, 165, 167, 168, 169, 170, 171, 172, 173, 174, 175, 176, 177, 178, 179, 180, 181, 183, 184, 185, 186, 187, 188, 189, 190, 191, 192, 193, 200, 201, 203, 205, 206, 208, 210, 211, 212, 213, 214, 216, 224, 226, 228, 231, 237, 240, 242, 243, 244, 250, 259, 260, 262, 263, 264, 265, 268, 269, 278, 279, 280, 281, 282, 283
Ardrey, Mrs (Elizabeth?) 16, 102, 104, 155, 157, 158, 159, 160, 161, 162, 163, 164, 165, 168, 170, 172, 178, 180, 182, 183, 184, 185, 186, 187, 188, 189, 190, 191, 201, 202, 203, 204, 212, 214, 217, 220, 222, 226, 227, 239, 254, 255, 259, 262, 269, 278, 290
Aynho, Northamptonshire 8, 11, 17, 40, 139, 194–200, 233, 234, 270, 271–272, 279

Bartholomew Fair 166
Bayly, Lewis 61, 72, 93, 124, 125, 127, 194, 202
bohee tea 319, 320, 388
bowls (ninepins) 139, 144, 150, 234, 240, 267, 338
Boyle Lectures 366

Bradford, Samuel 318, 319, 321, 323, 324, 331, 333, 334, 346, 359–360, 379, 398
Bray, Thomas 334n
Bridge House 389, 390, 391, 392, 394
Burnet, Gilbert, bishop of Salisbury 375, 390
Bury St Edmunds 66–67

Cambridge 94–97, 195, 244
camlet 18, 85, 133, 134, 135, 174, 216, 270, 273, 286
card games 8, 67, 75, 76, 83, 84, 85, 86, 87, 88, 89, 95, 97, 98, 99, 100, 101, 102, 103, 104, 105, 108, 109, 111, 113, 185, 189, 196, 197, 198, 200, 210, 219, 256, 257, 258, 268, 272, 275, 286, 287, 289, 292, 362, 376, 377, 384, 385, 386, 387
Catherine of Braganza 276, 288–289
chamois ('shamy') 112, 126, 127, 128, 129, 158, 159, 184, 185, 186, 187, 206, 207, 208, 209, 241, 260
Charitable Corporation 297, 315, 318, 333, 347, 358–359, 365; *see also* Higgs, William
Charles I 55n, 106n–107n
Charles II 74n, 194, 224, 276, 277, 289n
Charterhouse, London 301, 308, 309, 310, 313, 315, 317, 332, 348, 361, 362, 363, 364, 366, 367, 371, 372, 373, 378, 379, 382, 385, 387, 389, 396, 397, 403, 410, 413, 414, 417, 418, 420
Child, Dame Hester 378
Clifford, Lady Anne, countess of Dorset, Pembroke, and Montgomery 225
clothing 93, 102, 167, 193, 204, 232, 238, 268, 291, 312;
  belts 65, 73, 114, 137, 159, 160, 192, 206, 224
  breeches 82, 86, 90–91, 92, 100, 101, 102–103, 105, 106, 108, 112, 113, 114, 115, 116, 117, 118, 119–120, 123, 125, 126, 127, 128, 129, 136,

158, 159, 188, 206, 207, 208, 209, 227, 241, 257, 258, 260, 261, 276, 278, 403
cloaks 181
coats 75, 79, 81, 83, 84, 85, 86, 87, 88, 89, 90, 99, 110, 120, 121, 122, 123, 124, 125, 126, 127, 130, 131, 132, 133, 134, 135, 137–138, 155, 156, 182, 186, 187, 193, 200, 201, 202, 204, 207, 211, 216, 226, 244, 268, 270, 271, 275, 273, 286, 288, 291, 293, 328, 366, 368, 372, 405
cravats 59, 81, 91, 110, 124, 126, 156, 157, 163, 191, 192, 202, 225, 267, 276
cuffs 61, 70, 71, 79, 81, 83, 86, 90, 91, 120, 121, 127, 129, 136, 154, 155–156, 160, 162
gloves 59, 92, 93, 112, 114, 126, 166, 170, 179, 192, 202, 205, 209, 214, 257, 258, 284, 401
handkerchiefs 225, 319
hats 92, 125, 126, 170, 230, 252, 317, 321, 333, 334, 335, 343, 403, 404
lace 59, 81, 83, 90–91, 100, 105, 106, 108, 125, 126, 129, 136, 156, 191, 209, 227, 230, 252, 261, 290
linen 44, 53, 70, 72, 79, 84, 86, 87, 91, 93, 114, 129, 132, 145, 215, 221, 225, 237, 290
shirts 57, 78, 84, 85, 86, 87, 88, 89, 90, 108, 110, 111, 122, 123, 128, 129, 219, 220, 291
stockings 44, 46, 57, 60, 62, 68, 84, 88, 92, 109, 124, 126, 128, 129, 132, 143, 144, 150, 152, 157, 161, 169, 170, 171, 173, 184, 188, 190, 193, 202, 203, 205, 206, 212, 213, 215, 226, 227, 236, 239, 241, 244, 249, 252, 259, 268, 270, 281, 289, 291, 293, 299, 372, 401, 421
waistcoats 74, 75, 324
Cockayne, Brien, 2nd Viscount Cullen 11, 39, 57n, 110n, 158
Cocker, Edward 11, 13, 40, 41, 45
coffee houses 14, 25, 43, 52, 53, 57, 68, 96, 156, 174, 199, 270, 274, 287, 298, 300, 301, 302, 308, 309, 310, 311, 312, 316, 319n–320n, 321, 324, 330, 336, 337n, 342, 349, 355, 356, 357n, 362, 363, 364, 371, 372, 373, 378, 379n, 383, 384, 385, 389, 390, 391, 392, 394, 397, 400, 403, 408, 409, 415; Christian 323, 325, 328, 366; Guildhall 331, 409; King's Arms 343, 348, 390, 400, 403, 412; Nixon's 371n, 416, 419, 421; Queen's Arms 310, 329, 370, 378, 381, 386, 396, 399, 404, 408, 410, 413, 414, 416, 417, 418; Star 298, 303, 311, 313, 317, 322, 323, 324, 329, 330, 342, 345, 348, 357, 359, 360, 392, 401, 405, 414, 415, 420; Sun 312; Tom's 310, 311n, 318
Colchester Grammar School 13–14, 74n, 144n, 178n, 236n
Cooper, Anthony Ashley, 1st earl of Shaftesbury 243n, 258, 285n

dancing 50, 68, 86, 97, 98, 150, 166, 171, 197, 209, 210, 221, 246, 275, 291
dancing school 156, 204, 205, 206, 207, 208, 209, 210, 212, 213, 214, 217, 218, 219, 220, 221, 225, 226, 228, 236, 252, 256, 263, 267
Dedham, Essex 18, 43, 229, 232, 236, 238, 240, 242, 246, 247, 248, 249, 253, 254, 255, 259, 261, 264, 265, 266, 267, 268, 269
Deloney, Thomas 52n, 90
Donne, John 196, 344n
Doolittle, Thomas 66, 93, 94, 124, 125
draughts (boardgame) 256
Drexelius, Hieremias 43, 44, 136, 137, 211
dropsy (oedema) 21, 119, 407, 408

East India House 327, 364, 398
Elwes, Sir Gervase, 1st baronet 57, 94, 95, 98, 110
Etherege, George 141n
Eucharist (Sacrament) 53, 56, 93–94, 124–125, 153, 176, 196, 222, 233, 264, 267, 268, 285, 296, 306, 313, 321, 329, 331, 352, 353, 357, 361, 366, 371, 375, 377, 383, 389, 396, 398, 401, 407, 408, 418
Eusebius 60
Evance, Sir Stephen 377, 378, 390

fasting, fasts 55, 65, 77, 107, 137, 285, 380
Furly, John 46–47, 189n, 253

Gravesend 325, 327, 335–339, 340, 373, 392

Hale, Matthew 238, 239, 241, 242, 243, 244, 246, 247

INDEX

Hall, Joseph 245, 282
Hedges, Richard 28, 30, 312, 334, 359, 362
Hickeringill, Edmund (Colchester, All Saints) 82, 99, 101, 175, 176, 177, 200, 202, 205, 207, 215, 222, 224, 250, 266
Higgs, William 297, 298, 301, 302, 303, 308, 311, 313, 318, 322, 324, 325, 329, 330, 332, 333, 346, 347, 356, 357, 360, 365, 371, 372, 374, 381, 388–389, 402, 404, 407, 413, 420, 421
Holker family 304, 311, 312, 313, 319, 321, 335, 337, 338, 339, 367, 368, 400, 401, 407– 408, 419
Hooke, Robert 141n, 222n
Hyde, Edward, 3rd earl of Clarendon 332, 349n, 371, 404

Ibbot, Benjamin 320, 329, 360, 397
illnesses (primarily George Lloyd's) 55, 58, 114, 137, 164, 170, 176, 177, 185, 188, 195, 203, 211, 212, 214, 215, 217, 220, 226, 229, 230, 248, 250, 252, 264, 275, 279, 292, 316, 325, 328, 331, 335–336, 340–341, 342, 355, 362, 363, 364, 366, 371, 374, 381, 394, 406, 408, 413, 415, 417–419
inns 41, 42, 44, 67, 140, 142, 165, 166, 199, 256, 261, 266, 268, 269, 304n, 335, 337n, 370, 388; Black Swan (Holborn) 141; George (Colchester) 263; Red Lion (Colchester) 68, 177, 263n; Scole Inn 67, 247; Spread Eagle (Gracechurch St.) 305, 309, 313; Sun (Dedham) 265, 267, 269; (White) Bear (?Basinghall St.) 296, 301, 305, 345, 401; White Harte (Colchester) 45n, 132; 222, 231, 251, 263n; White Horse (Fleet St.) 343, 346, 348, 349, 350, 351, 364
insurance 418
Ipswich 67–8, 247
italic (chancery cursive, writing hand) 47, 49, 50, 152, 224, 231, 262

James, Frances 9, 31
James, Nicholas 9, 31, 307, 316, 320, 348, 388
Josephus 62, 193
Josselin, Ralph 63n

legal quays 141, 300, 329

Lexden 51, 52, 58, 59, 60, 62, 64, 65, 69, 77, 82, 83, 123, 126, 133, 137, 138, 144, 153, 157, 172
Lloyd, Elizabeth 4, 20, 30–32, 295–422 *passim*
Lloyd, George: *passim*;
　background:
　　identification of 2–3
　　survival of diary 3–4
　　parentage and ancestry 4–7
　　siblings 2–3, 7–9
　　education and upbringing 9–11
　　becomes schoolteacher 12–17
　　courtship and marriage 17–20
　　deaths of brothers 21–22
　　becomes Customs officer 22–25
　　becomes rent broker 25–30
　　final illness and death 30–32
　events in diary:
　　arrives and settles in Colchester 41–48
　　lodges with Strattons 48
　　establishes first school 50–54
　　visits Bury St Edmunds and Ipswich 66–68
　　begins family prayers with Strattons 84–85
　　meets Mr Ardrey 89
　　travels to Stoke-by-Clare, Suffolk 94–99
　　agrees with Ardrey to open a new school 129
　　first visit to London 138–142
　　second visit to London 165–166
　　agrees premises for new school 171
　　moves to lodge with Ardrey and opens new school 175–176
　　first visit to Aynho 194–199
　　third visit to London 199–200
　　bridesman at wedding 202–203
　　first visit to Lynford sisters at Dedham 229
　　fourth visit to London 232–234
　　second visit to Aynho 234–235
　　returns to London 235
　　learns Stratton is suing him 243
　　travels to Suffolk with Lynford sisters 247–248
　　settles dispute with Stratton 253–254
　　closes school 262–263
　　leaves Colchester for Newington Butts 269–270
　　third visit to Aynho 271–272
　　travels to Gravesend on Customs business 335–340

visits Lady Mathews at Windsor 350–351
  agrees to lodge with Mrs Hall 393–394, 397, 409
  moves in with Mrs Hall 411–412
  see also clothing; illnesses
Lloyd, John 2–3, 7, 9–10, 39, 54, 64, 129, 196, 270, 278, 280, 286, 287, 288, 289, 293, 294
Lloyd, Nicholas 2–11, 14, 17, 20, 21, 41–42, 50, 84, 101, 104, 114, 127, 129, 134, 138, 140, 152, 158, 196, 197, 198, 199, 232, 234, 235, 261, 262, 270, 271, 272, 273, 274, 275, 276, 277, 278, 279, 280, 281, 282, 283, 284, 285, 286, 287, 288, 290, 291, 292, 293, 294
London 1, 7, 8, 11, 12, 17, 18, 20, 23–31, 32, 39–40, 41, 45, 47, 50, 102, 104, 138–142, 153, 159, 165–166, 168, 188, 189, 198, 199–200, 228, 232–233, 234, 235, 237, 244, 263, 268, 270–271, 273–294, 295–422 *passim*
Longman, James, DD 40, 196, 197, 199
lotteries 297, 329, 349–350, 394, 395–396
Lucas, Sir Charles 47

Mapletoft, John 304, 310, 311, 314, 316, 319, 361, 365, 369, 371, 372, 373, 375, 378, 379, 380, 386, 394, 396, 398, 400, 401, 405, 407, 408
Mathews, Lady Ann 25–30, 297, 300, 301, 303, 305, 308, 312, 317, 320, 323, 325, 329, 330, 331, 343–344, 349, 350, 352, 354, 356, 357, 364, 370, 374–375, 376, 377, 379, 381, 382, 385, 386, 387, 389, 391–392, 403, 406, 415, 416, 418, 421
medicines (various) 78, 87, 88, 100, 111–116, 133, 177, 179, 188, 203, 210, 229–230, 244, 275, 302, 307, 315, 319, 320, 321, 325, 329, 331, 332, 336, 340, 342, 348, 355, 362, 363, 364, 365, 366, 368, 369, 374, 377, 383, 390, 391, 393, 394, 396, 397, 406, 408, 412, 413, 415, 417, 419, 421
Milton, John 280n
Monck, Christopher, 2nd duke of Albemarle 168, 170, 266
Moss, Robert 306, 308, 327, 380, 399
Mott, Samuel, Alderman 132, 179, 252
muslin 386

New Exchange 140, 277
Newington Butts, Surrey (now Southwark) 3, 11, 17, 18, 20, 40, 50, 139, 140, 141, 198, 233, 235, 261, 270–294 *passim*,
Northampton, Great Fire of 63

Pagett, John 140n
Pepys, Samuel 2n, 11, 17n, 32, 75n–76n, 78n, 125n–126n, 141n, 166n, 214n, 265n–266n, 267n, 275n, 276n, 277n, 281n, 288n–289n, 290n, 294n, 300n, 302n, 341n, 343n, 405n
periwigs 75, 76, 77, 92, 124, 159, 180, 182, 185, 187, 194, 198, 199, 200, 204, 216, 228, 232, 248, 309, 316, 326, 399, 401, 404, 406, 407, 413, 422
pounce (calligraphy) 49, 52, 79, 102, 145
Powell, Joseph (Colchester, St Mary-at-the-Walls) 219, 226, 227
Power, John, 9th Baron Power 297, 312, 329, 356, 360, 371–372, 373, 374
Practice of Piety, The, *see* Bayly, Lewis

Quarles, Francis 56

Raleigh, Sir Walter 280n
Rebow, Sir Isaac 44, 190
Reynolds Sr., Samuel 134, 162, 178, 220, 243, 256
Royal Exchange 140, 166, 277, 298, 312, 320, 355, 397

sagathy 402, 406
Sammes, Aylett 281
scurvy 119, 120
secretary (writing hand) 187, 262
Shaw, Sir John 168, 170, 223, 236, 243,
Shelton, William (Colchester, St James) 49, 76, 101, 107, 124, 127, 130, 132, 138, 147, 148, 153, 160, 168, 176, 178, 179, 181, 182, 184, 187, 188, 192, 193, 200, 202, 205, 208, 210, 211, 213, 215, 216, 218, 220, 221, 222, 223, 225, 230, 231, 236, 238, 239, 242, 246, 250, 251, 255, 257, 258, 260, 264, 266
Sherlock, Thomas, bishop of Bangor; of Salisbury; of London 412
shoes (boots etc.) 81, 93, 97, 98, 100, 110 124, 133, 135, 146, 149, 165, 180, 190, 200, 206, 226, 237, 242, 248, 253, 274, 318, 331, 365, 366, 402, 414, 415, 416, 420

INDEX

silk 83, 85, 114, 194, 270, 329, 367, 399, 404, 405, 406
Sion College 304n, 387n, 388
Smith, John (Colchester, St Mary-at-the-Walls) 41–42, 45, 56, 58, 61, 63, 66, 70, 72, 74, 77, 79, 94, 104, 106, 107, 109, 112, 116, 118, 120, 121, 123, 125, 127, 138, 144, 146, 148, 149, 151, 155, 156, 158, 160, 168, 170, 172, 173, 179, 185, 187, 203, 205, 206
Snape, Andrew 350, 410
Society for Promoting Christian Knowledge 304n, 334n
Society for the Propagation of the Gospel in Foreign Parts 304n, 334
Spira, Francis 107
Stanhope, George 307n
Stanley, William 358n
Stubbs, Philip (d.1738) 310
stuff (fabric) 114, 115, 123, 124, 125, 126, 129, 193, 278
suffrance (Customs) 390, 399
swords 78, 82, 83, 113, 126, 138, 191, 213, 236, 237, 239, 334–335, 375–376, 378, 380, 381

table games (tables, tick-tack, backgammon) 67, 98, 257, 258, 268
Taylor, Jeremy 1, 42, 55, 77, 87, 93, 107, 110, 120, 124, 137, 145, 146, 147, 148, 153, 161, 167, 183, 190, 196, 205, 206, 212, 221, 223, 225, 230, 231, 238, 239, 246, 263, 283, 285, 294
Thompson, Thomas (Colchester, St Peter) 43, 91, 92, 94, 99, 112, 114, 134, 136, 144, 148, 149, 151, 155, 157, 158, 161, 163

transire (Customs) 395, 399, 400
Trimnell, Charles, bishop of Norwich 319

velvet 370
Venetian treacle (theriac), *see* medicines
Vine Yard (Goswell Street) 28–29, 357, 362, 380, 383, 384, 385, 386, 388, 392, 393, 397, 401
viol 300
violin 2, 50, 52, 55, 56, 59, 62, 84, 85, 89, 90, 100, 102, 103, 104, 105, 106, 108, 109, 110, 111, 112, 115, 116, 117, 119, 120, 123, 125, 126, 127, 128, 129, 131, 132, 133, 134, 139, 142, 145, 146, 147, 148, 149, 157, 158, 167, 204, 207, 233, 236, 274, 282

Walker, Richard 8, 324, 333, 346, 358, 360, 396, 411, 417, 419, 422
watermen 311, 335, 367–368, 401
Waugh, John, bishop of Carlisle 319
Westminster 39n, 139, 140n, 142n, 233n, 277, 281, 288n
Wheely, John 44, 46, 47, 164, 184
Whitehall 274, 276–277n, 279, 284, 290n, 372
Whole Duty of Man, The 275
Wilde, Jonathan 375n
Wilson, Thomas, bishop of Sodor and Man 306, 313, 320, 321, 327
Windsor 348, 350–351, 352
Winchester College 5–6, 9, 39, 153, 233, 234n, 264
Wivenhoe, Essex 46, 60, 71, 131, 136, 137, 142, 144, 155, 163, 227, 254, 268–269
Wright, Samuel 361n